DAVID BUSCH'S
Sony® α a7R IV

GUIDE TO
DIGITAL PHOTOGRAPHY

DAVID D. BUSCH

David Busch's Sony® α a7R IV Guide to Digital Photography
David D. Busch

Project Manager: Jenny Davidson
Series Technical Editor: Michael D. Sullivan
Layout: Bill Hartman
Cover Design: Mike Tanamachi
Indexer: Valerie Haynes Perry
Proofreader: Mike Beady

ISBN: 978-1-68198-570-1
1st Edition (1st printing, March 2020)

© 2020 David D. Busch

All images © David D. Busch unless otherwise noted

Rocky Nook, Inc.
1010 B Street, Suite 350
San Rafael, CA 94901
USA
www.rockynook.com

Distributed in the UK and Europe by Publishers Group UK
Distributed in the U.S. and all other territories by Ingram Publisher Services

Library of Congress Control Number: 2019950821

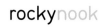

For Cathy

Acknowledgments

Thanks to everyone at Rocky Nook, including Scott Cowlin, managing director and publisher, for the freedom to let me explore the amazing capabilities of the Sony a7R IV in depth. I couldn't do it without my veteran production team, including project manager, Jenny Davidson, and series technical editor, Mike Sullivan. Also, thanks to Bill Hartman, layout; Valerie Hayes Perry, indexing; Mike Beady, proofreading; Mike Tanamachi, cover design; and my agent, Carole Jelen, who has the amazing ability to keep both publishers and authors happy.

About the Author

With more than 2.5 million books in print, **David D. Busch** is the world's #1 bestselling camera guide author, and the originator of popular series like *David Busch's Pro Secrets, David Busch's Compact Field Guides,* and *David Busch's Quick Snap Guides.* He has written dozens of hugely successful guidebooks for Sony and other digital SLR models, including the all-time #1 bestsellers for several different cameras, as well as many popular books devoted to photography, including *Mastering Mirrorless Photography.* As a roving photojournalist for more than 20 years, he illustrated his books, magazine articles, and newspaper reports with award-winning images. He's operated his own commercial studio, suffocated in formal dress while shooting weddings, and shot sports for a daily newspaper and an upstate New York college. His photos and articles have appeared in *Popular Photography, Rangefinder, Professional Photographer,* and hundreds of other publications. He's also reviewed dozens of digital cameras for CNet and other CBS publications.

When About.com named its top five books on Beginning Digital Photography, debuting at the #1 and #2 slots were Busch's *Digital Photography All-In-One Desk Reference for Dummies* and *Mastering Digital Photography.* Busch has had as many as 18 books listed in the Top 100 of Amazon.com's Digital Photography Bestseller list—simultaneously! Busch's 250-plus other published books include bestsellers like *Digital SLR Cameras and Photography for Dummies.*

Busch is a member of the Cleveland Photographic Society (www.clevelandphoto.org), which has operated continuously since 1887. Visit his website at http://www.sonyguides.com.

Contents

Preface

The Sony a7R IV, the latest edition of the company's high-resolution full-frame camera, is the most versatile E-mount mirrorless model the company has ever offered. Its remarkable 61 megapixels of resolution capture enough detail to satisfy the most discerning landscape, commercial, or portrait photographer's needs, and it can fire off continuous bursts at a 10-frames-per-second rate that make it a sports photographer's dream. With advanced autofocus, five-axis anti-shake image stabilization built into the camera body, and 4K video capabilities, the a7R IV comes close to being a "do-everything" model that is a jack of all trades—and master of them, as well.

In a few short years, Sony has gone from being a Nikon and Canon competitor that offered warmed-over Konica Minolta digital camera technology, to an acknowledged innovator with a lineup of cameras that are smaller, lighter, faster to focus, and loaded with cutting-edge features that many of us have been dreaming about. So, it's no wonder you're excited about your new Sony a7R IV. With all these features at your disposal, you don't expect to take good pictures with such a camera—you demand and anticipate *outstanding* photos.

Unfortunately, your gateway to pixel proficiency is dragged down by the limited instructions provided by Sony. Over the years, Sony has reduced the amount of useful information included in its printed guidebooks, often to a scant 100 pages or so, and relegated more detailed instructions to online HTML-based guides and PDF versions that are difficult to navigate. And, sad to say, not everything you need to know is included.

What you really need is a guide that explains the purpose and function of the cameras' basic controls, how you should use them, and *why*. That's what I am giving you in this book. If you want a quick introduction to focus controls, flash synchronization options, how to choose lenses, or which exposure modes are best, this book is for you. If you can't decide on what basic settings to use with your camera because you can't figure out how changing ISO or white balance or focus defaults will affect your pictures, you need this guide.

Introduction

With the a7R IV, Sony has packaged up the most alluring features of advanced digital SLRs and stuffed them into a compact, fully featured body, which boasts at least a few capabilities you won't find in cameras from other vendors. They include an innovative Pixel Shift capability, which captures 4 or 16 different images, each displaced from the last by a single pixel, and which are then combined in the free Imaging Edge software to provide the detail you'd expect to find in a sensor with the equivalent of up to 240 megapixels. Many of the a7R IV's other features are significant upgrades from previous models.

Of course, once you've confirmed that you made a wise purchase, the question comes up, *how do I use this thing?* All those cool features can be mind-numbing to learn, if all you have as a guide is the mediocre manual furnished with the camera. Basic functions and options are explained, but there's really very little about *why* you should use particular settings or features, and the organization may make it difficult to find what you need. Multiple cross-references may send you flipping back and forth between two or three sections of the book to find what you want to know. The basic manual is also hobbled by black-and-white line drawings and tiny pictures that aren't very good examples of what you can do.

Help is on the way. I sincerely believe that this book is your best bet for learning how to use your new camera, and for learning how to use it well. I've tried to make *David Busch's Sony Alpha a7R IV Guide to Digital Photography* comprehensive, but easy to comprehend. The roadmap sections use large, color pictures to show you where all the buttons and dials are, and the explanations of what they do are longer and more detailed. I've tried to avoid overly general advice, including the checklists and recipes you'll find in other manuals on how to take a "sports picture" or a "portrait picture" or a "travel picture." If you want to know where you should stand to take a picture of a quarterback dropping back to unleash a pass, there are plenty of books that will tell you that. This one concentrates on teaching you how to select the best autofocus mode, shutter speed, f/stop, or flash capability to take, say, a great sports picture under any conditions.

What You'll Learn

This book is aimed at Sony veterans as well as newcomers to digital photography. Both groups can be overwhelmed by the options the a7R IV offers, while underwhelmed by the explanations they receive in their user's manual, which some suspect was written by a Sony employee who last threw together instructions on how to operate a camcorder or DVD player.

Although this book's main focus is *still* photography, I *will* devote a lot of space to helping you get up to speed on using the a7R IV's video capabilities. After all, the a7R IV is capable of shooting awesome, professional-level movies, but extensive discussions about choosing between Internal UHD 4K30 and 1080p/120 fps recording, or technical information about S-Log3 gamma and display assist functions are beyond the scope of this book. Given that I expect that only a relatively small—albeit important—segment of the readers of this book want or require such information, I'm going with Vulcan philosopher Spock Prime's observation early in *The Wrath of Khan* that "Logic clearly dictates that the needs of the many outweigh the needs of the few."

Who Am I?

After spending many years as the world's most successful unknown author, I've become slightly less obscure in the past few years, thanks to a horde of camera guidebooks and other photographically oriented tomes. You may have seen my photography articles in the late, lamented *Popular Photography, Rangefinder, Professional Photographer,* and dozens of other photographic publications. But, first, and foremost, I'm a photojournalist and made my living in the field until I began devoting most of my time to writing books. Although I love writing, I'm happiest when I'm out taking pictures, which is why I spend many winters ensconced in the Florida Keys, dividing my time between writing books and taking photographs. You'll find images of many of these visual treats within the pages of this guide.

Like all my digital photography books, this one was written by someone with an incurable photography bug. I've worked as a sports photographer for an Ohio newspaper and for an upstate New York college. I've operated my own commercial studio and photo lab, cranking out product shots on demand and then printing a few hundred glossy 8 × 10s on a tight deadline for a press kit. I've served as a photo-posing instructor for a modeling agency. People have actually paid me to shoot their weddings and immortalize them with portraits. I even prepared press kits and articles on photography as a PR consultant for a formerly dominant (and now vestigial) Rochester, NY company. My trials and travails with imaging and computer technology have made their way into print in book form an alarming number of times, including hundreds of volumes on photographic topics. I teach classes and have branched out into online training courses.

Like you, I love photography for its own merits, and I view technology as just another tool to help me get the images I see in my mind's eye. But, also like you, I had to master this technology before I could apply it to my work. This book is the result of what I've learned, and I hope it will help you master your Sony a7R IV.

I'd like to ask a special favor: let me know what you think of this book. If you have any recommendations about how I can make it better, visit my website at www.sonyguides.com, click on the E-Mail Me tab, and send your comments, suggestions on topics that should be explained in more detail, or, especially, any typos. (The latter will be compiled on the Errata page you'll also find on my website.) I really value your ideas and appreciate it when you take the time to tell me what you think! Some of the content of the book you hold in your hands came from suggestions I received from readers like yourself. If you found this book especially useful, tell others about it. Visit http://www.amazon.com/dp/1681985705 and leave a positive review. Your feedback is what spurs me to make each one of these books better than the last, and if enough of you like what I've done, Rocky Nook may be moved to ask me to follow up with a new book the next time Sony introduces one of its photographic innovations. Thanks!

Meet Your Sony Alpha a7R IV

1

The Sony a7R IV *can* be incredibly easy to use, right out of the box, especially if you already have some experience with digital photography. As ridiculous as it may seem, this advanced camera can be used in point-and-shoot mode simply by holding down the mode dial release button and rotating the large mode dial on the top-right panel to select the Program (P) label or green Intelligent Auto icon. (See Figure 1.1.) If you've charged the battery, mounted a lens, and inserted a formatted memory card into the camera, flip the power switch to On. (It's concentric with the shutter release button on top of the camera.) I'll provide tips on performing these tasks later in this chapter, if you need help. Otherwise, you're ready to start taking your first pictures.

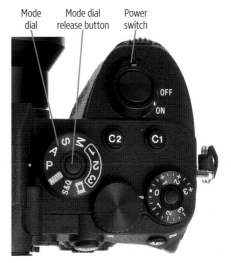

Mode dial   Mode dial release button   Power switch

Figure 1.1 Select Program or Auto and take a picture.

As you peer through the viewfinder or examine the monitor (the rear LCD screen), the scene your camera will capture is shown, with the current shooting mode displayed in the upper-left corner of the frame. Compose your image, and press the shutter release button when you're ready to take your first shot. That's all there is to it. The a7R IV is smart enough to produce a pretty good shot without much input from you. In this book, I'm going to help you go beyond *pretty good* to consistently great.

Although you can begin shooting as soon as you unbox your new camera, it's not a bad idea, once you've taken a few orientation pictures with your camera, to go back and review the basic operations of the a7R IV from the beginning—if only to see if you've missed something. This chapter is my opportunity to introduce new owners to the a7R IV and review the setup procedures for those among you who are already veteran users, and to help ease the more timid (even those few who have never before worked with an interchangeable-lens camera) into the basic pre-flight checklist that needs to be completed before you really spread your wings and take off. For the uninitiated, as easy as it is to use initially, your Sony a7R IV *does* have some dials, buttons, and menu items that might not make sense at first but will surely become second nature after you've had a chance to review the instructions in this book.

But don't fret about wading through a manual to find out what you must know to take those first few tentative snaps. I'm going to help you hit the ground running with this chapter (or keep on running if you've already jumped right in). If you *haven't* had the opportunity to use your a7R IV yet, I'll help you set up your camera and begin shooting in minutes. You won't find a lot of operational detail in this chapter. Indeed, I'm going to tell you just what you absolutely *must* understand, accompanied by some interesting tidbits that will help you become acclimated. I'll go into more depth and even repeat some of what I explain here in later chapters, so you don't have to memorize everything you see. Just relax, follow a few easy steps, and then go out and begin taking your best shots—ever.

DIFFERENT STROKES...

One of the challenges of writing a guidebook like this is satisfying the needs of both veteran E-mount users as well as newcomers to Sony cameras (which now includes the hordes who jumped to the Sony mirrorless world from other camera platforms). Believe it or not, while the a7R IV attracts both photo enthusiasts and professional photographers, a surprising number of less experienced shooters have found the a7R IV appealing, too.

So, whether you're an advanced shooter looking to improve your comfort level with the features of this well-designed (yet complex) camera or are looking forward to starting from a more modest level of photographic expertise, I hope you'll find the advice I'm about to offer in this chapter—or beyond—useful. If you like, you can zip right through the basics, and then dive into learning a few things you probably didn't know about your a7R IV. Sony veterans might want to skim through the material in this chapter and move on. I promise I didn't charge you extra for it; even in the days of digital publishing it's not possible to provide *only* the material a particular reader needs, and nothing else.

Your Out-of-Box Experience

Your Sony a7R IV comes in an attractive box filled with stuff, including a multi-purpose USB charging cable, basic instructions, some pamphlets, and a few other items. The most important components are the camera and lens, battery, charger, and, if you're the nervous type, the neck strap. You'll also need a Secure Digital card, as one is not included.

The first thing to do is to carefully unpack the camera and double-check the contents with the checklist on one side of the box. While this level of setup detail may seem as superfluous as the instructions on a bottle of shampoo, checking the contents *first* is always a good idea. It's better to know *now* that something is missing so you can seek redress immediately, rather than discover a few days later that the box didn't contain the cable protector—which keeps an accessory cable securely attached to the camera.

LENS NOMENCLATURE

In the discussion of lenses in the section that follows, you're going to find me describing certain E-mount lenses using their full, formal product names, which can be rather unwieldy. However, for the most part in this book, I'll use shorter, more compact nomenclature when there is little chance of confusion. For example, Sony offers several full-frame prime lenses in the 50-55mm focal length range. So, to be clear, I may need to refer to the Sony FE 50mm f/1.8, Sony Planar T* FE 50mm f/1.4 ZA, Sony Sonnar T* FE 55mm f/1.8 ZA, or Sony FE 50mm f/2.8 macro lens, as appropriate. Most of the time, a shorter version of the lens' name will do.

So, check the box at your earliest convenience, and make sure you have (at least) the following:

- **Sony a7R IV body.** This is hard to miss. The camera is the main reason you laid out the big bucks, and it is tucked away inside a nifty protective envelope you should save for re-use in case the camera needs to be sent in for repair. It almost goes without saying that you should check out the camera immediately, making sure the color LCD on the back isn't scratched or cracked, the battery compartment, memory card door, and connection port doors open properly; and, when a charged battery is inserted, and lens mounted, the camera powers up and reports for duty. Out-of-the-box defects in these areas are rare, but they can happen. It's probably more common that your dealer played with the camera or, perhaps, it was a customer return. That's why it's best to buy your camera from a retailer you trust to supply a factory-fresh camera.

- **Lens.** Depending on where you live, the Sony a7R IV may be available in several different configurations, often the body alone, or packaged in several different kits that included accessories such as the VG-C4EM Vertical Grip and NPA-MQZ1K Multi-Battery Adapter Kit. It was also available with the Sony FE 24-105mm f/4 G OSS lens ($1,300), Sony FE 28-70mm f/3.5-5.6 OSS lens (about $500), the Zeiss Vario-Tessar T* FE 24-70mm f/4 ZA OSS lens (about $1,200), or even the premium Sony FE 24-70mm f/2.8 GM (G Master) lens ($2,200).

  My recommendation: I already owned the Zeiss Vario-Tessar 24-70mm f/4, so I bought my a7R IV with the 24-105mm zoom. *You probably do not need both lenses* because the 24-105mm lens completely overlaps the range of the three 24/28-70mm optics. You might make an exception for the 24-70mm f/2.8 G-Master if you do a *lot* of shooting in the shorter focal length neighborhood and want a super-sharp lens with a fast f/2.8 maximum aperture.

  As the owner of a 61MP camera, you probably won't be satisfied with the low-cost 28-70mm f/3.5-5.6 OSS lens, as it's not the sharpest lens in the drawer. The Zeiss 24-70mm version is a bit better, and its constant maximum aperture gives you f/4 (rather than f/5.6) at the 70mm setting. The f/2.8 G-Master is the best of all, and my guess is that, despite it's greater bulk, will be the preferred lens among those investing in the a7R IV.

  Owning *any* lens in this particular zoom range is a matter of personal style and preference. Many shooters tend to "see" images as "wide-angle/perspective distortion/maximum depth-of-field" shots or, conversely, as "longer lens/selective focus" photos. If you are in either camp, eschewing all these lenses and putting the money toward a different lens is a good option. I use my Sony Vario-Tessar T* FE 16-35mm f/4 ZA OSS lens quite often and have been relying on the 24-105mm zoom more frequently as a "walk-around" lens.

- **Info-Lithium NP-FZ100 battery.** This is the power source for your Sony camera. Charge yours as soon as possible (as described next).

  My recommendation: Although the a7R IV's 2280 mAh battery is more than twice as powerful than the one furnished with Sony's original full-frame cameras (and the company's consumer-oriented APS-C models), it's smart, nay, *essential* to have more than one battery pack. Although relatively small in size, this camera gulps power, and, even with the generous standards Sony cites in its literature, each is likely to last for no more than 530 to 670 still shots or roughly 170 minutes of non-stop video capture. (The figures given vary depending on whether you are using the electronic viewfinder or LCD monitor screen to frame your image, plus other factors.) Buy *more*, and stick to Sony-brand products—even though third-party batteries have become available. Off-brand packs have been known to fail quickly, sometimes in potentially destructive ways.

- **Sony BC-QZ1 external charger.** This handy device (see Figure 1.2) allows you to recharge one battery while another is ensconced in your camera as you continue shooting.

  My recommendation: I strongly prefer the faster external charger to the alternative cable charging method, accomplished by plugging a USB cable into a computer or USB charger. However, an even better choice than the BC-QZ1 is the $400 NPA-MQZ1K Multi Battery Adapter Kit, described shortly.

- **Micro Type-C cable.** Use this USB cable to link your Sony to a computer when you need to transfer pictures but don't have an optional card reader accessory handy. While the camera is connected with the cable, the battery inside the body will also be charging. The USB cable can also be connected to an optional AC adapter (which can be the Sony AC-UUD12 adapter, or virtually any other 5V/2A smart device power cube) if you want to charge the battery using household power.

  My recommendation: An AC adapter is especially useful while traveling, as it eliminates the need to have a computer or laptop powered up to charge the battery. Note that you can use the Type-C cable plugged into the a7R IV's Type-C port, or a Micro B USB 2.0 cable inserted in the camera's Multi/Micro USB terminal. I'll list these other options in an upcoming section titled "Charging the Battery."

- **Shoulder strap.** Sony provides a suitable neck or shoulder strap, with the Sony logo subtly worked into the design.

  My recommendation: While I am justifiably proud of owning a fine Sony camera, I never attach the factory strap to my camera, and instead opt for a more serviceable strap from UPstrap (www.upstrap-pro.com). If you carry your camera over one shoulder, as many do, I particularly recommend UPstrap (shown in Figure 1.3). It has a patented non-slip pad that offers reassuring

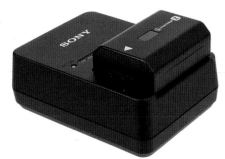

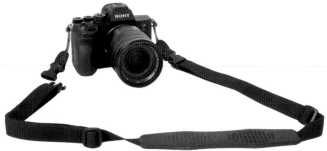

Figure 1.2 The Sony BC-QZ1 charger allows rejuvenating your battery outside the camera, so you can keep shooting with a spare battery.

Figure 1.3 Third-party neck straps, like this UPstrap model, are often preferable to the Sony-supplied strap.

traction and eliminates the contortions we sometimes go through to keep the camera from slipping off. I know several photographers who refuse to use anything else. If you do purchase an UPstrap, be sure to tell photographer-inventor Al Stegmeyer that I sent you hence. There are several different strap models, and Al will help you choose which one is best for you.

- **Multi Interface Shoe cap.** This plastic piece slides into the camera's multi interface shoe on top of the camera (what we used to call a "hot shoe") and protects the contacts from dirt, moisture, and damage when you don't have an electronic flash, microphone, or other accessory attached.

  My recommendation: If you are *very* careful about how you insert an external flash or microphone into the multi interface shoe, and avoid drenching moisture, you can remove this piece and leave it off for the rest of your life. I *have* lost shots while fumbling with protective covers and manage to lose the shoe cap with alarming frequency. If you misplace yours, USA shooters can get a replacement from www.laserfairepress.com for a few bucks.

- **FDA-EP18 eyepiece cup.** This rubber accessory is already installed on the electronic viewfinder eyepiece when you receive the camera; if you want to remove it, slide it up. It's not easily lost, but this cup fits a variety of Sony cameras, including the Sony a99 II and other Sony full-frame mirrorless cameras, so you can pick up a replacement for about $11.

- **Application software.** Sony no longer includes a software CD in the package. The first time you power up the camera, it will display the current URL for your country where you can download imaging software for the a7R IV. Be sure to get the new, free Imaging Edge software. It's a great RAW processor and editor and has a Remote application for tethered shooting (with your a7R IV connected to a laptop or other computer). It's also an essential tool for the camera's Pixel Shift feature, combining four individual photos to create a single ersatz 240.8-megapixel final image.

- **Printed instruction manual.** The camera comes with a skimpy 100-page basic instruction manual. A 698-page Help Guide to the camera's operation can be accessed online in HTML format or downloaded as a more useful PDF file from Sony's esupport.sony.com website. The box will also contain warranty and registration information, and assorted pamphlets listing available accessories, including, at the time I write this, a free copy of the Sony-specific Capture One Express from Phase One. You can upgrade that software to the full version for a modest fee.

- **Body cap.** This accessory will probably already be attached to the camera body if you purchase your a7R IV without a lens.

  My recommendation: Purchase an extra body cap. With mirrorless cameras like the a7R IV series, it is especially important not to leave the sensor unprotected. If you lose your body cap, mount a lens as a "body cap" until you purchase spares. A body cap is essential when packing your camera for compact travel. Owners in the USA will find cheap body and rear lens caps at www.laserfairepress.com, too. (Nobody gets rich selling these items for a few dollars, but these are provided as a service because a key previous source for them has gone out of business.)

- **Cable protector.** This gadget attaches to the left side of the a7R IV (as you hold the camera), and allows you to keep any combination of HDMI, USB Type-C, and Multi/Micro USB cables from detaching. This is an especially useful feature when saving movies to an external video recorder, as a loose cable is obviously more than an inconvenience when capturing movies live. (See Figure 1.4.)

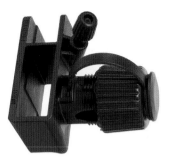

My recommendation: I'll show you how to attach this accessory in Chapter 2. While the cables usually fit snugly in the terminals without the protector, having one pull loose at an inopportune time while shooting video is annoying. However, when securely fastened, the protector also prevents removing the cables at

Figure 1.4 The cable protector keeps connections secure.

opportune times, as well; you can't just unplug the cables without detaching the protector as well. So, I tend to use it only when I know I will be shooting video for some time, or want to work tethered to a computer (usually to display what I am shooting when I run a workshop).

Initial Setup

The initial setup of your Sony is fast and easy. You just need to charge the battery, attach a lens (if that hasn't already been done), and insert a memory card. I'll address each of these steps separately, but if you already feel you can manage these setup tasks without further instructions, feel free to skip this section entirely. You should probably at least skim its contents, however, because I'm going to list a few options that you might not be aware of.

Battery Included

Your Sony a7R IV is a sophisticated hunk of machinery and electronics, but it needs a charged battery to function, so rejuvenating the NP-FZ100 lithium-ion battery pack should be your first step. A fully charged power source should theoretically be good for 530 shots (when using the power-hungry viewfinder) or 670 shots (when working with the more juice-frugal LCD monitor screen). Expect 105 minutes (or more) of typical video capture, which includes standby time, zooming, and turning the camera on or off from time to time. When shooting continuously, you may be able to stretch a single battery for as much as 170 minutes of continual video capture. Theoretically. I frequently (always) deplete my batteries more quickly than that. Sony's estimates are based on standard tests defined by the Camera & Imaging Products Association (CIPA). If you often use the camera's Wi-Fi feature (discussed later), you can expect to take even fewer shots before it's time for a recharge. This is an Info-Lithium battery, so the camera can display the approximate power remaining with a graphic indicator.

Remember that all rechargeable batteries undergo some degree of self-discharge just sitting idle in the camera or in the original packaging. Lithium-ion power packs of this type typically lose a small amount of their charge every day, even when the camera isn't turned on. Li-ion cells lose their power through a chemical reaction that continues when the camera is switched off. So, it's very likely that the battery purchased with your camera, even if charged at the factory, has begun to poop out after the long sea voyage on a banana boat (or, more likely, a trip by jet plane followed by a sojourn in a warehouse), so you'll want to revive it before going out for some serious shooting.

My recommendation: At roughly $400, the NPA-MQZ1K Multi-Battery Adapter Kit sounds pricey (it is!). However, it comes with two NP-FZ100 batteries (normally about $80 each), which means that, effectively, you're paying "only" $240 for the charger itself. The charger is extremely versatile: it can charge up to four NP-FZ100 batteries simultaneously but can be converted to a compact two-battery charger for use while traveling. (See Figure 1.5.)

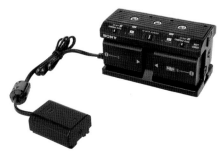

Figure 1.5 The NPA-MQZ1K Multi-Battery Adapter Kit lets you charge up to four batteries at once, or power your a7R IV using AC current.

Even better, the charger can serve as a power pack when outfitted with fully charged batteries. A dummy battery plugs into the battery compartment of the a7R IV (or, with a supplied adapter, into any E-mount camera that uses the puny NP-FW50 batteries). Two USB ports allow rejuvenating other devices that use USB cable charging (including your smartphone!). It has six standard 1/4"-20 mounting sockets so it can be mounted to support systems (like the cages videographers use to attach external viewfinders and other accessories).

I own eight NP-FZ100 batteries (so far). You won't need that many, but in addition to my a7R IV, I also own other cameras that use the same battery, including the a6600 and a9 II. I keep a fresh battery in the camera at all times. Nevertheless, I always check battery status before I go out to shoot, as some juice may have been siphoned off while the camera sat idle. I go to the Network 1 menu and turn Airplane Mode on (as described in Chapter 5) when I don't need Wi-Fi features.

THIRD-PARTY BATTERIES

I don't recommend using third-party batteries, even though they may cost one-third the price of Sony's own batteries. It makes little sense to risk damaging a $3,500 camera body just to save a few dollars on such a crucial component. I purchased several well-known NP-FZ100 clones when they were first introduced; they didn't work, and within a week the company had stopped selling them. All existing batteries were recalled or replaced.

Your a7R IV will display a compatibility warning message when many of these batteries are inserted. While the latest generation knock-offs seem to work better, many have reduced capacity, and there's no guarantee that the third parties selling them will be able to issue timely recalls if needed. While some owners have had no problems, and swear by their Wasabi, Watson, Neewer, or DTSE batteries, I don't think it's worth the risk.

Charging the Battery

While the included Sony BC-QZ1 external charger or optional NPA-MQZ1K multi-battery adapter should be your first choices, you have multiple other options, including charging the battery while it's still in the camera (best done when the camera is idle and not needed for shooting). You probably already own a suitable AC adapter/charger, in the form of any charging device you use for your smartphone, tablet, Kindle, or other electronic product. Their typical 5V/2A output will work fine. I also use a 22,000 mAh lithium-ion power "brick," which also can recharge my phone, my tablet, and, in a pinch (using an included cable) jump start a car. The brick comes with its own 12V DC charger, so I can keep it topped up using my vehicle's accessory outlet (what we used to call a "cigarette lighter" socket). I also have a more compact 5,000 mAh pack, about the size of a roll of quarters, that I keep in my camera bag.

When you're ready to charge the battery internally, turn the camera Off. Then, plug one end of the USB cable (with the smaller connector) into one of the two bottom ports on the left end of the a7R IV. A standard USB 2.0 Micro B cable can be plugged into the lower of the two, or a USB 3 Type-C cable into the one above it. (See Figure 1.6.) Plug the other end of either cable (with the familiar USB connector) into a computer's USB port, AC adapter, or battery-powered recharging device. Turn the camera On and you'll see a note that says USB Mode on the LCD screen; this confirms that the connection has been made.

Whether you charge from a computer's USB port or household power, a Charge light next to the camera's USB/charging ports glows yellow, without flashing. It continues to glow until the battery completes the charge and the lamp turns off. In truth, the full charge is complete about one hour *after* the charging lamp turns off, so if your battery was really dead, don't stop charging until the additional time has elapsed. Be sure to plan for charging time before your shooting sessions, because it takes several hours in a warm environment to fully restore a completely depleted battery.

If the charging lamp flashes after you insert an externally charged battery into the camera, that indicates an error condition. Remove it and re-insert it. To insert/remove it, slide the latch on the bottom of the camera, open the battery door, and press a blue lever in the battery compartment that prevents the pack from slipping out when the door is opened; then, ease the battery out. To insert it, do so with the contact openings facing into the compartment (see Figure 1.7).

Fast flashing that can't be stopped by re-inserting the battery indicates a problem with the battery. Slow flashing (about 1.5 seconds between flashes) means the ambient temperature is too high or low for charging to take place.

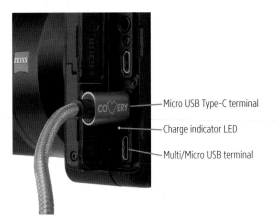

Figure 1.6 Charging through either the Multi/Micro terminal or Type-C USB terminal (as shown), takes several hours to provide a normal charge to a battery pack that was completely depleted, but can be performed through a USB connection to your computer, or with an appropriate power brick or AC adapter.

Micro USB Type-C terminal

Charge indicator LED

Multi/Micro USB terminal

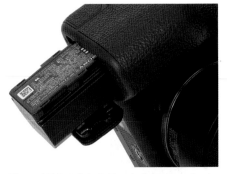

Figure 1.7 Install the battery in the camera; it only fits one way.

Charging the battery with the supplied BC-QZ1 external charger is even easier; just slide the battery in, connect to AC power, and the charger's yellow status light will begin to glow, accompanied by three green LEDs that illuminate progressively as charging proceeds, to let you know when the battery is fully charged. The yellow LED will extinguish when the cycle is over.

Final Steps

Your Sony a7R IV is almost ready to fire up and shoot. You'll need to select and mount a lens (if not previously done) and insert a memory card. Each of these steps is easy, and if you've used any similar camera in the past, such as a Sony or other model, you already know exactly what to do. I'm going to provide a little extra detail for those of you who are new to the Sony or interchangeable-lens camera worlds.

Mounting the Lens

My recommended lens mounting procedure emphasizes protecting your equipment from accidental damage and minimizing the intrusion of dust. Select the lens you want to use and loosen (but do not remove) the rear lens cap. I generally place the lens I am planning to mount vertically in a slot in my camera bag, where it's protected from mishaps but ready to pick up quickly. By loosening the rear lens cap, you'll be able to lift it off the back of the lens at the last instant, so the rear element of the lens is covered until then.

After that, remove the body cap that protects the camera's exposed sensor by rotating the cap toward the shutter release button. You should always mount the body cap when there is no lens on the camera, because it helps keep dust out of the interior of the camera. Unlike traditional dSLRs, these cameras have no mirror or closed shutter to protect the sensor.

Once the body cap has been removed, remove the rear lens cap from the lens, set the cap aside, and then mount the lens on the camera by matching the raised white alignment indicator on the lens barrel with the white dot on the camera's lens mount (see Figure 1.8). Rotate the lens away from the

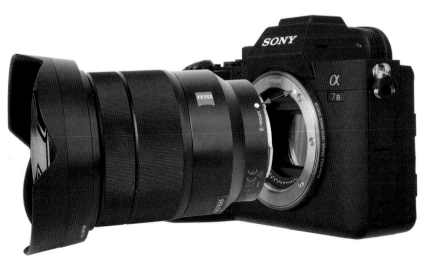

Figure 1.8 Match the raised white dot on the lens with the white dot on the camera mount to properly align the lens with the bayonet mount.

shutter release side of the camera until it seats securely and clicks into place. (Don't press the lens release button during mounting.) Some lenses ship with a hood. If that accessory is included, and if it's bayoneted on the lens in the reversed position (which makes the lens/hood combination more compact for transport), twist it off and remount with the rim facing outward (see Figure 1.9). A lens hood protects the front of the lens from accidental bumps, and reduces flare caused by extraneous light arriving at the front element of the lens from outside the picture area.

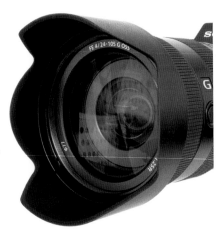

Turn on the Power

Locate the On/Off switch that is wrapped around the shutter release button and rotate it to the On position. The LCD display will be illuminated. If you bring the viewfinder up to your eye, a sensor will detect that action and switch the

Figure 1.9 A hood protects the lens from extraneous light and from accidental bumps, but not all lenses include this accessory.

display to the built-in electronic viewfinder instead. (You can disable this automatic switching in the FINDER/MONITOR setting within the Camera Settings II-07 (Display/Auto Review 1) menu, as I'll describe in Chapter 4. After one minute of idling (the default), the a7R IV goes into standby mode to save battery power. Just tap the shutter release button to bring it back to life. (You can select a longer time using the Power Save Start Time option in the Setup 2 menu, as I discuss in Chapter 5.)

When the camera first powers up, you may be asked to set the date and time. The procedure is self-explanatory (although I'll explain it in detail in Chapter 5). You can use the left/right directional buttons to navigate among the date, year, time, date format, and daylight savings time indicator, and use the up/down buttons to enter the correct settings. When finished, *press the control wheel center button* to confirm the settings and return to the menu system. Veteran users will know how to do this; if you're totally new to the E-mount system, I'll explain the control dials, wheels, and buttons in detail in Chapter 2.

Once the Sony a7R IV is satisfied that it knows what time it is, you will be viewing a live view of the scene in front of the lens—on the LCD screen or in the viewfinder when that is held up to your eye—whenever you turn the camera on. The view is superimposed with many items of data over the display; these provide a quick method for checking many current camera settings, including current shutter speed and aperture (f/stop), shooting mode, ISO sensitivity, and other parameters.

Adjusting the Diopter Setting

The a7R IV is equipped with a built-in electronic viewfinder or EVF, a small high-resolution (almost 5.7 million pixels) OLED (organic light-emitting diode) screen that can be used instead of the LCD screen for framing your photos or movies. A sensor detects your eye at the viewfinder and shuts off power to the LCD when you are using the EVF. Usually, when you're learning to use the camera's many features, you'll rely on the LCD screen's display, but when you're actually taking photos, you'll sometimes want to use the EVF instead. You can also use it to review your photos or video clips and navigate menu selections.

If you wear glasses and want to use the EVF without them, or if you find the viewfinder needs a bit of correction, rotate the diopter adjustment dial located to the right of the viewfinder window (and shown in Figure 1.10). Adjust the dial while looking through the viewfinder until the image appears sharpest.

Inserting a Memory Card

You can't take actual photos without at least one memory card inserted in your Sony camera, although if you have the Release without Card entry in the Camera Settings II-05 (Shutter/Steady-shot) menu set to Enable, you can pretend to shoot. In that case, if you don't have a card installed, the camera will sound as if it's taking a photo (when using the mechanical shutter, of course), and it will display that "photo." However, the image is only in temporary memory and not actually stored; you'll get a reminder about that with a flashing orange NO CARD warning at the upper left of the LCD. If you go back later and try to view that image, it will not be there. So, be sure you have inserted a compatible card with adequate capacity before you start shooting stills or videos.

The memory card slots are located beneath a door on the right side of the camera. Slide the door open, revealing two slots (see Figure 1.11). If you use only one memory card, you must insert it in the camera's primary slot, which, by default, is the upper slot (Slot 1). (I'll show you how to make Slot 2 the main slot in Chapter 6.)

SWITCHEROO

If you are upgrading from an earlier Sony full-frame interchangeable-lens camera, you'll want to know that the company switched the position of Slots 1 and 2 when designing the a7R IV. In previous models, the *lower* slot was Slot 1, and offered the fastest UHS-II transfer speeds. The upper slot, Slot 2, provided only UHS I transfer. Sony has installed the fast UHS-II slots in both positions, and assigned them new numbers. Both slots accept Secure Digital (SD), Secure Digital High Capacity (SDHC), or Secure Digital Extra Capacity (SDXC). The newest type of SD card, the super-high-capacity (and super-fast) SDXC type, at this writing, is available in capacities as high as 512GB. (**Note:** Unlike earlier models, the a7R IV does not support any type of Sony Memory Stick cards, including the Pro Duo or Pro-HG Duo cards.)

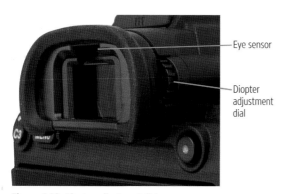

Figure 1.10 Diopter adjustment dial.

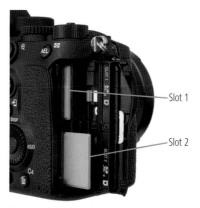

Figure 1.11 The memory cards are inserted in the slots on the side of the camera.

Given the fast continuous shooting speeds available with the a7R IV, you'll want to consider the speediest cards available, which, as I write this, are the Sony SF-G Series UHS-II U3 Class 10 SDXC memory cards, available in 128GB, 64GB, and 32GB capacities. They have a maximum 299 MB/second write speed (essential in order to transfer images from the a7R IV's built-in memory buffer to the card quickly). Poky write speeds can be infuriating when a "Processing" warning appears on your screen and you're unable to continue shooting or reviewing the images you've already taken until the buffer has emptied.

The Sony SF-G Series cards have a maximum read speed of 300MB/second, too. The latter spec is useful when it comes time to transfer your images from the memory card to your computer. Vendors typically tout their cards' read speed and downplay the write speed, which can be typically half as fast. With Sony's SF-G series, the card is wicked fast in both directions. (I suspect the 299/300 MB difference between write and read speeds is a marketing ploy to make sure consumers realize that both speeds are being shown.)

You should remove the memory card only when the camera is switched off. Insert an SD card with the label facing toward the front of the camera (as shown in Figure 1.11). In either case, the metal contacts go into the slot first; the card simply will not fit into the slot if it is incorrectly oriented.

Close the door, and your pre-flight checklist is done! (I'm going to assume you'll remember to remove the lens cap when you're ready to take a picture!) When you want to remove the memory card later, just press down on the card edge that protrudes from the slot, and the card will pop right out.

My recommendation: Size matters—when you're using a camera with a 61MP sensor. If you're buying new, rather than re-using old cards, I suggest eschewing 32GB cards and purchasing fast 64GB cards. With a 64GB card you can capture about 710 images in dual RAW/JPEG Fine formats (recommended for reasons I'll outline in Chapter 2), which is not an unreasonable amount for a day or two of intense shooting. Even though the a7R IV has two slots and can hold two cards, with smaller cards you still might find yourself swapping cards at inopportune times. And purchasing a more expensive 128GB memory card might tempt you to save a little with slower media. I do own both 128GB and 256GB memory cards, but they are, indeed, slower, so I load them in Slot 2 for backup purposes. I put nothing but Sony SF-G cards in Slot 1. (Full disclosure: Sony's black media are difficult to photograph, so I used another brand for Figure 1.11.) **Note:** Later in this book I'll show you how to store images on cards in both slots simultaneously. In these modes, the a7R IV decelerates to the speed of the slowest memory card.

There are three ways to create a blank memory card for your Sony a7R IV, and two of them are at least partially wrong. Here are your options, both correct and incorrect:

- **Transfer (move) files to your computer.** You'll sometimes decide to transfer (rather than copy) all the image files to your computer from the memory card (either using a direct cable transfer or with a card reader and appropriate software, as described later in this chapter). When you do so, the image files on the card can be erased leaving the card blank. Theoretically. This method does *not* remove files that you've labeled as Protected (by choosing Protect from the Playback menu during review), nor does it identify and lock out parts of your card that have become corrupted or unusable since the last time you formatted the card. Therefore, I recommend always formatting the card, rather than simply moving the image files. The only exception is when you *want* to leave the protected/unerased images on the card for a while longer, say, to share with friends, family, and colleagues.

- **(Don't) Format in your computer.** With the memory card inserted in a card reader or card slot in your computer, you can use Windows or Mac OS to reformat the memory card. Don't even think of doing this! The operating system won't necessarily arrange the structure of the card the way the camera likes to see it (in computer terms, an incorrect *file system* may be installed). In particular, cards larger than 32GB must be initialized using the exFAT format, and while your computer may offer exFAT as an option, it may default to a different scheme. The only way to ensure that the card has been properly formatted for your camera is to perform the format *in the camera itself*. The only exception to this rule is when you have a seriously corrupted memory card that your camera refuses to format. Sometimes it is possible to revive such a corrupted card by allowing the operating system to reformat it first, then trying again in the camera to restore the proper exFAT system.

- **Setup menu format.** Use the recommended method to format a memory card in the camera, as described next.

To format a memory card, just follow these steps. I'm going to suggest some basic navigation controls for those who are new to E-mount cameras. However, Sony gives you multiple ways to move around with its screens, and I'll show you how to do that in Chapter 2, where I'll also explain how to use the touch screen to specify a focus area. (Veteran users can use the method of their choice, including the rear multi-selector joystick.) For now, we'll just use the front and rear control dials to navigate.

1. **Press MENU.** When you press the MENU button, a menu screen will appear on the LCD monitor or electronic viewfinder. If you've previously selected a menu entry, the a7R IV will remember that and return to *that menu screen* with the most recently used item highlighted with an orange bar, as seen in Figure 1.12. However, in most cases the most recent menu may not be the one you want to use to format a memory card. To quickly move from one main menu tab to the next, rotate the *front* dial (just fore of the shutter release) to the left to move the highlight upward until only the tab at top is highlighted—if necessary. You can then rotate the *rear* dial to jump among the available tabs. (I'll explain these controls in more detail in Chapter 3.)

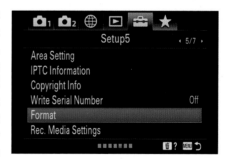

Figure 1.12 The Setup 5 menu.

2. **Navigate to the Setup tab.** Rotate the *rear* dial until the Setup tab (a yellow toolbox icon) is highlighted. Then use the *front* dial to move the orange highlighting down into the Setup menus.

3. **Navigate to the Setup 5 menu.** Use the rear dial to jump among the Setup tabs' menus until you arrive at the Setup 5 screen shown in the figure. Highlight Format, if necessary, and press the center of the control wheel to access the menu entry. (The relevant controls are shown in Figure 1.13.)

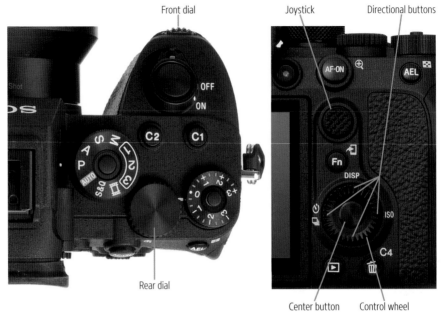

Figure 1.13 Navigation controls.

4. **Choose the slot.** Rotate the front or rear dials (it doesn't matter), or use the directional buttons or joystick, to highlight the slot containing the card you want to format. Press the control wheel center button.

5. **Format.** A display will appear asking if you want to delete all data. If you're sure you want to do so, press up/down to choose OK, and press the center button to confirm your choice. This will begin the formatting process.

Selecting a Shooting Mode

When it comes time to select the shooting mode and other settings on the a7R IV camera, you may start to fully experience the "feel" of the user interface. Thanks to the mode dial shown earlier in Figure 1.1, it's simple and quick to set a shooting mode. Just press the mode dial lock release button in the center of the dial, and rotate it to the position you want, such as P (Program Auto).

Hidden Scenes

There is a fully automatic shooting mode, Intelligent Auto. In that mode, the camera makes most of the decisions for you (except when to press the shutter). The a7R IV does not have a Scene position on the mode dial but does resort to these Scene-style settings when you use Intelligent Auto. Although you can't specify most settings on your own in Intelligent Auto mode, the a7R IV will evaluate your scene and switch to Portrait, Infant, Night Portrait, Night Scene, Backlight Portrait, Backlight, Landscape, Macro, Spotlight, Low Light, and Night Scene (Tripod) modes. (If you've disabled Face Detection, as described in Chapter 3, Portrait, Infant, Night Portrait, and Backlight Portrait scene modes are not available.) Scene detection may be incorrect if you're using the a7R

IV's digital zoom feature, discussed in Chapter 4. The available scene modes the camera may choose from are as follows:

- **Portrait.** With the Portrait setting, the camera uses settings to blur the background and sharpen the view of the subject, while using soft skin tones. External flash will fire in low light if you have attached it and powered it up.

- **Infant.** Optimizes settings for photographing small children, using bright, vivid colors.

- **Night Portrait.** Choose this mode when you want to illuminate a subject in the foreground with flash, but still allow the background to be exposed properly by the available light. Be prepared to use a tripod or to rely on the SteadyShot feature to reduce the effects of camera shake. If there is no foreground subject that needs to be illuminated by the flash, you may do better by using the Night Scene mode, discussed next. Remember that you must attach and power up the external flash before taking a shot if you want the flash to fire.

- **Night Scene.** This mode uses slower shutter speeds to provide a useful exposure, but without using flash. You should use a tripod to avoid the effects of camera shake that can be problematic with a slow shutter speed.

- **Backlight Portrait.** This is like the Portrait setting but compensates exposure for lighting coming from the rear.

- **Backlight.** Provides exposure compensation for backlight for subjects that are not portraits.

- **Landscape.** Select this scene mode when you want a maximum range of sharpness (instead of a blurred background) as well as vivid colors of distant scenes. External flash will never fire in this mode.

- **Macro.** This mode is helpful when you are shooting close-up pictures of a subject such as a flower, insect, or other small object. External flash will fire in low light if you have popped it into the up position, but the flash may be too bright for a subject that's very close to the camera.

- **Spotlight.** This setting compensates for subjects that are illuminated by a small, direct light source, as in stage performances and concerts.

- **Low Light.** This special mode is designed for use in low light. The camera will set a high ISO (sensitivity) level to enable it to use a fast shutter speed to minimize the risk of blurring caused by camera shake.

- **Night Scene (Tripod).** This mode also uses slower shutter speeds, including those long enough to make use of a tripod mandatory.

Other Modes

The mode dial also includes a Movie position, three semi-automatic modes, (Program, Aperture Priority, and Shutter Priority), which allow you to provide more input over the exposure and settings the camera uses, and a fully Manual mode. I'll provide tips on using these in Chapter 7. The other positions include S&Q (for slow-motion and quick-motion shooting), and three Memory Recall setting "slots" to register frequently used settings. I'll explain how to use the Memory settings in Chapter 3.

The mode dial options include:

- **P (Program auto).** This mode allows the a7R IV to make the basic exposure settings, but you can still override the camera's settings to fine-tune your image.
- **A (Aperture Priority).** Choose this mode when you want to use a particular lens opening (called an aperture or f/stop), especially to control how much of your image is in focus. The camera will set the appropriate shutter speed after you have set your desired aperture using the rear dial that's around the mode selector dial.
- **S (Shutter Priority).** This mode is useful when you want to use a particular shutter speed to stop action or produce creative blur effects. You dial in your chosen shutter speed with the rear dial, and the camera will set the appropriate aperture (f/stop) for you.
- **M (Manual).** Select this mode when you want full control over the shutter speed and the aperture (lens opening), either for creative effects or because you are using a studio flash or another flash unit not compatible with the camera's automatic flash metering. You also need to use this mode if you want to use the Bulb setting for a long exposure, as explained in Chapter 6. You select both the aperture (with the front dial) and the shutter speed aperture (with the rear dial on the camera back). There's more about this mode, and the others, in Chapter 6.
- **Movie.** Allows shooting movie clips. You can capture video in other exposure modes, just by pressing the red Movie button located to the right of the electronic viewfinder. While you can shoot movies with the camera set to PASM modes, this dial position gives you more options over your movie settings.
- **1/2/3 (Memory Recall).** These three positions on the mode dial, simply marked 1, 2, or 3, aren't actually exposure modes. Instead, they correspond to either of two different groups of settings that you've previously stored in an internal memory storage "slot" (register) numbered 1, 2, and 3. You can use the memory registers to set up the a7R IV for specific types of shooting scenes, and then retrieve those settings from the mode dial.
- **S&Q.** You can capture slow-motion and quick-motion video clips by moving the mode dial to this position and pressing the red Movie button. In the Camera Settings II-01 (Movie 1) menu's S&Q Settings entry, you can select Record Setting (60p, 30p, 24p) and frame rates in the S&Q Settings entry. If the a7R IV's 10-frames-per-second continuous shooting isn't fast enough for you, you can shoot video at up to 120 fps. which slows down motion by a 5X factor. Quick-motion rates of up to 60X normal speed can also be selected. I'll show you how to use these in Chapter 4.

Choosing a Metering Mode

You might want to select a particular exposure metering mode for your first shots, although the default high-tech Multi (short for multi-zone or multi-segment) metering is probably the best choice while getting to know your camera. If you want to select a different metering pattern, you must not be using Intelligent Auto; in that mode, the camera uses Multi metering and that cannot be changed. To change the metering mode, press the MENU button and navigate to the Camera Settings I menu, and thence to the Camera Settings I-09 menu to the Metering Mode entry. Press the center button,

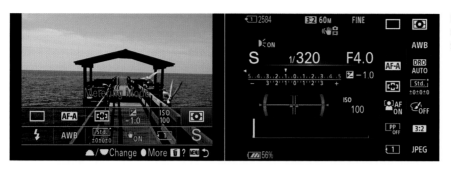

Figure 1.14 Function menu (left); Quick Navi screen (right).

then scroll up/down with the directional buttons to reach Multi, Center (for center weighted), Spot, Entire Screen Averaging, and Highlight metering selections. Press the center button to confirm your choice and return the camera to shooting mode. The metering options are as follows:

- **Multi metering.** In this standard metering mode, the camera attempts to intelligently classify your image and choose the best exposure based on readings from 1,200 different zones or segments of the scene. You can read about this so-called "evaluative" metering concept, as well as the other two options, in Chapter 7.

- **Center metering.** The camera meters the entire scene but gives the most emphasis (or weighting) to the central area of the frame.

- **Spot metering.** The camera considers only the brightness in a very small central spot, so the exposure is calculated only based on that area. You can set the size of the metering circle to Standard or Large, and either link the spot to a focusing point or fix it to the center position, as I'll explain in Chapter 7.

- **Entire Screen Averaging.** This mode sets exposure based on the mean value (in the arithmetic, rather than vengeful sense) of all the tones in the frame, which means the exposure will remain constant even if your subject moves around within the frame.

- **Highlight metering.** Emphasizes preserving tones in the highlights of an image to avoid overexposure, possibly at the expense of shadow detail. I'll show you how to balance exposures for lighter and darker images in Chapter 7.

OPTION OPTIONS

You'll soon find that your a7R IV gives you multiple ways to make adjustments. In this Quick Start chapter, I may show you just one way of selecting options. For example, you can select a metering mode using the Camera Settings I-09 menu, as described, or you can press the Fn button on the right side of the back of the camera and specify the metering method from the 12-item Function menu that pops up. (See Figure 1.14, left.) Alternatively, when the "Quick Navi" screen is shown on the LCD monitor, you can press the Fn button to change the metering mode as well as most of the other shooting settings. (See Figure 1.14, right.) I'll show you how to use the other optional methods in Chapter 2.

Choosing a Focus Mode

The focus mode can be selected using the Camera Settings I-05 menu entry or the Fn menu's Focus Mode (located second from the right in the top row of the Fn menu), or the Quick Navi screen. Focus mode is easy to understand; it determines *when* focus is established. The choices that are available when using P, A, S, or M mode are as follows:

- **Single-shot AF (AF-S).** This mode, sometimes called *single autofocus*, sets focus after you touch the shutter release button and the camera beeps to confirm focus (unless you've turned the beeps off). The active focus point(s) are shown in green on the screen and a green dot appears in the bottom-left corner of the display. The focus will remain locked as long as you maintain contact with the shutter release button, or until you take the picture. If the autofocus system is unable to achieve sharp focus (because the subject is too close to the camera, for example), the focus confirmation circle will blink. This mode is best when your subject is relatively motionless as when you're taking a portrait or landscape photo.

- **Continuous AF (AF-C).** This mode, sometimes called continuous servo or continuous tracking focus by photographers, sets focus when you partially depress the shutter button, but continues to monitor the frame and refocuses if the distance between the camera and the subject changes. (This allows it to continuously focus on a person walking toward you, for example.) No beep sound is provided. A green dot surrounded by two brackets (curved lines) appears to indicate that the camera is not having a problem achieving and maintaining focus. The brackets disappear when focus is achieved, leaving only the green dot. If the camera should fail to acquire focus, the green dot disappears, and the brackets remain. Continuous AF is a useful mode for photographing moving subjects.

- **Automatic AF (AF-A).** When using AF-A the a7R IV will switch between AF-S and AF-C to account for a subject that is moving intermittently. When shooting continuously, even if AF-A is set the camera will automatically shift into AF-C mode *after* the first exposure in the series.

- **DMF (Direct Manual Focus).** Allows you to manually adjust focus after autofocus has been confirmed, using the focus ring on the lens.

- **Manual Focus.** Focus by rotating the focus ring on the lens. The a7R IV offers magnification and Focus Peaking as aids to manual focus. I'll describe their use in Chapter 8.

Selecting a Focus Area

The Sony a7R IV is equipped with an advanced hybrid autofocus system using both phase detection and contrast detection. I'll explain what those are and how they work in detail in Chapter 8. In Intelligent Auto mode, the focus area that will set focus is selected automatically by the camera; in other words, the AF system decides which part of the scene will be in sharpest focus. In the semi-automatic P, A, and S mode, and in the manual M exposure modes, you can allow the camera to select the focus point automatically, or you can specify which focus point should be used with the Focus Area feature.

Set the camera to one of the four modes mentioned above and select Focus Area from the Camera Settings I-05 (AF1) menu. Focus Area can also be selected using the Function and Quick Navi menus. By default, it will be set to Wide (multi-point autofocus). Scroll up/down until you reach the option you want to use (see Figure 1.15) and press the center button to confirm your selection. (The button is located in the middle of the control wheel that resides to the immediate right of the LCD screen.) There are six autofocus area options, described in Chapter 8. Here's a brief overview of the options.

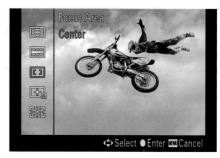

Figure 1.15 Choose Focus Area from this scrolling list.

- **Wide.** The a7R IV automatically chooses the appropriate focus area or areas; often several subjects will be the same distance from the camera as the primary subject. The active AF area or areas are then displayed in green on the LCD monitor or in the viewfinder, depending on which display you're using.

- **Zone.** In this mode, a frame that encompasses nine focus areas appears on the LCD while you're shooting. You can move this grid around the frame with the joystick controller shown in Figure 1.13 (*not* the directional buttons), and the camera will select which of the focus areas to use to focus within the zone you specify.

- **Center.** The camera *always* uses the focus area in the center of the frame, so it will focus on the subject that's closest to the center in your composition.

- **Flexible Spot.** After you select this option from Focus Area, you can use the joystick or left/right directional buttons to specify Small, Medium, or Large focus areas. Then, while viewing your subject, you can move the focus frame (rectangle) around the screen to your desired location, using the joystick. (But *not* the directional buttons. Those who have worked with previous Sony cameras that lack a joystick may need to get used to not using the directional buttons to move the AF area.) Adjust the focus frame so it covers the most important subject in the scene; I'll discuss this topic in more detail in Chapter 8, where I'll cover many aspects of autofocus (as well as manual focus), including some not covered in this Quick Start chapter.

- **Expand Flexible Spot.** Like standard Flexible Spot, in this mode, if the camera is unable to lock in focus using the selected focus point, it will also use the eight adjacent points to try to achieve focus.

- **Tracking.** In this mode, the camera locks focus onto the subject area that is under the selected focus spot when the shutter button is depressed halfway. Then, if the subject moves (or you change the framing in the camera), the camera will continue to refocus *on that subject*. You can select this mode *only* when the focus mode is set to Continuous AF (AF-C). You can activate it for any of the five focus area options described above. That is, once you've highlighted Lock-On AF on the selection screen, you can then press the left-right directional button and choose Wide, Zone, Center, Flexible Spot, or Expand Flexible Spot.

SWITCHING AF AREAS/POINTS

You can set separate AF points and AF areas for horizontal and two different vertical orientations (horizontal upside-down is not supported) using the Camera Settings I-05 (AF1) menu, and I'll show you how to use the Switch Vertical/Horizontal AF Area option in Chapter 8.

Other Settings

There are a few other settings you can make if you're feeling ambitious, but don't feel bad if you postpone using these features until you've racked up a little more experience with your Sony a7R IV. By default, these camera features will be at Auto, so the camera will make a suitable setting.

Adjusting White Balance and ISO

If you like, you can custom-tailor your white balance (overall color balance) and the ISO level (sensitivity) as long as you're not using Intelligent Auto. To start out, it's best to leave the white balance (WB) at Auto, and to set the ISO to ISO 200 for daylight photos or to ISO 400 for pictures on a

dark, overcast day or indoors when you'll be shooting with an external flash. You can adjust white balance with the White Balance entry in the Camera Settings I-12 (Color/WB/Img. Processing) menu; the ISO can be set either from the Camera Settings I-09 (Exposure 1) menu, after pressing the ISO section of the control wheel (the right directional button), or from the Function and Quick Navi menus. (So many optional options!)

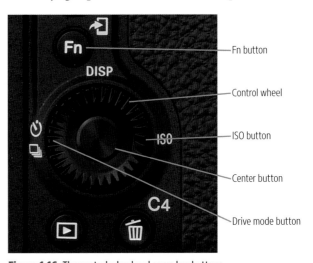

After accessing either feature, navigate (scroll) to make the desired setting with the directional buttons, joystick, or by rotating the control wheel. The control wheel and several of the most important buttons are shown in Figure 1.16.

Figure 1.16 The control wheel and some key buttons.

Using the Self-Timer

If you want to have time to get into the photo before the tripod-mounted camera takes the actual shot, the self-timer is what you need. You can select the self-timer using the Drive Mode button (the left directional button on the control wheel). Hold the Drive Mode button and rotate the control wheel to highlight either Self-Timer choice (described next). The dial also includes Single Shot, High-, Medium-, and Low-speed continuous, and various Bracketing options.

When the Drive Mode screen is visible, scroll up/down through the various options until you reach either the Self-timer (Single) or Self-timer CS (continuous) options. When the former is highlighted, press the directional buttons or joystick to choose 2-, 5-, or 10-second durations. With the Self-timer CS choice, you can also specify either 3 or 5 images to be taken after the timer elapses. Press the center button to confirm your choice and a self-timer icon will appear on the LCD monitor. Press the shutter release to lock focus and exposure and to start the timer. The self-timer lamp will blink, and the beeper will sound (unless you've silenced it in the menu) until the final two seconds when the lamp remains lit.

The multiple image option is handy if you are taking family group pictures with a few known inveterate blinkers to be pictured. Note that the self-timer setting is "sticky" and will still be in effect for multiple shots, even if you turn the camera off and power up again. When you're done using the self-timer, reset the camera to one of the other Drive Mode options.

Quick Start to Movie Making

I'm going to talk in more detail about your movie-making options with the a7R IV in Chapters 10 and 11. For now, though, I'll give you enough information to get started, in case a cinematic subject wanders into your field of view before you get to that chapter. The overrides you have set for certain aspects while shooting still photos will apply to the video clip that you'll record; these include exposure compensation, White Balance, any Creative Style, Metering Mode, Face Detection, D-Range Optimizer, and Lens Compensation. You'll even retain your aperture setting if the camera is in A mode or the shutter speed if it's in S mode. You also get access to the settings for the movie file formats (AVCHD, XAVC S HD, and XAVC S 4K modes we'll explore later in this book) and the resolution in the Record Setting item of the Camera Settings II section of the menu.

After you start recording, you can change the aperture or the shutter speed; either step will make your movie brighter or darker as you'll notice while viewing on the EVF or LCD while making the adjustments. However, you can also set plus or minus exposure compensation for that purpose while filming. The a7R IV provides an effective Continuous Autofocus in Movie mode and sound is recorded in stereo with the built-in mics located on the viewfinder housing on top of the camera.

Let's save the discussion of those aspects for Chapters 10 and 11. For the moment, let's just make a basic movie. With the camera turned on, aim at your subject and locate the red Movie record button located to the immediate right of the viewfinder. You don't have to switch to Movie mode using the mode dial; the Movie mode position simply gives you access to more movie-shooting controls, including the ability to adjust shutter speed and aperture.

Compose as you wish and press that button once to start the recording, and again to stop it; don't hold the button down. You can record for up to about 29 minutes consecutively if you have sufficient storage space on your memory card and charge in your battery. The camera will adjust the focus and exposure automatically, and you can zoom while recording, if you have a zoom lens attached to the camera.

After you finish recording a video clip, you can view it by pressing the Playback button at the lower right of the LCD screen, then pressing the Center button to start the movie displayed. While a movie is being played back, press the down button to access an operation panel with playback controls. (See Figure 1.17.) Highlight the control you want to use with the joystick or directional buttons. I'll explain the use of these buttons in more detail in Chapter 10. From left to right at the bottom of the figure, they are: Previous Movie File, Fast-Rewind, Pause/Resume, Fast-Forward, Next Movie File, Photo Capture, Sound Volume Adjustment, and Close Operation Panel.

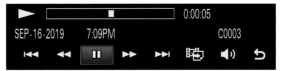

Figure 1.17 Movie playback options.

Reviewing the Images You've Taken

The Sony a7R IV has a broad range of playback and image review options. I'll cover them in more detail in Chapter 2. Initially, you'll want to learn just the basics for viewing still photos, so I'll assume you have taken only such images. Note that, as always, you have several options—the left/right edges of the control wheel, the joystick, and rear control dial can all be used to view the previous or next image. I'll stick to just one method in the list that follows. After shooting some video or JPEG and/or RAW photos, here's how to view them, using the controls shown in Figure 1.18:

- **Playback (Display the most recently taken image).** Press the Playback button. (It's the small button with a > symbol located to the lower right of the LCD monitor screen.) If you have shot both still photos as well as movie clips, the a7R IV will show both in playback mode. Just press the control wheel's center button to play the movie.

- **View a previous image.** Rotate the rear dial to the left.

- **View the next image.** Rotate the rear dial to the right.

- **Change information displayed.** While viewing a photo, press the DISP button (top directional button) repeatedly to cycle among the available displays: views that have no recording data, full recording data (f/stop, shutter speed, image quality/size, etc.), and a thumbnail image with histogram display. (I'll explain all these in Chapter 2.)

Figure 1.18 Review your images using the pertinent camera controls.

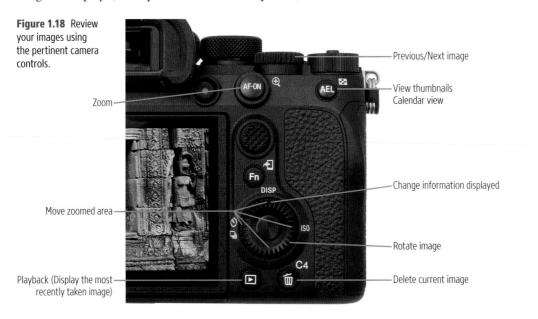

Zoom

Move zoomed area

Playback (Display the most recently taken image)

Previous/Next image

View thumbnails / Calendar view

Change information displayed

Rotate image

Delete current image

- **Delete current image.** Press the lower-right button, marked with a C4 (Custom 4) label and trash can icon, to delete the currently displayed image.

- **Rotate image.** While the image is displayed, press the MENU button and from the Playback 3 menu, select Rotate, followed by pressing the center button, to rotate the image on the screen 90 degrees. Successive presses of the center button rotate the image 90 degrees each time. (You won't likely need this feature unless you have disabled automatic rotation, which causes the camera to display your vertically oriented pictures already rotated. I'll explain how to activate/deactivate automatic rotation in Chapter 5.)

- **Zoom.** Press the AF-ON/Zoom button located to the right of the viewfinder window to zoom into the image. Rotating the control wheel on the back of the camera allows you to zoom in and out. You can also scroll around inside the image using the directional buttons. To exit this screen and return to normal view, press the MENU button.

- **Access thumbnail/calendar view.** While in Playback mode, press the AEL/Index button to display an index screen showing either 9 or 25 thumbnail images (select the number using the Image Index option in the Playback 3 menu). Keep scrolling downward to view the thumbnails of the next images (assuming you have shot lots of photos). Scroll to the thumbnail of the photo you want to view and press the center button; the photo will then fill the screen. In default Date View mode, the a7R IV arranges index images by date shot, and includes a calendar view you can use to look for pictures taken on a specific date. (See Figure 1.19.) (When the left bar of the playback screen is highlighted, press the center button to toggle between Calendar and Date View modes.) You can also choose to play back images using Folder View, or display only specific video file formats. I'll explain those options in more detail in Chapter 6.

VIEWING BURSTS

Capturing bursts of shots in continuous shooting modes produces a lot of separate images—up to 10 frames per second. Sony lets you speed up picture review by optionally "nesting" each burst sequence into a single "stack," which is represented by a single image overlaid on a "pile" icon. If you decide you do want to look at each image in the burst, press the center button to drill down into the stack, then press the left/right controls to view the images. Press center again to return to normal view. Enable the Display as Group in the Playback 3 menu to activate the stacking feature.

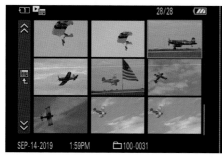 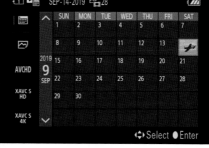

Figure 1.19 Viewing thumbnails (left) and calendar view (right).

Transferring Files to Your Computer

The final step in your picture-taking session will be to transfer the photos and/or movies you've taken to your computer for printing, further review, or editing. (You can also take your memory card to a retailer for printing if you don't want to go the do-it-yourself route.) Your a7R IV allows you to print directly to PictBridge-compatible printers, without downloading the photos to a computer and to create print orders right in the camera. It also offers an option for selecting which images to transfer to your computer.

For now, you'll probably want to transfer your images by either using the USB cable from the camera to the computer or by removing the memory card from the a7R IV and transferring the images with a card reader. The latter option is ordinarily the best, because it's usually much faster and doesn't deplete the camera's battery. However, you might need to use a cable transfer when you have the cable and a computer but no card reader. (You might be using the computer at a friend's home or the one at an Internet café, for example.)

Here's how to transfer images from a memory card to the computer using a card reader:

1. Turn off the camera.
2. Slide open the memory card compartment door and press on the card in Slot 1 or Slot 2, which causes it to pop up, so it can be removed from the slot. (You can see memory cards being removed in Figure 1.11.)
3. Insert the memory card into a memory card reader accessory that is plugged into your computer. Your installed software detects the files on the card and offers to transfer them. The card can also appear as a mass storage device on your desktop; in that case, you can open that and then drag and drop the files to your computer.

To transfer images from the camera to a Mac or PC computer using the USB cable:

1. Turn off the camera.
2. Open the lower port door on the left side of the camera (the upper door, marked with the candelabra-like USB symbol) and plug the USB cable furnished with the camera into the USB port inside that door.
3. Connect the other end of the USB cable to a USB port on your computer.
4. Turn on the camera. From this point on, the method is the same as in entry 3 in the card reader list above.

Wireless File Transfer

Your a7R IV is also equipped with built-in Wi-Fi which provides many options, including a method for wireless transfer of image files to a Mac or Windows computer when connected to a wireless network. This is a multi-faceted topic, so I won't begin to discuss it here; instead, you'll find full coverage in Chapter 5.

Your Camera Roadmap 2

Sony calls the official manual for the a7R IV a "Help Guide," which many take to mean that the average user needs a lot of help to use it. It's 698 pages long and includes page upon page of tiny black-and-white drawings impaled with dozens of callouts. Six pages are devoted just to *labeling* the 250-plus individual icons that can appear in the viewfinder and LCD screen. Seeking information about a specific feature is a lot like being presented with a world globe when what you really want is to locate the capital of Brazil.

I'll take a somewhat different approach in this book, particularly in this "roadmap" chapter. Rather than provide you with a satellite view, I'll give you a street-level map that includes close-up, full-color photos of the camera from several angles, with a smaller number of labels clearly pointing to each individual feature. And, I don't force you to flip back and forth among dozens of pages to find out what a component does. Each photo is accompanied by a brief description that summarizes the control's functions, so you can begin using it right away. *Only when a feature deserves a lengthy explanation do I direct you to a more detailed write-up later in the book.*

Using Cross-References

"I wish I could learn everything I need to know about a feature in one place!"

Some readers find cross-references inconvenient. They'd like to open the book to one page and read *everything* there is to know about using, for example, the bracketing feature. Unfortunately, it's not possible to explain everything there is to know about every button and control (or indeed, any feature of the a7R IV) with anything less than a mammoth 100-page chapter.

But it is possible to tell you what you absolutely *must* know to get started. So, if you're wondering what the right directional button on the control wheel does (it summons the ISO adjustment screen), I'll tell you up front, rather than have you flip to several pages. This book is not a scavenger hunt. But *after* I explain how to use the drive mode dial to select continuous shooting, I *will* provide a cross-reference to a longer explanation later in the book that clarifies the use of the various drive modes, the self-timer, and exposure bracketing. Unfortunately, it's impossible to understand some features without having a background in what related features do. Explanations of how to bracket exposures aren't useful for those who need to first understand all the available exposure options.

So, my strategy is to provide you with introductions in the earlier chapters, covering simple features completely, and relegating some of the in-depth explanations to later chapters. For veteran enthusiasts, the introductions may be all they need; less-experienced photographers will be glad I didn't make unwarranted assumptions about what they already know. Feedback from readers has told me that this kind of organization works best for the broadest possible audience working with a camera as sophisticated as the Sony a7R IV. (Remember, you were a beginner once, too, and can always skip any sections you like if you feel you won't benefit from a refresher.)

In all cases, however, by the time you finish this chapter, you'll have a good understanding of every control and of the various roles each can take on. I'll provide a lot more information about items in the menus and submenus in Chapters 3, 4, 5, and 6, but the following descriptions should certainly satisfy the button pusher and dial twirler in you.

Front View

When thinking about any given camera, we always imagine the front view. That's the view that your subjects see as you snap away, and the aspect that's shown in product publicity and on the box. The frontal angle is, essentially, the "face" of a camera like the Sony a7R IV. But, not surprisingly, most of the "business" of operating the camera happens *behind* it, where the photographer resides. The front of the camera has very few controls and features to worry about. These few controls are most obvious in Figure 2.1:

- **AF illuminator/Self-timer lamp.** This bright LED flashes while your camera counts down the 2-, 5-, or 10-second self-timer. In 5- and 10-second modes, the lamp blinks at a measured pace off and on at first, then switches to a constant glow in the final moments of the countdown. When the self-timer is set to 2 seconds, the lamp stays lit throughout the countdown. Stop the self-timer, once initiated, by pressing the shutter release a second time. This lamp also serves as the AF (autofocus) Illuminator, emitting its orange-red glow in dark conditions to help the camera's autofocus system achieve sharp focus. You can enable/disable the AF illuminator in the Camera Settings I-06 (AF2) menu. (You'll learn how to navigate menus in Chapter 3.)

Figure 2.1

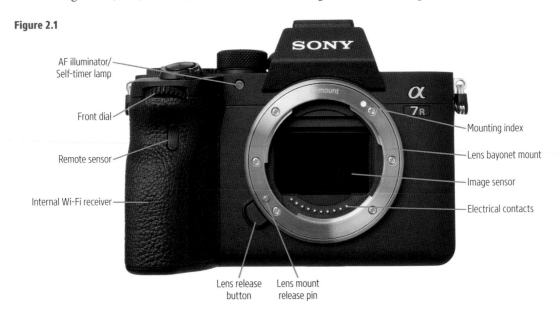

- **Front dial.** Adjusts various settings. It's often used in conjunction with the rear dial to control pairs of adjustments, such as shutter speed and aperture.

- **Remote sensor.** Detects infrared signals from the RMT-DSLR1 or RMT-DSLR2 Wireless Remote Commanders to take still pictures and (with the RMT-DSLR2 model only) to start/stop movie recording. Make sure the IR Remote Control entry in the Setup 3 menu is set to On. (That setting has no effect on the RMT-P1BT wireless remote commander, which is activated using the Network 2 menu, described in Chapter 5.) I'll show you how to adjust the various IR remote control options in Chapter 6.

- **Lens release button.** Press and hold this button to unlock the lens so you can rotate it to remove the lens from the camera.

- **Lens release pin.** Retracts when the release button is pressed, to allow removing the lens.

- **Mounting index.** Match this recessed, white index button with a similar white indicator on the camera's lens mount to line the two up for attaching the lens to the a7R IV.

- **Lens bayonet mount.** Grips the matching mount on the rear of the lens to secure the lens to the camera body. While some early E-mount cameras had relatively weak lens mounts, later models and the a7R IV have a sturdy mount fully capable of supporting many longer lenses. However, it's always a good idea to hold one hand under a very long lens and, if using a tripod or monopod, attach the support to the tripod socket of the lens (if available), rather than the one on the bottom of the a7R IV body.

- **Electrical contacts.** These metal contact points match up with a similar set of points on the lens, allowing for communication with the camera about matters such as focus and aperture.

- **Image sensor.** This fairly ordinary-looking little rectangle is the heart and soul of your digital camera. On the Sony camera, this EXMOR R sensor is a CMOS (complementary metal-oxide semiconductor) device, approximately 35.7×23.8 mm in size, with 61 megapixels of resolution.

- **Internal Wi-Fi receiver.** You can't access the Wi-Fi/Bluetooth antenna built into the hand grip of the a7R IV, but it's good to know where it is, so you don't accidentally wrap it in tin foil or something.

In Figure 2.2, left, you can see the terminals/ports hidden under the three port covers that provide a modicum of protection from dust and moisture for the six internal connectors. At right is the cable protector, which keeps your wired connectors firmly attached, as I'll describe shortly.

- **Microphone jack.** Allows connecting an external stereo microphone to provide better audio recording than the a7R IV's built-in mics.

- **PC/X flash sync terminal.** You can plug a dumb electronic flash unit, including studio flash, into this terminal, for manual operation only, as the only signal passed through this connection is a trigger for the strobe when the shutter opens. Note that the camera has no way of knowing that a flash is being used, so you must always remember to set the shutter speed to 1/250th second or slower (the a7R IV's *flash sync speed*, as described in Chapter 13). If you're using the electronic shutter for silent shooting, the top sync speed is 1/8th second.

- **Headphone jack.** You can monitor audio as you shoot video and listen to your movies during playback by plugging an external headphone into this jack.

Figure 2.2

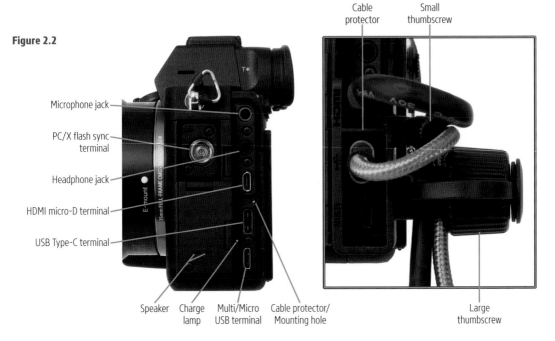

- **HDMI Micro-D terminal.** If you'd like to see the images from your camera on a television screen, you'll need to buy an HDMI cable (not included with the camera) to connect this port to an HDTV set or monitor. You can also link to an external video recorder when using DUAL REC mode to output 4K video to both the memory card and recorder. Be sure to get a Type-D cable; it has a male micro-HDMI connector at the camera end and a standard male HDMI connector at the TV end.

  The cable protector packaged with your camera (described later in this list) can be fitted to the mounting hole located in the lower center of the port cluster and used to keep the HDMI cable securely connected. Once the cable is connected, you can not only view your stored images on the TV in Playback mode, you can also see what the camera sees by viewing your TV screen. So, in effect, you can use your HDTV set as a large monitor to help with composition, focusing, and the like.

- **USB Type-C terminal.** You can use this USB 3 port (or the Multi/Micro USB 2.0 terminal described next) to connect the a7R IV to your computer. Sony provides a Type-C USB 3 cable with the camera. Either this connection or the USB 2.0 version can be used to upload images to a computer (although this USB 3.2 port is faster). You can also use either port to charge the battery while it's in the camera, and to upgrade the firmware to the latest version available for the a7R IV, using a file downloaded from the Sony support website. (www.esupport.sony.com.) The same port serves as a charging port when the USB cable is connected to a powered USB port on your computer or an AC charging adaptor or power pack, as I explained in Chapter 1.

- **Multi/Micro USB 2.0 terminal.** This connector can also be used to connect the a7R IV to your computer, or for charging the camera's battery, but uses the older (and slower) USB 2.0 protocol for camera/computer data transfer. Any USB 2.0 micro-B cable you have will work fine.
- **Cable protector/Mounting hole.** This threaded hole is used to attach the cable protector (see at left in Figure 2.2) so any combination of HDMI, USB Type-C, and Multi/Micro USB cables are kept from detaching. This is an especially useful feature when saving movies to an external video recorder, as a loose cable is obviously more than an inconvenience when capturing movies live.

  The protector is tricky to attach the first time you use it. Flip the two rear-most covers toward the front of the camera to open them. (That will give you access to those connectors when the protector is mounted.) Then, the bottom (the end opposite the chrome thumbscrew) of the cable protector slips into a ledge at the base of the lower port cover's opening. Turn the smaller, angled thumbscrew to secure the protector into the mounting hole. The large black thumbscrew can be removed to allow threading a cable downward, then replaced to secure the cable tightly.

- **Charge lamp.** This yellow LED flashes while battery charging is underway, and the camera is powered by an external source.
- **Speaker.** Sounds emanating from your camera emerge here.

The Sony a7R IV's Business End

The back panel of the Sony is where many of the camera's physical controls reside. There are roughly a dozen and a half of them, and, as I noted earlier, some can perform several functions, depending on the context.

Most of the controls on the back panel of the a7R IV are clustered on the right side of the body, with several located on the top edge. The key components labeled in Figure 2.3 include:

- **MENU button.** Press to enter the multi-tabbed menu system. This button also serves to exit many functions, including menu settings, and playback zoom. A Menu/Exit label will appear in the viewfinder or LCD in that case.
- **Viewfinder.** Look into this window to activate the eye-level electronic viewfinder (EVF), an internal OLED (organic LED) display with 5.76 million dots of resolution, and utilizing a Zeiss T* Coating to reduce reflections. On top of this, the a7R IV supports a customizable frame rate for this EVF, with options of either 60 fps or 120 fps.

  The viewfinder shows 100 percent of the frame at .78X magnification, making it equal or, I've found in most cases, *superior* to the optical viewfinders found in traditional digital SLR cameras. I actually like it much better in many circumstances, such as when shooting in dim light, when the view is quite bright. It's not as useful for continuous shooting as the camera may not show the previous image rather than a "live" view. You can frame your composition and see the information on the electronic viewfinder's display.

  While some shooters will use the rear-panel LCD monitor for framing their photos instead of the electronic viewfinder, the latter offers some benefits. On sunny days, when the LCD display is often obliterated by glare, the EVF is preferable. You might also want to use it for reviewing

Figure 2.3

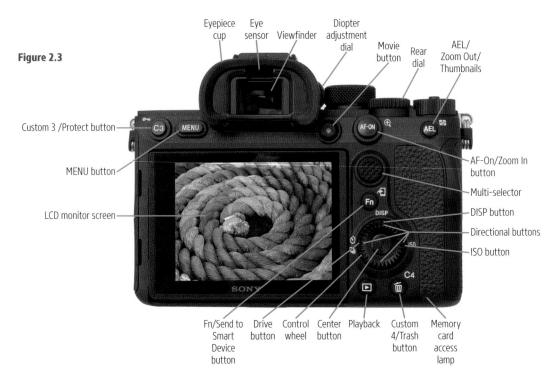

your images and video clips in Playback mode. Holding the camera pressed up against your face helps provide extra steadiness to reduce camera shake (and image blurring) at very slow shutter speeds. (Even the in-body 5-axis SteadyShot stabilization, or the optical SteadyShot included in some lenses, is not a panacea and is more effective when the camera is at least somewhat stable.) Both EVF and LCD monitors can be used with the camera's focus peaking and focus magnification features, which makes it easier to achieve sharp focus manually.

- **Movie button.** This button with a central red dot is located to the immediate right of the viewfinder window, where it's easy to access with your right thumb, but placed out of the way to avoid pressing it accidentally. This design was intended to minimize the risk of inadvertently starting to record a video clip. When you want to make a movie, there is no need to change the Shooting mode, or to fiddle with menu systems, as with some other cameras. Simply press the record button; when you're finished, press it again to stop recording. I'll discuss your movie-making options in Chapters 10 and 11.

- **Rear dial.** Adjusts various settings. It's often used in conjunction with the front dial to control pairs of adjustments, such as shutter speed and aperture.

- **Eye sensor.** This solid-state device senses when you (or anything else, unfortunately) approach the viewfinder; the camera then triggers a switch that turns off the back-panel LCD, activates the viewfinder screen, and starts the autofocus system. You can enable or disable either of these features, as I'll explain in Chapter 4.

- **Eyepiece cup.** This soft rubber frame seals out extraneous light when pressing your eye tightly up to the viewfinder, and it also protects your eyeglass lenses (if worn) from scratching.

- **Diopter adjustment dial.** As described in Chapter 1, you can spin this to adjust the built-in diopter correction to suit your vision. Since it's right beside the viewfinder window, it's a bit difficult to change the diopter setting while your eye is at the EVF, but it's worth taking the time to adjust it.

- **AF-ON/Zoom-In button.** This button has two modes, depending on whether you are in shooting mode or image playback mode:

  - **Shooting mode.** When you press this button in shooting mode, the a7R IV commences the auto-focus process. It's especially useful when you want to use back-button focus, as described in Chapter 8. (Back-button focus separates exposure lock from autofocus, allowing you to lock the exposure by pressing the shutter release halfway or you can re-compose at will, and later start AF only when you press a button on the back of the camera.)

  - **Playback mode.** While reviewing pictures in Playback mode, pressing this button activates the zoom feature and enlarges (magnifies) the full-screen image under review. When the image is magnified, you can rotate the control wheel to zoom in and out of the image, with 20 different levels of magnification. Once playback zoom is activated, you can also press the AF-ON/Zoom In button to enlarge further and the AEL/Zoom Out/Thumbnail button (described next) to zoom out. An Enlarge Image entry in the Playback 2 menu can also be used to activate the control wheel's zoom in/out feature but involves that extra step. To exit zooming, press the MENU button.

    Two options are available for the playback zoom feature found in the Playback 2 menu. Enlarge Initial Magnification can be set so the previous (most recent) zoom setting is used, or whether the standard magnification is applied. You may also select the initial position for the magnification window (as shown in the navigation box in the lower-left corner of the screen). Choose Focused Position to enlarge at the point used to focus the image, or Center to enlarge the center of the frame. For more Playback options, see Chapter 5.

- **AEL/Zoom Out/Thumbnail button.** This button also has two modes:

  - **Shooting mode.** Locks the exposure. The default behavior is to lock exposure *only* while the button is held down (AEL Hold). However, in the Custom Keys entries of the Camera Settings II-09 menu you can redefine the AEL button, so exposure is locked when the button is pressed once, and AE reactivated when the button is pressed a second time (AEL Toggle). See Chapter 4 for more information on redefining a host of the a7R IV's controls.

  - **Playback mode.** When an image under review is magnified, the Zoom Out button when pressed repeatedly reduces the magnification until the image is shown full frame again. In full-frame view, the button shows an Index display of thumbnail images (either 9 or 25 thumbnails, depending on your selection in the Image Index entry of the Playback 3 menu) and thence to Calendar view. These views were shown in Figure 1.19 in the previous chapter.

- **Custom 3/Protect button.** This button's dual features are not complicated. When shooting images, the C3 button changes Focus Mode (AF-S, AF-A, AF-C, Direct Manual Focus, and Manual Focus). In Playback mode, the button Protects or un-Protects the image being viewed, so it can/cannot be deleted. (Using the Format command overrides protection, however.) Both behaviors can be set to some other function using the Custom Key entry in the Camera Settings II-09 menu.

TIP As you'll learn, the control wheel and many buttons, including C1 and C2 (located on the top surface of the camera) as well as C3 and C4 (on the back panel), can be redefined to some other action, allowing you to tailor the camera's operation so it best suits your needs using the Camera Settings II-09 menu. However, keep in mind that customizing your camera's behavior can lead to confusion—both for you and for others you may allow to use the camera.

■ **Function/Send to Smartphone button.** In Shooting mode, press the Fn button to produce a screen with shooting setting options, as seen in Figure 2.4. By default, the 12 functions shown are displayed. However, as I'll describe in Chapter 4, you can choose exactly which functions you'd like to display; you aren't locked into 12. If you prefer, you can define a single row of six favorite functions or include some other number/combinations of choices. To adjust any of the functions, just follow these steps.

1. Press the Fn button and use the directional keys to highlight one of the options. **Note:** Exposure Compensation is available from the Function menu *only* when the Exposure Compensation dial on top of the camera (described later in this chapter) is set to zero.

2. When your setting is highlighted:

   • **Press the center button** to produce an adjustment screen with all the choices shown. You might need to do this as you are learning to use your camera and would like to see all your options arrayed in a vertical column. Then use the directional buttons to select the one you want. If a choice has multiple options, it will be accompanied by a right-pointing or left-pointing arrow. For example, when you choose the self-timer, you can press the left/right buttons to select timer durations of 2, 5, or 10 seconds.

   • **Optionally, you can rotate the control wheel** *or* **the front dial** to cycle among the available choices, which will appear one by one as you spin. Some of the choices have multiple options in this mode as well, which will appear on the screen below the main selections. Rotate the *rear* dial to select one of these.

3. Press the center button to confirm your choice. You'll be returned to the Function menu (press MENU to exit) or will exit the settings entirely.

Figure 2.4 Up to 12 user-selectable choices are available in the Function menu. This is the default layout.

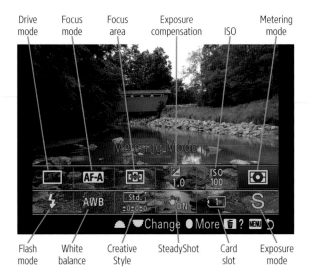

- **LCD monitor screen.** This swiveling screen can be used to preview images and to view them afterward, and to display/navigate menus. The LCD monitor has 3:2 proportions, which is perfect for previewing/shooting/reviewing stills. When you're shooting movies or using the 16:9 aspect ratio for stills, black bars appear at the top and bottom of the screen.

  You can set the LCD monitor brightness with an item in the Setup menu, to be discussed in Chapter 6; there's a special feature that provides a super-bright display, useful on bright days when the screen would otherwise be difficult to view. The monitor swivels upward or downward to provide a waist-level view (see Figure 2.5) or, by flipping the camera upside down, shoot images in "periscope" mode with the camera held overhead. The screen has limited touch functions, which I'll explain in the section that follows.

- **Playback button.** Displays the last picture taken. Thereafter, you can move back and forth among the available images by pressing the left/right directional buttons or spinning the control wheel (on the back of the camera) or front dial (on front of the camera) to advance or reverse one image at a time. To quit playback, press this button again. The a7R IV also exits Playback mode automatically when you press the shutter release button halfway (so you'll never be prevented from taking a picture on the spur of the moment because you happened to be viewing an image).

- **Multi-selector.** This joystick-like control serves as an all-purpose directional tool when navigating among menus, specifying a focus area within the frame when capturing images, and adjusting the zoomed area during playback. It can be pressed in the left/right/up/down directions and also diagonally. It's one of two controls that can be used in two modes; the other is the control wheel, described next.

  - **Menu mode.** Navigate among menu tabs and screens using the directional buttons. In menus, it serves as an Enter/OK button when you press down on it.

  - **Shooting mode.** Use the directional buttons to position focus point (when available) and press down to move the focus point/area to the center of the frame.

  - **Playback mode.** Directional buttons move the zoomed area around with the frame. Press down to exit zoomed view.

Figure 2.5 Tilting LCD.

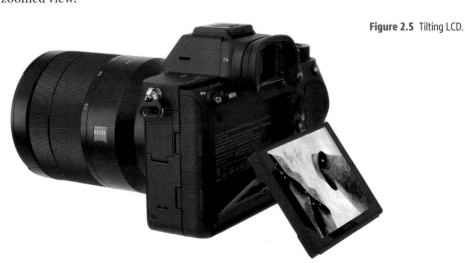

- **Control wheel.** This ridged dial, which surrounds the large center button, also has multiple functions, depending on the camera's mode. In both Shooting and Playback modes it can be useful for navigating menu screens to get to the item or option you want to use.

  The control wheel performs several important functions and is the other control on the camera that can be activated in two different ways: you can rotate the ridged part of the wheel to perform certain actions (such as navigation or setting exposure controls), and you can press on the various edges at top, bottom, left, and right. In that mode the edges serve as directional buttons for navigating through menu screens, for example. I'll explain the use of the "button" component of the control wheel in the entry that follows this one. The functions of the wheel itself include:

  - **Shooting mode.** By default, no function is assigned to the control wheel when shooting still photographs. However, you can redefine it to perform several optional functions if you like. Using the Custom Key entry of the Camera Settings II-09 menu, you can define the control wheel to move the AF point left/right or up/down, change the aperture, shutter speed, or ISO, or set white balance, exposure compensation, audio level, Creative Style, or Picture Effect. Note that all these can be readily adjusted using their default controls, but you can assign these functions to the control wheel if you prefer.

  - **Playback mode.** When reviewing images during playback, the control wheel always moves forward to the next image (when rotated clockwise) or to the previous image (when rotated counterclockwise). The rear dial and left/right buttons can also be used for that function. You cannot redefine the control wheel to do something else during playback.

- **Control wheel buttons (Playback mode).** During image review, the buttons along the edge of the control wheel are used for navigating. Keep in mind that many of the directional buttons' functions are also available using the multi-selector joystick. When an image is magnified in Playback mode, all four buttons and their diagonal counterparts can be used to move the viewing area around within the magnified image and within the index screens during playback. When the image is not magnified, the left/right buttons move to the previous/next image on your memory card in Playback mode.

YOUR CHOICE

Throughout this book, I'm using the terms directional buttons, directional controls, left/right button/control or similar navigational descriptions. In most cases, you can use either the multi-selector joystick or the directional buttons for navigation, and I will generally refer to them as directional controls rather than explicitly say *multi-selector joystick* or *left/right/up/down buttons*. Choose the method that works best for you.

- **Control wheel buttons (Shooting mode).** The center, left, and right directional buttons (but not the down button) also have a default specific purpose that activates when pressed, and that function is labeled on the area outside the wheel itself. You can also redefine any of these keys (including Down) using the Custom Keys entry in the Camera Settings II-09 menu, as described in Chapter 4.

Here's a summary of their default definitions:

- **Up key/DISP button.** The up key is labeled as DISP, for Display Contents, and it provides display-oriented functions, which vary depending on your Shooting/Playback mode:

  - **Shooting mode.** When the camera is in Shooting mode, press the DISP button repeatedly to cycle among the three screens that display data in the electronic viewfinder display or the six screens that display information about current settings on the LCD screen.

    The default display for the LCD is called Display All Info. This provides a full information display with a great deal of data overlaid over the live preview to show the settings in effect. The data provided when the camera is in a SCN mode or either Auto mode is quite limited; use P, A, S, or M mode to view all the available data in each display option.

    When you keep pressing the DISP button, the camera LCD cycles through other viewing modes, including No Display Info, which provides a few bits of data, a Graphic Display that shows the shutter speed and aperture on two related scales along with some recording information, and a basic display with a histogram in the bottom right of the screen. There is also a For Viewfinder/Quick Navi text information screen that omits the thumbnail and shows only shooting information. When you press the Fn button when the For Viewfinder screen is visible, you can then select and change settings, as I'll describe shortly. You can enable/disable each of these information displays using the DISP entry within the Camera Settings II-07 menu, as I'll explain in Chapter 4.

  - **Playback mode.** In Playback mode, the DISP button offers different display options, as you would expect. When viewing still images during playback, press the DISP button to cycle among the three available playback screens: full recording data, histogram with recording data, and no recording data. When displaying a movie on the screen, the DISP button produces only two screens: with or without recording information. There is no histogram display available.

- **Down button.** By default, the down key has no special function, but you can define one of your choices using the Custom Keys entry in the Camera Settings II-09 menu, as described in Chapter 4.

- **Left button/Drive mode button.** One press of this button in a compatible Shooting mode leads to a series of options that let you set the self-timer, enable the camera to shoot one frame at a time or continuously at a fast or very fast rate, or set up exposure bracketing. The latter causes the camera to automatically take a series of shots, varying the exposure for each to ensure you get the best exposure possible.

  When you scroll to the Self-timer or Bracket item, you can press the right key to adjust options for those drive modes, as discussed in Chapter 5.

- **Right button/ISO button.** When not helping you navigate to the right through menus and other screens, this button lets you activate the ISO screen in a compatible Shooting mode. You can then scroll up/down among the options by rotating the camera's rear dial or control wheel or by pressing the wheel's directional buttons.

- **Center button.** In shooting mode, the center button activates Eye AF, which tells the a7R IV to look for human eyes and focus on them. (You'll find more on autofocus in Chapter 8.) In Playback mode, it exits the zoom function, while when using menus, it serves as an OK/Enter button. You can redefine the center button's behavior during still shooting and movie modes, as I'll explain in Chapter 4.
- **Custom 4/Delete button.** This button enables/disables the touch screen when in Shooting mode (although you can specify another function using the Custom Keys feature). In Playback mode, the button serves as a delete key.
- **Memory card access lamp.** Flashes red while the memory card is being written to. It is located on the back of the camera, to the right of the C4/Trash button.

Introducing the Touch Screen/Pad

Sony has included a touch screen/pad in the a7R IV's arsenal of tools. The dual screen/pad nomenclature is applied because the touch feature can be used in two different ways: as a touch screen when you are using the LCD monitor to compose your photos and as a touch pad that you can tap when the camera is raised to your eye and you're using the electronic viewfinder. This section explains both modes and the options available once you've set up touch operations using the step-by-step instructions in Chapter 4.

Before you wax ecstatic, you'll want to know that the touch features are limited to the ability to specify a focus point when shooting stills and videos. You can't select menu entries, type in text, scroll through playback views, or pinch/expand with your fingertips to zoom in and out during image review. However, the touch focus feature is quite useful, especially when shooting movies, as it allows selecting a focus area with a gentle tap. Here are the two modes:

- **Touch screen.** When active and you're using the LCD monitor to compose, you can select a focus point or zone anywhere that the a7R IV is able to achieve autofocus (that is, most of the frame other than the edges). You can tap the screen or hold down your finger and slide the focus area around. A "Focus Cancel" message appears; press the center button to cancel your focus selection. A quick tap may not register; this function requires a firm press. I'll explain the various AF-area modes in Chapter 8.
- **Touch pad.** When touch pad mode is active and you're using the electronic viewfinder to compose, you can touch the LCD monitor screen to specify the focus area. You don't have to tap the exact area (actually, that's impossible, because you're not actually looking at the LCD). Instead, when you touch the pad, a focus point appears in the viewfinder *relative to the location on the LCD.* That is, if you tap the center of the sensitive area, the focus point appears in the center; tap to the right or left, and the focus area appears to the right or left side. As I'll explain shortly, that mode is needed because you can change the size of the sensitive area of the LCD screen. Once the focus area is displayed, keep your finger on the screen and slide it around to the position you want, using your view through the EVF as your reference.

Touch Options

Three touch options are available from the Setup 2 and 3 menus. I'm not going to explain how to navigate menus in this Quick Start. You can learn exactly how to enter touch screen options in Chapter 6. Here, I'll just quickly describe the adjustments you can make, and why.

- **Touch operation.** Here you can turn touch operation on or off. If you don't want to use the touch screen you can disable it to avoid moving your focus point when you accidentally touch it.
- **Touch panel/pad.** You can define whether the LCD-oriented Touch Panel or EVF-oriented Touch Pad, or *both* are active. Select Touch Panel Only, and the touch features operate only when you are composing using the LCD monitor; when you bring the camera up to your eye, the touch panel is disabled. Select Touch Pad Only, and touch features are disabled until you bring the camera up to your eye.
- **Touch pad settings.** This entry has three adjustments:
  - **Operation in vertical orientation.** You can specify whether touch controls are available when the camera is oriented in the vertical position (On), or only when the camera is held in horizontal orientation (Off). The touch feature can be a little awkward to use when rotated vertically, so some prefer to disable touch control for that mode.
  - **Touch position mode.** Specify whether touch functions operate using the *absolute* position on your screen (tap an exact position on the screen to move the focus point to the equivalent position on the sensor) or a *relative* position (tap the screen anywhere in the sensitive area, and then slide your finger to move the focus point in that direction from its current position).
  - **Operation area.** By default, the entire touch pad is sensitive when using the EVF, and that works well for most people. However, if your left eye is dominant (i.e., you're "left-eyed"), your nose will touch the screen, and the a7R IV registers that as a finger press. To fix that or to adjust for your personal preferences, you can limit sensitivity of the touch *pad* to the right *or* left 1/2 or 1/4 areas of the screen; or the upper-right, lower-right, upper-left, or lower-left corners. The "relative" orientation remains the same but is limited to that reduced area.

LCD Panel Data Displays

The Sony a7R IV provides a tilting and expansive 3-inch color LCD with high resolution to display everything you need to see, from images to a collection of informational data displays. Some of the data is shown only when you are viewing the Display All Info screen, but even then, not every item of data will be available all the time. (See Figure 2.6.) As discussed earlier, the electronic viewfinder display options provide much less data to avoid cluttering the live preview with numerals and icons during serious photography. **Note:** when you tilt the LCD monitor away from the camera body, the viewfinder is disabled, because the camera assumes you will be composing your image and performing other functions only with the LCD.

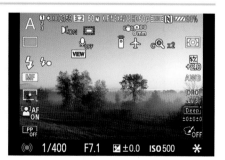

Figure 2.6 The Display All Info screen on the LCD.

While it is not possible to describe all the dozens and dozens of icons available for the LCD screen (indeed, it's not possible for *all* the icons shown in Figure 2.6 to appear simultaneously), you'll find all of them shown on pages 38 to 43 of the Sony Help Guide. The following is a description of the most important information that the camera can display in the LCD in Display All Info when it's set for P, A, S, or M mode; less data is available in other display modes and when other Shooting modes are being used. The For Viewfinder/Quick Navi text-only displays (shown only on the LCD monitor and not in the viewfinder) are pictured in Figures 2.7 and 2.8.

- **Shooting mode.** Shows whether you're using Program Auto, Aperture Priority, Shutter Priority, Manual, Panorama, one of the scene modes, or one of the two Auto modes.
- **Memory card/Uploading status.** Indicates whether a memory card is in the camera. (If you remove the card, a blinking NO CARD indicator will appear instead.) If the camera is connected using Wi-Fi, the indicator will display icons representing the upload status.
- **Exposures remaining.** Shows the approximate number of shots available to be taken on the memory card, assuming current conditions, such as image size and quality. When shooting a movie, the recordable time remaining is shown instead.
- **Aspect ratio/Image size.** Shows whether the camera is set for the default 3:2 aspect ratio or optional 4:3, 1:1, and wide-screen 16:9 aspect ratios (the image size icon changes to a "stretched" version when the aspect ratio is set to 16:9), and whether you're shooting Large-, Medium-, or Small-resolution images. When the camera is not set to the default 3:2 aspect ratio, wider black bands at the top and the bottom appear appropriate to the selected format.
- **Image quality.** Your image quality setting (JPEG Extra Fine, JPEG Fine, JPEG Standard, RAW, or RAW & JPEG) is displayed.
- **Frame rate/Movie recording settings.** These icons show what movie settings are in use, such as 60i FH (full HD video at 60i). I'll discuss your movie-making options, including file formats and size, in Chapter 10.
- **NFC active indicator.** Shows when your a7R IV is linked to another device using Near Field Communications.

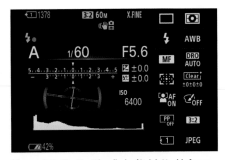

Figure 2.7 The For Viewfinder/Quick Navi information screen is available only for the LCD monitor and is not shown in the viewfinder.

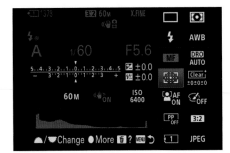

Figure 2.8 Change settings using the Quick Navi Function screen.

- **Battery status.** The remaining battery life (in percent) is indicated by this icon.
- **Metering mode.** The icons represent Multi, Center, or Spot metering. (See Chapter 9 for more detail.)
- **Flash exposure compensation.** This icon is shown whenever an external flash is active to indicate the level of flash exposure compensation, if any, that you have set.
- **White balance.** Shows current white balance setting. The choices are Auto White Balance, Daylight, Shade, Cloudy, Incandescent, Fluorescent, Flash, Color Temperature, and Custom. I'll discuss white balance settings and adjustments in Chapter 4.
- **Dynamic Range Optimizer.** Indicates the type of dynamic range optimization (highlight/shadow detail enhancement) in use: Off, Auto DRO, and levels 1–5 of DRO.
- **Creative Style.** Indicates which of the Creative Style settings (Standard, Vivid, Neutral, Clear, Deep, Light, Portrait, Landscape, Sunset, Night Scene, Autumn Leaves, Black-and-White, or Sepia) is being applied.
- **Picture effect.** Shows which of the special effects, such as Toy Camera, Pop Color, or Posterization, is being applied. I'll explain these options in Chapter 3.
- **SteadyShot indicator.** Provides information as to whether the image stabilizer is On or Off if you're using a lens with the SteadyShot mechanism and warns you that the shutter speed will be too long for the stabilizer to fully compensate for camera shake.
- **Flash charge in progress.** This lightning bolt icon appears on the screen when the flash unit is active; a solid orange dot beside it indicates the flash has recycled (charged) and is ready to fire.
- **AF illuminator status.** This icon appears when conditions are dark enough that the AF Illuminator will be needed to light up the area so that the autofocus system can operate properly.
- **Flash mode.** Provides flash mode information when an external flash is active. The possible choices are Flash Off, Autoflash, Fill Flash, Slow Sync, Rear Curtain, and Wireless. Not all these choices are available at all times. I'll discuss flash options in more detail in Chapter 13.
- **Drive mode.** Shows whether the camera is set for Single-shot, Continuous shooting, Continuous shooting, Self-timer, Self-timer with continuous shooting, or Exposure bracketing. There is one additional option available: Remote Commander, which sets up the camera to be controlled by an infrared remote control.
- **AE Lock.** Appears when autoexposure has been locked at the current setting.
- **ISO setting.** Indicates the sensor ISO sensitivity currently set, either Auto ISO or a numerical value. I'll discuss this camera feature in Chapter 9.
- **Exposure compensation.** This indicator shows the amount of exposure compensation, if any, currently set.
- **Aperture.** Displays the current f/stop set by the camera or, in Manual or Aperture Priority mode, as set by the user. If you're viewing the Graphic display, icons indicate that wider apertures produce less depth-of-field (a "blurry" background) while smaller apertures provide a greater range of acceptable sharpness (increasing the odds of a more distinct background).

- **Shutter speed.** Shows the current shutter speed, either as set by the camera's autoexposure system or, in Manual or Shutter Priority mode, as set by the user. If the camera's Graphic display is used, the screen illustrates that faster shutter speeds are better for action and slower speeds are fine for scenes with less movement.
- **Focus indicator.** Flashes while focus is underway, and turns a solid green when focus is confirmed.
- **Focus mode.** Shows the currently selected focus mode, such as AF-S, AF-C, DMF (Direct Manual Focus), or MF (Manual Focus), as explained in Chapter 9.
- **Focus area mode.** Displays the active focus area mode, such as Wide, Zone, Center, or Flexible Spot, as explained in Chapter 9.
- **Face Priority mode.** Shows status of Face Detection mode (on/off). When the feature is activated, the camera attempts to detect faces in the scene before it, and, if it does, it adjusts autofocus, exposure, and white balance accordingly. When the Face Registration feature is also in use, the camera can detect a face that you have registered as a favorite. The camera can also use Eye AF to locate and focus on human eyes found within the frame, as long as you're using Single Autofocus (AF-S). Autofocus options are discussed in more detail in Chapter 8.
- **Picture Profile.** If you've specified a picture profile image customization setting in the Camera Settings I-12, your choice (from PP1 to PP10) is indicated here. I discuss picture profiles in Chapter 3.
- **Zoom.** Shows when digital zoom modes are active.
- **Setting Effect.** Indicates whether the LCD shows the effects of any adjustments, including exposure, white balance, or Picture Effects in Shooting mode.
- **Database indicator.** This warning appears when your memory card's image database is full or has errors.
- **Audio recording.** Shows whether sound recording is enabled/disabled for movie shooting.
- **Airplane mode.** Appears when Airplane mode has disabled Wi-Fi and NFC communications.

Using the Quick Navi Function Menu

If you select the For Viewfinder screen by pressing the DISP button until it appears, the LCD monitor shows the For Viewfinder display, with only the data and no live view of the scene, as you can see in Figure 2.7. Press the Fn button to switch to the Quick Navi screen (see Figure 2.8). You can then use the multi-selector joystick or the left/right/up/down directional buttons to highlight any of the settings that are not grayed out.

Once an option is highlighted, you can rotate the control wheel to change its settings quickly or press OK (either the center button or multi-selector) to produce a screen with all the options. Use directional buttons and the OK button to select the option you want. The Quick Navi screen is, in effect, a more fully featured Function menu. When the Quick Navi display is visible on the LCD monitor, you must compose images using the electronic viewfinder.

Going Topside

The top surface of the a7R IV has several frequently accessed controls of its own. They are labeled in Figure 2.9:

- **Focal plane indicator.** Precision macro and scientific photography sometimes requires knowing exactly where the focal plane of the sensor is. The symbol etched on the top of the camera marks that plane.

- **Multi interface shoe.** This "standard" accessory shoe is used for electronic flash units and contains extra electrical contacts for use with Sony-brand microphones, such as the Sony ECM-XYSTM1 microphone, Sony-compatible electronic flash, and other accessories. However, it is also compatible with the ISO-518 hot shoe used by virtually all other camera manufacturers. While other flashes can be attached and fired, only Sony-compatible units can take advantage of wireless operation, through-the-lens (TTL) metering, and other options.

  The multi interface shoe replaces the non-standard Minolta-style proprietary "iISO" shoe used by Sony for many of its cameras until about 2012. The older shoe required adapters to use non-Sony accessories. The new multi interface connector can still be used with older Sony flash units and accessories, but it requires an adapter of its own for backward compatibility. If you own no older Sony electronic flash or accessories, you can simply move forward and purchase gear for the new, more standard hot shoe.

- **Stereo microphones.** A pair of microphones on the top panel of the camera can capture stereophonic audio while making movies.

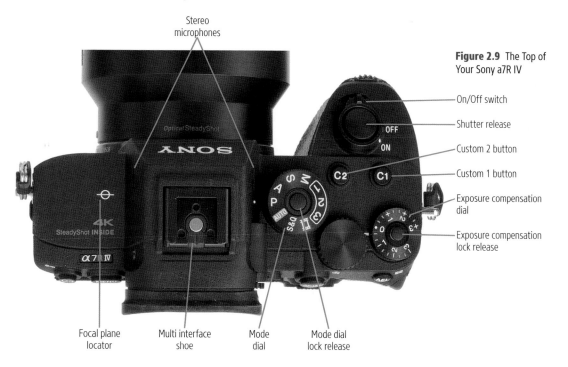

Figure 2.9 The Top of Your Sony a7R IV

- **Mode dial/Mode Dial Lock Release button.** Press the center Lock Release button and rotate this dial to select Shooting modes including Manual exposure, Shutter Priority, Aperture Priority, Program Auto, Intelligent Auto, Slow Motion/Quick Motion (S&Q), Movie mode, and the Memory Recall positions, numbered 1, 2, and 3 (which each allow you to choose predefined groups of settings for each, as described in Chapter 6).

- **Exposure Compensation dial.** Rotate this dial to add or subtract up to three stops' worth of exposure. The button in the center of the dial is used to lock or unlock it; with the button depressed, the exposure compensation dial is locked and cannot be accidentally (or intentionally) rotated.

- **On/Off switch.** Rotate to the right to turn the camera on; to the left to switch it off.

- **Shutter release button.** Partially depress this button to lock in exposure and focus. Press it all the way to take the picture. Hold this button down to take a continuous stream of images when the drive mode is set for Continuous shooting. Tapping the shutter release when the camera's power save feature has turned off the autoexposure and autofocus mechanisms reactivates both. When a review image or menu screen is displayed on the LCD, tapping this button removes that display, returning the camera to the standard view and reactivating the autoexposure and autofocus mechanisms.

- **Custom 1 button.** By default, this summons the white balance menu. The Custom 1 button can also be re-defined to perform any of several different functions, such as metering mode, creative style, drive mode, focus mode, flash mode, flash compensation, focus area, exposure compensation, and more than 50 (count 'em!) other behaviors. You can also select Not Set to deactivate it entirely. In Chapter 4, I'll show you how to redefine this button in the Custom Key Settings entry of the Camera Settings II-09 menu.

- **Custom 2 button.** By default, this button activates focus area (described in more detail in Chapter 8) but can be redefined to other functions.

The bottom panel of your a7R IV has only a few components, illustrated in Figure 2.10.

- **Tripod socket.** Attach the camera to the Sony VG-C4EM vertical grip, flash bracket, tripod, monopod, or other support using this standard receptacle. The socket is positioned roughly behind the optical center of the lens, a decent location when using a tripod with a pan (side rotating) movement, compared to an off-center orientation. For most accurate panning, the socket would ideally be placed a little forward (in *front* of the camera body) so the pivot point is located *under* the optical center of the lens, but you can't have everything. There are special attachments you can use to accomplish this if you like.

- **Vertical grip alignment holes.** These two small depressions located on either side of the battery door mate with matching nubs on the vertical grip to ensure correct alignment as the grip is attached to the bottom of the camera.

- **Battery compartment door.** Slide the door open to access the battery. This door can be removed when you attach an optional battery grip.

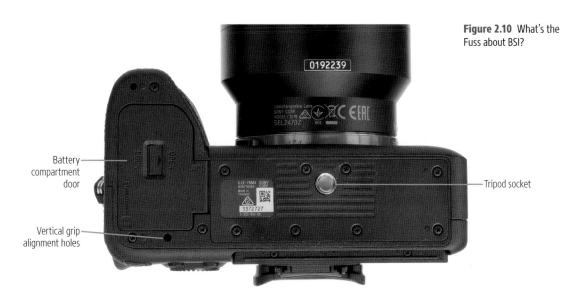

Figure 2.10 What's the Fuss about BSI?

Battery compartment door

Vertical grip alignment holes

Tripod socket

So far, I've given you an introduction to the most important physical components of your a7R IV—except for the camera's truly impressive sensor. Traditionally, packing more pixels into a given sensor size yields higher resolution, but results in smaller pixels with less surface area to gather light. So, the a7R IV's prodigious 61MP resolution surely must have required squeezing even tinier photosites into your camera's (roughly 36mm × 24mm) sensor, right?

Fortunately for us, not so! The Sony a7R IV has an innovative back-side illuminated (BSI) sensor. (Some call this sensor configuration *back-illuminated*, but the term *back-side illuminated* is the more common industry term.) This sensor gives the a7R IV remarkable low-light performance with reduced noise, compared to most other high-resolution sensors. The secret to all this good stuff is flipping the electronics around so the light-sensitive photosites are larger and closer to the incoming photons, thanks to the BSI configuration.

As I mentioned earlier, packing more light-gathering "pixels" (photodiodes) onto a sensor to produce high resolution requires using the tiniest "pixels" possible. Smaller pixels are less efficient at collecting light (photons) and processing the captured image to increase sensitivity results in more random artifacts. We call that "high ISO" noise. (A second type of visual noise is produced from long exposures.)

The a7R IV reduces high ISO noise by *increasing* the relative size of the photosites. That's possible because with a traditional front-illuminated sensor (shown at left in Figure 2.11), the chip's image-processing circuitry occupies much of the surface, leaving only a small photosensitive area at the bottom of a deep "well." Sony's BSI sensor reverses the position of the circuitry and photodiode components, so that a larger area can be occupied by the photosites, with the electronics positioned *underneath*, closer to the back of the camera, rather than closer to the rear of the lens. (See Figure 2.11, right.)

The figure shows a super-simplified rendition of what happens. (Actual sensors look nothing like this; the diagram includes only one set of three red, green, and blue photosites, is not to scale, and I

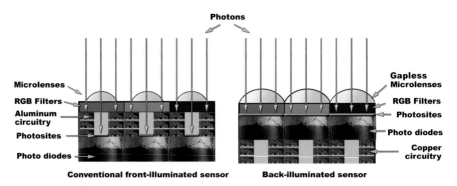

Figure 2.11 A conventional front-illuminated sensor (left), and a back-illuminated sensor (right).

show only three "beams" of light arriving at the sensor, when photons actually come from multiple directions.) With the conventional front-illuminated sensor at left, incoming light passes through microlenses that focus it on the photosites, which are located at the bottom of a well that resides between the on-chip aluminum circuitry. Even accounting for the microlens's focusing properties, the relative angles that result in light falling on the photosensitive area collected from the edges of the incoming image can be rather steep. Other photons (not shown) strike the sides of the wells or the area of the chip occupied by electronic circuitry and bounce back or around.

This limitation on the angle of incidence accounts for why vendors have been forced to develop "digital" lenses, which, unlike lenses designed for film cameras, focus light on the sensor from less steep angles. That explains, in general, why the a7R IV functions better in this regard than most other digital cameras when using older "non-digital" lenses.

At right in the figure is a representation of a back-illuminated sensor. Like the conventional sensor, it includes microlenses that focus the illumination before it passes through a red, green, or blue filter to the photosite. But because those photosites are larger, the minuscule focusing optics are larger, too, providing *gapless microlenses* that gather virtually all the illumination falling on the sensor. And, unlike the front-illuminated sensor, there is no deep well, and, without the need for intervening circuitry, the photosensitive area (shown in magenta for both types of sensors) is much larger. The electronics—faster copper (not aluminum) circuitry with lower resistance—have been moved to the back side of the sensor.

A typical conventional full-frame sensor captures only 30 to 80 percent of the light striking it, whereas a BSI sensor can grab nearly 100 percent of the photons. The angle of incidence is not nearly as crucial, making BSI sensors more similar in that respect to old-time film grain technology. The combination of larger photosensitive surface area and improved acceptable angles for incoming photons are the main factors in the Sony a7R IV's superior low-light performance. The speedy copper wiring and enhanced processing algorithms in the digital image processor chip also help—and give the camera its speedy continuous shooting speeds, as well. This camera is as close as you can get to a "do-everything" model, featuring high resolution, reduced noise, and continuous shooting suitable for the fastest action.

I don't normally venture so deeply into techie territory in my camera guides, but BSI sensors (which previously have been used in other devices with especially tiny sensors, such as cell phone cameras) will henceforth play a major part in enthusiast photography technology.

Camera Settings I Menu | 3

The a7R IV has a remarkable number of features and options you can use to customize the way your camera operates. Not only can you change settings used at the time the picture is taken, but you can adjust the way your camera behaves. This chapter and the next three will help you sort out the settings for all the menus. These include the Camera Settings I, Camera Settings II, Network, Playback, and Setup menus, plus the My Menu custom menu screen. This chapter details options with the Camera Settings I menu; the Camera Settings II menu will be covered in Chapter 4; the Network and Playback menus in Chapter 5; and the Setup and My Menu options will be addressed in Chapter 6.

Why four entire chapters just on the menus, when other sources may have just a single chapter with a line or two about each menu entry explaining what they do? As you're discovering, the a7R IV is an incredibly versatile camera with a mind-numbing number of different menu entries, many of which have submenus and multiple options. Even if you're a Sony veteran or an advanced photo enthusiast, you want more than just a brief explanation of what all the menu options do. You also need to know what they *don't* do, *when* to use each one, and, most importantly, when *not* to use them.

And, I'll bet, you purchased this book because you also wanted to know *my* personal preferences for settings and how I use these features. When I share what I know in person at workshops and other sessions with groups of photographers, I always tell them my informal motto: *I make terrible mistakes, so you don't have to!* I like to push cameras to their limits and, in the process, discover exactly what they can do, and what they can't.

So, like most of the rest of this book, Chapters 3 to 6 will cover both aspects in some detail. I'm not going to waste a lot of space on some of the more obvious menu choices in these chapters, especially those with only On/Off or Enable/Disable options. Instead, I'll concentrate on the more complex aspects of setup, such as autofocus. I'll start with an overview of using the camera's menus themselves.

Anatomy of the Menus

The menu system is quite easy to navigate. Pressing the MENU button takes you to a screen like the one shown in Figure 3.1. Rotate the front dial to move from one top-level menu tab to the next. Each tab is assigned a color: Camera Settings I (red), Camera Settings II (purple), Network (green), Playback (blue), Setup (yellow), and My Menu (gray). When a tab is active its highlight color will be bright, and the hues of the other tabs more subdued, as you can see in the figure.

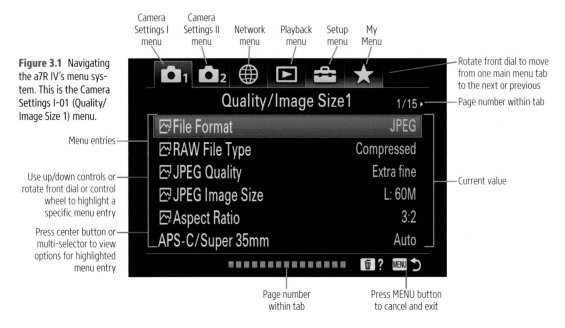

Figure 3.1 Navigating the a7R IV's menu system. This is the Camera Settings I-01 (Quality/Image Size 1) menu.

To navigate among menu entries:

- **Change tabs.** You can move from one main menu tab to another at any time by rotating the front dial clockwise (to move toward tabs on the right) or counter-clockwise (to move to the left). **Note:** Front dial tab navigation is an improvement new to the a7R IV; previous Sony full-frame models you may have used required the methods described next. It's usually much faster to just jump from tab to tab with the front dial.

  When only the tab is highlighted (that is, none of its entries are highlighted in orange), you can also move from one tab to the next by using any of the left/right controls, including the control wheel's directional buttons, by pressing the multi-selector left/right, or by rotating the rear dial.

  While navigating menu entries, when you navigate past the final entry within a tab, highlighting wraps around to the first entry on the next tab (or last entry on the previous tab, if you're navigating in the reverse direction).

- **Change menu pages.** Each main menu tab has multiple pages. When any entry in a menu tab is highlighted you can move from one page within that tab to the next using the left/right controls or rear dial. When you reach the last page of a tab's menus, additional movement wraps over to the first page of the next tab. The current page within a tab is shown by a numeric value (such as 1/14) and by a series of boxes at the bottom of the screen (you'll find both in Figure 3.1).

  For example, if you are using the Camera Settings I menu, the right key will take you from Camera Settings I-01 to Camera Settings I-02, and thence onward to the Camera Settings I-03 to I-15 tabs. Pressing the right key an additional time takes you onward to the Camera Settings II-01 page.

- **Select a menu entry.** To choose a menu entry within the pages of a main menu tab, use the up/down controls of the control wheel's directional buttons or the multi-selector joystick. You can also rotate the front dial or control wheel to highlight a specific menu entry.
- **Make adjustments.** When a menu entry is highlighted, press the control wheel's center button or the multi-selector to view options. After making adjustments, press the button again to confirm and exit, or MENU to cancel.

 TIP Reminder: Each of the main tabs may have several pages: the Camera Settings I menu has tabs 1 to 15; Camera Settings II menu has pages 1 to 11; Network has 4 pages; Playback menu has 3; and the Setup menu boasts pages 1 to 7. My Menu starts out with one page, but you may add additional pages to accommodate up to 30 entries. The advantage to having so many menu pages is that all the entries for a given page can be shown on a single screen, with no downward scrolling required.

Press the down button or rotate the front dial or the control wheel to move the highlighting down into the selected tab to the entry you want to work with. You can choose any item in the displayed page and press the center button to produce a screen where you can adjust the highlighted entry. While navigating any menu page, use the left/right keys or control wheel to move to the next page in that menu group, and then to wrap around to the first page in the next group.

Of course, not everything has to be set using these menus. The a7R IV has some convenient direct setting controls, such as the buttons of the control wheel that provide quick access to the drive modes, display information, and the ISO options. These and other buttons can be assigned other direct-access functions. These control features allow you to bypass the multi-tabbed menus for many of the most commonly used camera functions.

There is also a Function menu that appears when you press the Fn button, with a set of shooting setting options, as I described in Chapter 2. Although the Fn menu has a default set of 12 functions, you can redefine those entries as well. Your a7R IV offers a remarkable degree of customization. If a menu entry is unavailable, it will be "grayed out." Often this happens when you really *want* to use the feature, too. Scroll down to the grayed-out entry and press the center button. A help screen will generally pop up explaining what the problem is. Within this book, I'll also try to tell you the conditions that disable a particular feature, although there are so many possible interactions it is sometimes impossible to list them all. *A quick fix is to reset the camera to its default settings, as described in Chapter 6, to eliminate any conflicts.*

ABOUT THOSE ICONS

Menu entries are preceded by an icon, such as the "mountain" icon shown next to the first five entries in Figure 3.1. A mountain icon indicates that the particular menu entry applies *only* to still photography; an icon resembling a film frame shows that the menu entry applies *only* to movie making. Presumably, entries without any icon can be used with both. A few menu entries, such as Memory Recall, Proxy Recording, Slow and Fast Motion, Enlarge, and Language are preceded by their own graphic or text icons, and are apparently used just for decorative purposes.

Camera Settings I Menu Entries

Figure 3.1, earlier, shows the first screen of the Camera Settings I menu. As you can see, at most only a half-dozen items are displayed at one time. The items found in this menu are shown in Table 3.1.

File Format (Stills)

Options: RAW, RAW & JPEG, JPEG
Default: JPEG Fine
My preference: RAW & JPEG

This menu item lets you choose the file format setting that will be used by the a7R IV to store its still photo files. You have three options: RAW, RAW & JPEG, and JPEG. The two entries that follow this one allows you to specify the RAW file type (compressed or uncompressed), and JPEG quality (Extra Fine, Fine, and Standard). Sony has separated these options; some previous a7-series cameras combined format and quality in a single Image Quality entry.

Should you select RAW, JPEG, or both? You can elect to store only JPEG versions of the images you shoot, or you can save your photos as "unprocessed" RAW files, which consume several times as much space on your memory card. Or, you can store both file types at once as you shoot. Note that to open a RAW file, you must have an image editor or RAW processor capable of converting the RAW file to editable form. The free Sony Imaging Edge software can do this for you; Photoshop, Lightroom, Photoshop Elements, and other programs compatible with Adobe Camera Raw (ACR) can also make the conversion for you.

FOR USERS OF OLDER PHOTOSHOP VERSIONS

Adobe stopped upgrading its ACR software for the stand-alone (non–Creative Cloud/CC version) of Photoshop with Photoshop CS6. If that is your primary image editor, you'll need to use an external RAW processor, Adobe's free DNG Converter, or, my preference, MetaRAW ($49.95), which is available for both Windows and MacOS from www.thepluginsite.com. MetaRAW seamlessly "updates" the previous versions of Adobe Camera RAW by adding Adobe DNG converter capabilities to it when needed. As you import an "unsupported" RAW file, MetaRAW invisibly ushers the file through DNG converter (which must also be installed on your computer), and thence to ACR, where you can use Camera Raw's adjustments. You can use Adobe Camera Raw, Adobe DNG Converter, and MetaRaw's own converter for opening camera raw files. If one does not support a certain raw file, one of the others is used automatically.

Many photographers elect, as I do, to shoot *both* a JPEG and a RAW file (RAW & JPEG), so they'll have a JPEG version that might be usable as-is, as well as the original "digital negative" RAW file in case they will later want to make some serious editing of the photo with imaging software for reasons discussed shortly. If you use the RAW & JPEG option, the camera will save two different versions of the same file to the memory card: one with a .JPG extension, and one with the .ARW extension that signifies Sony's proprietary ARW RAW format that consists of raw data. (In Chapter 6, I'll show you how to save JPEG files to one slot, and RAW files to the other, using the Recording Mode sub-entry in the Setup 5 menu.)

TABLE 3.1 Camera Settings I Menus

QUALITY/IMAGE SIZE (PAGES 01-02)
File Format (Stills)
RAW File Type (Stills)
JPEG Quality (Stills)
JPEG Image Size (Stills)
Aspect Ratio (Stills)
APS-C/Super 35mm
Long Exposure Noise Reduction (Stills)
High ISO Noise Reduction (Stills)
Color Space (Stills)
Lens Compensation

SHOOT MODE/DRIVE (PAGES 03-04)
Drive Mode
Bracket Settings
Interval Shooting Functions
Pixel Shift Multi Shooting
Memory Recall
Memory
Select Media
Register Custom Shooting Set

AUTOFOCUS (PAGES 05-08)
Focus Mode
Priority Setting in AF-S
Priority Setting in AF-C
Focus Area
Focus Settings
Focus Area Limit
Switch Vertical/Horizontal AF Area (Stills)
AF Illuminator (Stills)
Face/Eye AF Settings
AF Tracking Sensitivity (Stills)
Aperture Drive in AF
AF with Shutter (Stills)
Pre-AF (Stills)
Eye-Start AF (Stills)
AF Area Registration (Stills)
Delete Registered AF Area (Stills)
Focus Frame Color
AF Area Auto Clear
Display Continuous AF Area
Phase Detect Area
Circulation of Focus Point
AF Micro Adjustment

EXPOSURE (PAGES 09-10)
Exposure Compensation
Reset Exposure Compensation
ISO Setting
Metering Mode
Face Priority in Multi Metering
Spot Metering Point
Exposure Step
AEL with Shutter
Exposure Standard Adjustment

FLASH (PAGE 11)
Flash Mode
Flash Compensation
Exposure Compensation Setting
Wireless Flash
Red Eye Reduction

COLOR/WHITE BALANCE/IMAGE PROCESSING (PAGES 12-13)
White Balance
Priority Setting in Auto White Balance
DRO
Creative Style
Picture Effect
Picture Profile
Shutter AWB Lock

FOCUS ASSIST (PAGE 14)
Focus Magnifier
Focus Magnifier Time
Initial Focus Magnification
AF in Focus Magnification (Stills)
Manual Focus Assist (Stills)
Peaking Setting

SHOOTING ASSIST (PAGE 15)
Anti-Flicker Shooting
Face Registration
Registered Faces Priority

JPEG vs. RAW

You'll sometimes be told that RAW files are the "unprocessed" image information your camera produces, before it's been modified. That's nonsense. RAW files are no more unprocessed than old-school camera film is after it's been through the chemicals to produce a negative or transparency. A lot can happen in the developer that can affect the quality of a film image—positively and negatively—and, similarly, your digital image undergoes a significant amount of processing before it is saved as a RAW file. Sony even applies a name (BIONZ) to the digital image processor used to perform this magic in Sony cameras.

A RAW file is closer in concept to a film camera's processed negative. It contains all the information, with no compression, no sharpening, no application of any special filters or other settings you might have specified when you took the picture. Those settings are stored with the RAW file, so they can be applied when the image is converted to JPEG or another format compatible with your favorite image editor. However, using RAW converter software such as Adobe Camera Raw (in Photoshop, Elements, or Lightroom) or Sony's Imaging Edge software (available for download from various Sony websites worldwide), you can override a RAW photo's settings (such as White Balance and Saturation) by applying other settings in the software. You can make essentially the same changes there that you might have specified in your camera before taking a photo.

Making changes to settings such as White Balance is a non-destructive process in a RAW converter since the changes are made before the photo is fully processed by the software program. Making a change in settings does not affect image quality, except for changes to exposure, highlight or shadow detail, and saturation; the loss of quality is minimal however, unless the changes you make for these aspects are significant. The RAW format exists because sometimes we want to have access to all the information captured by the camera, before the camera's internal logic has processed it and converted the image to a standard file format.

A RAW photo does take up more space than a JPEG and, in uncompressed mode, preserves all the information captured by your camera after it's been converted from analog to digital form. Since we can make changes to settings after the fact while retaining optimal image quality, errors in the settings we made in-camera are much less of a concern than in JPEG capture. When you shoot JPEGs, any modification you make in software is a destructive process; there is always some loss of image quality, although that can be minimal if you make only small changes or are skilled with the use of adjustment layers.

JPEG provides smaller files by compressing the information in a way that loses some image data. The lost data is reconstructed when you open a JPEG in a computer, but this is not a perfect process. If you shoot JPEGs at the highest quality (Extra Fine) level (JPEG Quality choices are explained below), the compression (and loss of data) is minimal; you might not be able to tell the difference between a photo made with RAW capture and a Large/Fine JPEG. If you use the lower quality level, you'll usually notice a quality loss when making big enlargements or after cropping your image extensively.

So, why don't we always use RAW? Although some photographers do save only in RAW format, it's more common to use either RAW plus the JPEG option or to just shoot JPEG and eschew RAW altogether. While RAW is overwhelmingly helpful when an image needs to be modified, working with a RAW file can slow you down significantly. The RAW images take longer to store on the memory card, so you cannot shoot as many in a single burst. Also, after you shoot a series, the camera must pause to write them to the memory card, so you may not be able to take any shots for a while (or only one or two at a time) until the RAW files have been written to the memory card. When you come home from a trip with numerous RAW files, you'll find they require more post-processing time and effort in the RAW converter, whether you elect to go with the default settings in force when the picture was taken or make minor adjustments.

Those who often shoot long series of photos in one session, or want to spend less time at a computer, may prefer JPEG over RAW. Wedding photographers, for example, might expose several thousand photos during a bridal affair and offer hundreds to clients as electronic proofs on a DVD. Wedding shooters take the time to make sure that their in-camera settings are correct, minimizing the need to post-process photos after the event. Given that their JPEGs are so good, there is little need for them to get bogged down working with RAW files in a computer. Sports photographers also avoid RAW files because of the extra time required for the camera to record a series of shots to a memory card and because they don't want to spend hours in extra post-processing. As a bonus, JPEG files consume a lot loss memory in a hard drive.

My recommendation: When shooting sports, I'll switch to shooting Large/Extra Fine JPEGs (with no RAW file) to minimize the time it takes for the camera to write a series of photos to the card; it's great to be able to take another burst of photos at any time, with little or no delay. I also appreciate the fact that I won't need to wade through long series of photos taken in RAW format.

In most situations however, I shoot virtually everything as RAW & JPEG. Most of the time, I'm not concerned about filling up my memory cards, as I usually carry at least three 64GB or 128GB memory cards with me. If I know I may fill up all those cards (say, on a long trip), I'll also carry a notebook computer and an external 2-terabyte hard drive to back up my files.

RAW File Type (Stills)

Options: Compressed, Uncompressed
Default: Compressed
My preference: Uncompressed

This option allows selecting either 12-bit compressed RAW format, or 14-bit uncompressed. I tend to favor the 14-bit uncompressed mode to avoid the artifacts that can appear in 12-bit compressed images. In practice, however, it's unlikely you'll notice the difference, and you may want to use the compressed format to save some storage space, as uncompressed RAW files, at about 120MB, are roughly twice the size of the compressed version (60MB). (JPEG files are even smaller, as noted next.)

JPEG Quality (Stills)

Options: Extra Fine, Fine, Standard
Default: Fine
My preference: Extra Fine

To reduce the size of your image files and allow more photos to be stored on a given memory card, the camera's processor uses JPEG compression to squeeze the images down to a smaller size. This compacting reduces the image quality a little, so you're offered your choice of Extra Fine, Fine, and Standard compression. Standard compression is quite aggressive; the camera discards a lot of data. While Fine is, well, just fine, you'll find that Extra Fine provides even better results, so it should really be your *standard* when shooting JPEG photos.

For most work, extra compression (or lower resolution, described next) is false economy. You never know when you might need that extra bit of picture detail. Your best bet is to have enough memory cards to handle all the shooting you want to do until you have the chance to transfer your photos to your computer or a personal storage device. In my tests, the typical JPEG Extra Fine, Fine, and Standard files were 42MB, 22MB, and 15MB in size, respectively.

JPEG Image Size (Stills)

Options: L, M, S
Default: L
My preference: L

Here you can choose between the a7R IV's Large, Medium, and Small settings for JPEG still pictures. The larger the size that's selected, the higher the resolution: the images are composed of more megapixels. Note that unlike some previous Sony full-frame cameras, you can specify JPEG Image Size even if you have selected RAW or RAW & JPEG for File Format. However, the a7R IV will always shoot Large RAW files, even if JPEG files are recorded in Medium or Small sizes.

As you scroll among the options, you'll note that the size for Large, Medium, and Small is shown in megapixels, as shown for the a7R IV in Table 3.2. The number of pixels will vary, depending on the *aspect ratio* you've chosen. (I'll explain aspect ratios next.)

For example, with the a7R IV, you'll get 60MP in Large mode using the 3:2 aspect ratio, and 54MP in Large mode using the 4:3 aspect ratio, 51MP with the 16:9 proportions, and 40MP when capturing square 1:1 images. If you are using the cropped APS-C/Super 35mm mode (explained in more detail in Chapter 12), with the a7R IV, the image is cropped, giving you a 26MP Large image at 3:2 aspect ratio, and proportionately smaller/lower resolution images in the other ratios. The a7R IV's resolutions at various sizes and with/without the APS-C/Super 35mm crop are shown in Table 3.2.

As I noted earlier, there are some limited advantages to using the Medium and Small resolution settings, and similar space-saving benefits accrue to the Standard JPEG compression setting. All these options help stretch the capacity of your memory card, so you can shoehorn quite a few more pictures onto a single card. That can be useful when you're away from home and are running out of storage, or when you're shooting non-critical work that doesn't require full resolution (such as photos taken for real estate listings, web page display, photo ID cards, or similar applications).

TABLE 3.2 Image Sizes Available

IMAGE SIZE	Megapixels 3:2 Aspect Ratio	Resolution 3:2 Aspect Ratio	Megapixels 4:3 Aspect Ratio	Resolution 4:3 Aspect Ratio	Megapixels 16:9 Aspect Ratio	Resolution 16:9 Aspect Ratio	Megapixels 1:1 Aspect Ratio	Resolution 1:1 Aspect Ratio
Full Frame								
Large (L)	60MP	9504 × 6336 pixels	54MP	8448 × 6336 pixels	51MP	9504 × 5344 pixels	40MP	6336 × 6336 pixels
Medium (M)	26MP	6240 × 4160 pixels	23MP	5552 × 4160 pixels	22MP	6240 × 3512 pixels	17MP	4160 × 4160 pixels
Small (S)	15MP	4752 × 3168 pixels	13MP	4224 × 3168 pixels	13MP	3984 × 2240 pixels	10MP	3168 × 3168 pixels
APS-C								
Large (L)	26MP	6240 × 4160 pixels	23MP	5552 × 4160 pixels	22MP	6240 × 3512 pixels	17MP	4160 × 4160 pixels
Medium (M)	15MP	4752 × 4160 pixels	13MP	4224 × 3168 pixels	13MP	4752 × 2672 pixels	10MP	3168 × 3168 pixels
Small (S)	6.5MP	3120 × 2080 pixels	5.8MP	2768 × 2080 pixels	5.5MP	3120 × 1752 pixels	4.3MP	2080 × 2080 pixels

Scroll to this Image Size menu item, press the center button, and scroll to the desired option: L, M, or S. Then press the center button to confirm your choice. As I noted, the actual size of the images depends on the aspect ratio you have chosen in the subsequent menu item (discussed below).

There are few reasons to use a size other than Large with this camera, even if reduced resolution is sufficient for your application, such as photo ID cards or web display. Starting with a full-size image gives you greater freedom for cropping and fixing problems with your image editor. An 800 × 600-pixel web image created from a full-resolution (large) original often ends up better than one that started out as a small JPEG.

Of course, the Medium and Small settings make it possible to squeeze more pictures onto your memory card. Indeed, the a7R IV images at Medium and Small resolution still amount to 26MP and 15MP, respectively, using the 3:2 aspect ratio. That's nothing to sneeze at; both approach the *maximum* of some very fine dSLR cameras that were available a few years ago. The smaller image sizes might come in handy in situations where your memory cards are almost full, and/or you don't have the opportunity to offload the pictures you've taken to your computer. For example, if you're on vacation and plan to make only 4 × 6-inch snapshot prints of the photos you shoot, setting a lower resolution will stretch your memory card's capacity. Even then, it makes more sense to simply buy and carry memory cards with higher capacity and use your a7R IV camera at its maximum resolution.

Aspect Ratio (Stills)

Options: 3:2, 4:3, 16:9, and 1:1 aspect ratios

Default: 3:2

My preference: 3.2; you can always crop to any of the others in your image editor

The aspect ratio is simply the proportions of your image as stored in your image file. The standard aspect ratio for digital photography is approximately 3:2; the image is two-thirds as tall as it is wide, as shown by the outer green rectangle in Figure 3.2. These proportions conform to those of the most common snapshot size in the USA, 4 × 6 inches. Of course, if you want to make a standard 8 × 10-inch enlargement, you'll need to trim some of the length of the image area since this format is closer to square; you (or a lab) would need 8 × 12-inch paper to print the full image area. The 3:2 aspect ratio was also the norm in photography with 35mm film.

If you're looking for images that will "fit" a wide-screen computer display, or a high-definition television screen, you can use this menu item to switch to a 16:9 aspect ratio, which is much wider than it is tall. The camera performs this magic by cutting off the top and bottom of the frame (as illustrated by the yellow boundaries in Figure 3.2) and storing a reduced resolution image (as shown in Table 3.2). Your 61MP image becomes a 51MP shot if you set the camera to shoot in 16:9 aspect ratio instead of using the default 3:2 option. If you need the wide-screen look, this menu option will save you some time in image editing, but you can achieve the same proportions (or any other aspect ratio) by trimming a full-resolution image with your software. The 16:9 option is most useful if you plan to take a *lot* of photos that will work best in that format. Only the JPEG version of a shot is cropped; the RAW file retains its full image area, which will be trimmed by your RAW converter when you import the image into your image editor.

Sony added two additional proportions to the a7R IV, 4:3, which is used by Micro Four Thirds cameras from Olympus and Panasonic, and the square 1:1 aspect ratio. Although the square format was popular during the film era for twin-lens reflexes and many professional cameras like early Hasselblads, it enjoyed a resurgence thanks to the popularity of Instagram. It's been calculated that more square Instagram photos are taken each day than for all other formats *combined*.

Figure 3.2 The 3:2 aspect ratio is shown by the outer green box. The yellow bars indicate the 16:9 aspect ratio; red bars indicate the 1:1 ratio; while the cyan dotted line represents the 4:3 aspect ratio.

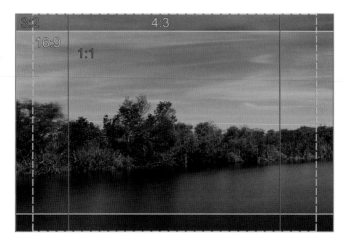

APS-C/Super 35mm

Options: On, Off, Auto
Default: Auto
My preference: N/A

This entry tells the a7R IV whether to automatically switch to the APS-C/Super 35mm "crop" mode when a lens not designed for full-frame coverage is mounted on the camera. (APS-C is a still-image format; Super 35mm is a movie format.) In Chapter 12, I'll fully explain crop mode, which effectively captures pictures using only the center portion of the image, corresponding to the APS-C area used by Sony cameras that are *not* full-frame models and for Super 35mm film mode. There are three options within this menu entry:

- **On.** The camera *always* captures only the APS-C size area. If you're using a non-FE E-mount lens, then the image will correspond to what you'd see with an ASP-C camera, such as the Sony a6600. The cropped image will have the same field of view as a lens with 1.5X the actual focal length. That is, if you're using the Sony 16-50mm f/3.5-5.6 power zoom "kit" lens often supplied with the a6600 and other models, the effective focal length will be 24-75mm, and the cropped image will have a resolution of 26MP on the a7R IV. Because the On setting always activates the cropping effect, even if you're using a full-frame FE lens (such as the Sony FE 70-200mm f/4 lens), the effective focal length will be 105-200mm. This APS-C crop "boost" works well with the a7R IV, because its 26MP image in crop mode in the 3:2 aspect ratio is still quite respectable.

- **Off.** With this setting, the camera *never* crops the image. If you are using a non-FE, non-full-frame lens, you'll probably end up with severe vignetting in the corners. (I'll show you this effect in Chapter 12.) I sometimes use this setting when working with lenses intended for APS-C cameras, because some lenses do cover the full frame (even if just barely) at some focal lengths.

- **Auto.** When you use this setting, the a7R IV will (often) detect whether you've mounted an FE or APS-C E-mount lens, and either crop or not crop as appropriate. It may not detect *all* E-mount lenses, particularly those from third-party vendors, so it's often safest to use the On option when you know you will be using an APS-C-type lens and want to avoid vignetting.

Long Exposure NR/High ISO NR (Stills)

Long Exposure NR: Options: On/Off; **Default:** On
High ISO NR: Options: Normal, Low, Off; **Default:** Normal
My preference: Off for both

I've grouped these two menu options together, the first two in the second page of the Camera Settings I (Quality/Image Size 2) menu (see Figure 3.3), because they work together, each under slightly different circumstances. Moreover, the causes and cures for noise involve some overlapping processes. Digital noise is that awful graininess that shows up as multicolored specks in images, and these menu items

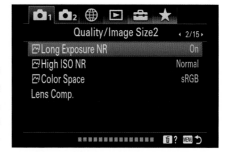

Figure 3.3 The Camera Settings I-02 (Quality/Image Size 2) menu page.

help you manage it. In some ways, noise is like the excessive grain found in some high-speed photographic films. However, while photographic grain is sometimes used as a special effect, it's rarely desirable in a digital photograph.

The visual noise-producing process is something like listening to music in your car, and then rolling down all the windows. You're adding sonic noise to the audio signal, and while increasing the volume may help a bit, you're still contending with an unfavorable signal-to-noise ratio that probably mutes tones (especially higher treble notes) that you really want to hear.

The same thing happens when the analog signal is amplified: You're increasing the image information in the signal but boosting the background fuzziness at the same time. Tune in a very faint or distant AM radio station on your car stereo. Then turn up the volume. After a certain point, turning up the volume further no longer helps you hear better. There's a similar point of diminishing returns for digital sensor ISO increases and signal amplification as well.

Your a7R IV can reduce the amount of grainy visual noise in your photo with noise reduction processing. That's useful for a smoother look, but NR processing does blur some of the very fine detail in an image along with blurring the digital noise pattern. These two menu items let you choose whether to apply noise reduction to exposures of longer than one second and how much noise reduction to apply (Normal or Low) when shooting at a high ISO level (at roughly ISO 1600 and above).

High ISO NR is grayed out when the camera is set to shoot only RAW format photos. The camera does not use this feature on RAW format photos since noise reduction—at the optimum level for any photo—can be applied in the software you'll use to modify and convert the RAW file to JPEG or TIFF. (If you shoot in RAW & JPEG, the JPEG images, but not the RAW files, will be affected by this camera feature.) As well, high ISO Noise Reduction is never applied when the camera is set to continuous shooting or continuous bracketing, or when the ISO is set to Multi Frame Noise Reduction.

Digital noise is also created during very long exposures. Extended exposure times allow more photons to reach the sensor but increase the likelihood that some photosites will react randomly even though not struck by a particle of light. Moreover, as the sensor remains switched on for the longer exposure, it heats up, and this heat can be mistakenly recorded as if it were a barrage of photons. To minimize the digital noise that can occur during long exposures, the a7R IV uses a process called "dark frame subtraction." After you take the photo, the camera fires another shot, at the same shutter speed, with the shutter closed to make the so-called dark frame. The processor compares the original photo and the dark frame photo and identifies the colorful noise speckles and "hot" pixels. It then removes (subtracts) them so the final image saved to the memory card will be quite "clean."

Context-Sensitive

The a7R IV has a novel "context-sensitive" noise-reduction algorithm that examines the image to identify smooth tones, subject edges, and textures, and apply different NR to each. This processing works best with areas with continuous tones and subtle gradations and does a good job of reducing noise while preserving detail. Because the BIONZ X digital processing chip is doing so much work, you may see a message on the screen while NR is underway. You cannot take another photo until the processing is done and the message disappears. If you want to give greater priority to shooting, set Long Exposure NR and High ISO NR to Off.

Long Exposure NR works well, but it causes a delay; roughly the same amount of time as the exposure itself. That would be a long 10 seconds after a 10-second exposure. During this delay the camera locks up, so you cannot take another shot. You may want to turn this feature off, as I do, to eliminate that delay when you need to be able to take a shot at any time. This feature is Off by default in continuous shooting and bracketing modes.

You might want to turn off noise reduction for long exposures and set it to a weak level for high ISO photos to preserve image detail. (NR processing blurs the digital noise pattern, but it can also blur fine details in your images.) Or, you simply may not need NR in some situations. For example, you might be shooting waves crashing into the shore at ISO 200 with the camera mounted on a tripod, using a neutral-density filter and long exposure to cause the pounding water to blur slightly. To maximize detail in the non-moving portions of your photos, you can switch off long exposure noise reduction.

It's also important to turn off noise reduction when taking interval photos, as explained in Chapter 9. For example, the long exposures needed to record star trails would trigger the dark frame subtraction process, producing a 30-second delay following each 30-second exposure in a continuous sequence. You'd want to disable noise reduction to allow shooting long exposures, one after another, to capture your star trails.

Color Space (Stills)

Options: sRGB, Adobe RGB
Default: sRGB
My preference: sRGB

The Sony a7R IV's Color Space option gives you two different color spaces (also called *color gamuts*), named Adobe RGB (because it was developed by Adobe Systems in 1998), and sRGB (supposedly because it is the *standard* RGB color space). These two color gamuts define a specific set of colors that can be applied to the images your a7R IV captures.

You're probably surprised that the Sony a7R IV doesn't automatically capture *all* the colors we see. Unfortunately, that's impossible because of the limitations of the sensor and the filters used to capture the fundamental red, green, and blue colors, as well as that of the phosphors used to display those colors on the LEDs in your camera and computer monitors. Nor is it possible to *print* every color our eyes detect, because the inks or pigments used don't absorb and reflect colors perfectly.

On the other hand, the a7R IV does capture quite a few more colors than we need. A 14-bit RAW image contains a possible 281 *trillion* different hues (16,384 colors per red, green, or blue channel), which are condensed down to a mere 16.8 million possible colors when converted to a 24-bit (eight bits per channel) image.

The set of colors, or gamut, that can be reproduced or captured by a given device (scanner, digital camera, monitor, printer, or some other piece of equipment) is represented as a color space that exists within the larger full range of colors. That full range is represented by the odd-shaped splotch of color shown in Figure 3.4, as defined by scientists at an international organization back in 1931. The colors possible with Adobe RGB are represented by the black triangle in the figure, while the sRGB gamut is represented by the smaller white triangle. The location of the corners of each triangle represent the position of the primary red, green, and blue colors in the gamut.

A third color space, ProPhoto RGB, represented by the yellow triangle in the figure, has become more popular among professional photographers as more and more color printing labs support it. While you cannot *save* images using the ProPhoto gamut with your a7R IV, you can convert your photos to 16-bit ProPhoto format using Adobe Camera RAW when you import RAW photos into an image editor. ProPhoto encompasses virtually all the colors we can see (and some we can't), giving advanced photographers better tools to work with in processing their photos. It has richer reds, greens, and blues, although, as you can see from the figure, its green and blue primaries are imaginary (they extend outside the visible color gamut). Those with exacting standards need not use a commercial printing service if they want to explore ProPhoto RGB: many inkjet printers can handle cyans, magentas, and yellows that extend outside the Adobe RGB gamut.

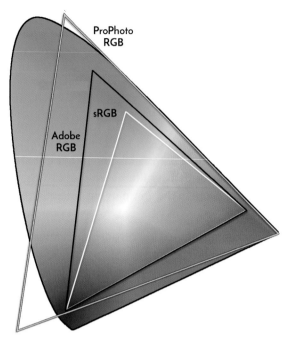

Figure 3.4 The outer curved figure shows all the colors we can see; the outlines show the boundaries of Adobe RGB (black triangle), sRGB (white triangle), and ProPhoto RGB (yellow triangle).

Regardless of which triangle—or color space—is used by the a7R IV, you end up with some combination of 16.8 million different colors that can be used in your photograph. (No one image will contain all 16.8 million! To require that many, only about two pixels of any one color could be the same in a 61-megapixel image!) But, as you can see from the figure, the colors available will be *different*.

Adobe RGB, like ProPhoto RGB, is an expanded color space useful for commercial and professional printing, and it can reproduce a wider range of colors. It can also come in useful if an image is going to be extensively retouched, especially within an advanced image editor, like Adobe Photoshop, which has sophisticated color management capabilities that can be tailored to specific color spaces. As an advanced user, you don't need to automatically "upgrade" your a7R IV to Adobe RGB, because images tend to look less saturated on your monitor and, it is likely, significantly different from what you will get if you output the photo to your personal inkjet. (You can *profile* your monitor for the Adobe RGB color space to improve your on-screen rendition using widely available color-calibrating hardware and software.)

While both Adobe RGB and sRGB can reproduce the exact same 16.8 million absolute colors, Adobe RGB spreads those colors over a larger portion of the visible spectrum, as you can see in the figure.

Think of a box of crayons (the jumbo 16.8 million crayon variety). Some of the basic crayons from the original sRGB set have been removed and replaced with new hues not contained in the original box. Your "new" box contains colors that can't be reproduced by your computer monitor, but which work just fine with a commercial printing press. For example, Adobe RGB has more "crayons" available in the cyan-green portion of the box, compared to sRGB, which is unlikely to be an advantage unless your image's final destination are the cyan, magenta, yellow, and black inks of a printing press.

The other color space, sRGB, is recommended for images that will be output locally on the user's own printer, as this color space matches that of the typical inkjet printer fairly closely. You might prefer sRGB, which is the default for the Sony a7R IV and most other cameras, as it is well suited for the range of colors that can be displayed on a computer screen and viewed over the Internet. If you plan to take your image file to a retailer's kiosk for printing, sRGB is your best choice, because those automated output devices are calibrated for the sRGB color space that consumers use.

BEST OF BOTH WORLDS

If you plan to use RAW+JPEG for most of your photos, go ahead and set sRGB as your color space. You'll end up with JPEGs suitable for output on your own printer, but you can still extract an Adobe RGB version from the RAW file at any time. It's like shooting two different color spaces at once—sRGB and Adobe RGB—and getting the best of both worlds.

Of course, choosing the right color space doesn't solve the problems that result from having each device in the image chain manipulating or producing a slightly different set of colors. To that end, you'll need to investigate the wonderful world of *color management*, which uses hardware and software tools to match or *calibrate* all your devices, as closely as possible, so that what you see more closely resembles what you capture, what you see on your computer display, and what ends up on a printed hardcopy. Entire books have been devoted to color management, and most of what you need to know doesn't directly involve your Sony a7R IV, so I won't detail the nuts and bolts here.

To manage your color, you'll need, at the bare minimum, some sort of calibration system for your computer display, so that your monitor can be adjusted to show a standardized set of colors that is repeatable over time. (What you see on the screen can vary as the monitor ages, or even when the room light changes.) I use the SpyderX Pro monitor color correction system from Datacolor (www.datacolor.com) for my computer's 32-inch main monitor, flanked by two 26-inch wide-screen LCD displays. The unit checks room light levels every five minutes and reminds me to recalibrate every week or two using a small sensor device, which attaches temporarily to the front of the screen and interprets test patches that the software displays during calibration. The rest of the time, the sensor sits in its stand, measuring the room illumination, and adjusting my monitors for higher or lower ambient light levels.

If you're willing to make a serious investment in equipment to help you produce the most accurate color and make prints, you'll want a more advanced system (up to $500) like the various other Spyder products from Datacolor or Colormunki from X-Rite (www.colormunki.com).

Lens Compensation

Options: Shading Compensation, Chromatic Aberration, Distortion Compensation: Auto, Off (for each)

Default: Shading/Chromatic Aberration: Auto; **Distortion:** Off

My preference: Auto for all three

This trio of submenus optimizes lens performance by compensating for optical defects; they're useful because very few lenses in the world are even close to perfect in all aspects. All three items work only with E-mount lenses and not when using A-mount lenses with an adapter accessory.

Shading

One key defect is caused by a phenomenon called *vignetting*, which is a darkening of the four corners of the frame because of a slight amount of fall-off in illumination at those nether regions. This menu option allows you to activate built-in "shading" compensation, which partially (or fully) compensates for this effect. Depending on the f/stop you use, the lens mounted on the camera, and the focal length setting, vignetting can be non-existent, slight, or may be so strong that it appears you've used a too-small hood on your camera. (Indeed, the wrong lens hood can produce a vignette effect of its own.)

Vignetting, even if pronounced, may not be much of a problem for you. I actually *add* vignetting, sometimes, in my image editor when shooting portraits and some other subjects. Slightly dark corners tend to focus attention on a subject in the middle of the frame. On the other hand, vignetting with subjects that are supposed to be evenly illuminated, such as landscapes, is seldom a benefit. Figure 3.5, left, shows an image without shading correction at top, and a corrected image at the bottom. I've exaggerated the vignetting a little to make it more evident on the printed page. Note that this effect is applied to both RAW and JPEG images.

Chromatic Aberration

The second defect involves fringes of color around backlit objects, produced by *chromatic aberration*, which comes in two forms: *longitudinal/axial*, in which all the colors of light don't focus in the same plane, and *lateral/transverse*, in which the colors are shifted in one direction. (See Figure 3.5, top right.) When this feature is enabled, the camera will automatically correct images taken with one of the supported lenses to reduce or eliminate the amount of color fringing seen in the final photograph. (See Figure 3.5, bottom right.)

Distortion

Distortion is the tendency of some lenses to bow outward (most often wide-angle lenses) or curve inward (found in some telephoto lenses). Figure 3.6, left, shows an exaggerated version of the outward-curving variety, called *barrel distortion,* exhibited by many wide-angle lenses—especially in fisheye optics, where the distortion is magically transformed into a feature. This feature works with most E-mount lenses, but not with all.

In Figure 3.6, right, you can see inward bowing, or *pincushion distortion,* as found in many telephoto lenses. Both types can be partially fixed using Photoshop's Lens Correction or Photoshop Elements'

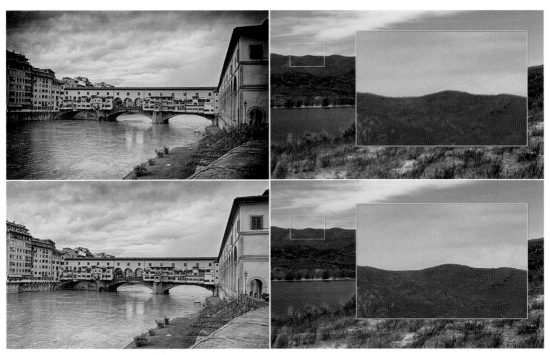

Figure 3.5 Vignetting (top left) is undesirable in a landscape photo, but the camera's shading correction feature can fix dark corners (bottom left). Lateral chromatic aberration, which shows as color fringes (top right), can also be corrected (bottom right).

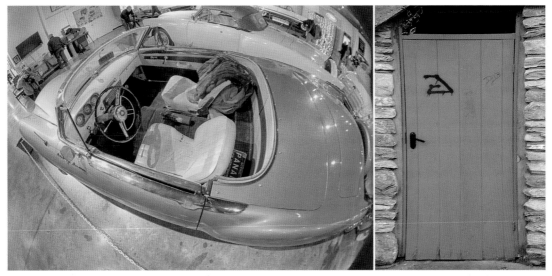

Figure 3.6 Left: Barrel distortion in wide-angle lenses becomes a useful feature with fisheye lenses. Right: Pincushion distortion causes straight lines at the edges of the frame to curve inward.

Correct Camera Distortion filters. Or, you can apply this in-camera feature to fix mild distortion. You should realize that correcting lens distortion involves warping pixels, mostly at the edges of the frame, providing a little less sharpness in those areas. The image area of your final picture will be slightly smaller than the frame you composed, and, during playback the active focus point is not shown in the review image.

In addition, applying distortion correction involves extra processing, which can reduce the number of consecutive shots possible. Because the correction is applied *after* you take the picture, the effect is not displayed on the screen when shooting in live view. (That is, Setting Effect is set to On in the Live View Display entry of the Camera Settings II-08 menu, as discussed in Chapter 4.)

Drive Mode

Options: Single Shooting; Cont. Shooting (Hi+, Hi, Mid, Lo); Self-timer (2/5/10 seconds); Self-timer Continuous (2/5/20 seconds with 3 or 5 shots); Continuous Bracket/Single Bracket (3, 5, or 9 images at 0.3/0.7/1.0 EV increments; 3 or 5 images at 2.0/3.0 EV increments); White Balance Bracket (Lo/Hi), DRO Bracket (Lo/Hi)

Default: Single Shooting

My preference: N/A

This is the first entry on the Camera Settings I-03 (Shoot Mode/Drive 1) page (see Figure 3.7). Just as with the Drive (left directional) button on the back of the camera, there are several choices available through this single menu item. Your choices include:

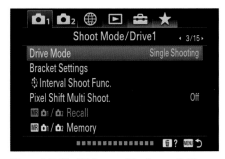

Figure 3.7 The third page of the Camera Settings I menu.

- **Single shooting.** Takes one shot each time you press the shutter release button. You must use this mode or one of the self-timer modes (described shortly) if you want to use the a7R IV's built-in Auto HDR (high dynamic range) feature or take a Bulb (long exposure) setting when working with Manual exposure.

- **Continuous Shooting.** Captures images at a rate of either 5 or 2.5 frames per second. When this option is highlighted, press the left/right directional buttons to switch among Hi+ (up to 10 fps), Hi (up to 8 fps), Mid (up to 6 fps), or Lo (up to 3 fps). The continuous speed will slow down if you're shooting uncompressed RAW, or when e-Front Curtain Shutter is set to Off when using Hi, Mid, or Lo speeds. The Hi+ speed is maintained, but the viewfinder/LCD monitor doesn't display the image in real time. You'll be viewing a slightly delayed image as the camera churns away capturing high-speed images. (Remember, you're shooting 10 frames per second at 61MP!)

  Focus and exposure can adjust during the burst if you set Focus Mode to Continuous AF and AEL w/Shutter to Off or Auto. However, when an f/stop smaller than f/8 is in use, focus is set for the first shot, and retained for subsequent images as long as you hold down the shutter button. Continuous shooting becomes slower when using flash, when the RAW file type is set to Uncompressed, or the e-Front Curtain Shutter is set to Off when using Hi, Mid, or Lo modes.

If you want to keep track of your remaining shots, the Continuous Shooting Length indicator can be activated using the Camera Settings II-08 (Display/Auto Review 2) menu entry, which I'll describe in Chapter 4. You'll find more on continuous shooting in Chapter 9.

- **Self-Timer (2 sec./5 sec./10 sec.).** Takes a single picture after two, five, or ten seconds have elapsed. When this choice is highlighted, press the left/right buttons to switch among the three durations.
- **Self-Timer Continuous.** The self-timer counts down, and then takes either 3 or 5 images, after delays of 2, 5, or 10 seconds. The left/right buttons cycle among the choices. You can cancel the timer by pressing the Drive button and selecting Single Shooting, or by tapping the shutter button a second time. Note that if you're using any of the continuous self-timer, continuous shooting, or continuous bracketing options, manual Bulb exposures produce an exposure time of 1/30th second.
- **Continuous Bracket.** Captures 3, 5, or 9 images in one burst when the shutter release is held down, bracketing them 0.3, 0.5, 0.7, or 1.0 stops apart. Increments of 2.0 or 3.0 stops apart are also available, but only 3 or 5 images can be taken. Use the left/right buttons to select the increment and number of shots.

  In Manual exposure (when ISO Auto is disabled), or in Aperture Priority, the shutter speed will change. If ISO Auto is set in Manual exposure, the bracketed set will be created by changing the ISO setting. In Shutter Priority, the aperture will change. Use continuous mode when you want all the images in the set to be framed as similarly as possible, say, when you will be using them for manually assembled high dynamic range (HDR) photos. You can use an external flash when continuous bracketing is active, but, because of the time required for the flash to recycle, you'll need to press the shutter button each time to take subsequent images (effectively switching the camera into Single Bracket mode, described next).

  Only the last shot in the set is displayed when using Auto Review. With all types of bracketing, the exposure/bracket scale at the bottom of the EVF or LCD monitor (in Display All Info mode) will display indicators showing the number of images shot and the relative amount of under-/overexposure. Don't forget that you can dial in exposure compensation, and *that* will affect the amount of over-/underexposure applied while bracketing. Continuous bracketing (and Single Bracketing) is disabled when using Intelligent Auto.

- **Single Bracket.** Captures one bracketed image in a set of 3, 5, or 9 shots each time you press the shutter release, bracketing them 0.3, 0.5, 0.7, 1.0 stops apart. Only 3 and 5 shots are available with the 2.0 or 3.0 EV increments. The left/right buttons are used to select the increment and number of shots. In this mode, you can separate each image by an interval of your choice. You might want to use this variation when you want the individual images to be captured at slightly different times, say, to produce a set of images that will be combined in some artistic way.

SELF-TIMER IN BRACKET MODES

You can set continuous and single bracket modes, and still make use of the self-timer. Access Bracket Settings (discussed next) and activate Self-Timer During Bracketing.

- **White Balance Bracket.** Shoots three image adjustments to the color temperature. While you can't specify which direction the color bias is tilted, you can select Lo (the default) for small changes, or Hi, for larger changes using the left/right buttons. Only the last shot taken is displayed during Auto Review.

- **DRO Bracket.** Shoots three image adjustments to the dynamic range optimization. While you can't specify the amount of optimization, you can select Lo (the default) for small changes, or Hi, for larger changes, using the left/right buttons. Again, only the last shot taken is displayed during Auto Review.

Bracket Settings

Options: Self-timer during Bracketing: Off, 2 sec., 5 sec., 10 sec.; Bracket Order: 0-+, -0+
Default: Off, 0-+
My preference: N/A

This item has two entries that let you customize how bracketing is applied.

- **Self-timer during bracketing.** You can choose delays of 2, 5, or 10 seconds before bracketing begins, or disable the self-timer during bracketing. This clever option solves a problem: how to use the self-timer (say, to avoid shaking a camera mounted on a tripod) when bracketing (which resides in the same Drive menu). With continuous bracketing, all exposures will be taken after the self-timer delay; if you're using single bracketing, the delay takes place before each shot in the bracket set is exposed.

- **Bracket order.** The default is metered exposure > underexposure > overexposure. However, if you're shooting photos that will later be manually assembled into an HDR photo, you might find it more convenient to expose in order of progressively more exposure: underexposure > metered exposure > overexposure. The order you choose will also be applied to white balance bracketing.

Interval Shooting Functions

Options: Interval Shooting, Shooting Start Time, Shooting Interval, Number of Shots, AE Tracking Sensitivity, Silent Shooting in Interval, Shoot Interval Priority
Default: Interval Shooting (Off), Shooting Start Time (1 second), Shooting Interval (3 seconds), Number of Shots (30), AE Tracking Sensitivity (Mid), Silent Shooting in Interval (On), Shoot Interval Priority (Off)
My preference: N/A

Interval (or *time-lapse*) shooting has had the distinction of long being one of the most desired features for Sony's E-mount mirrorless cameras. Until recently, you needed an external intervalometer device or a special app to capture individual shots at regular intervals—say, to take progressive photographs of a flower opening. Now, Sony has included this capability in some of its latest models. Your a7R IV can now capture a series of shots of the moon marching across the sky, or compile one of those extreme time-lapse picture sets showing something that takes a very, very long time, such as a building under construction.

You probably won't be shooting such construction shots, unless you have a spare a7R IV you don't need for a few months (or are willing to go through the rigmarole of figuring out how to set up your camera in precisely the same position using the same lens settings to shoot a series of pictures at intervals). However, other kinds of interval and time-lapse photography are entirely within reach. Best of all, with Sony's free Imaging Edge software, you can turn a series of time-lapse stills into a movie! I'll provide step-by-step instructions for capturing interval stills and time-lapse video in Chapter 9, and include tips on recommended intervals between shots. You'll also learn more about the seven major settings you have to work with, shown in Figure 3.8:

- **Interval shooting.** Choose On or Off to enable/disable the feature. You'll want to keep this setting at Off until you are ready to begin interval shooting.

- **Shooting start time.** Use this setting to delay the start of image capture, from 0 minutes 0 seconds (begin immediately) to 99 minutes, 59 seconds. Say you're planning on capturing a sunset and know that the best time to begin shooting will be in one hour. Specify 60 minutes and 0 seconds, set up your camera, and the a7R IV will begin taking your sequence at the designated time. You're free to do other things in the interim.

- **Shooting interval.** Specify how often an image should be captured. You might need an interval of 3 to 4 seconds to capture the march of fast-moving clouds across the sky, or prefer a more relaxed 10 to 12 seconds to shoot clouds with a slower pace. Intervals can range from 1 to 60 seconds between shots.

- **Number of shots.** This setting determines the total number of exposures in a time-lapse sequence. You can choose from 1 to 9999 shots. A message at the bottom of the screen will display how long it will take to capture the number of shots you specify using the shooting interval you've chosen. If you select the maximum 60 second interval and 9999 shots, your sequence will take almost just shy of one week to capture (166 hours and 36 minutes).

- **Autoexposure Tracking Sensitivity.** When the light levels are changing—say when capturing an entire day's activity, or something that happens fairly quickly, such as a sunset—you can specify whether the a7R IV adjusts exposure quickly, or slowly. Select from High, Mid (Medium), or Low sensitivity. Quick changes in exposure can be jarring, especially when combining shots into a time-lapse movie. You may want to experiment to see what works for your particular sequence, but the Mid setting should work for most projects. **Note:** if you *want* to see dramatic light shifts as your scene lightens or darkens, use Manual Exposure and set the shutter speed, ISO, and aperture to give the correct "normal" exposure (say, for mid-day when shooting a

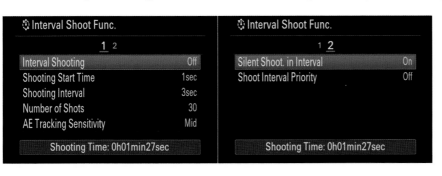

Figure 3.8 Interval Shooting options.

day-long series). The dawn/early morning and dusk/night exposures will have different degrees of underexposure—probably for a more dramatic effect.

- **Silent Shooting in Interval.** Choose On or Off. If you select On, the a7R IV will operate silently, which allows capturing your sequence in "stealth" mode if you need it. Silent shooting also makes the series of shots less intrusive in environments where low noise levels are prized—such as religious ceremonies, concerts, college libraries prior to finals week, or capturing a sleeping baby without interrupting parents' "quiet time."

- **Shoot Interval Priority.** When shooting sequences using Program or Aperture Priority modes, the a7R IV will adjust the shutter speed to provide the correct exposure. Unfortunately, when light levels are low, that may result in a shutter speed that is longer than the specified interval. That is, you may want to take a photo every two seconds, but the camera calculates that a four-second exposure is required.

If you select Off for this setting, when the a7R IV encounters a conflict, it will go ahead and expose for the correct amount of time, skipping the shot that would have taken place. This is the default behavior and often the best choice. In most cases, there is not enough subject motion between frames to result in a jarring effect. You're more likely to dislike having that conflicting image underexposed, which is what happens when this setting is On. When another interval exposure is due, the a7R IV will terminate the previous shot (underexposing it) and begin the next one on schedule. You might use the On option if you feel that just dropping the poorly exposed image from the sequence produces the best series.

Pixel Shift Multi Shooting

Options: Off; Shooting Intervals: [4 shots, 16 shots] [Shortest, 1, 2, 3, 4, 5, 10, 15, 30 seconds)
Default: Off
My preference: N/A

If 61MP resolution isn't enough for you, your a7R IV can capture images with greater effective resolution by grabbing 4 or 16 RAW images and then manipulating the pixels within them so every photo site captures red, green, and blue information, producing shots with up to 240MP of resolution. Sony's free Imaging Edge (Viewer) software combines the individual shots into your high-resolution final image.

You can also try a third-party solution, PixelShift2DNG, from LibRAW LLC, in versions for both Windows and Mac operating systems. It was headed for beta testing as I wrote this book, and may be available for purchase by the time this book is published. It purports to convert the a7R IV RAW files to Adobe's DNG format, handling both 4- and 16-image sequences. You can track the progress of this utility at https://www.fastrawviewer.com/Libraw-products.

Because your subject cannot move between shots, you'll need to mount the camera on a rock-solid tripod, so the 4 or 16 images can be aligned. This entry simply allows you to turn the Pixel Shift feature on or off and specify an interval between shots of Shortest, 1 to 5 seconds, plus 10, 15, or 30 seconds. The Shortest setting allows the camera to capture the shots continuously; the longer intervals are useful with electronic flash illumination: choose an interval that is longer than the recycling time of your flash. Pixel Shift Multi Shooting is explained in more detail in Chapter 9.

Memory Recall

Options: Select memory register to use. (Current physical slot, or M1, M2, M3, M4 on memory card.)
Default: None
My preference: N/A

Sony throws a curve ball by making its three Memory register entries as confusing as possible. They are listed in the Camera Settings I-03 and I-04 (Shoot Mode/Drive 1 and 2) menu in the wrong order and described in the Sony Help Guide in entirely different places (pages 292 and 427!). The menu icons are wrong, too, as shown earlier in Figure 3.7. The icons show Camera 1/Camera 2 and omit Camera 3. Before I describe how to use all three entries, I'm going to give you a quick overview of what each does.

The Memory feature allows you to save almost all the settings that you use for a particular shooting situation, including shutter speed and aperture (but *not* Program Shift adjustments), and then recall them quickly. There are three "slots" (labeled 1, 2, and 3) on the mode dial, and each slot can be loaded with default settings stored *in the camera*, or in four additional sets of settings you can store on a memory card, giving you seven groups of settings in all. The Memory feature lets you save custom-crafted sets that you can activate at any time. Simply activate the set that fits your current needs. For example, you might set up Register 1 with the settings you use while shooting volleyball in an indoor arena, Register 2 for use in landscape photography outdoors, and Register 3 for street photography. Whenever you encounter any of those three types of scenes, activate the memory channel with the suitable settings for that situation. You can then begin shooting immediately.

The three menu entries that you use to save and retrieve these memorized settings are as follows:

- **MR Recall.** This entry is grayed out if you haven't stored any settings. You'll be able to access Recall after you've stored some settings, using the MR Memory entry, described next.

  This setting is used to "load" one of the available settings into a specific 1, 2, or 3 register slot. If you want to use the settings already stored in the camera's memory for a particular slot, you don't need to use this menu entry. Just rotate the mode dial to the 1, 2, or 3 position.

  However, if you'd rather use one of the four *alternate* settings stored on your memory card, rotate the mode dial to the 1, 2, or 3 slots and then access MR Recall. (It's available only when the mode dial is set to one of the three numbered slots.) You can then use the multi-selector or left/right buttons to select M1, M2, M3, or M4. These settings reside on a memory card and are only available when that card is inserted in the a7R IV. I'll explain the storage process shortly.

- **MR Memory.** This entry allows you to store or *register* your camera's *current* settings to one of the three physical memory slots (1, 2, or 3) or to one of the four files (M1, M2, M3, or M4) on your memory card. Settings you've stored using the MR Memory entry become available to the MR Recall menu option.

- **MR Select Media.** This entry tells the a7R IV which memory card *slot* is active and contains the M1, M2, M3, or M4 settings files. In practice, that means you can store one group of four settings on one memory card, and a second group on the other card, and then switch between them.

Note that you can *store* sets of settings when using any shooting modes (using the MR Memory entry that follows). But to *recall* a set of stored settings, you *must* rotate the mode dial to one of the three Memory positions, marked with a 1, 2, or 3 on the dial and then either use the settings already stored or, optionally, use this menu entry to load the additional settings saved in M1, M2, M3, or M4 files on your memory card. I'll explain recalling settings here and show you how to store them under the next menu entry, Memory.

To recap, there are two ways to activate saved settings:

- **Mode dial.** Simply rotate the mode dial to the 1, 2, or 3 position. A set of settings for each of those positions is stored internally in the camera. When the mode dial is switched to 1, 2, or 3, the settings already loaded into that camera register automatically become active.

- **MR Recall.** This menu entry allows you to recall *additional* memory settings, numbered M1, M2, M3, and M4, which are stored on the memory card currently in the camera. You can load the M1, M2, M3, or M4 settings into the 1, 2, or 3 mode dial positions. That may be confusing at first, but the bottom line is that the a7R IV can use *any of three memory registers* (1, 2, and 3), but any of those three physical registers can be loaded with each of four sets of settings *on your current memory card*. Switch to the memory card in the other slot, and you can access four more! Remove your card (or reformat it), and those extra four settings are lost! (Smart move, Sony.)

SETTINGS LIBRARY

You can keep separate memory cards for each type of photography you like to do, and store M1, M2, M3, and M4 settings on each of them. But remember when you reformat the card, those settings are lost. The settings are stored in a folder on the card labeled /PRIVATE/SONY/SETTING with a subfolder for each different camera you use. The filenames end in .DAT.

To recall settings previously stored on your memory card using Memory Recall, just follow these steps:

1. **Rotate the mode dial to the 1, 2, or 3 positions.** Select the position you want to load settings into.
2. **Access the MR Recall entry.** Navigate to this menu entry. When you press the center button, a screen like the one shown at left in Figure 3.9 appears.
3. **Review your stored settings.** The 1 highlighted in orange in the figure indicates that the mode dial currently has been set to the 1 position, and the settings displayed show the values currently stored for that slot. While the 1 is highlighted, you can scroll down the list with the up/down controls and review all the settings that have been stored.
4. **Change to settings on memory card.** If you want to use settings stored on your memory card instead, highlight any of the M1, M2, M3, and M4 entries, which represent four different sets of settings registered to your card. You can review the M1 to M4 settings by scrolling, as described in Step 3. If no settings have been stored for a particular M1 to M4 register, the message No File appears.
5. **Confirm.** If a selected set is satisfactory, press the center button or multi-selector to confirm your choice and exit. Your settings are now active in the camera.

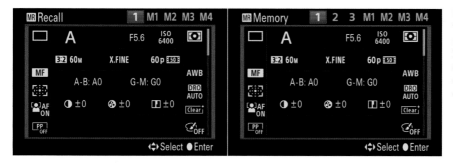

Figure 3.9 Recall settings stored on your memory card (left). Store settings in the 1, 2, or 3 mode dial positions, or as M1, M2, M3, or M4 on your memory card (right).

MR Memory

Options: Store settings on your memory card

Default: None

My preference: N/A

This entry registers your camera's current settings, either to one of the three physical memory registers (1, 2, or 3) within your a7R IV or to one of the card-based M1 to M4 files. The power of the memory feature stems from the fact that so many shooting settings can be saved for instant recall in any memory register.

Before you access the MR Memory item in the menu, make the desired settings in terms of camera operating mode, drive mode, ISO, white balance, exposure compensation, metering mode, and focus mode. Then, to save your current settings on your memory card to one of the physical slots in your camera, or in one of the M1, M2, M3, or M4 card-based sets, just follow these steps:

1. **Set up your camera.** Set your camera to the shooting mode and adjust the camera to use the settings you'd like to store. The register can preserve shooting mode, aperture, shutter speed, and settings from the Camera Settings I menu.

2. **Navigate to MR Memory entry.** Select the Memory entry in the Camera Settings I-03 (Shoot Mode/Drive 1) menu and press the center button. A screen like the one shown in Figure 3.9, right, appears.

3. **Review settings.** Use the up/down buttons to scroll through the current settings to make sure they are satisfactory. A great deal more information is available than is shown in the figure (note the scroll bar at right). You can press the up/down buttons to view additional screens with detailed listings of your current settings. Exit and change desired settings, then start again at Step 2.

4. **Choose Register.** Press the left/right buttons to select which of the memory locations you'd like to store your current settings in.

   - If you choose 1, 2, or 3, the settings will be loaded into the camera's physical memory and will be available regardless of which card is in the camera.
   - If you choose M1, M2, M3, or M4, the settings will be stored *on the memory card* and will be available *only* when that memory card resides in the camera.

5. **Proceed or cancel.** Press the center button to confirm and store your settings, or the MENU button to cancel.

6. **Activate register.** To use your stored settings, rotate the mode dial to Register 1, Register 2, or Register 3 (1, 2, or 3 on the mode dial).

MR Select Media

Options: Slot 1, Slot 2

Default: Slot 1

My preference: N/A

This entry is the first on the Camera Settings I-04 page (see Figure 3.10). It allows you to select which memory card slot contains the media with your M1 to M4 settings files. It does not have to be the memory card you are using to store your images. In fact, it is often a good idea to choose the *other* card slot, as that allows you to change your "main" card while retaining the stored settings in the other card. With that configuration you can also change the memory card with your M1 to M4 settings files as often as you like and keep shooting on your "main" card.

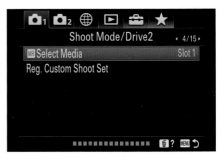

Figure 3.10 The Camera Settings I-04 page.

Register Custom Shooting Set

Options: Recall Custom Hold 1, 2, or 3

Default: Custom Hold 1

My preference: N/A

This function is an expansion of the Memory feature and available when using PASM exposure modes. It allows storing sets of settings for *temporary* recall at the press of a custom key, and lets you choose to store *some* settings and ignore others. You can register three groups of settings but can assign only one at a time to your defined key. The Custom Shooting set is active only while you are holding down the defined key; when you release it the a7R IV returns to its previous settings. You might want to use this feature to switch quickly and temporarily from one set of registered settings to another. Perhaps you're shooting landscapes and unexpectedly spy a rare raptor swooping by. If you've registered a set of parameters for "birds in flight" you can press your custom button, capture the bird, then release it and continue with your landscape shooting.

There are three available slots (Recall Custom Hold 1–3) and you can assign each of the three to a different button, giving you three settings available at the press of a defined button, three settings available from the 1, 2, and 3 physical mode dial positions, and four settings stored as M1 to M4 on your current memory card.

Here's how to use this feature, which is available only when PASM modes are active:

1. **Access this setting from the Camera Settings I-04 (Shoot Mode/Drive 2) menu.** The screen shown in Figure 3.11, left, appears.

2. **Choose registration number in which to store your settings.** Select from Custom Hold 1 to Custom Hold 3.

3. **Check current settings.** You can view the current settings of the camera. Only the settings that can be registered are shown. Use the up/down controls to scroll.

4. **Adjust or disable settings.** There are two columns in the settings display: Enabled/Disabled (represented by a checked/unchecked box) and setting name/and current setting. (See Figure 3.11, center.) The left/right controls switch you from the Enable/Disable column to the Setting Name/Setting column.

5. **To disable registration of a setting.** Highlight the left column of a setting listing and press the center button to add/remove the checkmark.

6. **To change a setting.** Highlight the right column of a setting listing and press the center button. A screen will appear with the available options. For example, for Shoot Mode you can switch from the current mode to Program Auto, Aperture Priority, Shutter Priority, or Manual exposure.

7. **Store settings.** Scroll down to the bottom of the screen and highlight Import Current Setting. Press the center button. The screen shown in Figure 3.11, right, appears.

8. **Register additional numbers.** Highlight Register to return to the screen seen in Figure 3.11, left, to register additional groups of settings.

9. **Assign a Custom Key.** To use this feature, you must assign a button to the Recall Custom Hold x (1, 2, or 3) behavior. Use the Custom Key entry in the Camera Settings II-09 (Custom Operation 1) menu, which I'll describe in Chapter 4. Note that you can define settings for all three Custom Hold registration numbers and can *define separate buttons* for each one. That means you can instantly (and temporarily) recall three additional sets of memory settings using custom keys, if you can spare that many from other duties.

10. **Use Custom Shooting Set.** Press the defined key to activate the Custom Hold settings assigned to that key, then press the shutter release down all the way to take a picture using those settings. When you release the custom key, your a7R IV will return to its previous settings.

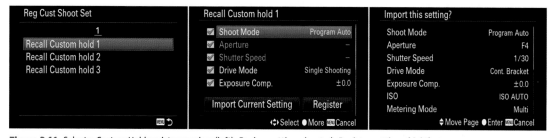

Figure 3.11 Select a Custom Hold register number (left). Review settings (center). Register settings (right).

Focus Mode

Options: Single-shot AF (AF-S), Automatic AF (AF-A), Continuous AF (AF-C), DMF (Direct Manual Focus), MF (Manual Focus)

Default: Single-shot AF (AF-S)

My preference: Automatic AF (AF-A)

This menu item is the first in the Camera Settings I-05 (AF 1) menu (see Figure 3.12). This menu item can be used to set the way in which the camera focuses. I'll discuss focus options in detail in Chapter 8.

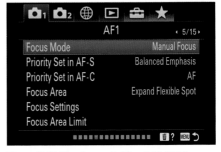

Figure 3.12 The Camera Settings I-05 (AF 1) menu.

- **Single-shot AF (AF-S).** With this default setting, the camera will set focus and it will keep that focus locked as long as you maintain slight pressure on the shutter release button even if the subject moves before you take the photo, the focus will stay where it was set. If you use this setting for still photos and then switch to Movie mode, the camera switches temporarily to AF-C.

- **Automatic AF (AF-A).** Begins to focus using AF-S but will switch to continuous autofocus (AF-C) if your subject is moving. This is a good all-purpose setting when you aren't sure whether your subject will suddenly begin moving around as you shoot.

- **Continuous AF (AF-C).** The camera will continue to adjust the focus if the camera-to-subject distance changes, as when a cyclist approaches your shooting position. The camera will constantly adjust focus to keep the subject sharply rendered. It uses predictive AF to predict the moving subject's position at the time you'll take the next shot and focusing at that distance. This option is useful when you're photographing sports, active children, animals, or other moving subjects, making it possible to get a series of sharply focused shots.

- **Direct Manual Focus (DMF).** Press the shutter button halfway down to let the camera start the focusing process; then, keeping the button pressed halfway, turn the focusing ring to fine-tune the focus manually. You might want to use DMF when you are focusing from a short distance on a small object and want to make sure the focus point is exactly where you want it. If you use this setting for still photos and then switch to Movie mode, the camera switches temporarily to AF-C.

- **Manual Focus (MF).** If you select Manual Focus, you turn the focusing ring on the lens to achieve the sharpest possible focus. With both DMF and Manual Focus, the camera will show you an enlarged image to help with the focusing process, if you have the MF Assist option turned on in the Camera Settings I-14 (Focus Assist) menu (described later).

Priority Set in AF-S/Priority Set in AF-C

Options: AF, Release, Balanced Emphasis
Default: Balanced Emphasis
My preference: Release

These are two separate entries, one for AF-S and one for AF-C autofocus, but functionally they are identical, differing only in the autofocus mode they are applied to. It makes sense to describe them together.

This feature lets you specify whether the camera *waits* to actually take the picture until it has achieved sharp focus (when using an autofocus mode, not manual focus mode); whether it takes the picture immediately, even if sharp focus is not guaranteed; or using a balanced approach somewhere between the two. For most kinds of candid photography, sports, or photojournalism, most of us would rather get the shot rather than lose a fleeting moment, and so Release is often your best choice. If you have a little more time, and the shot won't be affected by a short delay (perhaps half a second, on average), Balanced Emphasis, the default, will do the job. If you're looking for the best sharpness your camera can provide, the AF choice might be your best option. The choices are as follows:

- **AF.** The shutter is not activated until sharp focus is achieved. This is best for subjects that are not moving rapidly.
  - **AF-S.** When using AF-S, most prefer to set this to AF, because in this focus mode the subject is usually not moving rapidly, and it makes sense to allow a slight extra delay to get the best focus possible. However, I find that with the a7R IV, when equipped with a lens having a built-in focus motor, in combination with the hybrid AF system, focus is fast enough that I can choose Release instead. If your camera/lens combination is slower to focus, you'll want to stick with the AF setting.
  - **AF-C.** When working in AF-C focus mode, if you select AF, the a7R IV will continue to track your subjects' movement, but the camera won't take a picture until focus is locked in. An indicator in the viewing screen will flash green until focus can be achieved. You might miss a few shots, but you will have fewer out-of-focus images. Sports shooters probably won't choose AF priority for AF-C. Instead, they'll select release priority, discussed next.
- **Release.** When this option is selected, the shutter is activated when the release button is pushed down all the way, even if sharp focus has not yet been achieved. As I noted, I prefer this option for AF-C mode, as Continuous Focus focuses and refocuses constantly when autofocus is active, and even though an image may not quite be in sharpest focus, at least I got the shot. Use this option when taking a picture is more important than absolute best focus, such as fast action or photojournalism applications. (You don't want to miss that record-setting home run, or the pro-testor's pie smashing into the governor's face.) Using this setting doesn't mean that your image won't be sharply focused; it just means that you'll get a picture even if autofocusing isn't *quite* complete. If you've been poised with the shutter release pressed halfway, the camera probably has been tracking the focus of your image.

- **Balanced Emphasis.** In this mode, the shutter is released when the button is pressed, with a slight pause if autofocus has not yet been achieved. It can be selected for both AF-S and AF-C modes and is probably your best choice if you want a good compromise between speed of activation and sharpest focus. However, you would not want to use this setting if the highest possible continuous shooting rates are important to you.

Focus Area

Options: Wide, Zone, Center, Flexible Spot, Expand Flexible Spot, Tracking
Default: Wide
My preference: Wide for general use; Tracking Wide for sports and action

When the camera is set to Autofocus, use this menu option to specify where in the frame the camera will focus when you compose a scene in still photo mode, using the focus area selection you specify. I'll explain these options, the special requirements, and include illustrations of the focusing areas in Chapter 8.

- **Wide.** The camera uses its own electronic intelligence to determine what part of the scene should be in sharpest focus, providing automatic focus point selection. A green frame is displayed around the area that is in focus. Even if you set one of the other options, Wide is automatically selected in certain shooting modes, including both Auto and all SCN modes.

- **Zone.** Select one of nine focus areas (described in Chapter 9), and the camera chooses which section of that zone to use to calculate sharp focus. You can move the focus zone with the multi-selector joystick.

- **Center.** Choose this option if you want the camera to always focus on the subject in the center of the frame. Center the primary subject (like a friend's face in a wide-angle landscape composition); allow the camera to focus on it; maintain slight pressure on the shutter release button to keep focus locked; and re-frame the scene for a more effective, off-center, composition. Take the photo at any time and your friend (who is now off-center) will be in the sharpest focus. Use this option instead of manually selecting a focus point to quickly lock focus on the center of the frame, then press the defined AF lock button to fix the focus at that point so you can recompose the image as you prefer.

- **Flexible Spot.** This mode allows you to move the camera's focus detection point (focus area) around the scene to any one of multiple locations using the multi-selector joystick. When this option is highlighted, use the left/right directional buttons or control wheel to change the size range of the spot among Small (S), Medium (M), and Large (L).

  This mode can be useful when the camera is mounted on a tripod and you'll be taking photos of the same scene for a long time, while the light is changing, for example. Move the focus area to cover the most important subject, and it will always focus on that point when you later take a photo.

- **Expand Flexible Spot.** If the camera is unable to lock in focus using the selected focus point, it will also use the eight adjacent points to try to achieve focus. You can move the spot using the multi-selector joystick.

- **Tracking.** In this mode, the camera locks focus onto the subject area that is under the selected focus spot when the shutter button is depressed halfway. Then, if the subject moves (or you change the framing in the camera), the camera will continue to refocus *on that subject*. You can select this mode only when the focus mode is set to Continuous AF (AF-C). Note that Tracking is different from Center Tracking, discussed in this chapter, and in more detail in Chapter 8.

  This option is especially powerful because you can activate it for any of the five focus area options described above. That is, once you've highlighted Tracking on the selection screen, you can then press the left-right directional button and choose Wide, Zone, Center, Flexible Spot, or Expand Flexible Spot.

Focus Settings

Options: Move focus frame; select focus area

Default: None

My preference: Assign to a key of your choice using Custom Keys in the Camera Settings II-09 (Operation 1) menu.

Note that this entry is a *function* rather than a settings screen; that is, when invoked you can use the directional controls to move the focus zone/area around within the frame. As such, it is most convenient when it's summoned not by navigating to this menu entry, but by defining a Custom key to activate its function.

The Focus Settings function allows you to move the focus frame around when using the Zone focus area mode, or the focus spot when using Flexible Spot or Expand Flexible Spot area mode. It's not available when the a7R IV is set to Wide or Center area focus modes. It's most useful when you assign the function to a button using the Custom Key entry in the Camera Settings II-09 menu. When it's active, you can quickly make focus adjustments using the front and rear dials, and control wheel:

- In any Autofocus (AF-S, AF-A, AF-C) or Direct Manual focus mode:
  - **Front dial/up/down controls.** Moves the focus frame up/down.
  - **Rear dial/left/right controls.** Moves the focus frame left/right.
  - **Control wheel.** Rotating the wheel selects a specific focus area mode from any of the choices described in the Focus Area entry above.
- You can use Focus Settings in Manual focus mode, too:
  - **Front dial/up/down buttons.** Moves the magnified focus area up/down.
  - **Rear dial/left/right buttons.** Moves the magnified focus area left/right.
  - **Control wheel.** Rotating the wheel moves the magnified area up/down.

Focus Area Limit

Options: Wide, Zone, Center, Flexible Spot (Small, Medium, Large), Expand Flexible Spot, Tracking

Default: All available

My preference: Deactivate little-used focus area choices.

Experiencing too much of a good thing? This entry allows you to deactivate focus options that you rarely (or never) use, so that they don't appear when you select a focus area using the Focus Area entry (above), or use the Function menu's Focus Area option. Only the choices you enable will be shown; the others will be grayed out.

When you select this entry, the screen shown in Figure 3.13 appears. The check marks above each focus area indicates that that option is available. To disable/enable a particular focus area choice, highlight it using the directional buttons and press the center button to remove/add the check mark. The top row shows the non-tracking options (left to right): Wide, Zone, Center, Flexible Spot (Small), Flexible Spot (Medium), Flexible Spot (Large), and Expand Flexible Spot. The bottom row includes the Tracking counterparts of the exact same choices.

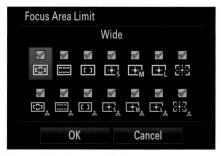

Figure 3.13 Focus Area Limit options.

That configuration gives you a great deal of flexibility. You can have one set of focus areas enabled for general use, and choose a different set when using the a7R IV's Tracking capabilities. In my case, I use the Flexible Spot: (Small) focus area frequently, but disable the Medium and Large options. However, when shooting sports and action, I use Tracking almost exclusively, so I disable *all* the Tracking choices except for Flexible Spot: (Small), (Medium), and (Large). So, all I need to do is press the Fn button, highlight Focus Area, and select Tracking. I can then switch among Small, Medium, or Large by pressing the left/right directional buttons.

But wait, there's more! As you'll learn in Chapter 4, you can assign the Switch Focus Area function to a Custom Key, using that entry in the Camera Settings II-09 menu. After you've enabled/disabled the Focus Area options to your liking, you can cycle among those that remain simply by pressing the assigned function key.

Switch Vertical/Horizontal AF Area

Options: Off, AF Point Only, AF Point+AF Area

Default: Off

My preference: Depends on subject

This is the first entry in the Camera Settings I-06 menu. (See Figure 3.14.) Here you can choose whether the Focus Area mode and the location of the focusing area within the frame adjusts when you change the camera's orientation from horizontal to vertical. It's especially useful when you

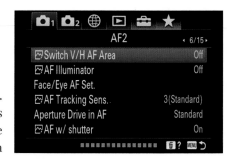

Figure 3.14 Camera Settings I-06 (AF 2) menu.

want to change orientation frequently for the same type of subject matter. For example, when I am photographing family and individual portraits I might shoot one set of images with the camera held horizontally to capture several members of a group, then rotate to use a vertical frame to capture a head-and-shoulders image of an individual. Many sports, such as basketball, involve the same sort of adjustment—a horizontal photo showing two or three players fighting for the ball, followed by a vertically oriented picture of a pair of roundballers going after a rebound off the boards.

Here are some things to consider:

- **You can/must set the Focus Area mode and/or focus point for each orientation individually.** That is, you must choose a Focus Area mode/focus point for horizontal orientation, then shift to each of the two vertical orientations and select a different location for either/both. If you don't specify a new location, the Focus Area and focus point remain where they were.

- **Only three orientations available.** They are horizontal, rotated 90 degrees clockwise with the shutter release on the lower half of the camera, and rotated 90 degrees from horizontal with the shutter release on the upper half of the camera. The horizontal/upside down orientation is the same as the conventional horizontal orientation. When the camera is pointed straight up (toward the sky) or straight down (towards your feet), the a7R IV has no idea about how it is otherwise oriented.

- **AF Area Mode/Focus Point Switching Disabled.** Changes in orientation are ignored if you are using Intelligent Auto, Movie, or S&Q Motion shooting modes. The feature is also disabled if you press the shutter halfway down (and then change orientations), and during autofocus, continuous shooting, self-timer countdown, or Focus Settings adjustments. Using the Focus Magnifier also disables the feature.

You have three options for this feature:

- **Off.** The Focus Area mode and Focus Point (Frame) remain the same regardless of camera orientation. If you've selected a particular Focus Area mode and you've placed the focus at the lower-left area of the frame when shooting horizontally (as seen in Figure 3.15, center), it will remain in the equivalent position when you rotate the a7R IV 90 degrees counter-clockwise (Figure 3.15, left), or 90 degrees clockwise. (See Figure 3.15, right.)

- **AF Point Only.** The Focus Area mode remains the same while the Focus Point adjusts to the camera orientation. (See Figure 3.16.)

- **AF Point+AF Area.** Both the Focus Area mode and Focus Point adjust, so you can use a different Focus Area mode for each orientation.

Figure 3.15 When the feature is turned off, the focus points remain in the same relative position as the camera is rotated.

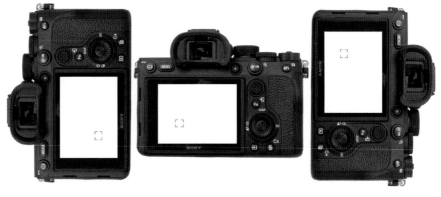

Figure 3.16 When switching is enabled, you can position the focus points in different locations within the frame for each of the three orientations. You can also optionally specify a different Focus Area mode for each presentation.

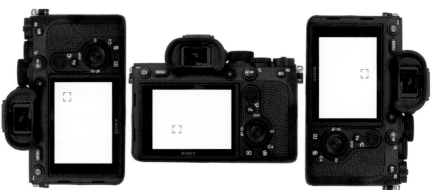

AF Illuminator (Stills)

Options: Auto, Off

Default: Auto

My preference: Auto

The AF illuminator is a light activated when there is insufficient light for the camera's autofocus mechanism to zero in on the subject. This light emanates from the same lamp on the front of the camera that provides the indicator for the self-timer. The extra blast from the AF illuminator provides a bright target for the AF system to help the camera set focus for subjects roughly no farther away than 10 feet. When you're shooting in environments so dark that conventional focusing is difficult, the a7R IV will ignore the focus area you've specified and instead focus on whatever the AF assist lamp is able to illuminate. This menu item is a still-photos-only option, as the illuminator does not operate while shooting conventional or Slow & Quick motion movies.

The default setting, Auto, allows the AF illuminator to work any time the camera judges that it is necessary. Turn it off when you would prefer not to use this feature, such as when you don't want to disturb the people around you or call attention to your photographic endeavors. The AF illuminator doesn't work when the camera is set for manual focus or when using AF-C or AF-A while the subject is moving. It is also disabled when using the Focus Magnifier, or one of the EA-LA adapters (which allow using A-mount lenses on the a7R IV).

Note: Some Sony flash units (currently only the HVL-F45RM) include a white LED video light that the a7R IV will use as an AF illuminator lamp if the flash is mounted on the camera and powered up.

Face/Eye AF Settings

Options: Face/Eye Priority in AF: On, Off; Subject Detection: Human/Animal; Right/Left Eye Select: Right, Left, Auto; Face Detect Frame Display: On, Off; Animal Eye Display: On, Off

Default: Face/Eye Priority in AF: On; Subject Detection: Human; Right/Left Eye Select: Auto; Face Detect Frame Display: On; Animal Eye Display: On

My preference: I use the defaults; this feature rocks!

When you're photographing people, the a7R IV can optionally look for faces and can base its autofocus decisions on the faces it locates. Even better, you can give certain countenances a higher priority than others by registering them with the camera, so, say, if your significant other is ensconced in the frame, the camera will favor that person as its AF focus (so to speak) over other humans in the frame. Further, the camera can locate human or animal eyes within your frame, and focus on them. Face/Eye detection can't be used with digital zoom, Sweep Panorama, the Focus Magnifier, the Posterization Picture Effect, Landscape/Night Scene/Sunset Scene modes, and 120p/100p movie or 120 fps/100 fps Slow & Quick Motion video. The Eye AF feature is unavailable when capturing all movies and Slow & Quick Motion clips.

Using this entry, you have the following choices (see Figure 3.17, left):

- **Face/Eye Priority in AF.** Choose On and the a7R IV can give a higher priority to detected faces. Select Off and AF will proceed without looking for faces. Up to eight faces, if present, may be detected. When autofocus is activated, the camera will attempt to focus on the eyes, if they are located within the active focus area. Note that when using Superior Auto, Face/Eye Priority is locked at On. **Note:** Enabling Face/Eye Priority does *not* mean the camera will automatically focus on those areas. See the sidebar that follows.

  The Eye AF portion of Face/Eye Priority AF may not function as expected with subjects which are rapidly moving, have long bangs, or closed eyes, or are wearing sunglasses. Shady conditions, backlight, and low-light situations can also hinder eye detection.

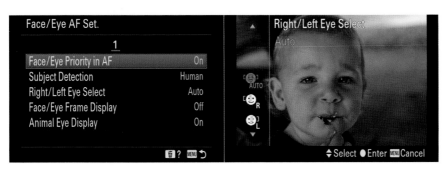

Figure 3.17 Face/Eye AF Settings (left). Choose Right Eye, Left Eye, or Auto selection (right).

- **Subject Detection.** When set to Human, the camera looks for human faces and eyes. If you choose Animal instead, it looks for animal eyes only; apparently creatures' faces are too varied to detect reliably.
- **Right/Left Eye Select.** Chooses whether to detect the left or right eye of the subject. Note that this feature uses the *subject's* eye, which may be on the opposite side from your perspective (that is, your subject's right eye is on the left side of your frame). (See Figure 3.17, right.)
- **Face Detection Frame Display.** The camera automatically shows a small white square around a human eye it is focusing on, and that frame will turn green when the subject is in focus. But you can *also* enable a frame around entire faces with this option. (If you want the frames to display, but disappear after a time, use AF Area Auto Clear, described later in this chapter.)

  Although the eye-focus box is helpful, I find the additional box around the face very useful and leave it on at all times so I know *exactly* what face(s) has been detected. When enabled, a gray selection box appears around detected faces. The box around the face used for autofocus turns white. If there are several faces in the frame and you've registered and prioritized some or all of them, the boxes around the other faces turn reddish-purple. (I'll show you how to register faces later in this chapter.) If you find the boxes distracting, you can turn them off, and face detection, if enabled as described earlier, will still be active.
- **Animal Eye Display.** Again, animal faces are not detected, but you can choose to have the camera place a frame around their eyes when they are found.

DETECTING VS. FOCUSING

For some unknown reason, Sony has thrown you a curve ball with this feature. Activating Face/Eye Priority in Autofocus means that your a7R IV will *detect* faces and eyes, but doesn't guarantee that it will automatically *focus* on them! The difference is so subtle, you may not notice. What actually happens is that when detection is enabled, the camera will prioritize focus on the face/eye it has found *if that face or eye is within the Focus Area you are using.* So, if you're using the Center focus area and your human subject happens to reside outside that area, the camera will helpfully detect a face/eye and display a frame around it, but will focus *only* on whatever is actually within the focus area.

You might not realize this, particularly if the actual subject you have focused on is located near to, but slightly in front of or behind a human. Further, most of our "people" shots have the person in the center of the frame, and, with some focus modes (such as Wide), the focus area is so large that your human may actually be in an appropriate location, anyway. But however, you should be aware of this distinction.

You *can* guarantee, at least, that Eye AF will be used, regardless of your selected Focus Area, by defining Eye AF to a Custom Key, as described next.

Customizing Eye AF

You can customize the eye detection component (Eye AF) of the feature by assigning a custom key to one of these two behaviors, or a different key to each of them. I'll show you how to set up custom keys in Chapter 4.

■ **Activate Eye AF with Custom Key.** The Eye AF function can be assigned to a key, and the a7R IV will detect and focus on the eye *as long as you are holding down the custom key*. The camera will search for human eyes within the entire frame, regardless of the Focus Area you've selected. Press the shutter release down all the way while holding the key to take the picture. This fixes the potential problem I described in the sidebar above. It also means that if you have a preferred Focus Area setting for a particular shooting session, you don't have to switch to another in order to make Eye AF function properly.

■ **Switch Eyes with Custom Key.** If your subjects are always facing you, then setting Right/Left Eye Select to Auto may be your best bet. That's because if you apply the Switch Right/Left Eye behavior to a custom key, should you not like the camera's eye selection, press and hold the defined key to temporarily switch focus to the other eye. Moreover, if you've told the a7R IV to always choose the Left (or Right) eye, you can switch to the alternate by pressing the key.

AF Tracking Sensitivity (Stills)

Options: 5 (Responsive) to 1 (Locked On)

Default: 3 (Standard)

My preference: 4

This feature determines how quickly the camera unlocks focus from the subject it is currently tracking and focuses instead on another subject that intervenes. For example, if you're shooting a football game as a running back is breaking through the line and a referee bolts along the sideline in front of you. With this feature set to Responsive, the camera will very quickly switch to the ref, and then should return its attention to the running back—but often, not quickly enough. A better choice would be to use Locked On, so that the camera briefly ignores the referee, who is likely to have moved on in a second or two. Focus tracking will remain on your running back. Your options include:

■ **Responsive.** At the 4 and 5 settings, the camera quickly responds to new subjects that cross the frame. This is the best setting to use for fast-moving subjects, such as sports or frenetic children, *as long as you don't expect intervening subjects*. The camera will smoothly follow your subjects. It works well when subjects within the frame are at significantly different distances.

■ **Standard.** At the 3 setting, response to movement is a bit slower, so that the camera doesn't constantly refocus as subjects move about the frame. This is the default and should be used when there is only moderate movement, and especially if the movement is across the width or height of the frame (rather than coming toward you or away from you), and when you're using a small f/stop, because the increased depth-of-field will eliminate the need for most re-focusing.

■ **Locked On.** At the 1 and 2 settings, the a7R IV will lock onto the initial subject and follow it until it leaves the frame. Use this setting when you know you'll have intervening subjects often and are certain that you want to ignore them. Many sports events, including football, soccer, and baseball, fall into this category.

Aperture Drive in AF

Options: Focus Priority, Standard, Silent Priority
Default: Standard
My preference: N/A

This setting determines whether and how much the aperture opens between shots, allowing you to choose whether you want the camera to operate more quietly or focus more accurately. Why is that even necessary? Well, if you're a photography veteran, you may wonder why Sony cameras, including the a7R IV, don't have a depth-of-field preview button. The short answer is that they don't need one, because, unlike most other models, these cameras always focus with the lens stopped down to the working f/stop ("taking aperture" in photo jargon) used to expose the picture.

When using cameras that keep the aperture wide open until the moment of exposure (when it stops down to take the picture), it's useful to have a depth-of-field preview that temporarily closes the aperture to the working f/stop. With the lens stopped down, you can see (more or less) exactly how much is in focus, and how much is not.

There are some advantages and disadvantages to having the lens already set to the taking aperture while composing your images. You *always* get to see the current depth-of-field; the a7R IV automatically brightens the view on the LCD or electronic viewfinder to compensate. (However, *exposure adjustments* do change the brightness of the display when Setting Effect On is enabled in the Live View Display entry of the Camera Settings II-08 menu.) In addition, because the camera doesn't have to keep opening and closing the aperture between shots, faster continuous shooting speeds are possible.

The downside is that it's more difficult to focus at smaller f/stops, even with your camera's hybrid phase detect/contrast detect AF system, as you'll learn in Chapter 8. At f/stops smaller than f/11 autofocus is not used between continuous shots when using the electronic shutter (to achieve the high speed of 10 frames per second). Instead, in that mode focus is fixed at that determined for the first shot. This entry offers three options for specifying exactly how the camera adjusts the aperture while shooting. Your choices are as follows:

- **Focus Priority.** When shooting continuously with the electronic shutter (but *not* Mechanical Shutter or Auto chosen for Shutter Type), the a7R IV will open slightly. Sony doesn't specify how much, but in my tests the lens does not necessarily open to its maximum aperture. With the wider aperture, the AF system can focus more quickly and accurately.

  There is a slight increase in noise with this setting, caused by the movement of the iris, the display may flicker, and the aperture level may not be displayed on the screen. The camera uses Standard instead of Focus Priority when not using continuous shooting, even if Focus Priority is set here.

- **Standard.** The a7R IV uses the working aperture to focus, and locks the aperture to the working f/stop of the first shot for subsequent continuous shots with the electronic shutter.

- **Silent Priority.** The f/stop doesn't change, even when an f/stop smaller than f/11 is set. Focusing may be slower, but the noise level is less than both Focus Priority and Standard settings. This option is available only when certain lenses are mounted on the camera. (Check with Sony for compatible optics. No list is available as I write this.)

AF with Shutter (Stills)

Options: On/Off
Default: On
My preference: N/A

As you know, a gentle touch on the shutter release button causes the camera to begin focusing when using an autofocus mode. There may be some situations in which you prefer that the camera not re-focus every time you touch the shutter release button, such as when you want to work with *back-button focus*, which I'll explain in detail in Chapter 8.

Let's say you are taking multiple pictures in a laboratory or studio with the subject at the same distance; you have no need to refocus constantly, and there is no need to put an extra burden on the autofocus mechanism and on the battery. But, you don't want to switch to manual focus. Instead, you can set AF w/Shutter to Off. From then on, the camera will never begin to autofocus, or to change the focus when the shutter release is pressed. You can still initiate autofocus by pressing the AF-On button or another key that you've assigned the AF-On function (as I'll describe later under Custom Keys). The AF-On button will start autofocus at any point, independent of the shutter release. Pressing the shutter release still locks *exposure,* unless you've disabled that function, too, using the AEL w/Shutter entry in the Camera Settings I-10 (Exposure 2) entry discussed later in this chapter.

Pre-AF (Stills)

Options: Off, On
Default: Off
My preference: N/A

This is the first entry in the Camera Setting I-07 (AF 3) menu. (See Figure 3.18.) It tells the camera to attempt to adjust the focus even before you press the shutter button halfway, giving you a head start that's useful for grab shots. When an image you want to capture appears, you can press the shutter release and take the picture a bit more quickly. However, this pre-focus process uses a lot of juice, depleting your battery more quickly, which is why it is turned off by default. Reserve it for short-term use during quickly unfolding situations where the slight advantage can be useful.

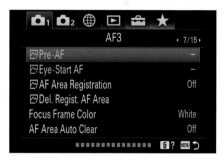

Figure 3.18 Camera Settings I-07 (AF 3) menu.

In my tests with the a7R IV and various lenses, Pre-AF can be a little slow to respond sometimes, but it does work with all autofocus modes and E-mount optics. If you find Pre-AF to be sluggish, say under low-light conditions, just press the shutter release halfway to commence autofocus manually.

Eye-Start AF (Stills)

Options: On, Off
Default: Off
My preference: Off

Note: This feature is available *only* when using the EA-LA2 or EA-LA4 adapters and a compatible A-mount lens. These two adapters are the counterparts to the LA1/LA3 (APS-C/Full frame) to allow using A-mount lenses on E-mount cameras like the a7R IV. However, unlike the odd-numbered versions, they contain their own semi-translucent mirror phase detect autofocus systems similar to those used in cameras like the Sony a77 II or a99 II. Both adapters include an autofocus motor built-in, so you can use A-mount lenses that *do not* have built-in motors.

When Eye-Start AF is turned On, the camera will start autofocusing the instant you move the viewfinder to your eye. The display on the LCD vanishes, the camera adjusts autofocus, and, if you're using any Shooting mode other than Manual exposure, it sets the shutter speed and/or aperture so you're ready to take the shot. You don't even need to touch the shutter release button or another button to summon autofocus. Of course, it's not magic. There is a sensor just above the viewfinder window that detects when your face (or anything else) approaches the finder.

This is useful because it increases the odds of capturing a fleeting moment. On the other hand, some people find this feature annoying. When it's On, the camera will begin to autofocus every time a stray hand or other object passes near the viewfinder. Also, if you're wearing the camera around your neck, you may hear a continuous clicking as the camera rubs against your body, triggering the focusing mechanism. When this happens frequently, it will consume a significant amount of battery power.

After experimenting with this feature, you may decide to turn Eye-Start AF off. After you do so, when using the a7R IV with the LA2/LA4 adapters, it reverts to its boring old behavior of not initiating focus until you partially depress the shutter button (or another defined button). Naturally, the electronic viewfinder will still activate when your eye (or anything else) is near the sensors (if the FINDER/MONITOR setting, described in Chapter 4, is set to Auto). But you won't get autofocus until you're certain you want AF to start.

AF Area Registration (Stills)

Options: Off, On
Default: Off
My preference: On

This is an absolute killer feature for sports photographers, as it allows you to switch from your current focus point to a pre-registered point—and then back to your original point—just by pressing a custom key. Say you're covering a baseball game and frequently alternate between photographing the batter or some other position and first base, where a lot of action takes place. If you've registered first base (as I'll describe shortly), you're free to focus elsewhere and then, when the batter makes contact and begins running toward first (or the pitcher decides to throw to first to cut off a base runner who's taken a lead), you can press the defined key and the focus point will instantly move back to the registered first base location within the frame.

To use this feature, just follow these steps:

1. **Activate AF Area Registration.** Navigate to this menu entry and choose On, then press the center button to confirm. A message will appear reminding you to register a specific focus area. I'll explain how to do that shortly. Press the center button again to exit to the menu.

2. **Access Custom Keys (Stills).** To relocate the focus point to a registered position, you'll need to define a custom button to do that. Access the Camera Settings II-9 (Custom Operations 1) menu and select the Custom Key (Stills) entry at the top of the list.

3. **Define a custom button.** Select an unused custom button to use and press the center button to view the behavior choices available. Several pages listing available functions can be displayed. Use the left/right buttons to scroll to the AF2 page within the definition screens for your selected key and choose how you want to enable the switch to the registered autofocus point. The three relevant options are as follows:

   - **Registered AF Area Hold.** Pressing the button switches to the registered location *only* while you hold the button down. When you release the custom key the focus point returns to your previous focus point. This option is useful if you want to be able to switch to the registered area only temporarily. If you find it awkward to manipulate two buttons at once (holding down your custom key, plus pressing the shutter release to take the picture), you may be better off switching back and forth using the toggle option described next.

   - **Registered AF Area Toggle.** Press and release the button to switch to the registered location and press it a second time to return to your previous focus point. Use this if you think you'll need to take several consecutive images using the registered point. Toggle is the only available option for the left, right, and down keys.

   - **Registered AF Area+AF On.** When the custom key is pressed the focus point switches to the registered area and autofocus is initiated. When you release the custom key, the focus point returns to its previous location. If you've registered first base you can then move the focus point to home plate and continue to capture the batter's efforts. Then, if action unfolds at first base, press the defined button and the a7R IV will switch to your registered focus point and focus. You can then continue to hold the key while pressing the shutter release down to take the picture. Release the button and the focus point returns to home plate. (You can avoid the need to hold down the button if you're using back-button focus, which decouples the AF activation feature from the shutter release.) This *sounds* complicated if you don't know how back-button focus works, but I'll explain it in more detail in Chapter 8.

4. **Registered focus frame appears.** When the defined custom key is pressed, the focus frame and points will flash in the viewfinder and on the LCD monitor.

AF Area Registration cannot be used when shooting movies or S&Q video, when using digital zoom or tracking, while focus is locked, or when you are focusing using the lens's focus ring or the a7R IV's Touch Focus feature.

Delete Registered AF Area (Stills)

Options: Delete, Cancel

Default: Cancel

My preference: N/A

Use this to delete a registered focus area. That prevents the camera from shifting to the previously defined area if you accidentally press the defined custom key.

Focus Frame Color

Options: White, Red

Default: White

My preference: Red

By default, the a7R IV shows the current focus frame in white, displaying the active points in green when focus is achieved. Many (including me) find the white frame difficult to discern with many subjects, particularly those that are bright or light in color. I prefer to see the frame highlighted in red, which seems more natural and provides a strong contrast.

AF Area Auto Clear

Options: Off, On

Default: Off

My preference: Off

It controls whether the focus area is shown all the time as you shoot, or whether it disappears a short time after focus is achieved. Choose On if you prefer having an uncluttered screen while you shoot. I prefer to have focus information available at all times, so I leave this setting at its default Off value.

Display Continuous AF Area

Options: On, Off

Default: On

My preference: On

This setting is the first in the Camera Settings II-08 (AF 4) menu. (See Figure 3.19.) This item determines whether the previewing display on the monitor or EVF shows the active Wide or Zone focus areas when you're using Continuous AF. It has no effect on their display if you're using Center or Flexible Spot in Continuous AF area modes, or autofocus modes other than AF-C.

Sometimes too much information can be distracting. That's especially true in AF-C mode, because if you've framed a moving subject, the camera can continue to change the

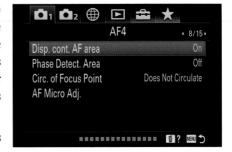

Figure 3.19 Camera Settings II-08 (AF 4) menu.

active focus areas if your subject is moving. In Wide mode, you may be treated to a dancing array of green rectangles squirming around on your screen as the a7R IV focuses and refocuses in anticipation of you eventually pressing the shutter release all the way down and taking a picture. I think that the constantly shifting focus requires less continual feedback about what focus areas are being used, so you may want to switch the feature off. In my case, I don't mind the display, and I tend to leave it on most of the time, even though it consumes a little more battery power.

Phase Detect. Area

Options: On, Off
Default: On
My preference: On

The a7R IV has 567 phase detection points embedded in its full-frame sensor. It allows you to enable or disable *display* of the phase detect area, in the form of a pair of brackets appearing on the screen to mark the portion of the frame where the points reside on the viewing screen when using compatible lenses. (Some compatible lenses may need a firmware update; check the Sony website for your country to view the latest list of compatible lenses and available lens firmware updates.) The area is not shown when the camera is set for APS-C crop mode, nor when shooting movies. If you happen to be using an autofocus lens attached using the LA-EA2 or LA-EA4 adapters for A-mount lenses, the adapter's phase detect points are used instead of the a7R IV's.

Circulation of Focus Point

Options: Does Not Circulate, Circulate
Default: Does Not Circulate
My preference: N/A

This setting simply determines whether you can only move the focus point within the image frame, or whether, when it reaches left, right, top, or bottom edges it wraps around to the opposite side. Unless you played too much *Pac-Man* in your youth, you will probably prefer Does Not Circulate.

AF Micro Adjustment

Options: AF Adjustment Setting, Amount, Clear
Default: None
My preference: N/A

If you've sprung for the $300 to $400 (in the US) required to purchase the optional LA-EA2 or LA-EA4 mount adapters and are using A-mount lenses on your a7R IV, you may find that some slight autofocus adjustment is necessary to fine-tune your lens. **Note:** I have noticed that my LA-EA adapters fit quite snuggly on my a7R IV, a much tighter fit than on my previous Sony full-frame cameras, probably due to the beefed-up lens mount flange. It sometimes requires a bit of effort to attach the adapter until it clicks, but I want to remind you that under no circumstances should you try to force the connection. It may be possible that slight tolerance differences have made your adapter and your camera not the best match. Seek help from Sony if you have a problem mounting an adapter—or any Sony lens to your a7R IV.

This menu item allows choosing a value from –20 (to focus closer to the camera) to +20 (to change the focus point to farther away). You can enable/disable the feature, and clear the value set for each lens. The camera stores the value you dial in for the lens currently mounted on the camera and can log up to 30 different lenses (but each lens must be different; you can't register two copies of the same lens). Once you've "used up" the available slots, you'll need to mount a lesser-used lens and clear the value for that lens to free up a memory slot. This adjustment works reliably only with Sony, Minolta, and Konica-Minolta A-mount lenses. I'll show you how to use this feature in Chapter 12.

A-MOUNT ADAPTERS ONLY

You'll note that no such adjustment is supplied for E-mount lenses. That's because the a7R IV calculates focus using *actual data collected at the sensor*—whether operating in contrast detect or phase detect mode. Front- or back-focus issues don't exist. The LA-EA2 and LA-EA4 adapters, on the other hand, use their separate SLT-style AF sensors, and slight alignment issues *can* make a difference. Sony recognizes this and has kindly provided this feature.

Exposure Compensation

Options: From +5 to –5

Default: 0.0

My preference: N/A

This is the first entry on the Camera Settings I-09 (Exposure 1) page (see Figure 3.20). It is one of three ways to specify exposure compensation:

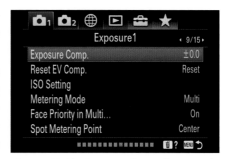

Figure 3.20 The Camera Settings I-9 (Exposure 1) menu.

- **This menu entry.** Here you can adjust EV values from +5 to –5 using the directional buttons, the multi-selector joystick, or by rotating the control wheel, rear dial, or front dial. It is available *only* when the Exposure Compensation dial on the top-right surface of the camera is set to 0.

- **Function menu.** Press the Fn button and navigate to the Exposure Compensation icon (located by default in the top row, fourth from the left). If the Exposure Compensation dial is set to 0, you can use the same controls described above to make adjustments.

- **Exposure Compensation dial.** If you elect to use the physical dial you can choose only values from +3 to –3. If those are a broad enough range for you (and most of the time that's all you'll really need), the dial is the fastest option. Any setting you make with the dial overrides an adjustment made with the menus. Remember to press the dial's lock button until it pops up to free the dial, then press down to lock it again if you don't want your setting to change accidentally.

Scroll until you reach the value for the amount of compensation you want to set to make your shots lighter (with positive values) or darker (with negative values). When shooting movies, only +2 to –2 values are valid. I'll discuss exposure compensation in more detail in Chapter 9.

Remember that any compensation you set with the physical dial will stay in place until you change it, even if the camera has been powered off in the meantime. It's worth developing a habit of checking your display to see if any positive or negative exposure compensation is still in effect; return to 0.0 before you start shooting. If you like, EV settings set using the two menu options can also be "sticky" and survive a power off/on cycle, using Reset EV Compensation (discussed next).

Exposure compensation cannot be used when the camera is set to Intelligent Auto. In Manual exposure mode, the EV settings only apply if ISO has been set to ISO Auto. The EV changes you make with the menus will be in either 1/3- or 1/2-EV increments, depending on the step size you specify in the Exposure Step entry, which I'll explain shortly. When using the physical dial, increments are locked at 1/3 EV steps.

Reset EV Compensation

Options: Reset, Maintain
Default: Reset
My preference: Reset

While EV compensation set using the physical dial is locked in until you rotate the dial to a different position, any adjustments you make using the menus can be automatically zeroed out when the camera is powered off. That ability, plus the broader +5 to –5 adjustment range is a good reason to use the (faster, but less flexible) dial. I like to use the default Reset option, as it eliminates a lot of unintended exposure errors caused when you're unknowingly using compensation set for an earlier subject. If you're shooting under the same conditions for a period of time and think you'll be turning the camera on and off frequently, use Maintain instead.

ISO Setting

Options: Fixed settings from 50 to 102400, plus ISO Auto, ISO Range Limits, ISO Auto Minimum Shutter Speed
Default: ISO Auto (ISO 100–12800); Range Limit: 50–102400; ISO Auto Minimum Shutter Speed: Standard
My preference: The defaults work best for general shooting, except I lower ISO Auto's top range to ISO 3200.

When you select ISO Setting from the menu, a screen appears with three choices: ISO, ISO Range Limit, and ISO Auto Minimum Shutter Speed. Earlier models spread some of these choices over several top-level entries, but Sony has combined them into one for the a7R IV. I'll address each of the subscreens separately.

ISO

This menu item can also be accessed by pressing the right (ISO) button on the control wheel. It allows you to use the ISO setting (sensor sensitivity) in one of two ways:

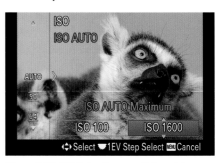

Figure 3.21 ISO Auto allows specifying minimum and maximum ISO sensitivity.

- **ISO Auto.** The Auto ISO setting is at the top of the scrolling list. When it's highlighted, press the right button and choose a minimum ISO to be used as well as the maximum ISO applied (which prevents the camera from taking a clutch of pictures at, say, ISO 25,600, unbeknownst to you). For general shooting, I use ISO 100 and ISO 3200 for my limits, as I mentioned. I sometimes lower the upper limit to ISO 1600 when I especially want to minimize noise, and raise the upper end to ISO 6400 or higher for indoor subjects (especially sports, which can benefit from faster shutter speeds and/or smaller f/stops). (See Figure 3.21.)

- **Fixed ISO settings.** You can select ISO settings from 50 to 102,400, and the camera will take all its shots at that sensitivity. Strictly speaking, ISO 100 is the lowest real sensitivity the camera can produce; that's the "native" sensitivity of the sensor. The 50/64/80 settings are "interpolated" and produce slightly higher contrast and lower quality. The a7R IV places horizontal bars above and below the number for those values as a "warning." Similarly, the same bars sandwich ISO settings above 32,000 to let you know that quality is reduced at the loftier settings.

  I recommend using the interpolated lower values only when you really need a lower sensitivity, say, to use a wider f/stop in very bright conditions, or when you want to use a slower shutter speed to intentionally produce blur of, perhaps, a waterfall. A neutral-density filter attached to your lens can also reduce the amount of light reaching the sensor. The upper extended settings are best reserved for situations where you really need high ISO sensitivity and are willing to accept the visual noise that results. I'll explain noise reduction in a little more detail in Chapter 7.

FAST FORWARD

If you're choosing fixed ISO settings and want to move quickly down the list, use the rear dial—which tells the a7R IV to jump in whole-stop leaps (i.e., from ISO 100 to 200 to 400) rather than the intermediate settings.

When making fixed ISO adjustments, you can scroll up and down the list in 1/3-stop increments with the up/down directional controls (the up/down buttons and multi-selector), and by rotating the control wheel or front dial. Rotate the rear dial to make adjustments in full 1 EV steps.

Your choices are restricted when you're using movies or S&Q video (only ISO 100 to 32,000, plus ISO Auto are available) or Intelligent Auto (ISO Auto is set automatically). Note too that ISO Auto is not available in M mode; you must set a numerical value. Settings up to 25,600 are available in still mode, and up to 12,800 for movies. (If you've selected a higher sensitivity when you switch to movie-making mode, the camera will automatically change to 12,800.)

Surprise! You can use ISO Auto in Manual exposure mode, giving you an "automatic" exposure mode. You still select the shutter speed and aperture and the a7R IV will increase or decrease ISO sensitivity to produce an appropriate metered exposure within the Minimum ISO and Maximum ISO settings you specify. The ISO Auto label will appear at lower right of the viewfinder or LCD monitor screen, indicating that sensitivity is being set automatically.

ISO Range Limit

If you want to intentionally restrict the ISO settings that are available (say, to avoid accidentally using settings you find are not usable from a quality standpoint), you can do that here. You can specify the minimum and maximum available ISO settings from 50–102,400. The a7R IV does let you set the minimum and maximum to the *same* figure, that is a Minimum of ISO 100 and a Maximum of ISO 100 (thus locking you into a single ISO sensitivity), but it is intelligent enough to keep you from setting a maximum that is lower than your minimum.

ISO Auto Minimum Shutter Speed

Use this entry with the a7R IV to specify the shutter speed that activates the ISO Auto feature described above. You'll want to use ISO Auto most frequently to avoid having the camera select a blur-inducing slow shutter speed when using P (Program Auto) or A (Aperture Priority) modes. (*You* always select the shutter speed yourself in S and M modes.) Depending on how well you can hand-hold the camera, or your level of trust for the lens and/or in-body image stabilization, you can choose which shutter speed you deem "too slow," and your a7R IV will boost the ISO sensitivity as required when ISO Auto is active. You can choose from values that the camera calculates, or supply a specific shutter speed, below which Auto ISO will start to do its stuff.

The camera-calculated minimum speeds are very cool because they are based on the focal length of your lens, giving you faster minimum speeds with telephoto lenses, and longer minimum speeds with wide angles. The Fast and Faster settings increase the minimum shutter speed by 1 and 2 stops (respectively) from the standard setting for a particular focal length. The Slow and Slower settings lower the minimum shutter speed for that focal length by 1 and 2 stops (respectively).

- **Faster/Fast.** When you highlight this entry, you can press the left/right directional buttons to choose among Faster and Fast, STD (Standard), Slow, or Slower. The a7R IV will activate ISO Auto at shutter speeds that are faster than the "standard" setting (which is calculated individually based on the focal length or zoom setting of your lens). This is a more conservative setting.

- **STD (Standard).** At this default value, the camera detects the current focal length/zoom setting and selects a minimum shutter speed that takes into account the effect the focal length has in magnifying the degree of blur. That is, a 200mm lens calls for higher shutter speeds than, say, a 50mm lens.

- **Slow/Slower.** This is a more liberal setting that allows slightly slower shutter speeds than specified by STD before ISO Auto kicks in. Use if you have an extraordinarily steady hand.

- **1/8000th–30 seconds.** You can bypass the camera's internal algorithm mumbo-jumbo and directly select a shutter speed that you want to use to activate ISO Auto. If you choose 1/8000th second, ISO Auto will effectively be active all the time (except when 1/8000th second is used as the shutter speed). Select 30 seconds, and ISO Auto will not activate at all.

Metering Mode

Options: Multi, Center, Spot (Standard, Large), Entire Screen Averaging, Highlight

Default: Multi

My preference: Multi

The metering mode determines how the camera will calculate the exposure for any scene. The camera is set by default to Multi, which is a multi-zone or multi-segment metering approach. No other options are available in Intelligent Auto mode or when you're using digital zoom. You'll find more information on these modes in Chapter 7, where exposure considerations are discussed in detail.

- **Multi.** Evaluates 1,200 individual segments of the scene using advanced algorithms; often, it will be able to ignore a very bright area or a very dark area that would affect the overall exposure. It's also likely to produce a decent (if not ideal) exposure with a light-toned scene such as a snowy landscape, especially on a sunny day. While it's not foolproof, Multi is the most suitable when you must shoot quickly and don't have time for serious exposure considerations. **Note:** When Face Priority in Multi Metering (discussed next) is On, this metering mode will base exposure on faces detected, if any.

- **Center.** Center-weighted metering primarily considers the brightness in a large central area of the scene, while still taking into account the average value of the rest of the frame. This approach ensures that a bright sky that's high in the frame, for example, will not severely affect the exposure. However, if the central area is very light or very dark in tone, your photo is likely to be too dark or too bright (unless you use exposure compensation).

- **Spot.** When using Spot metering, the camera measures only the brightness in a very small central area of the scene; again, if that area is very light or very dark in tone, your exposure will not be satisfactory; it's important to spot meter an area of a medium tone. Use this mode to zero in on a specific area of your image, such as a performer on a darkened stage.

  - **Size of spot.** When Spot is highlighted, press the left/right controls to change from a standard-size spot to a larger spot.

  - **Position of spot.** By default, the metering spot is placed in the center of the frame. You can optionally link the spot to the current focus point using the Spot Metering Point entry in the Camera Settings I-10 (Exposure 2) menu, discussed shortly.

- **Entire Screen Averaging.** The a7R IV calculates exposure based on the average brightness of the entire frame. This setting is useful if the overall scene has similar brightness values throughout; you can recompose slightly, or your subject can move within the frame and the exposure will not change.

- **Highlight.** In this mode, the camera adjusts the exposure to avoid blowing out the highlights, if at all possible. Use this setting if the highlights of a scene are the most important and you don't care if some shadow detail is lost. You can give Highlight metering some extra muscle by activating D-Range Optimizer or Auto HDR. The a7R IV will segment the image into small areas and analyze the difference between the light and dark areas, preserving the highlights but also keeping as much shadow detail as possible.

Face Priority in Multi Metering

Options: On, Off

Default: On

My preference: Off

When you choose On, this setting tells the a7R IV to adjust its Multi metering to prioritize exposure for any faces in the scene. Select Off, and the standard 1,200-zone evaluative metering system is used. For most shooting I disable this feature, as Multi metering does a good job of exposing so that faces and other parts of the image are well exposed. I turn it on when I am photographing individuals or groups and their surroundings are extra-bright or dark and I want to make sure the faces receive optimal exposure.

Spot Metering Point

Options: Center, Focus Point Link

Default: Center

My preference: Focus Point Link

If Focus Area is set to Flexible Spot or Expand Flexible Spot, and Spot metering is selected as the Metering Mode, then the Spot metering area can be linked to the focus point, rather than locked in the center. Just choose Focus Point Link here. If Center is selected instead, the focus point is locked in the center of the frame.

Note: Focus Point Link also works when Focus Area is set to Tracking: Flexible Spot or Tracking: Expand Flexible Spot, but the spot metering area is moved to the starting area and does not move once tracking begins. All these AF nuances are explained in Chapter 8.

Exposure Step

Options: 1/3 EV, 1/2 EV

Default: 1/3 EV

My preference: 1/3 EV

This setting is the first in the Camera Settings I-10 menu. (See Figure 3.22.) It specifies the size of the exposure change for both exposure compensation and flash exposure compensation. The 1/3-stop default allows fine-tuning exposure more precisely, while selecting 1/2 EV lets you make larger adjustments more quickly, which is useful when you are trying to capture more dramatic exposure changes. The actual difference between 1/3-stop and 1/2-stop changes is relatively small, so this setting is primarily a convenience feature that's most useful when you plan to, say, use exposure compensation and want to move from 0.0

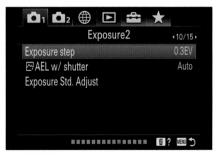

Figure 3.22 The Camera Settings I-10 (Exposure 2) menu.

to plus or minus several whole stops in bigger jumps. I'm never in that much of a hurry, so I opt for the greater precision of the 1/3 EV steps.

Autoexposure Lock with Shutter (Stills)

Options: Auto, On, Off

Default: Auto

My preference: On

This item allows the a7R IV to lock the exposure (as well as the focus in AF-S mode) when you apply light pressure to the shutter release button. Point the camera at your primary subject and maintain contact with the button while re-framing for a better composition. This technique will ensure that both focus and exposure are optimized for the primary subject. There are three modes to choose from:

- **Auto.** Adjusts focus and then locks in exposure in AF-S mode when you press the shutter release down halfway. In AF-A mode, the camera will do the same thing if the subject is stationary. If the subject is moving (that is, the camera switches to AF-C mode) or you are shooting continuously in burst mode, exposure is *not* locked. However, even if Auto is activated, pressing the AEL lock button overrides this behavior.

- **On.** Exposure is locked when you press the shutter release halfway.

- **Off.** Pressing the shutter release halfway locks only focus. Exposure is not locked when you press the shutter release halfway, and exposure will be adjusted automatically during continuous shooting. Exposure isn't locked until you press the shutter release down all the way to take the photo, or you press the AEL lock button. Use this setting when you prefer to lock exposure manually using the AEL button or when taking the actual picture.

  You might want to choose the Off option to lock focus on one subject in the scene while locking the exposure for an entirely different part of the scene. To use this technique, focus on the most important subject and keep the focus locked by keeping your finger on the shutter release button while you recompose. You can then point the lens at an entirely different area of the scene to read the exposure, and lock in the exposure with pressure on the AEL button. Finally, reframe for the most pleasing composition and take the photo.

  In your image, the primary subject will be in sharpest focus while the exposure will be optimized for the area that you metered. This technique makes the most sense when your primary subject is very light in tone like a snowman or very dark in tone like a black Lab dog. Subjects of that type can lead to exposure errors, so you might want to expose for an area that's a middle tone, such as grass. I'll discuss exposure in detail in Chapter 5; then, the value of this menu option will be more apparent.

Exposure Standard Adjustment

Options: Adjust Multi, Center, Spot, Entire Screen Averaging, or Highlight metering
Default: None
My preference: None

This setting is a powerful adjustment that allows you to dial in a specific amount of exposure compensation that will be applied to every photo you take using each of the five metering modes. No more can you complain, "My a7R IV always underexposes by 1/3 stop!" If that is the case, and the phenomenon is consistent, you can use this menu adjustment to compensate.

Exposure compensation is usually a better idea (does your camera *really* underexpose that consistently?), but this setting does allow you to "recalibrate" your camera yourself. You can fine-tune exposure separately for each of the metering modes. However, you have no indication that fine-tuning has been made, so you'll need to remember what you've done. After all, you someday might discover that your camera is consistently *over*exposing images by 1/3 stop, not realizing that your Exposure Standard Adjustment setting is the culprit.

In practice, it's rare that the a7R IV will *consistently* provide the wrong exposure in any of the five metering modes, especially Multi metering, which can alter exposure dramatically based on the camera's internal database of typical scenes. This feature may be most useful for Spot metering, if you always take a reading off the same type of subject, such as a human face or 18 percent gray card. Should you find that the gray card readings, for example, always differ from what you would prefer, go ahead and fine-tune optimal exposure for Spot metering, and use that to read your gray cards. To use this feature:

1. **Select Exposure Standard Adjustment.** Select this menu entry from the Camera Settings I-10 (Exposure 2) page.

2. **Consider yourself warned.** In the screen that appears, choose OK after carefully reading the warning that Sony insists on showing you every time this option is activated.

3. **Select metering mode to correct.** Choose Multi metering, Center, Spot, Entire Screen Averaging, or Highlight-weighted metering in the screen that follows by highlighting your choice and pressing the center button. You can set the standard adjustment separately for each exposure mode.

4. **Specify amount of correction.** Press the up/down buttons to dial in the exposure compensation you want to apply. You can specify compensation up to + 1 or –1 stops in increments of 1/6 stop, half as large a change as conventional exposure compensation. This is truly *fine-tuning*.

5. **Confirm your change.** Press the center button when finished to return to the previous menu. You can repeat the action to fine-tune the other exposure modes if necessary. When finished, press MENU to exit. **Note:** the values you set will survive using the Reset option of the Setting Reset entry in the Setup 7 menu but will be canceled if you choose Initialize instead.

Flash Mode

Options: Flash Off, Auto Flash, Fill Flash, Slow Sync., Rear Sync., Wireless

Default: Depends on shooting mode

My preference: N/A

The first entry in the Camera Settings I-11 (Flash) menu (see Figure 3.23), this item offers options for the several flash modes that are available. Not all the modes can be selected at all times, as shown in Table 3.3. I'll describe what these modes do, and the use of flash in detail in Chapter 13.

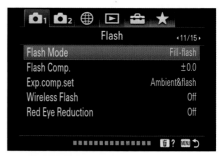

Figure 3.23 Flash Mode is the first entry in the Camera Settings I-11 (Flash) menu.

TABLE 3.3 Flash Modes

EXPOSURE MODE	FLASH OFF	AUTO FLASH	FILL FLASH	SLOW SYNC.	REAR SYNC.	WIRELESS	FLASH EXPOSURE COMPENSATION	RED-EYE REDUCTION
Intelligent Auto								
Program Auto								
Aperture Priority								
Shutter Priority								
Manual Exposure								

Flash Compensation

Options: –3 to +3 in 1/3 or 1/2 EV steps

Default: 0.0

My preference: N/A

This feature controls the flash output. It allows you to dial in plus compensation for a brighter flash effect or minus compensation for a subtler flash effect. If you take a flash photo and it's too dark or too light, access this menu item. Scroll up/down to set a value that will increase flash intensity (plus setting) or reduce the flash output (minus setting) by up to three EV (exposure value) steps. You can select between 1/3 and 1/2 EV increments in the Exposure Step entry described later in this chapter. Flash compensation is "sticky," so be sure to set it back to zero after you finish shooting. This feature is not available when you're using Intelligent Auto mode. I'll discuss this and many other flash-related topics in detail in Chapter 13.

Exp. Comp. Set

Options: Ambient & Flash, Ambient Only
Default: Ambient & Flash
My preference: Ambient & Flash

When this item is at the default setting, any exposure compensation value that you set will apply to both the ambient light exposure and to the flash exposure when using flash. You'd want to stick to this option in flash photography when you find that both the ambient-light exposure and the flash exposure produce an image that's too dark or too light. Setting plus or minus exposure compensation will affect both. However, in another situation when using flash, you might want to control only the brightness of the ambient light exposure and not the flash exposure.

The Ambient Only option allows you to control only the brightness of the background, such as a city skyline behind a friend when you're taking flash photos at night in a scene of this type. Setting exposure compensation will now allow you to get a brighter or a darker background (at a + and – setting, respectively) without affecting the brightness of your primary subject who will be exposed by the light from the flash. (Any exposure compensation you set will have no effect on the flash intensity.)

Wireless Flash

Options: Off, On
Default: Off
My preference: N/A

Sony is still playing catch-up in the electronic flash arena, having supported only optically triggered wireless flash until recently, but now offers radio-controlled wireless flash using the Sony AF-WRC1M/FA-WRR1 wireless radio commander/receiver combination or radio-compatible external flash units like the Sony HVL-45RM. This entry allows you to enable/disable both optical and radio wireless modes. I'll explain these and other flash options in Chapter 13.

Red Eye Reduction

Options: On, Off
Default: Off
My preference: Off

When flash is used in a dark location, red-eye is common in pictures of people, and especially of animals. Unfortunately, your camera is unable, on its own, to totally *eliminate* the red-eye effects that occur when an electronic flash bounces off the retinas of your subject's eyes and into the camera lens. The effect is worst under low-light conditions (exactly when you might be using a flash) as the pupils expand to allow more light to reach the retinas. The best you can hope for with this option is to *reduce* or minimize the red-eye effect. After all, the feature is called red-eye *reduction,* not red-eye *elimination.*

It's fairly easy to remove red-eye effects in an image editor (some image importing programs will do it for you automatically as the pictures are transferred from your camera or memory card to your computer). But, it's better not to have glowing red eyes in your photos in the first place.

To use this feature, you first have to attach an external flash to the multi interface shoe. When Red Eye Reduction is turned on through this menu item, the flash issues a few brief bursts prior to taking the photo, theoretically causing your subjects' pupils to contract, reducing the red-eye syndrome. It works best if your subject is looking toward the flash. Like any such system, its success ratio is not great.

White Balance

Options: Auto WB, Daylight, Shade, Cloudy, Incandescent, Fluorescent (4 options), Flash, Underwater Auto, C.Temp/Filter, Custom 1–3, Custom Setup

Default: Auto (AWB)

My preference: AWB

This is the first entry in the Camera Settings I-12 (Color/WB/Image Processing 1) menu. (See Figure 3.24.) The various light sources that can illuminate a scene have light that's of different colors. A household lamp using an old-type (not Daylight Balanced) bulb, for example, produces light that's quite amber in color. Sunlight around noon is close to white but it's quite red at sunrise and sunset; on cloudy days, the light has a bluish bias. The light from fluorescents can vary widely, depending on the type of tube or bulb you're using. Some lamps, including sodium vapor and mercury vapor, produce light of unusual colors.

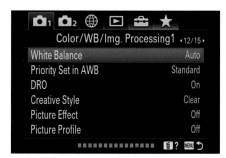

Figure 3.24 The Camera Settings I-12 (Color/WB/Image Processing 1) menu.

The Auto White Balance feature works well, particularly outdoors and under artificial lighting that's daylight balanced. Even under lamps that produce light with a slight color cast such as green or blue, you should often get a pleasing overall color balance. One advantage of using AWB is that you don't have to worry about changing it for your next shooting session; there's no risk of having the camera set for, say, incandescent light, when you're shooting outdoors on a sunny day.

The a7R IV also lets you choose a specific white balance option—often called a preset—that's appropriate for various typical lighting conditions, because the AWB feature does not always succeed in providing an accurate or the most pleasing overall color balance. Your choices include:

- **Daylight.** Sets white balance for average daylight.
- **Shade.** Compensates for the slightly bluer tones encountered in open shade conditions.
- **Cloudy.** Adjusts for the colder tones of a cloudy day.
- **Incandescent.** Indoor illumination is typically much warmer than daylight, so this setting compensates for the excessive red bias.

- **Fluorescent (four types).** You can choose from Warm White, Cool White, Day White, and Daylight fluorescent lighting.
- **Flash.** Suitable for shooting with the a7R IV's external electronic flash unit.
- **Underwater Auto.** Although you may find a vendor offering an underwater housing for your a7R IV, it's more likely that your "underwater" shooting will involve photographing fish and other sea life through the glass of an aquarium of the commercial variety. This setting partially tames the blue-green tones you can encounter in such environments (see Figure 3.25, left), producing a warmer tone that some (but not all) may prefer (see Figure 3.25, right).
- **C.Temp/Filter/Custom/Custom Setup.** These advanced features provide even better results once you've learned how to fine-tune color balance settings, which I'll explain in Chapter 9.

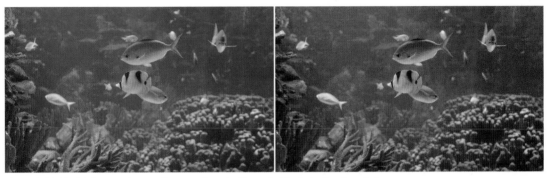

Figure 3.25 The Underwater Auto setting can reduce the blue cast of typical subsurface photos.

When any of the presets are selected, you can press the right button to produce a screen that allows you to adjust the color along the amber (yellow)/blue axis, the green/magenta axis, or both, to fine-tune color rendition even more precisely. The screen shown in Figure 3.26 will appear, and you can use the up/down and left/right controls to move the origin point in the chart shown at lower right to any bias you want. The amount of your amber/blue and/or green/magenta bias are shown numerically to the left of the chart. You'll find more information about White Balance in Chapter 9.

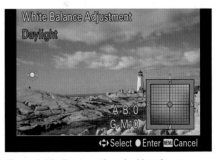

Figure 3.26 Fine-tune the color bias of your images using this screen.

My recommendation: If you shoot in RAW capture, though, you don't have to be quite as concerned about white balance, because you can easily adjust it in your software after the fact. Here again, as with ISO and exposure compensation, the white balance item is not available in Intelligent Auto mode; the camera defaults to Auto White Balance.

Priority Setting AWB

Options: Standard, Ambience, White
Default: Standard
My preference: Standard

You can finally exercise some control over Auto White Balance. This setting allows you to fine-tune how AWB works, producing "automatic" color balance that may more closely suit your personal taste than the default balance the a7R IV is initially set for. You have three choices:

- **Standard.** The camera makes its own adjustments for white balance, based on its interpretation of the colors it sees in your scenes. The a7R IV does a pretty good job of telling daylight from incandescent illumination and responding accordingly, and a fair job with other forms of illumination. This will work for you most of the time, although you'll want to use one of the presets or other white balance customizing features described above when appropriate.

- **Ambience.** Detects the light source and, if a naturally warm source is identified, will bias the color to keep warmer tones. Your interior photos, fireside chats, and similar scenes can keep their rosy colors. An indicator on your shooting settings screens will indicate that Ambience (or White) bias is being used.

- **White.** The reverse of Ambience, this setting tries to preserve whites in scenes with warm color temperatures.

DRO

Options: DRO Off; DRO Auto (Auto or Levels 1–5)
Default: DRO Auto
My preference: DRO Off

The brightness/darkness range of many images is so broad that the sensor has difficulty capturing detail in both bright highlight areas and dark shadow areas. That's because a sensor has a limited dynamic range. However, the a7R IV is able to expand its dynamic range using extra processing when dynamic range optimization (DRO) is active. It's on by default at the Auto level where the camera evaluates the scene contrast and decides how much extra processing to apply; this is the only available setting in Intelligent Auto mode. In other modes, you can turn DRO off, or set it manually to one of five intensity levels.

When the DRO Auto option is highlighted, you can press the left/right controls to set the DRO to a specific level of processing, from 1 (weakest) to 5 (strongest). You'll find that DRO can lighten shadow areas; it may darken bright highlight areas too, but not to the same extent. By level 3, the photos you take will exhibit much lighter shadow areas for an obviously wide dynamic range; DRO Auto will never provide such an intense increase in shadow detail.

Creative Style

Options: Standard, Vivid, Neutral, Portrait, Landscape, Black & White; adjustable versions of these, plus Clear, Deep, Light, Night, Autumn, Sepia, and Sunset

Default: Standard

My preference: Standard

This option gives you six basic Creative Styles with fixed combinations of contrast, saturation, and sharpness. Each of these basic styles display a prefix number on the screen: 1: Standard, 2: Vivid, 3: Neutral, 4: Portrait, 5: Landscape, 6: B&W. Each of the basic styles *also* appears a second time (without the number prefix) and with the addition of Clear, Deep, Light, Night, Autumn, Sepia, and Sunset. You can adjust the contrast, saturation, and sharpness of each style using the left/right controls to choose an attribute, and the up/down controls to adjust that attribute. You can apply Creative Styles when you are using any shooting mode except Intelligent Auto.

Sony has made Creative Styles a little confusing by providing both a numbered listing of the six basic styles, plus a second, unnumbered list that includes the basic styles and seven more. But there is method to this madness. You can adjust *all 13* styles to suit your preferences. Effectively, that means you can have *two* Standard/Vivid/Neutral/Portrait/Landscape/B&W styles, both the basic, numbered version and the non-numbered variation. I discuss the use of Creative Styles in Chapter 9.

Picture Effect

Options: Off, Toy Camera, Pop Color, Posterization (Color, B&W), Retro Photo, Soft High-key, Partial Color (Red, Green, Blue, Yellow), High-Contrast Monochrome

Default: Off

My preference: Off

This camera feature allows you to create JPEG photos with special effects provided by the camera's processor in JPEG capture mode (but not in RAW or RAW & JPEG) when the camera is in P, A, S, or M mode. It's not available for use when shooting movies. Scroll through the options in this item and watch the change in the preview image display that reflects the effect that each option can provide if you activate it; if you find one that looks interesting, press the center button or touch the shutter release button to confirm your choice and return to shooting mode.

When some effects are highlighted, left/right triangles will appear next to their label, indicating you can press the left/right keys to select an option available for that effect. Not all provide this extra benefit.

Your options are:

- **Toy Camera.** Produces images like you might get with a Diana or Holga "plastic" camera, with vignetted corners, image blurring, and bright, saturated colors. It's at Normal by default but when you press the left/right buttons you can select Normal, Cool, Warm, Green, or Magenta.

- **Pop Color.** This setting adds a lot of saturation to the colors, making them especially vivid and rich looking. When used with subjects that have a lot of bright colors, the effect can be dramatic. Duller subjects gain a more "normal" appearance; try using this setting on an overcast day to see what I mean.

- **Posterization.** This option produces a vivid, high-contrast image that emphasizes the primary colors (as shown in Figure 3.27, top) or in black-and-white, with a reduced number of tones, creating a poster effect. The default rendition is Color, but a monochrome option also appears if you press the left/right controls.

- **Retro Photo.** Adds a faded photo look to the image, with sepia overtones.

- **Soft High-key.** Produces bright images.

- **Partial Color.** Attempts to retain the selected color of an image, while converting other hues to black-and-white. (See Figure 3.27, center.) It's set at Red by default, indicating that photos will retain red tones, but you can also choose Blue, Green, or Yellow.

- **High-Contrast Monochrome.** Converts the image to black-and-white and boosts the contrast to give a stark look to the image. (See Figure 3.27, bottom.)

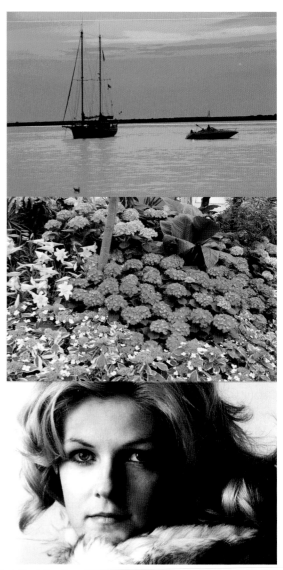

Figure 3.27 From top: Posterization, Partial Color, and High-Contrast Monochrome.

Picture Profile

Options: Picture Profiles PP1–PP10, Off
Default: Off
My preference: Off

Picture Profiles are a great tool for advanced movie shooters. You can customize the picture quality, including color and gradation of your movies by defining the parameters included in each of ten different Picture Profiles. To make these adjustments, connect the camera to a TV or monitor using the HDMI port, and use the picture on the screen as a guide while making your changes. After connecting the camera to your HDTV/monitor, navigate to this menu entry and select which Picture Profile you want to modify. Press the right button to access the index screen, then press the up/down buttons to select the parameter to be changed. Then make your adjustments and press the center button to confirm.

Even a short course in how each of the parameters affects video images, and a discussion of how to select the best settings would require a chapter or two of technical discussion and is thus beyond the scope of this book. I'm going to provide a quick listing of each type of setting for a reminder; your Sony manual provides more information about each of these. The ten Picture Profile presets already have default values:

- **PP1:** Example setting using [Movie] gamma
- **PP2:** Example setting using [Still] gamma
- **PP3:** Example setting of natural color tone using the [ITU709] gamma
- **PP4:** Example setting of a color tone faithful to the [ITU709] standard
- **PP5:** Example setting using [Cine1] gamma
- **PP6:** Example setting using [Cine2] gamma
- **PP7:** Example setting using [S-Log2] gamma
- **PP8:** Example setting using [S-Log3] gamma with the Picture Profile's Color Mode set to [S-Gamut3.Cine]
- **PP9:** Example setting using [S-Log3] gamma with the Picture Profile's Color Mode set to [S-Gamut3]
- **PP10:** Example setting for HDR Movies using [HLG2] gamma

The list that follows is not for the faint-of-heart. As I noted, you can find entire books and motion picture school classes on color grading and adjusting these parameters:

- **Black Level.** Sets the black level (–15 to +15). Black level is the level of brightness at which no light is emitted from a screen, resulting in a pure black screen. Adjustment of this parameter ensures that blacks are seen as black, and not a dark shade of gray.
- **Gamma.** Selects a gamma curve, a formula which corrects for the nonlinear relationship between the brightness (*luminance*) captured by a sensor and the brightness of the image as it's displayed on a monitor. In other words, correction is needed to make what you see on a screen more closely resemble what the camera captured in real life. You can choose from 14 different gamma curves.

- **Black Gamma.** Corrects gamma in low-intensity areas, using Range and Level controls.
- **Knee.** Sets "knee point" and slope for video signal compression to prevent overexposure by limiting signals in high-intensity areas of the subject to the dynamic range of your camera. In short, a higher knee level produces more detail in the highlights; a lower knee level produces fewer details in the highlights. Your adjustments include:
  - **Mode.** In Auto mode, the knee point and slope are set automatically; in Manual mode, they are set manually.
  - **Auto Set.** Even when the Mode is set to Auto, you can still choose maximum point for the knee point, from 90 to 100 percent, and Sensitivity, from High, Medium, or Low.
  - **Manual Set.** When Mode is set to manual, you specify a knee point (75 to 105 percent), and Slope from gentle (–5) to steep (+5).
- **Color Mode.** Sets type and level of colors, from among Movie, Still, Cinema, Pro, ITU-709 Matrix, Black & White, and S-Gamut, S-Gamut3.Cine, S-Gamut3, PT-2020, and 709.
- **Saturation.** Sets the color saturation, from –32 to +32 values.
- **Color Phase.** Sets the color phase (–7 to +7).
- **Color Depth.** Sets the color depth for each color phase.
- **Detail.** Sets parameters including Level, and Detail adjustments including Mode, Vertical/Horizontal Balance, B/W Balance, Limit, Crispning (sic), and Hi-Light Detail.
- **Copy.** Copies the settings of the picture profile to another picture profile number.
- **Reset.** Resets the picture profile to the default setting. You cannot reset all picture profile settings at once.

Shutter AWB Lock (Stills)

Options: Shutter Halfway Down, Continuous Shooting, Off
Default: Off
My preference: Off

This is the only entry in the Camera Settings I-13 (Color/WB/Image Processing 2) menu. (Not shown.) As described earlier, your a7R IV actually has *two* Auto White Balance controls—the standard AWB setting and Underwater Auto. Each selects the appropriate white balance for their respective conditions. However, neither auto white balance option is perfect; you may find that white balance adjustments may occur as you hold the shutter release down halfway, or during continuous shooting. If color consistency between individual shots is important, you can tell the camera to *lock* color balance temporarily. These are the settings:

- **Shutter Halfway Down.** If you choose this setting, the camera will always lock the white balance at its current setting whenever AWB or Underwater Auto are active and the shutter release is half-pressed. If the Drive mode is Continuous, when you press the shutter release down all the way and hold it down, the white balance is locked for the entire sequence.

- **Continuous Shooting.** White balance is locked *only* during continuous shooting. Either Auto WB setting may continue to make adjustments when the shutter release is half-pressed.
- **Off.** White balance may change during a half-press or continuous shooting when either of the two Auto white balance presets are enabled. (The non-auto fixed presets, of course, do not change until you adjust them.)

Focus Magnifier

Options: Activate
Default: Off
My preference: N/A

This is the first entry in the Camera Settings I-14 (Focus Assist) menu. (See Figure 3.28.) If you like to focus manually, this is a very useful aid, one of several that Sony generously offers to enhance the chore of achieving sharp focus without using autofocus features. While you will probably find the focus magnifier most useful when using manual focus, it is also available when using autofocus. I'm going to explain its use in MF mode first. To use the Focus Magnifier for manual focus, just follow these steps:

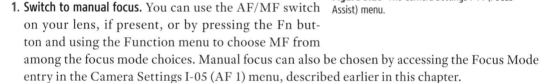

Figure 3.28 The Camera Settings I-14 (Focus Assist) menu.

1. **Switch to manual focus.** You can use the AF/MF switch on your lens, if present, or by pressing the Fn button and using the Function menu to choose MF from among the focus mode choices. Manual focus can also be chosen by accessing the Focus Mode entry in the Camera Settings I-05 (AF 1) menu, described earlier in this chapter.

2. **Access Focus Magnifier.** You can activate the Focus Magnifier from this menu entry, but it's usually more convenient to assign the magnification behavior to a custom key, as I'll explain in Chapter 4. When activated, the image will be enlarged within a screen like the one shown in Figure 3.29, left.

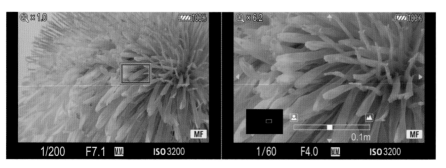

Figure 3.29 The Focus Magnifier can be zoomed from 1X (left) to 5.9X (right) and 11.9X.

3. **Press the center of the multi-selector to zoom in.** The image first is enlarged to 5.9X and then to 11.9X. (A third press exits magnified view.) A navigation window appears at lower left showing an orange rectangle that represents the current location of the blown-up section (as seen in Figure 3.29, right). You can also use the control wheel's center button to zoom in.

4. **Adjust the magnified area.** A quartet of triangles surrounds the image, indicating that you can move the enlarged window around with the frame. Press and release the multi-selector button or the center button, and then use the left/right/up/down directional controls to move the enlarged area.

5. **Center the magnifier.** You can press the Trash button to center the magnified section back in the center of the frame.

6. **Manually focus.** Rotate the lens's focus ring to achieve sharp focus. A scale along the bottom of the screen shows the approximate focus distance.

7. **Take the picture.** When you press the shutter release down all the way to take the picture, Focus Magnification is canceled when you're using manual focus.

8. **(Optional) Return to autofocus.** Remember to return to autofocus when you no longer want to focus on your subject manually.

TOUCH FOCUS

Your a7R IV's touch screen may be a faster way to invoke the Focus Magnifier. You'll need to enable Touch Operation, which is found in the Setup 2 menu. I'll explain all the settings for the touch screen in Chapter 6. When enabled, simply double tap the LCD monitor to select the area to focus on. You can then use a finger on the monitor screen to drag the focused area around. Double tap the monitor again to exit (if you're using manual focus) or by pressing the shutter release down halfway (if you're using the Focus Magnifier with autofocus). You'll need to enable the Focus Magnifier for autofocus using the AF in Focus Magnification entry of this menu, which I'll explain a few menu entries after this one.

Focus Magnifier Time

Options: 2 sec., 5 sec., No Limit

Default: 2 sec.

My preference: 5 sec.

This entry can be used to specify the length of time that the Focus Magnifier will magnify the image during manual focusing. If you find that it takes you longer than two seconds to manually focus using MF Assist, you can change the time to five seconds, or to No Limit; the latter will cause the image to remain magnified until you tap the shutter release button (you don't need to actually take a picture), press the center button/multi-selector button again to return to full frame, or double tap the LCD monitor if you have enabled Touch Operation.

Initial Focus Magnification (Stills)

Options: 1.0X, 5.9X (or 3.9X in APS-C/Super 35mm mode)
Default: 1.0X
My preference: 5.9X

You can specify the initial magnification presented when the Focus Magnifier is invoked. The default is 1.0X (no magnification), which is fine if your first step is frequently to move the magnification window around in the frame before zooming in. At 1.0X, you see the entire frame and can position the window anywhere you like. I prefer to skip that step and jump right in at 5.9X, which usually positions the window close enough that I can go ahead and move it within the frame if I want. The 5.9X magnification is automatically used if you have enabled Touch Operation and double tap the LCD monitor to zoom in. If you're using APS-C/Super 35mm crop mode, the initial focus magnification is 3.9X instead of 5.9X.

AF in Focus Magnification (Stills)

Options: On, Off
Default: Off
My preference: Off when not shooting macro/close-up images

As I mentioned earlier, the Focus Magnifier works just fine in autofocus mode. You can use it to view an enlarged image to confirm that correct focus has been achieved automatically, or to fine-tune focus when working with Direct Manual Focus (DMF) mode.

Once you've enabled the AF focus magnification option, activate the Focus Magnifier as described earlier and adjust the enlarged area using the directional controls and the navigation box. Avoid positioning the enlarged area at the edges of the frame, as the camera may be unable to focus at those positions. When you're ready, press the shutter release halfway. In any AF mode or DMF, the a7R IV will focus on the center of the enlarged area. If you're using DMF, you can fine-tune focus with the lens's focus ring. Then press the shutter release down all the way to take the photo.

Autofocus using focus magnification cannot be used when shooting movies; when the Focus mode is set to AF-C; when using AF-A and continuous shooting or a shooting mode other than P, A, S, or M. The feature is also disabled when using one of the EA-LA mount adapters. Certain autofocus features are disabled when using the focus magnifier, including Eye-AF, Center Tracking, Eye-Start AF, Pre-AF, and Face Priority in AF.

Manual Focus Assist (Stills)

Options: On, Off

Default: On

My preference: On

Forget about the need to activate the Focus Magnifier manually. Set this entry to On and any time you are using manual focus or manual focus in the DMF mode, the a7R IV will automatically enlarge the screen so you can better judge by eye whether the important part of your subject is in sharp focus. As you begin to focus manually by rotating the focus ring on the lens, the image on the LCD will appear at 5.9X its normal size (press the multi-selector or center button to zoom in to 11.9X). This version of the Focus Magnifier is available only for still photography. You can then scroll around the image using the directional controls. As with the manually activated Focus Magnifier, this feature makes it easier to check whether the most important subject area is in the sharpest focus. When you stop turning the focus ring, the image on the LCD display will revert back to normal (non-magnified) so you can see the entire area that the camera will record. You can turn this feature Off however, if you find that you don't need it, and adjust the magnifier time-out using Focus Magnifier Time, the entry described previously.

Peaking Setting

Options: Peaking Display (On, Off); Peaking Level (High, Mid, Low); Peaking Color (Red, Yellow, White)

Default: Off, Mid, White

My preference: On, High, Red

This is a useful manual focusing aid (available only when focusing in Manual and Direct Manual modes) that's difficult to describe and to illustrate. You're going to have to try this feature for yourself to see exactly what it does. *Focus peaking* is a technique that outlines the area in sharpest focus with a color; as discussed below, that can be red, white, or yellow. The colored area shows you at a glance what will be very sharp if you take the photo at that moment. If you're not satisfied, simply change the focused distance (with manual focus). As the focus gets closer to ideal for a specific part of the image, the color outline develops around hard edges that are in focus. You can choose how much peaking is applied (High, Medium, or Low), select a specific accent color (Red, Yellow, or White), or turn the feature off.

Peaking Color allows you to specify which color is used to indicate peaking when you use manual focus. White is the default value, but if that color doesn't provide enough contrast with a similarly hued subject, you can switch to a more contrasting color, such as red or yellow. (See Figure 3.30.)

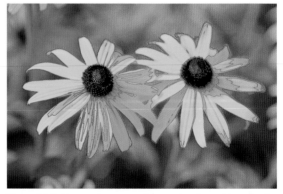

Figure 3.30 You can choose any of three colors for peaking color (for manual focus), but only if you have activated the Peaking Level item. For these blossoms, red was a better choice than white or yellow.

Anti-Flicker Shooting (Stills)

Options: Off, On

Default: Off

My preference: Off, unless shooting under flickering light source

This is the first of only three entries in the Camera Settings I-15 (Shooting Assist) menu. (See Figure 3.31.) Novice sports photographers often ask me why shots they take in certain gymnasiums or arenas have inconsistent exposure, wildly varying color, or banding. The answer is that certain types of artificial lighting actually have a blinking cycle that is imperceptible to the eye, but which the camera can capture. This setting, when enabled, detects the frequency (it's optimized for 100 to 120 Hz illumination) of the light source that is blinking, and takes the picture at the moment when the flicker has the least effect on the final image. It cannot be used in live view or movie shooting.

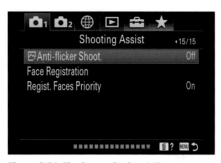

Figure 3.31 The Camera Settings I-15 menu.

You may experience a slight shutter release time lag as the camera "waits" for the proper instant, and your continuous shooting speed may be reduced, which makes this setting a necessary evil for sports and other activities involving action. Your results may vary when using P or A modes, because the shutter speed can change between shots as proper exposure requires. You're better off using S or M mode, so the shutter speed remains constant.

A handy Flicker warning will appear, alerting you that the feature is enabled, except in Intelligent Auto mode. This feature may not work as well with dark backgrounds, a bright light within the image area, when using wireless flash, and under other shooting conditions. I recommend taking test shots to see how effective the feature is under the light source you are working with. The feature is not available at all when using Bulb exposures or shooting movies. If you have Priority Set in AF-S, or AF-C is set to Release or Balanced Emphasis, the camera will focus and shoot immediately when you press the shutter release down all the way. You'll need to use a half-press first to give Anti-Flicker a chance to do its thing.

Face Registration

Options: New Registration, Order Exchanging, Delete, Delete All

Default: None

My preference: N/A

When you access this entry, the screen shown in Figure 3.32 (left) appears. The top option, New Registration, allows you to log up to eight different faces. For best results, line up your victim (subject) against a brightly lit background to allow easier detection of the face. A white box appears that you can use to frame the face. (See Figure 3.32, right.) Press the shutter button. A confirmation message appears (or a Shoot Again warning suggests you try another time, usually because you need to frame the face better). When Register Face? appears, choose Enter or Cancel, and press the MENU button to confirm.

Figure 3.32 Face Registration has four options (left). Capture an image of the face you want to register (right).

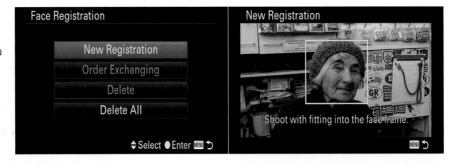

The Order Exchanging option allows you to review and change the priority in which the faces appear, from 1 to 8. (See Figure 3.33.) The a7R IV will use your priority setting to determine which face to focus on if several registered faces are detected in a scene. For example, place close family members high on your list, and relegate that annoying brother-in-law to last place. You can also select a specific face and delete it from the registry (say, you broke up with your significant other!) or delete *all* faces from the registry (your SO got custody of the camera). Face data remains in the camera when you delete individual faces but is totally erased when you select Delete All.

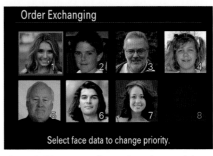

Figure 3.33 You can change the order—and therefore the priority—assigned to each face.

Registered Face Priority

Options: On, Off

Default: On

My preference: Off

This entry simply tells the a7R IV whether it should give a higher priority to registered faces during the autofocus process when Face Priority in AF (discussed earlier) has been set to On.

Camera Settings II Menu | 4

Additional shooting options are available from the Sony a7R IV's Camera Settings II menu. These settings are adjustments that you generally don't make during a particular shooting session but need to tweak more often than those in the Setup menu, which is described in Chapter 6. This menu has some very cool features, including the ability to assign as many different behaviors to a variety of buttons and controls on your camera or lens. Sony has moved many menu items for the a7R IV when compared to its predecessor a7-series cameras, grouping some (but not all) related settings together more logically.

Camera Settings II Menu Entries

Figure 4.1 shows the first screen of the Camera Settings II menu. As you can see, at most only a half-dozen items are displayed at one time. The items found in this menu are shown in Table 4.1.

Exposure Mode (Movies)

Options: Program Auto, Aperture Priority, Shutter Priority, Manual Exposure

Default: Program Auto

My preference: Program Auto works well for me when shooting movies.

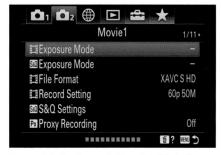

Figure 4.1 The Camera Settings II-1 (Movie 1) menu.

This setting is the first on the Camera Settings II-01 (Movie 1) menu. It is available only when the mode dial is in the Movie position and allows you to specify which exposure mode is used (from among P, S, A, and M options) when shooting movies; the mode you select can be different from the one set for still photography or S&Q modes.

TABLE 4.1 Camera Settings II Menus

MOVIE (PAGES 01-04)	SHUTTER/STEADYSHOT (PAGE 05)	CUSTOM OPERATION (PAGES 09-11)
Exposure Mode (Movies)	Silent Shooting (Stills)	Custom Key (Stills)
Exposure Mode (S&Q)	e-Front Curtain Shutter	Custom Key (Movies)
File Format (Movies)	Release without Lens	Custom Key (Playback)
Record Setting (Movies)	Release without Card	Function Menu Settings
S&Q Settings (S&Q)	SteadyShot	My Dial Settings
Proxy Recording	SteadyShot Settings	Dial Setup
AF Drive Speed (Movies)	**ZOOM (PAGE 06)**	Av/Tv Rotate
AF Track Sensitivity (Movies)	Zoom	Dial EV Compensation
Auto Slow Shutter (Movies)	Zoom Setting	Function Ring (Lens)
Initial Focus Magnification (Movies)	Zoom Ring Rotate	Function of Touch Operations
Audio Recording	**DISPLAY/AUTO REVIEW (PAGES 07-08)**	MOVIE Button
Audio Recording Level		Lock Operation Parts
Audio Level Display	DISP Button	Audio Signals
Audio Out Timing	FINDER/MONITOR	
Wind Noise Reduction	Finder Frame Rate (Stills)	
Marker Display (Movies)	Zebra Setting	
Marker Settings (Movies)	Grid Line	
Video Light Mode	Exposure Setting Guide	
Movie with Shutter	Live View Display	
	Continuous Shooting Length	
	Auto Review	

Exposure Mode (S&Q Motion)

Options: Program Auto, Aperture Priority, Shutter Priority, Manual Exposure

Default: Program Auto

My preference: Program Auto

This setting is identical to the previous entry, except that it applies only to S&Q (Slow-motion and Quick-motion) capture and is grayed out if the mode dial is not set to the S&Q position. As before, the mode you select here can be different from the one set for still photography or movie shooting modes.

File Format (Movies)

Options: XAVC S 4K, XAVC S HD, AVCHD

Default: XAVC S HD

My preference: AVCHD

The a7R IV offers full HD (high-definition) video recording in the AVCHD format. Advanced video shooters can also choose from the XAVC S 4K or XAVC S HD formats, which support faster recording speeds for improved quality, as I'll explain in Chapter 10.

By default, movies are recorded in XAVC S HD, but this menu item allows you to switch to XAVC S 4K AVCHD. Note that AVCHD clips are limited to roughly 2GB in size; when your movie file reaches that limit, the a7R IV will continue recording using a new file that it creates automatically.

In all cases, you'll need a fast memory card of at least 64GB capacity to support the higher frame rates possible with the XAVC S pro formats. The XAVC S 4K format is especially demanding because of its ultra-high 3840 × 2160–pixel resolution (roughly four times that of full HD). If you're using an external recorder, video monitor, or other device using the a7R IV's HDMI connection, as discussed in Chapter 12, the real-time image is *not* displayed on the camera's LCD monitor as you shoot. It is shown only on the external display.

Sony has made a significant change in how 4K movies are captured compared to the previous model a7R III:

- **APS-C/Super 35 Set to Off.** The camera captures 4K video using the full width of the sensor, using pixel-binning, a technique that combines information from adjacent pixels to create one super-pixel with reduced noise. However, each frame ends up with less detail, despite the improvement in noise characteristics.

- **APS-C/Super 35 Set to Auto or On.** The a7R IV captures video in crop mode, without binning, and with better resolution. As with the still photography APS-C mode, explained in Chapter 12, the crop "multiplies" the effective focal length of the lens, so your wide-angle settings are less wide, and longer focal length settings have a more telephoto effect.

  To complicate things, the crop factor isn't the same 1.5X used for still photography. It amounts to 1.6X for 24p footage (or 25p for users in Europe and other countries that use PAL instead of NTSC), and 1.8X for 30p video capture. The effect is most noticeable for wide-angle shots: a 28mm lens or zoom setting "becomes" roughly 45mm at 24p and the equivalent of about 50mm at 30p. Not wide at all!

  I'll explain recording formats, frame rates, and NTSC/PAL in more detail in Chapters 10 and 11.

Record Setting (Movies)

Options: Varies

Default: XAVC S: 60p 50M

My preference: XAVC S: 60p 50M

This item allows you to choose from various options if you are using XAVC S 4K, XAVC S, or AVCHD. Your choices are shown in the left-hand column of Table 4.2. Note that the frame rates apply to countries using the NTSC system, such as the US, Japan, and some other countries. For countries that use the PAL system, 25, 50, and 100 frame rates replace 30, 60, and 120 fps, respectively. I'll explain frame rates, scanning, and bit rates in Chapters 10 and 11. All the terminology and concepts will make more sense when you read Chapters 10 and 11, which provide more of an education on many aspects of movie making.

TABLE 4.2 Camera Settings II Menus

	RECORD SETTING	BIT RATE	RESOLUTION
XAVC S 4K	30p 100M/25p 100M	100 Mb/sec	3840 × 2160
	30p 60M/25p 60M	60 Mb/sec	3840 × 2160
	24p 100M	100 Mb/sec	3840 × 2160
	24p 60M	60 Mb/sec	3840 × 2160
XAVC S	60p 50M/50p 50M	50 Mb/sec	1920 × 1080
	60p 25M/50p 25M	25 Mb/sec	1920 × 1080
	30p 50M/25p 50M	50 Mb/sec	1920 × 1080
	30p 16M/25p 16M	16 Mb/sec	1920 × 1080
	24p 50M/50p 50M	50 Mb/sec	1920 × 1080
	120p 100M/100p 50M	100 Mb/sec	1920 × 1080
	120p 60M/100p 60M	60 Mb/sec	1920 × 1080
AVCHD	60i 24M/50i 24M (FX)	24 Mb/sec	1920 × 1080 interlaced
	60i 17M/50i 17M (FH)	17 Mb/sec	1920 × 1080 interlaced

S&Q Settings (S&Q Motion)

Options: Record Setting: 60p, 30p, 24p (NTSC); Frame Rate: 120, 60, 30, 15, 8, 4, 2, 1 frames per second

Default: 30p, 120 fps

My preference: N/A

This is a great feature if you want to shoot some slow-motion movies as a special effect, analyze the dynamics of a particular motion, or speed up a sequence to provide a humorous herky-jerky appearance. Sony's implementation of high/slow frame rate photography, which it now calls slow-motion/quick-motion, allows you to capture a *silent* (no sound) slow-motion video at up to 120 frames-per-second rate (100 fps for PAL). It will play back 4X or 5X slower, depending on whether you select

30p/25p or 24p as your Record Setting option within this menu entry. You can also record at slower speeds (down to 1 frame per second) for speeded-up, Charlie Chaplinesque footage. Here are your options, and how it works:

- **Record setting.** This parameter is labeled a bit misleadingly. It determines the *playback* speed of your video clip and, therefore, how much of a slow-motion/fast-motion effect you will see when viewing the movie. Your choices are 60p, 30p, or 24p when using the NTSC television system. Think of this setting as a *factor,* which, when dividing the Frame Rate, determines the motion effect you get. All will become clear in a moment.

- **Frame rate.** Here you select the number of frames per second captured in S&Q mode. You can select 120, 60, 30, 15, 8, 4, 2, and 1 frames per second. (Scroll down to find the last two options.) When the frames per second is divided by the record setting, you will arrive at the slow-motion effect or speed factor. I'll show you some typical results next.

Slow-Motion

When you capture video at any frame rate and then play it back at a *slower* frame rate, the result is slow-motion. For example, if you choose 120 fps for the Frame Rate, a 10-second video will include 1,200 individual frames (120 fps × 10). If you've chosen 30 fps for your Record Setting, those frames will require 40 seconds to play back (1,200 frames divided by 30). The playback time is increased 4X. Other playback times involve different amounts of slow-motion: 24 fps gives you 5X playback. (When shooting at 120 fps, the 60 fps Record Setting is not available.) Table 4.3 shows the amount of slow motion you get with each combination of frame rates from 30 to 120, and playback settings of 60, 30, and 24 frames per second.

Quick-Motion

Frame rates *slower* than 30 fps gives you speeded-up quick-motion instead of slow-motion. For example, with a Frame Rate of 4 frames per second you'll capture just 40 frames in 10 seconds. When viewed at a Record Setting of, say, 24 fps that 10-second clip will be compressed into only 1.7 seconds of viewing time. Obviously, because of the speed-up factor, you'll get the maximum effect when you shoot longer sequences that can be displayed very, very quickly. Look over Table 4.3, and the explanation that follows to calculate your own slow-/quick-motion effects.

TABLE 4.3 Slow-Motion/Quick-Motion Effects

CAPTURE FRAME RATES	60P PLAYBACK	30P PLAYBACK	24P PLAYBACK
120 fps	Not possible	4X slow-motion	5X slow-motion
60 fps	1X standard speed	2X slow-motion	2.5X slow-motion
30 fps	2X quick-motion	1X standard speed	1.25X quick-motion
15 fps	4X quick-motion	2X quick-motion	1.6X quick-motion
8 fps	7.5X quick-motion	3.75X quick-motion	3X quick-motion
4 fps	15X quick-motion	7.5X quick-motion	6X quick-motion
2 fps	30X quick-motion	15X quick-motion	12X quick-motion
1 fps	60X quick-motion	30X quick-motion	24X quick-motion

To calculate the *slow-motion* effects you can look forward to, multiply any of the figures labeled "slow-motion" by the number of seconds captured in your original clip. For example, if you shot a two-minute, 120 fps sequence and played it back at 30p (4X slow-motion) you'd need 8 minutes to watch the whole thing. Going the other way, a two-minute clip captured at 4 fps and played back at 30p, would zip by in four seconds of frantic action.

Obviously, in real life you probably won't be shooting slow-motion video for two whole minutes (a golf swing or sports action sequence can be captured in a few seconds), and will be shooting quick-motion, time-lapse-like clips (such as a blooming flower or the march of the stars across the night sky) for longer periods so you'll have time to enjoy what you see. As you work with this cool feature, you may have to experiment to see which combination of frame rate capture speeds and the three possible playback speeds work best for you in a given situation. Also, keep in mind that many video-editing programs can handle clips captured at various frame rates and output them at a different rate for playback.

All movies are recorded in XAVC S HD format, and, as noted earlier, are silent. When shooting slow-motion video, TC Run and TC Output (under TC/UB Settings, described later), and 4K Output Selection are disabled. And, obviously, fast frame rates require shorter shutter speeds, so be ready to boost your ISO settings if necessary to cope.

Proxy Recording

Options: On, Off
Default: Off
My preference: Off

If you like, you can record a compact, low-bit-rate version of your XAVC S movies simultaneously while capturing your main movie. Although lower in quality, these "proxy" recordings are suitable for emailing, display on a smartphone or tablet, or uploading online.

While capturing your full HD (1920 × 1080) video, the a7R IV also saves a standard HD (1280 × 720) version at a paltry 9 Mb/second, using the same frame rate (that is, 60/50p, 30/25p, or 24p) selected for the main video. You must use the XAVC S HD record setting with a frame rate other than 120/100p. A "Px" label appears over a main movie's icon during image review to indicate that a proxy movie was recorded at the same time (the proxy itself cannot be displayed or edited in-camera). Any time you delete the main movie from your memory card the proxy is erased, too.

AF Drive Speed (Movies)

Options: Fast, Normal, Slow
Default: Normal
My preference: Normal for most scenes, Fast for sports and action

This entry is the first in the Camera Settings II-02 (Movie 2) menu (shown in Figure 4.2). It is a mov-ies-only setting for the a7R IV that is used to adjust how quickly the camera focuses while capturing video. It's used in conjunction with AF Track Sensitivity (Movies), described next. Unlike stills, when focus changes while shooting movies it is apparent in the clip and can be undesirable. Your three options are as follows:

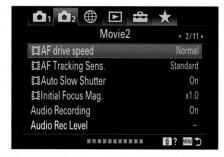

Figure 4.2 The Camera Settings II-2 (Movie 2) menu.

- **Fast.** The camera focuses as quickly as possible, but with slightly less precision. This setting is good for sports, action, photojournalism, and street photography, and any situation where it's important to keep the main subjects in focus as they move around. In such situations, the automatic focus adjustments add to the feeling of following the action; any delay in refocusing would be disconcerting.

- **Normal.** The AF responds smoothly to subject movement by refocusing gradually. With scenes that are not filled with constant action, this mode may be the least noticeable to the viewer.

- **Slow.** Focusing is much less speedy and is a good choice if your subjects are moving at a constant rate of speed and direction. This setting will allow the a7R IV to smoothly follow focus. Choose Slow to be on the safe side in such situations, particularly when using older lenses that are themselves somewhat pokey in achieving focus.

AF Track Sensitivity (Movies)

Options: Responsive or Standard

Default: Standard

My preference: Standard

This entry works hand-in-hand with the AF Drive Speed entry above. It is another movies-only setting and determines how quickly the camera unlocks focus from the subject it is currently tracking and focuses instead on another subject that intervenes. For example, if you're shooting a video of a child or grandchild enjoying a playground and another kid unexpectedly darts between you and your youngster, you don't want the camera to switch to the intervening subject. With this feature set to High, the camera will very quickly switch to the other youth, and then should return its attention to your child—but often, not quickly enough. A better choice would be to use Normal, so that the camera briefly ignores the other kid, who is likely to have moved on. Focus tracking will remain on the intended "star" of your video. Your options include:

- **Responsive.** The camera quickly responds to new subjects that cross the frame. This is the best setting to use for fast-moving subjects, such as sports or frenetic children, *as long as you don't expect intervening subjects*. The camera will smoothly follow your subjects, especially if AF Drive Speed has been set to Fast, too.

- **Standard.** Response to movement is a bit slower, so that the camera doesn't constantly refocus as subjects move about the frame. This is the default and should be used when there is only moderate movement, and especially if the movement is across the width or height of the frame (rather than coming toward you or away from you), and when you're using a small f/stop, because the increased depth-of-field will eliminate the need for most re-focusing.

Auto Slow Shutter (Movies)

Options: On, Off

Default: On

My preference: Off

When shooting movies in very dark locations, the best way to ensure that the video clips are bright is to use a slow shutter speed. When this menu item is On, the camera can automatically switch to a slower shutter speed than its default. This is a useful feature, since it works in any camera operating mode; there's no need to use S mode and set a slow shutter speed yourself in dark locations. I like to leave it off, because when I am capturing video with a slow shutter speed, I want to make sure I have the camera mounted on a tripod, and the need to activate this feature manually is a reminder to me that I need to do so.

Initial Focus Magnification (Movies)

Options: 1X, 4X

Default: 1.0X

My preference: 4X

You can specify the initial magnification presented when the Focus Magnifier is invoked while shooting movies. It's equivalent to the corresponding still photography setting in the Camera Settings I-14 menu. The default is also 1.0X (no magnification), but the optional zoomed-in choice is 4X. The default is fine if your first step is frequently to move the magnification window around in the frame before zooming in. At 1.0X, you see the entire frame and can position the window anywhere you like. I usually want to enlarge the image to 4X so I can study focus.

Audio Recording

Options: On, Off

Default: On

My preference: On

Use this item to turn off sound recording when you're shooting videos, if desired. In most cases you'll want to leave the setting On, to capture as much information as possible; the audio track can be deleted later, if desired, with software. However, there could be occasions when it's useful to disable sound recording for movies, for example, if you know ahead of time that you will be dubbing in other sound, or if you have no need for sound, such as when panning over a vista of the Grand Canyon. At any rate, this option is there if you want to use it.

Audio Recording Level

Options: Levels from 0 to 31

Default: 26

My preference: On

You can adjust the recording level of the camera's built-in or external microphones using this entry, which also enables/disables the audio level overlay on the screen while movies are captured. To use this feature, just follow these steps:

1. Rotate the mode dial to the Movie position.
2. Navigate to the Camera Settings II-02 menu, highlight Audio Rec Level, and press the center button.
3. The screen shown in Figure 4.3 appears. Rotate the front or rear dials or control wheel or use the left/right controls to adjust the volume level up or down. There are 32 different levels, from 0 to 31.
4. Press the center button to confirm and exit the screen.
5. Alternatively, you can use the up/down buttons to highlight Reset to return the recording level to the default value. Then press MENU to exit.
6. If Audio Recording and Audio Level Display are set to On, an overlay appears at the lower left of the EVF or LCD monitor showing the current audio levels for the left/right channels (Ch1/Ch2).

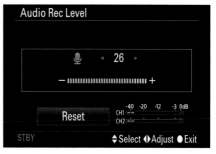

Figure 4.3 Set Audio level.

Audio Level Display

Options: On, Off

Default: On

My preference: N/A

This entry is the first in the Camera Settings II-03 menu. (See Figure 4.4.) It is available only when the mode dial is set to the Movie position. It enables/disables display of audio level indicator bars, so you can monitor sound recording levels visually. The volume bars do not appear when Audio Recording is set to Off, or the DISP setting is set to No Disp. Info., or you are recording slow-motion or quick-motion video. When in movie standby mode, the bars will display so you adjust the sound level before starting to capture.

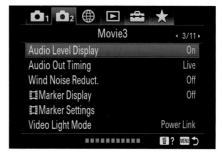

Figure 4.4 The Camera Settings II-03 (Movie 3) menu.

Audio Out Timing

Options: Live, Lip Sync

Default: Live

My preference: Live

With the a7R IV, *audio out* refers to the sound signal you hear when monitoring the recording through the camera's headphone jack. In this mode, the sound you hear may be slightly out of sync with the video, because the video must be processed by the camera's digital processing chip before you see it on the LCD or EVF. Using an external microphone may contribute to this delay. Sony offers two different audio modes that can ignore or compensate for this lag.

- **Live mode.** If you are not using headphones and are listing to the audio in real time, this setting allows you to hear the sound being recorded in real time, with no delay. Use this mode if you are watching the action in the scene directly, rather than viewing it through the viewfinder or on the LCD monitor.
- **Lip Sync mode.** In this mode, the audio and video shown while the movie is being captured are delayed by the same amount and will be in sync with each other if you monitor using headphones in conjunction with the EVF or LCD.

Wind Noise Reduction

Options: On, Off

Default: Off

My preference: Off

Designed to muffle the howling sound produced by a loud wind passing over the built-in microphones, this item (when On) is for use when recording video. It's off by default because Wind Noise Reduction (provided by the camera's processor) does degrade sound quality, especially bass tones, and the recording volume is reduced. I recommend setting it to On only when shooting in a location with loud wind noises.

Marker Display (Movies)

Options: On, Off

Default: Off

My preference: N/A

When shooting video that will end up being displayed in other than HDTV's 16:9 ratio, it's useful to know exactly where the boundaries of other types of frames are, so the image can be composed to keep important subject matter contained within those boundaries. This setting lets you turn the display of any of four different types of markers on or off, as described in the Marker Settings entry that follows.

Marker Settings (Movies)

Options: Center, Aspect Ratio, Safety Zone, Guideframe

Default: All marker settings Off

My preference: N/A

This entry allows you to choose which markers are displayed during video capture. You can select any or all of the following, if you like, although using more than one or two markers is likely to be confusing. Your choices (shown in Figure 4.5) are as follows:

- **Center—On/Off.** Whether or not the center marker is shown in the middle of the shooting screen. The default value is Off.
- **Aspect Ratio—Off/4:3/13:9/14:9/15:9/1.66:1/1.85:1/2.35:1.** This activates a marker showing your preferred aspect ratio. The default is Off.
- **Safety Zone—Off/80%/90%.** Sets the safety zone display that represents the standard range that can be received by a household standard-definition television.
- **Guideframe—On/Off.** Enables/disables a guide frame that can be used to verify whether a subject is parallel or perpendicular.

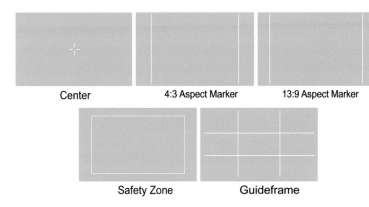

Center   4:3 Aspect Marker   13:9 Aspect Marker

Safety Zone   Guideframe

Figure 4.5 Video guide markers.

Video Light Mode

Options: Power Link, REC Link, REC Link & Standby, Auto

Default: Power Link

My preference: Auto

Sony offers video lighting units for its camcorders and digital cameras, such as the HVL-LE1 (about $250), which is a battery-operated LED video light. This menu entry allows you to control when the light illuminates. Your choice is a matter of personal preference, depending on how you operate. Your choices are as follows:

- **Power Link.** Turns on when the camera is powered up, and off when the camera is powered down. Use this if you'll be shooting more or less continually and don't need to save battery power between sequences.

- **REC Link.** Video light turns on when movie recording starts, and off when you stop capture. This setting will preserve your battery. I like to use it when I definitely want to use the video light at all times during movie capture, such as when I am shooting exclusively indoors, or am outdoors and want some fill light to illuminate shadows for close-ups.

- **REC Link & STBY.** Illuminates when movie capture is underway and dims at other times. Operates like the previous choice but stretches the life of your battery.

- **Auto.** The video light turns on under dim lighting conditions. You might want to use this if you intend to shoot movies under both dim and bright lighting conditions (say, indoors and out) and want the light to come on only under reduced illumination.

Movie with Shutter

Options: On, Off
Default: Off
My preference: Off

This is the only entry in the Camera Settings II-04 (Movie 4) menu. (Not shown in a figure.) Your a7R IV gives you the option of using the shutter release to start and stop shooting movies as an alternate to the Movie button located to the right of the viewfinder. Select On, and either button can be used; choose Off, and only the movie button will activate/stop movie capture. It's usually easier to find the shutter release, which is larger and located on top of the camera, when your eye is up to the viewfinder. It's easy to press the AF-ON or even AEL button by mistake. If your current session will be confined to video capture, you'll probably decide that using the shutter button will be more convenient.

I like this option when I am capturing movies hand-held. If the a7R IV is mounted on a tripod and I am generally framing, composing, or focusing using the LCD monitor, I'll usually use either the Movie button or a remote release like the Sony RMT-DSLR2 or Sony RM-VPR1 to stop/start video capture. (The latter two help avoid camera motion from "stabbing" the Movie button with a finger.)

Silent Shooting (Stills)

Options: On, Off
Default: Off
My preference: Off

This is the first entry in the Camera Settings II-05 (Shutter/Steady Shot) menu. (See Figure 4.6.) Because the a7R IV model has an electronic front curtain shutter (described next), you can take still photographs without the audible clunk that the physical shutter makes. Silent Shooting is available only in P, S, A, or M shooting modes.

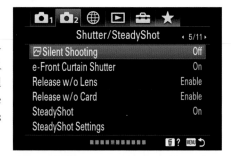

Figure 4.6 The Camera Settings II-05 (Shutter/SteadyShot) menu.

However, the most important limitation of silent shooting is that you can't use electronic flash when in this mode.

There's a whole list of other functions that are not available in quiet mode. You can't use it when making Bulb exposures, using Auto HDR, Picture Effect, or Picture Profile settings, nor when using Long Exposure noise reduction. It's also disabled if you have the electronic front curtain shutter enabled. Bracket shooting is not available when shooting RAW or RAW & JPEG formats when you've specified Uncompressed for your JPEG format.

You can turn the silent shutter feature on or off using this menu entry. Note that even with silent shutter activated, the camera will not be totally silent. The opening and closing of the aperture as the f/stop changes may make a faint noise, and the focusing motor and zoom motor (in power zoom lenses) may also be heard. However, I've spooked a few colleagues when they saw me take a picture and could not hear the familiar shutter click.

The "rolling shutter" in silent shooting mode (the camera records the 6,336 lines in a full-resolution image, one line after another) may produce distortion with moving subjects, because as a subject crosses the frame, the portion at the top of the frame will be in a different position from the part of the subject at the bottom of the frame. This "Jell-o" effect may be most noticeable when shooting uncompressed RAW images. To reduce the distortion, change the RAW file type to Compressed, and use continuous shooting. You'll get the best results, however, capturing in JPEG mode.

e-Front Curtain Shutter

Options: On, Off
Default: On
My preference: N/A

This feature reduces the lag time between when you press the shutter, and when the picture is actually taken. It can also reduce a certain type of blurring due to slight camera motion when the physical shutter "clunks" open. When set to On, the electronic front shutter curtain is used by the camera at the start of the exposure, rather than the mechanical shutter. (The physical rear shutter curtain is still used to conclude the exposure.)

Although e-front curtain shutter usually works very well, when you are using an unusually wide aperture, such as the Sony/Zeiss T* FE 55mm f/1.8 ZA lens, for example, and a very fast shutter speed, areas of the photo may exhibit a secondary (ghost) image and bokeh (the out-of-focus portion of the image) may be affected. When that happens, set this menu item to Off and the camera will use only its mechanical shutter mechanism, and the problem will not occur. Sony also recommends turning the e-curtain Off when you are using a lens made by another manufacturer, as exposure may be uneven or incorrect.

The problems pop up because the e-curtain is, in effect, *too* fast. It reduces the shutter lag to the point that the iris may not have sufficient time to close completely before the exposure begins. So, the f/stop used at the beginning of the exposure can be different from the one used for the rest of the exposure (after the iris closes down to the correct aperture completely). The overall exposure will thus be incorrect, regardless of shutter speed. In addition, at higher shutter speeds, *exposure grading* can occur. At those higher speeds, the "slit" (the gap between the front and rear curtains) is increasingly small as the shutter speed becomes faster, and parts of the image exposed initially will receive more exposure than those exposed later.

Exposure grading is worse with lenses that need a longer time to close their irises, and so is more likely with non-Sony lenses, older Sony lenses, and Sony/Minolta/third-party A-mount lenses used with one of the LA-EA adapters. The irises of those lenses aren't designed to respond at the speeds demanded by an electronic front curtain shutter. In addition, even theoretically compatible lenses may have slower iris response due to dust/grit infiltration. You'll want to use newer, good condition E-mount lenses, or adapted lenses that are manually stopped down to the "taking" aperture prior to exposure.

Release w/o Lens

Options: Disable, Enable
Default: Enable
My preference: Enable

By default, the a7R IV will refuse to try to take a photo when a lens is not mounted on the camera; this is a logical setting, especially for distracted folks who fail to notice that they have a lensless camera body hanging around their necks. If you chose Enable, however, the camera will open its shutter when you depress the shutter release button when no lens is mounted. This option will be useful if you attach the camera to some accessory such as a telescope or a third-party optic that's not recognized as a lens. I prefer to select Enable, because I frequently use oddball third-party and "foreign" lenses on my camera, such as my favorite Lensbaby distortion lens or a fisheye lens designed with a different camera mount.

Release w/o Card

Options: Disable, Enable
Default: Enable
My preference: Disable

The ability to trip the shutter without having a memory card installed is not especially useful, unless you want to hand your camera to someone for demonstration purposes and do not want to give them the capability of actually taking a picture. This happens frequently at trade shows, where vendors want you to try out their equipment, but would prefer you not leave the premises with any evidence/image samples, especially if the memory card in question belongs to the vendor rather than you.

On the contrary, it's more likely that you'd prefer to have your own camera inoperable if you've forgotten to insert a memory card. It's easy to miss the orange No Card warning that flashes when the non-picture is taken. Disabling release when a card is absent can help you avoid losing a card (you removed it to load some pictures onto someone else's computer) or having to sheepishly ask the bride and groom if they would be willing to re-stage their wedding.

SteadyShot

Options: On, Off
Default: On
My preference: On

Sony introduced in-body image stabilization (IBIS) with its a7 II-series cameras. So, the a7R IV has both in-body image stabilization (the awesome 5-axis SteadyShot that so many of us are crazy about), and the ability to use optical image stabilization (Optical SteadyShot or OSS) built into certain lenses. Both systems work well with each other and can be used simultaneously. If for some reason you want to disable SteadyShot, you can use this menu entry. Some lenses, like the Sony FE 24-105 f/4 G OSS have an Optical SteadyShot On/Off Switch. If so, this menu setting is not available.

SteadyShot is on by default to help counteract image blur that is caused by camera shake, but you should turn it off when the camera is mounted on a tripod, as the additional anti-shake feature is not needed, and slight movements of the tripod can sometimes "confuse" the system. In other situations, however, I recommend leaving SteadyShot turned on at all times.

SteadyShot Settings

Options: Auto, Manual (8mm–1000mm)
Default: Manual, 8mm
My preference: Auto

This setting allows the camera to adjust the behavior of SteadyShot, based on the amount of image stabilization typically required at particular focal lengths. That is, telephoto lenses "magnify" camera shake and thus can benefit from more aggressive image stabilization. Indeed, this aspect is one reason why in-lens IS is often touted as superior to in-body stabilization. Your a7R IV gives you the opportunity to benefit from both! This setting is not available if you have disabled SteadyShot using the entry above. If your lens has Optical SteadyShot, settings can only be changed using the control on the lens.

- **Auto.** When this default setting is chosen, the camera receives focal length information electronically from the lens and can activate the appropriate amount of SteadyShot anti-shake.
- **Manual.** You can enter the focal length of the lens or the zoom position from the range 8mm to 1000mm. This is especially useful if you're working with a teleconverter, which produces magnification beyond that which the camera can detect from the supplied lens data alone. It's also a good option if you are using a lens (possibly a "foreign" lens with an adapter) that cannot communicate focal length to the a7R IV.

Zoom

Options: Smart or ClearImage Zooming in shooting mode

Default: None

My preference: None

This is the first entry in the Camera Settings II-06 (Zoom) menu. (See Figure 4.7.) The feature adds an ersatz "power zoom" control to the a7R IV, which otherwise lacks one. It's useful once you understand what it does and how it works, but Sony has done its best to make the feature as confusing as possible.

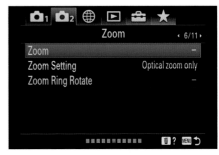

Figure 4.7 The Camera Settings II-6 (Zoom) menu.

Some other cameras in the Sony mirrorless lineup, such as the a5100, have a physical zoom lever located concentrically with the shutter release. None of the a7R IV-series models has this feature. But, in effect, you still have *five* different ways to zoom while you're taking still photographs or movies.

This list will sort out the options for you:

- **Optical zoom with zoom ring.** Zoom lenses always have a ring around their barrel that can be rotated back and forth to zoom in or out on your subject. The sole exception might be a few lenses that have a power zoom lever that takes the place of the zoom ring.

- **Optical Power Zoom.** Certain E-mount lenses include a PZ (power zoom) designation in their name. These include several APS-C format Sony lenses, and the Sony 28-135mm FE PZ F4 G OSS full-frame E-mount power zoom lens. They all have a zooming motor built in that can be activated by sliding a switch on the lens barrel itself. Alternatively, you can zoom these lenses using a camera's zoom switch (if you own an APS-C model that has one).

- **Smart Zoom.** This is one of three zoom options that take you beyond the true optical zoom range of your lens into the realm of digitized zooming, which produces a zoom *effect* by taking the pixels in the center of the original image and filling the frame with them.

  Smart Zoom is available *only* when you have set the camera to M (medium) or S (small) image size. It provides a limited amount of zooming, but, technically, requires no quality-reducing interpolation. The camera simply produces each "zoomed" image by cropping the photo to the zoomed size. The resolution of your final image corresponds to the resolution of the Medium or Small image size, as explained in Chapter 2. When using Smart Zoom, an S label appears in the viewfinder or LCD monitor zoom scale to indicate that the feature is in effect.

- **ClearImage Zoom.** When using this option, some quality is lost, as this kind of zooming doesn't produce any actual additional information; it just *interpolates* the pixels captured optically to simulate a zoomed-in perspective. Pixels are created to fill the frame at the resolution of the given Image Size setting (Large, Medium, or Small). ClearImage Zoom has many options, and

I'll explain them later in this chapter. When a zoom scale is shown in the viewfinder or on the LCD monitor, a C label appears whenever you leave optical zooming behind and enter the Clear-Image realm. When ClearImage Zoom is used alone, you'll typical achieve 1X to 2X magnifications *over and above* whatever optical zoom setting you've used. At Medium and Small image size settings, you can zoom up to 3X and 4X, respectively.

- **Digital Zoom.** This option gives you even higher magnifications than ClearImage Zoom, with an additional decrease in image quality. When a zoom scale is shown in the viewfinder or on the LCD monitor, and a D label appears when you are using digital zoom. I'll explain the options later in the chapter. When Digital Zoom is active, it takes up where ClearImage Zoom leaves off, giving you up to 4X magnification *beyond* the optical zoom focal length you've selected when using Large image size. At Medium image size, you can zoom up to 6.1X; with Small image size, up to 8X.

Using Zoom

My basic recommendation is to use optical zoom only most of the time, and this feature might not be available. If you've set the camera for Optical Zoom Only in the Zoom Settings entry which follows this one, then this Zoom feature is not available at all if Image Size is set to Large. If ClearImage Zoom is set to On, you can use ClearImage zooming; if Digital Zoom is set to On, you can use both. When Image Size is set to Medium or Small, then Smart Zoom is also available for all three Zoom Settings options. After you've sorted out which of the zoom methods you want to use, using the Zoom feature while shooting is fairly easy. Just follow these steps:

1. **Navigate to the Camera Settings II-06 (Zoom) menu.** Select Zoom and press the center button.
2. **Preview image.** A live view of your sensor image appears in the EVF and LCD monitor, with a zoom scale at lower right, as shown in Figure 4.8.
3. **Zoom in or out.** You can rotate the control wheel or use the left/right directional controls to zoom in or out.
4. **Change zoom steps.** Press the up/down controls to change the size of the zoom increment, from 1X to 1.4X and thence all the way up to 8X, depending on whether you've selected Large, Medium, or Small as your image size.
5. **Confirm or cancel.** When you're satisfied with the zoom level, press the center button to confirm, or the MENU button to cancel. You can then continue to shoot at the new zoomed magnification.

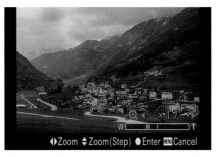

Figure 4.8 The zoom scale shows the amount of magnification and type of zoom in use.

Zoom Setting

Options: Optical Zoom Only, ClearImage Zoom, Digital Zoom
Default: Optical Zoom Only
My preference: Optical Zoom Only

The a7R IV series has three different types of zoom settings: Optical Zoom, ClearImage Zoom, and Digital Zoom, and you can choose any *one* of them here. My preference is to stick with optical zoom only. I own lots of great lenses, and don't hesitate to switch to one of them when I need some extra reach. Neither ClearImage nor Digital Zoom give me the image quality I am looking for. However, if you don't own a lens with enough telephoto magnification and/or don't need the best quality for some applications, the two electronic zoom modes are available.

They are most practical with a camera like the a7R IV, as its 61-megapixel sensor has resolution to waste. Of course, you can always shoot without the electronic zoom features and crop to the effective magnification you want in your image editor. ClearImage Zoom and Digital Zoom are not available when Image Quality is set to RAW or RAW & JPEG. When working with those ersatz zooms, the metering mode is locked at Multi, and Focus Area setting is disabled (the focus area frame in the zoomed image is shown by a dotted line).

Zoom Ring Rotate

Options: Left/Right (Wide-Tele), Right/Left (Wide-Tele)
Default: Left (W), Right (T)
My preference: N/A

This setting controls whether power zooming (with PZ-designated lenses that have a power zoom feature) proceeds from wide-angle to telephoto settings when the zoom control is pressed from left to right, or in the reverse direction, from right to left. The setting is compatible only with power zoom lenses that support this feature.

DISP Button

Options (Monitor): Graphic Display, Display All Info., No Disp. Info., Histogram, Level, For Viewfinder, Monitor Off
Options (Viewfinder): Graphic Display, Display All Info., No Disp. Info., Histogram, Level
My preference: Activate all but Graphic Display

This is the first entry in the Camera Settings II-07 (Display/Auto Review 1) menu. (See Figure 4.9.) Use this item to specify which of the available display options will—and will not—be available in Shooting mode when you use the LCD or viewfinder and press the DISP button to cycle through the various displays. Choose from Monitor or Viewfinder and mark or unmark the screens you want to enable or

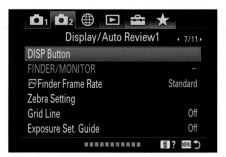

Figure 4.9 The Camera Settings II-07 (Display/Auto Review 1) menu.

disable. The Monitor selection includes a For Viewfinder option that displays a text/graphic display of your current settings on the back-panel LCD.

You can use this menu item to deselect one or more of the display options, so it/they will never appear on the LCD when you press the DISP button. To make that change, scroll to an option and press the center button to remove the check mark beside it. Naturally, at least one display option must remain selected. If you de-select all of them, the camera will warn you about this and it will not return to Shooting mode until you add a check mark to one of the options. If you turn the camera off while none are selected, the camera will interpret this as a Cancel command and return to your most recent display settings.

The same screens shown at left in Figure 4.10 are also available for the electronic viewfinder, except For Viewfinder and Monitor Off. (See Figure 4.10, right.) The viewfinder versions have some slight differences; for example, at the bottom of the viewfinder version is an analog exposure indicator. You can select a different set of displays for the viewfinder and monitor. That is, you can choose to view the plain-vanilla No Display Info view in the EVF and Display All Info on the LCD monitor. Here's a recap of the available display options for the monitor.

- **Graphic Display.** When selected, this display shows basic shooting information, plus a graphic display of shutter speed and aperture (except when Sweep Panorama is the mode in use). If you learn how to interpret it, you'll note that it indicates that a fast shutter speed will freeze motion, that a small aperture (large f/number) will provide a great range of acceptably sharp focus, and other information of this type. (See Figure 4.11, left.)

- **Display All Info.** The default screen when you first turn the camera on, this option displays data about current settings for a complete overview of recording information. (See Figure 4.11, right.) Not all the information in the figure may be displayed at one time, and there are additional icons not shown because they occupy the same space on the screen as another indicator.

- **No Disp. Info.** Despite its name, this display option provides the basic shooting information as to settings, in a conventional size. (See Figure 4.12, left.)

- **Histogram.** Activate this option if you want to be able to view a live luminance histogram to assist you in evaluating the exposure before taking a photo, a feature to be discussed in Chapter 9. The basic shooting data will appear in addition to the histogram. (See Figure 4.12, right.)

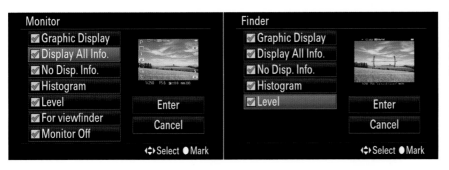

Figure 4.10 Select which display screens are shown on the LCD monitor (left) or viewfinder (right).

Figure 4.11 Graphic
Display (left); Display All
Information (right).

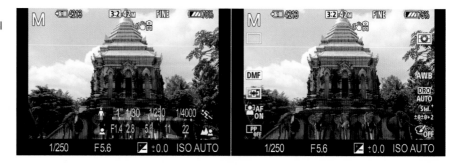

Figure 4.12 The No
Display Information
(left); Histogram Display
(right).

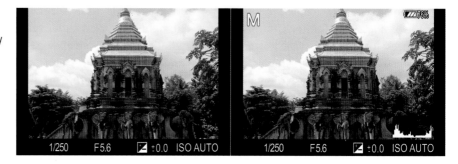

- **Level.** This display shows how much the camera is rotated around the lens axis (horizontal tilt) as well as how far it is tilted forward and backward. When the camera is not perfectly level, orange indicators show the amount of forward/backward and horizontal tilt. (See Figure 4.13.) When the camera is level in both directions, the indicators turn green. (See Figure 4.14.)
- **For Viewfinder.** This display can be shown only on the LCD monitor. When visible, you can press the Fn button to produce the Quick Navi screen, which I explained in Chapter 2. (See Figure 4.15.)
- **Monitor Off.** When this option is selected, pressing the DISP button eventually takes you to a blank monitor screen, which you might need to use when a brightly lit LCD is distracting or intrusive.

Figure 4.13 Orange
indicators show the
amount of tilt.

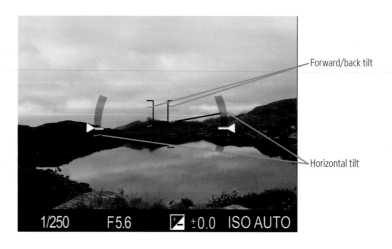

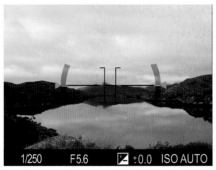

1/250   F5.6   ±0.0   ISO AUTO

Figure 4.14 When the camera is level, the indicators turn green.

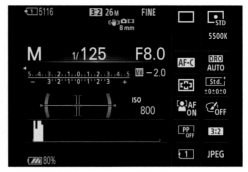

Figure 4.15 For Viewfinder Display.

FINDER/MONITOR

Options: Auto, Viewfinder, Monitor

Default: Auto

My preference: N/A

This also uses the eye sensor located above the viewfinder window, but it controls only whether the camera turns off the LCD and switches the view to the viewfinder when your eye comes near the EVF. With the default setting of Auto, the screen goes blank and the viewfinder activates when your eye (or any other object) approaches the Eye-Start sensor. Helpfully, the eye sensor is *disabled* when you tilt the LCD monitor away from the camera body, presumably because in that mode you'll be working exclusively with the LCD and do not want the a7R IV to switch to viewfinder mode if your hand (or any other object) passes in front of the sensor.

Switch to the Viewfinder or Monitor options and the eye sensor no longer initiates a switch from one display to the other. The display is then *always* sent to the viewing device you selected, and the other one is turned off. You might want to use the Monitor option if you are doing work involving critical focusing using the LCD, and as you examine the screen closely, your face will frequently be close to the back of the camera where the Eye-Start sensor might detect it. Or, perhaps, you are shooting at a concert or other venue where the bright LCD can be distracting to others. Choose Viewfinder, and the shooting preview, menus, photos displayed for review during playback, and so forth will be shown only in the EVF.

Of course, if you disable automatic switching between the two, you'll still want to have the option of activating the viewfinder or monitor displays manually. To do that, you'll need to assign the FINDER/MONITOR switching function to a key. I'll show you how to do that later in this chapter, when I describe the Custom Key option in the Camera Settings II-09 (Custom Operation) menu.

Finder Frame Rate (Stills)

Options: Standard, High

Default: Standard

My preference: Standard

The a7R IV sports an advanced 5.76 million dot UXGA (Ultra-XGA) OLED Tru-Finder electronic viewfinder, and includes a Zeiss T* coating to reduce reflections. To reduce a slight jerkiness in the EVF when shooting action, you can switch from the default Standard (60 fps) frame rate to a blistering High (120 fps) rate that displays fast-moving subjects more smoothly. The tradeoff is a reduced resolution view at the highest frame rate. Standard is automatically invoked when reviewing images or video in playback mode, when viewing using an HDMI connection, or when the temperature inside the camera body is high. I tend to stick with the higher-resolution Standard frame rate, except when tracking sports or action subjects.

Zebra Setting

Options: On, Off, IRE 70, 75, 80, 85, 90, 95, 100, 100+

Default: Off, **Zebra Level:** 70

My preference: 80

This feature warns you when highlight levels in your image are brighter than a setting you specify in this menu option. It's somewhat comparable to the flashing "blinkies" that digital cameras have long used during image review to tell us, after the fact, which highlight areas of the image we just took are blown out.

Zebra patterns are a much more useful tool, because you are given an alert *before* you take the picture and can specify exactly how bright *too bright* is. The Zebra feature has been a staple of professional video shooting for a long time, as you might guess from the moniker assigned to the unit used to specify brightness: IRE, a measure of video signal level, which stands for *Institute of Radio Engineers.*

When you want to use Zebra pattern warnings, access this menu entry and specify an IRE value from 70 to 100, or 100+. Once you've been notified, you can adjust your exposure settings to reduce the brightness of the highlights, as I'll describe in Chapter 7.

So, exactly how bright *is* too bright? A value of 100 IRE indicates pure white, so any Zebra pattern visible when using this setting (or 100+) indicates that your image is extremely overexposed. Any details in the highlights are gone and cannot be retrieved. Settings from 70 to 90 can be used to make sure facial tones are not overexposed. Generally, Caucasian skin generally falls in the 80 IRE range, with darker skin tones registering as low as 70, and very fair skin or lighter areas of your subject edging closer to 90 IRE. Once you've decided the approximate range of tones that you want to make sure do *not* blow out, you can set the camera's Zebra pattern sensitivity appropriately and receive the flashing striped warning on the LCD of your camera. (See Figure 4.16.) The pattern does not appear in output to a device through the HDMI port, nor in your final image, of course—it's just an aid to keep you from blowing it, so to speak.

Grid Line

Options: Rule of 3rds Grid, Square Grid, Diag.+Square Grid, Off
Default: Off
My preference: Off

This feature allows you to activate one of three optional grids, so it's superimposed on the LCD or EVF display. The grid pattern can help you with composition while you are shooting architecture or similar subjects. I sometimes use the Rule of Thirds grid to help with composition, but you might want to activate another option when composing images of scenes that include diagonal, horizontal, and perpendicular lines. (See Figure 4.17.)

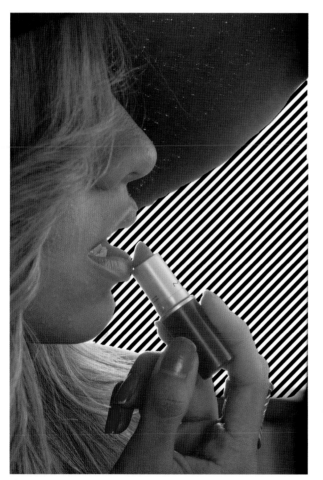

Figure 4.16 The flashing stripes show an area is overexposed.

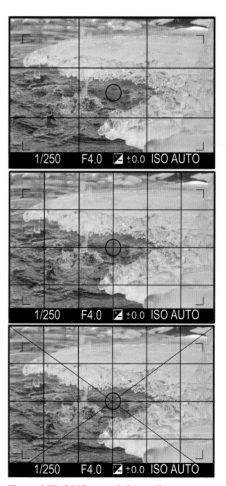

Figure 4.17 Grid lines can help you align your images on the LCD or EVF.

Exposure Setting Guide

Options: On, Off

Default: Off

My preference: On

This feature is of most use to those with poor eyesight, but a convenience for all. All it does is show a scrolling scale on the LCD or viewfinder with an enlarged rendition of the current shutter speed or aperture highlighted in orange. It more or less duplicates the display of both that already appears on the bottom line of the screen, but in a larger font and with the next/previous setting flanking the current value. In Aperture Priority, the scale shows f/stops. In Shutter Priority, you see shutter speeds. In Program mode, both are visible. When using Manual exposure, a single scrolling line appears showing shutter speed *or* aperture, depending on whether you rotate the rear or front dials. I like to leave it switched on, as the display is a reminder of which parameter I'm fooling with at the moment.

Live View Display

Options: Setting Effect ON, Setting Effect OFF

Default: Setting Effect ON

My preference: Setting Effect ON, unless using flash in manual mode

This is the first entry in the Camera Settings II-08 (Display/ Auto Review 2) menu (see Figure 4.18). As a mirrorless camera, the a7-series cameras are always in a "live view" mode, showing you what the sensor sees. This entry lets you specify whether the camera should apply any exposure settings or effects that you've selected to the image before presenting it to you as a preview.

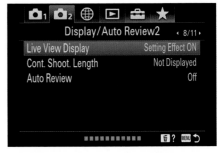

Figure 4.18 The Camera Settings II-08 menu.

There are times when you don't want to see the effects of the settings you've made on the screen/EVF. For example, when you are using flash in manual mode, the camera has no way of knowing exactly how much light will be illuminating your scene. That f/16 aperture may be ideal for a shot exposed by your studio strobes, but the a7R IV will, when Setting Effect is set to ON, show you a preview based on the ambient light, rather than the flash. The result? Your viewfinder or LCD monitor image is very, very dim. You'll want to select Setting Effect OFF so the camera will boost the electronic image to viewable levels.

When Setting Effects are active, the live view display in the EVF or the LCD reflects the *exact* effects of any camera features that you're using to modify the view, including as exposure compensation and white balance. In that mode, this allows for an accurate evaluation of what the photo will look like and enables you to determine whether the current settings will provide the effects you want.

The ON option can be especially helpful when you're using any of the Picture Effects, because you can preview the exact rendition that the selected effect and its overrides will provide. It's also very useful when you're setting some exposure compensation, as you can visually determine how much lighter or darker each adjustment makes the image. And when you're trying to achieve correct color balance, it's useful to be able to preview the effect of your white balance setting.

If you'd like to preview the image without the effect of settings visible, you can set this feature to OFF. Naturally, the display will no longer accurately depict what your photo will look like when it's taken. So, for most users, ON is the most suitable option. Unfortunately, this setting has caused more than a few minutes of head-scratching among new users who switch to Manual exposure mode and find themselves with a completely black (or utterly white) screen. The black screen, especially, may fool you into thinking your camera has malfunctioned.

Continuous Shooting Length

Options: Always Display, Shooting-Only Display, Not Displayed
Default: Not Displayed
My preference: Shooting-Only Display when shooting action

Your a7R IV has a much larger buffer than its predecessor, the a7R III, and can store an impressive 68 full-resolution 61MP JPEG or RAW photos (or 30 uncompressed 14-bit RAW files) before it fills, slowing down the camera while images are dumped to your memory card. (A message, "SLOW," appears on the screen.) At 10 frames per second, you might encounter a full buffer with a burst of less than 8 seconds. This entry can enable a useful "thermometer"-type indicator at the left side of the screen that graphically shows the status of the a7R IV's buffer. You can choose Always Display, which pops up the indicator any time the camera is set to Continuous Shooting. In that mode, it also serves as a reminder that you're shooting bursts. I prefer to use Shooting-Only Display, but only when I am photographing sports or other action. If I'm just using continuous shooting to allow me to take short bursts of shots—say, when photographing urban street scenes—it's screen clutter that I don't need. You can dispense with the indicator entirely by selecting Not Displayed.

Auto Review

Options: Off, 2 sec., 5 sec., 10 sec.
Default: Off
My preference: N/A

When this item is set to 2, 5, or 10 seconds, the camera can display an image on the LCD or viewfinder for your review immediately after the photo is taken. (When you shoot a continuous or bracketed series of images, only the last picture that's been recorded will be shown.) During this display, you can press the Zoom In button to get a closer look at your image, delete a disappointing shot by pressing the Delete button, or cancel picture review by tapping the shutter release button or performing another function. (You'll never be prevented from taking another picture because you were reviewing images.) This option can be used to specify whether the review image appears for 2, 5, or 10 seconds, or not at all.

Depending on how you're working, you might want a brief display, or you might prefer to have time for a more leisurely examination (when you're carefully checking compositions). Other times, you might not want to have the review image displayed at all, such as when you're taking photos in a darkened theater or concert venue, and the constant flashing of images might be distracting to others. Turning off picture review or keeping the duration short also saves battery power. You can always review the last picture you took at any time by pressing the Playback button.

Custom Key (Stills)

Options: More than 100 different definitions for Control Wheel, Custom Buttons 1, 2, 3, 4, Multi-selector Center Button, Center Button, Left/Right/Down Buttons, AF-ON Button, AEL Button, Focus Hold Button (on lens)

Default: Various

My preference: N/A

This is the first entry on the Camera Settings II-09 (Custom Operation 1) menu. (See Figure 4.19.) It allows customization of as many as 11 buttons of the camera, the control wheel, and one additional button, Focus Hold, found on some lenses. Indeed, the following is a list of the only buttons on the camera that you *cannot* redefine to perform some other function:

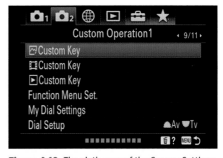

Figure 4.19 The ninth page of the Camera Settings II menu.

- **Shutter release.** It is always used to take a picture and will initiate autofocus if you haven't assigned AF-ON and other AF functions to a different key.

- **Up directional button.** It is used to change your information display in shooting and Playback modes, and as a directional button in menus.

- **Playback button.** Activates picture review.

- **Fn (Function) button.** (Almost) always summons the Function menu, and in Playback mode sends the current image to a smart device. However, you *can* redefine the Fn button to FTP Transfer when in Playback mode (only).

- **Movie button.** Starts/stops movies. However, you can specify whether you want the button to commence video capture always, or only when the mode dial is set to the Movie position.

Your custom key definitions override any default definitions for those buttons when in Shooting mode; they retain their original functions in Playback mode (unless you redefine them, as I'll describe shortly). Because button definition is such a personal choice, I steer away from recommending particular definitions for each of the buttons, even though certain functions can be accessed *only* by assigning them to a custom key setting. Our fingers and agility vary, so, while buttons like the AF-ON button are traditionally used for something like back-button focus, you may prefer to assign that function to a different key.

When assigning definitions to keys, keep in mind that certain behaviors can be used *only* if you have made them available using a custom key definition. For example, if you want to use the Bright Monitoring feature, which temporarily turns the Live View Setting Effect to Off to increase the brightness level of the screen in dark locations, you must assign it to a key.

Each of the customizable buttons (except the down button) have a default behavior assigned for shooting mode, listed below. In Movie mode, these buttons have the exact same behavior, unless you choose a different option. In Playback mode, only the Fn button and C1–C3 buttons can be redefined, with Custom 3 having the only default behavior (Protect).

- Custom 1: White Balance
- Custom 2: Focus Area
- Custom 3: Focus Mode; (Protect in Play-back mode)
- Custom 4: Touch Operation Select
- Multi-selector Center button: Focus Standard
- AEL button: AEL Hold

- AF-ON button: AF ON
- Control Wheel: Not Set
- Control Wheel Center button: Not Set
- Left button: Drive Mode
- Right button: ISO
- Down button: Not Set
- Up button: DISP (Not customizable)
- Focus Hold (on lens): Focus Hold

Basic Functions

These functions are all available for Custom buttons 1, 2, 3, 4, and the AF-ON and Focus Hold buttons. The whole list, *except* for In-Camera Guide, can be assigned to the multi-selector center button, control wheel center button, and AEL buttons. In all cases, choosing Not Set deactivates that button.

The functions for the controls appear on four pages of listings, each page dedicated to a specific set of programmable custom keys. The first page is shown in Figure 4.20.

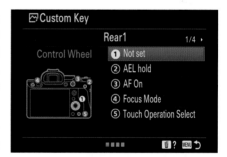

Figure 4.20 Four pages display the available assignable functions.

The basic functions include:

- File Format
- JPEG Quality
- JPEG Image Size
- Aspect Ratio
- APS-C/Super 35/Full Frame
- Drive Mode
- Self-timer During Bracket
- Interval Shooting
- Pixel Shift

- Memory Recall
- Recall Custom Hold 1
- Recall Custom Hold 2
- Recall Custom Hold 3
- Focus Mode
- AF/MF Control Hold
- AF/MF Ctrl Toggle
- Focus Standard
- Focus Area
- Switch Focus Settings

- Focus Settings
- Register AF Area Hold
- Register AF Area Toggle
- Register AF Area+AF-ON
- Tracking On
- Face Priority in AF
- Eye AF
- Subject Detection
- Switch Right/Left Eye

- Face/Eye Frame Display Selection
- AF Tracking Sensitivity
- Aperture Drive in AF
- AF On
- Focus Hold
- Exposure Comp
- ISO
- ISO Auto Min SS
- Metering Mode
- Face Priority in Multi Metering
- AEL Hold
- AEL Toggle
- AEL Spot Hold
- AEL Spot Toggle
- Flash Mode
- Flash Compensation
- Wireless Flash
- FEL Lock Hold
- FEL Lock Toggle
- FEL Lock/AEL Hold
- FEL Lock/AEL Toggle
- White Balance
- Priority Set in AWB
- AWB Lock Hold

- AWB Lock Toggle
- DRO
- Creative Style
- Picture Effect
- Picture Profile
- Focus Magnifier
- Peaking Display Selection
- Peaking Level
- Peaking Color
- Anti-Flicker Shooting
- In-Camera Guide
- Movie
- S&Q Frame Rate
- Audio Rec Level
- Audio Level Display
- Marker Display Settings
- Silent Shooting
- SteadyShot
- SteadyShot Adjustments
- SteadyShot Focal Length
- Zoom
- Aperture Preview
- Shot Result Preview
- FINDER/MONITOR Selection
- Finder Frame Rate

- Zebra Display Select
- Zebra Level
- Grid Line
- Live View Display Selection
- Bright Monitoring
- My Dial 1 During Hold
- My Dial 2 During Hold
- My Dial 3 During Hold
- My Dial 1 -> 2 -> 3
- Toggle My Dial 1
- Toggle My Dial 2
- Toggle My Dial 3
- Audio Signals
- Sent to Smartphone
- FTP Transfer
- Playback
- Monitor Brightness
- Gamma Display Assist
- Touch Operation Select
- TC/UB Display Switch
- Prioritize Record Media
- MENU
- Display My Menu
- Not Set

New Assignable Functions

If you're upgrading from an earlier Sony camera with custom keys, you'll be interested in knowing which of the functions listed above are new for the a7R IV. Most of them have been implemented as a way of better using new features. Here is a list of the new menu functions:

- **Interval Shooting.** If you find yourself using the new Interval Shooting feature frequently, and think it's a pain to navigate to the Camera Settings I-03 menu every time, you can assign a custom key of your choice to jump immediately to the interval photography settings.

- **Face/Eye Priority in AF.** Assign this function to one of the available keys to enable/disable giving higher priority to detected faces. You'll find this capability especially useful to turn the feature off when your subjects include faces that may be difficult for the a7R IV to detect (often people with long bangs or wearing sunglasses) or in difficult lighting conditions (shade, backlight, or low-light scenes).

- **Subject Detection.** If pet or animal photography is a big part of your shooting, you switch back and forth between Human and Animal eye detection more frequently than your average photographer. Assign Subject Detection to a custom key, and you can toggle back and forth between the two modes at the press of a button.

- **AF Tracking Sensitivity.** Sports photographers will like the ability to quickly change how fast the camera responds to new subjects entering the frame. Assign the function to a custom key, and you can switch to responsive, standard, or locked on settings, as described in Chapter 3.

- **Aperture Drive in AF.** If you need quiet operation in certain environments, you can assign a key to enable or disable this feature, described earlier in this chapter.

- **MENU.** I find the MENU button easy to find, even in the dark, as it's located to the immediate left of the viewfinder. If you often make adjustments while viewing through the viewfinder, you might prefer having a second menu button that can be accessed with the camera up to your eye. Assign MENU to the C1 or C2 buttons, and you can summon menus by moving your trigger (shutter) finger from the shutter release position to either of the two top-panel custom keys.

- **My Dial Assignments.** You can assign up to three different behaviors to the control wheel and/or control dial, and return them to their default functions quickly. The custom functions let you activate the alternate behavior by holding the button down, switching among the three dial assignments by spinning a control, and toggling one of the three on or off. I'll explain this feature later in the chapter.

Other Buttons

The other buttons have limitations on the functions that can be assigned to them. In all cases, selecting Not Set deactivates that button.

- **Left, Right, Down buttons.** All the basic functions listed above are available, except for the following behaviors, which require holding the button down to access the feature. They are: Recall Custom Hold 1, Recall Custom Hold 2, Recall Custom Hold 3, AF/MF Control Hold, Focus Standard, Register AF Area Hold, Register AF Area+AF-ON, Eye AF, AF On, Focus Hold, AEL Hold, AEL Spot Hold, FEL Lock Hold, FEL Lock/AEL Hold, In-Camera Guide, Aperture Preview, Shot Result, and Preview.

- **Control Wheel.** The *only* functions that can be assigned to the rotation of the control wheel for Shooting mode are Move AF Point Left/Right, Move AF Point Up/Down, Aperture, Shutter Speed, ISO, White Balance, Creative Style, Picture Effect, Audio Recording Level, and Not Set.

- **Center button.** All the basic functions can be assigned, plus Standard, which leaves the control wheel at its standard behavior as an OK/Enter button.

VARIATIONS ON A THEME

You have several options for assigning the very useful autoexposure lock (AEL) functions to one of the definable keys.

- **AEL Hold.** Exposure is locked while the button is held down.
- **AEL Toggle.** The AEL button can be pressed and released, and the exposure remains locked until the button is pressed again.
- **Center Point AEL Hold.** Exposure is locked on the center point of the frame while the button is held down.
- **Center Point AEL Toggle.** Toggles exposure lock on/off using the center point of the frame.

Other Useful Key Definitions

Here are some other possible custom key definitions you might find useful:

- **FINDER/MONITOR switch.** If you turn off automatic switching between finder and monitor, you'll want to have a button that will quickly toggle between the two. The down button has no default behavior, and FINDER/MONITOR is a good choice.
- **Fast ISO change.** Assign ISO to the control wheel, and as you shoot you can spin the wheel to adjust your ISO setting on the fly. While the a7R IV's Auto ISO feature works well (especially when you're shooting fast and quickly), at times the photographer can do a better job of adjusting sensitivity to suit the task at hand.
- **More pairs.** The control wheel and its center button can also be assigned pairs of related functions. For example, if you've set the control wheel to change ISO sensitivity, the center button can be used to specify ISO Auto Minimum Shutter Speed when you select ISO Auto with the wheel. Image Size/Quality is another good pair for the wheel/center button combination.
- **Freed-up keys.** Once you assign ISO to the control wheel, that leaves the right button, formerly used to set ISO, free for a new definition. You could assign it to Metering Mode or another function.

Custom Key (Movies)

Options: More than 100 different definitions for Control Wheel; Custom Buttons 1, 2, 3, 4; Multi-selector Center Button; Center Button; Left/Right/Down Buttons; AEL Button; Focus Hold Button (on lens)

Default: Follow Custom (Stills)

My preference: N/A

You can assign *different* functions to each of the customizable controls when shooting movies, assuming you have such a need and an excellent memory. The default definition for those controls is Follow Custom (Stills), which uses whichever behaviors you have assigned using the Custom Key (Stills) entry.

Custom Key (Playback)

Options: Definitions for Custom Buttons 1, 2, and 3, plus Fn/Send to Smartphone button

Default: Varies

My preference: N/A

Only a limited number of controls and functions are available using this entry. The Custom 1, 2, and 3 buttons can be assigned behaviors during Playback, most of them options from the Playback menu itself. C1 and C2 follow the setting made for Stills/Movie mode (unless you choose another behavior), while C3 has a default setting of Protect during image review. The Fn button, which by default sends the displayed image to your smartphone, can also be defined to switch to FTP settings.

Function Menu Settings

Options: 53 different Function menu settings, plus Not Set

Default: Top row: Drive Mode, Focus Mode, Focus Area, Exposure Compensation, ISO, Metering mode; Bottom row: Flash Mode, Flash Compensation, White Balance, Creative Style, Prioritize Record Media, Shoot Mode

My preference: N/A

When you press the Fn button when in Shooting or Movie modes, a screen like the one shown in Figure 4.21 pops up, with six settings each in two rows arrayed along the bottom. The default options are illustrated. This entry allows you to change the function of any of the 12 positions in the Function menu, so you can display only those you use most, and arrange them in the order that best suits you. There are 53 different functions available, plus Not Set. Browse through the list below and decide which 12 you want to display on the Function menu.

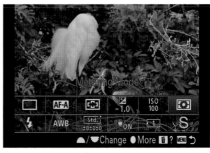

Figure 4.21 Function menu default settings.

When you highlight Function Menu Set. and press OK, the screen appears shown in Figure 4.22, left. The screen has an entry for each of the positions in the top row and bottom row, along with the current function with the still photo version at the top and movie Function Menu at the bottom. Highlight the position you want to modify and press OK. You can then select from among the

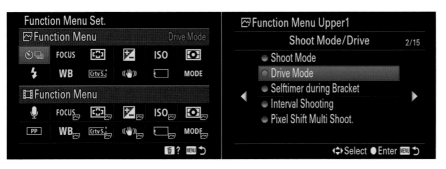

Figure 4.22 Choose Function Menu entry to edit (left). Select from available options (right).

options from a screen like the one shown in Figure 4.22, right. All the available options are explained in detail elsewhere in this book:

- File Format
- JPEG Quality
- JPEG Image Size
- Aspect Ratio
- APS-C/Super 35 Shooting
- Shoot Mode
- Drive Mode
- Self-timer During Bracket
- Interval Shooting
- Pixel Shift Multi Shooting
- Focus Mode
- Focus Area
- Face/Eye Priority in AF
- Subject Detection
- Left/Right Eye Select
- Face/Eye Frame Display
- AF Tracking Sensitivity
- Aperture Drive in AF
- Exposure Compensation

- ISO
- ISO Auto Minimum Shutter Speed
- Metering Mode
- Face Priority in Multi Metering
- Flash Mode
- Flash Compensation
- Wireless Flash
- White Balance
- Priority Set in AWB
- DRO
- Creative Style
- Picture Effect
- Picture Profile
- Peaking Display
- Peaking Level
- Peaking Color
- Anti-Flicker Shooting

- S&Q Frame Rate
- Audio Recording Level
- Audio Level Display
- Marker Display
- Silent Shooting
- SteadyShot
- SteadyShot Adjust
- SteadyShot Focal Length
- Finder Frame Rate
- Zebra Display
- Zebra Level
- Grid Line
- Live View Display
- Audio Signals
- Gamma Display Assist
- Touch Operation
- Prioritize Record Media
- Not Set

Note that you can select Not Set to leave a position blank if you want to unclutter your screen, or even duplicate an entry in multiple positions, accidentally or on purpose. Don't underestimate the power of this function. You can, in effect, create your own pop-up Function menu using any of more than four *dozen* different functions.

My Dial Settings

Options: Three separate definitions each for control wheel and control dial

Default: Not Set

My preference: N/A

This is an extremely versatile feature, which allows you to temporarily assign a different behavior to the control wheel and/or control dial, and still return them to their default functions easily. Most of the time in shooting mode, you'll want to use the wheel/dial to control shutter speed or aperture. But a quick spin of the dial/wheel can be convenient for making other settings, such as ISO or white balance adjustments. You can assign that alternate function to one of those controls, and then recall it by pressing a Custom Key that you've defined (as described above).

When you access this entry, a screen similar to the one shown in Figure 4.23 appears. The right column shows the front dial, rear dial, and control wheel. The right three columns show the current values for the three definitions for each, called My Dial 1, My Dial 2, or My Dial 3. Before you have added any definitions, each of the current settings will be Not Set, represented by double-dashes like the ones at right in the figure.

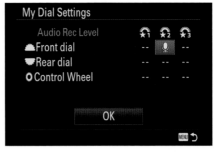

Figure 4.23 My Dial Settings.

Note: Each of the three My Dial settings can define actions for front dial, rear dial, and control wheel, but you do not have to define a function for all three. For example, you could use My Dial 1 to assign a particular function to the control wheel, but leave the front and rear dials at Not Set (which means they would retain their default behaviors).

To assign a definition, just follow these steps:

1. **Access My Dial Setup.** The settings screen appears.

2. **Choose your control and My Dial register.** Use the directional buttons to highlight My Dial 1, My Dial 2, or My Dial 3, either in the front dial, rear dial, or control wheel rows.

3. **Press the center button.** A set of screens will appear with five pages that encompass the possible functions that can be assigned.
   - Move AF Point Left/Right
   - Move AF Point Up/Down
   - Aperture
   - Shutter Speed
   - Exposure Compensation
   - ISO
   - White Balance
   - Color Temperature
   - Creative Style
   - Picture effect
   - Audio Recording Level
   - Not Set

4. **Press the center button to confirm.** You can then repeat steps 2 and 3 to define additional My Dial registers.

5. **Highlight OK.** Press OK to exit.

6. **Assign My Dial 1, 2, or 3 to a Custom Key.** Use the Custom Key (Stills) entry described earlier to assign the temporary behavior to the button you will use to switch to the alternate function. You have three different modes for activating the feature:
   - **My Dial 1 (or 2, or 3) During Hold.** When you press the assigned Custom Key, the alternate function for the specified My Dial register is active. As soon as you release it, the wheel/dial resumes its default function.
   - **My Dial 1→2→3.** When you press and hold the Custom Key, rotating that control switches among each of the registers in turn, and then wraps around to the first. Think of this as a meta-control: instead of activating a particular My Dial register and its settings, it allows you to quickly cycle among all three of them, each with their own set of settings. I suspect only those who

truly need a larger number of alternate actions for the control wheel and control dial will really need this (and I don't envy them the learning curve required to remember which My Dial settings contain which customized functions).

- **Toggle My Dial 1 (or 2, or 3).** The specified My Dial register is activated when the Custom Key is pressed, and deactivated when the Custom Key is pressed again. Use this if you need to turn on particular features for a period of time, and then return to the controls' default operation with a second key press.

Dial Setup

Options: Reverse functions

Default: Front Dial: Aperture; Rear Dial: Shutter Speed

My preference: N/A

By default, in Manual exposure mode the front dial controls the f/stop, and the rear dial adjusts the shutter speed. This entry allows you to reverse those functions for Manual exposure only if you prefer. (Either the front or rear dials can be used to adjust shutter speed [in Shutter Priority mode] and aperture [in Aperture Priority mode].) You may have a special reason for wanting to reverse the dial directions, but you're better off leaving it alone.

Av/Tv Rotate

Options: Normal, Reverse functions

Default: Normal

My preference: N/A

This is the first entry of the Camera Settings II-10 (Custom Operation 2) menu. (See Figure 4.24.) It lets you specify the direction of rotation of the front and rear dials, plus the control wheel when using them to adjust the aperture or shutter speed. When the default Normal is in effect, rotating the appropriate dial clockwise produces a smaller f/stop or faster shutter speed; rotating counterclockwise sets a larger f/stop or slower shutter speed. Choose Reverse, and clockwise rotation sets a larger f/stop or slower shutter speed, while counterclockwise produces a smaller f/stop or faster shutter speed. This is a personal preference setting.

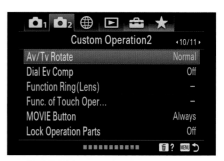

Figure 4.24 Camera Settings II-10 (Custom Operation 2) menu.

Dial EV Compensation

Options: Off, Front Dial, Rear Dial
Default: Off
My preference: N/A

If you like, you can use the front *or* rear dial to control exposure compensation whenever the exposure compensation dial is set to zero. Or, select Off and neither will have the Ev comp function. Assigning the exposure compensation behavior to a dial overrides any other function you might have defined for that dial. Moreover, dialing in exposure comp with a dial takes priority over any exposure compensation you might have set using a menu. In Manual exposure mode, the defined dial is disabled if ISO sensitivity is set to ISO Auto.

Function Ring (Lens)

Options: Power Focus, APS-C/Super 35-Full-frame Select
Default: Front Dial: Aperture; Rear Dial: Shutter Speed
My preference: N/A

Sony has begun introducing lenses with an additional "Function" control ring, including the FE 400mm f/2.8 GM (SEL400F28GM) and FE 600mm f/4 GM OSS, which ring in at roughly $12,000 and $13,000, respectively. An accompanying select switch on these lenses has three positions: Preset, Function, and Off. Here's a quick explanation:

- **Preset.** In this position, pressing the SET button on the lens (see Figure 4.25) memorizes a desired focus point. The present focus plane can be recalled instantly using the function ring. That's an important feature for sports photography and other scenes with rapid movement. Importantly, the preset focus point can be specified and recalled whether the photographer is using autofocus or manual focus, and can be outside any focus limit range currently active.

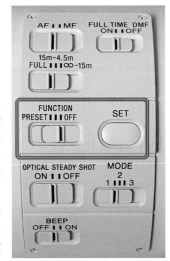

- **Function.** In this position, the function ring can be assigned a specific function.

  - The Power Focus function uses focus-by-wire technology to move the focusing plane toward infinity when the function ring is rotated to the right, and closer when the function ring is rotated to the left. However, the speed at which focus is adjusted is determined by the amount of function ring rotation. This allows smooth focus shift for movies. Think of it as power "zoom" for focusing.

  - The APS-C/Super 35-Full Frame Select function switches quickly between cropped and full-frame modes, allowing you to make the adjustment using a lens control rather than using the menus or a custom-defined key on the camera body.

Figure 4.25 The Function ring's mode can be selected with these controls.

- **Off.** The function ring does nothing.

Function of Touch Operations

Options: Touch Shutter, Touch Focus, Touch Tracking

Default: Touch Focus

My preference: Touch Tracking

As I noted in Chapter 2, the a7R IV's touch screen can operate in three different modes: Touch Shutter, Touch Focus, and Touch Tracking. You can have only one mode active at a time, but their functions overlap enough that one of the three will likely do the job for you. This entry allows you to activate the mode you prefer. To recap:

- **Touch Shutter.** Tap the screen to specify the focus point. The camera will then immediately take a picture. While Touch Shutter is enabled, you can activate it or deactivate it by tapping the icon at the upper-right corner of the screen. You can tell Touch Shutter is enabled when the orange bar appears to the left of the Touch icon.

  This mode is most useful when you're composing your image using the LCD monitor. Just tap to take a single picture, or keep touching the screen when Drive Mode is set to Continuous Shooting to capture a burst. This mode is unavailable when using the viewfinder, or Movie, S&Q Motion, or Manual Focus modes; when using Digital or Clear Image Zoom; and when Focus Area is set to Digital or Clear Image Zoom.

- **Touch Focus.** Tap the LCD screen and select a focus point or zone anywhere that the a7R IV is able to achieve autofocus (that is, most of the frame other than the edges).

  - **Tap the LCD screen.** The camera will focus at that point. Or slide your finger around the screen to move the focus area around within the frame. You can do this whether composing on the LCD monitor or looking through the viewfinder.

  - **Double tap the LCD screen.** In Manual Focus mode, a double-tap on the LCD activates the focus magnifier.

  In autofocus mode, the a7R IV will focus when you press the shutter release down halfway. You can deactivate touch focus by pressing the center button, or by tapping the "cancel focus" icon (a pointing finger with an X next to it) that appears at upper right on the screen. A quick tap may not register; this function requires a firm press.

  This mode is not available for autofocus activation when Focus Area is set to Flexible Spot or Expand Flexible Spot, but you can still move the focus frame around. In Movie mode, Spot Focus can be used with the LCD only. Touch Focus is not available when using Digital Zoom or with A-mount lenses when using the LA-EA2 or LA-EA4 adapters.

- **Touch tracking.** In this mode, you can specify a subject that will be tracked by tapping the LCD monitor. Tracking will start and continue until you press the center button or tap the Cancel Tracking icon in the upper-right corner of the LCD monitor. The camera will focus on the tracked subject when you press the shutter release down halfway. Note that this feature is not available in Manual Focus modes; with Smart, Clear Image, or Digital zoom features; and when using the LA-EA2 or LA-EA4 lens adapters. It is also disabled in Movie mode when Record Setting is set to 120p/100p.

MOVIE Button

Options: Always, Movie Mode Only
Default: Always
My preference: Always

Movie recording can be started in any operating mode by pressing the Movie record button. This feature is on by default, but if you find that you occasionally press the button inadvertently, you might want to choose the Off option. After you do so, pressing the button will have no effect; when you want to record a movie, you'll need to rotate the mode dial to the Movie position. I prefer Always, because I find that impromptu video-capture situations are more frequent than accidental movie start-ups.

Lock Operation Parts

Options: Off, Multi-Selector Only, Dial+Wheel, All
Default: Off
My preference: Off

If you want to avoid accidentally changing settings by inadvertently using the front/rear dials, multi-selector, or control wheel, you can implement this locking option. Choose Lock and the specified dial or dials are frozen whenever the Fn button is pressed and held down. A "Locked" indicator appears on the screen. If the default Off option is selected, pressing the Fn button has no effect on the controls. You can choose to freeze the multi-selector (only), the front/rear control dials *plus* control wheel, or all four controls.

Audio Signals

Options: On, Off
Default: On
My preference: Off

This is the only entry on the Camera Settings II-11 (Custom Operation 3) menu page. (Not shown in a figure.) This setting enables and disables the beeping/chirping sounds the camera makes when various operations happen, such as achieving autofocus or the self-timer countdown. Most of the time I don't require the feedback and, on the contrary, want to blend in without calling attention to myself, so I disable the noises. The self-timer countdown is especially noticeable, even in environments with a moderate amount of noise. Couple this setting with Silent Shooting and you can often take pictures virtually unnoticed.

Network and Playback Menus

5

Your a7R IV is equipped with a built-in wireless communication system that includes a whole collection of impressive abbreviations, acronyms, and buzzwords—and functions to match! Wi-Fi, NFC, Bluetooth, and FTP have arrived, so you can easily and quickly transfer files from your camera to a smartphone or computer, upload to Facebook, control your camera remotely, and perform other tasks. This chapter provides an introduction to connecting your camera to other devices using the Network menu. Then, we'll move on to the Playback menu to discuss some of the options available when reviewing images.

Using the Network Menu

This section explains the basic functions on the Network menu, in order, although you probably won't be *using* them in this order. For example, you should make Wi-Fi Settings or assign a name to a device in the Network 2 menu *before* you use the functions in the Network 1 menu. (Both menus are shown in Figure 5.1.) I'll summarize all the entries first, and then later cover the major options in logical/functional order rather than the order they appear in the menus. Detailed networking/information technology topics and software operation discussions are beyond the scope of this book, which is primarily a *photography* tome, not a software tutorial, so some sections may provide just an overview. Consult the PlayMemories Home and Imaging Edge/Imaging Edge Mobile help files for detailed descriptions of how to transfer, post process, and organize your stills and videos. Because the Network menu entries are *functions,* the settings all relate to your own camera/device configuration, so I won't provide any **My Preference** notes for them.

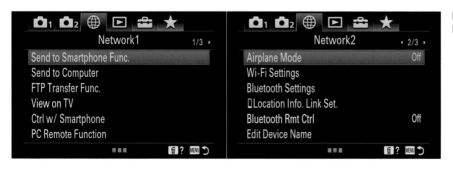

Figure 5.1 The Network 1 and 2 menus.

The Network menu contains the entries shown in Table 5.1.

TABLE 5.1 Network Menu

Send to Smartphone Function	PC Remote Function	Bluetooth Remote Control
Send to Computer	Airplane Mode	Edit Device Name
FTP Transfer Function	Wi-Fi Settings	Import Root Certificate
View on TV	Bluetooth Settings	Security (Ipsec)
Control with Smartphone	Location Info Link Settings	Reset Network Settings

Send to Smartphone Function

Options: Send to Smartphone (Select on This Device, Select on Smartphone); Sending Target (Proxy Only, Original Only, Proxy & Original)

Using the Imaging Edge Mobile app (which replaces the PlayMemories Mobile app you may have used with your previous Sony camera) on your smart device, you can transfer from your memory card still photographs, XAVC S video or their proxies (shot at 60p or lower), proxies of 4K and XAVC S videos shot at 100p or faster, and slow- or quick-motion movies. This entry lets you specify whether the files to be transferred are selected on the camera or on the smart device, and whether you transfer the original file only, or, in the case of videos, a proxy (lower-quality, faster transfer) movie only, or both the original and proxy. (See Chapter 4 for a description of proxy recordings in the Camera Settings II-01 menu.)

The Imaging Edge Mobile app on your device allows you to choose the Image Copy Size for stills, original, 2MB, or VGA, so you can speed up transfer, if necessary, by selecting a smaller file size. RAW files are converted to JPEG before transmission. 4K video, XAVC S movies recorded at 120/100p, and AVCHD movies cannot be transferred at all. Only the proxy movies can be sent. Be aware that your smart device may not be able to play back some files; even if they transfer fine, your phone or tablet may not be able to display them. That's a limitation of the destination device, not your a7R IV. You may need to find a third-party gallery app for your Android or iOS device that can handle a wider variety of files.

Note that when the Fn button's Playback behavior is set to its default value, pressing it while a still image or movie is displayed summons the Send to Smartphone function, bypassing this menu. If you don't transmit to your smart device often, you can safely redefine the Fn button to another behavior for Playback, as this menu entry is always available.

Send to Computer

Options: Select Media: Slot 1, Slot 2

This entry starts the transfer of all the images on your memory card, or a particular folder, to your computer using the PlayMemories Home application *on your computer.* The camera will attempt to use the Wi-Fi connection you've established earlier, or a USB connection if you link the a7R IV to your computer with a USB cable. PlayMemories Home is the Windows/Mac counterpart to the Imaging Edge Mobile (previously PlayMemories Mobile) app on your smart device. Don't confuse the two! Once the USB connection is established, PlayMemories Home will provide instructions on completing the transfer. Proxy movies cannot be transferred using this facility.

Software Shuffle

Sony is constantly updating its free software, which may cause some confusion, especially since it has done a little renaming of some key applications as they are upgraded. For advanced editing functions offered by Imaging Edge and PlayMemories Home, consult the official documentation provided by Sony. As I noted in the introduction, I'm devoting the pages allotted for this book to functions and features of the a7R IV camera and its key accessories, rather than software tutorials and advanced networking procedures.

Here's a quick summary of the available software:

- **Imaging Edge.** This is the suite of three applications that runs on Mac and Windows computers. The trio includes Viewer (for browsing, filtering images by rating, and creating time-lapse movies); Edit (used to crop/straighten images, adjust their brightness and color, and convert RAW files into JPEG or TIFF formats); and Remote (for taking photos with a camera tethered by USB cable to your computer). Note that Remote has an additional function of creating higher resolution images by combining four shots using Pixel Shift Multi shooting, as I write this currently available only on Sony's a7R III and a7R IV full-frame E-mount cameras.

- **PlayMemories Home (Mac and Windows).** This older software (which I think will eventually be folded into the Imaging Edge suite), allows you to manage and perform simple edits on your PC or Mac. Shared features of the versions available when this book was written include:
  - Import images from the camera into your computer.
  - Playback and view images imported into your computer.
  - Organize/search images by camera/lens used, or other attributes.
  - Share images by uploading them to the PlayMemories Online cloud.
  - Edit movies by trimming or merging them.
  - Add effects including background music and subtitles to movies.

- **PlayMemories Home (Windows version only).** Some functions are available only with the Microsoft Windows version of the PlayMemories software:
  - Organize and view images/videos on the computer on a calendar by shooting date.
  - Edit and correct images through trimming and resizing.
  - Create Blu-ray or AVCHD discs for XAVC S-format movies. You must have a Blu-ray/DVD burner to create the discs.
  - Upload images to a network service over an internet connection.

VERSION FLUX

Sony is in the midst of revising its software to account for the latest 64-bit platforms for both Windows and Mac computers, as well as for new features added to its newest cameras. As a result, both the PlayMemories Home and Imaging Edge Windows/Mac OS available after March 2020 may have different functions from those I describe in this book. The latest PlayMemories Home software as I write this is Version 6.0.00 (Windows, 64-bit) and 5.5.01 (Mac OS 10.12-10.14, 32-bit). Note that Sony supports the Macintosh version on Sierra, High Sierra, and Mojave releases only. From macOS Catalina forward, only 64-bit applications can be used. Sony has not announced (yet) whether a new version of PlayMemories Home (for the Mac) will be introduced when the 5.5.01 release is discontinued.

- **Imaging Edge Mobile.** This is a replacement for PlayMemories Mobile on your smart device; indeed, if you already have the previous app on your device, it will be automatically replaced the next time you perform an update. Its functions include Remote Shooting (to preview, change settings, and take photos with your smart device) and Transfer Images/Movies (you can select files to transfer from the smart device or the a7R IV). As noted above, the functions/features of the Imaging Edge Mobile app may change by the time this book is published. In addition, the app has had problems in some areas with iOS 13.0 (and later versions).

FTP Transfer Function

Options: FTP Transfer, Display FTP Result, Select FTP Server, Define FTP Server 1–3

IT techies who understand FTP server functions can transfer images from the camera to a networked FTP (File Transfer Protocol) server, view the results, select which server to send to, and define up to three different FTP servers. Only JPEG and RAW files can be transferred using FTP. Sony offers a detailed 57-page FTP Help Guide (much too long to summarize here!) through its website: https://helpguide.sony.net/di/ftp/v1/en/index.html.

View on TV

Options: Connect to TV; Slideshow settings.

You don't need to hardwire your network-enabled smart TV to the a7R IV to transfer still images. This entry allows you to set up displays and slide shows wirelessly, selecting images, the display interval, playback size, and any special effects. Movies cannot be transferred using this facility. Operations controlled from the TV vary by model, so you'll need to consult your DLNA-compatible smart TV's manual to make the best use of this feature.

The HDTV and camera must be logged into the same Wi-Fi access point. Then, press the Play button on the camera, followed by the MENU button. Navigate to this menu entry, and press the Center button. The camera will search for the Wi-Fi connection to your HDTV, connect, and then commence playback. You can then press the left/right directional buttons to move from one image to another, and the down button to switch playback devices or adjust slideshow options.

Control with Smartphone

Options: Control with Smartphone (On, Off); Display QR Code; Always Connected (On, Off)

You can control your camera using your smart device and a Wi-Fi connection. This entry turns the feature on or off, displays a QR code to quickly link the camera and device, and specifies whether, once activated, the camera remains connected to the smartphone at all times (draining your battery significantly), or maintains the link only when you connect manually.

PC Remote Function

Options: PC Remote: (On, Off); PC Remote Connect Method: (USB, Wi-Fi Direct, Wi-Fi Access Point); Pairing

This entry allows you to take control of your camera from a computer connected either using Wi-Fi or a USB link. It includes three menu pages with seven sub-entries. I'll explain how to use this feature's options in more detail later in this chapter.

Airplane Mode

Options: On, Off

Enables/disables wireless functions. Use this to save power, or when required (as when boarding an airplane). Note that NFC, if active, uses negligible power and that Wi-Fi connections consume power only while the camera is connected to a network, so that ordinarily you do not need to use Airplane Mode.

Wi-Fi Settings

Options: WPS Push, Access Point Settings, Frequency Band, Display Wi-Fi Information, SSID/PW Reset

This entry includes features for connecting the a7R IV to a Wi-Fi access point, either semi-automatically using WPS Push, or by manually registering by entering the SSID name of the access point and entering security information. You can choose whether to use your Wi-Fi network's standard 2.4GHz band, or the faster 5GHz band (if available from your router). You can also view the device's detailed information, including IP address, DNS server, and MAC Address.

SSID/PW Reset deletes the current SSID and password. You might want to do this for security reasons (say, you load/give/sell your a7R IV to someone else) or need to start over in registering your camera with a network. Reset Network Settings removes all network settings from the camera.

Bluetooth Settings

Options: Bluetooth Function (On, Off); Pairing; Display Device Address

Your a7R IV can access the GPS information available from your smartphone and embed that data in your image files using low-energy Bluetooth connectivity. Use this, and you no longer have to wonder where you took a photo; the GPS data can be displayed by many applications, including Lightroom's Map tab. This entry allows you to turn off Bluetooth sharing, pairing your phone with your camera, and displaying the device's address. Keep in mind that when you initialize your camera, as described in Chapter 6, pairing settings are canceled as well.

Location Information Link Setting

Options: Location Info Link, Auto Time Correction, Auto Area Adjustment

This entry allows the a7R IV to access the location information from your smartphone, after you've enabled Bluetooth connectivity in the previous entry. One of the cool features is to use the Auto Time Correction option to allow your smartphone's (very) accurate time information to be used to set the time and date used by your camera. It's the "let's synchronize our watches" version for the 21st century. You can also activate Auto Area Adjustment, so the camera "knows" where it is and uses the correct time zone. Turn this on if you want to embed in your image files the local time when you took a picture; turn if off if you'd prefer the time reflect your "back home" norm.

Bluetooth Remote Control

Options: On/Off

The Sony RMT-P1BT remote control operates by Bluetooth LE (low-energy) radio signals, and became compatible with the a7R IV beginning with the June 2019 Version 2.0 firmware upgrade. This remote, at a little less than $80, is not as inexpensive as infrared remote controls, drains much less juice from your camera, has a range of about 16 feet, and isn't dazzled by bright sunlight (which can give IR remotes fits). It can start/stop movie recording, too.

Edit Device Name

Options: Change Device Name

By default, the label applied to your camera is ILCE-RM4. You can change it to something else, if, say, you own three or four a7R IV's and want to differentiate between them—or simply want to personalize your camera's "name."

Import Root Certificate

Options: Import certificate from Slot 1 or Slot 2

This is the first entry on the third page of the Network menu (see Figure 5.2). Encrypted communications with an FTP server may require verification using a root certificate. This entry allows you to import that certificate, which you have stored on Slot 1 or Slot 2. You'll find detailed instructions on using this FTP function in the Sony FTP Help Guide, described earlier.

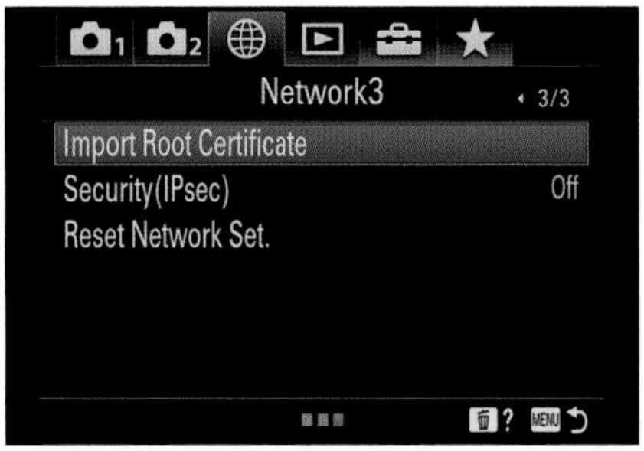

Figure 5.2 The Network 3 menu.

Security (Ipsec)

Options: On, Off; Destination IP Address, Shared Key

This entry allows you to encrypt the data when your a7R IV and computer are linked through a Wi-Fi connection. Most a7R IV owners will have no need for this extra layer of security. Are you really concerned about someone stealing your information when you transfer your photos to your laptop while relaxing at Starbucks? If that's the case, you need to implement even more layers of security, because if a hacker tries to access your computer, safeguarding the photos therein are the least of your worries.

Reset Network Settings

Changes all network settings to their factory defaults and reboots your a7R IV. It is not available when PC Remote is On.

Remotely Controlling Your Camera

If you're using a computer to connect to your camera, the PC Remote function in the Network 1 menu is the easiest, fastest way to shoot tethered. You can also shoot remotely using the Imaging Edge Mobile software, which you can download from your country's Sony website. For casual remote-control shooting, whether you want to exercise some creative options (to get unusual viewpoints), you are stalking wildlife, or are a double-naught spy, your smartphone and camera will do the job.

Once you've connected your camera to the smartphone, there are a limited number of settings you can make from the smartphone, but you can always use the controls *on the camera itself* to make additional adjustments. You can change White Balance, switch from single to continuous shooting, select an f/stop or shutter speed if using Aperture Priority or Shutter Priority (respectively), or select both f/stop and shutter speed when using Manual exposure. Tap the "shutter button" icon at bottom of the app screen and take a picture. If you have specified Always Connected under the Control with Smartphone entry in the Network 1 menu, you'll always be ready to go when the camera and smartphone are in proximity.

Using PC Remote

As I noted, your second option for controlling your camera remotely is using the PC Remote function found in the Network 1 menu. While it seems complex—chiefly because it has its own three pages of submenu screens—it's actually quite easy to use. That's especially true if you are able to use a USB connection rather than Wi-Fi link, which I recommend. The USB connection is much easier to set up and is typically faster, although it requires using a computer instead of your smart device. This section will show you everything you need to know to begin shooting your camera by remote control using the PC Remote entry. Just follow these steps:

1. **Access PC Remote.** In the Network 1 menu, select the PC Remote entry and press the center button. The first of three screens will appear, shown in Figure 5.3.

2. **Activate PC Remote.** Access the PC Remote sub-entry and select On. You'll be returned automatically to the original screen.

3. **Specify connection.** Access the PC Remote Connection Method entry and choose USB (my recommendation), Wi-Fi Direct, or Wi-Fi Access Point from the screen that appears. (See Figure 5.4.)

   - **USB.** Connect your computer to the a7R IV with a USB cable.

   - **Wi-Fi Direct.** This method will let you connect your computer directly to the a7R IV's built-in access point. The first time you use this connection, you'll be directed to view the connection information you'll need to link up. The Wi-Fi Direct Information entry at the top of the PC Remote Function's second menu page will provide you with a screen like the one shown in Figure 5.5. You'll then use your operating system (Mac or Windows) Wi-Fi connection dialog boxes to make the connection using that information.

   - **Wi-Fi Access Point.** Select this option and you can specify a Wi-Fi Access point on your computer's network that your camera and computer can share.

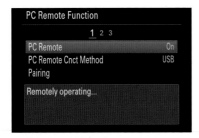

Figure 5.3 PC Remote Function menu.

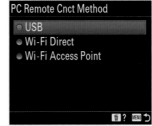

Figure 5.4 Select connection method.

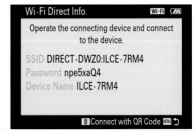

Figure 5.5 Use the direct connection information to link your computer to the camera's Wi-Fi access point.

4. **Choose Still Image Save Destination.** This option is on the second PC Remote Function page (see Figure 5.6). Select PC only, PC+Camera, or Camera only. Opt for PC only if you will be doing a lot of shooting and don't want to let your memory card fill up. Choose PC+Camera to automatically back up your shots to two locations. With Camera only, no images are saved on your computer.

5. **Set RAW+J PC Save Image options.** This is available only if you've selected PC+Camera as your still image destination, and RAW & JPEG as your File Format. You can save both RAW & JPEG to the computer, JPEG only (for faster transfer; especially important if you are using Wi-Fi rather than a faster USB connection), or RAW only.

6. **PC Save Image Size.** Choose to store images on the computer in their original size, or in a smaller 2MP size that's quicker to transfer. (See Figure 5.7.)

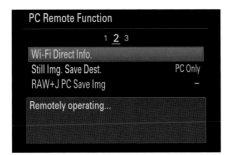

Figure 5.6 The second page of the PC Remote Function menu.

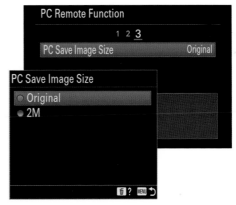

Figure 5.7 Choose original or compact 2MP image size for transfer.

Once you've set up your connection, launch the Imaging Edge Remote application. Double-click on the connection you want to see (see Figure 5.8, upper left) and the Remote application will appear. A live image as seen through the a7R IV's lens appears and a panel with all the settings you can make is shown at far right in the figure.

You can control most shooting aspects, including shooting mode, shutter speed, aperture, ISO settings, and exposure compensation, along with file format, aspect ratio, white balance, focus settings, and more. A live histogram is shown, and you can specify the folder where your files are stored on your computer.

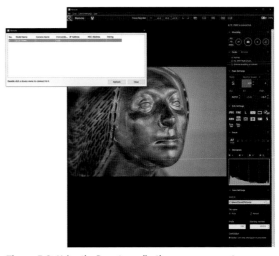

Figure 5.8 Using the Remote application on your computer.

Making a Wireless Connection

For this section, I'm basing my descriptions in this chapter on the assumption that you are *not* an IT specialist, and don't need (or want) to compare the advantages of WEP versus WPA security, would rather not set IP addresses yourself, and don't care much about root certificates. Alternatively, I will assume that if you *are* an IT specialist and find these topics compelling, you already know most of what you need and would rather not hear it from me, again. As Thoreau once said, "Simplify, simplify!" (but without explaining the redundant "Simplify.")

If you want to connect using your smartphone or tablet, the first thing you should do is venture over to your smart device's app store and download the Imaging Edge Mobile app, which I described earlier in this chapter. (If you already have the older PlayMemories Mobile app, it will be upgraded to the newer version during your next update.) Then follow the instructions that follow for connecting through NFC or Wi-Fi. The a7R IV has an additional option for linking your smartphone to the camera through Bluetooth so GPS information can be embedded in your photographs.

Camera/Device: NFC Connection

If you have an Android device, connecting with NFC is your simplest option. NFC stands for *Near Field Communication*, a wireless access method found in Android-based smartphones and tablets. It's not available with iOS devices, although Apple Pay uses it to send your money hither and yon. Once you've installed the Imaging Edge Mobile app on your device, linking the a7R IV and the device is as simple as tapping the area on your phone containing its transceiver with the camera's transceiver (located under the "N" mark on the right side). Just follow these steps:

1. Turn on NFC on your smart device. Cancel any sleep or lock-screen functions so the device will not disconnect before you are finished shooting.

2. Access the Control w/Smartphone entry in the camera's Network 1 menu and make sure the feature is On.

3. Power up the a7R IV. The NFC "N" mark will display on the camera's screen, indicating that NFC is available.

4. Tap the matching NFC mark on the camera with your device for several seconds. If either the camera or phone are in a third-party case, you may need to remove the case to make the connection.

5. Once connected, the Imaging Edge Mobile application on the phone should launch automatically.

6. You can now preview the a7R IV's image on your smartphone, take pictures using it as a remote control, and transfer your shots from the camera to your device.

7. To transfer images, choose Send to Smartphone Functions from the Network 1 menu, select Send to Smartphone, and select images. Use NFC to connect the camera to the phone if not already linked.

Camera/Device: Wi-Fi Connection

Wi-Fi connections are slightly more complicated and can be used both for Android and iOS smartphones. Just follow these steps:

1. Make sure Ctrl w/Smartphone is set to On in the Network 1 menu.

2. Choose Connection in the same menu. The a7R IV will display a QR code on the LCD monitor.

3. Launch Imaging Edge Mobile. You'll see a screen like the one at left in Figure 5.9. Tap Scan QR Code of the camera.

4. A screen appears (see Figure 5.9, center). Choose whether to scan the Wi-Fi QR Code, or the NFC code of the camera. You can dismiss this screen from appearing again by choosing Don't Show This Again from the screen that pops up next.

5. A capture window will appear on the smartphone. Center it over the code on the LCD monitor of the a7R IV to allow the smartphone to capture the code. (See Figure 5.9, right.)

6. If your phone requires installing a profile, follow the remaining instructions to add it. You may have to enter your device's passcode and confirm installation. **Note:** if you have problems making a Wi-Fi connection (especially with iOS 13 and later), try resetting your device's Network Connections and in its General settings delete any Profile that may have been set up for your camera.

7. When installation is complete, you will be instructed to select the a7R IV's "hot spot" as your Wi-Fi connection, and then restart Imaging Edge Mobile.

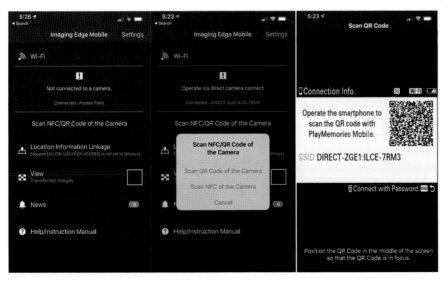

Figure 5.9 Connecting using Imaging Edge Mobile.

Using WPS Push

Wi-Fi Protected Setup (WPS) works only when you're in range of a network provided by a wireless router that is equipped with a WPS button. Not all are. Examine your router and look for a button labeled WPS, or with a 🔗 symbol. Or, find the owner's manual for your router or use a Google search (try "*routername* manual PDF") to locate the WPS button, if one is available. Some routers that support WPS provide it with software instead of a physical button; in that case, you'll need to access the router's control panel using a computer and then click the button on the WPS page. The WPS Push tactic is great, but it would not work at a Wi-Fi hotspot in a supermarket, for instance, since the network owner is unlikely to use the WPS feature for hundreds of customers.

WHAT'S WPS?

The abbreviation WPS indicates Wi-Fi Protected Setup. This is a security standard that makes it easier and quicker to connect a device, including your a7R IV, to a wireless home network. It eliminates the need to key in the password. Because it's possible for an aggressive hacker to recover the WPS PIN number, some experts suggest turning the router's WPS feature off when you're not actually using it; this may not be possible with all router models but check the owner's manual for the one you own.

Just follow these steps:

1. **Access Network 1 menu and choose Wi-Fi Settings.** If your router provides WPS, scroll to the WPS Push item in the camera's Wi-Fi settings menu and press the center button.

2. **Press the router's WPS button.** A screen will appear advising you to press the router's WPS button within 2 minutes. When you press the button (or use the software to do so), the camera should be able to establish connectivity.

3. **Confirm registration.** Once the connection is established, a screen reporting "Registered. SSID *network name*" appears. Press the center button to confirm.

Registering Manually

You can also select an access point manually when within range of a wireless network; you'll need to know the network password, if one is in place, to do so. Just follow these steps:

1. **Access the Network 2's Wi-Fi entry and scroll to Access Point Set.** Press the center button. A Wi-Fi Standby screen will appear confirming that the camera is searching for available access points.

2. **Wait for the camera to find your network.** The a7R IV will find the nearby access points (networks) in less than a minute. (See Figure 5.10.) If there is more than one network or available access point, all of those found will be shown. If your smartphone has a hotspot feature and it's turned on, that "network" may appear as well.

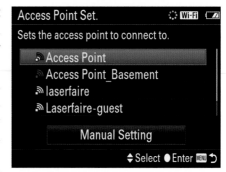

Figure 5.10 Access Point Settings can be used to select an access point/hotspot. The camera displays the available networks that are within range.

When several networks are displayed, some may belong to nearby businesses or your neighbors, and you can ignore them (their signal strength is probably weaker than your own network in any case, even if your neighbor's network is not protected by a password). In my case, my wireless router resides in my office; in other, more distant rooms is a wired access point, and, on the second floor, a wireless repeater. Scroll to the one you intend to use and press the center button to confirm.

3. **Input the password (if necessary).** The next screen that appears may have a field for entering your network password, if your router/access point is set up to require one. If not, proceed to Step 4. Otherwise, press the center button and a virtual keyboard will appear. Using this keyboard, enter the password for your network. The keyboard works a bit like the physical multi-tap keyboard found on some (older) cell phones. Use the directional buttons to highlight a letter group, such as abc, def, ghi, and press the center button once to enter the first character in the group, twice for the second character, three times for the third character, and four times for the fourth. Some of the virtual keys allow you to backspace, delete characters, and toggle between uppercase and lowercase. When finished, highlight OK and press the center button.

4. **IP Address Setting.** The next screen will appear, showing the IP Address Setting as Auto and Priority Connection as Off. These defaults should work perfectly. Select OK and press the center button. A screen will appear showing the camera trying to connect to the network.

   If the Auto IP Address Setting option does not work, and you have some networking expertise, change from Auto to Manual, and a screen appears that allows you to enter the IP address, Subnet Mark, and Default Gateway. You can safely leave the Priority Connection parameter set to Off. Fortunately, you probably won't have to resort to these additional steps.

5. **Confirm connectivity.** After the Wi-Fi connectivity has been made, a screen will appear confirming that your network has been registered. The screen will look like the one in Figure 5.10, but an orange dot will appear next to the connected network. If you get a screen with a note stating *cannot authenticate*, or that the *input value is invalid*, you'll need to start again at step 1; make sure you have the correct password for the network and be extra careful when keying it in. Remember that when a capital letter is required, you must use the shift feature (an arrow pointing upward) on the virtual keyboard.

6. **Try it again later.** After you have established Wi-Fi connectivity, you can revert to using the a7R IV as usual; a touch of the shutter release button returns it to shooting mode. The camera will retain the connection to the network until you turn it off or it goes into power-saving sleep mode; Wi-Fi is then temporarily disconnected. When you're ready to use Wi-Fi again, activate the a7R IV while in range of the same network, scroll to Access Point Settings in the Wireless menu, and press the center button. The camera will quickly find your network to re-establish Wi-Fi connectivity.

If you're connecting to a public Wi-Fi hotspot, the steps should be the same, but you'll most likely find a screen that requires you to agree to the hotspot's terms and conditions. Some hotspots may not require you to enter a password.

Selecting an Access Point Manually

If the desired access point (network) is not displayed on the screen as described in Step 2 above, you may need to enter it yourself. Just follow these steps:

1. **Choose Manual Setting.** Scroll down to Manual Setting and press the center button. The screen shown in Figure 5.11 appears.

2. **Select Manual Registration.** Press the center button to begin the manual registration process. The screen shown in Figure 5.12 appears.

3. **Enter SSID.** On the Manual Registration screen, there's a field for entering the SSID name of the access point (network) you plan to use. Press the center button when this field is visible, and the virtual keyboard appears. Enter the data. When you're finished press the center button.

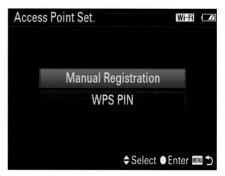

Figure 5.11 Manual registration requires you to complete extra steps.

4. **Change Security (if necessary).** Again, if you have some networking expertise, you'll know if the security setting on your router is WPA (Wi-Fi Protected Access, the default), WEP (Wired Equivalent Privacy, an older, easily "hacked" protection scheme), or None (effectively, no security). If you want to change the Security setting, highlight that field and press the center button. Select your choice and press the MENU button to return.

5. **Enter password.** The next screen will ask for your password, which you can enter using the virtual keyboard.

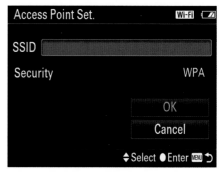

Figure 5.12 Enter the SSID (network/access point name).

6. **Enter WPS PIN (if necessary).** If your WPS connection requires a PIN, you can enter it.

Take care not to lose the network connection by inadvertently using the Initialize or the Reset Network Settings item of the Wireless menu. If you do so, the camera will eliminate all your network settings and you'll need to repeat the steps in this section.

Connecting with Bluetooth

The good news is that Sony has finally brought simple Bluetooth LE connections to its camera line, allowing you to share GPS data from your phone with the a7R IV. You can use devices with Android 5.0 versions or later compatible with Bluetooth 4.0 and later; and Apple devices including iPhone 4s (and later) or iPad (3rd generation and later). The camera will embed the data in the EXIF image information, making it available for mapping and other applications that can access it.

I love Bluetooth—my smartphone is linked to my vehicle's hands-free calling feature, the soundbar on my smart TV, and the remote control I use to snap photos with my iPhone's camera. My Fitbit tells my health app how well I slept the night before using a Bluetooth connection, and my wireless headphones allow me to listen to music or take calls without removing the phone from my pocket. When I play "music," (I've been told it's debateable) my bass guitar "talks" to my amp from 16 feet away, with no cable required.

The bad news—and it isn't really bad—is that you need to temporarily forget your traditional way of connecting to a new Bluetooth device. Do not try to pair your a7R IV with your smart device using your smart device's Settings screen. If you accidentally do so, you'll need to use your phone's Bluetooth Forget Device command and start over. Your a7R IV connects to your phone or tablet using the Imaging Edge Mobile app and can't link up any other way. Make sure your Bluetooth Remote Control setting, described earlier, is set to Off. While your camera can be paired with as many as 15 different devices, it can share location information with only one smartphone and can't connect to two devices simultaneously. Then, just follow these steps (and remember that when you use the Setup menu's Initialize command, your Bluetooth connects are removed, too):

1. Select Bluetooth Settings from the Network 2 menu. The screen shown at left in Figure 5.13 appears.

2. Highlight Pairing and press the center button. The screen shown at right in Figure 5.13 pops up.

3. Launch the Imaging Edge App. Choose Location Image Linkage to produce the screen shown at left in Figure 5.14.

4. Select OK and the screen shown at right in Figure 5.14 appears. It displays any cameras you've already linked (in my case a Sony a6400 that I purchased early in 2019), and currently non-paired cameras, including my a7R IV. Highlight the a7R IV's label (it appears as ILCE-7RM4) and choose OK to begin pairing.

5. Imaging Edge and your camera will link up.

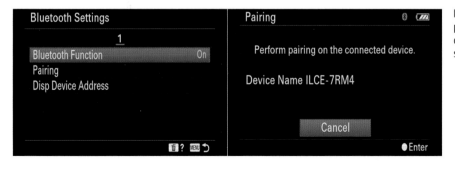

Figure 5.13 Select pairing (left) and the camera will display the screen shown at right.

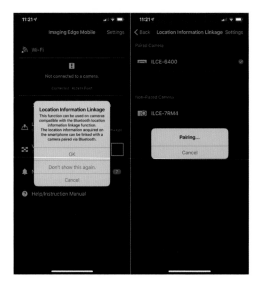

Figure 5.14 Choose Location Information Linkage (left) then choose the a7R IV camera to begin pairing (right).

6. The matching Location Information Linkage menu entry in the camera's menu system, which I described earlier in this chapter, allows your a7R IV to automatically set itself to the correct time, and determine your current geographical area. You'll never have to adjust your Date/Time and Area Setting entries in the Setup 4 menu as long as you keep your phone linked to the camera.

7. If you encounter difficulties, make sure your phone/tablet's Bluetooth is enabled, Airplane Mode on the camera is Off, and the camera is not connected to other devices. Choose Reset Network Settings in the Network 3 menu and try pairing again.

Viewing Images on a TV

As with any current digital camera, it's possible to view JPEG photos and video clips on an HDTV when you connect the a7R IV to the TV using an HDMI cable. This is an extra-cost accessory. Buy the Type-D cable with a micro HDMI connector at one end (for plugging into the camera) and a conventional HDMI plug (to connect to the TV's HDMI port) at the other. An inexpensive cable is fine; there's no need to pay more for one of the premium brands unless you need a cable that's longer than about 6 feet. Make the cable connection and you can now display photos and movies on the oversized screen.

After the Wi-Fi connection has been made with a Digital Living Network Alliance/DLNA-compatible (network-enabled or Wi-Fi Direct–enabled) HDTV, you can use this menu item, on the second screen of Wireless options. Use it to display photos on the HDTV without cable connection after Wi-Fi connectivity has been confirmed. The benefit of Wi-Fi Direct is that you do not need to register your access point on the camera before doing so; in other words, the TV need not be connected to the network if you are using Wi-Fi Direct. Movie clips cannot be transferred to a TV for display over Wi-Fi; to show those, connect the camera to the HDTV using an optional Type-D HDMI cable.

Use the menu options to instruct the camera as to which device (TV) it should send to, which photos to display (all or only those in a specific folder), and whether the display time should be long or short if using the slide show feature. Press the center button if you do want to use the slide show feature. At any time, you can move to another image for the display by scrolling to the left or right.

It's also possible to transfer JPEG photos, but not videos, to an HDTV without cable connection. If you have a networked TV (or a network-friendly game machine such as PlayStation or Xbox), you can view the images in your camera on that display without using the HDMI cable.

Of course, the HDTV must be DLNA (Digital Living Network Alliance) compliant and it must first be connected to your home network via Wi-Fi as per the instructions that came with the device. The a7R IV must also be communicating with your network via Wi-Fi, of course. (Use the steps provided earlier.)

 TIP There is an exception to the DLNA rule. Some HDTVs are Wi-Fi Direct enabled; if yours is, then it need not be connected to your network.

There are simply too many types of Wi-Fi-enabled HDTVs to provide full specifics on exactly how you'll transfer JPEGs to the device. Sony's published documents specifically recommend their Bravia HDTV, as you might expect, but you can use any DLNA- (or Wi-Fi Direct–) enabled TV. A Bravia HDTV does provide a few extra display features that are possible only when using a Sony camera.

In any event, start by accessing the View on TV item in the camera's Network 1 menu and press the center button. The camera will confirm the Wi-Fi connection to your network and it will search for a compatible TV. Be sure to consult your TV's instructions for setting the media display component to receive information from the camera. When connectivity with the TV has been confirmed, you can begin the sharing process using connection controls like those described earlier in this chapter.

Sending Files to a Smart Device

To transfer files from your camera to a smartphone or tablet, the device must be running the free Imaging Edge Mobile app for Android or iOS; you can get it from your usual app store. After you have downloaded the app (for iOS or Android) and are running it in your smart device, you can send one or more images to the smart device. (The app, and hence the camera's Wi-Fi features like this one, are not available in a few countries where many aspects of Internet use are restricted.) This feature does not work for video clips.

1. **Turn on the camera and the smart devices.** Launch the Imaging Edge app and ensure that both the a7R IV and the smart device have been connected, as described earlier.

2. **Access an image you want to transfer.** Press Playback and navigate to a file you want to transfer. Press the Send to Smartphone (Fn) button. If your camera and device are not connected, the camera will offer to make the connection and display a QR code that can be scanned using the Imaging Edge Mobile app on your device.

3. **Choose image(s) to transfer.** A screen like the one in Figure 5.15 appears asking whether you want to transfer the currently displayed image, all still photos with this date, or multiple images. When you press the center button after choosing This Image or All With This Date, the camera will connect to your device and begin executing the transfer.

Note: All With This Date will be offered even if you have changed View Mode to Folder View or one of the movie modes in the Playback 3 menu (described later in this chapter). If you want to send images spanning more than one date, select Multiple Images. You can

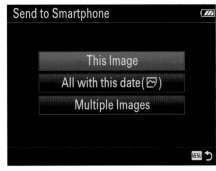

Figure 5.15 Choose which images to transfer.

then review any image on your memory card and mark it by pressing the center button. When finished selecting multiple images, press MENU to execute.

4. **View images.** After the smart device has completed importing files from the a7R IV, you can view the thumbnails on its screen. Naturally, you can enlarge any photo so it fills the device's screen.

5. **Use the smart device to share photos, etc.** You can now use any of the smart device's capabilities: modify any of the images, send it to friends via e-mail, upload it to any website, and so on.

Note that you can also send photos from your camera to your smart device using the Send to Smartphone Functions entry of the Network 1 menu. (See Figure 5.16, left.) That method has additional options.

- **Selection platform.** You can choose whether to select the photos you want to send from your smart device, or from your camera. If you elect to choose them from the smart device, the a7R IV will download thumbnails for you to preview while making your selection.

- **Movies or proxies.** You can also choose whether to transfer movies by sending only the original video clip, its proxy (if you opted to record one), or both proxy and original. (See Figure 5.16, right.)

- **Connect during Power Off.** If you activate this feature, transfer will continue even if you have flipped the a7R IV's power switch to the off position. Transferring many files can take a long time, and you may want to avail yourself of this option, but keep in mind that this mode will consume a lot of power while your camera is otherwise "inactive."

Figure 5.16 Select additional parameters.

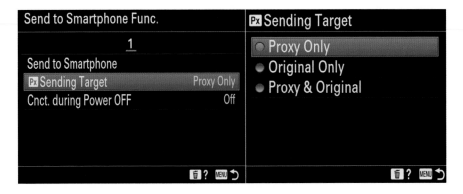

Specialized Capabilities

Sony is erecting a big tent for users of its most advanced cameras, such as the a7R IV and a9 II. Some of these are most useful only to a smaller number of users who are themselves more technically oriented. So, as I've noted earlier, the available space in this book is devoted to photography and photographic techniques. Photo editing and organizing software, including Photoshop, Lightroom, and Imaging Edge are covered only to the extent required. Some other features, including those leveraging computer technology, are beyond the scope of this book.

For example, transfer to a remote FTP server is an extremely useful feature for the more technically oriented types among us, especially for photojournalists who want to upload still images to their organizations for immediate editing and distribution. Considerable knowledge of the technology is required, and beyond the scope of this book, but Sony offers an additional FTP Help Guide described earlier in this chapter.

If you are a sports photographer or photojournalist, you also might have need of Sony's Transfer and Tagging Add-On, an application for smartphones and tablets that works in conjunction with Imaging Edge Mobile and imagingedge.sony.net. It can transfer JPEG images from the camera to a smart device as you shoot, and thence to an FTP server, along with captioning information (IPTC metadata) that can be input through voice memos that are automatically converted to text. It enables resizing, compressing, and cropping images en route to the FTP server, and includes a Caption Glossary to correct pre-registered words. Not all mobile devices are compatible, and some functions require a special USB cable. This, too, is a complex function that's beyond the scope of this book.

Playback Menu

This menu controls functions for deleting, protecting, displaying, and printing images. **Tip:** While you can access the Playback menu at any time using the Menu system, you can bring it up on your screen more quickly just by pressing the Playback button first, then the MENU button, which causes the *most recent* Playback menu page you've accessed to appear. The entries available in the three Playback menus are shown in Table 5.2.

TABLE 5.2 Playback Menu

Protect	Photo Capture	Select Playback Media
Rotate	Enlarge Image	View Mode
Delete	Enlarge Initial Magnification	Image Index
Rating	Enlarge Initial Position	Display as Group
Rating Set (Custom Key)	Continuous Playback for Interval	Display Rotation
Specify Printing	Playback Speed for Interval	Image Jump Setting
Copy	Slide Show	

Protect

Options: Multiple Images, All with Current View Mode, Cancel All Images

This is the first entry in the Playback menu. (See Figure 5.17.) You might want to protect certain images or movie clips on your memory card from accidental erasure, either by you or by others who may use your camera from time to time. This menu item enables you to tag one or more images or movies for protection, so a delete command will not delete it. (Formatting a memory card deletes everything, including protected content.) This menu item also enables you to cancel the protection from all tagged photos or movies. If all you want to do is protect/unprotect the image currently on the screen, just press C3 during playback, a white key ("locked") icon will appear overlaid on the image.

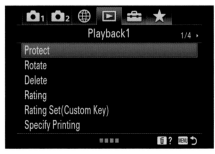

Figure 5.17 Playback 1 menu.

To use this feature, make sure to specify whether you want to do so for stills or movies; use the View Mode item in the Playback 3 menu (described later) to designate the desired view mode. There, you can select from Date View, Folder View (Still), AVCHD View, XAVC S HD View, or XAVC S 4K View to see only items matching that parameter.

Then, access the Protect menu item, choose Multiple Images, and press the center button. An image (or thumbnail of a movie) will appear; scroll among the photos or videos using the control wheel to reach the photo you want to tag for protection; press the center button to tag it with an orange check mark at the left of the image. (If it's already tagged, pressing the button will remove the tag, eliminating the protection you had previously provided.)

After you have marked all the items you want to protect, press the MENU button to confirm your choice. A screen will appear asking you to confirm that you want to protect the marked images; press the center button to do so. Later, if you want, you can go back and select the Cancel All Images option to unprotect all the tagged photos or movies.

Rotate

Options: None

When you select this menu item, you are immediately presented with a new screen showing the current or most recently reviewed image along with an indication that the center button can be used to rotate the image. (This feature does not work with movies.) Scroll left/right to reach the image you want to rotate. Successive presses of the center button will now rotate the image 90 degrees at a time. The camera will remember whatever rotation setting you apply here. You can use this function to rotate an image that was taken with the camera held vertically, when you have set Display Rotation to Manual. Press the MENU button to exit.

Delete

Options: Multiple Img., All with Current View Mode

Sometimes we take pictures or video clips that we know should never see the light of day. Maybe you were looking into the lens and accidentally tripped the shutter. Perhaps you really goofed up your settings. You want to erase that photo *now,* before it does permanent damage to your reputation as a good photographer. Unless you have turned Auto Review off in the Camera Settings II-08 (Display/Auto Review 2) menu, you can delete a photo immediately after you take it by pressing the Trash key (Delete button). Also, you can use that method to delete any individual image that's being displayed on the screen in Playback mode.

However, sometimes you need to wait for an idle moment to erase all pictures that are obviously not "keepers." I sometimes do this during halftime when shooting sports, to eliminate a series of continuous shots I know were a waste of storage space. This menu item makes it easy to remove selected photos or video clips (Multiple Images), or to erase all the photos or video clips taken, sorted by your currently active view mode (such as folder or date). (Change the type of view using the View Mode option, described later.) Note that there is no delete method that will remove images tagged as Protected.

To remove one or more images (or movie files), select the Delete menu item, and use the up/down directional buttons, front dial, rear dial, or the control wheel to choose the Multiple Images option. Press the center button, and the most recent image *using your currently active view* (Date View, Folder View [Still], Folder View [MP4], or AVCHD View) will be displayed on the LCD.

Scroll left/right through your images and press the center button when you reach the image you want to tag for deletion; a check mark then appears beside it and an orange check mark appears in the left of the screen. You can press the DISP button to see more information about a particular image. You can also press the AEL/Thumbnail button to view thumbnails of multiple images and select them in that mode.

The number of images marked for deletion is incremented in the indicator at the lower-right corner of the LCD, next to a trash can icon. When you're satisfied (or have expressed your dissatisfaction with the really bad images), press the MENU button, and you will be asked if you're sure you want to proceed. To confirm your decision, press the center button. The images (or video clips) you had tagged will now be deleted. If you want to delete *everything* on the memory card, it's quicker to do so by using the Format item in the Setup menu.

Rating

Options: One to five stars, Off

This setting lets you apply a quality rating to still images (but not movies) you've shot. You can also use the rating system to represent some other criteria. Simply select this menu item (or define a custom key as a dedicated Rating button, as described next). You can use this entry to give images one, two, three, four, or five stars, or turn the rating off. The Image Jump function (described later in this chapter) can display only images that have been given a specific rating, or any rating at all.

Suppose you were photographing a track meet with multiple events. You could apply a one-star rating to jumping events, two stars to relays, three stars to throwing events, four stars to hurdles, and five stars to dashes. Then, using the Image Jump feature, you could review only images of one type. I personally find this type of use more helpful than simply critiquing my own work.

With a little imagination, you can apply the rating system to all sorts of categories. At a wedding, you could classify pictures of the bride, the groom, guests, attendants, and parents of the couple. If you were shooting school portraits, one rating could apply to first grade, another to second grade, and so on. Given a little thought, this feature has many more applications than you might think. Ratings can be used to specify images for a slide show, too, or to select images in Digital Photo Professional.

To use the Ratings menu entry, follow these steps:

1. Choose the Rating menu item.
2. The most recently viewed image appears.
3. Press the center button, and an icon appears, flanked by left/right triangles. (See Figure 5.18, left.)
4. Use the left/right controls to scroll among Off, and the individual star settings available. (You can specify which ratings can be applied, as I'll describe shortly.)
5. Press MENU to confirm and exit.
6. The star rating (if any) that you've applied will henceforth be overlaid on the image each time you review it.

Figure 5.18   You can apply one to five stars or turn ratings off (left). If you rarely use a particular star value, you can deactivate it when using a Custom Key.

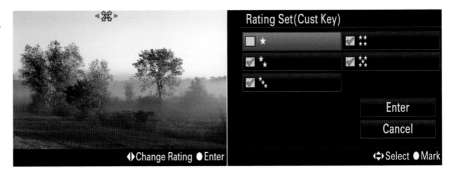

Rating Set (Custom Key)

Options: Activate any (or all) star ratings

This is a clever option that allows you to specify *which* star ratings can be applied when rating images using a defined Custom Key for the Rating function. For example, if you're rating by quality and don't deign to mark your really bad images, you can disable the * or ** star values. Thereafter, you'll only need to consider ***, ****, or ***** ratings.

For this to work, you must apply the Rating behavior to a custom key of your choice, as I described in Chapter 4. After that, you can visit this menu entry, shown in Figure 5.18, right, and highlight individual star values. Press the center button to mark/unmark them, then highlight Enter and press the center button again to confirm and exit. When rating an image using the Custom Key, just press the key multiple times. The ratings change to the next available value each time you press the key. (This should be your default way of applying ratings!)

Specify Printing

Options: Multiple Images, Cancel All, Print Setting

Most digital cameras are compatible with the DPOF (Digital Print Order Format) protocol, which enables you to tag JPEG images on the memory card (but not RAW files or movies) for printing with a DPOF-compliant printer; you can also specify whether you want the date imprinted as well. Afterward, you can transport your memory card to a retailer's digital photo lab or do-it-yourself kiosk or use your own DPOF-compatible printer to print out the tagged images in the quantities you've specified.

Choose multiple images using the View Mode filters described earlier to select to view either by Date or by Folder. Press the center button to mark an image for printing with an orange check mark, and the MENU button to confirm when you're finished. The Print Setting entry lets you choose to superimpose the date onto the print. The date will be added during printing by the output device, which controls its location on the final print.

Copy

Options: Copy all images in current view mode to other card

This menu entry is the first in the Playback 2 menu (see Figure 5.19). The ability to work with two memory cards is a great feature. One of the best uses for your two slots is to make back-up images while traveling, or at any other time that your computer isn't easily accessible. Here are some examples of what I do:

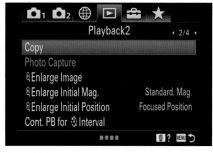

Figure 5.19 Playback 2 menu.

- **Make a copy.** Use this Copy facility to make a copy of images you shot on one card to your second card.

- **Make copies to distribute.** I bought a bunch of 8GB memory cards for $4 each and find it's quick and easy to make multiple copies of photos, not for backup, but for distribution either on the spot, say, to provide models I've hired with some raw (not RAW) images or to send by snail mail to colleagues, friends, or family. No computer required!

- **Leave your laptop or external storage at home.** When I use a camera with dual memory card slots, I leave my hard disk/personal storage device with its built-in reader or my laptop at home more often. If I am going to be gone for only a day or two, it's easier to just make copies in the camera, and not bother with another external device.

The process is simple: just select Copy and the a7R IV will take all the images visible *in your current View Mode* and copy them from the memory card slot that you specified using Select Playback Media (described later in this chapter) to the other memory card slot. Note that the process takes a while, especially if you have many images, so you should be prepared to wait, and have a fully charged battery installed. Use the View Mode entry to choose the type of files to copy, using Date View, Folder View (Still), Folder View (MP4), AVCHD View, XAVC S HD View, or XAVC S 4K View. You can interrupt transfer at any time (say, a UFO lands nearby) by pressing the center button to cancel.

If you have any XAVC S movies on the source card, you will not be able to copy them to a card that is not fast enough to support XAVCS S video. When that conflict happens, you'll see a message: "Cannot copy in the current memory card combination. Insert an SDXC Class 10 or USH-I/UHS II compatible memory card in the slot of the device where the copies are to be saved." Substitute another card, or switch to a View Mode that excludes XAVC S clips.

Photo Capture

Options: Capture video frame

This menu entry can be accessed only when you're playing back a video clip. You can use it to extract a still frame from a movie you've captured. Just follow these steps:

1. **Select the movie.** In Playback mode, navigate to the movie you want to clip from.
2. **Press MENU.** Choose Photo Capture from the Playback 2 menu. The first frame of the video will appear, along with a display offering playback controls.
3. **Play video.** Press the center button to start playback of the video at normal speed.
4. **Pause.** Press the center button again to pause playback when you reach the approximate location containing the desired frame.
5. **Select frame.** Use one of the following controls to navigate to the exact frame you want to extract:
   - **Up button.** Plays back slowly so you can monitor the action easily.
   - **Forward/Reverse.** Press the left/right buttons to move to the next frame/previous frame.
   - **Down button.** Saves the currently displayed frame to your memory card.

Enlarge Image

Options: Zoom In, Zoom Out

Whenever you are playing back still images (not movies), you can use this menu entry to magnify the image. (You can also double tap the touch screen to zoom in.) The a7R IV will try to zoom in on the point used to focus the image, if possible, and will zoom into the center of the frame if not. Press the Index/Reduce/AEL button to zoom out, and the Magnify/AF-MF button to zoom in. The MENU button exits. Use the control wheel to zoom in and out, and you can scroll around inside the enlarged image using the control wheel's directional controls. Rotate the front or rear dials to view the next or previous image (respectively) at the same magnification. Press MENU or the center button to exit. The initial magnification of the image is set using the entry that follows.

Enlarge Initial Magnification

Options: Standard Magnification, Previous Magnification

Here you can choose the initial magnification used by the Enlarge Image entry. Use Standard Magnification to always see any image you magnify at the same zoom level. This is a good choice if you magnify from time to time to closely examine an image and may want to zoom in or out to view more or less of your subject matter. When you select Previous Magnification, the enlargement resumes at the most recent level used. For example, if you are checking focus of your images as you shoot and zooming in tightly, it's convenient to return to the same zoom level for each successive image.

Enlarge Initial Position

Options: Focused Position, Center

By default, whenever you magnify an image during playback, the a7R IV centers the enlargement around the area in the frame where focus was achieved. That's often the best choice, because when evaluating an image during playback, focus is the parameter most often checked. However, I prefer the enlargement positioned in the center of the frame, so I can move the magnifying window around anywhere I like. That setting potentially minimizes the amount of "travel" if the previous area I examined is located some distance in the frame from my new area of interest.

Continuous Playback for Interval

Options: Plays back interval shots

Use this setting to play back a sequence of images you captured using the Interval feature described in Chapter 9, or when shooting with the Continuous drive mode. Select the image or image group you want to view, and then press the center button to display the images. Press the center button again to pause during playback, or to resume playback. Change the playback speed by rotating the control dial or control wheel while you are watching. You can also adjust playback speed using the menu entry described next. If you want to create a movie from the sequence, use the Imaging Edge software, as outlined in Chapter 9.

Playback Speed for Interval

Options: Playback speeds from 1 (Slow) to 9 (Fast)

This is the first entry in the Playback 3 menu. (See Figure 5.20.) While you can adjust the speed of playback for interval sequences while viewing them (as described above), you can also set a value to be used automatically. You can still speed up or slow down while watching your sequence. The camera accomplishes playback speed by skipping frames, depending on the speed requested. The faster playback goes, the jerkier the motion will appear.

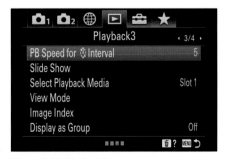

Figure 5.20 Playback 3 menu.

Slide Show

Menu Options: Repeat (On/Off), Interval: 1 second, 3 seconds, 5 seconds, 10 seconds, 30 seconds

Use this menu option when you want to display all the still images on your memory card in a continuous show. You can display still images in a continuous series, with each one displayed for the amount of time that you set. Choose the Repeat option to make the show repeat in a continuous loop. After making your settings, press the center button and the slide show will begin. You can scroll left or right to go back to a previous image or go forward to the next image immediately, but that will stop the slide show. The show cannot be paused, but you can exit by pressing the MENU button.

Select Playback Media

Options: Slot 1, Slot 2

Your a7R IV has two memory card slots, with useful labels on the reverse side of the memory card door to help you sort them out. You can specify which slot has precedence when reviewing images. Select either Slot 1 or Slot 2 here to register your preference.

- **See images on preferred card.** Once you've selected a slot, when you press the Playback button, images in that card matching your current view mode will be displayed. If no images are available in that view, a sidebar appears at the left of the LCD/viewfinder. You can press the up/down buttons to change to a different view mode.
- **Card not inserted.** If you press Playback and no card is inserted in your preferred slot, you'll see a message "No memory card inserted. Slot #."
- **Switching slots.** To change active *playback* slot, you'll need to use this menu entry. Note that if you want to change the active *recording* slot to use during shooting, you can define a button for the Select Recording Media behavior with the Custom Key (Shooting) entry in the Camera Settings II-09 menu, as described in Chapter 4.

View Mode

Options: Date View, Folder View (Still), AVCHD View, XAVC S HD View, XAVC S 4K View

Adjusts the way the camera displays image/movie files, which is useful for reviewing only certain types of files, or for deleting only particular types, as described above. You can elect to display files by Date View, Folder View (still photos only), AVCHD View (just AVCHD movies), or XAVCS clips in both HD (high-definition) and 4K modes.

Image Index

Options: 9, 25

You can view an index screen of your images on the camera's LCD by pressing the down directional button (Index button) while in Playback mode. By default, that screen shows up to 9 thumbnails of photos or movies; you can change that value to 25 using this menu item. Remember to use the View Mode menu item first, to identify the folder that the index display should access; by default, it will show thumbnails of still photos, but you might want to view thumbnails of your movie clips instead. When viewing an index, highlight the bar at the left side of the screen and use the control wheel's directional controls to move quickly among available thumbnails. Press the center button to switch View Mode quickly.

Display as Group

Options: On, Off

If you shoot sports, you'll love this feature. The a7R IV is smart enough to know that when you shoot a burst of images in continuous shooting mode it would be helpful to group them all together. That makes it easy to evaluate the first shot in a particular set of images captured sequentially, without having to wade through all of them. When set to On, the camera groups images in a burst together, and overlays a "stack" icon on the group, so you'll know you are viewing/evaluating only the first image in that burst. The View Mode must be set to Date View to use this feature. Set this option to Off and you'll be shown every picture you captured, one by one, during image review.

Display Rotation

Options: Auto, Manual, Off

This is the first of only two entries in the Playback 4 menu (see Figure 5.21). You can use this function to determine whether a vertical image is rotated automatically during picture review. If you want to rotate the image more, use the Rotate entry.

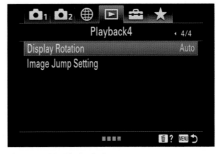

Figure 5.21 Playback 4 menu.

- **Auto.** The image will be shown in the orientation indicated by information in the image, no matter how the camera itself is rotated during picture review. For example, a vertical image will be shown in the correct orientation, as shown at top left in Figure 5.22 when the camera is held horizontally. It will be shown smaller in size to fit the long dimension of the image into the short dimension of the screen. Rotate the camera 90 degrees, and the a7R IV will automatically rotate the photo so it's *still* shown in the correct orientation, but it will now fill the LCD screen, as you can see in Figure 5.11, top right.

- **Manual.** With this setting, the image is always displayed on the LCD in the same orientation it was taken. That is, a vertically oriented photo will be displayed in a smaller size, just as it is when using Auto, as shown at center left in Figure 5.22. However, when you rotate the camera during picture review, the a7R IV does *not* automatically rotate the image at the same time, so it will be shown with an incorrect orientation (see Figure 5.22, center right).

- **Off.** With this setting, both vertical and horizontal images are displayed to fill the screen as much as possible with the image. Vertical shots are larger, as shown at bottom left in Figure 5.11, but the camera must be rotated to view them in the correct orientation (see Figure 5.22, bottom right).

Figure 5.22 Display Rotation configurations.

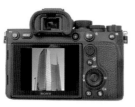
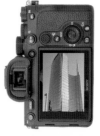

Display Rotation: Auto

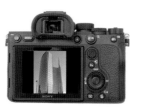
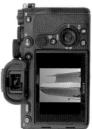

Display Rotation: Manual

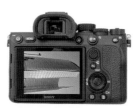
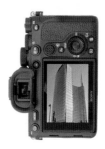

Display Rotation: Off

Image Jump Setting

Options: Select Dial (Front, Rear); Image Jump Method (One by One, Protect Only, Rating Only [All]), Rating Only (1–5 stars, or Without Rating Only)

You can select which dial to use when scrolling among images during playback. The default method, One by One, is usually most convenient, but it would have been nice if Sony had provided options other vendors use that allow jumping ahead by 10 or 100 images. This feature is much better than nothing, as you can elect to jump only between Protected images, images that have been rated, or images with particular star ratings. That allows you to "mark" images that you want to evaluate later, using either the protection attribute or a star rating.

Setup and My Menus

6

Even more options are available from the Sony a7R IV's Setup menu, providing control over adjustments that you typically won't change during a particular shooting session. For example, you can fine-tune the brightness of the LCD monitor or viewfinder, change your HDMI parameters to direct your camera's output to an external screen or recorder, and enter copyright information to be embedded in each image file. I'll wind up this chapter with a description of how you can build your own list of commands using the My Menu feature.

Setup Menu

Other than the Format and Cleaning mode commands listed below, you probably won't make frequent changes using any of these settings. Language, date/time, power-saving options, and many others are likely to be "set and forget" adjustments over the long term. The complete list of entries, and the Setup menu pages where you will find them, is in Table 6.1.

TABLE 6.1 Setup Menu

PAGE 01	PAGE 03	PAGE 05
Monitor Brightness	Touch Panel/Pad	Area Setting
Viewfinder Brightness	Touch Pad Settings	IPTC Information
Finder Color Temperature	Demo Mode	Copyright Info
Gamma Display Assistance	TC/UB Settings	Write Serial Number
Volume Settings	IR Remote Control	Format
Delete Confirm	HDMI Settings	Recording Media Settings
PAGE 02	**PAGE 04**	**PAGE 06**
Display Quality	4K Output Selection (Movies)	File/Folder Settings (Stills)
Power Save Start Time	USB Connection	File Settings (Movies)
Auto Power Off Temperature	USB LUN Setting	Recover Image Database
NTSC/PAL Selector	USB Power Supply	Display Media Information
Cleaning Mode	Language	Version
Touch Operation	Date/Time Setup	**PAGE 07**
		Save/Load Settings
		Setting Reset

Monitor Brightness

Options: Manual, Sunny Weather
Default: Manual
My preference: Manual

This is the first entry on the Setup 1 menu. (See Figure 6.1.) When you access this menu item, two controls appear. The first is a Brightness bar (shown just above the grayscale/color patches in Figure 6.2). It's set to Manual adjustment by default but press the center button and you can change it to Sunny Weather for a brighter display. You might resort to this setting if you're shooting outdoors in bright sun and find it hard to view the LCD even when shading it with your hand.

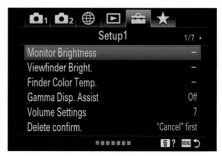

Figure 6.1 The first page of the Setup menu.

If you set it to Sunny Weather, the LCD brightness will automatically increase, making the display easier to view in very bright light. This makes the display unusually bright and less suitable for judging exposure and color, so use it only when it's really necessary. In such bright conditions, you're usually better off using the electronic viewfinder. Remember too that it will consume a lot more battery power, so have a spare battery available.

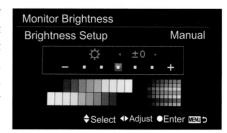

Figure 6.2 Adjust monitor brightness.

The grayscale steps and color patches can be used as you manually adjust the screen brightness using the left/right directional buttons. Scroll to the right to make the LCD display brighter or scroll to the left to make the LCD display darker, in a range of plus and minus 2 (arbitrary) increments. As you change the brightness, keep an eye on the grayscale and color chart to visualize the effect your setting will have on various tones and hues. The zero setting is the default and it provides the most accurate display in terms of exposure and color, but you might want to dim it when the bright display is distracting while shooting in a dark theater, perhaps. A minus setting also reduces battery consumption but makes your photos appear to be underexposed (too dark).

I prefer to choose Manual but then leave the display at the zero setting. This ensures the most accurate view of scene brightness on the LCD for the best evaluation of exposure while previewing the scene before taking a photo.

Viewfinder Brightness

Options: Auto, Manual

Default: Auto

My preference: Manual+1

This entry is similar to Monitor Brightness control but adds an Auto setting that adjusts the viewfinder's output based on the a7R IV's reading of the ambient light falling on the full-frame sensor. No Sunny Weather option is available, but I still like a slightly brighter viewfinder, so I prefer Manual with a +1 boost. A notice will appear on the LCD monitor advising you to look through the viewfinder and make your settings.

Finder Color Temperature

Options: +2 to –2

Default: 0

My preference: N/A

While looking through the viewfinder, press the left/right buttons to adjust the color balance of the finder to make it appear warmer (using the left button) or colder/bluer (using the right button), according to your preference.

Gamma Display Assist

Options: Off, Auto, S-Log2→709 (800%), S-Log3→709 (800%), HLG (BT.2020), HLG (709)

Default: Off

My preference: N/A

As you'll learn in Chapter 10, the a7R IV is capable of recording movies using Picture Profiles (which were introduced in Chapter 3). These profiles can use gamma correction to extend the dynamic range (range of tones from black to white) recorded during video capture. Movies captured using gamma profiles appear to be very low in contrast until processed using software on your computer. As a result, reviewing these clips in the camera can be difficult. This menu entry allows selecting options that will adjust the display of extended dynamic range clips so they appear *in the camera* with a more normal look, which is useful if you use live view to evaluate your captures. The display is not changed if you're viewing through a device such as an external monitor plugged into the HDMI port, and you'll still need to process the video in your video-editing software.

You can turn Gamma Display Assist off, allow the camera to select an appropriate adjustment automatically, or manually set the assist feature to use the gamma you are using. Your choices include S-Log2 and S-Log3, and two HLG (Hybrid Log Gamma) settings, which are used for delivery of video to high dynamic range TVs that are currently the rage. These are a bit esoteric for the average a7R IV user who isn't heavily into professional-quality video capture.

Volume Settings

Options: 0–15

Default: 7

My preference: N/A

This menu item affects only the audio volume of movies that are being played back in the camera (and not the beeps or other noises the a7R IV emits). When you select Volume Settings, the camera displays a scale of loudness from 0 to 15; scroll up/down to the value you want to set, and it will remain in effect until changed.

You might want to use this menu item to pre-set a volume level that you generally prefer. However, you can also adjust the volume whenever you're displaying a movie clip, to set it to just the right level. To do so, press the down directional button and use the up/down directional buttons to raise or lower the volume.

Delete Confirm

Options: Delete First, Cancel First

Default: Cancel First

My preference: Delete First

Determines which choice is highlighted when you press the trash button to delete an image. The default Cancel First is the safer option, as you must deliberately select Delete and then press the center or trash buttons to actually remove an image. Delete First is faster; press the trash button, then the center button, and the unwanted image is gone. You'd have to scroll down to Cancel if you happened to have changed your mind or pressed the trash button by mistake.

Display Quality

Options: Standard (60 fps), High (120 fps)

Default: Standard

My preference: Standard, except when shooting sports

This is the first entry on the second page of the Setup menu. (See Figure 6.3.) You can specify the image quality of the EVF display, switching from the default Standard of 60 fps to High, which at 120 fps uses more battery power and reduces the resolution of the display. While you might discern a small difference when viewing on an external monitor, most of the time the camera display isn't reliable for judging images anyway, so sticking to Standard quality is usually your best bet. However, if you shoot sports in continuous mode, you might want to use High Quality to reduce the tiny lag in displaying the image in the viewfinder.

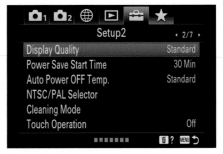

Figure 6.3 The Setup 2 menu.

Power Save Start Time

Options: 30 minutes, 5 minutes, 2 minutes, 1 minute, 10 seconds

Default: 1 minute

My preference: 5 minutes

Although the NP-FZ100 battery is more powerful than the one used in the a7R IV's predecessor, you'll still want to avoid wasting juice when the camera is idle. This item lets you specify the exact amount of time that should pass before the camera goes to "sleep" when the eye sensor next to the viewfinder window indicates you're not actively taking photos. The default of 1 minute is a short time, useful to minimize battery consumption. You can select a much longer time before the camera will power down, or a much shorter time. I use 5 minutes most of the time to avoid having to "waken" the camera frequently. If I'm wandering around with long periods of time between shots or the camera is mounted on a tripod, I may set it to 2 or 5 minutes. In street photography or sports mode, I use 30 minutes to make sure my camera will always be ready for action. But, of course, I tend to carry at least two spare batteries with me at all times, and in a pinch will use my RavPower 16,750 mAh power pack linked to the camera with a USB-C cable for long-term non-stop shooting.

You'll need to keep in mind that this setting will be ignored if the camera is linked to an external monitor or video recorder through the HDMI port, and shutoff will be postponed while you are uploading images over a Wi-Fi connection.

Auto Power Off Temperature

Options: Standard, High

Default: Standard

My preference: Standard

Your camera may overheat if operated continuously (as when shooting movies) for periods of time and continued use after that point can result in damage. The a7R IV can turn itself off when its internal temperature gets too high, which is particularly useful if the camera is mounted on a tripod so that your hands don't feel the increasing warmth. Shooting 4K video, for example, can generate a lot of heat and deplete your battery rather quickly. This option allows you to stretch the safe operating time by switching from the default Standard mode to High (which allows operation when the camera is hotter than normal). Sony recommends not holding the camera in your hands when you've activated the High setting.

NTSC/PAL Selector

Options: NTSC, PAL

Default: Depends on the country where the camera is sold

My preference: N/A

Allows you to switch the camera between the two major television video systems, NTSC (used in North and South America, Korea, Japan, and some other Pacific countries), and PAL, which is used in Europe, the Middle East, and elsewhere. To switch from one video system to another, Sony says you must be using a memory card that was formatted while the camera was using that video system. You'll be prompted to reformat the card or use a different card. However, the a7R IV *does not* reformat the card for you (whew!). However, if you try to shoot a video using the "new" system, you should be forced to reformat. A message appears asking you to reformat the card in the current slot the first time you try to record a movie in the new video system.

Your camera will be set up at the factory to default to the video system used in your country. If you switch to the alternate system, the start-up screen will display a message "Running on NTSC" or "Running on PAL" to make sure you're aware of the change. Note that a few countries in South America (Brazil, Argentina, Paraguay, and Uruguay) use a modified PAL system, while others, including Bulgaria, France, Greece, Guiana, Iran, Iraq, Monaco, Russia, and Ukraine use a third system, called SECAM.

Cleaning Mode

Options: Enter, Cancel

Default: Cancel

My preference: N/A

Access this entry when you want to use the camera's auto image sensor cleaning feature. You'll hear a buzzing sound as the camera gives the sensor a good shake. Your tip-off that the sensor needs cleaning will be blurry spots and artifacts that show up in less detailed areas of the image (such as the sky) in photos taken at small f/stops (the extra depth-of-focus makes them more obvious). If the a7R IV's own sensor cleaning isn't sufficient, you can use a "rocket"-style blower, special sensor cleaning brushers, or wet-wipe swabs available online and from photo retailers.

Touch Operation

Options: On, Off

Default: Off

My preference: On, once you've mastered touch controls

This entry allows you to disable touch operations completely. You should leave touch operation Off until you've practiced using the feature; otherwise, the touch pad/panel's functions can be confusing.

Touch Panel/Pad

Options: Touch Panel+Pad, Touch Panel Only, Touch Pad Only

Default: Touch Panel Only

My preference: Touch Panel+Pad

This is the first entry on the third page of the Setup menu. (See Figure 6.4.) As I described in Chapter 2, the a7R IV has a touch-sensitive LCD. With this setting, you can define whether the LCD-oriented Touch Panel or EVF-oriented Touch Pad, or *both* are active. The dual screen/pad modes are used because the touch feature can be used in two different ways: as a touch *screen* or *panel* when you are using the LCD monitor to compose your photos, and as a touch *pad* that you can tap when the camera is raised to your eye and you're using the electronic viewfinder.

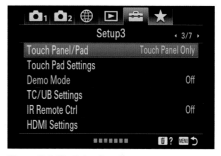

Figure 6.4 The Setup 3 menu.

Unfortunately, the touch features are limited to the ability to specify a focus *point* when shooting stills and videos. You still have to press the shutter release halfway or the AF-ON button (or other defined key) to initiate focus. You can't select menu entries, type in text, scroll through playback views, or pinch/expand with your fingertips to zoom in and out during image review. However, the touch focus feature is quite useful, especially when shooting movies, as it allows selecting a focus area with a gentle tap. There are two modes:

- **Touch screen.** When active and you're using the LCD monitor to compose, you can select a focus point or zone anywhere that the a7R IV is able to achieve autofocus (that is, most of the frame other than the edges). You can tap the screen or hold down your finger and slide the focus area around. Cancel your focus selection by pressing the center button. A quick tap may not register; this function requires a firm press. I'll explain the various AF-area modes in Chapter 8.

- **Touch pad.** When touch pad mode is active and you're using the electronic viewfinder to compose, you can touch the LCD monitor screen to specify the focus area. You don't have to tap the exact area (actually, that's impossible, because you're not actually looking at the LCD). Instead, when you touch the pad, a focus point appears in the viewfinder *relative to the location on the LCD*. That is, if you tap the center of the sensitive area, the focus point appears in the center; tap to the right or left, and the focus area appears to the right or left side. As I'll explain shortly, that mode is needed because you can change the size of the sensitive area of the LCD screen. Once the focus area is displayed, keep your finger on the screen and slide it around to the position you want, using your view through the EVF as your reference.

Select whether you want the touch screen *and* touch pad, or only one to be used, depending on your preference.

Touch Pad Settings

Options: Operation in Vertical Orientation: On, Off; Touch Position Mode: Absolute Position, Relative Position; Operation Area: Whole screen, Right/Left half of screen, upper/lower right/left corners

Default: Operation in Vertical Orientation: On; Touch Position Mode: Absolute Position; Operation Area: Whole screen

My preference: N/A

Additional settings that relate only to the touch pad configuration can be selected from this menu entry:

- **Operation in Vertical Orientation.** Here you can specify whether touch controls are available when the camera is oriented in the vertical position (On), or only when the camera is held in horizontal orientation (Off).
- **Touch Position Mode.** Choose Absolute Position, to allow you to quickly move the focusing frame to a distant position on the LCD. This setting automatically changes the Operation Area (described next) to encompass the full screen. Use Relative Position to move the focus point relative to the location on the LCD.
- **Operation Area.** By default, the entire touch pad is sensitive when using the EVF. However, if your *ocular dominance* favors your left eye (i.e., you're "left-eyed"), you may be more comfortable choosing an active area on the left side of the screen that avoids contact with your nose. The "relative" orientation remains the same, but is limited to that reduced area. However, if you selected Absolute Position for the Touch Position above, the entire screen is used, regardless of your setting here.

Demo Mode

Options: On, Off
Default: Off
My preference: N/A

This is a semi-cool feature that allows your camera to be used as a demonstration tool, say, when giving lectures or showing off at a trade show. When activated, if the camera is idle for about one minute it will begin showing a protected AVCHD movie, which is not impressive on the camera's built-in LCD, but can have a lot more impact if the camera is connected to a large-screen HDTV through the HDMI port.

You may not have seen this feature discussed much in other guides; they tend to dismiss it as a retailer-only feature. But it can be quite useful. Previously, it could only be activated when using the optional AC-PW20 AC Adapter, but I've found that it works perfectly if you connect your a7R IV to an external power source through a USB port. My RavPower pack is perfect, and doubles as a power source for time-lapse images.

If you're properly equipped, just follow these steps:

1. Use the File Format entry in the Camera Settings II-1 (Movie 1) menu and select AVCHD as the movie format, as explained in Chapter 3. Demo Mode works only with AVCHD files.

2. Shoot the clip that you want to use as your demonstration, in AVCHD format.

3. In the Playback 3 menu, access the View Mode and select AVCHD View so that only AVCHD videos will appear.

4. In the Playback 1 menu, choose Protect and select the demo clip, which must reside on Slot 1, and must be the video with the oldest recorded date and time. (If you have some older clips on your card, you should move or delete them.)

5. Connect the camera to the optional AC-PW20 AC adapter or to a power source using the USB-C port. Because Demo Mode uses a lot of juice, it operates only when one of these external power sources is connected.

6. Demo Mode will no longer be grayed out in the Setup 2 menu. Select it and choose On.

7. After about one minute of idling, the demo clip will begin playing. Note that, because the external source is connected, your automatic power-saving setting is ignored, and Demo Mode will not operate if no movie file is stored on your memory card.

TC/UB Settings

Options: TC/UB Display Settings, TC Preset, UB Preset, TC Format, TC Run, TC Make, TC/UB Time Rec.

Default: TC/UB Display Settings: Counter; TC Preset: 00:00:00:00; UB Preset: 00:00:00:00; TC Format: DF; TC Run: Rec Run; TC Make: Preset; TC/UB Time Rec.: Off

My preference: N/A

The Time Code (TC) and User Bit (UB) settings are information that can be embedded and used to sync clips and sound when editing movies, especially those captured by multiple cameras. I'll describe this advanced feature in a little more detail in Chapter 11, including what each of these options do, but pro movie-making techniques are largely beyond the scope of this book.

IR Remote Control

Options: On, Off

Default: Off

My preference: N/A

The a7R IV can be operated at distances of about 20 feet (indoors) or 6 feet (outdoors in full sunlight) using infrared signals using the Sony RMT-DSLR1 and RMT-DSLR2 Wireless Remote Commander controls. It can also be triggered with an array of third-party remotes, and smartphones with an infrared transmitter and accompanying remote control app on your smart device.

Constantly "looking" for the IR signal using the sensor on the front of the camera can sap battery power (because the a7R IV does not go into power save mode), so it's wise to turn the remote control feature on only when it's actually needed. Choose On, and you can take pictures using the Shutter, 2

Sec., Start/Stop buttons on the RMT-DSLR1/2 controls, plus the Movie button found on the RMT-DSLR2 control. The RMT-DSLR1 model cannot be used to shoot movies; the RMT-DSLR2 remote can be used to activate movie shooting as long as the Movie button on the camera is not set to Movie Mode Only in the Camera Settings II-10 menu.

For best performance, make sure a lens hood or other object doesn't interfere with the IR signal reaching the a7R IV's sensor. If the camera is set for an autofocus mode, the a7R IV will attempt to focus when you press the Shutter or 2 Sec. buttons. If it cannot focus, the picture won't be taken.

Note: The IR remote control cannot be used while the Bluetooth Remote Control setting in the Network 2 menu is set to On.

HDMI Settings

Options: HDMI Resolution, 24/60p Output, HDMI Info. Display, TC Output, REC Control, CTRL for HDMI

Default: HDMI Resolution: Auto; 24/60p Output: 60p; HDMI Info. Display: On; TC Output: Off; CTRL for HDMI: On

My preference: N/A

You can view the display output of your camera on a high-definition television (HDTV) when you connect it to the a7R IV if you make the investment in an HDMI cable (which Sony does not supply); get the Type C with a mini-HDMI connector on the camera end. (Still photos can also be displayed using Wi-Fi, without cable connection.) When connecting HDMI-to-HDMI, the camera automatically makes the correct settings. If you're lucky enough to own a TV that supports the Sony Bravia synchronization protocol, you can operate the camera using that TV's remote control when this item is On. Just press the Link Menu button on the remote, and then use the device's controls to delete images, display an image index of photos in the camera, display a slide show, protect/unprotect images in the camera, specify printing options, and play back single images on the TV screen.

- **HDMI Resolution (Auto, 2160/1080p, 1080p, 1080i).** The camera can adjust its output for display on a high-definition television when at the Auto setting. This usually works well with any HDTV. If you have trouble getting the image to display correctly, you can set the resolution manually here to 2160/1080p (for 4K and Full HD), 1080p, or 1080i. I had to make a manual selection so my BlackMagic Intensity Shuttle (a screen capture device) could accept my a7R IV's output. (The Intensity Shuttle requires 1080i.)

- **24p/60p Output.** You can select either 60p or 24p output to the HDMI port when connected to a 1080 60i–compatible device and Record Setting (described in Chapter 4) has been set to 24p 24M (FX), 24p 17M (FH), or 24p 50M. The frames of the 24p video are duplicated to play back at a 60 fps rate. If a different setting was used, this setting is ignored, and the output conforms to the HDMI Resolution setting above instead.

- **HDMI Info. Display.** Choose On or Off. Choose On if you want the shooting information to display when the camera is connected to an HDTV television/monitor or other device using an HDMI cable. For example, I left this setting On when capturing screen shots of live view images, so all the overlaid icons appear. Select Off if you don't want to show the shooting information on the display.

- **TC Output.** Choose on or off to enable/disable including time code in the HDMI output signal. Use On if you are outputting to professional video equipment and want to include the time code information. Note that the time code is *data* and will not actually appear on the screen. If this setting is on and you are sending the signal to a television or some other device, the image may not appear properly. Change this setting to off when outputting to devices not equipped to handle TC information.

- **REC Control.** This setting is available only when TC Output is set to on. Choose on or off. The setting allows you to start and stop REC Control–compatible external video recorders connected to the camera. A REC or STBY icon will be displayed on the camera's screen as appropriate.

- **CTRL for HDMI.** This option can be useful when you have connected the camera to a non-Sony HDTV and find that the TV's remote control produces unintended results with the camera. If that happens, try turning this option Off, and see if the problem is resolved. If you later connect the camera to a Sony Bravia sync-compliant HDTV (vendors other than Sony also use it), set this menu item back to On. Be aware that not all so-called Bravia-friendly devices conform completely, so you should be prepared to turn the function off if necessary.

4K Output Selection (Movie)

Options: Memory Card+HDMI, HDMI Only (30p), HDMI Only (24p), HDMI Only (25p)
Default: Memory Card+HDMI
My preference: N/A

This is the first entry in the Setup 4 menu. (See Figure 6.5.) When your a7R IV is connected to an external video recorder or playback device and set to Movie mode, you can use this setting to specify how 4K movies are recorded and output. Note that when using one of these choices, the camera's movie counter does not appear on the screen. Your choices are as follows:

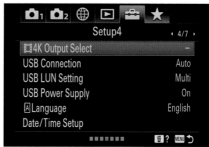

Figure 6.5 The Setup 4 menu.

- **Memory Card+HDMI.** A 4K movie in 30p is saved on the camera's internal memory card (in compressed format at a maximum transfer rate of 100 Mb/sec) *and* output to the external device (uncompressed, at up to 147 Mb/sec.). Use this if you want two copies of your video, including one on the memory card. **Reminder:** Use a fast memory card for these huge files!

- **HDMI Only (30p).** A 4K movie in 30p is output only to the external device, and not recorded on your memory card. HDMI Info. Display is disabled.

- **HDMI Only (24p).** A 4K movie in 24p is output only to the external device. HDMI Info. Display is disabled.

- **HDMI Only (25p).** If the NTSC/PAL Selector described earlier is set to PAL, you can use this option to shoot a 4K movie in 25p, and output only to the external device. HDMI Info. Display is disabled.

USB Connection

Options: Auto, Mass Storage, MTP, PC Remote

Default: Auto

My preference: N/A

This entry allows you to select the type of USB connection protocol between your camera and computer.

- **Auto.** Connects your camera to your computer or other device automatically, choosing either Mass Storage or MTP connection as appropriate.
- **Mass Storage.** In this mode, your camera appears to the computer as just another storage device, like a disk drive. You can drag and drop files between them. When you are applying a firmware update (as described in Chapter 14), the installation utility will prompt you to make sure the camera is set to this mode.
- **MTP.** This mode, short for Media Transfer Protocol is a newer version of the PTP (Picture Transfer Protocol) that was standard in earlier cameras. It allows better two-way communication between the camera and the computer and is useful for both image transfer and printing with PictBridge-compatible printers. Slot 1 is used for the connection.
- **PC Remote.** This setting is used with Sony's new Imaging Edge software to adjust shooting functions and take pictures from a linked computer.

USB LUN Setting

Options: Multi, Single

Default: Multi

My preference: Multi for PCs, Single for Macs

This setting specifies how the camera selects a Logical Unit Number when connecting to a computer through the USB port. Normally, you'd use Multi with the USB Connection set to MTP; the camera will adjust the LUN automatically as necessary. If you've set USB Connection (above) to Mass Storage, each of the two memory card slots in your camera appear on your computer as an individual device, and a third "drive" will appear named PMHOME, a vestigial folder used only by the camera itself. Use Single to lock in a LUN if you have trouble making a connection between your camera and a particular computer or device. PlayMemories Home software will usually not work when this setting is active. But don't worry; Single is rarely necessary.

USB Power Supply

Options: On, Off

Default: On

My preference: On

When set to On, the camera receives charging power from a connected computer or other device through the micro USB cable link. Use this setting if you want to charge the a7R IV's battery when connected to a computer or other device. Set to Off, and power is not supplied. You'd want to use this to avoid draining power from the computer host. Although I frequently connect my camera to a desktop computer, if I am using a laptop, I set this to Off, as I have plenty of NP-FZ100 batteries and recharging the laptop is sometimes inconvenient. You'll want to leave this On if you're using an external power pack.

Language

Options: English, French, Italian, Spanish, Japanese, Chinese languages

Default: Language of country where camera is sold

My preference: N/A

If you accidentally set a language you cannot read and find yourself with incomprehensible menus, don't panic. Just find the Setup menu, the one with the red toolbox for its icon, and scroll down to the line that has a symbol that looks like an alphabet block "A" to the left of the item's heading. No matter which language has been selected, you can recognize this menu item by the "A" icon. Scroll to it, press the center button to select this item, and scroll up/down among the options until you see a language you can read.

Date/Time Setup

Options: Year, Day, Month, Hour, Minute, Date Format, Daylight Savings Time

Default: None

My preference: N/A

Use this option to specify the date and time that will be embedded in the image file along with exposure information and other data. Having the date set accurately also is important for selecting movies for viewing by date. Use the left/right directional buttons to navigate through the choices of Daylight Savings Time On/Off; year; month; day; hour; minute; and date format. You can't directly change the AM/PM setting; you need to scroll the hours past midnight or noon to change that setting. Use the up/down directional buttons or rotate the control wheel to change each value as needed.

Area Setting

Options: World time zones

Default: None

My preference: N/A

This is the first entry in the Setup 5 menu. (See Figure 6.6.) When you select this option, you are presented with a world map on the LCD monitor. Use the left/right directional buttons to scroll until you have highlighted the time zone that you are in. Once the camera is set up with the correct date and time in your home time zone, you can use this setting to change your time zone during a trip, so you will record the local time with your images without disrupting your original date and time settings. Just scroll back to your normal time zone once you return home.

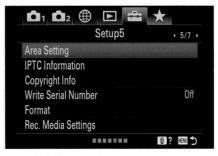

Figure 6.6 The Setup 5 menu.

IPTC Information

Options: Write IPTC Info, Register IPTC Info

Default: Disabled

My preference: N/A

This entry allows you to enable or disable embedding of IPTC (International Press Communications Council) metadata in your JPEG and RAW files. The IPTC standard is the most widely used standard used by news and photo agencies, photojournalists, libraries, and museums. You can load, edit, save, and register specifications using a free utility available from Sony, the IPTC Metadata Preset (https://www.sony.net/iptc/help/). Professional journalists should investigate Sony's Transfer and Tagging Add-On, a smart device app that works in conjunction with Imaging Edge Mobile to streamline transfer of images and IPTC information to your smart device as you shoot. It operates with both Wi-Fi and transfer using a special USB cable connecting the camera and your device. To embed IPTC information, just follow these steps:

1. **Launch the IPTC Metadata Preset.** Your computer will display a screen something like the one shown in Figure 6.7.

2. **Enter your default information.** For general use, you will want to enter information only for the fields shown at the bottom of the figure, under Image Rights. These include photographer's name, title, URL, copyright notice, and credit line. You can embed this information in all the photos you take.

3. **Enter shoot-specific data (optional).** If you will be taking many pictures for a particular project, you can optionally add more information about a specific series or individual image. Photojournalists might find this especially useful, but most of us can skip entering these minutiae.

4. **Save preset.** You'll need to save the information entered to your computer, a memory card, or both.

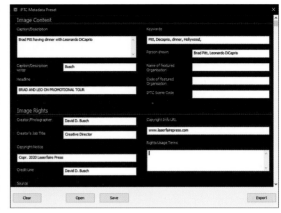

- Click Save in the utility and specify a storage location on your computer. You can later retrieve your settings using the Open command in the utility to revise, edit, or create a new version.
- Click Export to store the metadata on a memory card. Insert the card into a card reader, first. A dialog box will appear allowing to select the drive representing your memory card. (The card will usually appear as a USB card in your file manager.)

Figure 6.7 Sony IPTC Metadata Preset utility.

5. **Copy to camera.** You'll next need to transfer the information to the a7R IV in order to make it available for embedding in your photos. With a memory card containing the information loaded into one of the camera's slots, navigate to the IPTC Information entry in the Setup 5 menu and choose Register IPTC Info.

6. **Select media.** From the screen that appears, select either Slot 1 or Slot 2 to specify the card containing your IPTC metadata. Press MENU to confirm. The data will be recorded in the camera's memory, *overwriting any existing IPTC data* that may already have been there. **Note:** You can store separate IPTC data on different memory cards and choose which one to write to the camera's register.

7. **Highlight Write IPTC Info.** Select On to enable embedding the IPTC data you have just registered to your images.

Copyright Info

Options: Write Copyright Info, Set Photographer, Set Copyright, Display Copyright Info
Default: Off
My preference: Add all information

Your choices include:

- **Write Copyright Info.** Turn On to embed copyright information in your image file; Off to disable this feature. If you choose On, a copyright symbol will appear on the shooting screen to indicate that copyright data is being written to the image file.
- **Set Photographer.** Enter the name of the photographer. Highlight this and press the center button to move to the next screen, where a blank line appears. Highlight that and press the center button, and the text entry screen appears. It functions much like the multi-tap cell phone keypads in the pre-smartphone era: highlight a button and press the center button multiple times to enter

a particular character. For example, if you highlight the "abc" button, pressing once inserts an a, twice a b, and three times a c. When finished, highlight OK and press the center button to return to the initial screen, where you can highlight OK again and press the center button a last time to confirm.

- **Set Copyright.** Define your copyright terms, such as *Cpr. 2020 David D. Busch*. Strictly speaking, "Cpr." should be used rather than a lowercase c between two parentheses. Text is entered as described above.
- **Disp. Copyright Info.** Displays whatever copyright information you've specified.

Write Serial Number

Options: On, Off
Default: Off
My preference: On—but you probably will prefer Off

When enabled, the a7R IV will embed your camera's unique serial number in the EXIF data for a particular image. That will help you identify which camera was used to capture a particular image. Back in the days when news organizations had large photo staffs and a pool of equipment that was sometimes (or often) shared among photographers, this would have been a killer feature (along with IPTC info) for providing a digital photo trail. Today, it is more likely to be used by individual shooters who own more than one a7R IV (or other Sony cameras with the Serial Number feature). I happen to be one of them: it's also available with my Sony a9 and a9 II cameras (but not with my earlier a7R III).

Format

Options: OK, Cancel
Default: None
My preference: N/A

As you'd guess, you'll use Format to re-format your memory card while it's in your a7R IV. To proceed with this process, choose the Format menu item and select "OK" and press the center button to confirm, or Cancel to chicken out.

Use the Format command to erase everything on your memory card and to set up a fresh file system ready for use. This procedure removes all data that was on the memory card and reinitializes the card's file system by defining anew the areas of the card available for image storage, locking out defective areas, and creating a new folder in which to deposit your images. It's usually a good idea to reformat your memory card in the camera (not in your camera's card reader using your computer's operating system) before each use. Formatting is generally much quicker than deleting images one by one. Before formatting the card, however, make sure that you have saved all your images and videos to another device; formatting will delete everything, including images that were protected.

Recording Media Settings

Options: Prioritize Recording Media (Slot 1, Slot 2); Recording Mode (Standard; Simultaneous modes for Stills, Movies, Stills/Movies; Sorted for RAW/JPEG, JPEG/RAW, Stills Movies); Auto Switch Mode (On, Off)

Default: Prioritize: Slot 1; Recording Mode: Standard; Auto Switch Mode: Off

My preference: N/A

This entry has three options that specify how the memory cards in your camera should be used. They include specifying which slots to use, what types of files should be saved on specific card slots, and what to do when switching from one card slot to another. Your choices, shown in Figure 6.8, are as follows:

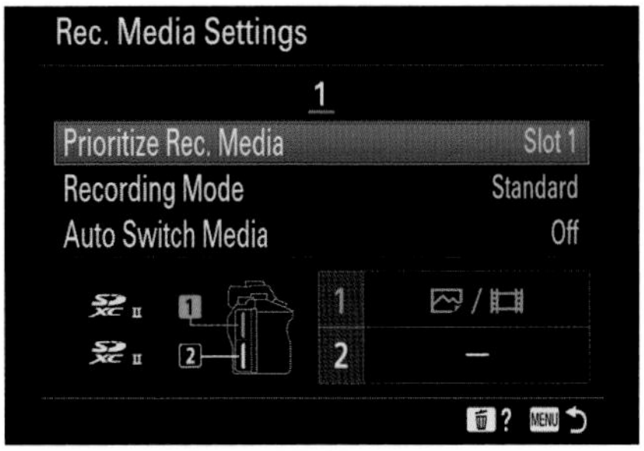

Figure 6.8 Your Recording Media Settings options.

- **Prioritize Recording Media.** Use this to specify the memory card that your image and movie files are stored on by default.

- **Recording Mode.** This slightly confusing entry (because of its multiple options) is actually simple to understand. Here you choose whether you save files to two cards (for in-camera backup) or split various types of files between the two cards. Your choices include:

  - **Standard.** All files are stored on the slot you specify using Prioritize Recording Media (above).

  - **Simultaneous (Stills).** Still photos are stored on *both* memory cards (excellent for backup), while movies are stored on your default (prioritized) slot.

  - **Simultaneous (Movies).** Movies are stored on *both* memory cards, while stills are stored on your default slot. Use this if you are shooting video primarily and want to back up your work.

  - **Simultaneous (Stills/Movies).** Both still photographs and movies are stored on both slots. As with any of the other two "simultaneous" (backup) modes, storing files on both cards at the same time will slow down your continuous shooting speed.

  - **Sort (RAW/JPEG).** RAW photos are stored on your default slot, and JPEG files on the other card. This option and the next allows you to keep both file types separate. Because JPEG files are smaller than RAW files, you may be able to get away with using a memory card with less capacity in your alternate slot.

  - **Sort (JPEG/RAW).** JPEG images are stored on your default slot, and RAW files on the other. Note that in this case, and the previous one, if you are only shooting JPEG or only RAW, only the file type you are actually capturing will be saved to the appropriate memory card; the other card will be ignored.

  - **Sort (Stills/Movies).** Still photos are stored on your default slot, and movies on the other card.

- **Auto Switch Media.** This option determines what happens when a memory card fills, or you have inserted a card into only one of the two available slots. Your choices are as follows:
  - **Off.** The a7R IV only stores files on the available card. If it fills, you will no longer be able to capture images.
  - **On.** When your main card is full, the camera switches to the other card slot automatically. However:
    - If you've set simultaneous (backup) recording (above), the a7R IV stops capturing images when *either* memory card is full. You can simply remove the full card, and the camera starts recording to the other card, but it's a better idea to replace the full card with one with available capacity. In that case, the a7R IV will resume normal operation until either of the two cards fills up.
    - If you've set recording of RAW and JPEG files to different cards, or stills and movies to different cards, the a7R IV also stops capturing images when *either* memory card is full. If you replace the depleted card, *both* types of files will be stored on the remaining card. Insert a non-full card, and the a7R IV will resume storing the files on separate cards until either of them fills up again.

File/Folder Settings (Stills)

Options: File Number (Series, Reset), Set File Name (DSC, User Entry), Select Recording Folder, New Folder, Folder Name (Standard Form, Date Form)

Default: File Number: Series; Set File Name: DSC; Select Recording Folder: Current folder; New Folder: N/A; Folder Name: Standard Form

My preference: N/A

This entry is the first in the Setup 6 menu (see Figure 6.9). It allows you to specify when file numbers are reset to zero, choose the first three letters of your camera's filenames, choose a folder to store images in, create a new folder, and select the format for your folders. Figure 6.10 shows the array of options in the File/Folder Settings submenu. I'll explain each of them separately.

Although your camera will create new folders automatically as needed, you can create a new folder at any time, and switch among available folders already created on your memory card. (Of course, a memory card must be installed in the camera.) This is an easy way to segregate photos by folder.

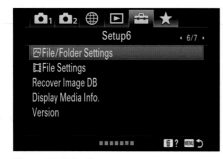

Figure 6.9 Setup 6 menu

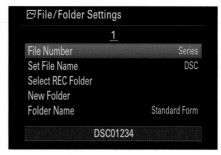

Figure 6.10 File/Folder Settings

For example, if you're on vacation, you can change the Folder Name convention to Date Form (described below). Then, each day, create a new folder (with that date as its name), and then deposit that day's photos and video clips into it. A highlighted bar appears; press the up/down buttons to select the folder you want to use and press the center button.

File Number (Folder)
Options: Series, Reset
Default: Series
My preference: Series

The default for the File Number item is Series, indicating that the a7R IV will automatically apply a file number to each picture that you take, using consecutive numbering; this will continue over a long period of time, spanning many different memory cards, and even if you reformat a card. Numbers are applied from 0001 to 9999; when you reach the limit, the camera starts back at 0001. The camera keeps track of the last number used in its internal memory. So, you could take pictures numbered as high as 100–0240 on one card, remove the card, and insert another, and the next picture will be numbered 100–0241 on the new card. Reformat either card, take a picture, and the next image will be numbered 100–0242. Use the Series option when you want all the photos you take to have consecutive numbers (at least, until your camera exceeds 9999 shots taken).

If you want to restart numbering back at 0001 frequently, use the Reset option. In that case, the file number will be reset to 0001 *each* time you format a memory card or delete all the images in a folder, insert a different memory card, create a new folder, or change the folder name format (as described in the next menu entry). I do not recommend this since you will soon have several images with exactly the same file number. However, if you import your images to your computer using a utility that renames the files as they are copied, you won't have duplicate file number/names if you specify a unique prefix each time you transfer.

Set File Name
Options: Choose three-character prefix
Default: DSC
My preference: 7R4

This entry allows you to specify the first three characters in the filename applied to your images. The a7R IV, like other cameras in the Sony product line, automatically applies a name like _DSC0001.jpg or DSC_0001.arw to your image files as they are created. You can use this menu option to change the names applied to your photos, but only within certain strict limitations. In practice, you can change only three of the eight characters, the *DSC* portion of the filename. The other five are mandated either by the Design Rule for Camera File System (DCF) specification that all digital camera makers adhere to or to industry conventions.

DCF limits filenames created by conforming digital cameras to a maximum of eight characters, plus a three-character extension (such as .jpg, .nef, or .wav in the case of audio files) that represents the format of the file. The eight-plus-three (usually called 8.3) length limitation dates back to an evil and frustrating computer operating system that we older photographers would like to forget (its initials are D.O.S.), but which, unhappily, lives on as the wraith of a file-naming convention.

Of the eight available characters, four are used to represent, in a general sense, the type of camera used to create the image. By convention, one of those characters is an underscore, placed in the first position (as in _DSCxxxx.xxx) when the image uses the Adobe RGB color space, and in the fourth position (as in DSC_xxxx.xxx) for sRGB and RAW files. That leaves just three characters for the manufacturer (and you) to use. The remaining four characters are used for numbers from 0000 to 9999, which is why your a7R IV "rolls over" to DSC_0000 again when the 9999-number limitation is reached.

Because the default DSC characters don't tell you much, don't hesitate to change them to something else. I use 7R4 for my a7R IV. (See Figure 6.11, left.) You can change the three characters to anything else that suits your purposes. You must use capital letters, numbers, or underscores, with the exception that you cannot use an underscore as the *first* character in your filename; it's reserved for AdobeRGB files. You could not use _R4, for example. The text entry screen is shown in Figure 6.11, right.

You might prefer to use your initials (DDB_ or JFK_, for example), or even customize for particular shooting sessions (EUR_, GER_, FRA_, or JAP_ when taking vacation trips). You can also use the filename flexibility to partially overcome the 9999 numbering limitation. You could use the template 7R1_ to represent the first 10,000 pictures you take with your a7R IV, and then 7R2_ for the next 10,000, and 7R3_ for the 10,000 after that.

This capability is especially useful for those who own more than one camera, whether it's a Sony model or another brand that also defaults to the DSC nomenclature. It's often important to know exactly *which* camera produced a given image, particularly when you discover some sort of problem in your photos and would like to pin down which camera is the culprit.

This file-renaming feature assumes that you don't rename your image files in your computer. In a way, file naming verges on a moot consideration, because, they apply *only* to the images as they exist in your camera. After (or during) transfer to your computer, you can change the names to anything you want, completely disregarding the 8.3 limitations (although it's a good idea to retain the default extensions). If you shot an image file named DSC_4832.jpg in your camera, you could change it to Paris_EiffelTower_32.jpg later.

Figure 6.11 Set a File Name (left); the text entry screen (right).

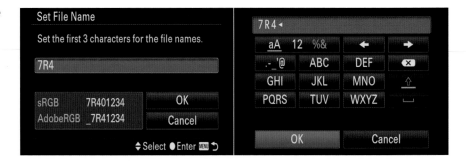

Select Recording Folder

Options: Choose from among available folders

Default: None

My preference: N/A

This entry allows you to choose which of the folders *that have already been created* within the *currently selected slot* is used to store images as you create them. You can select the recording folder only if Folder Name is set to Standard Form, as described shortly.

I like to use this capability to keep various images separate while they still reside on my memory card. For example, if I am working on two different projects, I can store images for one project in a particular folder, switch to a different folder for the second project, and switch back to the original one at any time. When traveling, I may spend a few hours shooting wildlife, then spend some time photographing landscapes before moving on to a different location to continue taking wildlife photos. I assign the Select Recording Folder to a Custom Key, and can switch back and forth more quickly than alternate methods, such as swapping memory cards in and out, or changing from Slot 1 to Slot 2 and back again.

New Folder

Options: N/A

Default: None

My preference: N/A

This item will enable you to create a brand-new folder. Press the center button, and a message like "10100905 folder created" or "102MSDCF folder created" appears on the LCD. The alphanumeric format will be determined by the Folder Name option you've selected (and described next), either Standard Form or Date Form.

This entry allows you to create a new storage folder in the currently selected slot (but only if Folder Name is set to Standard Form, as described shortly). Although your camera will create new folders automatically as needed, you can create a new folder at any time, and switch among available folders already created on your memory card, using the Select Recording Folder entry described above.

As I mentioned earlier, using multiple folders is an easy way to segregate photos. For example, if you're on vacation, you can change the Folder Name convention to Date Form (described next). Then, each day, create a new folder (with that date as its name), and then deposit that day's photos and video clips into it. A highlighted bar appears; press the up/down buttons to select the folder you want to use and press the center button.

Folder Name

Options: Standard Form, Date Form

Default: Standard Form

My preference: N/A

If you have viewed one of your memory card's contents on a computer, you noticed that the top-level folder on the card is always named DCIM. Inside it, there's another folder created by your camera. Different cameras use different folder names, and they can co-exist on the same card. For example, if your memory card is removed from your Sony camera and used in, say, a camera from another vendor that also accepts Secure Digital cards, the other camera will create a new folder using a different folder name within the DCIM directory.

By default, the a7R IV creates its folders using a three-number prefix (starting with 100), followed by MSDCF. As each folder fills up with 9999 images, a new folder with a prefix that's one higher (say, 101) is used. So, with the "Standard Form," the folders on your memory card will be named 100MSDCF, 101MSDCF, and so forth. As I noted earlier, the camera *must* be set to Standard Form if you want to be able to specify a folder using the Select Recording Folder entry described earlier.

However, you can also select Date Form instead, and the a7R IV will use a *xxxymmdd* format, such as 10010904, where the initial *100* is the folder number, the following *1* is the last digit of the year (2021), 09 is the month, and 04 is the day of that month. If you want the folder names to be date-oriented, rather than generic, use the Date Form option instead of Standard Form. This entry allows you to switch back and forth between them for folder creation (using the New Folder entry described above).

 TIP   Whoa! Sony has thrown you a curveball in this folder switching business. Note that if you are using Date Form naming, you can *create* folders using the date convention, but you can't switch among them when Date Form is active. If you *do* want to switch among folders named using the date convention, you can do it. But you have to switch from Date Form back to Standard Form. *Then* you can change to any of the available folders (of either naming format). So, if you're on that vacation, you can select Date Form, and then choose New Folder each day of your trip, if you like. But if, for some reason, you want to put some additional pictures in a different folder (say, you're revisiting a city and want the new shots to go in the same folder as those taken a few days earlier), you'll need to change to Standard Form, switch folders, and then resume shooting. Sony probably did this to preserve the "integrity" of the date/folder system, but it can be annoying.

File Settings (Movies)

Options: File Number: (Series, Reset); Series Counter Reset; File Name Format: (Standard, Title, Date+Title, Title+Date); Title Name Settings

Default: File Number: Series; File Name Format: Standard

My preference: N/A

You have four options with this movies-only entry, and I'll describe them separately.

File Number

This command functions like the File Number setting for still photos, described above. The default for the File Number item is Series (consecutive numbering), using the scheme I outlined. Or, use Reset to *automatically* set the video's file number to 0001 *each* time you format a memory card or delete all the images in a folder, or insert a different memory card. You can also reset the counter manually, as described next. Remember that if you reset automatically, you may end up with several video clips that use the same number. A solution is to use the File Name Format (described shortly), that allows you to embed a title and/or date in the filename.

Series Counter Reset

The Series Counter Reset entry can be used to *manually* reset the series counter to zero when the File Number option is set to Series. In other words, you can reset the counter to zero at any time, and the camera will then continue to use the Series option (described above) until you manually reset the next time, or change File Number to Reset to commence automatically reinitializing the numbering.

File Name Format

All the numbering and resetting options can be confusing, but Sony gives you a better way of naming your movie clips. You can embed the name (which you can choose) or both the name and date in the filename of your movie. Your options for filename format include:

- **Standard.** The movie filename begins with C, as in C0001, C0002, and so forth. You might want to use this if you don't shoot many movie clips and don't need to be able to segregate them using additional information.

- **Title.** The movie filename begins with a title you specify (as described shortly), followed by the file number. This setting makes it easy to sort your videos by title using your computer operating system's Sort feature.

- **Date+Title.** The movie filename begins with the date, followed by the title. If you're shooting several clips with the different titles, you can sort them in chronological order with this setting. Perhaps you're shooting several different subjects and need to know the order in which they were captured.

- **Title+Date.** When you're working on a project that includes several different video clips, using this filename format allows you to sort that project's movies chronologically; any additional projects will also be sorted chronologically, separate from the others.

Title Name Settings

This entry is found on the second page of the File Settings screen. It allows you to create a title used by the Date+Title and Title+Date options described above. You can enter the title using up to 37 upper/lowercase characters on an input screen similar to the one shown at right in Figure 6.11. You'll end up with a title like the one seen in Figure 6.12.

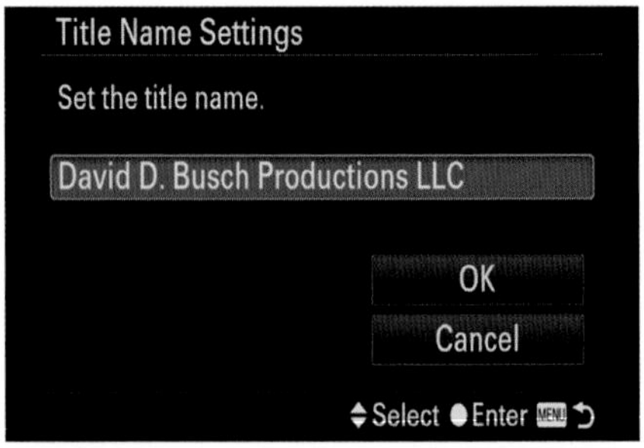

Recover Image Database

Options: Select Media, OK, Cancel

Default: Slot 1

My preference: N/A

> **Title Name Settings**
>
> Set the title name.
>
> David D. Busch Productions LLC
>
> OK
>
> Cancel
>
> ♦ Select ● Enter MENU ↩

Figure 6.12 Your title can include up to 37 characters.

The Recover Image DB function is provided in case errors crop up in the camera's database that records information about your movies. According to Sony, this situation may develop if you have processed or edited movies on a computer and then re-saved them to the memory card that's in your camera. I have never had this problem, so I'm not sure exactly what it would look like. But, if you find that your movies are not playing correctly in the camera, or the camera reports that the image database is corrupt, try this operation. Highlight this menu option and press the center button, and the camera will prompt you, "Check Image Database File?" Press the center button to confirm, or the MENU button to cancel. You may also encounter this if using a card that includes images recorded using another camera, as it will not contain a Sony image database.

Display Media Information

Options: Select Media

Default: Slot 1

My preference: N/A

This entry gives you a report of how many still images and how many movies can be recorded on the memory card that's in the camera, given the current shooting settings. This can be useful, but that information is already displayed on the screen when the camera is being used to shoot still photos (unless you have cycled to a display with less information), and the information about minutes remaining for movie recording is displayed on the screen as soon as you press the Record button. But, if you want confirmation of this information, this menu option is available.

Version

Options: None
Default: N/A
My preference: N/A

Select this menu option to display the version number of the firmware (internal operating software) installed in your camera. From time to time, Sony updates the original firmware with a newer version that adds or enhances features or corrects operational bugs. When a new version is released, it will be accompanied by instructions, which generally involve downloading the update to your computer and then connecting your camera to the computer with the USB cable to apply the update. It's a good idea to check occasionally at the Sony website, www.esupport.sony.com, to see if a new version of the camera's firmware is available for download. (You can also go to that site to download updates to the software that came with the camera, and to get general support information.)

Certification Logo (Non-US/Canada Models Only)

Options: None
Default: N/A
My preference: N/A

This information-only entry displays various certification logos indicating the camera has met specifications mandated by other countries. It's included in cameras intended for non-US/Canada sales so that the logos can be tailored for specific areas through firmware updates, rather than printed notices on the bottom of the cameras themselves.

Save/Load Settings

Options: Load, Save
Default: Load
My preference: N/A

This is the first of only two entries on the Setup 7 menu (not shown in a figure). Consider this entry an extension of the Memory Recall feature of the a7R IV. It allows you to save current camera settings to a memory card. You can save up to 10 settings, named CAMSET01 through CAMSET10, and which are always stored on the card in Slot 1. At some later time, you can load them back into the camera, and thence store them in the a7R IV's Memory Recall registers if you like. In effect, you can have many, many more stored settings than is available with the Memory Recall feature (described in Chapter 3). You could dedicate several memory cards just to store your settings, if you like. (If you use low-capacity memory cards, it would cost you very little to use them for nothing else.) Settings that can be saved are shown in Table 6.2.

There are some limitations, of course. You cannot load or save settings when the camera's mode dial is set to the 1, 2, or 3 Memory positions. In addition, there are some settings that cannot be saved (in other words, the a7R IV retains those settings even when the new ones are loaded).

TABLE 6.2 Settings That Can Be Saved

CAMERA SETTINGS 1	CAMERA SETTINGS 2	PLAYBACK MENU
MR Recall	Zoom	View Mode
MR Memory	Network	**SETUP MENU**
AF Micro Adjustments	FTP Transfer Functions	Language
White Balance: Custom 1, 2, 3	Wi-Fi Settings	Date/Time Setup
Face Registration	Edit Device Name	Area Setting
	Import Root Certificate	IPTC Information
	Security (Ipsec)	Copyright Information

Setting Reset

Options: Camera Settings Reset, Initialize
Default: N/A
My preference: N/A

If you've made a lot of changes to your camera's settings, you may want to return the features to their defaults, so you can start over without manually going back through the menus and restoring everything. This menu item lets you do that. Your choices are as follows:

- **Camera Settings Reset.** Resets the main parameters in the Camera Settings I and II menus to their default values. Your Fn settings remain.
- **Initialize.** Resets *all* Camera Settings I and II adjustments to their default settings, including the time/date and downloaded applications, but *not* including any AF Micro Adjustments or Wi-Fi settings you may have entered.

My Menu

Options: Add Item, Sort Item, Delete Item, Delete Page, Delete All
Default: None
My preference: N/A

The My Menu feature lets you create your own customized menu containing the entries you use most often, which can save you a lot of time wading through the a7R IV's many pages of menu tabs and entries. Of course, since you can create up to five My Menu screens, each with as many as five menu items, you can find you've created your own maze of entries—but, at least, it is *your* maze. Virtually any menu entry from the other main menu tabs (except for the Playback menu) and View on TV can be added to your personalized menu. The My Menu system can be handy and quick to access (if one of your My Menu pages was the one you used last, it will pop up first when you press the MENU button). But you might have used a different menu, so it would have been helpful to be able to assign My Menu to a custom key. Pay attention, Sony!

The first time you access My Menu, no custom pages will exist, so you'll see a screen similar to the one in the screen shown at left in Figure 6.13, except all the entries except Add Item will be grayed out. Press the center button, and you'll be shown a screen with a list of menu entries (see Figure 6.13, right). Use the left/right controls to scroll among available menu pages, and up/down controls to highlight a particular entry you want to add. Press the center button and you'll be given the opportunity to choose which page to add it to, numbered from 1 through 5. (See Figure 6.14, left.)

You don't need to fill up one page before starting another one. Conceivably, you could have five My Menu pages, each with a single entry. After you've created a new My Menu page, the command function page (Add, Sort, etc.) moves to the end of the line, eventually becoming Page 6 when the other five My Menu pages have been created. Each newborn My Menu page will look something like Figure 6.14 (right), but with your personal entries included. The additional options available include:

- **Sort.** Highlight a My Menu item and press the center button. You can then use the up/down controls to move it within its current menu, or the left/right controls to transport it to a different My Menu page.

- **Delete Item/Delete Page/Delete All.** Highlight an entry or page and press the center button to remove that item or page from My Menu. Delete All will remove all your My Menu items so you can start from scratch.

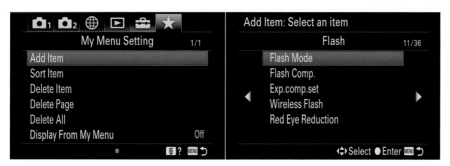

Figure 6.13 My Menu functions (left). Add an item (right).

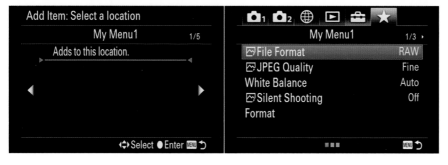

Figure 6.14 Specify a position (left). A sample My Menu page (right).

Nailing the Optimum Exposure

7

Left to its own devices, your a7R IV can do an excellent job of providing the proper exposure for most scenes. But even a camera as smart as the a7R IV frequently can benefit from intelligent input. For example, when you shoot with the main light source behind the subject, you end up with *backlighting*, which can result in an overexposed background and/or an underexposed subject. The Sony a7R IV recognizes backlit situations nicely, and, in most cases, can properly base exposure on the main subject using the default Multi metering mode, producing a decent photo.

But, as a creative photographer, there will be many instances where you would rather *not* have automatic correction for backlighting. What if you *want* to underexpose the subject, to produce a silhouette effect? The a7R IV does a poor job of exposing intentional silhouettes and will end up producing unwanted detail in what should have been inky black areas of your image. Fortunately, the camera has metering modes and other exposure options that allow you to produce the image you are looking for. If you're looking for an extensive exposure range, options like the a7R IV's built-in DRO feature can adjust your exposure as you take photos, preserving detail in the highlights and shadows as required. Your Sony a7R IV also has the capability of *fine-tuning* exposure separately for each of the metering modes, so you can consistently add or subtract a little exposure to suit your creative tastes.

In the most basic sense, exposure is all about light. Exposure can make or break your photo. Correct exposure brings out the detail in the areas you want to picture, providing the range of tones and colors you need to create the desired image. Poor exposure can cloak important details in shadow or wash them out in glare-filled featureless expanses of white.

This chapter discusses using the full range of the camera's various shooting modes and exposure controls, so you'll be better equipped to override the default settings when you want to, or need to, and achieve spot-on exposures that produce the exact image you are looking for, every time.

Getting a Handle on Exposure

You're probably well aware of the traditional "exposure triangle" of aperture (quantity of light, light passed by the lens), shutter speed (the amount of time the shutter is open), and the ISO sensitivity of the sensor—all working *proportionately* and *reciprocally* to produce an exposure. The trio is itself affected by the amount of illumination that is available to work with. So, if you double the amount of light, increase the aperture by one stop, make the shutter speed twice as long, or boost the ISO setting 2X, with any one of those changes you'll get exactly twice as much exposure. Similarly, you can *increase* any of these factors while *decreasing* one of the others by a similar amount to keep the same exposure.

Working with any of the three controls involves trade-offs. Larger f/stops provide less depth-of-field, while smaller f/stops increase depth-of-field (and potentially at the same time can *decrease* sharpness through a phenomenon called *diffraction*). Shorter shutter speeds do a better job of reducing the effects of any camera/subject motion, while longer shutter speeds make that motion blur more likely. Higher ISO settings increase the amount of visual noise and artifacts in your image, while lower ISO settings reduce the effects of noise. (See Figure 7.1.)

Exposure determines the look, feel, and tone of an image, in more ways than one. Incorrect exposure can impair even the best-composed image by cloaking important tones in darkness, or by washing them out so they become featureless to the eye. On the other hand, correct exposure brings out the detail in the areas you want to picture and provides the range of tones and colors you need to create the desired image. However, getting the perfect exposure can be tricky, because digital sensors can't capture all the tones we are able to see. If the range of tones in an image is extensive, embracing both inky black shadows and bright highlights, the sensor may not be able to capture them all. Sometimes, we must settle for an exposure that renders most of those tones—but not all—in a way that best suits the photo we want to produce. You'll often need to make choices about which details are important, and which are not, so that you can grab the tones that truly matter in your image. That's part of the creativity you bring to bear in realizing your photographic vision.

Figure 7.1 The traditional exposure triangle includes aperture, shutter speed, and ISO setting.

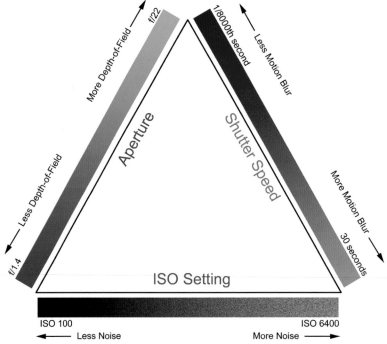

For example, look at the two bracketed exposures presented in Figure 7.2. For the image at top left, the highlights are well exposed, but everything else in the shot is seriously underexposed. The version at the top right, taken an instant later with the tripod-mounted camera, shows detail in the shadow areas, but the highlights are completely washed out. The camera's sensor simply can't capture detail in both dark areas and bright areas in a single shot. With digital camera sensors, it's tricky to capture detail in both highlights and shadows in a single image, because the number of tones, the *dynamic range* of the sensor, is limited.

One solution is to resort to a technique called High Dynamic Range (HDR) photography. I produced the image shown at the bottom of the figure by merging the two original shots using a Photoshop/Photoshop Elements feature called Merge to HDR. There are also specialized software tools like Photomatix (about $100 from www.hdrsoft.com) and HDR Efex Pro as part of the Nik Collection

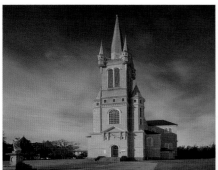
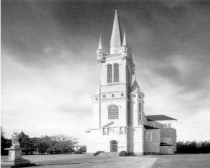

Figure 7.2 At top left, exposure for the highlights loses shadow detail. At top right, exposure for the highlights washes out the background. Bottom, combining the two exposures produces the best compromise.

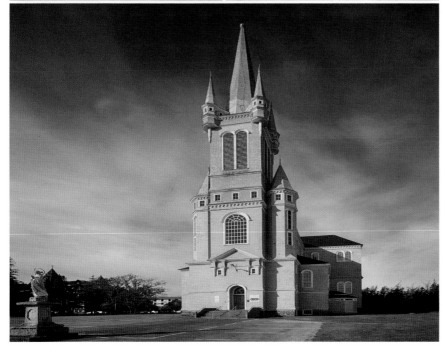

($149, but frequently discounted), formerly distributed by Google, and since 2017 available from DxO (https://nikcollection.dxo.com) or Aurora HDR ($39.95 from https://skylum.com/aurorahdr).

I'll explain more about HDR photography, and how to explore it using the bracketing features of your a7R IV later in this chapter. For now, though, I'm going to concentrate on showing you how to get the best exposures possible without resorting to such tools.

To understand exposure, you need to appreciate the aspects of light that combine to produce an image. Start with a light source—the sun, a household lamp, or the glow from a campfire—and trace its path to your camera, through the lens, and finally to the sensor that captures the illumination. Here's a brief review of the things within our control that affect exposure, listed in "chronological" order (that is, as the light moves from the subject to the sensor):

- **Light at its source.** Our eyes and our cameras—film or digital—are most sensitive to that portion of the electromagnetic spectrum we call visible light. That light has several important aspects that are relevant to photography, such as color and harshness (which is determined primarily by the apparent size of the light source as it illuminates a subject). But, in terms of exposure, the important attribute of a light source is its intensity. We may have direct control over intensity, which might be the case with an interior light that can be brightened or dimmed. Or, we might have only indirect control over intensity, as with sunlight, which can be made to appear dimmer by introducing translucent light-absorbing or reflective materials in its path.

- **Light's duration.** We tend to think of most light sources as continuous. But, as you'll learn in Chapter 13, the duration of light can change quickly enough to modify the exposure, as when the main illumination in a photograph comes from an intermittent source, such as an electronic flash.

- **Light reflected, transmitted, or emitted.** Once light is produced by its source, either continuously or in a brief burst, we are able to see and photograph objects by the light that is reflected from our subjects toward the camera lens; transmitted (say, from translucent objects that are lit from behind); or emitted (by a candle or television screen). When more or less light reaches the lens from the subject, we need to adjust the exposure. This part of the equation is under our control to the extent we can increase the amount of light falling on or passing through the subject (by adding extra light sources or using reflectors), or by pumping up the light that's emitted (by increasing the brightness of the glowing object).

- **Light passed by the lens.** Not all the illumination that reaches the front of the lens makes it all the way through. Filters can remove some of the light before it enters the lens. Inside the lens barrel is a variable-sized diaphragm that dilates and contracts to produce an aperture that controls the amount of light that enters the lens. You, or the Alpha's autoexposure system, can vary the size of the aperture to control the amount of light that will reach the sensor. The relative size of the aperture is called the f/stop. (See Figure 7.3, which is a graphic representation of the relative size of the lens opening, not an actual photo of the aperture of a lens.)

- **Light passing through the shutter.** Once light passes through the lens, the amount of time the sensor receives it is determined by the camera's shutter; this mechanism can remain open for as long as 30 seconds (or even longer if you use camera's Bulb setting) or as briefly as 1/8000th second.

■ **Light captured by the sensor.** Not all the light falling onto the sensor is captured. If the number of photons reaching a particular photosite doesn't pass a set threshold, no information is recorded. Similarly, if too much light illuminates a pixel in the sensor, then the excess isn't recorded or, worse, spills over to contaminate adjacent pixels. We can modify the minimum and maximum number of pixels that contribute to image detail by adjusting the ISO setting. At higher ISO levels, the incoming light is amplified to boost the effective sensitivity of the sensor.

F/STOPS AND SHUTTER SPEEDS

Especially if you're new to advanced cameras, it's worth quickly reviewing some essential concepts. For example, the lens aperture, or f/stop, is a ratio, much like a fraction, which is why f/2 is larger than f/4, just as 1/2 is larger than 1/4. However, f/2 is actually *four times* as large as f/4. (Think back to high school geometry where we learned that to double the area of a circle, you multiply its diameter by the square root of two: 1.4.)

The full f/stops available with an f/2 lens are f/2, f/2.8, f/4, f/5.6, f/8, f/11, f/16, and f/22. Each higher number indicates an aperture that's half the size of the previous number. Hence, it admits half as much light as the one before. Figure 7.3 shows a simplified representation. (Of course, you can also set intermediate apertures with the a7R IV, such as f/6.3 and f/7.1, which are the 1/3-stop increments between f/5.6 and f/8.)

Shutter speeds are actual fractions (of a second), so that 1/60, 1/125, 1/250, 1/500, 1/1000, and so forth represent 1/60th, 1/125th, 1/250th, 1/500th, and 1/1000th second. Each higher number indicates a shutter speed that's half as long as the one before. (And yes, intermediate shutter speeds can also be used, such as 1/640th or 1/800th second.) To avoid confusion, Sony uses quotation marks to signify long exposures: 0.8", 2", 2.5", 4", and so forth; these examples represent 0.8-second, 2-second, 2.5-second, and 4-second exposures, respectively.

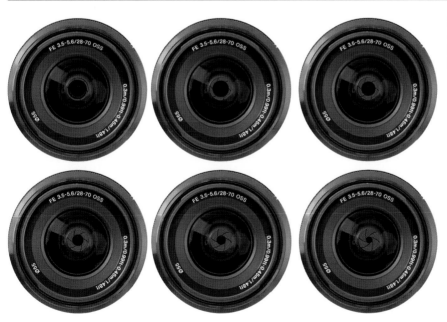

Figure 7.3 Top row (left to right): f/3.5, f/5.6, f/8; bottom row: f/11, f/16, f/22.

As we'll see however, changing any of those aspects in P, A, or S mode does not change the actual exposure; that's because the camera also makes changes when you do so, in order to maintain the same exposure. That's why Sony provides other methods for modifying the exposure in those modes.

Equivalent Exposure

One of the most important aspects in this discussion is the concept of "equivalent exposure." This term means that exactly the same amount of light will reach the sensor at various combinations of aperture and shutter speed. Whether we use a small aperture (large f/number) with a long shutter speed or a wide aperture (small f/number) with a fast shutter speed, the amount of light reaching the sensor can be exactly the same. Table 7.1 shows equivalent exposure settings using various shutter speeds and f/stops; in other words, any of the combination of settings listed will produce exactly the same exposure.

TABLE 7.1 EQUIVALENT EXPOSURES

SHUTTER SPEED	F/STOP	SHUTTER SPEED	F/STOP
1/30th second	f/22	1/1000th second	f/4
1/60th second	f/16	1/2000th second	f/2.8
1/125th second	f/11	1/4000th second	f/2
1/200th second	f/8	1/8000th second	f/1.4
1/500th second	f/5.6		

When you set the camera to P mode, it sets both the aperture and the shutter speed that should provide a correct exposure, based on guidance from the light metering system. In P mode, you cannot change the aperture or the shutter speed individually, but you can shift among various aperture/shutter speed combinations by rotating the rear dial, providing what is called *program shift*. (If you use program shift, an asterisk will appear next to the P on your display screens to let you know you've made an adjustment.) If you change the ISO, the camera will set a different combination automatically. As the concept of equivalent exposure indicates, the image brightness will be exactly the same in every photo you shoot with the various combinations because they all provide the same exposure.

In Aperture Priority (A) and Shutter Priority (S) modes, you can change the aperture or the shutter speed, respectively. The camera will then change the other factor to maintain the same exposure. I'll cover all of the operating modes and the important aspects of exposure with each mode in this chapter.

F/STOPS VERSUS STOPS

In photography parlance, *f/stop* always means the aperture or lens opening. However, for lack of a current commonly used word for one exposure increment, the term *stop* is often used. In the past, EV (Exposure Value) served this purpose, and was used as a measure of the total sensitivity range of a device such as a light meter, but exposure value and its abbreviation have since been inextricably intertwined with its use in describing exposure compensation. In this book, when I say "stop" by itself (no *f/*), I mean one whole unit of exposure, and am not necessarily referring to an actual f/stop or lens aperture. So, adjusting the exposure by "one stop" can mean changing to the next shutter speed increment (say, from 1/125th second to 1/200th second) or the next aperture (such as f/4 to f/5.6). Similarly, 1/3-stop or 1/2-stop increments can mean either shutter speed or aperture changes, depending on the context. Be forewarned.

How the a7R IV Calculates Exposure

Your camera calculates exposure by measuring the light that passes through the lens and reaches the sensor, based on the assumption that each area being measured reflects about the same amount of light as a neutral gray card that reflects a "middle" gray of about 12 to 18 percent reflectance. (The photographic "gray cards" you buy at a camera store have an 18 percent gray tone; your camera is calibrated to interpret a somewhat lighter 12 percent gray. I'll explain more about this later.) That "average" 12 to 18 percent gray assumption is necessary, because different subjects reflect different amounts of light. In a photo containing, say, a white cat and a dark gray cat, the white cat might reflect five times as much light as the gray cat. An exposure based on the white cat will cause the gray cat to appear to be black, while an exposure based only on the gray cat will make the white cat appear washed out.

This is more easily understood if you look at some photos of subjects that are dark (they reflect little light), those that have predominantly middle tones, and subjects that are highly reflective. I'm not going to use actual cats but, rather, will include a more human figure in the frame (which is more common, unless you're a cat photographer), accompanied by a card with a trio of gray reference patches. The next figure shows what you would end up with if you exposed a set of photographs using a different gray patch for each.

Correctly Exposed

The image shown in Figure 7.4, left, represents how a photograph might appear if you inserted the patches shown at bottom left into the scene, and then calculated exposure by measuring the light reflecting from the middle gray patch, which, for the sake of illustration, we'll assume reflects approximately 12 to 18 percent of the light that strikes it. The exposure meter in the camera sees an object that it thinks is a middle gray (the middle patch), calculates an exposure based on that, and the patch in the center of the strip is rendered at its proper tonal value. Best of all, because the resulting exposure is correct, the black patch at left and white patch at right are rendered properly as well.

Figure 7.4 Exposure based on the middle-gray tone in the center of the card is accurate (left). Metering the black square, the black patch looks gray, the gray patch appears to be a light gray, and the white square is seriously over-exposed (center). With exposure calculated from the white patch, the photo is underexposed (right).

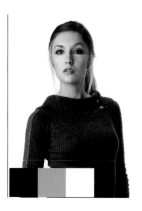 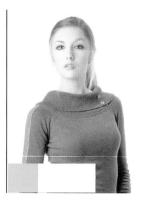 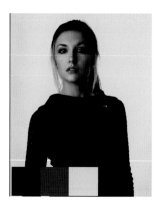

When you're shooting pictures with your a7R IV camera, and the meter happens to base its exposure on a subject that averages that "ideal" middle gray, then you'll end up with similar (accurate) results. The camera's exposure algorithms are concocted to ensure this kind of result as often as possible, barring any unusual subjects (that is, those that are backlit, or have uneven illumination). The camera has five different metering modes (described in an upcoming section), each of which is equipped to handle certain types of unusual subjects, as I'll outline.

Overexposed

Figure 7.4, center, shows what would happen if the exposure were calculated based on metering the leftmost, black patch, which is roughly the same tonal value of the darkest areas of the subject's hair. The light meter sees less light reflecting from the black square than it would see from a gray middle-tone subject, and so figures, "Aha! I need to add exposure to brighten this subject up to a middle gray!" That lightens the "black" patch, so it now appears to be gray.

But now the patch in the middle that was *originally* middle gray is overexposed and becomes light gray. And the white square at right is now seriously overexposed and loses detail in the highlights, which have become a featureless white. Our human subject is similarly overexposed. You should always be *aware* when overexposure occurs but note that it's not *always* a bad thing. Some slight overexposures add a dreamy look to an image; once you know how the rules are derived, you'll know how and when to break them.

Underexposed

The third possibility in this simplified scenario is that the light meter might measure the illumination bouncing off the white patch and try to render *that* tone as a middle gray. A lot of light is reflected by the white square, so the exposure is *reduced*, bringing that patch closer to a middle gray tone. The patches that were originally gray and black are now rendered too dark. Clearly, measuring the gray card—or a substitute that reflects about the same amount of light—is the only way to ensure that the exposure is precisely correct. (See Figure 7.4, right.)

As you can see, the ideal way to measure exposure is to meter from a subject that reflects 12 to 18 percent of the light that reaches it. If you want the most precise exposure calculations, the solution is to use a stand-in, such as the evenly illuminated gray card I mentioned earlier. But, because the standard Kodak gray card reflects 18 percent of the light that reaches it and, as I said, your camera is calibrated for a somewhat lighter 12 percent tone, you would need to add about one-half stop *more* exposure than the value metered from the card. Of course, in most situations, it's not necessary to do this. Your camera's light meter will do a good job of calculating the right exposure, especially if you use the exposure tips in the next section. But, I felt that explaining exactly what is going on during exposure calculation would help you understand how your camera's metering system works.

In some very bright scenes (like a snowy landscape or a lava field), you won't have a mid-tone to meter. Another substitute for a gray card is the palm of a human hand (the backside of the hand is too variable). But a human palm, regardless of ethnic group, is even brighter than a standard gray card, so instead of one-half stop more exposure, you need to add one additional stop. That is, if your meter reading is 1/500th of a second at f/11, use 1/500th second at f/8 or 1/200th second at f/11 instead. (Both exposures are equivalent.)

Or, you might want to resort to using an evenly illuminated gray card mentioned earlier. Small versions are available that can be tucked in a camera bag. Place it in your frame near your main subject, facing the camera, and with the exact same even illumination falling on it that is falling on your subject. Then, use the Spot metering function (described in the next section) to calculate exposure.

In serious photography, you'll want to choose the *metering mode* (the pattern that determines how brightness is evaluated) and the *exposure mode* (determines how the appropriate shutter speed and aperture is set). I'll describe both aspects in later sections.

ORIGIN OF THE 18 PERCENT "MYTH"

Why are so many photographers under the impression that camera light meters are calibrated to the 18 percent "standard," rather than the true value, which may be 12 to 14 percent, depending on the vendor? You'll find this misinformation in an alarming number of places. I've seen the 18 percent "myth" taught in camera classes; I've found it in books, and even been given this wrong information from the technical staff of camera vendors. (They should know better—the same vendors' engineers who design and calibrate the cameras have the right figure.)

The most common explanation is that during a revision of Kodak's instructions for its gray cards in 1977, the advice to open up an extra half stop was omitted, and a whole generation of shooters grew up thinking that a measurement off a gray card could be used as-is. Kodak restored the proviso in 1997 during the next update of the instructions but by then it was too late.

EXTERNAL METERS CAN BE CALIBRATED

The light meters built into your camera are calibrated at the factory. But if you use a hand-held incident or reflective light meter, you *can* calibrate it, using the instructions supplied with your meter. Because a hand-held meter *can* be calibrated to the 18 percent gray standard (or any other value you choose), my rant about the myth of the 18 percent gray card doesn't apply.

The Importance of ISO

Another essential concept when discussing exposure, ISO control allows you to change the sensitivity of the camera's imaging sensor. Sometimes photographers forget about this option, because the common practice is to set the ISO once for a particular shooting session (say, at ISO 100 or 200 for bright sunlight outdoors, or ISO 800 or 1600 when shooting indoors) and then forget about ISO. Or some shooters simply leave the camera set to ISO Auto. That enables the camera to change the ISO it deems necessary, setting a low ISO in bright conditions or a higher ISO in a darker location. That's fine, but sometimes you'll want to set a specific ISO yourself. That will be essential sometimes, since ISO Auto cannot set the highest ISO levels that are available when you use manual ISO selection. Indeed, when shooting movies, only ISO settings from ISO 200 to ISO 32000 can be set.

 TIP When shooting in the Program (P), Aperture Priority (A), and Shutter Priority (S) modes, all discussed soon, changing the ISO does not change the exposure. If you switch from using ISO 100 to ISO 1600 in A mode, for example, the camera will simply set a different shutter speed. If you change the ISO in S mode, the camera will set a different aperture, and in P mode, it will set a different aperture and/or shutter speed. In all of these examples, the camera will maintain the same exposure. If you want to make a brighter or a darker photo in P, A, or S mode, you would need to set + or – exposure compensation, as discussed later.

However, when you use the Manual (M) mode, changing the ISO also changes the exposure, as discussed shortly.

The camera provides the best possible image quality in the ISO 50 to 400 range. We use higher ISO levels such as ISO 1600 in low light and ISO 6400 in a very dark location because it allows us to shoot at a faster shutter speed. That's often useful for minimizing the risk of blurring caused by camera shake, which can occur even with 5-axis image stabilization in the camera body and optical image stabilization (OSS) built into many lenses. And, of course, you must also contend with movement of the subject, which no amount of image stabilization will fix.

Although you can set a desired ISO level yourself, the a7R IV also offers an ISO Auto option. When enabled, the camera will select an ISO that should be suitable for the conditions: a low ISO on a sunny day and a high ISO in a dark location. In Intelligent Auto, ISO Auto is the only available option. Over the past few years, there has been something of a competition among the manufacturers of digital cameras to achieve the highest ISO ratings. The highest announced ISO numbers have been rising annually, from 1600 to 3200 and 6400; a few cameras even allow you to choose a sensitivity setting that tops 1.6 *million*. Sony is a bit more conservative, but the a7R IV offers all of the ISO options you're ever likely to need, up to 104200. Obviously, the loftiest numbers come at the cost of increased contrast and grain.

Choosing a Metering Method

The Sony a7R IV has five different schemes for evaluating the light received by its exposure sensors. The quickest way to choose among them is to assign Metering Mode to a key using the Custom Key settings in the Camera Settings II-09 menu, as described in Chapter 4. Then, you can press the defined key to produce the Metering Mode screen; then scroll up/down among the options. Without a custom key, the default method for choosing a metering mode is to use the Camera Settings II-09 (Exposure 1) setting (see Figure 7.5), the Function menu, or the Quick Navi menu.

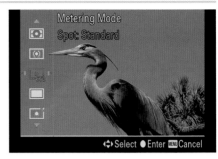

Figure 7.5 The a7R IV cameras provide five options for metering mode: Multi (the default), Center, Spot, Entire Screen Averaging, and Highlight (left, top to bottom).

Multi Metering

In this "intelligent" (multi-segment) metering mode, the a7R IV measures the illumination falling on all the pixels in the sensor, but slices up the frame into 1,200 different zones, as shown at left in Figure 7.6. The camera evaluates the measurements to make an educated guess about what kind of picture you're taking, based on examination of exposure data derived from thousands of different real-world photos. For example, if the top section of a picture is much lighter than the bottom portions, the algorithm can assume that the scene is a landscape photo with lots of sky. This mode is the best all-purpose metering method for most pictures. A typical scene suitable for Multi metering is shown at right in Figure 7.6.

The Multi system can recognize individual elements in a very bright scene and it can automatically increase the exposure to reduce the risk of a dark photo. This will be useful when your subject is a snow-covered landscape or a close-up of a bride in white. Granted, you may occasionally need to use a bit of exposure compensation, but often, the exposure will be close to accurate even without it. (In my experience, the Multi system is most successful with light-toned scenes on bright days. When shooting in dark, overcast conditions, it's more likely to underexpose a scene of that type.)

Multi-segment metering is especially suitable for people. If you activate Face Priority in Multi Metering in the Camera Settings I-09 (Exposure 1) menu, the a7R IV will use any detected faces to calculate exposure. The 61MP sensor has enough resolution to allow detecting eyes, noses, and mouths, and thus confirm to its satisfaction that humans are in the photo (and contain detail that

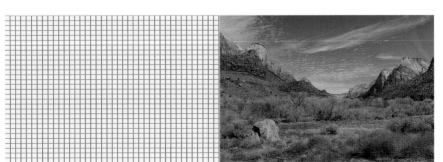

Figure 7.6 Multi metering uses 1,200 zones and is suitable for complex scenes like this one.

should be preserved, possibly at the expense of other areas, such as sky or background). If human faces are also located within the current autofocus area, the a7R IV will consistently try to preserve detail in those faces. You can disable face detection if you're shooting landscapes.

The Multi metering mode is best for most general subjects, because it can intelligently analyze a scene and make an excellent guess of what kind of subject you're shooting a great deal of the time. The camera can tell the difference between low-contrast and high-contrast subjects by looking at the range of differences in brightness across the scene. Because the a7R IV has a fairly good idea about what kind of subject matter you are shooting, it can underexpose slightly when appropriate to pre-serve highlight detail when image contrast is high. (It's often possible to pull detail out of shadows that are too dark using an image editor, but once highlights are converted to white pixels, they are gone forever.)

Center-weighted Metering

This (center-weighted) metering was the only available option with cameras some decades ago. In this mode you get conventional metering without any "intelligent" scene evaluation. The light meter considers brightness in the entire frame but places the greatest emphasis on a large area in the center of the frame, as shown at left in Figure 7.7, on the theory that, for most pictures, the main subject will not be located far off-center.

Of course, Center metering is most effective when the subject in the central area is a mid-tone. Even then, if your main subject is surrounded by large, extremely bright or very dark areas, the exposure might not be exactly right. (You might need to use exposure compensation, a feature discussed shortly.) However, this scheme works well in many situations if you don't want to use one of the other modes for scenes like the one shown at right in Figure 7.7.

Spot Metering

This mode confines the reading to a very small area in the center of the image, as shown at left in Figure 7.8. When Spot is highlighted, you can press the left/right controls to choose from a standard-size spot, or a larger one.

By default, the spot is located in the center of the frame, unless you use the Spot Metering Point entry of the Camera Settings I-09 (Exposure 1) menu to link it to the current focus area. However, when you use the Flexible Spot or Expand Flexible Spot focus area options, the spot metering will *always* be at the area where the camera sets focus. So, you have the option of linking the exposure spot to the focus area *all* of the time, or only when using the two Flexible Spot settings.

The Spot meter does not apply any "intelligent" scene evaluation. Because the camera considers only a small target area, and completely ignores its surroundings, Spot metering is most useful when the subject is a small mid-tone area. For example, the "target" might be a tanned face, a medium red blossom, or a gray rock in a wide-angle photo; each of these is a mid-tone.

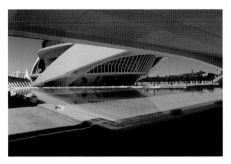

Figure 7.7 Center-weighted metering calculates exposure based on the full frame but emphasizes the center area.

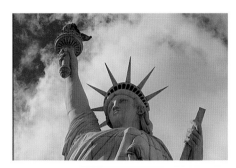

Figure 7.8 Spot metering calculates exposure based on a spot that's only a small percentage of the image area, such as this statue's face.

The Spot metering technique is simple if you want to Spot meter a small area that's dead center in the frame. If the "target" is off-center, you would need to point the lens at it and use the AE Lock technique discussed later in this chapter. (Lock exposure on your target before re-framing for a better composition so the exposure does not change.) For Figure 7.8, right, Spot metering was used to base the exposure on the Statue of Liberty's face.

If you Spot meter a light-toned area or a dark-toned area, you will get underexposure or overexposure, respectively; you would need to use an override for more accurate results. On the other hand, you can Spot meter a small mid-tone subject surrounded by a sky with big white clouds or by an indigo blue wall and get a good exposure. (The light meter ignores the subject's surroundings so they do not affect the exposure.) That would not be possible with Center-weighted metering, which considers brightness in a much larger area.

Entire Screen Averaging

This option tells the a7R IV to simply measure all the illumination in the frame and calculate exposure based on the average value. (See Figure 7.9, left.) That may not lead to the optimal exposure for an image (if some large very bright or very dark areas are present), but it does have one advantage: because only the average reflectance is used, the exposure will not change as your subjects move around in the frame. The woman's hands shown at right in Figure 7.9 darted back and forth as she worked, but the exposure remained constant for several successive images.

Figure 7.9 When using Entire Screen Averaging, the exposure will not change if a subject, such as this artisan's fast-moving hands, moves within the frame.

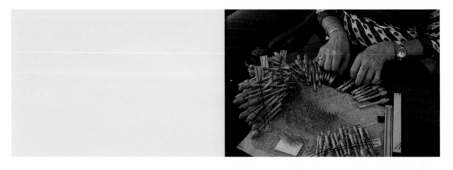

Figure 7.10 Highlight-weighted metering will help avoid overexposure of subjects surrounded by dark areas.

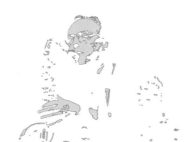

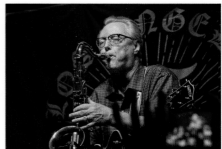

Highlight-weighted Metering

This choice pays special attention to the highlights of an image. Figure 7.10, left, doesn't really show the active metering area, but is a graphical representation of what areas are most important in the photo at right in the figure. If your subject is surrounded by very dark areas, this metering method will help avoid overexposure.

Highlight metering is *not* a spot metering mode, despite its icon, which is the same as the Spot icon, with an asterisk added. With this mode, the camera's Exmor processor seeks out highlight areas of your image and bases exposure on a setting that will keep those highlights from being overexposed. Less emphasis ("weight") is given to non-highlight areas.

So, if you're shooting spotlit performers on-stage at a concert or play, the a7R IV can calculate the correct exposure using the performers, and ignoring, for the most part, the dark surroundings. You'd have your choice of measuring exposure in Spot mode, as described in the previous section, placing the metering spot on the performer's face or shirt, or, you could select Highlight-weighted metering and allow the camera to identify the performer when figuring exposure. Your results might be similar with either, depending on how well you "placed" the Spot area and how cleverly the a7R IV sorts out your subject from the background. I tend to use Spot mode when the area I want to meter is clearly defined, and Highlight-weighted when there is a range of highlights.

> **INSTANT SWITCHING**
>
> If you frequently use one metering method, but occasionally like to switch to another method on the fly, you can redefine one of the a7R IV's custom keys to change to your alternate mode at the press of a button, using the Custom Keys feature I explained in Chapter 4.
>
> The really cool thing is that you can define one button for, say, Center-weighted metering, another one for Spot metering, and then set the main metering mode switch to Matrix, and thus be able to switch among those on a whim. I've done this as a way to compare the exposure settings of the metering methods while composing a single image in the viewfinder. I've also found the capability useful when I'm, say, working with Multi metering and want to zero in on a particular area of the frame temporarily using Spot metering.

Choosing an Exposure Mode

After you set a desired metering mode, you have several methods for choosing the appropriate shutter speed and aperture, semi-automatically or manually. Just press the mode dial's center lock button and spin the mode dial to the exposure mode that you want to use. Your choice of which is best for a given shooting situation will depend on aspects like your need for extensive or shallow depth-of-field (the range of acceptably sharp focus in a photo) or the desire to freeze action or to allow motion blur. The semi-automatic Aperture Priority and Shutter Priority modes discussed in the next section emphasize one aspect of image capture or another, but the following sections introduce you to all four of the modes that photographers often call "creative."

Aperture Priority (A) Mode

When using the A mode, you specify the lens opening (aperture or f/stop) with the front or rear dial. After you do so, the camera (guided by its light meter) will set a suitable shutter speed considering the aperture and the ISO in use. If you change the aperture, from f/5.6 to f/11, for example, the camera will automatically set a longer shutter speed to maintain the same exposure, using guidance from the built-in light meter. (I discussed the concept of equivalent exposure earlier and provided the equivalent exposure chart.)

Aperture Priority is especially useful when you want to use a particular lens opening to achieve a desired effect. Perhaps you'd like to use the smallest aperture (such as f/22) to maximize depth-of-field (DOF), to keep the entire subject sharp in a close-up picture. Or, you might want to use a large aperture (small f/number like f/4) to throw everything except your main subject out of focus, as in Figure 7.11. Maybe you'd just like to "lock in" a particular f/stop, such as f/8, because it allows your lens to provide the best optical quality. Or, you might prefer to use f/2.8 with a lens that has a maximum aperture of f/1.4, because you want the best compromise between shutter speed and optical quality.

Aperture Priority can even be used to specify a *range* of shutter speeds you want to use under varying lighting conditions, which seems almost contradictory. But think about it. You're shooting a soccer game outdoors with a telephoto and want a relatively fast shutter speed, but you don't care if

Figure 7.11 Use Aperture Priority mode to "lock in" a wide aperture (denoted by a large f/number) when you want to blur the background.

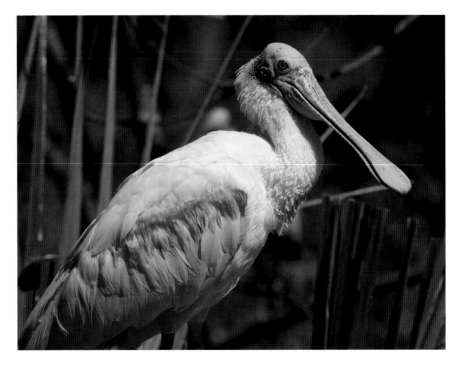

the speed changes a little should the sun duck behind a cloud. Set your camera's shooting mode to A, and adjust the aperture using the front or rear dial until a shutter speed of, say, 1/1000th second is selected at the ISO level that you're using. (In bright sunlight at ISO 400, that aperture is likely to be around f/11.) Then, go ahead and shoot, knowing that your a7R IV will maintain that f/11 aperture (for sufficient DOF as the soccer players move about the field) but will drop down to 1/800th or 1/500th second if necessary should a light cloud cover part of the sun.

When the camera cannot provide a good exposure at the aperture you have set, the shutter speed numeral will blink. That indicator warns that the camera is unable to find an appropriate shutter speed at the aperture you have set, considering the ISO level in use and over- or underexposure will occur. That's the major pitfall of using Aperture Priority: you might select an f/stop that is too small or too large to allow an optimal exposure with the available shutter speeds.

Here are a couple of examples where you might encounter a problem. Let's say you set an aperture of f/2.8 while using ISO 400 on an extremely bright day (perhaps at the beach or in snow); in this situation, even your camera's fastest shutter speed might not be able to cut down the amount of light reaching the sensor to provide the right exposure. (The solution here is to set a lower ISO or a smaller aperture, or both, until the blinking stops.) Or, let's say you have set f/16 in a dark arena while using ISO 100; the camera cannot find a shutter speed long enough to provide a correct exposure so your photo will be underexposed. (In low light, the solution is to manually set a higher ISO or a wider aperture, or both, until the orange shutter speed indicator turns white again.) Aperture Priority is best used by those with a bit of experience in choosing settings. Many seasoned photographers leave their camera set on Aperture Priority all the time.

When to use Aperture Priority:

- **General landscape photography.** The a7R IV is a great camera for landscape photography, of course, because its high resolution allows making huge, gorgeous prints, as well as smaller prints that are filled with eye-popping detail. Aperture Priority is a good tool for ensuring that your landscape is sharp from foreground to infinity, if you select an f/stop that provides maximum depth-of-field.

  If you use A mode and select an aperture like f/11 or f/16, it's your responsibility to make sure the shutter speed selected is fast enough to avoid losing detail to camera shake, or that the a7R IV is mounted on a tripod. One thing that new landscape photographers fail to account for is the movement of distant leaves and tree branches. When seeking the ultimate in sharpness, go ahead and use Aperture Priority, but boost ISO sensitivity a bit, if necessary, to provide a sufficiently fast shutter speed, whether shooting hand-held or with a tripod.

- **Specific landscape situations.** Aperture Priority is also useful when you have no objection to using a long shutter speed, or, particularly, *want* the a7R IV to select one. Waterfalls are a perfect example. You can use A mode, set your camera to ISO 100, use a small f/stop, and let the camera select a longer shutter speed that will allow the water to blur as it flows. Indeed, you might need to use a neutral-density filter to get a sufficiently long shutter speed. But Aperture-priority mode is a good start.

- **Portrait photography.** Portraits are the most common applications of selective focus. A medium-large aperture (say, f/5.6 or f/8) with a longer lens/zoom setting (in the 85mm-135mm range) will allow the background behind your portrait subject to blur. A *very* large aperture (I frequently shoot wide open with my 85mm f/1.8 lens) lets you apply selective focus to your subject's *face*. With a three-quarters view of your subject, as long as her eyes are sharp, it's okay if the far ear or her hair is out of focus.

- **When you want to ensure optimal sharpness** All lenses have an aperture or two at which they perform best, providing the level of sharpness you expect. That's usually about two stops down from wide open, and thus will vary depending on the maximum aperture of the lens. My 85mm f/1.8 is good wide open, but it's even sharper at f/2.8 or f/4; I shoot my 70-200mm f/4 wide open at concerts, but, if I can use f/5.6 instead, I'll get better results. A relatively slow lens with, say, an f/5.6 maximum aperture at the telephoto end, really needs to be set at f/11 if I crank it out to its maximum focal length. Aperture Priority allows me to use each lens at its very best f/stop.

- **Close-up/Macro photography** Depth-of-field is typically very shallow when shooting macro photos, and you'll want to choose your f/stop carefully. Perhaps you might want to use a wider stop to emphasize your subject. Or, you might need the smallest aperture you can get away with to maximize depth-of-field. Aperture Priority mode comes in very useful when shooting close-up pictures. Because macro work is frequently done with the camera mounted on a tripod, and your close-up subjects, if not living creatures, may not be moving much, a longer shutter speed isn't a problem. Aperture Priority can be your preferred choice.

Shutter Priority (S) Mode

Shutter Priority is the inverse of Aperture Priority. You set the shutter speed you'd like, using the front or rear dial, and the camera sets an appropriate f/stop considering the ISO that's in use. When you change the shutter speed, the camera will change the aperture to maintain the same (equivalent) exposure using guidance from the built-in light meter. Shutter Priority mode gives you some control over how much action-freezing capability your digital camera brings to bear in a particular situation. In other cases, you might want to use a slow shutter speed to add some blur to a sports photo that would be mundane if the action were completely frozen (see Figure 7.12).

Take care when using a slow shutter speed such as 1/8th second, because you'll potentially get blurring from camera shake unless you're using a tripod or other firm support. Of course, this applies to any mode, but in most modes the camera displays a blinking camera shake warning icon when the shutter speed is long. That indicator does not blink in S mode, however, perhaps because Sony assumes that users of Shutter Priority are aware of the potential problem caused by camera shake. The in-body 5-axis image stabilization and SteadyShot stabilizer in OSS-designated lenses are useful but they cannot work miracles.

As in Aperture Priority, you can encounter a problem in Shutter Priority mode; this happens when you select a shutter speed that's too long or too short for correct exposure under certain conditions. I've shot outdoor soccer games on sunny fall evenings and used Shutter Priority mode to lock in a 1/1000th second shutter speed, only to find that my camera refused to produce the correct exposure when the sun dipped behind some trees and there was no longer enough light to shoot at that speed, even with the lens wide open.

In cases where you have set an inappropriate shutter speed, the aperture numeral will blink. When might this happen? Let's say you set 1/15th second shutter speed while using ISO 400 on that extremely bright day; in this situation, even the smallest aperture available with your lens might not

Figure 7.12 Set a slow shutter speed when you want to introduce blur into an action shot, as with this panned image of a base runner.

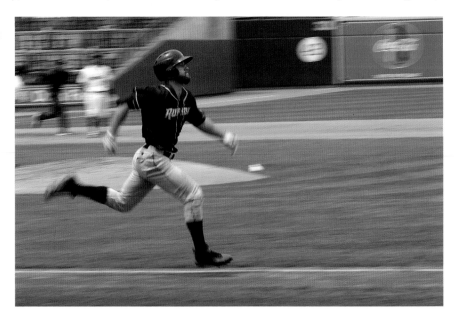

be able to cut down the amount of light reaching the sensor to provide a correct exposure. (The solution here is to set a lower ISO or a faster shutter speed, or both, until the blinking stops.) Or, let's say you have set 1/250th second in the arena while using ISO 100; your lens does not offer an aperture that's wide enough to enable the camera to provide a good exposure so you'll get the blinking and your photo will be underexposed. (In low light, the solution is to set a higher ISO or a longer shutter speed, or both, until the blinking stops.)

When to use Shutter Priority:

- **To reduce blur from subject motion.** Set the shutter speed of the a7R IV to a higher value to reduce the amount of blur from subjects that are moving. The exact speed will vary depending on how fast your subject is moving and how much blur is acceptable. You might want to freeze a basketball player in mid-dunk with a 1/1000th second shutter speed or use 1/200th second to allow the spinning wheels of a motocross racer to blur a tiny bit to add the feeling of motion.

- **To add blur from subject motion.** There are times when you want a subject to blur, say, when shooting waterfalls with the camera set for a one- or two-second exposure in Shutter Priority mode.

- **To add blur from camera motion when *you* are moving.** Say you're panning to follow a base runner. You might want to use Shutter Priority mode and set the a7R IV for 1/60th second, so that the background will blur as you pan. The shutter speed will be fast enough to provide a sharp image of the athlete, as shown in Figure 7.12.

- **To reduce blur from camera motion when *you* are moving.** In other situations, the camera may be in motion, say, because you're shooting from a moving train or auto, and you want to minimize the amount of blur caused by the motion of the camera. Shutter-priority is a good choice here, too.

- **Landscape photography hand-held.** If you can't use a tripod for your landscape shots, you'll still probably want the sharpest image possible. Shutter-priority can allow you to specify a shutter speed that's fast enough to reduce or eliminate the effects of camera shake. Just make sure that your ISO setting is high enough that the a7R IV will select an aperture with sufficient depth-of-field, too.

- **Concerts, stage performances.** I shoot a lot of concerts with my 70-200mm f/4 lens, and have discovered that, when vibration reduction is taken into account, a shutter speed of 1/160th second is fast enough to eliminate camera shake that can result from hand-holding the camera with this lens, and also to avoid blur from the movement of all but the most energetic performers. I use Shutter-priority and set the ISO so the camera will select an aperture in the f/4–5.6 range.

Program Auto (P) Mode

The Program mode uses the camera's built-in smarts to set an aperture/shutter speed combination, based on information provided by the light meter. If you're using Multi metering, the combination will often provide a good exposure. Rotate the front or rear dial and you can switch to other aperture/shutter speed combinations, all providing the same (equivalent) exposure. The P on the screen changes to P*. You can't use Program Shift when working with flash. To reverse Program Shift, change to another exposure mode (you can immediately switch back to P mode) or turn the camera off.

In the unlikely event that the correct exposure cannot be achieved with the wide range of shutter speeds and apertures available, the shutter speed and aperture will both blink. (The solution is to set a lower ISO in bright light and a higher ISO in dark locations until the blinking stops.) The P mode is the one to use when you want to rely on the camera to make reasonable basic settings of shutter speed and aperture, but you want to retain the ability to adjust many of the camera's settings yourself. All overrides and important functions are available, including ISO, white balance, metering mode, exposure compensation, and others.

When to use Program mode:

- **When you're in a hurry to get a grab shot.** The a7R IV will do a pretty good job of calculating an appropriate exposure for you, without any input from you.
- **When you hand your camera to a novice.** Set the a7R IV to P, hand the camera to your friend, relative, or *trustworthy* stranger you meet in front of the Eiffel Tower, point to the shutter release button and viewfinder, and say, "Look through here, and press this button."
- **When no special shutter speed or aperture settings are needed.** If your subject doesn't require special anti- or pro-blur techniques, and depth-of-field or selective focus aren't important, use P as a general-purpose setting. You can still make adjustments to increase/decrease depth-of-field or add/reduce motion blur with a minimum of fuss.

Making Exposure Value Changes

Sometimes you'll want a brighter or darker photo (more or less exposure) than you got when relying on the camera's metering system. Perhaps you want to underexpose to create a silhouette effect or overexpose to produce a high-key (very light) effect. It's easy to do so by using the a7R IV's exposure compensation features, available only in P, S, A, M, Panorama, and Movie modes. There are several ways to set exposure compensation:

- **Exposure compensation dial.** This dial, located at the right end of the top surface of the camera, is the fastest method for adding/subtracting exposure. It can be rotated to provide plus or minus three stops of exposure in one-third stop increments. Only plus/minus 2 stops are available when using Movie mode.

  In Manual exposure mode, exposure compensation can be dialed in only when ISO Auto is activated, as the camera will leave your shutter speed and aperture settings undisturbed and add or subtract exposure by changing ISO sensitivity instead. The exposure compensation dial can be locked/unlocked by pressing the button in its center. When unlocked, you can easily spin it with your thumb while shooting. However, the dial has click detents and is not likely to rotate accidentally, so you may only want to lock it when you absolutely don't want the setting to change accidentally.

  Note: When you set exposure compensation using this physical dial, it overrides and cancels any EV settings you make using the three optional methods described next. See the section "Which EV Method?" for a more detailed description.

- **Exposure Compensation menu.** If you want additional exposure compensation, venture to the Camera Settings I-09 (Exposure 1) menu, where the Exposure Comp. entry will let you set plus or minus five stops of exposure using the front or rear dials or control wheel. This option is not available if you've made a setting with the exposure compensation dial; its menu entry will be grayed out.

- **Function menu.** Unless you've redefined your Function menu to remove it, exposure compensation can also be applied by pressing the Fn button. The exposure compensation entry's default position is at the far right of the top row of functions. The Function menu entry also lets you choose up to five stops of compensation. **Note:** the Quick Navi screen can be used only to set Flash Exposure Compensation.

- **Define a key.** If you like, you can define a key as your exposure compensation button, using the Custom Keys feature described in Chapter 4. When I feel I am going to be making many exposure compensation settings, I define the down directional button as the exposure compensation button. Then, I can press the down button and rotate the control wheel to make quick adjustments.

Which EV Method?

The relationship between the EV dial and the menu/custom key options for setting exposure compensation can be tricky until you learn how it works. Here's a quick summary.

- **When to use the EV dial.** Using the EV dial has its advantages and disadvantages:
  - **Speed.** If you find you need to add or subtract exposure in a hurry, the EV dial is very fast. You can completely avoid a dive into the slower menu system. The EV dial overrides and *cancels* any EV setting you've made using the menu settings. (So when you return the dial to the zero position, any previous EV changes you've entered from the menus are changed to zero as well.)
  - **Accessibility.** The EV dial is easy to find and spin in the dark, when you're wearing gloves, or otherwise want to avoid locating buttons and navigation controls.
  - **Limited Range.** You can only change EV settings within a range of +/- 3 stops. In most cases, however, that will be sufficient.
  - **Sticky.** EV settings you've dialed in are always sticky. They are not cancelled when you power down the camera. That can be an advantage if you want to retain your settings over an extended shooting session, or a disadvantage when you forget to return the dial to zero when the EV adjustment is no longer need.
- **When to set EV with menus.** Here are some advantages of using the menus for EV:
  - **Longer range.** The Function menu and the Exposure Compensation setting in the Camera Settings I-09 menu each allow you to make adjustments of +/- 5 stops. You might need this range when shooting a set of images for later merging using high dynamic range (HDR) processing, or when you want to seriously over- or underexpose images in creative ways.
  - **Set/Forget Options.** Menu settings for Exposure Compensation can be sticky, or not, at your discretion. If you tend to forget to zero out your adjustments at the end of a session, select On for Reset EV Compensation in the Camera Settings 1 (Exposure) menu, and your setting will be canceled as soon as you power off your a7R IV. However, that automatic reset means you *shouldn't* turn your camera off until you are finished using your current settings. If you'll be powering down the camera during a session, either disable automatic reset or use the EV dial.

In my experience, adding exposure compensation is the option that's most often necessary. I'll often set +2/3 when using Multi metering if the camera underexposed my first photo of a light-toned scene. With Center-weighted or Spot metering, +1.3 or an even higher level of plus compensation is almost always necessary with a light-toned subject. Since the camera provides a live preview of the scene (when Setting Effect is turned on), it's easy to predict when the photo you'll take is likely to be obviously over- or underexposed. When the histogram display is on, you can make a more accurate prediction about the exposure; I'll discuss this feature shortly. Of course, you can also use plus compensation when you want to intentionally overexpose a scene for a creative effect.

You won't often need to use minus compensation. This feature is most likely to be useful when metering a dark-toned subject, such as close-ups of black animals or dark blue buildings, for example. Since these dark-toned subjects lead the camera to overexpose, set –2/3 or –1 compensation (when using Multi metering) for a more accurate exposure. (The amount of minus compensation that you need to set may be quite different when using the other two metering modes.) Minus compensation can also be useful for intentionally underexposing a scene for a creative effect, such as a silhouette of a sailboat or a group of friends on a beach.

As I noted above, any exposure compensation you set will remain active for all photos you take afterward, unless you've activated Reset EV Compensation in the Camera Settings I-09 (Exposure 1) menu, as described in Chapter 3. The camera provides a reminder as to what value is currently set in some display modes. Turning the a7R IV off and then back on does not set compensation back to zero; when you no longer need to use it, be sure to do so yourself, or enable the Reset option. If you inadvertently leave it set for +1 or –1, for example, your photos taken under other circumstances will be over- or underexposed.

Manual Exposure (M) Mode

Part of being an experienced photographer comes from knowing when to rely on your a7R IV's automation (including Intelligent Auto and P modes), when to go semi-automatic (with Shutter Priority or Aperture Priority), and when to set exposure manually (using M). Some photographers actually prefer to set their exposure manually. This is quite convenient, as the camera is happy to provide an indication of when your settings will produce over- or underexposure, based on its metering system's judgment. It can even indicate how far off the "correct" (recommended) exposure your photo will be at the settings you have made.

I often hear comments from novices first learning serious photography claiming that they must use Manual mode in order to take over control from the camera. While a back-to-basics approach does force you to learn photographic principles, it's not always necessary. For example, you can control all important aspects when using semi-automatic A or S mode as discussed in the previous sections. This allows you to control depth-of-field (the range of acceptable sharpness) or the rendition of motion (as blurred or as frozen). You can set a desired ISO level; that will not change the exposure. You would use exposure compensation when you want a brighter or a darker photo.

Manual mode provides an alternative that allows you to control the aperture and the shutter speed and the exposure simultaneously. For example, when I shot the outdoor sculpture in Figure 7.13, I was not getting exactly the desired effect with A or S mode while experimenting with various levels

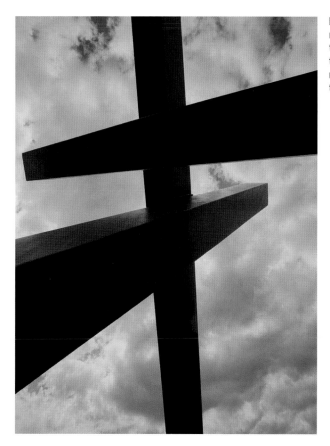

Figure 7.13 Manual mode allowed setting the exact exposure for this silhouette shot, by metering the subject and then underexposing.

of exposure compensation. So, I switched to M mode, set to ISO 100, and then set an aperture/shutter speed that might provide the intended exposure. After taking a test shot, I changed the aperture slightly and the next photo provided the exposure for the interpretation of the scene that I wanted.

Manual mode is also useful when working in a studio environment using multiple flash units. The additional flash units are triggered by slave devices (gadgets that set off the flash when they sense the light from another flash, or, perhaps from a radio or infrared remote control). In some cases, M mode is the only suitable choice. Your camera's exposure meter doesn't compensate for the extra illumination, and can't interpret the flash exposure at all, so you need to set the aperture and shutter speed manually.

The Basic M Mode Technique

Depending on your proclivities, you might not need to use M mode very often, but it's still worth understanding how it works. Here are your considerations:

- Rotate the mode dial to M.
- Use the front dial to adjust aperture and the rear dial to adjust shutter speed (unless you've swapped their functions, as described in Chapter 4). The setting that is currently active will be highlighted in orange.

- If you have Exposure Settings Guide in the Camera Settings II-07 (Display/Auto Review 1) menu set to On, enlarged labels showing the changing shutter speed or aperture will be displayed near the bottom of the screen, unless you choose the Graphic display mode with the DISP button. In that case, scales will show the current shutter speed and aperture at the same time.

- Any change you make to either factor affects the exposure, of course, so if you have Live View Display in the Camera Settings II-07 (Display/Auto Review 2) menu set to Setting Effect ON, you'll see the display getting darker or brighter as you change settings.

- If the display you're viewing includes the histogram graph, that will provide an even better indication of the exposure you'll get as you set different apertures or shutter speeds. I'll explain histograms later in this chapter.

- A guide at the bottom of the Monitor or viewfinder indicates exposure. To use the suggested exposure, adjust the shutter speed or f/stop until the MM guide reads ±0.0.

Long Exposures

You can specify exposures as long as 30 seconds when using P, A, or S modes. In Manual exposure mode, you can select B (for bulb exposure), located *after* the 30-second option. Bulb cannot be selected when using Silent Shooting, or when Drive mode is set to Continuous Shooting, Self-Timer Continuous, or Continuous Bracketing. If you try to shoot a bulb exposure in those modes, the a7R IV will use a 30-second exposure instead.

In Bulb mode, you can press and hold the shutter release button, and the shutter will remain open as long as the button is depressed. Standing there with your finger on the trigger, so to speak, can produce vibration, so I prefer to use a wired release with a locking button, such as the Sony RM-VPR1 ($50).

Adjusting Exposure with ISO Control in M Mode

As mentioned in the previous section, changing the ISO level is another method of changing the exposure in M mode, whether you adjust it yourself manually or activate Auto ISO and let the camera do it for you when you add or subtract exposure compensation.

Most photographers control the aperture and/or shutter speed exclusively to adjust exposure, sometimes forgetting about the option to adjust ISO. The common practice is to set the ISO once for a particular shooting session (say, at ISO 100 outdoors on a bright day or ISO 1600 when shooting indoors). There is also a tendency to use the lowest ISO level possible because of a concern that high ISO levels produce images with obvious digital noise (such as a grainy effect). However, changing the ISO is a valid way of adjusting exposure in M mode, particularly with the a7R IV, which produces good results at relatively high ISO levels that create grainy, unusable pictures with some other camera models.

I find myself using ISO adjustment as a convenient alternate way of adding or subtracting EV (exposure values) when shooting in Manual mode. For example, if I've selected a manual exposure with both f/stop and shutter speed suitable for my image using, say, ISO 400. I can change the exposure in full-stop increments by pressing the ISO button (right directional button) and spinning the front/rear dials or control wheel one click at a time. The difference in image quality/noise is not much different at ISO 200 or ISO 800 than at ISO 400, and this exposure control method allows me to shoot at my preferred f/stop and shutter speed while retaining control of the exposure. Indeed, if you've activated ISO Auto (discussed next), you can specify your desired shutter speed and aperture and the a7R IV will tweak the ISO sensitivity to provide an appropriate exposure. Effectively, you've turned Manual into a semi-automatic mode, while still being able to specify the aperture and shutter speed.

Or, perhaps, I am using Shutter Priority mode and the metered exposure at ISO 400 is 1/500th second at f/11. If I decide on the spur of the moment I'd rather use 1/500th second at f/8, I can press the ISO button and quickly switch to ISO 200. Of course, it's a good idea to monitor your ISO changes, so you don't end up at ISO 6400 or above accidentally; a setting like that will result in more digital noise (graininess) in your image than you would like. Higher ISO levels are necessary only when shooting in a very dark location where a fast shutter speed is important; this might happen during a sports event in a dark arena, for example.

Using ISO Auto

ISO Auto is a powerful feature, available in PSAM and Movie modes. In your camera's Fn and Camera Settings I-09 menu page, it's designated as ISO Auto. ISO Auto provides two major benefits. First, if the shutter speed and aperture settings in use won't provide a proper exposure, ISO Auto can adjust the ISO setting to compensate. Second, you can use ISO Auto to "lock in" a particular shutter speed or aperture (or both, in Manual mode), and use ISO sensitivity to compensate for changing or low-light conditions.

In the first case, suppose you were shooting a moving subject in Aperture Priority mode and your selected f/stop would result in a shutter speed of 1/8th second at ISO 400. All the image stabilization in the world can't protect you from blur caused by *subject* movement. If you were using ISO Auto with the a7R IV (only) and had specified a minimum shutter speed of 1/30th second in the Camera Settings I-09 (Exposure 1) menu (as described in Chapter 3), the camera's exposure system would automatically increase ISO from 400 to 1600. Most of us would prefer a slight increase in noise from the ISO boost than a blurry photograph.

With the a7R IV, the minimum (slowest) shutter speed allowed before ISO Auto kicks in has no effect when you're using Shutter Priority, as the shutter speed you choose is locked in. But in Program and Aperture Priority modes, you can choose that minimum. If you were shooting action and wanted to ensure that P and A modes would try to use a shutter speed of 1/250th second or faster, you could select that speed as the minimum speed before ISO Auto would increase sensitivity. If you were shooting subjects with little movement, you might select 1/8th second and count on the camera and/or lens's image stabilization to give you sharp results. For most general applications, a minimum of 1/30th second should work well.

We're not done yet. ISO Auto also allows you to choose a *minimum* and *maximum* ISO speed to be used. If you want to avoid noise, you could set the Minimum ISO to 100 and the Maximum to 800, and still gain the benefits of using ISO Auto. If you wouldn't mind seeing a little noise, you could set the Maximum somewhat higher. Coupled with Minimum Shutter speed (with the a7R IV), ISO Auto gives you quite a bit of flexibility in controlling the range of shutter speeds and apertures used.

And, as I mentioned earlier, in Manual Exposure mode you can use ISO Auto in a special way. As you might expect, in Manual Exposure mode, the shutter speed and aperture are selected by you and fixed at those settings until you change them. However, if ISO Auto is active, you can add or subtract exposure compensation, as described earlier, by rotating the exposure compensation dial on top of the camera, or by using the menu, Function menu, or a physical ISO control.

Exposure Bracketing

While exposure compensation lets you adjust exposure, sometimes you'll want to quickly shoot a series of photos at various exposures in a single burst. Doing so increases the odds of getting one photo that will be exactly right for your needs and is particularly useful when assembling high dynamic range (HDR) composite images manually. This technique is called bracketing.

Years ago, before high-tech cameras became the norm, it was common to bracket exposures when shooting color slide film especially, by taking three (or more) photos at different exposures in Manual mode. Eventually, exposure compensation became a common feature as cameras gained semiautomatic modes; it was then possible to bracket exposures by setting a different compensation level for each shot in a series, such as 0, –1, and +1 or 0, –1/3, and +2/3.

Today, cameras like the a7R IV give you a lot of options for automatically bracketing exposures. When Bracket is active, you can take a series of consecutive photos: one at the metered ("correct") exposure, and others with more or less exposure. Figure 7.14 shows an image with the metered exposure (center), flanked by exposures of 2/3 stop more (left), and 2/3 stop less (right).

Bracketing cannot be performed when using Intelligent Auto mode. If flash is used, you must take the photos one at a time, manually, rather than in a continuous burst. Exposure bracketing can be used with both RAW and JPG capture. When it's set, the camera will fire the shots in a sequence if you keep the shutter release button depressed; you can also decide to shoot the photos one at a time.

Bracketing is activated using the Drive settings, which can be found in the Camera Settings I-03 (Shoot Mode/Drive) menu, Function menu, and summoned by pressing the left directional button or some other button you've defined as the Drive button. Four different bracketing modes can be selected: continuous bracket, single bracket, white balance bracket, and DRO (dynamic range optimizer) bracket. In the Bracket Settings entry on the same menu page, you can specify Self-Timer During Bracketing and Bracket Order, as explained in Chapter 4.

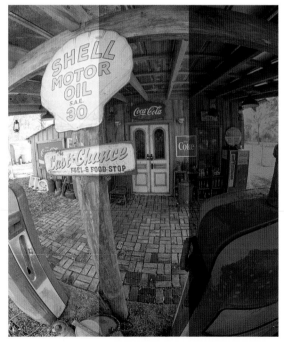

Figure 7.14 Metered exposure (center) accompanied by bracketed exposures of 2/3 stop more (left) and 2/3 stop less (right).

Continuous Bracketing

This mode captures three, five, or nine images in one burst when the shutter release is held down, bracketing them 0.3, 0.7, or 1.0 stops apart. Increments of 2.0 or 3.0 stops are also available, but only 3 or 5 images can be taken. These larger increments are especially useful when capturing images you'll combine later in your image editor to produce a high dynamic range (HDR) image. Use continuous bracketing when you want all the images in the set to be framed as similarly as possible, say, when you will be using them for manually assembled high dynamic range (HDR) photos.

When you highlight Cont. Bracket. in the Drive menu, the left/right buttons are used to select the increment between shots and the number of shots. In Manual Exposure (when ISO Auto is disabled), or in Aperture Priority, the shutter speed will change. If ISO Auto is set in Manual Exposure, the bracketed set will be created by changing the ISO setting. In Shutter Priority, the aperture will change. You can use flash when continuous bracketing is active, but, because of the time required for the flash to recycle, you'll need to press the shutter button each time to take subsequent images (effectively switching the camera into Single Bracket mode, described next). Continuous Bracketing (and Single Bracketing) is disabled when using Intelligent Auto.

Only the last shot in the set is displayed when using Auto Review. With all types of bracketing, the exposure/bracket scale at the bottom of the EVF or LCD monitor (in Display All Info mode) will display indicators showing the number of images shot and the relative amount of under- or overexposure.

Don't forget that you can dial in exposure compensation, and *that* will affect the amount of over/underexposure applied while bracketing, too. You can bracket your exposures based on something other than the base (metered) exposure value. Set any desired exposure compensation, either a plus or a minus value. Then set the Bracketing level you want to use. The camera will bracket exposures as over, under, and equal to the *compensated* value.

Single Bracketing

This mode captures one bracketed image in a set of 3, 5, or 9 shots each time you press the shutter release, bracketing them 0.3, 0.7, or 1.0 stops apart. Only 3 and 5 shots are available with the 2.0 EV or 3.0 EV increments. The left/right buttons are used to select the increment and number of shots. In this mode, you can separate each image by an interval of your choice. You might want to use this variation when you want the individual images to be captured at slightly different times, say, to produce a set of images that will be combined in some artistic way.

HDR ISN'T HARD

The 1.0 EV to 3.0 EV options are the ones you might try first when bracketing if you plan to perform High Dynamic Range magic later on in Photoshop (with Merge to HDR), Elements (with Photomerge), or with another image editor that provides an HDR feature. That will allow you to combine images with different exposures into one photo with an amazing amount of detail in both highlights and shadows. To get the best results, mount your camera on a tripod, shoot in RAW format, and use BRK C3.0EV to get three shots with 3 EV of difference in exposure.

White Balance Bracketing

In this mode, the camera shoots three images, each with a different adjustment to the color temperature. While you can't specify which direction the color bias is tilted, you can select Lo (the default) for small changes, or Hi, for larger changes using the left/right buttons. Only the last shot taken is displayed during Auto Review.

DRO Bracketing

This mode takes three images, with Lo (the default) or High adjustments to the dynamic range optimization. Use the left/right buttons to specify the degree of adjustment. Again, only the last shot taken is displayed during Auto Review.

Dealing with Digital Noise

Visual noise is that random grainy look with colorful speckles that some like to use as a visual effect, but most consider to be objectionable. That's because it robs your image of detail even as it adds that "interesting" texture. Noise is caused by two different phenomena: high ISO levels and long exposures. The a7R IV offers a menu item to minimize both types. In Chapter 3, I discussed the Camera Settings I-02 (Quality/Image Size 2) menu items that you can use to modify the noise reduction processing; you might want to review the sections about High ISO NR and Long Exposure NR as a refresher.

High ISO Noise

Digital noise commonly appears when you set an ISO above ISO 1600 with the a7R IV. High ISO noise appears as a result of the amplification needed to increase the effective sensitivity of the sensor. While higher ISOs do pull details out of dark areas, they also amplify non-signal information randomly, creating noise.

High ISO Noise Reduction is very useful, although at default, it also tends to make images slightly softer as blurring the noise pattern also blurs some intricate details. The higher the ISO, the more aggressive the processing will be, depending on whether you've specified Normal or Low. The Low level for NR provides images that are more grainy but with better resolution of fine detail. Even if you've chosen Off, the camera still applies some noise reduction.

High ISO NR is grayed out when the camera is set to shoot only RAW-format photos. The camera does not use this feature on RAW-format photos since noise reduction—at the optimum level for any photo—can be applied in the software you'll use to modify and convert the RAW file to JPEG or TIFF. (If you shoot in RAW & JPEG, the JPEG images, but not the RAW files, will be affected by this camera feature.) I'll discuss Noise Reduction with software in more detail in the next section.

Figure 7.15 shows two pictures that I shot at ISO 6400. For the first, I used the default (Normal) High ISO NR, and for the second shot, I set the NR to Off. (I've exaggerated the differences between the two slightly so the grainy/less grainy images are more evident on the printed page. The halftone screen applied to printed photos tends to mask these differences.)

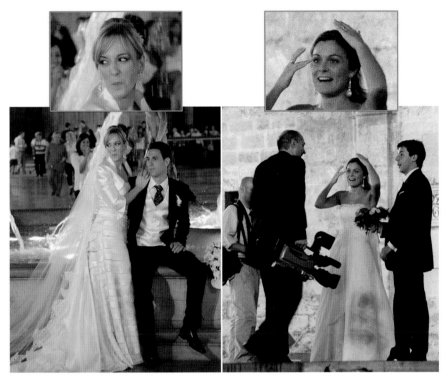

Figure 7.15 The Normal level for High ISO NR (left) produces a smoother (less grainy) image than one made with High ISO NR turned off (right).

Long Exposure Noise

A similar digital noise phenomenon occurs during long time exposures, which allow more photons to reach the sensor, increasing your ability to capture a picture under low-light conditions. However, the longer exposures also increase the likelihood that some pixels will register as random, "phantom," photons, often because the longer an imager collects photos during an exposure, the hotter it becomes, and that heat can be mistaken by the sensor as actual photons. The camera tries to minimize this type of noise automatically; there is no separate control you can adjust to add more or less noise reduction for long exposures.

CMOS imagers like the one in the a7R IV, contain millions of individual amplifiers and A/D (analog to digital) converters, all working in unison though the BIONZ X digital image processor chip. Because these circuits don't necessarily all process in precisely the same way all the time, they can introduce something called fixed-pattern noise into the image data.

Long exposure noise reduction is used with JPEG exposures longer than one full second. (This feature is not used on RAW photos and in continuous shooting or bracketing modes.) When it's active, long exposure noise reduction processing removes random pixels from your photo, but some of the image-making pixels are unavoidably vanquished at the same time.

It's possible that you prefer the version made without NR, and you can achieve that simply by shooting RAW. Indeed, noise reduction can be applied with most image-editing programs. You might get even better results with an industrial-strength product like Nik Dfine, part of the Nik collection, or Topaz DNoise or Enhance (www.topazlabs.com). You can apply noise reduction to RAW photos with Sony's Image Data Converter or any other versatile converter software. Some products are optimized for NR with unusually sophisticated processing, such as Photo Ninja (www.picturecode.com) and the $129 DxO Photolab (www.dxo.com).

Using Dynamic Range Optimizer

Dynamic Range Optimizer (DRO) is a feature you can select from the Camera Settings I-12 (Color/ WB/Image Processing 1) menu or the Function menu, as explained in Chapter 3. When enabled, the camera will examine your images as they are exposed, and, if the shadows appear to have detail even though they are too dark, will attempt to process the image so the shadows are lighter, with additional detail, without overexposing detailed highlights. The processed image is always saved as a JPEG, so if you are shooting RAW you won't notice a difference.

Here is how the DRO feature works:

- **DRO Off.** No optimization. You're on your own; the camera will not apply extra processing even to your JPEG photos. Of course, if you are shooting RAW (or RAW & JPEG) photos, you can apply DRO effects to your photo when converting it with the downloadable Image Data Converter SR software. (Other programs have different tools for lightening shadow areas and/or darkening highlight areas.) Use Off when shooting subjects of normal contrast, or when you want to capture an image just as you see it, without modification by the camera.

- **DRO.** Press the left/right buttons after scrolling to DRO Auto and you can then set a specific intensity level for the Dynamic Range Optimizer, from Level 1 through Level 5.

  If you do not want to set a specific level, simply scroll to DRO Auto and allow the camera to decide on the amount of increased dynamic range. With the Auto setting, the camera dives into your image, looking at various small areas to examine the contrast of highlights and shadows, making modifications to each section to produce the best combination of brightness and tones with detail. In my experience, Auto provides a mid-level of DRO that's worth leaving on at all times.

 TIP The primary method for DRO processing is lightening the dark tones and mid tones of an image. The higher the level of DRO you set, the more significantly the processor will lighten those areas; that causes digital noise to be more and more noticeable, especially in photos made at ISO 800 and at higher ISO levels. This is one reason why you would not always want to set Level 4 or 5 for DRO, particularly when using a high ISO setting. The other reason is that very high DRO produces a somewhat unnatural-looking effect with all shadow areas lighter than "normal." Auto and Levels 1 to 3 retain the most natural-looking effect.

When you activate DRO, you have your choice of specifying the aggressiveness of the processing (from Level 1 through Level 5), in which case it will *always* be applied at the level you specify. Or, you can set the feature to Auto and let the camera decide the ideal amount of optimization (or even when to apply it at all). Auto is usually your best choice, because the camera is pretty smart about choosing which images to process, and which to leave alone. Indeed, the camera's programming usually does a better job than a similar feature available in the Image Data Converter SR software you may have installed on your computer.

Figure 7.16 shows an image with DRO turned off, and using Level 1, Level 3, and Level 5 optimization. (The differences between, say, Level 1 and 2, or 2 and 3 are subtle and wouldn't show up well on the printed page, so I skipped the even-numbered levels.) The printed page also doesn't show that DRO tends to increase the amount of noise in an image as it works more aggressively; it's usually a good idea to avoid using the feature at high ISO levels where noise tends to be a real problem under any conditions.

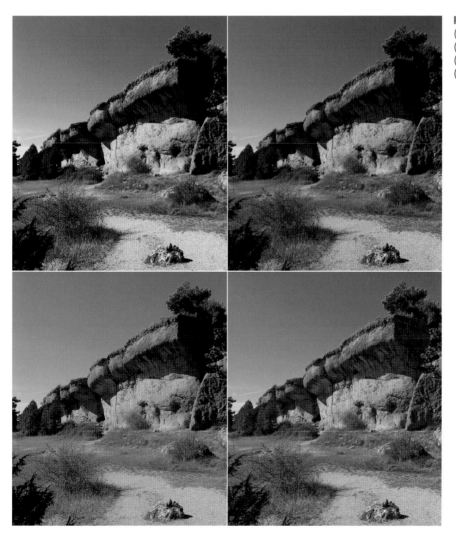

Figure 7.16 DRO Off (upper left); Level 1 (upper right); Level 3 (lower left); and Level 5 (lower right).

Working with HDR

High dynamic range (HDR) photography is quite the rage these days, and entire books have been written on the subject. It's not really a new technique—film photographers have been combining multiple exposures for ages to produce a single image of, say, an interior room while maintaining detail in the scene visible through the windows.

It's the same deal in the digital age. Suppose you wanted to photograph a dimly lit room that had a bright window showing an outdoors scene. Proper exposure for the room might be on the order of 1/60th second at f/2.8 at ISO 200, while the outdoors scene probably would require f/11 at 1/400th second. That's almost a 7 EV step difference (approximately 7 f/stops) and well beyond the dynamic range of any digital camera, including the Sony a7R IV cameras. (An additional problem, of course, is the mixed illumination: daylight outdoors and probably tungsten or fluorescent lamps indoors. Pro photographers sometimes gel the windows with corrective film so that inside/outside illumination matches.)

Until camera sensors gain much higher dynamic ranges (which may not be as far into the distant future as we think), special tricks like DRO and HDR photography will remain basic tools. With the Sony a7R IV you must shoot HDR the old-fashioned way—with separate bracketed exposures that are later combined in a tool like Photomatix or Adobe's Merge to HDR image-editing feature. Auto HDR, found in some other Sony cameras, is not supported by this one.

Bracketing and Merge to HDR

Creating HDR images manually is not difficult. You simply shoot individual images either by manually bracketing or using the camera's auto bracketing modes, described earlier in this chapter.

Although my goal in this book is to show you how to take great photos *in the camera* rather than how to fix your errors in Photoshop, the Merge to HDR Pro feature in Adobe's flagship image editor (and a variation also found in Photoshop Elements) is too cool to ignore. The ability to have a bracketed set of exposures that are identical except for exposure is key to getting good results with this Photoshop feature, which allows you to produce images with a full, rich dynamic range that includes a level of detail in the highlights and shadows that is almost impossible to achieve with digital cameras.

When you're using Merge to HDR Pro, you'd take several pictures, some exposed for the shadows, some for the middle tones, and some for the highlights. The exact number of images to combine is up to you. Four to seven is a good number. Then, you'd use the Merge to HDR Pro command to combine all of the images into one HDR image that integrates the well-exposed sections of each version. Here's how.

The images should be as identical as possible, except for exposure. So, it's a good idea to mount the camera on a tripod, use a remote release, and take all the exposures in one burst. Just follow these steps:

1. **Set up the camera.** Mount the camera on a tripod.
2. **Set the camera to shoot a bracketed burst with an increment of at least 2 EV.** You can use auto bracketing or manually change the exposure between shots. In Manual mode, make sure Auto ISO is off,

and you adjust exposures *only* by changing the shutter speed. You should be very careful when you make the adjustment to avoid jostling the camera.

3. **Choose an f/stop.** Set the camera for Aperture Priority and select an aperture that will provide a correct exposure at your initial settings for the series of manually bracketed shots. *And then leave this adjustment alone!* You don't want the aperture to change for your series, as that would change the depth-of-field and, potentially, the image size of some elements. You want the camera to adjust exposure *only* using the shutter speed.

4. **Choose manual focus.** You don't want the focus to change between shots, so set the camera to manual focus, and carefully focus your shot.

5. **Choose RAW exposures.** Set the camera to take RAW files, which will give you the widest range of tones in your images. (This is an advantage of manually creating HDR files; the camera's Auto HDR feature can't be used when RAW or RAW+JPEG is active.)

6. **Take your bracketed set.** Press the button on the remote (or carefully press the shutter release or use the self-timer) and take the set of bracketed exposures.

7. **Continue with the Merge to HDR Pro steps listed next.** You can also use a different program, such as Photomatix or Nik software, if you know how to use it.

DETERMINING THE BEST EXPOSURE DIFFERENTIAL

How do you choose the number of EV/stops to separate your exposures? You can use histograms, described at the end of this chapter, to determine the correct bracketing range. Take a test shot and examine the histogram. Reduce the exposure until dark tones are clipped off at the left of the resulting histogram. Then, increase the exposure until the lighter tones are clipped off at the right of the histogram. The number of stops between the two is the range that should be covered using your bracketed exposures. Note that if you want to override the +/- 3 stop limitation of auto bracketing, you can add or subtract exposure compensation. That will bias the exposures in the direction you choose. For example, if autobracketing in Aperture Priority mode would produce exposures of 1/125th, 1/250th, and 1/500th second, you can set EV to –2 and get 1/30th-, 1/60th-, and 1/125th-second exposures instead.

The next steps show you how to combine the separate exposures into one merged high dynamic range image.

1. **Copy your images to your computer.** If you use an application to transfer the files to your computer, make sure it does not make any adjustments to brightness, contrast, or exposure. You want the real raw information for Merge to HDR Pro to work with. Your three images might look something like the trio stacked at the left side of Figure 7.17.

2. **Activate Merge to HDR Pro.** Choose File > Automate > Merge to HDR Pro.

3. **Select the photos to be merged.** Use the Browse feature to locate and select your photos to be merged. You'll note a check box that can be used to automatically align the images if they were not taken with the camera mounted on a rock-steady support. This will adjust for any slight movement of the camera that might have occurred when you changed exposure settings.

Figure 7.17 Three bracketed images (left) can be combined to produce the merged HDR image (right).

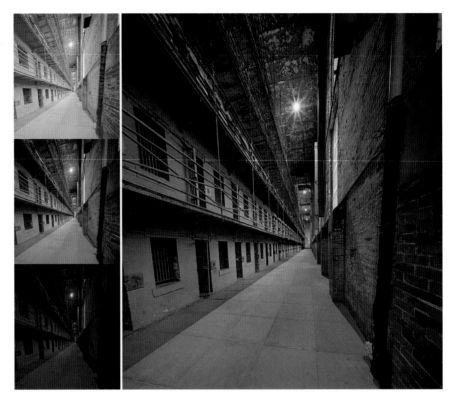

4. **Choose parameters (optional).** The first time you use Merge to HDR Pro, you can let the program work with its default parameters. Once you've played with the feature a few times, you can read the Adobe Help files and learn more about the options than I can present in this non-software-oriented camera guide.

5. **Click OK.** The merger begins.

6. **Save.** Once HDR merge has done its thing, save the file to your computer.

If you do everything correctly, you'll end up with a full-range high dynamic range photo, like the one shown at right in Figure 7.17. What if you don't have the opportunity, inclination, or skills to create several images at different exposures, as described? If you shoot in RAW format, you can still use Merge to HDR, working with a *single* original image file. What you do is import the image into Photoshop several times, using Adobe Camera Raw to create multiple copies of the file at different exposure levels.

For example, you'd create one copy that's too dark, so the shadows lose detail, but the highlights are preserved. Create another copy with the shadows intact and allow the highlights to wash out. Then, you can use Merge to HDR to combine the two and end up with a finished image that has the extended dynamic range you're looking for. (This concludes the image-editing portion of the chapter. We now return you to our alternate sponsor: photography.)

Exposure Evaluation with Histograms

While you may be able to improve poorly exposed photos in your image-editing software or with DRO or HDR techniques, it's definitely preferable to get the exposure close to correct in the camera. This will minimize the modifications you'll need to make in post-processing, which can be very time-consuming and will degrade image quality, especially with JPEGs. A RAW photo can tolerate more significant changes with less adverse effects, but for optimum quality, it's still important to have an exposure that's close to correct.

Instead, you can use a histogram, which is a chart displayed on the camera's screen that shows the number of tones that have been captured at each brightness level. Two types of histograms are available, a "live" histogram that appears at the lower-right corner of the screen in Shooting mode, and a larger, more detailed version that appears in Histogram mode during playback. The live version can help you make exposure decisions as you shoot, whereas the playback version is useful in determining corrections to be made before you take your next shot. I'll explain both versions, but first it's useful to understand exactly what you're seeing when you view a histogram.

The Live Histogram

The camera's live histogram offers the most reliable method for judging the exposure as you shoot (although the Zebra feature described in Chapter 4 can be used to isolate specific problems involving blown highlights). A pair of live histograms are also available for display for both the viewfinder and monitor; activate both with the DISP Button (MONITOR/FINDER) item in the Camera Settings II-07 menu, as discussed in Chapter 4. After activating, press the DISP button a few times to reach the display that includes the histogram, which will be shown at lower right in the viewfinder and LCD monitor screens.

In Shooting mode, you'll get a luminance (brightness) histogram that shows the distribution of tones and brightness levels across the image given the current Camera Settings I setting, including exposure compensation, Dynamic Range Optimizer (DRO) level in use, or the aperture, shutter speed, and ISO that you have set if using Manual mode. This live histogram (displayed before taking a photo) is useful for judging whether the exposure is likely to be satisfactory or whether you should use a camera feature to modify the exposure. When the histogram looks better, take the photo. I'll show you how to evaluate histograms later in this chapter.

The Playback Histograms

You can view histograms in Playback mode, too; press the DISP button until the display shown in Figure 7.18 appears. The top graph, called the luminance or brightness histogram, is conventional, showing the distribution of tones across the image. Each of the other three histograms is in a specific color: red, green, and blue. That indicates the color channel you're viewing in that histogram: red, green, or blue. These additional graphs allow you to see the distribution of tones in the three individual channels. It takes a lot

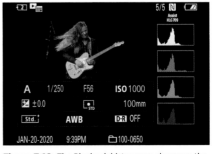

Figure 7.18 The Playback histograms show you the tonal distribution of a photo you've already taken.

of expertise to interpret those extra histograms and, frankly, the conventional luminance histogram is the only one that many photographers use.

As a bonus in Playback mode, another feature is available when the histograms are visible: any areas of the displayed image that are excessively bright, or excessively dark, will blink. This feature, often called "blinkies," warns that you may need to change your settings to avoid loss of detail in highlight areas (such as a white wedding gown) or in shadow areas (such as a black animal's fur). The camera also includes the Zebra feature to indicate overexposure, as discussed in Chapter 4. You can use the histogram information along with the flashing blinkie and Zebra alerts to guide you in modifying the exposure, and/or setting the DRO feature (discussed earlier), before taking the photo again.

Tonal Range

Histograms help you adjust the tonal range of an image, the span of dark to light tones, from a complete absence of brightness (black) to the brightest possible tone (white), and all the middle tones in between. Because all values for tones fall into a continuous spectrum between black and white, it's easiest to think of a photo's tonality in terms of a black-and-white or grayscale image, even though you're capturing those tones in three separate color layers of red, green, and blue.

Because your images are digital, the tonal "spectrum" isn't really continuous: it's divided into discrete steps that represent the different tones that can be captured. Figure 7.19 may help you understand this concept. The gray steps shown range from 100 percent gray (black) at the left, to 0 percent gray (white) at the right, with 20 gray steps in all (plus white).

Along the bottom of the chart are the digital values from 0 to 255 recorded by your sensor for an image with 8 bits per channel. (8 bits of red, 8 bits of green, and 8 bits of blue equal a 24-bit, full-color image.) Any black captured would be represented by a value of 0, the brightest white by 255, and the midtones would be clustered around the 128 marker. The actual scale may be "finer" and record say, 0 to 4,094 for an image captured when the a7R IV is capturing RAW images with 14 bits per channel.

Grayscale images (which we call black-and-white photos) are easy to understand. Or, at least, that's what we think. When we look at a black-and-white image, we think we're seeing a continuous range of tones from black to white, and all the grays in between. But, that's not exactly true. The blackest black in any photo isn't a true black, because *some* light is always reflected from the surface of the print, and if viewed on a screen, the deepest black is only as dark as the least-reflective area a computer monitor can produce. The whitest white isn't a true white, either, because even the lightest

Figure 7.19 A tonal range from black (left) to white (right) and all the gray values in between.

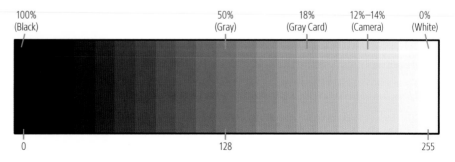

areas of a print absorb some light (only a mirror reflects close to all the light that strikes it), and, when viewing on a computer monitor, the whites are limited by the brightness of the display's LCD or LED picture elements. Lacking darker blacks and brighter, whiter whites, that continuous set of tones doesn't cover the full grayscale tonal range.

The full scale of tones becomes useful when you have an image that has large expanses of shades that change gradually from one level to the next, such as areas of sky, water, or walls. Think of a picture taken of a group of campers around a campfire. Since the light from the fire is striking them directly in the face, there aren't many shadows on the campers' faces. All the tones that make up the *features* of the people around the fire are compressed into one end of the brightness spectrum—the lighter end.

Yet, there's more to this scene than faces. Behind the campers are trees, rocks, and perhaps a few animals that have emerged from the shadows to see what is going on. These are illuminated by the softer light that bounces off the surrounding surfaces. If your eyes become accustomed to the reduced illumination, you'll find that there is a wealth of detail in these shadow images.

This campfire scene would be a nightmare to reproduce faithfully under any circumstances. If you are an experienced photographer, you are probably already wincing at what is called a *high-contrast* lighting situation. Some photos may be high in contrast when there are fewer tones and they are all bunched up at limited points in the scale. In a low-contrast image, there are more tones, but they are spread out so widely that the image looks flat. Your digital camera can show you the relationship between these tones using a *histogram*.

Histogram Basics

Your a7R IV's histograms are a simplified display of the numbers of pixels at each of 256 brightness levels, producing an interesting mountain range effect. Although separate charts may be provided for brightness and the red, green, and blue channels, when you first start using histograms, you'll want to concentrate on the brightness histogram.

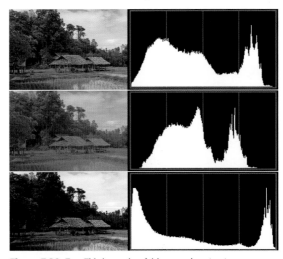

Each vertical line in the graph represents the allocation of pixels in the image for each brightness value, from 0 (black) on the left to 255 (white) on the right. Although histograms are most often used to fine-tune exposure, you can glean other information from them, such as the relative contrast of the image. Figure 7.20, top, is a simplified rendition of a histogram of an image having normal contrast. In such an image, most of the pixels are spread across the image, with a healthy distribution of tones throughout the

Figure 7.20 Top: This image has fairly normal contrast, even though there is a peak of light tones at the right side representing the sky. Center: This low-contrast image has all the tones squished into one section of the grayscale. Bottom: A high-contrast image produces a histogram in which the tones are spread out.

midtone section of the graph. That large peak at the right side of the graph represents all those light tones in the sky. A normal-contrast image you shoot may have less sky area, and less of a peak at the right side, but notice that very few pixels hug the right edge of the histogram, indicating that the lightest tones are not being clipped because they are off the chart.

With a lower-contrast image, like the one shown in Figure 7.20, center, the basic shape of the previous histogram will remain recognizable, but gradually will be compressed together to cover a smaller area of the gray spectrum. The squished shape of the histogram is caused by all the grays in the original image being represented by a limited number of gray tones in a smaller range of the scale.

Instead of the darkest tones of the image reaching into the black end of the spectrum and the whitest tones extending to the lightest end, the blackest areas of the scene are now represented by a light gray, and the whites by a somewhat lighter gray. The overall contrast of the image is reduced. Because all the darker tones are actually a middle gray or lighter, the scene in this version of the photo appears lighter as well.

Going in the other direction, increasing the contrast of an image produces a histogram like the one shown in Figure 7.20, bottom. In this case, the tonal range is now spread over the entire width of the chart, but, except for the bright sky, there is not much variation in the middle tones; the mountain "peaks" are not very high. When you stretch the grayscale in both directions like this, the darkest tones become darker (that may not be possible) and the lightest tones become lighter (ditto). In fact, shades that might have been gray before can change to black or white as they are moved toward either end of the scale.

The effect of increasing contrast may be to move some tones off either end of the scale altogether, while spreading the remaining grays over a smaller number of locations on the spectrum. That's exactly the case in the example shown. The number of possible tones is smaller and the image appears harsher.

Understanding Histograms

The important thing to remember when working with the histogram display in your a7R IV is that changing the exposure does *not* change the contrast of an image. The curves illustrated in the previous three examples remain exactly the same shape when you increase or decrease exposure. I repeat: The proportional distribution of grays shown in the histogram doesn't change when exposure changes; it is neither stretched nor compressed. However, the tones as a whole are moved toward one end of the scale or the other, depending on whether you're increasing or decreasing exposure. You'll be able to see that in some illustrations that follow.

So, as you reduce exposure, tones gradually move to the black end (and off the scale), while the reverse is true when you increase exposure. The contrast within the image is changed only to the extent that some of the tones can no longer be represented when they are moved off the scale.

To change the *contrast* of an image, you must do one of four things:

- **Change the a7R IV's contrast setting** using the menu system. You'll find these adjustments in your camera's Creative Styles feature, as discussed in Chapter 9.

- **Use your camera's shadow-tone "booster."** As previously discussed, D-Range Optimizer can also adjust contrast.

- **Alter the contrast of the scene itself,** for example, by using a fill light or reflectors to add illumination to shadows that are too dark.

- **Attempt to adjust contrast in post-processing** using your image editor or RAW file converter. You may use features such as Levels or Curves (in Photoshop, Photoshop Elements, and many other image editors), or work with HDR software to cherry-pick the best values in shadows and highlights from multiple images.

Of the four of these, the third—changing the contrast of the scene—is the most desirable, because attempting to fix contrast by fiddling with the tonal values is unlikely to be a perfect remedy. However, adding a little contrast can be successful because you can discard some tones to make the image more contrasty. However, the opposite is much more difficult. An overly contrasty image rarely can be fixed, because you can't add information that isn't there in the first place.

What you *can* do is adjust the exposure so that the tones *that are already present in the scene* are captured correctly. Figure 7.21, top, shows the histogram for an image that is badly underexposed. You can guess from the shape of the histogram that many of the dark tones to the left of the graph have been clipped off. There's plenty of room on the right side for additional pixels to reside without having them become overexposed. So, you can increase the exposure (either by changing the f/stop or shutter speed or by adding an EV value) to produce the corrected histogram shown in Figure 7.21, center.

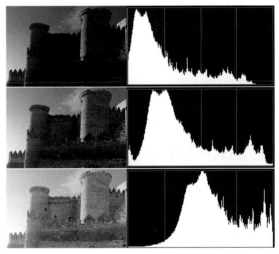

Conversely, if your histogram looks like the one shown in Figure 7.21, bottom, with bright tones pushed off the right edge of the chart, you have an overexposed image, and you can correct it by reducing exposure. In addition to the histo-

Figure 7.21 Top: A histogram of an underexposed image may look like this. Center: Adding exposure will produce a histogram like this one. Bottom: A histogram of an overexposed image will show clipping at the right side.

gram, the a7R IV has its Highlights and Zebra options, which, when activated, shows areas that are overexposed with flashing tones (often called "blinkies"). Depending on the importance of this "clipped" detail, you can adjust exposure or leave it alone. For example, if all the dark-coded areas in the review are in a background that you care little about, you can forget about them and not change the exposure, but if such areas appear in facial details of your subject, you may want to make some adjustments.

In working with histograms, your goal should be to have all the tones in an image spread out between the edges, with none clipped off at the left and right sides. Underexposing (to preserve highlights) should be done only as a last resort, because retrieving the underexposed shadows in your image editor will frequently increase the noise, even if you're working with RAW files. A better course of action is to expose for the highlights, but, when the subject matter makes it practical, fill in the shadows with additional light, using reflectors, fill flash, or other techniques rather than allowing them to be seriously underexposed.

A traditional technique for optimizing exposure is called "expose to the right" (ETTR), which involves adding exposure to push the histogram's curve toward the right side *but not far enough to clip off highlights.* The rationale for this method is that extra shadow detail will be produced with a minimum increase in noise, especially in the shadow areas. It's said that half of a digital sensor's response lies in the brightest areas of an image, and so require the least amount of amplification (which is one way to increase digital noise). ETTR can work, as long as you're able to capture a satisfactory amount of information in the shadows.

Exposing to the Right

It's easier to understand exposing to the right if you mentally divide the histogram into fifths (unfortunately, the a7R IV's histogram uses quarters instead). And, for the sake of simplicity and smaller numbers, assume you're shooting in 14-bit RAW. Any 14-bit image can record a maximum of 16,383 different tones per channel. However, each fifth of the histogram does *not* encompass 3,277 tones (one-fifth of 16,383).

Instead, the right-most fifth, the highlights, shown in Figure 7.25, accounts for fully *half*, or 50 percent of the tones; the next fifth accounts for 1/4 (25 percent); and so on, with 1/8th, 1/16th, and 1/32nd assigned to the remaining fifths. These "fifths" are fuzzy rather than hard boundaries. But note that in the left-most area, approximately only 512 different tones are captured. When processing your RAW file, there are only 512 tones to recover in the shadows, which is why boosting/amplifying them increases noise. (The effect is most noticeable in the red and blue channels; your sensor's Bayer array has twice as many green-sensitive pixels as red or blue.)

Instead, you want to add exposure—as long as you don't push highlights off the right edge of the histogram—to brighten the shadows. Because there are approximately 8,192 tones available in the highlights, even if the RAW image *looks* overexposed, it's possible to use your RAW converter's Exposure slider (such as the one found in Adobe Camera Raw) to bring back detail captured in that surplus of tones in the highlights. This procedure is the exact opposite of what was recommended for

Figure 7.22 Tones are not evenly allocated throughout a histogram.

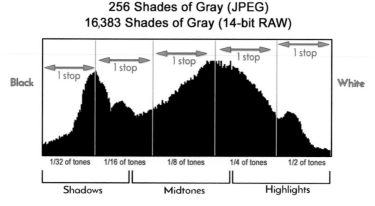

film of the transparency variety—it was fairly easy to retrieve detail from shadows by pumping more light through them when processing the image, while even small amounts of extra exposure blew out highlights. You'll often find that the range of tones in your image is so great that there is no way to keep your histogram from spilling over into the left and right edges, costing you both highlight and shadow detail. Exposing to the right may not work in such situations. A second school of thought recommends *reducing* exposure to bring back the highlights, or "exposing to the left." You would then attempt to recover shadow detail in an image editor, using tools like Adobe Camera Raw's Exposure slider. But remember, above all, that this procedure will also boost noise in the shadows, and so the technique should be used with caution. In most cases, exposing to the right is your best bet.

Dealing with Channels

The more you work with histograms, the more useful they become. One of the first things that histogram veterans notice is that it's possible to overexpose one channel even if the overall exposure appears to be correct. For example, flower photographers soon discover that it's really, really difficult to get a good picture of a red rose. The exposure looks okay—but there's no detail in the rose's petals. (See Figure 7.23, left.) The image's histogram will show you why: typically, you'll find a peak at the right edge that indicates that highlight information has been lost. In fact, the green channel is often blown, too, and so the green parts of the flower also lack detail. Only the blue channel's histogram may be entirely contained within the boundaries of the chart, and, on first glance, the white luminance histogram at top of the column of graphs may appear to be fairly normal.

Any of the primary channels—red, green, or blue—can blow out all by themselves, although bright reds seem to be the most common problem area. More difficult to diagnose are overexposed tones in one of the "in-between" hues on the color wheel. Overexposed yellows (which are very common) will be shown by blowouts in *both* the red and green channels. Too-bright cyans will manifest as excessive blue and green highlights, while overexposure in the red and blue channels reduces detail in magenta colors. As you gain experience, you'll be able to see exactly how anomalies in the RGB channels translate into poor highlights and murky shadows.

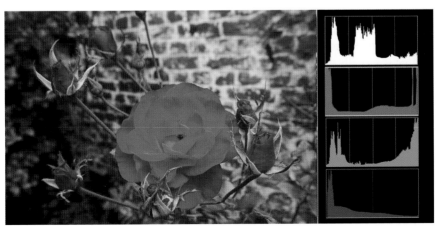

Figure 7.23 When the red channel is "blown," red portions of an image may lack detail (left), as indicated by the highlight peak in the red channel's histogram (right).

The only way to correct for color channel blowouts is to reduce exposure. As I mentioned earlier, you might want to consider filling in the shadows with additional light to keep them from becoming too dark when you decrease exposure. In practice, you'll want to monitor the red channel most closely, followed by the blue channel, and slightly decrease exposure to see if that helps. Because of the way our eyes perceive color, we are more sensitive to variations in green, so green channel blowouts are less of a problem, unless your main subject is heavily colored in that hue. If you plan on photographing a frog hopping around on your front lawn, you'll want to be extra careful to preserve detail in the green channel, using bracketing or other exposure techniques outlined in this chapter.

Fine-Tuning Exposure

When all else fails—that is, when you find your camera *consistently* over- or underexposes when using a particular exposure mode—you can recalibrate the a7R IV to produce images more to your liking. No more can you complain, "My a7R IV always underexposes by 1/3 stop!" If that is actually the case, and the phenomenon is consistent, you can use this custom menu adjustment to compensate.

Exposure compensation is usually a better idea (does your camera *really* underexpose that consistently?), but this setting does allow you to adjust your a7R IV's behavior yourself. Your dialed-in modifications will survive a reset. However, you have no indication that fine-tuning has been made, so you'll need to remember what you've done. After all, you someday might discover that your camera is consistently *over*exposing images by 1/3 stop, not remembering that you've made the adjustment.

In practice, it's rare that the Sony a7R IV will *consistently* provide the wrong exposure in any of the metering modes, especially Multi metering, which can alter exposure dramatically based on the a7R IV's internal database of typical scenes. This feature may be most useful for Spot metering, if you always take a reading off the same type of subject, such as a human face or gray card. Should you find that the gray card readings, for example, always differ from what you would prefer, go ahead and fine-tune optimal exposure for Spot metering, and use that to read your gray cards.

The Exposure Standard Adjustment feature is your key to fine-tuning your camera's exposure. It allows you to dial in a specific amount of exposure compensation that will be applied to every photo you take using each of the metering modes. No more can you complain, "My a7R IV always underexposes by 1/3 stop!" If that is actually the case, and the phenomenon is consistent, you can compensate using the Exposure Standard Adjustment entry in the Camera Setting I-10 (Exposure 2) menu. I provided step-by-step instructions for fine-tuning exposure in Chapter 3 and will not duplicate that information here.

Mastering Autofocus Options

8

The autofocus system found in the Sony a7R IV is one of its most innovative features. The camera has the ability to lock in on subjects, track their motion, switch to face detection/tracking, then progress to even more precise eye detection—and then backtrack to the other methods as movement continues through the frame. That's particularly impressive because, when mirrorless digital cameras were introduced, autofocus was something they weren't particularly good at.

Indeed, the mirrors found in traditional SLRs had two distinct advantages: they allowed previewing an image through an optical viewfinder, and made it possible to direct some of the incoming illumination to a separate electronic autofocus system. At the moment of exposure, focus was locked, and the mirror flipped up out of the way, allowing the light to pass through the camera body to the film or digital sensor. Autofocus was fast, and reasonably accurate.

Of course, the mirror system had its own set of drawbacks. Moving mirrors are noisy and bulky, and increase the distance between the lens mounting flange and the film or sensor, resulting in larger cameras. Mirror-based viewing systems also mean that autofocus can't take place during exposure, which is particularly problematic when capturing video. Those mirrors were, at best, a kluge introduced to allow previewing an image through the same lens used to take the picture; early cameras had no mirrors, nor did the first 35mm cameras (dating from the first Leica prototypes of 1913). Compact models with mirrors for previewing images didn't start to make in-roads until just before World War II, and mirrorless cameras from Leica and others were prized for their light weight, smaller size, and quietness for another 30 to 35 years.

We eventually became so accustomed to the limitations of single-lens reflex models with mirrors that the first digital mirrorless cameras seemed very limited, especially when it came to autofocus. The initial generations of mirrorless cameras from Sony and other vendors had to use a slower AF method, based on what the sensor sees. But that was then, and this is now. Sony has combined the slow, but inherently very accurate method of autofocus, called *contrast detection,* with a much speedier *phase detection* system to produce a single "4D" (Sony's terminology) *hybrid* AF system that combines speed with accuracy and exceptional tracking capabilities.

However, there is still one logistical problem to overcome: the camera doesn't really know, for certain, *what* subject *you* want to be in sharp focus. It may select an object and lock in focus with lightning speed. (Sony claims 0.02-second response in some cases.) However, the focus plane isn't guaranteed to be your intended center of interest in your photograph. Or, the camera may lock focus too soon, or too late. This chapter will help you understand the options available with your Sony a7R IV so you can help the camera understand what you want to focus on, when, and maybe even why.

Getting into Focus

Learning to use the a7R IV's autofocus system is easy, but you do need to fully understand how the system works to get the most benefit from it. Once you're comfortable with autofocus, you'll know when it's appropriate to use the manual focus option, too. The important thing to remember is that focus isn't absolute. For example, some things that appear to be in sharp focus at a given viewing size and distance might not be in focus at a larger size and/or closer distance. That family portrait hanging over the mantle may look fine when you're seated on the sofa, but it appears less sharp when examined from two feet away.

In addition, the goal of optimum focus isn't always to make things look sharp. For some types of subjects, not all of an image needs be sharp. Controlling exactly what is sharp and what is not is part of your creative palette. Use of depth-of-field characteristics to throw part of an image out of focus while other parts are sharply focused is one of the most valuable tools available to a photographer. But selective focus works only when the desired areas of an image are in focus properly. For the digital camera photographer, correct focus can be one of the trickiest parts of the technical and creative process.

As I said in the introduction to this chapter, there are two major focusing methods used by modern digital cameras: *phase detection*, used by all digital cameras with mirrors, including the fixed-mirror Sony models like the a77 II; and *contrast detection*, which was the primary focusing method employed by all mirrorless models until very recently.

Contrast Detection

Contrast detection relies on examining the image formed on the sensor, and how it works is illustrated, if over-simplified, in Figure 8.1. At top in the figure, the transitions between the edges of the vertical wood grain grooves are soft and blurred because of the low contrast between them. The traditional contrast detection autofocus system looks only for contrast between edges, and those edges can run in any direction. At the bottom of the figure, the image has been brought into sharp focus, and the edges have much more contrast; the transitions are sharp and clear. Although this example is a bit exaggerated so you can see the results on the printed page, it's easy to understand that when maximum contrast in a subject is achieved using contrast detection, it can be deemed to be in sharp focus.

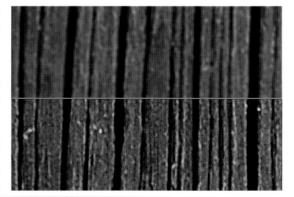

Figure 8.1 Using the contrast detection method of autofocus, a camera can evaluate the increase in contrast in the edges of subjects, starting with a blurry image (top) and producing a sharp, contrasty image (bottom).

Contrast detection works best with static subjects, because it is inherently slower and not well-suited for tracking moving objects. Contrast detection works less well in dim light, because its accuracy depends on its ability to detect variations in brightness and contrast. You'll find that contrast detection works better with faster lenses, too, because larger lens openings admit more light that can be used by the sensor to measure contrast. Despite its limitations, you'll find that contrast detection is *more accurate* than phase detection, so Sony's hybrid system uses it to fine-tune focus after phase detection has achieved *approximate* focus (more quickly).

Phase Detection

In the a7R IV, phase detection is built into pixels embedded in the sensor and combines with contrast detection to give us, potentially, the best of both worlds. Phase detection is also used in a different way when you use A-mount (rather than E-mount) lenses attached to the optional LA-EA2 or LA-EA4 A-mount lens adapters. Both adapters have their own built-in phase detection autofocus systems that bypass and replace the hybrid AF technology built into your camera.

With phase detection, each autofocus sampling area is divided into two halves. The two halves are compared, much like (actually, exactly like) a two-window rangefinder used in surveying, weaponry, and non-SLR cameras such as the venerable Leica M film models. The contrast between the two images changes as focus is moved in or out, until sharp focus is achieved when the images are "in phase," or lined up. Figure 8.2 can help you visualize how this works.

Figure 8.3 is another way of visualizing phase detection. (This is a greatly simplified view just for illustration purposes.) In Figure 8.3 (top left), a typical horizontally oriented focus sensor is looking

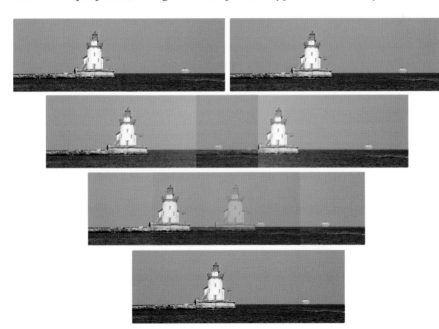

Figure 8.2 Phase detection "lines up" portions of your image using rangefinder-like comparison to achieve focus.

at a series of parallel vertical lines in a weathered piece of wood. The lines are broken into two halves by the sensor's rangefinder prism, and you can see that they don't line up exactly; the image is slightly out of focus. The rangefinder approach of phase detection tells the camera exactly how much out of focus the image is, and in which direction (focus is too near, or too far), thanks to the amount and direction of the displacement of the split image.

The camera can snap the image into sharp focus and line up the vertical lines, as shown in Figure 8.3, top right, in much the same way that rangefinder cameras align two parts of an image to achieve sharp focus. Even better, because it knows the amount of focus travel needed, the camera is able to adjust the speed of the lens's AF motor to move the lens elements slowly or quickly, depending on how much focus adjustment is needed.

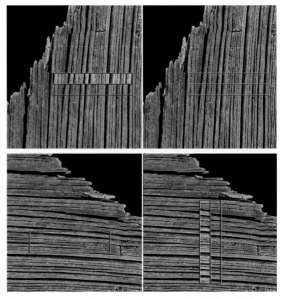

Figure 8.3 When an image is out of focus, the split lines don't align precisely (top left); phase detection can be used to align vertical features of an image and achieve sharp focus quickly (top right).

HORIZONTAL PROBLEMS

You should know that each of these sensors consist of a tiny horizontal array of pixels (represented by the red and green rectangles at top in the figure) and do the best job of detecting vertical lines that intersect them at a 90-degree angle. These vertical-sensitive sensors also do a fairly good job lining up diagonally oriented features. But they are less effective when faced with horizontal features, such as the rotated example shown at bottom left in Figure 8.3. The solution would be to include some vertically oriented, horizontal-line-sensitive sensors (as in Figure 8.3, bottom right), but Sony didn't need to do this, as the a7R IV's complementary contrast detection fine-tuning system handles horizontal features well. However, with very difficult subjects, if you find yourself photographing something with predominant horizontal lines, you can improve your results by rotating the camera to better align the a7R IV's PDAF sensors with your subject.

As with any rangefinder-like function, accuracy is better when the "base length" between the two images is larger, so the two split images have greater separation. (Think back to your high school trigonometry; you could calculate a distance more accurately when the separation between the two points where the angles were measured was greater.) For that reason, phase detection autofocus is more accurate with larger (wider) lens openings than with smaller lens openings, and, with the Sony a7R IV, may not work at all when the f/stop is smaller than f/8 (Sony says f/9 or smaller). Obviously, the "opposite" edges of the lens opening are farther apart with a lens having an f/2.8 maximum aperture than with one that has a smaller, f/5.6 maximum f/stop, and the base line is much longer. The camera is able to perform these comparisons and then move the lens elements directly to the point of correct focus very quickly, in milliseconds.

Because of the speed advantages of phase detection, makers of mirrorless cameras have been adding on-chip phase detection points to their sensors. Sony, because it designs and makes its own sensors, has been able to do a stellar job with this. The a7R IV has a whopping 567 phase detection pixels embedded in its sensor.

Comparing the Two Hybrid Components

Sony a7R IV autofocus uses both phase detection autofocus (PDAF) and contrast detection autofocus (CDAF) to provide a combination of fast and accurate AF, covering roughly three-quarters of the frame. Figure 8.4 shows the layout of the autofocus points and zones used.

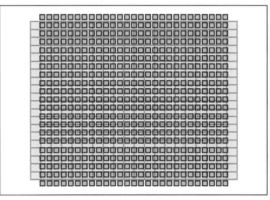

- **Contrast detection zones.** The blue boxes in Figure 8.4 represent the 425 areas of the sensor used by the a7R IV when deploying contrast detection in full-frame mode. Notice that a large area of the frame is covered by the contrast-sensitive areas of the sensor.

Figure 8.4 Autofocus zones for phase detection (green boxes) and contrast detection (blue shaded area).

- **Phase detection points.** The 567 phase detection points of the a7R IV, represented by the green rectangles in the figure, are spread over a wide area.

- **Crop mode coverage.** One often-overlooked advantage of using the a7R IV APS-C/Super 35 crop mode is that both the CDAF and PDAF areas are larger, because the outside area of the sensor is cropped out. The contrast detection zones fill virtually the entire cropped frame. Even though the image is cropped, 325 PDAF points are available when using a full-frame lens in APS-C mode. Sony says that if you use an APS-C lens (designed for cameras like the Sony a6600), 247 PDAF points are used. This effective extended coverage can be important for sports photographers, who may have subjects in all parts of the image.

The hybrid autofocus system uses both types of AF. The process begins by rapidly focusing using PDAF, because the rangefinder approach always tells the camera whether to move focus closer or farther, and by approximately how much. No hunting is required, which is often the case with phase detection, which needs to tweak the focus point until it settles on the sharpest position.

Once the PDAF has done its stuff, contrast detection kicks in, using its finicky but more accurate focusing capabilities to fine-tune focus. So, you end up with speedy initial focus (PDAF) and slightly slower final adjustments (CDAF), providing a perfect hybrid compromise. That's why Sony didn't switch to phase detection completely. Here's a quick rundown of the advantages of a hybrid system:

- **Contrast detection works with more image types.** Contrast detection doesn't require subject matter to have lines that are at angles to the PDAF points to work optimally, as phase detection does. Any subject that has edges running in any direction can be used to achieve sharp focus.

- **Contrast detection can focus on larger areas of the scene.** Whereas phase detection focus can be achieved *only* at the points that fall on one of the special autofocus sensor pixels, with contrast detection much larger portions of the image can be used as focus zones. Focus is achieved with the actual sensor image, so focus point selection is simply a matter of choosing which part of the sensor image to use. (This point is highlighted by the fact, discussed below, that in Flexible Spot mode, you can move the Autofocus Area to many parts of the sensor, whereas with a phase detection system, you can move the Autofocus Area only to a small number of specific locations where the special autofocus sensors used for phase detection are located.)

- **Contrast detection can be more accurate with some types of scenes.** Phase detection can fall prey to the vagaries of uncooperative subject matter: if suitable lines aren't available, the system may achieve less than optimal focus. In addition, accuracy decreases as the maximum aperture baseline used for calculations becomes smaller. A lens with a maximum aperture of f/5.6 will focus with less accuracy than one with an f/1.8 maximum aperture. Contrast detection focus is more clear-cut. In most cases, the camera is able to determine clearly when sharp focus has been achieved.

- **Phase detection "knows" which direction to focus.** The split image seen by phase detection sensors reveal instantly whether focus is too close or too far. As I mentioned earlier, there is no need to "hunt" for the focus point, as the AF system can immediately adjust in the proper direction. That boosts focus speed considerably.

- **Phase detection "knows" how far out of focus a subject is.** The separation between the two halves of the image let the AF system know whether the subject is grossly out of focus, or whether only a slight adjustment is needed. That means faster autofocus, too.

- **Phase detection isn't as dependent on scene brightness.** As long as the split images are illuminated well enough for the AF system to make an evaluation, greater or lesser amounts of light don't have as much of an effect on speed and accuracy. Remember, the reason phase detection systems operate less well at smaller f/stops is because the baseline diameter of the aperture is smaller.

- **Sony's 4D high-density tracking can follow moving subjects.** The a7R IV's phase detection system can achieve focus quickly (even when shooting continuously at 11 frames per second), whether your subject is moving horizontally or vertically (what Sony calls *area*), toward you, or away from you (*depth* in Sony-speak). To those three dimensions, the system adds the fourth dimension of time (which the company labels as *steadfast*), so focus can be maintained as it changes position. The 4D AF also deploys *high-density* tracking to zero in on moving subjects, using focus areas that are smaller than the 425 phase detection sensor areas shown in Figure 8.5.

 NOTE **Compatible lenses.** Not all lenses are compatible with the phase detection component. Older lenses, and lenses that need to be updated using firmware, don't support phase detection, which in turn blocks use of the Automatic AF, AF Track Duration, and AF Drive Speed features explained in Chapter 3. A-Mount lenses used with the LA-EA2 or LA-EA4 adapters do not support focal plane phase detection, although most can be used with their own phase detection.

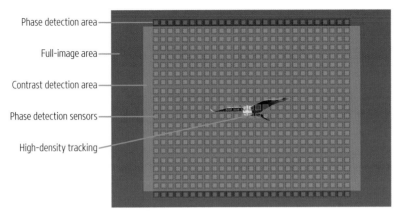

Phase detection area

Full-image area

Contrast detection area

Phase detection sensors

High-density tracking

Figure 8.5 Within the image frame are phase detection areas consisting of 425 pixels embedded in the sensor, 567 contrast detection zones, and high-density tracking areas that can follow your subject as it moves.

Focus Modes and Options

Now that you understand the fundamental principles of how the a7R IV achieves focus, let's discuss the practical application of these principles to your everyday picture-taking activities by setting the various modes and options available for the autofocus system. We'll also discuss the use of manual focus, and when that method might be preferable to autofocus.

As you've come to appreciate by now, the a7R IV offers many options for your photography. Focus is no exception. Of course, as with other aspects of this camera, you can set the shooting mode to either Auto option or a scene mode such as Sports Action, and the camera will do just fine in most situations, using its default settings for autofocus. But, if you want more creative control, the choices are there for you to make.

FOCUS MODES/FOCUS AREA MODES

Your camera has a lot of modes! To keep the various focus options straight, remember that *focus modes* determine *when* the camera focuses: either once or continuously using autofocus, or manually. *Focus area modes* determine *where* in the frame the a7R IV collects the information used to achieve autofocus.

So, no matter what shooting mode you're using, your first choice is whether to use autofocus or manual focus. Yes, there's also a Direct Manual Focus (DMF) option, discussed in Chapter 3, but that still provides autofocus, with the option of *fine-tuning* focus manually before taking the shot. Manual focus presents you with great flexibility along with the challenge of keeping the image in focus under what may be difficult conditions, such as rapid motion of the subject, darkness of the scene, and the like. Later in this chapter, I'll cover manual focus as well as DMF. For now, I'll assume you're going to rely on the camera's conventional AF mode.

The Sony a7R IV has three basic AF modes: AF-S (Single-shot autofocus) and AF-C (Continuous autofocus), as well as Automatic AF (AF-A), which switches between the two other modes as required. Once you have decided on which of these to use, you also need to tell the camera how to select the area used to measure AF. In other words, after you tell the camera *how* to autofocus, you also have to tell it *where* to direct its focusing attention. I'll explain both *AF modes* and *AF area modes* in more detail later in this chapter.

MANUAL FOCUS

When you select manual focus (MF) in the Focus Mode entry in the Camera Settings I-05 menu, using the Function menu, Quick Navi screen, or by switching using a defined button, the a7R IV lets you set the focus yourself by turning the focus ring on the lens. There are some advantages and disadvantages to this approach. While your batteries will last slightly longer in manual focus mode, it will take you longer to focus the camera for each photo. And unlike older 35mm film SLRs, digital cameras' electronic viewfinders and LCDs are not designed for optimum manual focus. Pick up any advanced film camera and you'll see a big, bright viewfinder with a focusing screen that's a joy to focus on manually. So, although manual focus is still an option for you to consider in certain circumstances, it's not as easy to use as it once was. I recommend trying the various AF options first and switching to manual focus only if AF is not working for you. And then be sure to take advantage of the focus peaking feature and the automatic frame enlargement (MF Assist), which can make it easier to determine when the focus is precisely on the most important subject element. And remember, if you use the DMF mode, you can fine-tune the focus after the AF system has finished its work.

Focus Pocus

Back in the pre-AF days, manual focusing was problematic because our eyes and brains have poor memory for correct focus, which is why your eye doctor must shift back and forth between sets of lenses and ask, "Does that look sharper or was it sharper before?" in determining your correct prescription. Similarly, manual focusing involves jogging the focus ring back and forth as you go from almost in focus, to sharp focus, to almost focused again. The little clockwise and counterclockwise arcs decrease in size until you've zeroed in on the point of correct focus. What you're looking for is the image with the most contrast between the edges of elements in the image.

The Sony a7R IV can assess sharpness quickly, and it's also able to remember the progression perfectly, making the entire process fast and precise. Unfortunately, even this high-tech system doesn't really know with any certainty *which* object should be in sharpest focus. Is it the closest object? The subject in the center of the frame? Something lurking *behind* the closest subject? A person standing over at the side of the picture? Many of the techniques for using autofocus effectively involve telling the camera exactly what it should be focusing on.

Adding Circles of Confusion

But there are other factors in play, as well. You know that increased depth-of-field brings more of your subject into focus. But more depth-of-field also makes autofocusing (or manual focusing) more difficult because the contrast is lower between objects at different distances. So, autofocus with a 300mm lens (or zoom setting) may be easier than at a 16mm focal length (or zoom setting) because the longer lens has less apparent depth-of-field. By the same token, a lens with a maximum aperture of f/1.8 will be easier to autofocus (or manually focus) than one of the same focal length with an f/4 maximum aperture, because the f/4 lens has more depth-of-field and a dimmer view. It's also important to note that lenses with a maximum aperture smaller than f/5.6 would give your Sony Alpha's autofocus system fits, because the smaller opening (aperture) would allow less light to enter or to reach the autofocus sensor.

To make things even more complicated, many subjects aren't polite enough to remain still. They move around in the frame, so that even if the camera's lens is sharply focused on your main subject, the subject may change position and require refocusing. An intervening subject may pop into the frame and pass between you and the subject you meant to photograph. You (or the camera) have to decide whether to focus on this new subject, or to remain focused on the original subject. Finally, there are some kinds of subjects that are difficult to bring into sharp focus because they lack enough contrast to allow the camera's AF system (or our eyes) to lock in. Blank walls, a clear blue sky, or other low-contrast subject matter may make focusing difficult even with the hybrid AF system.

If you find all these focus factors confusing, you're on the right track. Focus is, in fact, measured using something called a *circle of confusion*. An ideal image consists of zillions of tiny little points, which, like all points, theoretically have no height or width. There is perfect contrast between the point and its surroundings. You can think of each point as a pinpoint of light in a darkened room. When a given point is out of focus, its edges decrease in contrast and it changes from a perfect point to a tiny disc with blurry edges (remember, blur is the lack of contrast between boundaries in an image). (See Figure 8.6.)

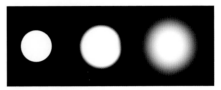

Figure 8.6 When a pinpoint of light (left) goes out of focus, its blurry edges form a circle of confusion (center and right).

If this blurry disc—the circle of confusion—is small enough, our eye still perceives it as a point. It's only when the disc grows large enough that we can see it as a blur rather than as a sharp point that a given point is viewed as being out of focus. You can see, then, that enlarging an image, either by displaying it larger on your computer monitor or by making a large print, also magnifies the size of each circle of confusion. Moving closer to the image does the same thing. So, parts of an image that may look perfectly sharp in a 5 × 7–inch print viewed at arm's length, might appear blurry when blown up to 11 × 14 inches and examined at the same distance. Take a few steps back, however, and the image may look sharp again.

To a lesser extent, the viewer also affects the apparent size of these circles of confusion. Some people see details better at a given distance and may perceive smaller circles of confusion than someone standing next to them. For the most part, however, such differences are small. Truly blurry images will look blurry to just about everyone under the same conditions.

Technically, there is just one plane within your picture area, parallel to the back of the camera (actually the sensor) that is in sharp focus. That's the plane in which the points of the image are rendered as precise points. At every other plane in front of or behind the focus plane, the points show up as discs that range from slightly blurry to extremely blurry. In practice, the discs in many of these planes will still be so small that we see them as points, and that's where we get depth-of-field: the range of planes that includes discs that we perceive as points rather than blurred splotches. The size of this range increases as the aperture is reduced in size and is allocated roughly one-third in front of the plane of sharpest focus, and two-thirds behind it. (See Figure 8.7.)

Figure 8.7 The focused plane (the butterfly's wing) is sharp, but the area behind (the leaf above it) is blurred because the depth-of-field (the range of acceptably sharp focus) is shallow in this image.

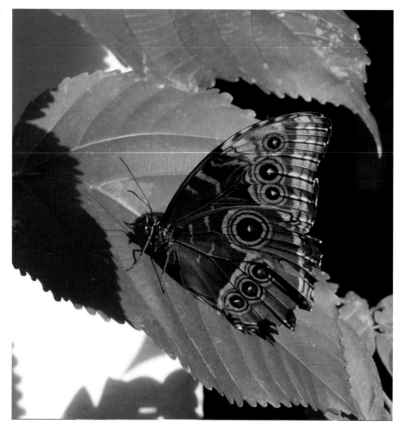

Your Focus Mode Options

Manual focus can come in handy, as I'll explain later in this chapter, but autofocus is likely to be your choice in the great majority of shooting situations. Choosing the right AF mode and the way in which focus points are selected is your key to success. Using the wrong mode for a particular type of photography can lead to a series of pictures that are all sharply focused—on the wrong subject.

FOCUS INDICATOR

At the lower-left corner of your screen, you'll find a green focus confirmation indicator that's active while focusing is underway. It consists of a round green disk which may have rounded brackets at either side. If the *disk glows steadily*, the image is in focus. Only the disk appears when using AF-S; in AF-C mode, the disk is surrounded by the brackets and indicates that the focus plane may change if the subject moves. If the *brackets are flashing and no disk appears*, focusing is in progress; if the *disk is flashing*, focusing has failed. (See Figure 8.8.)

Figure 8.8 The focus indicator icon shows focus status.

Steady: Image in focus (AF-S)

Flashing: Focus has failed

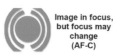
Image in focus, but focus may change (AF-C)

Focus in progress

But autofocus isn't some mindless beast out there snapping your pictures in and out of focus with no feedback from you. There are several settings you can modify to regain a fair amount of control. Your first decision should be which of the autofocus modes to select: Single-shot (AF-S), Continuous AF (AF-C), or Automatic AF (AF-A). DMF first uses autofocus, and then allows you to fine-tune focus manually. Press the MENU button, go to the Camera Settings I-05 menu, and navigate to the line for Focus Mode. Press the center button, then highlight your autofocus mode choice from the submenu, and press the center button again. You can also set autofocus mode using the Quick Navi screen or by pressing the Fn button and using the Function menu.

In the next sections, I'm going to describe all five focus modes, so you'll understand exactly what types of subjects each is intended for. However, as you'll learn, the a7R IV's AF system is so sophisticated that you can generally set up your camera as I'll explain later in this chapter in a section called "Magic AF," and then forget about twiddling with autofocus thereafter. I'll list a few settings you can make that will let the a7R IV easily nail autofocus under most conditions more than 90 percent of the time.

Single-Shot AF (AF-S) Mode

With Single-Shot AF (AF-S), the camera will lock in focus when you press the shutter release (or defined AF start button) and will not adjust focus if your subject moves or you change the distance between you and your subject, as long as you hold down the button.

In AF-S mode, focus is locked. By keeping the button depressed halfway, you'll find you can reframe the image by moving the camera to aim at another angle; the focus (and exposure) will not change. Maintain pressure on the shutter release button and focus remains locked even if you recompose, or if the subject begins running toward the camera, for example.

 TIP In this chapter, I'm assuming that you're using P, A, S, or M mode where you have full control over the camera features. This is important because the camera will use only AF-S in either Intelligent Auto mode. And it will set Continuous AF (AF-C) only in Movie mode, regardless of what focus mode you've selected for still images.

When sharp focus is achieved in AF-S mode, the solid green focus indicator appears in the lower-left corner of the screen and you'll hear a little beep. One or more green focus confirmation frames will also appear to indicate the area(s) of the scene that will be in sharpest focus.

For non-action photography, AF-S is usually your best choice, as it minimizes out-of-focus pictures (at the expense of spontaneity). Because of the small delay while the camera zeroes in on correct focus, you might experience slightly more shutter lag. This mode uses less battery power than Continuous AF.

If you have set the a7R IV for Pre-AF in the Camera Settings I-07 menu, you may notice something that seems strange: the camera's autofocus mechanism will begin seeking focus even before you touch the shutter release button. In this mode, no matter which AF method is selected, the camera will continually alter its focus as it is aimed at various subjects, *until* you press the shutter release button halfway. At that point, the camera locks focus, in Single-shot AF mode.

When using AF-S or AF-C (described next), you can specify focus priority, from AF (wait until the subject is in sharp focus), Release (take the picture *now* even if not in perfect focus), and Balanced Emphasis (compromise!). I explained these options in more detail in Chapter 3.

Continuous AF (AF-C) Mode

When Continuous AF is active, focus is constantly readjusted as your subject (or you) move. The difference between Single-shot AF and Continuous AF comes at the point the shutter release button (or defined focus start button) is pressed halfway. (See the discussion of *back-button focus* later in this chapter.)

Switch to this mode when photographing sports, young kids at play, and other fast-moving subjects. In this mode, the camera can lock focus on a subject if it is not moving toward the camera or away from your shooting position; when it does, you'll see a green circle surrounded by brackets. (There will be no beep.) But if the camera-to-subject distance begins changing, the camera instantly begins to adjust focus to keep it in sharp focus, making this the more suitable AF mode with moving subjects.

Automatic AF (AF-A) Mode

The camera begins using AF-S, and switches to AF-C if the subject begins moving. Use this mode when you're not certain that your subject will begin moving, and you'd like to take advantage of AF-S, as described earlier, until the subject does move. You might use AF-A to photograph a sleeping pet, which, if awakened by the activity, might respond with sudden movement.

Direct Manual Focus (DMF) Mode

The camera focuses using AF-S mode, then uncouples the focus motor so you can fine tune focus (if necessary) manually. For best results, use this mode with focus peaking enabled to provide you with visual feedback as you adjust.

Manual Focus

No autofocus at all. You're on your own in deciding when the image is in sharp focus but provided with extra tools, such as the focus indicator in the lower-left corner of the screen (shown earlier in Figure 8.8), focus peaking, and the a7R IV's focus magnification features.

Focus or Release Priority?

The current focus plane is fixed and cannot be changed at a certain point in the picture-taking process. With AF-S mode, that point is when you press the shutter release halfway. As long as you keep your finger on the button, the camera will not refocus until you press down all the way, or take your finger off the release. In AF-C mode, the camera will focus, but will continue to refocus as long as the shutter release is held down halfway. Focus is *not* locked until you press down all the way to take a picture.

In either mode, when you simply press the shutter release down all the way, focus activation, locking, and picture taking take place one after the other—but still happen in the order I just described. That's where focus/release priority come into play. When the shutter release is pressed down all the way in a continuous motion, do you want the camera to wait until sharp focus is achieved—even if that means missing the exact instant you wanted to capture? Or do you want to have the a7R IV go ahead and take the picture anyway, even if there is a possibility that the image isn't perfectly focused? I explained the priority options in Chapter 3, but here's a recap to using the Priority Set in AF-S/AF-C entries in the Camera Settings I-05 menu:

- **AF Priority.** The shutter is not activated until sharp focus is achieved. You can choose the AF Priority option for both AF-S and AF-C modes individually. Use AF Priority for subjects that are not moving rapidly. The a7R IV's AF system is fast enough that the slight delay should be negligible. However, if you're using an A-mount lens that does not have a built-in AF motor with the EA-LA adapter, you can experience a significant delay. Sports shooters and others who depend on capturing the decisive moment and can countenance no delay at all generally use Release Priority, discussed next.

- **Release Priority.** When this option is selected, the shutter is activated when the release button is pushed down all the way in both AF-S and AF-C modes, even if sharp focus has not yet been achieved. I prefer this option for AF-C mode, as Continuous Focus focuses and refocuses constantly when autofocus is active, and even though an image may not quite be in sharpest focus, at least I am able to get my shot. Using Release Priority does *not* mean that your image won't be sharply focused; it just means that you'll get a picture even if autofocusing isn't *quite* complete. If you've been poised with the shutter release pressed halfway, the camera probably has been tracking the focus of your image. And keep in mind that the a7R IV's AF system is *very* speedy.

- **Balanced Emphasis.** In this mode, the shutter is released when the button is pressed, with a slight pause if autofocus has not yet been achieved. It can be selected for both AF-S and AF-C modes, and is probably your best choice if you want a good compromise between speed of activation and sharpest focus. However, you would not want to use this setting if the highest possible continuous shooting rates are important to you.

Autofocus Magnified

A very cool way to improve your AF accuracy is to use autofocus in conjunction with the Focus Magnifier that you probably work with most often when manually focusing. Just follow these steps:

1. **Turn on AF in Focus Magnifier** in the Camera Settings I-13 menu (as described in Chapter 3).
2. **Define a key,** such as the C1 button as the activating button for Focus Magnifier. (Or access the feature directly from the Camera Settings I-14 menu.)
3. **Activate Focus Magnifier.** An orange box will appear on the screen. Use the directional buttons to position the orange box over the area you want to bring into focus.
4. **Press the center button.** The Focus Magnifier will enlarge the image contained within the orange box.
5. **Activate AF.** Press the shutter release halfway to activate autofocus (or use another key you may have defined to perform that function, say, if you're using back-button focus as described later in this chapter).
6. **AF focus commences.** The a7R IV will use the current AF settings to focus on the area you've selected with the orange box.

Choosing the AF Area

So far, you have allowed the camera to choose which part of the scene will be in the sharpest focus using its focus detection points called *AF areas* by Sony. However, you can also specify a single focus detection point that will be active. Use the Function menu, or press the MENU button, navigate to the Focus Area item in the Camera Settings I-05 menu, press the center button, and select one of the options. Press the center button again to confirm. The Custom 2 (C2) button will summon Focus Area if you haven't redefined it to another behavior. Here is how the AF Area options work:

- **Wide.** The camera chooses the appropriate focus area(s) in order to set focus on a certain subject in the scene. There are no focus indicators visible on the screen until you press the shutter release button halfway. At that point, in AF-S mode the camera displays one or more green focus indicators to show what area(s) of the image it has used to set focus on. In AF-C mode, the indicators will continue to flicker around the frame while the camera refocuses as necessary. If Face Detection is active, the AF system will prioritize faces when making its decision as to where it should set focus. You'll see multiple focus indicators when several parts of the scene are at the same distance from the camera. When most of the elements of a scene are at roughly the same distance, the camera displays a single, large green focus bracket around the entire edge of the screen. Even if you set one of the other options, Wide is automatically selected in Intelligent Auto mode. Use this mode to give the camera complete control over where to focus. (See Figure 8.9.)

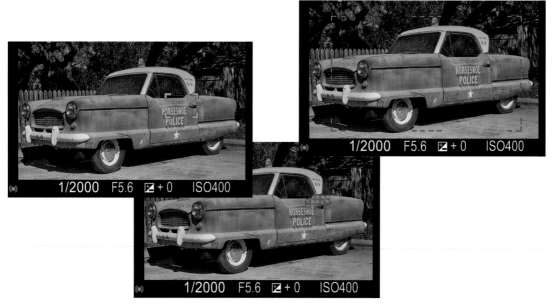

Figure 8.9 With Wide AF Area, the camera either displays a large green bracket indicating that most of the scene is at the same distance to the camera (left), or it displays one or more smaller brackets to indicate the specific area(s) of the scene that will be in sharpest focus (lower center). If the camera decides that all areas of the frame should be considered, a bracket around the entire focusing area is shown (upper right).

You can set Display Continuous AF Area in the Camera Settings I-08 menu if you want to see the focus area displayed as you use AF-C. Indeed, if you're working with AF-C, you'll see the high-density points "dance" as the a7R IV continually refocuses as your subject or camera moves.

- **Zone.** Brackets representing nine different focus zones are shown on the screen—three at the top left, center, and top right of the frame, three in the equivalent positions at the bottom, and three in the middle. Each zone is populated by a 9 × 9 array of PDAF focus points. You can move the focus zone by holding down the defined Focus Settings button (the default is C2) and then using the multi-selector joystick to shift the array to one of the nine overlapping areas. Select one of those nine focus zones, and the camera chooses which sections within that zone to use to calculate sharp focus. (See Figure 8.10). Those individual focus points will be highlighted in green. Use this mode when you know your subject is going to reside in a largish area of the frame and want to allow the a7R IV to select the exact focus point within your designated zone.

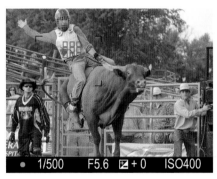

Figure 8.10 In Zone mode, brackets represent a focus zone, and you can move the zone to nine different locations on the screen. The camera selects one or more focus points within that array.

- **Center.** Activate this AF area and the camera will use only a single focus detection point in the center of the frame to set focus. Initially, a pair of black focus brackets appears on the screen. Touch the shutter release button and the camera sets and locks focus on the subject in the center of the image area; the brackets then turn green to confirm the area that will be in the sharpest focus in your image. (See Figure 8.11.) Choose this option if you want the camera to always focus on the subject in the center of the frame. Center the primary subject (like a friend's face in a wide-angle landscape composition), allow the camera to focus on it, maintain slight pressure on the shutter release button to keep focus locked, and re-frame the scene for a more effective, off-center, composition. Take the photo at any time and your friend (who is now off-center) will be in the sharpest focus.

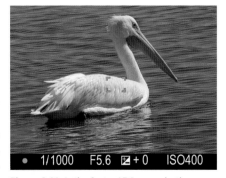

Figure 8.11 In the Center AF Area mode, the camera displays the focus brackets in the center of the screen; the brackets turn green after focus has been set.

- **Flexible Spot.** This mode enables you to move the camera's focus detection point (focus area) around the scene to any one of multiple locations, using the directional buttons. When opting for Flexible Spot, you can use the left/right buttons to choose Small, Medium, or Large spots, which changes the size of the focus brackets in the frame. This mode can be useful when the camera is mounted on a tripod and you'll be taking photos of the same scene for a long time, while the light is changing, for example. Move the focus area to cover the most important subject, and it will always focus on that point when you later take a photo.

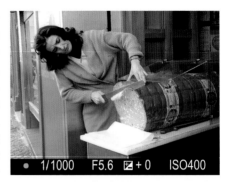

Figure 8.12 When the Flexible Spot AF Area mode is initially selected, the active focus detection point is delineated with indicators that turn green when focus is confirmed and locked. Use the multi-selector or touch screen to specify location of the spot.

Use the multi-selector joystick to move the brackets around the screen, which allows great versatility in the placement of the active focus detection point. (See Figure 8.12.) Adjust the brackets until they cover the most important subject area and touch the shutter release button. The brackets will turn green and the camera will beep to confirm that focus has been set on the intended area.

- **Expand Flexible Spot.** If the camera is unable to lock in focus using the selected focus point, it will also use the eight adjacent points to try to achieve focus.

- **Tracking AF.** In this mode, the camera locks focus onto the subject area that is under the selected focus spot when the shutter button is depressed halfway. Then, if the subject moves (or you change the framing in the camera), the camera will continue to refocus *on that subject*. You can select this mode only when the focus mode is set to Continuous AF (AF-C).

  This option is especially powerful, because you can activate it for any of the focus area options described above. That is, once you've highlighted Lock-On AF on the selection screen, you can then press the left-right directional button and choose Wide, Zone, Center, Flexible Spot, or Expand Flexible Spot. The camera will lock on a subject, using one of those area modes to follow it. (See Figure 8.13 and the explanation which follows in the next section.)

  You cannot use this option if the mode dial is set to Movies or S&Q quick-/slow-motion video shooting movies. I'll describe Tracking AF, along with eye/face recognition in more detail in the section that follows this one.

MOVING THE FOCUS FRAME

You can move the focus frame/point in either of two ways: use the multi-selector joystick when working with an AF mode that allows you to specify the focus area, or, if touch operations are enabled, by tapping the touch screen to indicate the focus point and/or dragging the focus point on the screen to the desired location. In manual focus mode, the same controls move the magnified focus area. If you assign Focus Standard to the multi-selector center button, pressing it will move the focusing frame back to the center of the screen.

Just as you're limited in the use of the AF mode in certain operating modes, there's a limitation with AF Area as well. For example, Flexible Spot is not available for selection in Intelligent Auto mode; the camera will always use Multi as the AF Area mode.

Tracking and Focusing on Subjects, Faces, and Eyes

The a7R IV's tracking capabilities are awesome enough on their own. The camera's upgraded face and eye detection augments the plain vanilla tracking capabilities enough that it can be considered one of the most significant improvements this camera boasts (aside from its 61MP sensor).

Tracking AF is not limited to following and focusing on faces or eyes, of course; it can track any moving subject. In general, you can turn it on and forget it. It does, however, only work in still photography mode; you can't use it when shooting movies. One thing to keep in mind is that it's sometimes difficult to track subjects other than humans; if your chosen subject happens to be near a face (say, an active pet, when you have the Animal subject option turned off), the a7R IV's AF system will sometimes jump to the face/eyes, and begin tracking it, instead. The desired subject needn't be physically near the face; proximity in two-dimensions is sufficient to fool the AF system. Perhaps you want to photograph a close-up of a bride's hand wearing her new wedding ring, with the groom smiling in the background. If the groom's face is "close" enough to the ring in the frame, instead of a sharp photo of the bridge's hand and a smiling groom (who you wanted to be out of focus for creative effect), you end up with a sharp husband and blurry wedding ring.

Tracking may not work if the subject is moving too quickly, is too small or too large to be isolated effectively, has only reduced contrast against its background, or if the ambient light is too dark or changes dramatically while you're tracking. I'm going to show you how to use the basic tracking feature first, then go into detail about the new face/eye detection features.

To use Tracking AF, just follow these steps:

1. **Choose AF-C.** Tracking works only when you are using continuous autofocus because, well, it refocuses continually.
2. **Activate Tracking AF.** Use the Function menu and choose Focus Area. Scroll down to the bottom of the list of modes and highlight Tracking AF.
3. **Choose Focus Area Mode.** Using Tracking AF does *not* mean you lose access to the four AF area modes. With Tracking AF highlighted, use the left/right controls to select Wide, Zone, Center, Flexible Spot, or Expand Flexible Spot. That will give you both Tracking AF *and* the area mode you prefer. If you switch from AF-C to AF-S, you lose the lock-on capabilities, and the camera just reverts to whatever focus area mode you select here.

4. **Select subject to track.** Your subject will be within the selected autofocus area.
   - **Tracking: Wide.** The camera selects the focus area and subject to track.
   - **Tracking: Center.** Frame the scene so the subject you want to track is under the center focus point.
   - **Tracking: Flexible Spot.** You can use the multi-selector joystick to position the Small, Medium, or Large Flexible Spot over the subject.
   - **Tracking: Expand Flexible Spot.** You can use the multi-selector joystick to position the Small, Medium, or Large Flexible Spot over the subject. (See Figure 8.13, left.)

5. **Start tracking.** When you activate focus by pressing the shutter release halfway, the camera will use your selected focus area option to lock in focus, as always. However, now, once focus has been locked, the camera will *track* your subject as it roams around the screen. You'll see the green focus area box moving as your subject moves (or you reframe the image with the camera). (See Figure 8.13, right.) If a face is detected, a tracking rectangle around the face will be shown. (You'll learn more about face detection in an upcoming section.)

Figure 8.13 Left: Place the focus point on the object the camera should track, and press the shutter release to activate tracking. Right: When Tracking is active, the camera maintains focus on your preferred target, tracking it as it moves around the scene.

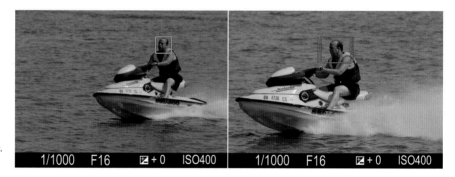

Face Detection and Eye AF Overview

As hinted already, the a7R IV has a couple more tricks up its sleeve for setting the AF area. The camera can detect faces and eyes, lets you select which eye to track, and can differentiate between humans and animals—and it can do all that at high speed! You can turn Face Priority on or off, and activate visible frames around the faces the a7R IV detects. This enables the camera to attempt to identify any human faces in the scene. If it finds one or more faces, the camera will surround each one (up to eight in all) with the highest priority face outlined in white, and the others in either gray (if an unregistered face) or purple (if you have previously registered that face). In AF-S mode, an additional frame will be placed on the eyes of your subject, if detected. Press the shutter release halfway and the camera focuses on the highest priority face.

You can also specify Face Priority in Multi Metering and the a7R IV will not only try to focus on faces, it will base its exposure on them as well. In Chapter 3, I explained how to register and prioritize faces using entries in the Camera Settings I-15 menu. Face Detection is available only when you're using AF and when the Focus Area is set to Wide and the Metering mode is set to Multi, the defaults. So, if the Face Detection Settings option is grayed out on the Camera Settings I menu, check those other settings to make sure they are in effect. Face Detection in the a7R IV works well enough that you can leave it on all the time. It's also an ideal choice if you need to hand the camera to someone to photograph you and your family or friends at an outing in the park. However, it really comes in useful when you couple it with Eye AF.

Face/Eye Detection is disabled when using digital zoom features, the focus magnifier, and the Posterization Picture Effect. It's also unavailable when shooting movies with the 120p/100p Record Setting, S&Q slow-motion movies at 120/100 frames per second, or when capturing 4K movies at 30/25p 100M, 30/25p 60M, or when you output 4K movies to both your camera's internal memory card and HDMI port.

Making Your Face/Eye Detection Settings

The key Face/Eye Detection settings are found in several different menus. This section will help you find and adjust all of them. I'll show you how to tell the a7R IV to base its AF decisions on faces, give certain faces a higher priority, and explain how to switch back and forth between detecting human eyes and those of animals.

Your first stop should be the Face/Eye AF Settings menu entry, originally shown in Figure 3.17 in Chapter 3 of this book. The sub-screen has five entries:

- **Face/Eye Priority in AF.** The entry has two choices: On or Off. When set to Off, the camera gives no special priority to faces detected within the frame. Perhaps you're shooting landscapes or other scenes and don't want the camera to fixate on any faces it detects.

  Alternatively, choose On and the a7R IV will give a higher priority to detected faces. Up to eight faces, if present, may be detected. When autofocus is activated, the camera will attempt to focus on the eyes, if they are located within the active focus area. Note that when using Superior Auto, Face/Eye Priority is locked at On.

  The Eye AF portion of Face/Eye Priority AF may not function as expected with subjects which are rapidly moving, have long bangs, closed eyes, or are wearing sunglasses. Shady conditions, backlight, and low-light situations can also hinder eye detection. Keep in mind that if the a7R IV is unable to focus on human eyes in the frame for some reason, it will fall back to focusing on the human's *face* instead. (This is useful with humans who have their eyes closed, are wearing some kinds of glasses, or who have hair that obscures their eyes. You can generally count on having to manually focus Saul "Slash" Hudson.)

A USEFUL BUG

As I noted in Chapter 3, you should keep in mind that activating Face/Eye Priority in Autofocus with this entry means that your a7R IV will give priority to *detecting* faces and eyes, but doesn't guarantee that it will automatically *focus* on them! In practice, what happens is that the camera will prioritize focus on faces/eyes found—but *only* if that particular face or eye resides within *the Focus Area you are using*. In other words, if you're using the Center focus area and your human subject happens to reside outside the center area, the camera will helpfully detect a face/eye and display a frame around it, but will focus *only* on whatever is actually within the focus area.

   It's easy to overlook this discrepancy, especially if the subject you want to focus on is located near to, but in front of or behind a human. Further, most of our "people" shots have the person in the center of the frame, and, with some focus modes (such as Wide), the focus area is so large that your human may actually be in an appropriate location, anyway. However, you should be aware of this distinction.

   As you'll learn shortly, the "bug" is actually a *feature*. As I point out in the "Magic AF: Set and Forget" section coming up, separating the Face/Eye detection from Face/Eye implementation comes in useful. If you need to work around it, however, use Eye AF, which zeroes in and focuses on detected eyes, regardless of your selected focus area. I assign Eye AF to a Custom Key for that purpose.

- **Subject Detection.** When set to Human, the camera looks for human faces and eyes. If you choose Animal instead, it looks for animal eyes only; as, to date, the faces of other types of living creates vary too much for existing technology to detect with any reliability. It's generally safe to leave this setting at Human, unless you happen to be at a zoo, photographing the Westminster Kennel Club show, or engaged in other animal-intensive activities. (Animal eye detection works great, by the way.)

- **Right/Left Eye Select.** Chooses whether to detect the left or right eye of the human subject (the option is not available when Animal is selected for Subject Detection). Note that this feature uses the *subject's* eye, which may be on the opposite side from your perspective (that is, your subject's right eye is on the left side of your frame). In general, it usually doesn't matter which eye the camera scrutinizes. If you don't care (which will usually be the case), select Auto instead of Right or Left, and the a7R IV will do a good job of finding the closest eye for you.

   One really cool thing to do (because you can!) is to assign Switch Right/Left Eye to a Custom Key in the Camera Settings II-09 menu, just to have the power to alternate eyes on the fly if you feel the need.

- **Face Detection Frame Display.** When activated, the camera automatically shows a small white square around a human eye it is focusing on, and that frame will turn green when the subject is in focus. But you can *also* enable a frame around entire faces with this option. (If you want the frames to display, but disappear after a time, use AF Area Auto Clear, described later in this chapter.)

   Although the eye-focus box is helpful, I find the additional box around the face very useful and leave it on at all times so I know *exactly* what face(s) have been detected. When enabled, a gray selection box appears around detected faces. The box around the face used for autofocus turns white. If there are several faces in the frame and you've registered and prioritized some or all of them, the boxes around the other faces turn reddish-purple. (I'll show you how to register faces later in this chapter.) If you find the boxes distracting, you can turn them off, and face detection, if enabled, as described earlier, will still be active.

- **Animal Eye Display.** Again, animal faces are never detected, but you can choose to have the camera place a white frame around their eyes when they are found. The frame appears as soon as the eye is detected; it turns green when you press the shutter release halfway to start autofocus. If you've set the display to off, no white frame is shown, but the green frame will appear when you initiate focus. The frames appear only when Animal is selected for Subject Detection. You might find the display reassuring if you're wondering whether the camera knows you have an animal in your sights, but I find the a7R IV does a good enough job that I generally leave this turned off.

Other Important Face/Eye Settings

There are several other settings you need to keep in mind when using Face/Eye Detection. They were fully explained in Chapter 3, and I won't repeat that information here. But this recap should remind you:

- **Face Priority in Multi Metering.** Since the a7R IV does such a good job in finding faces, you might as well leverage that capability to improve your exposure metering, too, when you're photographing people. This entry in the Camera Setting I-07 menu tells the a7R IV to adjust its Multi metering to prioritize exposure for any faces in the scene. It works especially well for street photography and some kinds of performances.

- **Face Registration.** This entry in the Camera Settings I-15 menu allows you to prioritize faces of friends, associates, family members, and anyone you suspect is stalking you. You can enter faces (say, a new friend), delete registered faces (say, your stalker is arrested), and change the order of their priority (your brother-in-law never paid back that money he owed you).

- **Registered Faces Priority.** This lets you enable or disable priority assigned to registered faces.

- **Eye AF.** The Custom Key definition entry in the Camera Settings II-09 menu can be your best friend when you want to customize the way your a7R IV uses features like Eye AF. Assign the Eye AF function to a key, and the a7R IV will detect and focus on the eye *as long as you are holding down the custom key.* As I noted earlier, the camera will search for human eyes within the entire frame, regardless of the Focus Area you've selected. Press the shutter release down all the way while holding the key to take the picture. It also allows you to use one Focus Area setting, and instantly bypass that selection by activating Eye AF. I also noted that you can assign a key to Right/Left Eye select, bypassing the Auto setting for that feature if your subject tends to not face you consistently.

Magic Autofocus—Set and Forget

I gave this chapter the title *Mastering Autofocus Options* for a reason. Your Sony a7R IV has an incredible number of autofocus adjustments—many of them new to Sony mirrorless cameras introduced in 2019 and later (or provided as a firmware update to earlier models like the a7R III and a9). My goal, to this point, has been to help you learn about all those options so you'll understand exactly what you can do to fine-tune the a7R IV's incredible AF features under a variety of situations.

The good news is that your camera's AF system is so robust, you may not need to implement many features for about 90 percent of your shooting. This section will explain some basic adjustments you can set, and then forget, for most of your shooting. The a7R IV can do an excellent job of achieving focus under most conditions; my camera stumbles only under very low-light environments, insanely active sports, or with challenging subjects like birds in flight. Not that it can't perform well in those situations, but you can still benefit from the AF options described earlier in this chapter.

Here's the secret of "magic" autofocus, which I think you'll find will work very well nearly all of the time, thanks to the a7R IV's generous array of phase detection AF points embedded in the sensor, 425 contrast detect zones, and the pure power of its Bionz X microprocessor.

- **Set your AF mode to AF-C.** Leave it there. Advanced users don't need the "automatic" AF-A mode, which is inconsistent. You might need AF-S if you want to lock focus on a particular subject. I'm going to show you how you can leave the camera set on AF-C and temporarily switch from AF-C to AF-S when you hold down a Custom Key.

- **Set AF Area mode to Tracking: Flexible Spot M.** Thereafter, you can move the box representing the focus spot around the screen with the multi-selector joystick. Half-press the shutter release button and the a7R IV will begin tracking whatever is under the spot location as long as you continue to hold the shutter button.

  Here's the cool part: if there is a human in the area you decide to track, the a7R IV will add Face/Eye detection to improve its AF performance. If the area you track does *not* have a human, the camera will track that object instead. It will continue to detect faces and eyes, but won't automatically focus on them. This is the "feature" I noted in the "A Useful Bug" sidebar earlier. Most other camera brands with face detection don't give you this flexibility. It makes it possible to track objects that are *not* human without disabling face detection—as long as the human face isn't *too* close to the tracked subject.

- **Activate Face/Eye Priority in AF.** I showed you how to do this in the previous section.

- **Set Subject Detection to Human and Right/Left Eye Detect to Auto.** Change these only if you have a reason to switch to Animal or specific eye detection.

- **Enable Face Detection Frame Display.** You'll appreciate the extra feedback and reassurance.

- **Begin to enjoy amazingly accurate AF.** You may find you rarely have to make most of the adjustments described earlier in this chapter—although you'll be able to once you've learned how and when to use each of them.

- **If you need to lock focus** switch to manual focus, or temporarily switch to AF-S using the technique described next.

Your AF-C to AF-S Switch

Sony doesn't offer a Custom Key definition to toggle between AF-C and AF-S, but you can do the next best thing—define a button so that the camera switches to AF-S *while you hold down the button* and then switches back to AF-C once you release it.

The procedure is fairly simple. Just follow these steps:

1. **Access Register Custom Shoot Set.** Navigate to this entry, located on the Camera Settings I-04 page, and originally described in Chapter 3.

2. **Select a Custom Shoot Set to register.** I selected Recall Custom Hold 1. Press the center button to enter the setup screen. (See Figure 8.14.)

3. **Unmark all but two settings.** A wide variety of camera settings can be registered, but for this application we don't want to mess with most of your camera's settings. We only want to change the Focus Mode and Focus Area settings, and only while the defined Custom Key is pressed. Scroll through the list and unmark all of them except for Focus Mode and Focus Area.

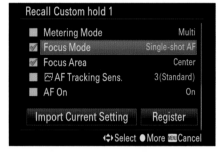

Figure 8.14 Recall Custom 1 screen.

4. **Specify each of the two.** Highlight Focus Mode and select Single-Shot AF from the screen that appears. Then Highlight Focus Area, and choose Center.

5. **Select Register.** Scroll down to the bottom of the settings list and highlight Register. Press the center button to confirm your settings, and MENU to exit.

6. **Navigate to the Camera Settings II-09 menu** and choose Custom Key (Stills).

7. **Define the button you want to use** to switch temporarily to AF-S. I chose the Multi-Selector Center Button, which is on the second page of the Custom Key button options.

8. **When your button is highlighted** press the center button, and in the screen that appears navigate to the Recall Custom Hold 1 option. It was located on Page 2 of 27 for my chosen button.

9. **Press enter to confirm.** Then press MENU to exit.

That's all there is to it. Henceforth, AF-C, Tracking, and Face/Eye Detection will by default be active and provide amazing AF performance under most circumstances. If you want to switch to AF-S to lock in focus on a specific subject, just press your defined Custom Key (in my case the multi-selector button) *and hold it down.* Then, press the shutter release halfway. The a7R IV will use Single-Shot (AF-S) to focus *and* the Focus Area will be set to the center of the screen. The camera will lock focus as long as you keep the Custom Key and shutter release depressed. To return to AF-C and your other previous AF settings, just release the Custom Key.

Understanding Aperture Drive in AF

If you used digital SLRs prior to switching to mirrorless cameras, there may be a difference in the way your new camera's aperture behaves when focusing. Single-lens reflex cameras have traditionally focused with the lens aperture set to its maximum (widest) position. That provides a big, bright image and the shallowest depth-of-field the lens is capable of at that focal length. At the moment of exposure, the lens stops down to the "taking" or *shooting* aperture (which is specified by you or the camera's autoexposure system) and the mirror flips up so the shutter can open and take the photo.

The iris of your a7R IV behaves in a much more complicated way. That's necessary because your image preview is produced from the actual sensor image, whether you are using the viewfinder or LCD monitor, and the image you see is affected by how large or how small the current aperture is. The camera's designers made some trade-offs in how the aperture opens and closes before and during exposure. Here's a quick description:

- **AF-S mode.** When using Single Shot AF, the camera has plenty of time to achieve focus, so in what Sony calls Standard mode, AF is achieved with the aperture set to wide open (but *not* wider than f/2, if you happen to be using, say, a lens with an f/1.4 maximum aperture).
- **AF-C mode.** When using Continuous AF, in Standard mode, the iris remains closed down during focus. The camera's AF mechanism has a dimmer view (but can brighten the display for your benefit). However, by retaining the shooting aperture during the constant focusing and refocusing that happens during Continuous AF, your a7R IV avoids the rapid opening/closing of the iris, and its attendant noise. The downside is that under low-light conditions or when the shooting aperture is small, both the CDAF and PDAF systems are handicapped.

The Aperture Drive in AF entry in the Camera Settings I-06 menu provides a partial solution. Sony retains the Standard aperture drive system I just described, but adds new Focus Priority and Silent Priority modes you can select. Here are the differences.

- **Standard Mode.** This default mode performs as I've described above. Most people will want to retain that setting under most circumstances.
- **Focus Priority.** At this setting AF-S functions as before, but AF-C mode is forced to focus *nominally* wide open (and never wider than f/2). In practice, the camera doesn't necessarily dilate the iris all the way; it partially opens, depending on light levels. That means in bright daylight the aperture may not open much at all, because the camera has enough illumination to focus quickly without resorting to a wider f/stop. Under darker conditions, the iris tends to open much wider for focusing, which means AF can be significantly faster under low-light conditions.

  Unfortunately, while AF is faster, this Focus Priority setting introduces a certain amount of shutter lag—the time between when you press the shutter down all the way, and when the picture is actually taken. If you want to improve AF under low light and can accept some shutter lag, give this setting a try.

- **Silent Priority.** The a7R IV *always* focuses at the shooting aperture, in both AF-S and AF-C focus modes, avoiding the noise of the iris opening and closing repeatedly.

Using Manual Focus

Manual focus is not as straightforward as with an older manual focus 35mm SLR equipped with a focusing screen optimized for this purpose and a readily visible focusing aid. But Sony's designers have done a good job of letting you exercise your initiative in the focusing realm, with features that make it easy to determine whether you have achieved precise focus. It's worth becoming familiar with the techniques for those occasions when it makes sense to take control in this area.

Here are the basic steps for quick and convenient setting of focus:

- **Select Manual Focus.** After you do so (in the Focus Mode entry in the Camera Settings I-05 menu), the letters MF will appear in the LCD display when you're viewing the default display that includes a lot of data. (You can change display modes by pressing the DISP button.)

- **Aim at your subject and turn the focusing ring on the lens.** As soon as you start turning the focusing ring, the image on the LCD is enlarged (magnified) to help you assess whether the center of interest of your composition is in focus. (That is, unless you turned off this feature, called MF Assist, through the Camera Settings I-14 menu.) Use the up/down/left/right directional controls to move around the magnified image area until you're viewing the most important subject element, such as a person's eyes. Turn the focusing ring until that appears to be in the sharpest possible focus.

  The enlargement lasts two seconds before the display returns to normal; you can increase that with the MF Assist Time menu item. In situations where you want to use manual focus without enlargement of the preview image, you can turn this feature off in the Camera Settings II menu, using the MF Assist item.

- **If you have difficulty focusing, zoom in if possible and focus at the longest available focal length.** If you're using a zoom lens, you may find it easier to see the exact effect of slight changes in focus while zoomed in. Even if you plan to take a wide-angle photo, zoom to telephoto and rotate the ring to set precise focus on the most important subject element. When you zoom back out to take the picture, the center of interest will still be in sharp focus.

- **Use Peaking of a suitable color.** On by default in Shooting mode, focus peaking provides a colored overlay around edges that are sharply focused; this makes it easier to determine when your subject is precisely focused. The overlay is white, but you can change that to another color when necessary. The alternate hue may be needed to provide a strong contrast between the peaking highlights and the color of your subject. Access the Peaking Setting entry in the Camera Settings I-14 menu to adjust the color. To make the overlay even more visible, select High in the Peaking Level item; you can also turn peaking Off with this item, if desired.

■ **Consider using the DMF option.** Another option is DMF, or Direct Manual Focus. Activate it and the camera will autofocus with Single-shot AF and lock focus when you press the shutter release button halfway. As soon as focus is confirmed, you can turn the focusing ring to make fine-tuning adjustments, as long as you maintain slight pressure on the shutter release button. The MF Assist magnification will be activated immediately.

This method gives you the benefit of autofocus but gives you the chance to change the exact point of focus, to a person's eyes instead of the tip of the nose, for example. This option is useful in particularly critical focusing situations, when the precise focus is essential, as in extremely close focusing on a three-dimensional subject. Because depth-of-field is very shallow in such work, you'll definitely want to focus on the most important subject element, such as the pistil or stamen inside a large blossom. This will ensure that it will be the sharpest part of the image.

Back-Button Focus

Once you've been using your camera for a while, you'll invariably encounter the terms *back focus* and *back-button focus* and wonder if they are good things or bad things. Actually, they are *two different things,* and are often confused with each other. *Back focus* is a bad thing and occurs when a particular lens consistently autofocuses on a plane that's *behind* your desired subject. Fortunately, that's a malady only cameras with outboard AF sensors have, so you won't experience back or front focus unless you're using an EA-LA2 or EA-LA4 A-mount adapter.

Back-button focus, on the other hand, is a tool you can use to separate two functions that are commonly locked together—exposure and autofocus—so that you can lock in exposure while allowing focus to be attained at a later point, or vice versa. It's a *good* thing, although using back-button focus effectively may require you to unlearn some habits and acquire new ways of coordinating the action of your fingers.

As you have learned, the default behavior of your camera is to set both exposure and focus (when AF is active) when you press the shutter release down halfway. When using AF-S mode, that's that: both exposure and focus are locked and will not change until you release the shutter button or press it all the way down to take a picture and then release it for the next shot. In AF-C mode, exposure is locked and focus is set when you press the shutter release halfway, but the a7R IV will continue to refocus if your subject moves for as long as you hold down the shutter button halfway. Focus isn't locked until you press the button down all the way to take the picture. In AF-A mode, the camera will start out in AF-S mode but switch to AF-C if your subject begins moving.

What back-button focus does is *decouple* or separate the two actions. You can retain the exposure lock feature when the shutter is pressed halfway, but assign autofocus *start* and/or autofocus *lock* to a different button. So, in practice, you can press the shutter button halfway, locking exposure, and reframe the image if you like (perhaps you're photographing a backlit subject and want to lock in exposure on the foreground, and then reframe to include a very bright background as well).

But, in this same scenario, you *don't* want autofocus locked at the same time. Indeed, you may not want to start AF until you're good and ready, say, at a sports venue as you wait for a ballplayer to streak into view in your viewfinder. With back-button focus, you can lock exposure on the spot where you expect the athlete to be and activate AF at the moment your subject appears. The a7R IV gives you a great deal of flexibility, both in the choice of which button to use for AF, and the behavior of that button. You can *start* autofocus, *lock* autofocus at a button press, or *lock it while holding the button.* That's where the learning of new habits and mind-finger coordination comes in. You need to learn which back-button focus techniques work for you, and when to use them.

Back-button focus lets you avoid the need to switch from AF-S to AF-C when your subject begins moving unexpectedly. Nor do you need to use AF-A and *hope* the camera switches when appropriate. You retain complete control. It's great for sports photography when you want to activate autofocus precisely based on the action in front of you. It also works for static shots. You can press and release your designated focus button, and then take a series of shots using the same focus point. Focus will not change until you once again press your defined back button.

Want to focus on a spot that doesn't reside under one of the a7R IV's focus areas? Use back-button focus to zero in focus on that location, then reframe. Focus will not change. Don't want to miss an important shot at a wedding or a photojournalism assignment? If you're set to *focus priority*, your camera may delay taking a picture until the focus is optimum; in *release priority* there may still be a slight delay. With back-button focus you can focus first and wait until the decisive moment to press the shutter release and take your picture. The a7R IV will respond immediately and not bother with focusing at all.

Activating Back-Button Focus

To enable back-button focus, just follow these steps:

1. **Select an AF-ON button.** The a7R IV's built-in AF-ON button performs this function by default, but if you don't care for its location next to the viewfinder, you can redefine the AEL button or another key to have the AF-ON behavior. In the Camera Settings II-09 menu, select Custom Key Settings (Stills) and define the button of your choice.

2. **Turn off shutter button AF activation.** In the Camera Settings I-06 menu, set AF/w Shutter to Off. When you want to disable back-button focus (temporarily or permanently), change it back to On.

That's all there is to it. Henceforth, pressing the shutter release will *not* activate autofocus. Autoexposure metering will still be initiated by pressing the button halfway, as long as the AEL/w Shutter is set to Auto or On (and not Off) and pressing it all the way takes a picture.

Useful Menu Items for AF

I discussed how to set all the autofocus options, which are scattered among the Camera Settings I and Camera Settings II menus, plus how to define Custom Keys to activate certain features in Chapters 3 and 4. If you need a recap, here is a list of the a7R IV autofocus features that you should keep in mind. I'll recap the most important aspects here, as a quick guide to help you locate the longer discussions. Table 8.1 provides some guidelines for particular types of subjects if you don't want to rely on my "Magic AF" recommendation. Remember that some of these are also available in the Function menu.

- **AF Illuminator (Stills).** This Camera Settings I-06 menu item is set at Auto by default, indicating that the illuminator on the front of the camera will provide a burst of light in a dark location when using in AF-S mode. That provides a bright target for the autofocus system. Turn this feature off when you feel the red burst might be intrusive.

- **Face Registration.** Mentioned briefly earlier in this chapter, this Camera Settings I-15 menu item is quite versatile and was described in Chapter 3. You can register up to eight faces that should get priority in terms of autofocus and then specify the order of priority from the most important faces to the least important.

  To register a face, point the camera at the person's face, make sure it's within the large square on the screen, and press the shutter release button. Do so for several faces. When you're taking a photo of a scene that contains more than one registered face, the camera will prioritize faces based on which were the first to be registered in the process you used.

  Take advantage of the Order Exchanging option of this menu item so the faces you consider the most important are prioritized. When you access it, the camera displays the registered faces with a number on each; the lower the number the higher the priority. You can now change the priority in which the faces will be recognized, from 1 (say your youngest child) to 8 (perhaps your cousin twice removed). You can also use the Delete or the Delete All options to delete one or more faces from the registry, such as your ex and former in-laws.

- **Face/Eye AF Settings (Camera Settings I-06).** Allows turning Face/Eye Detection priority on/off, specifying Human or Animal subjects, selecting right or left eyes, turning face frames on/off, and displaying a frame around animal eyes.

- **Focus Mode (Camera Settings I-05).** Choose focus modes from AF-S, AF-C, AF-A, DMF, and MF.

- **Priority Set AF-S/AF-C (Camera Settings I-05).** Select whether focus is *release priority* (take picture immediately, even if sharp focus not achieved) or *focus priority* (don't take picture until sharp focus locked in). You can also choose *balanced emphasis* as a compromise between the two. Separate entries for AF-S and AF-C.

- **Focus Area (Camera Settings I-05).** Select the number and location of autofocus points used, from Wide, Zone, Center, Flexible Spot, and Expanded Flexible Spot.

- **Focus Area Limit (Camera Settings I-05).** Choose which focus area modes are available.

TABLE 8.1 Focus Guidelines

SUBJECT	FOCUS MODE	FOCUS AREA	PRIORITY SETUP	LOCK-ON AF	TRACKING DRIVE SPEED	TRACKING DURATION	FACE DETECTION	EYE AF
Portraits	AF-S	Flexible Spot	AF	Off	Fast	3	On	Yes
Street photography	AF-C	Wide	Balanced Emphasis	On	Fast	3	On	As needed
General sports action	AF-C	Expanded Flexible Spot	Release	On	Fast	1	Off	No
Birds in flight	AF-C	Expanded Flexible Spot	Balanced Emphasis	On	Fast	5	Off	No
Football, soccer, basketball	AF-C	Expanded Flexible Spot	Release	On	Fast	1	Off	Off
Kids, pets	AF-C	Zone	Balanced Emphasis	On	Fast	2	On	Yes
Track events, auto racing	AF-C	Wide	Release	On	Fast	3	Off	No
Landscapes	AF-S	Wide	AF	Off	Slow	3	Off	No
Concerts, performances	AF-S	Flexible Spot	AF	Off	Fast	3	On	Yes

- **Focus Settings (Camera Settings I-05).** Adjust specific focus area with the front dial and multi-selector joystick and focus type of focus area with the control wheel.

- **Switch Vertical/Horizontal AF Area (Camera Settings 1-06).** Specify different AF areas for horizontal and two vertical camera orientations.

- **AF Track Sensitivity (Stills) (Camera Settings I-06).** Select tracking response from 1 (locked on) to 5 (responsive).

- **AF System (Camera Settings I-06).** When using an A-mount lens and adapter, specify whether PDAF or CDAF is used.

- **AF with Shutter (Camera Settings I-06).** Choose On to start AF when the shutter is pressed halfway, or Off to decouple AF start from shutter release.

- **Pre-AF (Stills) (Camera Settings I-07).** Enables/disables AF initiation even before a button is pressed.

- **Eye-Start AF (Stills) (Camera Settings I-07).** When using a compatible A-mount lens and adapter, autofocus is initiated when you put your eye up to the viewfinder.

- **AF Area Registration (Stills) (Camera Settings I-07).** Allows setting a preassigned AF area location to a custom key.

- **Delete Registered AF Area (Camera Settings I-07).** Removes a pre-defined registered AF area that you no longer want to use.

- **AF Area Auto Clear (Camera Settings I-07).** Determines whether the autofocus area is displayed all the time, or only briefly before disappearing.
- **Display Continuous AF Area (Camera Settings I-08).** Enables/disables display of AF areas during continuous autofocus.
- **Phase Detect Area (Camera Settings I-08).** Displays the phase detection area when used with compatible lenses.
- **Circulation of Focus Point (Camera Settings I-08).** Enables/disables wrap-around of focus point/frame as you move them toward the edges of the frame.
- **AF Micro Adjustment (Camera Settings I-08).** Fine-tune autofocus for specific A-mount lenses when used with EA-LA2 or EA-LA4 adapters.
- **AF Drive Speed (Movies) (Camera Settings II-02).** Choose between slow and accurate AF, or fast and slightly less accurate in video mode.
- **AF Track Sensitivity (Movie) (Camera Settings II-02).** Adjust how long the a7R IV waits to refocus on intervening objects when shooting movies.
- **Focus Magnifier (Camera Settings I-14).** Enlarges image during manual focus.
- **MF Assist (Camera Settings I-14).** Turns manual focus magnifier on or off.
- **Focus Magnifier Time (Camera Settings I-14).** Length of time focus magnifier remains active.
- **Peaking Setting (Camera Settings I-14).** Turn peaking on or off, set the level (strength) of the effect, and the color of the outline.

Advanced Techniques

9

Of the primary foundations of great photography, only one of them—the ability to capture a compelling image with a pleasing composition—takes a lifetime (or longer) to master. The art of *making* a photograph, rather than just *taking* a photograph, requires an aesthetic eye that sees the right angle for the shot, as well as a sense of what should be included or excluded in the frame; a knowledge of what has been done in the medium before (and where photography can be taken in the future); and a willingness to explore new areas. The more you pursue photography, the more you will learn about visualization and composition. When all is said and done, this is what photography is all about.

The other basics of photography—equally essential—involve more technical aspects: the ability to use your camera's features to produce an image with good tonal and color values; to achieve sharpness (where required) or unsharpness (when you're using selective focus); and to master appropriate white/color balance. It's practical to learn these technical skills in a time frame that's much less than a lifetime, although most of us find there is always room for improvement. You'll find the basic information you need to become proficient in each of these technical areas in this book.

The final and most rewarding stage comes when you begin exploring advanced techniques that enable you to get stunning shots that will have your family, friends, and colleagues asking you, "How did you *do* that?" These more advanced techniques deserve an entire book of their own, but there is plenty of room in this chapter to introduce you to some clever things you can do with your a7R IV.

Exploring Ultra-Fast Exposures

Fast shutter speeds (such as 1/1000th second) can stop action because they capture only a tiny slice of time: a high-jumper frozen in mid-air, perhaps. The Sony a7R IV has a top shutter speed of 1/8000th second for ambient light exposures. Electronic flash can also freeze motion by virtue of its extremely short duration—as brief as 1/50000th second or less. When you're using flash, the short duration of the actual burst of light can freeze a moving subject; that can also give you an ultra-quick glimpse of a moving subject when the scene is illuminated only by flash.

The a7R IV is fully capable of immobilizing all but the very fastest movement if you use a shutter speed of 1/8000th second (without flash). The top speeds are generally overkill when it comes to stopping action; I can rarely find a situation where even 1/4000th second is required to freeze high-speed motion. For example, each of the images shown in Figure 9.1 required a shutter speed of just 1/2000th second to freeze the action.

Figure 9.1 A shutter speed of 1/2000th second will freeze most action.

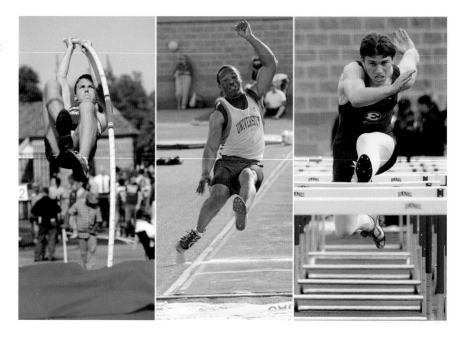

Virtually all sports motion can be frozen at 1/2000th second or a slower shutter speed, and for many sports a shutter speed of 1/500th of a second or even much slower is actually preferable—for example, to allow the wheels of a racing automobile or motorcycle, or the propeller on a classic aircraft, to blur realistically.

There may be a few situations where a shutter speed faster than 1/4000th second is required. If you wanted to use an aperture of f/1.8 at ISO 100 outdoors in bright sunlight, say to throw a background out of focus with the shallow depth-of-field available at f/1.8, a shutter speed of 1/4000th second would more than do the job. You'd need a faster shutter speed only if you set a higher ISO, and you probably wouldn't do that if your goal were to use the widest aperture possible. Under *less* than full sunlight, I doubt you'd even need to use a shutter speed of 1/4000th second in any situations you're likely to encounter.

Electronic flash works well for freezing the motion of a nearby subject when flash is the only source of illumination. Since the subject is illuminated for only a split second, you get the effect that would be provided by a very fast shutter speed and also the high level of light needed for an exposure. This feature can be useful for stopping the motion of a nearby subject.

Of course, as you'll see in Chapter 13, the tiny slices of time extracted by the millisecond duration of an electronic flash exact a penalty. To use flash, the a7R IV employs a shutter speed no faster than 1/250th second, which is the fastest shutter speed—called sync speed—in conventional flash photography with your a7R IV camera.

You can have a lot of fun exploring the kinds of pictures you can take using very brief exposure times, whether you decide to take advantage of the action-stopping shutter speeds (between 1/1000th and 1/8000th second) or the brief burst of light from flash that can freeze the motion of a nearby subject.

Here are a few ideas to get you started:

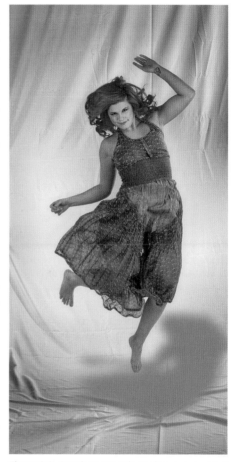

- **Take revealing images.** Fast shutter speeds can help you reveal the real subject behind the façade, by freezing constant motion to capture an enlightening moment in time. Legendary fashion/portrait photographer Philippe Halsman used leaping photos of famous people, such as the Duke and Duchess of Windsor, Richard Nixon, and Salvador Dali, to illuminate their real selves. Halsman said, *"When you ask a person to jump, his attention is mostly directed toward the act of jumping and the mask falls so that the real person appears."* Try some high-speed portraits of people you know in motion to see how they appear when concentrating on something other than the portrait. (See Figure 9.2.)

- **Create unreal images.** High-speed photography can also produce photographs that show your subjects in ways that are quite unreal. A helicopter in mid-air with its rotors frozen or a motocross cyclist leaping over a ramp, but with all motion stopped so that the rider and machine look as if they were frozen in mid-air, makes for an unusual picture. (See the frozen rotors at top in Figure 9.3.) When we're accustomed to seeing subjects in motion, seeing them stopped in time can verge on the surreal.

- **Capture unseen perspectives.** Some things are *never* seen in real life, except when viewed in a stop-action photograph. MIT professor Dr. Harold Edgerton's famous balloon burst photographs were only a starting point for the inventor of the electronic flash unit.

Figure 9.2 Fast shutter speeds can freeze your subject at the top of a jump.

Freeze a hummingbird in flight for a view of wings that never seem to stop. Or, capture the splashes as liquid falls into a bowl, as shown in Figure 9.4. No electronic flash was required for this image (and wouldn't have illuminated the water in the bowl as evenly). Instead, a clutch of high-intensity lamps bounced off a green card and an ISO setting of 1600 allowed the camera to capture this image at 1/2000th second.

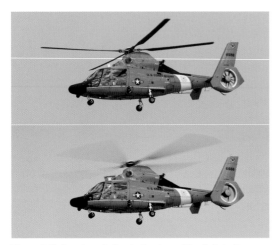

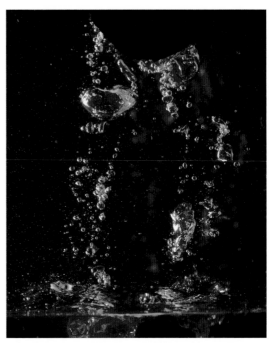

Figure 9.3 Freezing a helicopter's rotors with a fast shutter speed makes for an image that doesn't look natural (top); a little blur helps convey a feeling of motion (bottom).

Figure 9.4 A large amount of artificial illumination and an ISO 1600 setting made it possible to capture this shot at 1/2000th second without use of electronic flash.

Long Exposures

Longer exposures are a doorway into another world, showing us how even familiar scenes can look much different when photographed over periods measured in seconds. At night, long exposures produce streaks of light from moving, illuminated subjects like automobiles or amusement park rides, as you can see in Figure 9.5. Or, you can move the camera or zoom the lens to get interesting streaks from non-moving light sources, such as holiday lights. Extra-long exposures of seemingly pitch-dark subjects can reveal interesting views using light levels barely bright enough to see by. At any time of day, including daytime (in which case you'll often need the help of neutral-density filters to make the long exposure practical), long exposures can cause moving objects to vanish entirely, because they don't remain stationary long enough to register in a photograph.

Because the a7R IV produces such good images at longer timed exposures (and at even longer bulb exposures), and there are so many creative things you can do with long-exposure techniques, you'll want to do some experimenting. Get yourself a tripod or another firm support and take some test shots with long exposure noise reduction both enabled and disabled in the Setup menu (to see whether you prefer low noise or high detail) and get started.

As I noted in Chapter 7, you can make exposures as long as 30 seconds when using P, A, or S modes. In Manual exposure mode, bulb exposures can be even longer. The Bulb option is not available if you're using Silent Shooting, or any mode that captures multiple images with the single press of the shutter release, such as continuous shooting, self-timer (continuous), or continuous bracketing. In

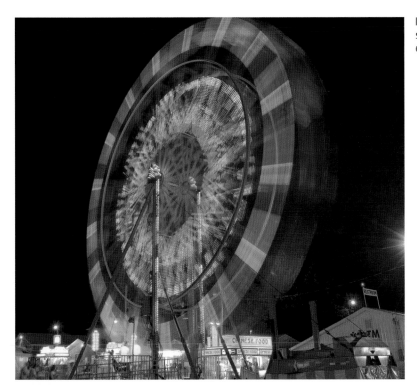

Figure 9.5 Long exposures can produce interesting streaks of light.

bulb mode, hold down the shutter release for the duration of the exposure, or use a wired release with a locking button, such as the Sony RM-VPR1 ($50).

If you want to experiment with long exposures, here are some things to try:

- **Make people invisible.** One very cool thing about long exposures is that objects that move rapidly enough won't register at all in a photograph, whereas the subjects that remain stationary are portrayed in the normal way. That makes it easy to produce people-free landscape photos and architectural photos at night, or even in full daylight if you use one or more dark neutral-density filters to allow an exposure of at least a few seconds. At ISO 100 and f/16, for example, a pair of 8X (three-stop) neutral-density filters will allow you to make an exposure of nearly two seconds on a sunny day. Overcast days and/or even more neutral-density filtration would work even better if daylight people-vanishing is your goal. They'll have to be walking *very* briskly and across the field of view (rather than directly toward the camera) for this to work. At night, it's much easier to achieve this effect with the 20- to 30-second exposures that are possible in low light without any filter.

- **Create streaks.** If you aren't shooting for total invisibility, long exposures with the camera on a tripod can produce some interesting streaky effects. Even a single 8X ND filter will let you shoot at f/22 and 1/6th second in daylight. Indoors, you can achieve interesting streaks with slow shutter speeds, which is a technique I often use when photographing ballet dancers.

 TIP Neutral-density filters are gray (non-colored) filters that reduce the amount of light passing through the lens, without adding any color or effect of their own.

- **Produce light trails.** At night, car headlights, taillights, and other moving sources of illumination can generate interesting light trails. Your camera doesn't even need to be mounted on a tripod; hand-holding the camera for longer exposures adds movement and patterns to your trails. If you're shooting fireworks, a longer exposure—with the camera on a tripod—may allow you to combine several bursts into one picture.

- **Blur waterfalls, etc.** You'll find that waterfalls and other sources of moving liquid produce a special type of long-exposure blur, because the water merges into a fantasy-like veil that looks different at different exposure times, and with different waterfalls. Cascades with turbulent flow produce a rougher look at a given longer exposure than falls that flow smoothly. Although blurred waterfalls and rapids have become almost a cliché, there are still plenty of variations for a creative photographer to explore.

- **Show total darkness in new ways.** Even on the darkest, moonless nights, there is enough starlight or glow from distant illumination sources to see by, and, if you use a long exposure, there is enough light to take a picture, too. I was visiting a Great Lakes park hours after sunset but found that a several-second exposure revealed the skyline scene shown in Figure 9.6, even though in real life, there was barely enough light to make out the boats in the distance. Although the photo appears as if it were taken at twilight or sunset, in fact the shot was made at 10 p.m.

Figure 9.6 A long exposure transformed this night scene into a picture apparently taken at dusk.

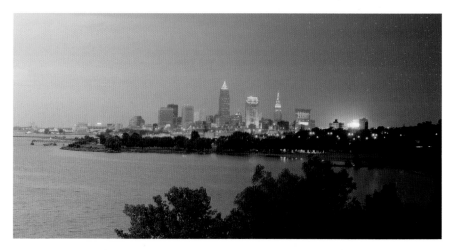

Continuous Shooting

The a7R IV's continuous shooting modes are indispensable for the sports photographer, and useful for anyone photographing an event in which, even if you have lightning-fast reflexes, a decisive moment may occur a fraction of a second after you've completed an exposure. The a7R IV is capable of capturing images continuously at *up to* (and note that qualification) 10 frames per second, so you can shoot consecutive images non-stop until the camera's buffer fills. At an air show I covered earlier this year, I took more than 1,000 images in a couple hours. I was able to cram hundreds of Large/Fine JPEGs on a single memory card. That's a lot of shooting. Given an average burst of about eight images per sequence at the camera's highest frame (nobody really takes 15 to 20 shots or more of one pass, even with a slow-moving biplane as shown in Figure 9.7), I was able to capture more than 100 different sequences like the one shown before I needed to swap cards. For some types of action (such as football), even longer bursts come in handy, because running and passing plays often last 5 to 10 seconds; there's also a change in character as the action switches from the quarterback dropping back to pass or hand off the ball, then to the receiver or running back trying to gain as much yardage as possible. (See Figure 9.8.)

To use the a7R IV's continuous advance mode, press the drive button (left directional button), access the Function menu, or go to the Drive Mode entry in the Camera Settings I-03 menu. Then navigate to the Cont. Shooting option. Press the left/right buttons to select Hi+ (10 fps), Hi (8 fps), Mid (6 fps), or Lo (3 fps). The camera takes advantage of the electronic front curtain shutter to produce the highest frame rates, and actually slows down in Hi, Mid, or Lo modes if you have turned it off.

If you set the AF mode (in the Function submenu) to AF-C (Continuous autofocus) and AEL w/ Shutter in the Camera Settings I-10 menu to Off or Auto, then autofocus will be available in all continuous drive modes, but only as long as the subject is covered by the active focus detection point(s). This feature is useful when a moving subject is approaching the camera or moving away from it; the a7R IV will continuously adjust to focus on the subject as the distance changes, so the entire set of photos should be sharply focused. When using Hi+, Hi, or Mid, and an f/stop smaller than f/8 (f/11 and beyond), the a7R IV focuses for the first image in a burst, then keeps that focus point for subsequent shots. Moreover, in Hi+ and Hi modes, the image is not displayed in real time (you see a previous shot); in Mid or Lo modes, you'll be looking at the actual image as it is captured.

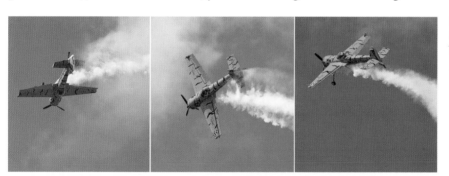

Figure 9.7 Air shows make a perfect subject for continuous bursts.

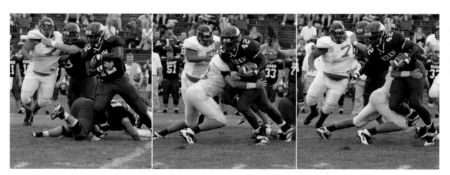

Figure 9.8 Continuous shooting allows you to capture an entire sequence of exciting moments as they unfold.

Surprise! Your a7R IV is fast enough to shoot continuously even when capturing RAW, although the shooting speed will be slower if you're grabbing uncompressed RAW images. In addition, at the Hi+ setting, the camera captures 12-bit RAW rather than full-range 14-bit RAW files to reduce the size of the files it must write to the memory card. However, the buffer is large enough to handle up to 68 images in a burst without pausing for both RAW, JPEG, and RAW & JPEG files. Its capacity drops to 30 images, though for uncompressed RAW/uncompressed RAW & JPEG.

The reason the cameras cannot let you shoot hundreds of photos in a single burst is that continuous images are first shuttled into the a7R IV's internal memory buffer, then doled out to the memory card as quickly as the card can write the data. Technically, the a7R IV takes the data received from the digital image processor and converts it to the output format you've selected—either JPEG, RAW, or both—and deposits it in the buffer ready to store on the card.

The internal "smart" buffer can suck up photos much more quickly than the memory card and, indeed, some memory cards are significantly faster or slower than others. When the buffer begins to fill, the framing speed slows significantly; eventually the buffer fills and then you can't take any more continuous shots until the a7R IV has dumped some of them to the card, making more room in the buffer.

Remember that if you need a reminder of how much space remains in your buffer, you can opt to display the Continuous shooting length indicator using the entry in the Camera Settings II-08 menu, as explained in Chapter 4. Continuous shooting may be disabled if your battery level is low.

Customizing White Balance

Back in the film days, both color transparency and color negative ("print") films were standardized, or balanced, for a particular "color" of light. Most were balanced for daylight but you could also buy "tungsten" balanced color negative and transparency film for shooting under incandescent lamps that produced light of an amber color. This type of film had a bluish color balance, intended to moderate the effect produced by light that was amber. Digital cameras like the Sony a7R IV can be adjusted for specific white balance options suitable for particular types of illumination.

This is important because various light sources produce illumination of different "colors," although sometimes we are not aware of the difference. Indoor illumination tends to be somewhat amber when using light bulbs that are not daylight balanced, while noonday light outdoors is close to white, and the light early and late in the day is somewhat red/yellow.

White balance is measured using a scale called color temperature. Color temperatures were assigned by heating a theoretical "black body radiator" (which doesn't reflect any light; all illumination comes from its radiance alone) and recording the spectrum of light it emitted at a given temperature in degrees Kelvin. So, daylight at noon has a color temperature in the 5,500- to 6,000-degree range. Indoor illumination is around 3,400 degrees. Hotter temperatures produce bluer images (think blue-white hot) while cooler temperatures produce redder images (think of a dull-red glowing ember). Because of human nature, though, bluer images are actually called "cool" (think wintry day) and redder images are called "warm" (think ruddy sunset), even though their color temperatures are reversed.

Take a photo indoors under warm illumination with a digital camera sensor balanced for cooler daylight and the image will appear much too red/yellow. An image exposed outdoors with the white balance set for incandescent (tungsten) illumination will seem much too blue. These color casts may be too strong to remove in an image editor from JPEG files. Of course, if you shoot RAW photos, you can later change the WB setting to the desired value in RAW converter software; this is a completely "non-destructive" process so full image quality will be maintained.

Mismatched white balance settings are easier to achieve accidentally than you might think, even for experienced photographers. I'd just arrived at a Dwight Yoakam concert after shooting some photos indoors with electronic flash and had manually set WB for Flash. Then, as the concert began, I resumed shooting using the incandescent stage lighting—which looked white to the eye—and ended up with a few shots like Figure 9.9, left. Eventually, I caught the error during picture review and changed my white balance. Another time, I was shooting outdoors, but had the camera white balance still set for incandescent illumination. The excessively blue image is shown in Figure 9.9, right.

The Auto White Balance (AWB) setting, available from the White Balance entry in the Camera Settings I-12 menu, Function menu, or a key defined with that function, examines your scene and chooses an appropriate value based on its perception of the color of the illumination and even the colors in the scene. However, the process is not foolproof (with any camera). Under bright lighting conditions, it may evaluate the colors in the image and still assume the light source is daylight and balance the picture accordingly, even though, in fact, you may be shooting under extremely bright incandescent illumination. In dimmer light, the camera's electronics may assume that the

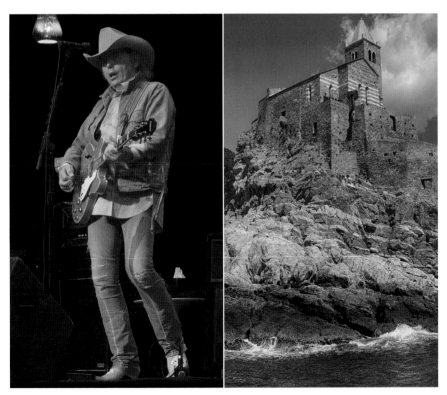

Figure 9.9 An image exposed indoors with the WB set for electronic flash will appear too reddish (left); using the incandescent setting outdoors makes an image too blue (right).

illumination is tungsten, and if there are lots of reddish colors present, set color balance for that type of lighting. With mercury vapor or sodium lamps, correct white balance may be virtually impossible to achieve with any of the so-called presets. In those cases, you should use flash instead, or Custom WB with JPEGs, or shoot in RAW format and make your corrections after importing the file into your image editor with a RAW converter.

The a7R IV provides many WB presets, each intended for use in specific lighting conditions. You can choose from Daylight, Shade, Cloudy, Incandescent (often called Tungsten by photographers), four types of Fluorescent (Warm White, Cool White, Day White, and Daylight), and Flash. However, the a7R IV also offers a method for setting a desired color temperature/filter as well as a custom WB feature.

The Daylight preset provides WB at 5,200K, while the Shade preset uses 7,000K to give you a warming effect that's useful in the bluish light of a deeply shaded area. The chief difference between direct sun and an area in shade, or even incandescent light sources, is nothing more than the proportions of red and blue light. The spectrum of colors used by the a7R IV is continuous, but it is biased toward one end or the other, depending on the white balance setting you make.

However, some types of fluorescent lights produce illumination that has a severe deficit in certain colors, such as only particular shades of red. If you looked at the spectrum or rainbow of colors encompassed by such a light source, it would have black bands in it, representing particular wavelengths of light that are absent. You can't compensate for this deficiency by adding all tones of red. That's why the fluorescent setting of your Sony may provide less than satisfactory results with some kinds of fluorescent bulbs. If you take many photographs under a particular kind of non-compatible fluorescent light, you might want to investigate specialized filters intended to be mounted on your lens for use under various types of fluorescent light, available from camera stores, or develop skills in white balance adjustment using an image editor or RAW converter software program. However, you do get four presets for fluorescent WB with the a7R IV and one of these should provide close to accurate white balance with the common types of lights.

It's when you find that AWB and the various presets simply cannot produce pleasing white balance in certain lighting conditions that you'll need the other options (discussed shortly): use the white balance adjustment feature, set a specific color temperature, or calibrate the WB system to set a custom white balance.

Fine-Tuning Preset White Balance

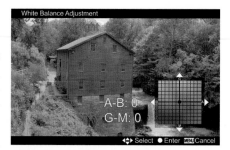

After you scroll to any of the WB options (AWB, Daylight, Shade, etc.), pressing the right directional button reveals the White Balance Adjustment screen, with a grid, shown in Figure 9.10. This feature allows you to fine-tune the white balance by biasing it toward certain colors. Use any of the four directional keys to move the orange dot (cursor) from the center of the grid: upward to bias the WB toward green (G), downward toward magenta (M), right toward amber (A), or left toward blue (B). You can move the cursor

Figure 9.10 Use this feature when you want to fine-tune white balance when using AWB or any of the presets.

seven increments (although Sony doesn't reveal exactly what those increments are) in any of the four directions.

Naturally, you can also move the orange dot to any point within the grid: toward amber/magenta, for example. While biasing the WB, examine the scene in the LCD or viewfinder preview display; stop making adjustments when the white balance looks fine. Tap the shutter release to escape from the WB settings adjustments. Let's look at the options in more detail:

- **Cooler or warmer.** Pressing the left/right directional buttons changes the white balance to cooler (left) or warmer (right) along the blue/amber scale. There are seven increments, and the value you "dial in" will be shown in the upper-left corner of the screen as an A-B value (yes, the labels are *reversed* from the actual scale at the right side of the screen). The red dot will move along the scale to show the value you've selected. Typically, blue/amber adjustments are what we think of as "color temperature" changes, or, "cooler" and "warmer." These correspond to the way in which daylight illumination changes: warm at sunrise and sunset, very cool in the shade (because most of the illumination comes from reflections of the blue sky) and at high noon. Indoor light sources can also be cooler or warmer, depending on the kind of light they emit.

- **Green/magenta bias.** Press the up/down buttons to change the color balance along the green (upward) or magenta (downward) directions. Seven increments are provided here, too, and shown as vertical movement in the color balance matrix at the right of the screen. Color changes of this type tend to reflect special characteristics of the light source; certain fluorescent lights have a "green" cast, for example.

- **Either or both.** Because the blue/amber and green/magenta adjustments can be made independently, you're free to choose just one of them, or both if your fine-tuning requires it.

- **Never mind.** If you want to cancel all fine-tuning and shift back to neutral, just press the MENU button to cancel. The red dot in the color chart will be restored to the center position.

Setting White Balance by Color Temperature

If you want to set a specific white balance based on color temperature, choose C. Temp/Filter in the White Balance menu and press the right button. You'll next see a display of color temperatures arrayed along the bottom of the screen. Press the right button a second time to view an adjustment screen similar to the one shown in Figure 9.10, but with a scrolling list of color temperatures displayed along the right edge of the screen. Here's how to use this feature.

- **Change color temperature.** Rotate the control wheel on the camera back to select a specific color temperature in 100K increments, from 2,500K (a level that makes your image much bluer, to compensate for amber illumination) to 9,900K (a level that makes images much redder to correct for light that is extremely blue in color). The live preview changes as you scroll to give you an indication as to the white balance you can expect at any K level. If you have a color temperature meter accessory, or reliable tips that guide you in making the optimal setting, this WB feature will be particularly useful. Even if you don't have that accessory or useful information, you may want to experiment with this setting using the live preview, especially if you are trying to achieve creative effects with color casts along the spectrum from blue to red.

- **Fine-tune the color temperature.** In addition to color temperature, you can change the blue/amber or green/magenta bias, exactly as described earlier; move the cursor in any direction with the directional keys. If you change your mind, press the MENU button to cancel the bias adjustments you've made.

This feature corresponds to the use of CC (Color Compensation) filters that were used to compensate for various types of lighting when shooting film. When you use C. Temp/Filter, the color filter value you set takes effect in conjunction with the color temperature you set. In other words, both of these settings work together to give you very precise control over the degree of color correction you are using.

Setting a Custom White Balance

If you often shoot in locations that are illuminated by artificial light of unusual colors, the best bet is to set a custom white balance. This calls for teaching (calibrating) the WB system to render white as white under a specific type of illumination. When white is accurately rendered, other colors will look accurate as well. You can use this feature under more common types of lighting too; it's very useful under tungsten lamps, for example, when the Incandescent WB option does not adequately correct for the amber color of the light. Custom WB is the most accurate way of getting the right color balance, short of having a special meter that gives you a precise reading of color temperature. It's easy to do with the a7R IV. Just follow these steps:

1. Navigate to White Balance in the Camera Settings I-12 or Function menus.
2. Use the directional buttons or the control wheel to scroll up/down through the list of white balance options until the Set icon is highlighted. Don't select the Custom 1, Custom 2, or Custom 3 entries, located just above it. These are white balance memory register "slots" you can use to store customized white balance settings.
3. Press the center button. The LCD will display a message telling you to press the shutter button to capture the white balance data. (Custom 1, 2, and 3 are used later to *choose* a custom WB setting you have saved; Custom Set *creates* that setting.)
4. Point the camera at a white object (such as a sheet of white paper) large enough to fill the small circle that's displayed in the center of the frame. Your target must be in the same light as the subject you plan to photograph, not in some entirely different part of the scene where the illumination is different.
5. Press the shutter release button. The target (such as the sheet of white paper) that you had aimed at, as well as the custom white balance data, appears on the LCD or EVF screen. (The image is not recorded to the memory card.)
6. The white balance of the target you photographed will appear at the bottom of the screen, along with an invitation to choose one of the three registers to store that setting. Rotate the control wheel to specify the register and press the center button to enter it and return to live view.
7. Press the center button to return to the live view on the LCD. Henceforth, you can select that Custom register to load a particular set of white balance parameters.

Using Creative Styles

This option, located in the Camera Settings I-12 menu, gives you six basic Creative Styles with fixed combinations of contrast, saturation, and sharpness. They each have a number prefix on the screen: 1: Standard, 2: Vivid, 3: Neutral, 4: Portrait, 5: Landscape, 6: B&W. Each *also* appears a second time (without the number prefix) and with the addition of Clear, Deep, Light, Sunset, Night Scene, Autumn Leaves, and Sepia. You can adjust the contrast, saturation, and sharpness of the non-numbered versions using the left/right buttons to choose an attribute, and the up/down buttons to adjust that attribute. You can apply Creative Styles when you are using any Shooting mode except Intelligent Auto, or any of the scene modes. When working with Creative Styles, you can *adjust* the parameters within each preset option to fine-tune the rendition. First, look at the "stock" creative styles, each labeled with the number prefix:

- **1: Standard.** This is, as you might expect, your default setting, with a good compromise of sharpness, color saturation, and contrast. Choose this, and your photos will have excellent colors, a broad range of tonal values, and standard sharpness that avoids the "over sharpened" look that some digital pictures acquire.

- **2: Vivid.** If you want more punch in your images, with richer colors, heightened contrast that makes those colors stand out, and standard sharpness, this setting is for you. It's good for flowers, seaside photos, any picture with expanses of blue sky, and on overcast days where a punchier image can relieve the dullness.

- **3: Neutral.** Reduces saturation and sharpness to produce images with more subdued tones. Use this if you plan on tweaking your photos in an image editor and you want a basic image without any of the enhancements of the other styles.

- **4: Portrait.** You'll get reduced saturation, contrast, and sharpness for a more "gentle" rendition that often works well for people pictures, especially skin tones. This style is a good choice if you're planning on fine-tuning those aspects of your JPEG photos in your computer and don't want the camera to overdo any of them.

- **5: Landscape.** As with the Vivid setting, this option boosts saturation (especially in blues and greens) and contrast to give you rich scenery and purple mountain majesties, even when your subject matter is located far enough from your camera that distant haze might otherwise be a problem. There's extra sharpness, too, to give you added crispness when you're shooting fall colors, for example.

- **6: B&W.** This is useful if you want to shoot monochrome photos in the camera, so you won't need to modify color photos in software. This style will allow you to change the contrast and sharpness, but not the saturation (because there are no colors to saturate).

As mentioned earlier, those six are repeated without the number prefix, and augmented with seven additional Creative Styles:

- **Clear.** Sony recommends this style for "clear tones" and "limpid colors" in the highlights, especially when you're capturing "radiant light." The description is a bit artsy, but I've found this style useful for foggy mornings and other low-contrast scenes.

- **Deep.** Darker and more somber images result from this style.

■ **Light.** Recommended for bright, uncomplicated color expressions. I like it for high-key images with lots of illumination and few shadows.

■ **Sunset.** Accentuates the red tones found in sunrise and sunset pictures.

■ **Night Scene.** Contrast is adjusted to provide a more realistic night-time effect.

■ **Autumn Leaves.** Boosts the saturation of reds and yellows for vivid fall colors.

■ **Sepia.** Provides a warm brownish, old-timey tone to images.

To adjust the level of Sharpness, Contrast, and/or Color Saturation for any Creative Style, scroll to a style you want to use (in the Camera Settings I-12 menu) and use the left/right keys to display a line at the bottom of the screen showing the available adjustments of the three parameters. Use the left/right directional buttons to scroll among Sharpness, Contrast, and Color Saturation. With the parameter you want to modify highlighted, press the up/down directional buttons to change the values in a range of –3 to +3. Press the center button to confirm. Here is a summary of how changing the parameters in a Creative Style will affect your images:

■ **Sharpness.** Increases or decreases the contrast of the edge outlines in your image, making the photo appear more or less sharp, depending on whether you've selected 0 (no sharpening), +3 (extra sharpening), to –3 (softening). Remember that boosting sharpness also increases the overall contrast of an image, so you'll want to use this parameter in conjunction with the contrast parameter with caution.

■ **Contrast.** Compresses the range of tones in an image (increase contrast from 0 to +3) or expands the range of tones (from 0 to –3) to decrease contrast. Higher-contrast images tend to lose detail in both shadows and highlights, whereas lower-contrast images retain the detail but appear more flat and dull, without any snap.

■ **Color Saturation.** You can adjust the richness of the color from low saturation (0 to –3) to high saturation (0 to +3). Lower saturation produces a muted look that can be more realistic for certain kinds of subjects, such as humans. Higher saturation produces a more vibrant appearance but can be garish and unrealistic if carried too far. Boost your saturation if you want a vivid image, or to brighten up pictures taken on overcast days. (Remember, however, Vivid and Landscape provide high saturation even at the zero level.) As I noted earlier, saturation cannot be changed for the Black & White Creative Style.

To modify Creative Styles, just follow these steps:

1. **Access the Creative Style menu.** Use the Camera Settings I-12 menu entry or press the Fn button and navigate to the Creative Style entry.

2. **Choose a style to apply.** In the Creative Style screen, the styles are shown in the left-hand column. (You must scroll down to see all of them.) If you want to modify one of the styles shown, press up/down to highlight that style, and press the center button to activate it.

3. **Select a parameter to modify.** You can adjust the contrast, saturation, and sharpness of any of the styles in the left column. Highlight the style you want to adjust/replace and press the right directional button.

4. **Select an attribute to change.** The icons at the bottom of the image area represent (left to right): Image Style, Contrast, Saturation, and Sharpness. Press left/right to highlight the attribute you'd like to modify.

5. **Enter your adjustments.** To change the style that appears in the box you selected at left, highlight the Image Style icon and press up/down to choose one of the 13 styles.

6. **Make other adjustments.** To modify the currently selected style, press left/right to highlight Contrast, Saturation, or Sharpness, described earlier, then press up/down to add/subtract from the default zero values.

7. **Confirm and exit.** Press the center button to confirm your changes. If you redefined one of the six slots, that style will appear in the listing in the left column henceforth and can be selected quickly by following Steps 1 and 2 above.

Don't confuse the Picture Effects feature with the Creative Styles. The Picture Effects are intended to provide special effects in-camera, such as Pop Color, Posterization, and Soft Focus. Since I have discussed them in detail in Chapter 3, I won't do so here.

Pixel Shift

If 61MP resolution isn't enough, your a7R IV features an amazing Pixel Shift Multi Shooting capability that can mimic the amount of detail you might expect from a sensor with a whopping 240 megapixels! The limitations: the camera takes 4 or 16 separate pictures that are merged in the free Sony Imaging Edge software, and they must be captured with the a7R IV rock-steady on a tripod, and I strongly recommend using a remote release.

 WARNING These large files can be quite taxing on your computer's resources. The 240MP test shot I use as an example in this chapter measured 19,008 × 12,672 pixels and occupied 690MB of space on my hard disk drive when converted to TIF format—almost 12X the disk real restate commanded by the same scene captured as an .ARW raw file!

If you intend to work with these massive styles frequently, it may be worth upgrading the amount of RAM in your computer. I already had Adobe Photoshop running as quickly as possible on my 2TB solid-state boot drive, so I added a second SSD internally and designated it as Photoshop's "scratch" disk. Now Photoshop is able to perform most operations on my a7R IV's image files without resorting to slow magnetic memory frequently.

The secret behind the pixel shift process is that your a7R IV doesn't actually have 61MP of resolution in the first place. It does have 61MP worth of pixels, but each pixel can only detect one color—red, green, or blue. When you capture a conventional picture, about 15MP are sensitive *only* to blue light, another 15MP detect only red light, and 30MP are sensitive to green light. Even though each pixel captures only one of the three RGB colors, by examining the values of surrounding pixels, the a7R IV can make a pretty good guess as to the actual color of a particular pixel through an interpolation process called *demosaicing*. The algorithms may tell the camera that a pixel captured by a green-sensitive photosite is probably red or blue instead. This works fairly well, but, as you might think, isn't perfect.

Figure 9.11 shows a small section of a Bayer array, named after Kodak scientist Dr. Bryce Bayer, who patented the technology in 1976. He specified using twice as many green elements as red or blue to

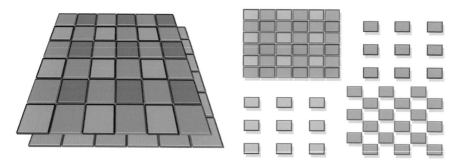

Figure 9.11 A section of a Bayer array (left) and relative distribution of the red, green, and blue filters (right).

simulate human vision, which, in daylight, combines two different types of cells in the retina that are most sensitive to green light. At left, I've superimposed the array's red, green, and blue microfilters over a representation of the photosensitive layer beneath, which is colored gray for the illustration. At right in the figure, I show how the pixels are arranged: every other pixel is green, and the remaining pixels are red or blue, alternating rows.

While each pixel detects only one of the primary colors in ordinary shooting, the pixel shift process fixes this deficiency by capturing *multiple* images, shifting the sensor slightly between shots so that each photosite has the opportunity to read each of the primary colors in turn. In four-shot mode, the camera captures four separate images. The first shot produces the standard image that results from non-shift mode. Then, the sensor moves by one pixel after each of three more images to capture information such that all colors are captured by every photosite. The result is a higher degree of detail without the need to "guess" which colors each pixel represents.

In 16-image pixel-shift mode, the a7R IV also starts by shooting four images centered around one pixel. Then, the camera shifts the sensor *half a pixel* sideways and takes four more images; then half a pixel more for an additional four images. The process is done two more times, giving you 16 separate images that can be processed to provide the detail you'd get from a 240-megapixel sensor. That's a huge amount of information, prodigious enough that the camera cannot process it internally (and you wouldn't want to wait that long between shots even if it could). So, the Imaging Edge Viewer's software interprets these multiple shots for you, to produce a single image in which every pixel reflects the actual color of your subject. You get more detail and potentially more accurate color at the cost of a little post-processing.

Capturing Your Images

Pixel shift works *only* with non-moving, static subjects, and neither the camera nor subject matter can move *at all* during the sequence of exposures. For that reason, you'll get the best results shooting indoors, as there are many factors outdoors that can cause subject/camera movement, even when a tripod is used. For example, you'd need to pay special attention to foliage; if there is any breeze at all, the leaves on trees will move. Using a high shutter speed may help somewhat, but, like MPG, your actual results may vary considerably between different sets of shots when working outdoors.

The plane of focus must not change, either, so you should use manual focus. The exposure itself should be constant, so I recommend manual exposure when using ambient lighting, as long as the illumination itself remains constant. Outdoors, swiftly moving clouds can cause changes in lighting, and indoors you'll find that fluorescent and other non-incandescent sources flicker slightly. I've found that Sony's electronic flash units work well, even in automatic exposure mode, and can provide consistent illumination between shots (if you set the interval between them appropriately, as described in Step 4 below).

FLASH NOTE

When using a dedicated flash unit, the a7R IV's flash sync speed (explained in Chapter 13) *is automatically fixed at 1/8th second*, because the pixel shift mode uses the camera's electronic shutter. If you are using a "dumb" flash, such as a studio flash unit connected through the a7R IV's PC/X connection (described in Chapter 2) or with a trigger attached to the camera's flash/accessory shoe, you should set the shutter speed to 1/8th second manually.

Keep in mind that if you *are* using a "dumb" flash, change the Live View Display entry in the Camera Settings II-08 menu to Off. Otherwise, the a7R IV will base the preview image on the exposure provided by the ambient light, and may produce a viewfinder/monitor image that is too dark.

To capture a pixel shift image, just follow these steps:

1. **Activate.** In the Camera Settings I-03 menu, access the Px. Shift Multi Shoot. entry.

2. **Select parameters.** A screen will appear allowing you to choose among Off, Shoot 4 Shots, or Shoot 16 Shots.

3. **Number of shots.** I recommend starting with four-shot sequences to help you master the pixel-shift feature. The exposures are made quickly, and the files are smaller and are combined faster in Imaging Edge's Viewer module. You'll rapidly see how and where your technique can be improved.

4. **Interval between shots.** When your choice of 4 or 16 shots is highlighted, use the left/right controls to choose the amount of delay between shots. Your options:

   • **Shortest.** Use this default setting to capture all the images continuously, one after another. This is usually your best choice, because it minimizes the chance of even slight movement of your subject between shots.

   • **Delays of 1–30 seconds.** You can also select specific delays of up to 30 seconds. Select a longer pause if you plan to use flash. Just set the time for the amount of time it takes for your flash to recycle; you can err on the side of caution if using battery-powered units, which may have varying recycle times.

5. **Check your lighting.** Indoors, I use incandescent light or flash instead of fluorescent illumination; the flickering such lighting causes can produce banding in your image. Keep in mind that softer lighting (such as that produced by umbrellas, softboxes, diffusers, or bounce lighting) reduces glare but may mask that extra detail you're looking for. More contrasty illumination (generally, direct lighting) can emphasize detail—and also any defects in your subject matter.

6. **Set your exposure.** Manually set your exposure for ambient light and illumination from a "dumb" (say, studio-type) flash. The shutter speed should be 1/8th second or slower. If you're using a dedicated flash unit, the camera will set the shutter speed for you.

7. **Mount your camera on a rock-solid tripod.** If possible, use only the legs of the tripod to achieve the shooting elevation you want, and avoid raising the center column. Lock all the tripod's positional controls. If you're using a lightweight tripod, suspend your camera bag or another weight from the center column to steady it. In my tests I discovered that even almost imperceptible movement (which can be produced simply by pressing the a7R IV's shutter release too vigorously) can ruin a series. The tip-off: a slight amount of blurring in the first shot of a series, or a "ghost" image from ambient light when using flash, compared to the additional exposures, taken after short delay.

8. **Some settings are automatic.** You can turn SteadyShot off if you like, but when Pixel Shift is active it is automatically disabled. The a7R IV also switches to silent shooting (again, to reduce camera vibrations) and uncompressed RAW, regardless of how you have the camera set. As I've noted twice before, silent shooting requires a shutter speed no faster than 1/8th second if you're using electronic flash.

9. **Manually focus to get the sharpest possible image.** Your extra resolution is wasted if you haven't focused properly. I use the Focus Magnifier (found in the Camera Settings I-14 menu) to ensure tack-sharp focus.

10. **Connect the a7R IV to a remote release device or cable.** You'll want to eliminate any camera shake caused by pressing the shutter release manually. I use the Sony RM-VPR1 remote control with the multi-terminal cable. Do this even if you plan to expose using electronic flash. During my tests *without* a remote release, I noticed that in the first shot of each sequence, the main exposure from the flash was augmented by some ambient light "ghost images" (explained in Chapter 13). My solution was to use the RM-VPR1 remote *and* reduce the room's ambient light for good measure.

11. **Trigger the shutter to take your 4 or 16 images.** Don't touch the camera between shots.

Processing Your Pixel-Shift Exposures

Once you've captured your images, transfer them to your computer and launch the Imaging Edge software (which you can download from the Sony website in your country). Then, just follow the steps that follow. (You can also use LibRaw's PixelShift to DNG software, which was still in beta testing when this book was written, to combine images.) (See Figure 9.12.)

1. **In the Viewer module,** browse to your images in the panel shown at left in Figure 9.13, which features a directory/folder tree.

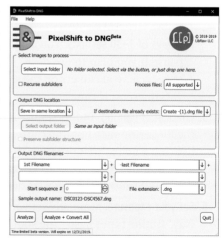

Figure 9.12 You can also use LibRaw's PixelShift to DNG software to combine images.

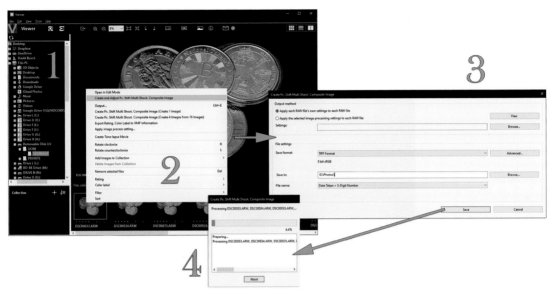

Figure 9.13 1. Navigate to the folder containing your images. 2. Choose pixel-shift processing. 3. Enter parameters. 4. Watch as images are combined.

2. **Choose images to process.** Select one image of the 4 (or 16). The software "knows" which of the additional images belong to the complete sequence, so you don't have to select them individually. Right-click and select Create and Adjust Px. Shift Multi Shoot.

3. **Enter parameters.** In general, you can set the parameters once and use them for future pixel-shift processing if you want to standardize:

    • **Output method.** Click Apply Each RAW File's Own Settings to Each RAW file. You'd use the alternate only if you wanted a specific set of adjustments and follow the instructions to override your original settings.

    • **File settings.** Select the Save Format for the combined image. I often use TIFF, because it can be opened by virtually all image-editing software utilities. Choose ARQ, which is Sony's proprietary pixel-shift format if you want to be able to access a full range of adjustments in Imaging Edge or Lightroom. The latest versions of Lightroom can open ARQ files, with support added after the a7R IV's Mark III predecessor introduced the feature.

    • **Save In.** You can select a directory/folder to store your images, and a filename convention (either the original filename, or a combination of filename, date, and a number).

4. **Click Save.** A dialog will pop up showing you the images are being combined, and you'll be notified when the process is completed.

The software will create a composite image with the resolution shown in Figure 9.14. It's difficult to illustrate just how detailed the processed images are on the printed page, but you'll be amazed when you try this feature for yourself.

Figure 9.14 The final composite image (top); an enlargement of the original image (lower left); and the pixel-shift version (lower right).

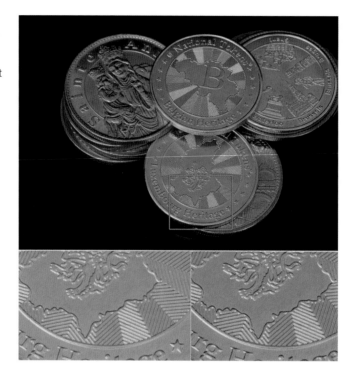

Interval Shooting

I introduced you to interval shooting in Chapter 3, where I listed all the options and settings in the Camera Settings I-03 menu's Interval Shooting Function entry. As I noted there, with previous Sony cameras, this very popular feature has previously required a special app or external device to trigger successive shots over a specific period of time. Today, interval shooting is built right into your a7R IV's capabilities (and has been added to some earlier Sony models via a firmware upgrade).

This section will help you get the most from this capability, and provide some ideas for setting up and capturing your own sequences. There is a lot more to interval shooting than you might think.

Here are a few ideas to get you started:

- **Time-lapse nature movies.** Although interval shooting captures a series of *still* images, which you can view one at a time, it's easy to combine a set of consecutive exposures to create a time-lapse movie. This technique is often used to good effect in nature films, such as Walt Disney's pioneering *The Living Desert*. I'll show you how to create a time-lapse movie later in this chapter.

- **Star trails.** You don't need interval shooting to capture images of the heavens—a long exposure will suffice. However, still photos of the sky longer than a certain length produce blurry images (even if the camera is mounted on a tripod), due to the rotation of the Earth and the apparent "movement" of the stars. You can, however, use interval photography to capture a series of sharp star images over a period of time and combine them into a sweeping star trail image. I'll show you how to do that later in this chapter, as well.

- **Sunsets.** I shoot plenty of sunset photos, particularly in Florida during the winter, and find that images taken at different times as the sun sinks below the horizon often look dramatically different. Interval shooting is particularly useful for capturing the elusive "green flash," a phenomenon in which the sun changes color (usually green, but other colors are possible) for one or two seconds. If you take one photo every second or two for a long enough period, you have a better chance of capturing the green flash—if it happens at all. (It doesn't always appear.)

  The green flash is caused by the separation of the light into different colors as it is refracted through the thickest section of atmosphere (much like the way a prism or raindrops creates a rainbow). The shorter wavelengths of blue, indigo, and violet are scattered by the atmosphere, while the longer red, orange, and yellow colors are absorbed, making the "middle" color, green, most visible for a few seconds. (I *knew* that the mnemonic ROY G. BIV would come in handy after elementary school!)

- **Capture the decisive moment.** You know deer and other wildlife wander into your backyard to munch on the delectables in your garden during the daytime. It would almost be worth the loss of lettuce to capture a few images of them—but you don't have four or five hours to waste waiting for them to show up. (I know erecting a "Deer Crossing" sign doesn't work; it appears the animals either can't read, or ignore them.) Instead, set up your camera (indoors, and shoot through a window if you wish), take a series of photos, and then review them to find your prize photo.

- **Documentation.** Use your imagination, and you'll discover dozens of ways to document things using sequences of photos take at intervals. Wondering how hard your friends worked at helping you re-roof your garage? You can capture an entire workday with shots taken every ten minutes or so to create a hilarious series showing who spent the most time hammering, and who took the most frequent beer breaks (and ended up hammered). How often do you toss and turn at night? A dim nightlight can provide enough illumination to capture images at intervals and see if you slept like a log, or rolled like one.

- **Self-portraits.** You can use your self-timer to take a self-portrait or two—but what if you wanted to shoot 30 or 40 shots of you mugging for the camera or assuming different poses? Choose an interval of 10 seconds or more, and you can take as many consecutive photos of yourself—or someone else—without the need to press the shutter button each time.

Interval Shooting Checklist

Interval photography is not a technique where you can get your best shots by winging it. The shooting process can be—and usually is—lengthy, so you don't want to spend two hours driving to a location, then 10 minutes or 10 hours capturing a sequence to discover poor planning has ruined your final results. This section provides some tips for preparing for your interval or time-lapse shooting session.

- **Know your subject.** If you plan to shoot a sunset, make sure you know exactly *when* the sun will set, so you can arrive early enough to set up your equipment and adjust your camera. You can Google the necessary information, but an app for Android and iOS devices called The Photographer's Ephemeris can tell you exactly when a celestial event will occur, and even provide you with a map that will help you calculate your best location. If, say, you want to shoot the sun setting

behind a lighthouse, the app will tell you the precise spot to stand, and when. If you're capturing the ebb and flow of tides, you'll need to know the time of high and/or low tides at a specific
location. Don't forget to scout the location ahead of time, too.

- **Use a sturdy tripod.** If you don't have a sturdy tripod, take along an empty sack (I use the lightweight mesh bags that oranges come in), fill it with rocks when you arrive at your location, and
hang it from the center column of your tripod to add ground-hugging weight. Successful interval
photography calls for a camera that doesn't move between shots so the successive images show
what has changed between intervals. That's not to say that some interesting photos can't be
taken by panning and/or moving the camera between intervals. You want to avoid *unwanted*
movement, and save intentional movement for experimental photography.

- **Have a fully charged battery or another power source.** Interval photography drains the a7R IV's batteries at an alarming pace. For long sequences, you'll want to use a charged battery or external
power. Turn off picture review to reduce power consumption.

- **Make sure the camera is protected** from the elements, accidents, and theft.

- **Consider Disabling Long Exposure Noise Reduction.** As you'll recall from Chapter 3, when Long Exposure NR is enabled, the a7R IV takes an additional dark "comparison" frame using the same
exposure time so sensor noise can be removed. If you're taking a 20-second exposure at intervals
of less than 40 seconds, you do *not* want the camera to follow the original shot with an additional
20-second dark frame. That's true whenever the total time required for the original/dark frame
exposures is longer than your interval. You'll have to accept a little noise to maintain your shooting rate. Of course, if you are taking a 20-second exposure once a minute, there's no problem
and Long Exposure NR can be left on.

- **Focus manually.** There aren't many common interval-shooting situations in which I'd want to have
focus change from shot to shot. Perhaps you're expecting a herd of deer to cavort through your
garden and would like the camera to attempt to focus on the nearest beast. Most of the time,
however, consistent manual focus is best. Choose whether you want to focus on the foreground,
middle range, or background, and set your focus point there. If you're capturing photos of, say,
a flower opening, use the Focus Magnifier to help you choose the precise plane of focus. Depth-
of-field can be used creatively with small apertures (to increase the range of sharpness) or large
f/stops (to allow selective focus).

- **Manual exposure—or not?** If you set exposure manually, each picture you take will use the same
ISO, f/stop, and shutter speed setting. If the light remains even during the sequence, that can be
a good thing. If the light changes (say, throughout a day), that can be bad, or distracting, or, in
some cases, add a certain desirable look. Your a7R IV's Interval Photography setting for Autoexposure Tracking Sensitivity can be used to fine-tune exposure. If autoexposure is active, you
can specify a fast response to changes (High), or opt for slower adjustments using the Medium
or Low sensitivity settings.

Know that quick changes in exposure can be distracting, especially when combining shots into
a time-lapse movie. If you *want* to see dramatic light shifts as your scene lightens or darkens,
use Manual Exposure and set the shutter speed, ISO, and aperture to give the correct "normal"
exposure.

- **Choose an interval.** The time *between* each shot can be important. If you wait too long, you may miss an important event; choose a very brief interval, and you can end up with too many photos that are almost identical and lacking in the time-lapse effect. The interval is especially important if you intend to combine your shots into a time-lapse movie. With, say, slow-moving clouds, one shot every 10 seconds may produce a majestic march across the sky; fast-moving clouds can require taking one picture every three to five seconds. Sunsets work best with 30-second intervals; I get good results using 60-second gaps between shots when shooting the stars.

  To add Charlie Chaplin–like movement to pedestrians, one shot every second or two does the job. (Fun fact: The cameras used for Chaplin's comedies were hand-cranked at frame rates of around 14 to 16 frames per second; when projected at the eventual standard of 24 fps, the motion was speeded up. To compensate, Chaplin later had some frames duplicated in printing to simulate the 24 fps rate—while the motion was less frenetic, it became jerkier in the process.)

- **Choose number of shots to capture.** For practical reasons, you need to know how long it will take to capture your sequence. When you've chosen an interval and number of shots, the a7R IV displays the total elapsed time, but common sense will tell you that if you are shooting one frame every 10 seconds (six per minute), if you want to capture 60 minutes' worth of action, you'll need to take 360 shots. Conversely, if you plan to convert your images into a movie, you'll know that, at, say, 30 frames per second, your 360 images will provide a movie only 12 seconds in length! Obviously, for time-lapse movies, you'll probably be capturing a lot more than 360 images; the a7R IV allows as many as 9999 frames—about 5.5 minutes' worth at 30 fps.

- **Choose your start time.** Use this setting to delay the start of image capture, from 0 minutes, 0 seconds (begin immediately) to 99 minutes, 59 seconds. While you may want to begin shooting immediately, you should still set a short delay (say 20 seconds) as a start time so the camera can settle down in its tripod perch. If you want to begin capturing an event, say, a sunset, in 10 minutes, you can specify that much of a delay, and spend the intervening time setting up other cameras, performing other tasks, or chatting with your companions about how great your photos are going to be.

A REMINDER

The interval cannot be shorter than the shutter speed; for example, you cannot set one second as the interval if the images will be taken at two seconds or longer.

Settings Recap

I detailed all seven major settings for the Interval Shooting Functions entry of the Camera Settings I-03 menu in Chapter 3. Here's a quick recap:

- **Interval shooting.** Choose On or Off to enable/disable the feature. You'll want to keep this setting at Off until you are ready to begin interval shooting.
- **Shooting start time.** Use this setting to delay the start of image capture, from 0 minutes, 0 seconds (begin immediately) to 99 minutes, 59 seconds.
- **Shooting interval.** Specify how often an image should be captured.

- **Number of shots.** This setting determines the total number of exposures in a time-lapse sequence. You can choose from 1 to 9999 shots. A message at the bottom of the screen will display how long it will take to capture the number of shots you specify using the shooting interval you've chosen.

- **Autoexposure Tracking Sensitivity.** Select from High, Mid (Medium), or Low sensitivity.

- **Silent Shooting in Interval.** Choose On or Off. If you select On, the a7R IV will operate silently, which allows capturing your sequence in "stealth" mode if you need it.

- **Shoot Interval Priority.** When shooting sequences using Program or Aperture Priority modes, the a7R IV will adjust the shutter speed to provide the correct exposure. That may result in a shutter speed that is longer than the specified interval. Choose Off for this setting and the a7R IV will go ahead and expose for the correct amount of time, skipping the shot that would have taken place.

  Choose On, and when another interval exposure is due, the a7R IV will terminate the previous shot (underexposing it) and begin the next one on schedule. You might use the On option if you feel that just dropping the poorly exposed image from the sequence produces the best series. You may be able to avoid the underexposure by activating Auto ISO Sensitivity, and selecting a minimum shutter speed that is shorter than the interval time. In that case, the camera will increase the ISO setting (if necessary) to produce the correct exposure using the automatically selected shutter speed. The chief drawback is that increasing the ISO automatically may also increase the amount of noise in your image. Significant changes in graininess may detract from your sequence or time-lapse movie.

Viewing Your Interval Sequences

You can view your sequences as if they were a time-lapse movie in the camera. You can also create an actual time-lapse movie from your photos; I'll describe that in the section following this one. To view your sequence as a movie in the camera, just follow these steps:

1. **Choose speed.** In the Playback 3 menu, select Playback Speed for Interval and choose a speed from 1 (slow) to 9 (fast).

   - **At the slowest speed**, the a7R IV will display each frame you took one after the other, so you'll see every image captured. The apparent speed of motion will be determined by length of the interval between each frame, and, to a certain extent, the size of the image file. That is, motion captured with larger intervals will appear to be moving faster, so sequences shot at 10-second intervals will seem "slower" than those taken at 20-second intervals. In addition, you may need to take into account how many images can fit into the camera's buffer as they are displayed. Images captured in Large JPEG Extra Fine format may take longer to display than those captured in Small JPEG Standard format. In most cases, the difference in speed will be much less than the difference caused by the interval.

   - **At faster speeds,** the a7R IV "skips" frames, playing back every second, third, fourth, etc. image, producing faster apparent motion, but also resulting in a jerkier appearance. In effect, faster playback speeds decreases the interval between shots.

2. **Select Continuous Playback.** Navigate to the Continuous Playback for Interval entry in the Playback 2 menu. Scroll to the sequence of images you captured, and press the center button. The camera will display the images in order quickly, at the speed you've specified.

Time-Lapse Movies

It's easy to convert your sequence of images into a time-lapse movie. All you need is the Viewer module from the free Imaging Edge software suite. It can quickly convert your individual frames into a Full HD (1920 × 1080) or Ultra HD (3840 × 2160) MP4 video clip. Just follow these steps.

1. **Deposit sequence in a folder.** Copy all the frames you want to use to a new folder on your computer. You'll find it easier to select them if they are located in their own folder. Your images can be RAW or JPEG files.

2. **Launch Viewer.** The left-hand panel displays your computer's directory tree. Select the drive and folder that contain your files.

3. **Sort files.** In the Viewer's Tools menu, choose Sort > Sort by Date and Time Taken.

4. **Select All.** Press Control-A (Command-A on a Mac) to select all the files in the folder. Note that you must have at least 15 images to create a time-lapse movie.

5. **Commence processing.** In the Tools menu, choose Create Time Lapse Movie (see Figure 9.15, left).

6. **Select options.** The screen shown at right in Figure 9.15 appears. There are four adjustments you can make.

   - **Output method.** In general, you can leave the Apply Each RAW File's own settings to each RAW file marked. The app will use the parameters you specified in the camera for white balance, etc. If, for some reason, the RAW settings differ among your files, you can apply the parameters for an image you select (say, the first one in a sequence) and apply them to all subsequent frames.

   - **Save Format.** Here you can choose a color space and/or compression level for your video. I recommend going with the defaults. If you needed an extra-high-quality movie, you could change to Compression Level 1.

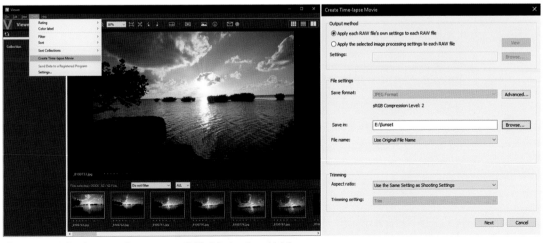

Figure 9.15 Select images and start process (left). Select options (right).

- **Save To.** Select a folder to save your video to, and specify a filename. You can use the original filename or select various combinations of Date Taken, Date and Time Taken, and a 5-digit number generated by the program.

- **Trimming.** Here you can specify the aspect ratio of your movie. For greatest compatibility with other video you may want to add or intercut, choose the 16:9 ratio standard for HD movies. You can also select 4:3, 3:2, or 1:1 aspect ratios, or tell the program to use whatever proportions the a7R IV was set to when the stills were captured.

7. **Click Next.** If you're working with JPEG still photos instead of RAW images, the program will suddenly come to the conclusion that no further processing (adjusting white balance and so forth) is required, and tell you "Some of the selected images will not be processed because they do not have to be developed or are in unsupported formats." Ignore this message if Sony's programmers haven't corrected this bug in your current release of the Imaging Edge software. The program will tell you which files it skipped (basically, all your JPEG images), and invite you to click Next once again to proceed.

8. **Edit settings.** The Edit screen, shown at left in Figure 9.16, appears. It has several options that you can reveal from drop-down lists.

- **Time Lapse Setting.** This panel is shown at far left in Figure 9.16. You can adjust playback speed from 1X to 16X, and view the total time recorded, although with the most recent copy of Viewer that I used, the speed didn't seem to vary as described. Look for a fix in a future update of the software.

- **Music.** Allows you to select music tracks on your computer, and to download additional music from Sony's website (see Figure 9.16, center right).

- **Music Settings.** Here you can balance the volume of the music you added with the soundtrack already recorded on your video. That allows you to have the music predominate, fade in, fade out, and/or loop continuously during playback. (see Figure 9.16, far right).

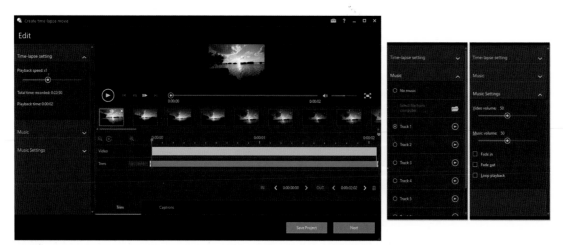

Figure 9.16 Edit time-lapse settings (left); add music (center right); select music settings (far right).

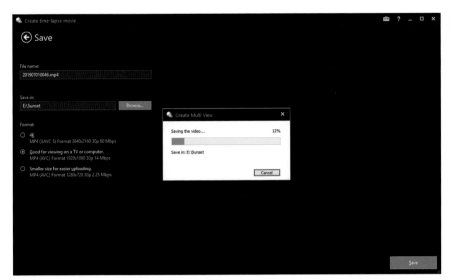

Figure 9.17 Choose filename, folder, and movie format.

9. **Save your work or produce a movie.** You can stop working at this point and return to this point by clicking Save Project. It's a good idea to do this, just in case your final video needs to be tweaked and redone. When you're ready to produce your time-lapse clip, click Next.

10. **Specify filename, folder, and format.** When the Save screen shown in Figure 9.17 appears, you can type in a new filename for your movie, specify a different directory to save your file in, or choose one of three movie formats:

   - **4K.** This choice produces a 2160p/30 fps MP4 video clip in XAVC S format. (You can read about various video formats and parameters in Chapter 10.) You'll need a 4K-compatible display to view this UHD movie.

   - **Good for Viewing on a TV or Computer.** This is usually your best choice, as it delivers a 1080p/30 fps MP4 file in AVC format, viewable on any HDTV or modern-day computer screen that can handle Full HD.

   - **Smaller Size for Easier Uploading.** Choose this to create a Standard HD 720p/30 fps MP4 clip in AVC format. This creates a much smaller file that can be transferred over the Internet, and uploaded to YouTube more easily.

11. **Click Save.** The program will create your video clip and store it in the specified folder. The process may take some time, but a progress bar (seen at center in Figure 9.17) will keep you updated.

Star Trails

Star trails are another great application for interval shooting. As I noted earlier, you can shoot the night sky using long exposures with your a7R IV mounted on a tripod. However, because of the rotation of the Earth, longer exposures will record the apparent motion of the celestial objects through the sky, producing a light trail. If you use a very, very long exposure, the light trail will record as continuous streaks, centered around the Polaris (the North Star) in the northern hemisphere and

Sigma Octantis (which is, unfortunately, too dim to be easily seen with the naked eye) in the southern hemisphere.

Such long exposures can result in excessive noise and sensor overheating, so it's more common for photographers to take a series of individual exposures and combine them to produce a single star trail image. If you want your stars to appear as reasonably sharp points, you'll need to keep the exposure short enough that their movement in the sky isn't apparent. Fortunately, there's a simple formula you can use to calculate that exposure time, the "500 Rule." Divide 500 by the focal length of your lens to determine the longest exposure (in seconds) before stars start to produce a blurred trail. For example, with a 50mm lens, the longest exposure would be 10 seconds (500 divided by 50). Capturing the complete canopy of stars generally requires a wider viewing perspective. With a the 16mm wide-angle setting exposures could be as long as roughly 30 seconds.

For Figure 9.18, I set my camera to ISO 200, and used a basic exposure of 30 seconds at f/5.6. I selected an interval of 32 seconds and 170 total exposures, which totals about 90 minutes. Noise reduction was OFF! Then, I followed these steps, using Photoshop:

1. **Transfer files to a folder.** Select a folder on your computer, and copy all your files to that location.
2. **In Photoshop:** Choose Files > Scripts > Load Files into Stack.
3. **Browse to folder.** Click the Browse button and navigate to the folder where your images are stored.
4. **Click OK.** Photoshop will create a file with one layer for each of your captured images.
5. **Select All layers.** Then click Layer Blending Options from the Layers palette, and choose Lighten.
6. **Flatten image.** You'll want to flatten your image (the multi-layer file will be huge!). You'll end up with an impressive star trail image.

Figure 9.18 Capturing a star trail.

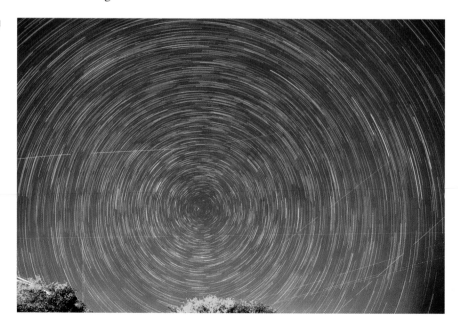

Movie-Making Basics 10

As we've seen during our exploration of its features so far, the a7R IV is superbly equipped for taking still photographs of very high quality in a wide variety of shooting environments. But this camera's superior level of performance is not limited to stills. It's highly capable in the movie-making arena as well. It can shoot Full HD (high-definition) and 4K (ultra-high-definition) clips. Sony has also provided overrides for controlling all important aspects of a video clip.

So, even though you may have bought your camera primarily for shooting stationary scenes, you acquired a device that's also great for recording high-quality video clips. Whether you're looking to record informal clips of the family on vacation, the latest viral video for YouTube, or a set of scenes that will be painstakingly crafted into a cinematic masterpiece using editing software, the a7R IV will perform admirably.

This camera can shoot HD video at 1920 × 1080 resolution using Sony's AVCHD encoding, plus MP4 video, which allows both 1920 × 1080 full HD and 1280 × 7210 standard HD. It can also capture HD video in the newer XAVC S format. The a7R IV adds the ability to capture superior 4K video *internally* using XAVC S 4K.

The camera also uses something called *Picture Profiles*, to tailor color, saturation, sharpness, and some video-centric attributes. You can visualize Picture Profiles as Creative Styles for video. This chapter will show you the fundamentals of shooting video; in the next chapter, you'll learn about some of your camera's more advanced features, including the XAVC S format in HD and 4K options.

This chapter and the next deal with conventional video; S&Q (slow- and quick-motion video) settings were explained in Chapter 4.

Some Fundamentals

Recording a video with the a7R IV is extraordinarily easy to accomplish—just press the black button with the red dot located on the back of the camera to the immediate right of the viewfinder window. Sony has placed it there to minimize the chance that you'll start recording a movie accidentally. That's because video can be captured in *any* exposure mode; there's no need to activate a special Movie mode. After you press the button, the camera will confirm that it's recording with a red REC and numerals showing the elapsed time in the EVF and LCD monitor. Press the button again when you want to stop recording.

Before you start, though, there are some settings to prepare the camera to record the scene the way you want it to. I'll show you how to optimize your settings before you start shooting video, but here are some considerations to be aware of as you get started. Many of these points will be covered in more detail later in this chapter:

- **Use the right card.** Because movie capture is, basically, full-time "continuous" shooting, you'll need to use a memory card with sufficient capacity and a fast enough write speed to handle the streams of video you'll be shooting. I recommend SDXC memory cards 64GB or larger. Keep in mind that both of the a7R IV's slots support speedy UHS-II memory cards.

- **Avoid extraneous noise.** Try not to make too much noise when changing camera controls or when using a conventional zoom lens's mechanical zooming ring (power zooms with a zoom lever on the lens are typically relatively quiet). And don't make comments that you will not want to hear on the audio track.

- **Minimize zooming.** While it's great to be able to use the zoom for filling the frame with a distant subject (especially the power zoom on lenses equipped with that feature), think twice before zooming. The sound made by a mechanical zoom ring rotating will be picked up and it will be audible when you play a movie. (As I noted, lenses with power zoom are virtually silent.) As well, remember that any more than the occasional minor zoom will be very distracting to friends who watch your videos. And while digital zoom will definitely degrade video quality, the effect is minimized when shooting video because your final video frame (in Full HD mode) will be just 1920×1080 pixels. Digital zoom *is* useful as a way of mimicking a power zoom, as, when activated in the Camera Settings II-06 Zoom Setting entry, you can "zoom" quietly and digitally by pressing the right button, and then pressing and holding again to zoom continuously. (You can't do this if you have a lens with a power zoom lever.)

- **Use a fully charged battery.** A fresh battery will allow about one hour of filming at normal (non-winter) temperatures, but that can be shorter if there are many focus adjustments.

- **Keep it cool.** Video quality can suffer terribly when the imaging sensor gets hot so keep the camera in a cool place. When shooting on hot days especially, the sensor can get hot more quickly than usual; when there's a risk of overheating, the camera will stop recording and it will shut down about five seconds later. A thermometer icon will appear on the screen as a warning. Give the sensor time to cool down before using the camera again. This limitation generally won't affect serious movie-makers, who tend to shoot a series of short scenes that are assembled into a finished movie with an editor. But if you plan to set up your camera and photograph your kid's school pageant non-stop for an hour, you're out of luck.

- **Press the Movie button.** You don't have to hold it down. Press it again when you're done to stop recording. It's recessed so you will not press it inadvertently.

Preparing to Shoot Video

First, here's what I recommend you do to prepare for a *basic* recording session. More advanced detail settings will be addressed later:

- **Choose your file format.** Go to the File Format entry in the Camera Settings II-01 menu (as discussed in Chapter 3) and select the file format for your movies. (The mode dial must be set to Movie mode to access this entry.) You can set it to AVCHD, XAVC S HD, or, with the a7R IV, XAVC S 4K. File formats determine the transfer rate (roughly equivalent to JPEG compression), which, with resolution, determines the quality of your video. You'll learn more about these formats later.

- **Choose record setting.** Also, in the Camera Settings II-01 menu, you'll find the Record Setting item, which allows you to choose the size, frame rate, and image quality for your movies. Tables 10.1 to 10.4 later in this chapter spell out your choices.

  Which of the many options should you choose? It depends in part on your needs. If your plan is to primarily shoot videos that you'll show to friends and family on an HDTV set, choose AVCHD. For more professional productions, you'll want to select XAVC S HD or XAVC S K. I'll explain the differences later.

- **Activate proxy recording (optional).** If you are shooting an XAVC S or AVCHD movie, you can elect to record a lower 9 Mb/sec. bit-rate (reduced quality) Standard HD (1280 × 720) movie simultaneously, giving you a video optimized for viewing on a smart device or website. Use the Proxy Recording entry in the Camera Settings II-01 menu. You'll definitely want to use a larger memory card when working with this option. When you review your images, the proxy video isn't displayed, viewable, or editable in the camera; the "main" movie will have a Px indicator overlaid on its icon to show you that the clip is paired with a proxy counterpart. Deleting or protecting the main clip deletes/protects the proxy at the same time.

- **Preview the movie's aspect ratio for stills.** In the Aspect Ratio entry of the Camera Settings I-01 menu, the proportions default to 3:2, but you can change that to 4:3, 16:9, or 1:1. *The setting in this item won't affect your video recording.* Setting the aspect ratio options will merely cause the camera to display the *preview* of the scene when you are shooting stills, before you start movie recording, in the format that will be used for the video clip. This gives you a better feel for what will be included in the frame after you press the record button.

- **Turn on autofocus.** Make sure autofocus is turned on through the Focus Mode entry of the Camera Settings I-05 menu. You also have the option of using manual focus, or even Direct Manual Focus, with focus peaking.

■ **Try Flexible Spot AF Area.** As in still image making, you can use the Flexible Spot AF Area (discussed in Chapter 8) while recording a video clip. This feature is most suitable for a static scene you'll record with the camera on a tripod, where an important small subject is off-center and will remain in the same location. By placing the AF Area exactly on that part of the scene, you'll be sure that the focus will remain on the most important part of the scene during the entire recording. (In truth, you could use manual focus for the same purpose.)

If you decide to try this, compose the scene as desired before pressing the record button. Set the Focus Area to Flexible Spot in the Camera Settings I-05 menu. Brackets will appear on the screen, indicating the current location of the active focus detection point. Move the brackets with the directional buttons so they cover the primary subject and press the center button to confirm. You can now begin recording the video, confident that the focus will always be on your primary subject (assuming it does not move while you're recording).

■ **Set useful functions.** Before you start recording, you can set a desired ISO, white balance, Creative Style, Picture Profiles (explained in the next chapter), a Picture Effect (for special effects), any of the three metering modes, and the level of exposure compensation. You can also set an override in the Creative Style for a specific level of sharpness, contrast, and saturation, if desired, or use a Picture Profile for more advanced parameters. The DRO feature will not be available, however. You'll recall that these functions are not available in fully automatic modes; if you set them while using another mode and then switch to a fully automatic mode for recording the video, the camera will revert back to the defaults.

■ **Decide on a shooting mode.** You can choose an exposure mode (P, S, A, or M) for your movies, either using a menu entry or by rotating the mode dial.

The P mode works well, allowing the camera to set the aperture/shutter speed and giving you access to the other features discussed above. Program shift (to other aperture/shutter speed combinations) can be used before you start recording, but it will not be available during actual recording.

You might prefer to use Aperture Priority (A) mode for full control over the specific aperture; in that case, you can preset a desired aperture and you can also change it anytime while recording. Be careful however, especially if you have set a specific ISO level. If you switch to a very small aperture while recording in low light, your movie clip may darken; this is particularly likely if you're using a low ISO level. And if you switch to a very wide aperture on a sunny day, especially if using a high ISO, your video will become too bright. Of course, you can see the change in brightness in the live view display before recording a movie and while you're recording.

Switch to S mode if you want control over the shutter speed; this is a more advanced technique in Movie mode. You can preset a shutter speed and you can change it while recording. Again, be careful as to your settings to avoid a very dark or overly bright video, especially if you have set a specific ISO level. The live view display before and during recording will help to guide you. I don't recommend using the Manual (M) mode initially but you might want to experiment with it later.

■ **Press the record button.** You don't have to hold it down. Press it to start recording and press it again when you're done. Shoot a short test clip and view it to make sure that the settings you made are producing the overall effect you want. If not, change some settings (White Balance or Creative Style or Exposure Compensation, for example) and try again.

Steps During Movie Making

Once you have set up the camera for your video session and pressed the Movie button, you have done most of the technical work that's required of you for basic movie clips. Now your task is to use your skills at composition, lighting, scene selection, and, perhaps, directing actors, to make a compelling video production.

- **Zoom, autofocus, and autoexposure all work.** If you're new to the world of high-quality still cameras that also take video, you may just take it for granted that functions such as autofocus continue to work normally when you switch from stills to video. But until recently, most such cameras performed weakly in their video modes; they would lock their exposure and focus at the beginning of the scene, and you could not zoom while shooting the video. The a7R IV has no such handicaps, and, in fact, it is especially capable in these areas.

  Indeed, this camera allows you to choose any exposure mode, including Manual exposure, Auto ISO, shutter speed, and aperture. You can change settings while shooting, and lock exposure with the AEL button.

  Autoexposure works very well, modifying the exposure as the scene brightness changes; the method used depends on the metering mode that you're using. You can zoom to your heart's content (though I recommend that you zoom sparingly). Best of all, AF-C autofocus works like a charm; the camera can track moving subjects and quickly snap them back into sharp focus with speedy continuous AF. Manual focus is also available, with focus peaking to help you zero in on a focus plane. Don't limit yourself based on the weaknesses of past cameras; the a7R IV opens up new horizons of video freedom.

- **Exposure compensation works while filming.** I found this feature to be quite remarkable. Although the autoexposure system works very well (especially with Multi metering) to vary the aperture when the ambient lighting changes, you can certainly dial in exposure compensation when you need to do so or want to do so for a certain effect. You could even use this function as a limited kind of "fade to black" in the camera, though you probably won't be able to fade quite all the way to black.

  If the preview display (when Live View Display is set to Setting Effect On in the Camera Settings II-08 menu) suggests that your movie will be dark (underexposed) and if it does not get brighter after you set plus compensation, there's another problem: the camera cannot provide a good exposure for the movie at the ISO that you have set (as discussed earlier). Switch to a higher ISO level until the brightness is as desired or switch to ISO Auto to enable the camera to set a higher ISO level to prevent the "underexposure."

- **Use AE Lock instead.** Occasionally, you may find that you start having an exposure problem during recording; this might happen when pointing the lens toward a light-tone area that causes the camera to begin underexposing. While plus compensation will allow you to increase brightness, it's preferable to use the defined AE Lock button (either the physical AEL button or one you specify using Custom Keys in the Setup menu) to maintain a pleasing exposure during the entire video clip.

Why would you need this feature? Let's say you're filming entertainers against grass and foliage, but you're moving the camera and will soon be filming a second group against a white sky. As soon as you do so, the backlighting will cause the video to get darker. Don't let that happen. Before pointing the lens toward the backlit area, press AEL and keep it depressed. This will prevent the exposure from changing as you point the lens toward the backlit part of the scene. This is preferable to waiting until an underexposure problem starts and then setting plus exposure compensation that suddenly makes the video brighter.

■ **Don't be a flash in the pan.** With HD video, there is a possibility of introducing artifacts or distortion if you pan too quickly. (This effect is called rolling shutter distortion or the "Jell-O effect.") That is, because of the way the lines of video are displayed in sequence, if the camera moves too quickly in a sideways motion, some of the lines may not show up on the screen quickly enough to catch up to the rest of the picture. As a result, objects in your video can become somewhat distorted or you may experience a jiggling effect and/or loss of detail. So, if at all possible, make your pans smooth and steady, and slow them down to a comfortable pace.

More About Frame Rates and Bit Rates

Both videos and stills are captured in much the same way, but the technology used for the sensor can cause problems that are most evident when shooting movies. To understand why, it's necessary to understand the difference between a *rolling shutter* and a *global shutter*, and how *interlacing* differs from *progressive scan.*

An image (still or video) captured by the sensor consists of rows and columns of pixels. With the a7R IV, there are 6,336 different rows, each row consisting of 9,504 individual pixels. A "rolling" shutter captures each row one after the other, so that, effectively, the pixels in the top row are captured at a different moment in time than those in the bottom row. This gap is very brief, and typically isn't noticeable in still photographs. But with video this difference can manifest itself as anomalies such as wobble when the camera is moving or vibrating, skew (which is a diagonal bending of an image due to wobble), smear (produced when part of the image, such as an automobile tire, is rotating), and other defects.

A "global" shutter, on the other hand, captures the entire image in one instant, eliminating these problems. Although your a7R IV *does* have a rolling shutter, the high speed of its sensor (aided by the improved on-sensor copper wiring of the 61MP sensor) and BIONZ digital image processing chip minimizes the rolling shutter effects.

Frame Rates

That leads us to progressive scanning versus interlacing. With a rolling shutter, line-by-line scanning during capture and playback can be done in one of two ways. With *interlaced scanning,* odd-numbered lines (lines 1, 3, 5, 7, and so forth) are captured with one pass, and then the even-numbered lines (2, 4, 6, 8, and so forth) are grabbed. With the 1080/60i format, roughly 60 pairs of odd/even line scans, or 60 *fields* are captured each second. (The actual number is 59.94 fields per second.)

Interlaced scanning was developed for and works best with analog display systems such as older television sets. It was originally created as a way to reduce the amount of bandwidth required to transmit television pictures over the air. Modern LCD, LED, and plasma-based HDTV displays must de-interlace a 1080i image to display it. (See Figure 10.1.)

Newer displays work better with a second method, called *progressive scanning* or *sequential scanning,* and progressive scan modes are the only choices when shooting XAVC S video. Instead of two interlaced fields, the entire image is scanned as consecutive lines (lines 1, 2, 3, 4, and so forth). This happens at a rate of 120, 60, 30, or 24 frames per second (not fields). (All these numbers apply to the NTSC television system used in the United States, Canada, Japan, and some other countries; other places use systems like PAL, where the nominal scanning figures are 100/50/25 rather than 120/60/30. The 24 fps rate applies to both NTSC and PAL.)

One problem with interlaced scanning appears when capturing video of moving subjects. Half of the image (one set of interlaced lines) will change to keep up with the movement of the subject while the other interlaced half retains the "old" image as it waits to be refreshed. Flicker or *interline twitter* results. That makes your progressive scan (p) options a better choice for action photography. Interlaced video frame rates are indicated with an (i) designation; for example, within the AVCHD choices, 60i 24M (FX) indicates interlaced video, while 60p 28M (PS) represents progressive scan video. (I'll explain the 24M/28M part in the next section.)

Computer-editing software like Final Cut Pro can handle either type, and convert between them (although AVCHD, XAVC S 4K, and XAVC S HD may not be compatible with the other software you own). The choice between 24 fps and 60 fps (NTSC), or 25 fps and 50 fps (PAL) is determined by what you plan to do with your video. The short explanation is that, for technical reasons I won't

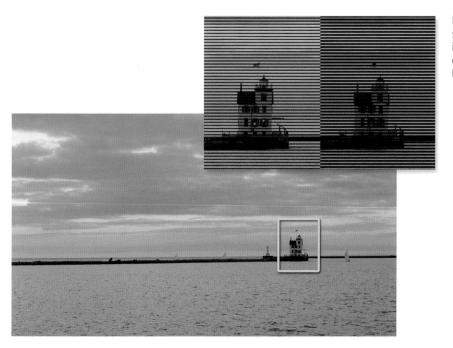

Figure 10.1 The inset shows how lines of the image alternate between odd and even in an interlaced video capture.

go into here, shooting at 24 fps (or 25 fps) gives your movie more of the so-called "cinematic" look that film would produce, excellent for showing fine detail. However, if your clip has moving subjects, or you pan the camera, 24 fps (or 25 fps) can produce a jerky effect called "judder." The 60 fps (or 50 fps) option produces a home-video look that some feel is less desirable, but which is smoother and less jittery when displayed on an electronic monitor. I suggest you try both and use the frame rate that best suits your tastes and video-editing software.

ABOUT 120/100P

You'll note that when shooting XAVC S HD, you can select 120p (at 100Mbs transfer rates; NTSC only) or 120/100p (at 60Mbs transfer rate; both NTSC and PAL). These high frame rates—amounting to 120 and 100 frames per second—produce video that can be converted to play back at conventional speeds, either 30/25 fps (four times slower than recorded) or 24 fps (five times slower than recorded; NTSC only). Specify the playback speed using the Movie/HFR entry of the Camera Settings II-01 menu, as explained in Chapter 3. The slow-motion video that results can be used for special effects, including clichés like two long-lost lovers running toward each other on a beach.

Bit Rates

Bit rates represent the speed of transfer from your camera to your memory card or external video recorder. The higher the bit rate, the more demands made on your media in storing that data quick enough to keep pace with the video capture. Higher average bit rates range from 6 Mbps (megabits per second) for 1280 × 720 (720p) MP4 movies, to as much as 28 Mbps maximum for AVCHD, 60p full-HD clips. When using XAVC formats, the demands are even higher: 50 Mbps with XAVC S HD and 60 to 100 Mbps with XAVC S 4K (with the a7R IV only). Tables 10.1 to 10.4 show the frame rates, bit rates, and resolution of the various recording settings for video. Note that frame rates of 30/25, 60/50, and 120/100 represent NTSC/PAL systems, respectively.

TABLE 10.1 XAVC S 4K

RECORD SETTING	RESOLUTION	BIT RATE
30p/25p 100M	3840 × 2160	Approx. 100 Mbps
30p/25p 60M	3840 × 2160	Approx. 60 Mbps
24p 100M (NTSC only)	3840 × 2160	Approx. 100 Mbps
24p 60M (NTSC only)	3840 × 2160	Approx. 60 Mbps

TABLE 10.2 XAVC S HD

RECORD SETTING	RESOLUTION	BIT RATE
60p/50p 50M	1920 × 1080	Approx. 50 Mbps
30p/25p 50M	1920 × 1080	Approx. 50 Mbps
24p 50M (NTSC only)	1920 × 1080	Approx. 50 Mbps
24p 50M (NTSC only)	1280 × 720	Approx. 50 Mbps
120p/100p 50M	1280 × 720	Approx. 50 Mbps

TABLE 10.3 AVCHD

RECORD SETTING	RESOLUTION	BIT RATE
60i/50i 24M (FX)	1920 × 1080	Approx. 24 Mbps
60i/50i 17M (FH)	1920 × 1080	Approx. 17 Mbps
60p/50p 28M (PS)	1920 × 1080	Approx. 28 Mbps
24p/25p 24M (FX)	1920 × 1080	Approx. 24 Mbps
24p/25p 17M (FH)	1920 × 1080	Approx. 17 Mbps

TABLE 10.4 MP4

RECORD SETTING	RESOLUTION	BIT RATE
60p/50p 28M	1920 × 1080	Approx. 28 Mbps
30p/25p 16M	1920 × 1080	Approx. 16 Mbps
30p/25p 6M	1280 × 720	Approx. 6 Mbps

Choosing Metering/Exposure Modes

You can use Multi, Center, or Spot metering when shooting movies. I recommend sticking with Multi metering, unless you have a special reason for, say, Spot metering, as I explained in Chapter 7. Next, you'll want to select exposure mode, from among Program, Aperture Priority, Shutter Priority, or Manual. Rotate the mode dial to the Movie position and specify which of these modes is used for movies using the Movie/S&Q Motion entry or Exposure Mode entry in the Camera Settings II-01 menu page, as explained in Chapter 4. The mode you select will be used when the mode dial is in the Movie position. Of course, using the Movie position on the mode dial isn't mandatory, as you can use any exposure mode for movie recording.

- **Program mode.** The P mode works well for movies, allowing the camera to set the aperture/shutter speed. Program shift (to other aperture/shutter speed combinations) can be used before you start recording, but it will not be available during actual recording.

- **Aperture Priority.** You might prefer to use Aperture Priority (A) mode for full control over the specific aperture; in that case, you can preset a desired aperture and you can also change it anytime while recording. However, remember that your shutter speed may change in Aperture Priority mode, and when shooting movies, it is often desirable to use a specific shutter speed (as I'll explain in an upcoming section).

- **Shutter Priority.** Switch to S mode if you want control over the shutter speed; this is a more advanced technique in Movie mode. You can preset a shutter speed and you can change it while recording. Again, be careful as to your settings to avoid a very dark or overly bright video, especially if you have set a specific ISO level. The live view display before and during recording will help to guide you. I recommend Shutter Priority highly, especially for beginners.

- **Manual Exposure.** Manual exposure may be best when you want to maintain tight control over shutter speed and aperture, say, to maintain exposure as lighting conditions change, or to keep the same depth-of-field in a scene under changing conditions.

As you work, you'll discover that the a7R IV's Zebra feature in the Camera Setting II-07 (Display/ Auto Review 1) menu, as explained in Chapter 4, can be a marvelous aid in monitoring your exposure. If you are using Shutter Priority, as I recommended, you'll have the shutter speed fixed and, based on what you see in the viewfinder or LCD monitor and Zebra display feedback, adjust the aperture or ISO sensitivity to get the exposure you want. As I explained in Chapter 4, you can adjust the Zebra feature's threshold setting, perhaps specifying 95% so that you're alerted only when the brightest highlights start to clip (making the stripes less distracting) or use 85% so you'll know when human skin starts to be overexposed. Zebra display may not work for you when using S-Log2/S-Log3 gamma settings (described later in this chapter), as those very low contrast renditions don't lend themselves to that kind of monitoring.

Should you need to adjust exposure from what the camera recommends, exposure compensation works quite well while filming. Although the autoexposure system does a good job (especially with Multi metering) to vary the aperture when the ambient lighting changes, you can certainly dial in exposure compensation when you need to do so or want to do so for a certain effect. You could even use this function as a limited kind of "fade to black" in the camera, though, as I mentioned earlier, you probably won't be able to fade quite all the way to black.

If the preview display (when Live View Display is set to Setting Effect On in the Camera Setting II-08 menu) suggests that your movie will be dark (underexposed) and if it does not get brighter after you set plus EV compensation, there's another problem: the camera cannot provide a good exposure for the movie at the ISO that you have set (as discussed earlier). Switch to a higher ISO level until the brightness is as desired or switch to ISO Auto to enable the camera to set a higher ISO level to prevent the "underexposure." You can also "lock" exposure to keep the same exposure settings as lighting changes or you reframe your scene.

Stop That!

Both Manual Exposure and Shutter Priority modes allow you to explicitly choose a shutter speed. You might think that setting your camera to a faster shutter speed will help give you sharper video frames. But the choice of a shutter speed for movie making is a bit more complicated than that. As you might guess, in most cases it's best to leave the shutter speed at 1/30th or 1/60th second and allow the overall exposure to be adjusted by varying the aperture and/or ISO sensitivity.

Effectively, you're better off working in Shutter Priority mode, so that the aperture or ISO settings are your only way of adjusting the exposure. A "slow" 1/30th or 1/60th second shutter speed doesn't mean your movies will have the same amount of blur that a typical still photograph will have using those shutter speeds. We don't normally stare at a video frame for longer than 1/30th or 1/24th second, so while the shakiness of the *camera* can be disruptive (and often corrected by your camera's in-lens and in-body image stabilization), if there is a bit of blur in our *subjects* from movement, we tend not to notice. Each frame flashes by in the blink of an eye, so to speak, so a shutter speed of 1/30th or 1/60th second works a lot better in video than it does when shooting stills. Even shots with lots of movement, such as the frame shown in Figure 10.2, are often sufficiently sharp at 1/60th second.

Higher shutter speeds actually introduce problems of their own. If you shoot a video frame using a shutter speed of 1/250th second, the actual moment in time that's captured represents only about 12 percent of the 1/30th second of elapsed time in that frame. Yet, when played back, that frame occupies the full 1/30th of a second, with 88 percent of that time filled by stretching the original image to fill it. The result is often a choppy/jumpy image, and one that may appear to be *too* sharp.

The reason for that is more social imprinting than scientific: we've all grown up accustomed to seeing the look of Hollywood productions that, by convention, were shot using a shutter speed that's half the reciprocal of the frame rate (that is, 1/48th second for a 24 fps movie). Movie cameras use a rotary shutter (achieving that 1/48th second exposure by using a 180-degree shutter "angle"), but the effect on our visual expectations is the same. For the most "film-like" appearance, use 24 fps and 1/60th second shutter speed.

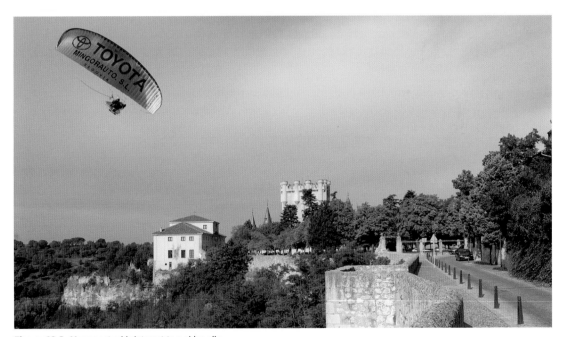

Figure 10.2 Movement adds interest to a video clip.

Faster shutter speeds do have some specialized uses for motion analysis, especially where individual frames are studied. The rest of the time, 1/30th or 1/60th of a second will suffice. If the reason you needed a higher shutter speed was to obtain the correct exposure, use a slower ISO setting, or a neutral-density filter to cut down on the amount of light passing through the lens. A good rule of thumb is to use 1/60th second or slower when shooting at 24 fps; 1/60th second or slower at 30 fps; and 1/125th second or slower at 60 fps.

In choosing between 30p and 60p, there are several considerations. The 30p frame rate allows you to use a reduced ISO setting for improved grain compared to 60p at a higher ISO value. That's an advantage under low light. However, as I mentioned earlier, at 60p you can safely use a higher shutter speed of 1/125th second, which can produce smoother video of moving subjects. Video editors can *transcode* 60p video to give you 30p video (with files suitable for uploading to websites) as well as the 60i video you might need for DVD/Blu-Ray productions.

Choosing an Autofocus Mode

As I said in Chapter 8, you'll generally want sharp focus in your image—somewhere—but exactly where and how focus is achieved can be an important part of your creative process. On the one hand, while shooting certain types of scenes—particularly action scenes—you'll want the camera to automatically retain focus on your main subjects and keep them tightly in focus. Other times, you'll want to use selective focus to emphasize a subject and de-emphasize the background, or "pull" focus to dramatically change the focus (so to speak) of the scene, say, refocusing to cause a blurry subject to suddenly come into sharp relief.

As with still photography, you have both manual focus and autofocus tools at your disposal, which allow you to specify *when* to focus and what to focus on. An important step before shooting is to ensure autofocus is turned on through the Focus Mode entry of the Camera Settings or Function menus. Only Continuous AF (AF-C) and Manual Focus (MF) can be used when shooting movies. Here are some points to consider.

- **AF-C or MF.** If the mode dial is in the Movie position, only AF-C and MF are available.
- **Presto change-o.** If the mode dial is *not* in the Movie position, and you have selected a focus mode other than AF-C or MF, when you begin shooting movies, the a7R IV will automatically switch to AF-C.
- **Lock focus.** As video is captured, the a7R IV's Continuous autofocus will refocus as you move the camera, or subjects in the frame change location. To lock focus, press the shutter release halfway, or use a key you've assigned that function. When you release the button, the camera will refocus. Ordinarily, it does an excellent job of not refocusing constantly, and changes focus only when the a7R IV detects camera or subject movement.
- **Manual focus.** If you prefer manual focus, you'll need to set it before commencing video capture. I find that manual focus is fine for situations such as a stage play where the actors will usually be at roughly the same distance to your position during the entire performance, and for more professional productions where precise focus is a must, or when changing focus during a shot (*focus*

pulling) is used creatively. In other cases, however, you'll probably want to rely on the camera's effective full-time continuous autofocus ability while recording a video clip.

■ **Focus area modes.** You can use all focus area modes, as described in Chapter 8, except for Tracking AF. Center Lock-On, however, can be used. Try Flexible Spot AF. As in still image making, you can use the Flexible Spot AF Area (also discussed in Chapter 8) while recording a video clip. This feature is most suitable for a static scene you'll record with the camera on a tripod, where an important small subject is off-center and will remain in the same location.

By placing the Focus Area exactly on that part of the scene, you'll be sure that the focus will remain on the most important part of the scene during the entire recording. (In truth, you could use manual focus for the same purpose.) If you decide to try this, compose the scene as desired before pressing the record button. Set the Focus Area to Flexible Spot in the Camera Settings I-05 menu. When you press the center button (or designated Focus Standard button), locator brackets will appear on the screen, indicating the current location of the active focus detection point. Move the bracket with the directional buttons so they cover the primary subject and press OK (the center button) to confirm. You can now begin recording the video, confident that the focus will always be on your primary subject (assuming it does not move while you're recording).

Tips for Movie Making

I'm going to close out this introductory movie chapter with a general discussion of movie-making concepts that you need to understand as you move toward more polished video production. In the chapter that follows, I'll explain some of the a7R IV's features that allow you to produce more sophisticated movies. Here are some basic tips:

■ **Keep things stable and on the level.** Camera shake's enough of a problem with still photography, but it becomes even more of a nuisance when you're shooting video. While the a7R IV's in-body five-axis stabilization and stabilizer found in lenses with the OSS designation can help minimize this, neither can work miracles. Placing your camera on a tripod will work much better than trying to hand-hold it while shooting. One bit of really good news is that compared to pro dSLRs, the a7R IV can work very effectively on a lighter tripod, due to the camera's light weight. On windy days however, the extra mass of a heavy tripod is still valuable.

■ **Use a shooting script.** A shooting script is nothing more than a coordinated plan that covers both audio and video and provides order and structure for your video. A detailed script will cover what types of shots you're going after, what dialogue you're going to use, audio effects, transitions, and graphics.

■ **Plan with storyboards.** A storyboard is a series of panels providing visuals of what each scene should look like. While the ones produced by Hollywood are generally of very high quality, there's nothing that says drawing skills are important for this step. Stick figures work just fine if that's the best you can do. The storyboard just helps you visualize locations, placement of actors/actresses, props, and furniture, and also helps everyone involved get an idea of what you're trying to show. It also helps show how you want to frame or compose a shot. You can even shoot a series of still photos and transform them into a "storyboard" if you want, such as in Figure 10.3.

Today's audience is used to fast-paced, short-scene storytelling. In order to produce interesting video for such viewers, it's important to view video storytelling as a kind of shorthand code for the more leisurely efforts print media offers. Audio and video should always be advancing the story. While it's okay to let the camera linger from time to time, it should only be for a compelling reason and only briefly.

It only takes a second or two for an establishing shot to impart the necessary information. For example, many of the scenes for a video documenting a model being photographed in a rock 'n' roll music setting might be close-ups and talking heads, but an establishing shot showing the studio where the video was captured helps set the scene.

- **Provide variety.** Provide variety too. Change camera angles and perspectives often and never leave a static scene on the screen for a long period of time. (You can record a static scene for a reasonably long period and then edit in other shots that cut away and back to the longer scene with close-ups that show each person talking.)

- **When editing, keep transitions basic!** I can't stress this one enough. Watch a television program or movie. The action "jumps" from one scene or person to the next. Fancy transitions that involve exotic "wipes," dissolves, or cross fades take too long for the average viewer and make your video ponderous.

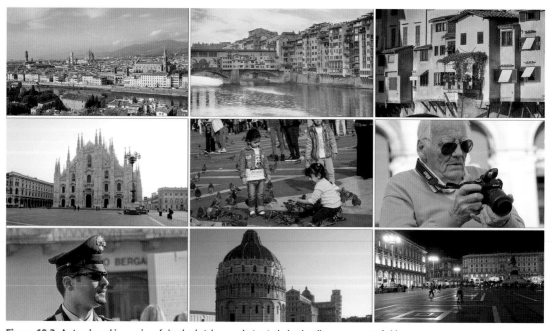

Figure 10.3 A storyboard is a series of simple sketches or photos to help visualize a segment of video.

Composition

In movie shooting, several factors restrict your composition, and impose requirements you just don't always have in still photography (although other rules of good composition do apply). Here are some of the key differences to keep in mind when composing movie frames:

- **Horizontal compositions only.** Some subjects, such as basketball players and tall buildings, just lend themselves to vertical compositions. But movies are generally shot and shown in horizontal format only. (Unless you're capturing a clip with your smartphone; I see many vertically oriented YouTube videos.) So, if you're shooting a conventional video and interviewing a local basketball star, you can end up with a worst-case situation like the one shown in Figure 10.4. If you want to show how tall your subject is, it's often impractical to move back far enough to show him full-length. You really can't capture a vertical composition. Tricks like getting down on the floor and shooting up at your subject can exaggerate the perspective but aren't a perfect solution.

- **Wasted space at the sides.** Moving in to frame the basketball player as outlined by the yellow box in Figure 10.4 means that you're still forced to leave a lot of empty space on either side. (Of course, you can fill that space with other people and/or interesting stuff, but that defeats your intent of concentrating on your main subject.) So, when faced with some types of subjects in a horizontal frame, you can be creative, or move in *really* tight. For example, if I was willing to give up the "height" aspect of my composition, I could have framed the shot as shown by the green box in the figure and wasted less of the image area at either side.

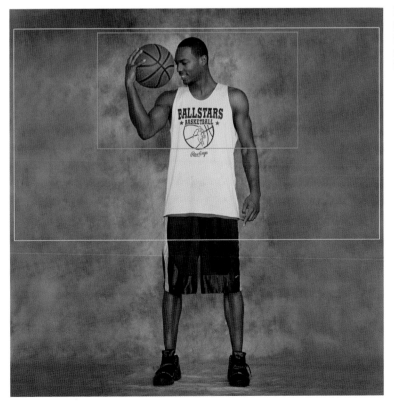

Figure 10.4 Movie shooting requires you to fit all your subjects into a horizontally oriented frame.

- **Seamless (or seamed) transitions.** Unless you're telling a picture story with a photo essay, still pictures often stand alone. But with movies, each of your compositions must relate to the shot that preceded it, and the one that follows. It can be jarring to jump from a long shot to a tight close-up unless the director—you—is very creative. Another common error is the "jump cut" in which successive shots vary only slightly in camera angle, making it appear that the main subject has "jumped" from one place to another. (Although everyone from French New Wave director Jean-Luc Goddard to Guy Ritchie—Madonna's ex—have used jump cuts effectively in their films.) The rule of thumb is to vary the camera angle by at least 30 degrees between shots to make it appear to be seamless. Unless you prefer that your images flaunt convention and appear to be "seamy."

- **The time dimension.** Unlike still photography, with motion pictures there's a lot more emphasis on using a series of images to build on each other to tell a story. Static shots where the camera is mounted on a tripod and everything is shot from the same distance are a recipe for dull videos. Watch a television program sometime and notice how often camera shots change distances and directions. Viewers are used to this variety and have come to expect it. Professional video productions are often done with multiple cameras shooting from different angles and positions. But many professional productions are shot with just one camera, and with careful planning you can do just fine with your a7R IV camera.

Here's a look at the different types of commonly used compositional tools:

- **Establishing shot.** Much like it sounds, this type of composition, as shown at top left in Figure 10.5, establishes the scene and tells the viewer where the action is taking place. Let's say you're shooting a video of your offspring's move to college; the establishing shot could be a wide shot of the campus with a sign welcoming you to the school in the foreground. Another example would be for a child's birthday party; the establishing shot could be the front of the house decorated with birthday signs and streamers or a shot of the dining room table decked out with party favors and a candle-covered birthday cake. In this case, I wanted to show the studio where the video was shot.

- **Medium shot.** This shot is composed from about waist to head room (some space above the subject's head). It's useful for providing variety from a series of close-ups and also makes for a useful first look at a speaker. (See Figure 10.5, top right.)

- **Close-up.** The close-up, usually described as "from shirt pocket to head room," provides a good composition for someone talking directly to the camera. Although it's common to have your talking head centered in the shot, that's not a requirement. In the middle left image in Figure 10.5, the subject was offset to the right. This would allow other images, especially graphics or titles, to be superimposed in the frame in a "real" (professional) production. But the compositional technique can be used with a7R IV videos, too, even if special effects are not going to be added.

- **Extreme close-up.** When I went through broadcast training, this shot was described as the "big talking face" shot and we were actively discouraged from employing it. Styles and tastes change over the years and now the big talking face is much more commonly used (maybe people are better looking these days?) and so this view may be appropriate. Just remember, the a7R IV is capable of shooting in high-definition video and you may be playing the video on a high-def

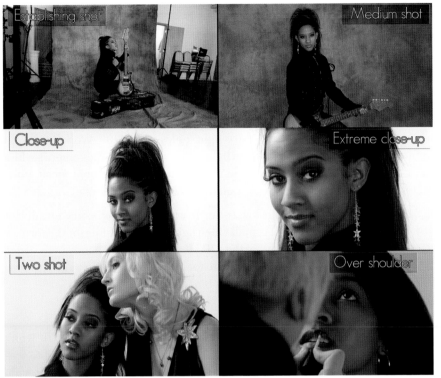

Figure
10.5 Establishing shot (upper left); Medium shot (upper right); Close-up (middle left); Extreme close-up (middle right); Two shot (lower left); Over-the-shoulder shot (lower right).

TV; be careful that you use this composition on a face that can stand up to high definition. (See middle right, Figure 10.5.)

- **"Two" shot.** A two shot shows a pair of subjects in one frame. They can be side by side or one subject in the foreground and one in the background. This does not have to be a head-to-ground composition. Subjects can be standing or seated. A "three shot" is the same principle except that three people are in the frame. (See Figure 10.5, lower left.)

- **Over-the-shoulder shot.** Long a composition of interview programs, the "over-the-shoulder shot" uses the rear of one person's head and shoulder to serve as a frame for the other person. This puts the viewer's perspective as that of the person facing away from the camera. (See Figure 10.5, lower right.)

Lighting for Video

Much like in still photography, how you handle light pretty much can make or break your videography. Lighting for video can be more complicated than lighting for still photography, since both subject and camera movement are often part of the process.

Lighting for video presents several concerns. First off, you want enough illumination to create a useable video. Beyond that, you want to use light to help tell your story or increase drama. Let's take a better look at both.

Illumination

You can significantly improve the quality of your video by increasing the light falling in the scene. This is true indoors or out, by the way. While it may seem like sunlight is more than enough, it depends on how much contrast you're dealing with. If your subject is in shadow (which can help him from squinting) or wearing a ball cap, a video light can help make him look a lot better.

Lighting choices for amateur videographers are a lot better these days than they were a decade or two ago. An inexpensive incandescent video light, which will easily fit in a camera bag, can be found for $15 or $20. You can even get a good-quality LED video light for less than $100. Work lights sold at many home improvement stores can also serve as video lights since you can set the camera's white balance to correct for any color casts. You'll need to mount these lights on a tripod or other support, or, perhaps, to a bracket that fastens to the tripod socket on the bottom of the camera.

Much of the challenge depends upon whether you're just trying to add some fill light on your subject versus trying to boost the light on an entire scene. A small video light will do just fine for the former. It won't handle the latter. Fortunately, the versatility of the a7R IV comes in quite handy here. Since the camera shoots video in Auto ISO mode, it can compensate for lower lighting levels and still produce a decent image. For best results though, better lighting is necessary.

Creative Lighting

While ramping up the light intensity will produce better technical quality in your video, it won't necessarily improve the artistic quality of it. Whether we're outdoors or indoors, we're used to seeing light come from above. Videographers need to consider how they position their lights to provide even illumination while up high enough to angle shadows down low and out of sight of the camera.

When considering lighting for video, there are several factors. One is the quality of the light. It can either be hard (direct) light or soft (diffused) light. Hard light is good for showing detail, but it can also be very harsh and unforgiving. "Softening" the light, but diffusing it somehow, can reduce the intensity of the light but make for a kinder, gentler light as well.

While mixing light sources isn't always a good idea, one approach is to combine window light with supplemental lighting. Position your subject with the window to one side and bring in either a supplemental light or a reflector to the other side for reasonably even lighting.

Lighting Styles

Some lighting styles are more heavily used than others. Some forms are used for special effects, while others are designed to be invisible. At its most basic, lighting just illuminates the scene, but when used properly it can also create drama. Let's look at some types of lighting styles:

- **Three-point lighting.** This is a basic lighting setup for one person. A main light illuminates the strong side of a person's face, while a fill light lights up the other side. A third light is then positioned above and behind the subject to light the back of the head and shoulders. (See Figure 10.6, left.)

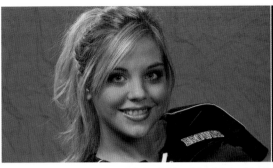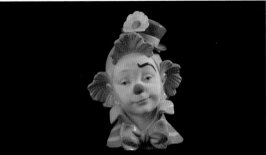

Figure 10.6 With three-point lighting (left) and flat lighting (right).

- **Flat lighting.** Use this type of lighting to provide illumination and nothing more. It calls for a variety of lights and diffusers set to raise the light level in a space enough for good video reproduction, but not to create a particular mood or emphasize a particular scene or individual. With flat lighting, you're trying to create even lighting levels throughout the video space and minimize any shadows. Generally, the lights are placed up high and angled downward (or possibly pointed straight up to bounce off of a white ceiling). (See Figure 10.6, right.)
- **"Ghoul lighting."** This is the style of lighting used for old horror movies. The idea is to position the light down low, pointed upward. It's such an unnatural style of lighting that it makes its targets seem weird and ghoulish.
- **Outdoor lighting.** While shooting outdoors may seem easier because the sun provides more light, it also presents its own problems. As a general rule of thumb, keep the sun behind you when you're shooting video outdoors, except when shooting faces (anything from a medium shot and closer) since the viewer won't want to see a squinting subject. When shooting another human this way, put the sun behind her and use a video light to balance light levels between the foreground and background. If the sun is simply too bright, position the subject in the shade and use the video light for your main illumination. Using reflectors (white board panels or aluminum foil–covered cardboard panels are cheap options) can also help balance light effectively.

Audio

When it comes to making a successful video, audio quality is one of those things that separates the professionals from the amateurs. We're used to watching top-quality productions on television and in the movies, yet the average person has no idea how much effort goes in to producing what seems to be "natural" sound. Much of the sound you hear in such productions is actually recorded on carefully controlled sound stages and "sweetened" with a variety of sound effects and other recordings of "natural" sound.

Your a7R IV has a pair of stereo microphones on its top surface, able to capture Dolby Digital Audio. You can plug an external microphone into the mic jack on the left side of the camera, or work with a microphone designed specifically for Sony cameras, such as the (roughly $110) Sony ECM-XYST1M mic (see Figure 10.7). Hook up Sony's ECM-B1M shotgun mic or XLR-K3M XLS adapter kit with a pro microphone; you'll get professional audio quality that can match any dedicated camcorder.

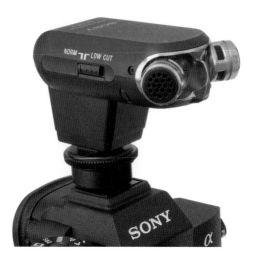

Figure 10.7 An external microphone can significantly improve your audio quality.

If you stick with the built-in microphones, you must be extra careful to optimize the sound captured by those fixed sound-grabbers. You will find an Audio Recording entry in the Camera Settings II-02 menu (it just turns sound on or off), along with an Audio Recording Level and Audio Level display entry. In the Camera Settings II-03 menu, you'll find an Audio Out Timing entry (to compensate for a delay when viewing live video through the a7R IV's HDMI port), and a Wind Noise Reduction on/off entry. The latter is a low-cut filter feature that can further reduce wind noise; however, this processing feature also affects other sounds, making a wind screen on the microphone itself far more useful. Your camera options were explained in Chapter 4.

Tips for Better Audio

Since recording high-quality audio is such a challenge, it's a good idea to do everything possible to maximize recording quality:

- **Turn off any sound makers you can.** Little things like fans and air handling units aren't obvious to the human ear but will be picked up by the microphone. Turn off any machinery or devices that you can plus make sure cell phones are set to silent mode. Also, do what you can to minimize sounds such as wind, radio, television, or people talking in the background.

- **Make sure to record some "natural" sound.** If you're shooting video at an event of some kind, make sure you get some background sound that you can add to your audio as desired in postproduction.

- **Consider recording audio separately.** Lip-syncing is probably beyond most of the people you're going to be shooting, but there's nothing that says you can't record narration separately and add it later. It's relatively easy if you learn how to use simple software video-editing programs like iMovie (for the Macintosh) or Windows Movie Maker (for Windows PCs). Any time the speaker is off-camera, you can work with separately recorded narration rather than recording the speaker on-camera. This can produce much cleaner sound.

Lens Craft

I'll cover the use of lenses with the a7R IV in more detail in Chapter 12, but a discussion of lens selection when shooting movies may be useful at this point. In the video world, not all lenses are created equal. The two most important considerations are depth-of-field, or the beneficial lack thereof, and zooming. I'll address each of these separately.

Depth-of-Field and Video

Have you wondered why professional videographers have gone nuts over still cameras that can also shoot video? The producers of *Saturday Night Live* could afford to have Alex Buono, their director of photography, use the niftiest, most-expensive high-resolution video cameras to shoot the opening sequences of the program. Instead, Buono opted for a pair of digital SLR cameras. One thing that makes digital still cameras so attractive for video is that they have relatively large sensors. That provides two benefits compared to cameras with a smaller sensor. In addition to improved low-light performance, the large chip allows for unusually shallow depth-of-field (a limited range of acceptable sharpness) for blurring the background; this effect is difficult or impossible to match with most professional video cameras since they use smaller sensors.

As you'll learn in Chapter 12, a larger sensor calls for the use of longer focal lengths to produce the same field of view, so, in effect, a larger sensor allows for making images with reduced depth-of-field. And *that's* what makes cameras like the a7R IV attractive from a creative standpoint. Shallow depth-of-field makes it easier to blur a cluttered background to keep the viewers' eyes riveted on the primary subject. Your camera, with its larger sensor, has a distinct advantage over consumer camcorders in this regard, and even does a much better job than professional video cameras.

Zooming and Video

When shooting still photos, a zoom is a zoom is a zoom. The key considerations for a zoom lens used only for still photography are the maximum aperture available at each focal length ("How *fast* is this lens?"), the zoom range ("How far can I zoom in or out?"), and its sharpness at any given f/stop ("Do I lose sharpness when I shoot wide open?").

When recording video, the priorities may change, and there are two additional parameters to consider. The first two I listed, lens speed and zoom range, have roughly the same importance in both still and video photography. Zoom range gains a bit of importance in videography, because you can always/usually move closer to shoot a still photograph, but when you're zooming during a shot most of us don't have that option (or the funds to buy/rent a dolly to smoothly move the camera during capture). But, oddly enough, overall sharpness may have slightly less importance under certain conditions when shooting video. That's because the image changes in some way many times per second (30/60 times per second), so any given frame doesn't hang around long enough for our eyes to pick out every single detail. You want a sharp image, of course, but your standards don't need to be quite as high when shooting video.

Here are the considerations:

- **Zoom lens maximum aperture.** The "speed" of the lens matters in several ways. A zoom with a relatively wide maximum aperture (small f/number) lets you shoot in lower light levels with fewer exposure problems. A wide aperture like f/1.8 also enables you to minimize depth-of-field for selective focus. Keep in mind that with most zooms, the maximum aperture gets smaller as you zoom to longer focal lengths. A variable-aperture f/3.5 to 5.6 lens like the power zoom kit lens, offers a fairly wide f/3.5 maximum aperture at its shortest focal length but only f/5.6 worth of light capturing ability at the long end. Zooms with a wide and constant (not variable) maximum aperture such as f/2.8 are available, but they are larger, heavier, and more expensive.

- **Power zoom.** An ideal movie zoom should have a power zoom feature, and that's available with Sony lenses with the PZ designation. PZ lenses offer smooth, silent zooming that's ideal for video shooting. Mechanical zooming with other lenses during capture can produce jerky images, even with vibration reduction turned on. If you own a remote with a zoom button, such as the RM-VPR1, I recommend using that with your PZ lenses for smoother zooming. As I mentioned earlier, you can also mimic power zoom using the a7R IV's digital zoom feature.

- **Zoom range.** Use of zoom during actual capture should not be an everyday thing, unless you're shooting a kung-fu movie. However, there are effective uses for a zoom shot, particularly if it's a "long" one from wide angle to telephoto. Most of the time, you'll use the zoom range to adjust the perspective of the camera *between* shots, and a longer zoom range can mean less trotting back and forth to adjust the field of view. Zoom range also comes into play when you're working with selective focus (longer focal lengths produce shallower depth-of-field) or want to expand or compress the apparent distance between foreground and background subjects. A longer range gives you more flexibility.

- **Linearity.** Interchangeable lenses may have some drawbacks, as many photographers who have been using the video features of their digital SLRs have discovered. That's because lenses with mechanical zooming are rarely linear unless they were specifically designed for shooting movies. Rotating the zoom ring manually at a constant speed doesn't always produce a smooth zoom. There may be "jumps" as the elements of the lens shift around during the zoom. Keep that in mind if you plan to zoom during a shot and are using a non-linear lens. In practice, those include virtually all the lenses at your disposal, aside from power zoom lenses, a special E-mount cine lens, or a cine lens in an entirely different mount that you can use with your a7R IV with an optional third-party adapter.

Advanced Video Features **11**

As I've noted several times in this book, the a7R IV boasts professional-level video features not found in most consumer- or even some pro-oriented digital still cameras. Many of those looking for an advanced Sony camera for video may prefer a dedicated camcorder, like the Sony PXW-FS5M2 4K XDCAM Super 35mm Compact camcorder (about $4,750), which uses E-mount lenses, or the 4K-capable Sony AX1 Professional Handycam ($4,500), which has a fixed 20X zoom lens. Even so, the a7R IV is no slacker when it comes to capturing clips that can be assembled into polished video productions.

This chapter will introduce you to some of the most important concepts you'll need to learn as you continue your educational journey toward professional cinematography. Some of this will seem a little technical to those who are just learning about video, so if you're not going to be venturing into serious movie making soon, you might want to skim through this chapter simply to gain some background. As I mentioned when I talked about the a7R IV's backside illuminated sensor, I don't normally venture this deeply into tech territory in my books, but the a7R IV isn't an ordinary camera!

More on Sensors and Crop Factors

In Chapter 10, I described some of the reasons why the large sensor size of a full-frame still camera provides video shooters with some selective focus advantages when compared to the much smaller sensor found on many professional video cameras in the past. I'll be explaining the concept of *crop factor* in detail in Chapter 12. Both aspects are important in the video world, but with a few variations caused by the differences in how video is captured and used.

However, unlike the Mark III, the a7R IV uses a 1.6X crop to give 24p footage and 1.8X crop for 30p. So, while the crop modes are still marked as 'Super35,' it'll actually be a little more difficult to get a wide-angle field-of-view, even if you resort to dedicated Super35 or APS-C lenses.

Sensor Size

Sensor size is important because smaller sensors use lenses with shorter focal lengths to fill their frames, and the shorter the focal length, the larger the depth-of-field. That's why point-and-shoot cameras (or smartphones), with their minuscule sensors, can produce acceptably sharp images for subjects located a few inches from the lens out to infinity. Conversely, because a normal lens on an APS-C camera is in the 38mm range, and on a full-frame camera is roughly 55mm, a full-frame camera like the a7R IV has less depth-of-field for the same field of view.

Selective focus is a definite creative plus for videographers. We've all seen shots in which focus initially emphasizes some foreground object that's sharply rendered, and then the camera operator pulls focus out to a more distant subject, which suddenly appears in great detail. Larger sensors make such techniques easier, which is why current video cameras are often segregated into *small sensor* and *large sensor* categories. The Sony PX1 camcorder I mentioned earlier has a large APS-C sensor, measuring 23.6mm × 13.3mm, while the Sony AX1 Professional Handycam has a smaller $^1/_{2.3}$-inch sensor. (Video cameras dating back to the dawn of television have used the diameter of the video tube as a measurement.)

Figure 11.1 shows the relative size of the 4K and/or full HD capture area of some typical sensor sizes, starting with the a7R IV's full-frame sensors at upper left, the "small" sensor of typical pro cameras and the $^1/_{2/3}$-inch sensor of Sony's least expensive pro camera at right, and an APS-C sensor and the RED Raven "large" sensor shown at the bottom. Note that the 4K/Full HD Area region shown in the figure applies *only* when the a7R IV is *not* set to APS-C/Super 35 mode. Your camera is capable of shooting 4K video using both full-frame *and* cropped sensor modes. Although labeled APS-C/Super 35, the a7R IV in that mode actually uses a somewhat tighter 1.6X crop when shooting 24p video and a 1.8X crop when capturing 30p video. In still photography mode, APS-C/Super 35 uses a 1.5X crop factor. The effect becomes more apparent when you're looking for a wide-angle perspective. A 20mm focal length has the equivalent full-frame field of view as a 30mm setting with a 1.5X crop, but 32mm at 1.6X and 36mm at 1.8X. Although equivalent changes seem small, replacing a 20mm wide perspective with 30mm to 36mm fields of view can be important when space is tight. (That is, you are unable to back up a few feet to compensate for the crop.) I'll explain more about the crop factor in the next section.

Figure 11.1 Relative video capture areas for example sensor sizes.

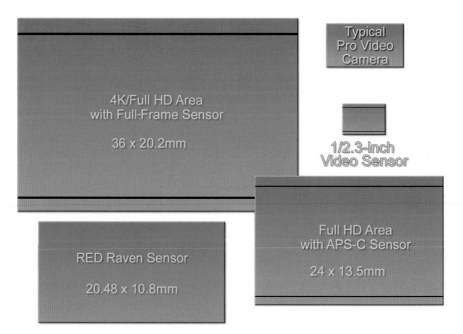

Crop Factor

The *crop factor* is important because with any given lens, the field of view will vary depending on how much of that lens's coverage area is used to capture video. (If you're completely unfamiliar with crop factors, skip ahead to Chapter 12 and read about them.) Still photos can be shot in both vertical or horizontal orientations, and most often using the 3:2 aspect ratio used outside the Micro Four Thirds (4:3) world. So, the crop factor for stills is calculated by comparing the diagonal measurement of the frame with the diagonal of the traditional 35mm frame.

For video, clips are normally captured with the camera in a horizontal orientation (at least, outside the realm of the smartphone), and the proportions or aspect ratio of the video frame can vary, with 16:9 being the standard for standard HD, full HD, and 4K (Ultra HD) video (and beyond).

The 16:9 proportions work out to roughly 1.78:1, which is close enough to the 1.85:1 widescreen cinema aspect ratio that it's easy to show movies captured in either aspect ratio on displays compatible with either. Given the 16:9 standard, it's common to represent the resolution of a video image by its horizontal measurement and scanning method: that is, 720p, 1080p, and 4K (actually 3,840 pixels with your Sony a7R IV camera; 4,096 pixels with some other 4K devices) for progressive scan (p) video.

Your full-frame sensor provides a 1X crop factor for video when shooting Standard HD (720p), Full HD (1080p), or 4K (3840p). Sensors with smaller areas produce various crop factors, based, not on the sensor's diagonal measurement, but the relative *width* of the sensor area, compared to the full frame. Super 35 is a popular format for video and is available with your a7R IV. By comparing the widths of the sensor area, we can arrive at a crop factor of roughly 1.6/1.8X when shooting in APS-C/Super 35mm mode with the a7R IV. (See Figure 11.2.) (Those are nominal values; the exact crop factors are 1.58 and 1.84, respectively.)

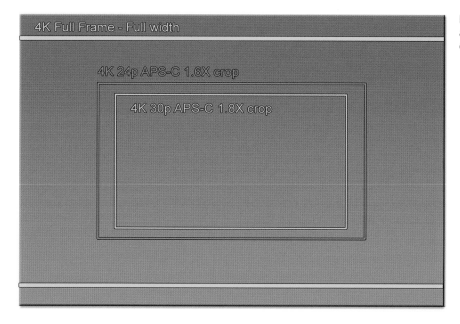

Figure 11.2 Full-frame and Super 35/APS-C crops of the Sony sensor.

There are subtle differences between shooting video in full frame versus Super 35/APS-C modes. Both capture more pixels than needed, but process them differently, using pixel binning and over-sampling, respectively. These two processes are *different,* regardless of what you may have heard, even though they are often incorrectly used interchangeably:

- **Full-frame mode.** Video shot in full-frame mode grabs pixels across the full width of the sensor, combining them using a process called *pixel binning*, which takes clumps of red, green, and blue pixels and merges them with others of the same color to create a larger "pixel" at a reduced resolution, resulting in faster capture with reduced noise. The remaining pixels are then *demo-saiced,* which interprets the colors of adjacent pixels to produce a full-color image even though each physical pixel actually is sensitive to only one of the three primary colors.

- **Super 35/APS-C mode.** In this mode, the a7R IV captures pixels within the smaller APS-C-sized area of the sensor, which results in the 1.6X (for 24p video) or 1.8X (for 30p video) field-of-view crops. However, it *oversamples*, grabbing more pixels than required for the final video frame. That large number of pixels is demosaiced *first*, and *then* downsized to the required size. Because oversampling happens *after* the RGB pixels have been analyzed and demosaiced, the process allows for better capture of details for a sharper final image.

In practice, the image quality difference is not great, but still can be important when capturing ultra-high-definition 4K video. You'll probably want to shoot in full-frame mode to avoid the crop factor under most circumstances, and switch to Super 35/APS-C mode when you actually need the 1.6/1.8X field-of-view crop or must have the sharpest possible image.

But should you be shooting full high-definition movies, or ultra-high-definition (4K) video? If your memory card (which should be a 64GB or larger SDXC card) or external recorder like the Atomos Shogun, can handle the data rates, 4K is alluring, even if your movies will never be viewed in anything other than 1080p format. All that extra detail is hard to resist.

Video gurus who have studied the Sony cameras have concluded that the a7R IV's Super 35 4K video provides the most detailed movies with the best dynamic range and noise characteristics. As I described earlier, each pixel within the Super 35 image area is captured, producing more information than is required for even a 4K video frame, and then downscaled. Paradoxically, this oversampling means that Super 35 4K has better detail than 4K video produced from the a7R IV's full-frame 61MP sensor.

Conversely, when using 1080p instead of 4K, the full-frame video typically has more detail than 1080p shot using the Super 35/APS-C setting. If full HD shooting is your intent, you're better off reserving Super 35/APS-C format for those times when you want to take advantage of the 1.6/1.8X crop factors to increase the reach/magnification of your lenses, say, for wildlife photography or sports. In all cases, though, 4K video in either full-frame or Super 35/APS-C mode is superior to what you get using 1080p alone. Your video will still be better if shot in 4K and then downscaled to 1080p. The choice is yours.

Other Important Parameters

But wait, as they say, there's more! The last sections of this chapter will explain some of the other technical details of shooting video, providing enough detail, I hope, to get you reading more complex tomes that cover this information in depth.

Frame Guides

Frame guides are a useful way of visualizing the area that will be captured within a larger visible display. In ancient times, interchangeable-lens rangefinder film cameras that used an optical viewfinder would have bright frame outlines appear, often automatically when a particular lens was mounted on the camera, and sometimes through the use of an attachment that fit over the built-in viewfinder. In the digital age, frame guides have been popular with digital cameras that use an optical viewfinder, providing a masked off display to preview the actual image area that will be captured in crop or video modes. Cameras with electronic displays, like the a7R IV, don't necessarily need frame guides, because the capture area can be enlarged and masked off electronically to show only the actual image area.

Even so, frame guides are a popular tool for videographers, because they allow viewing the area outside the actual frame that will be captured (the "look-around area") so you can monitor moving subjects before they enter the frame. In professional productions, it's useful to look at the region outside the captured frame to detect when boom microphones, careless crew members, or other objects threaten to intrude on the frame.

The a7R IV cameras offer a variety of frame guides that can be turned on or off in the Camera Settings II menu, including grid lines, aspect ratios, frame center markings, and "safety" areas. These markers appear *only* on the EVF or LCD monitor, and not in the captured video itself (see Figure 11.3 for example placement).

- **Marker Display.** This Camera Settings II-03 menu entry works in conjunction with the Marker Settings option (described next), and simply turns settings on or off.

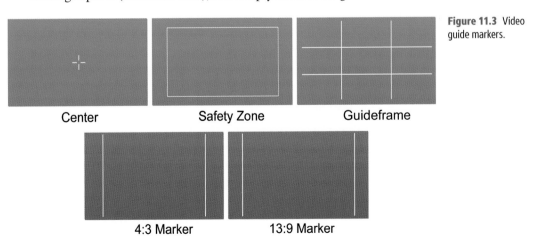

Figure 11.3 Video guide markers.

Center   Safety Zone   Guideframe

4:3 Marker   13:9 Marker

- **Marker Settings.** This menu entry allows you to specify Center, Aspect Ratio, Safety Zone, or Guide frame. Each can be specified individually, and turned on or off independently, so you can display any, all, or none.

  - **Center.** This crosshair can be used to determine whether your subject is placed in the exact center of the screen.

  - **Aspect Ratio.** Use these guides to frame your image so the important subject matter is contained within a desired aspect ratio, or to frame the image for later cropping to that aspect ratio. You can select among 4:3, 13:9, 14:9, 15:9, 1.66:1, 1.85:1, or 2.35:1. These conform to various movie formats in common use. (*Star Wars*, for example, was filmed in CinemaScope, with a 2.35:1 aspect ratio.)

  - **Safety Zone.** It's common to shoot movies knowing in advance that they will be cropped down eventually for display in a slightly different format. The director simply makes sure that the important parts of the frame are included in the "safety zone" that will never be cropped out. For example, you wouldn't want to put two characters who are talking to each other at opposite ends of the entire frame but would instead locate them in the safety zone so both would be visible. Your camera's safety zone display can be set for 80 percent or 90 percent of the frame to represent the area that will always be shown when the movie is viewed on a standard HDTV.

  - **Guideframe.** This grid is used to help you determine whether horizontal and vertical lines are skewed and can also be used as a Rule of Thirds guide for composition.

Time Codes and User Bits

The Time Code (TC) and User Bit (UB) settings are information that can be embedded and used to sync clips and sound when editing movies. Advanced video shooters find SMPTE (Society of Motion Picture and Television Engineers)-compatible time codes embedded in the video files to be an invaluable reference during editing. To oversimplify a bit, the time system provides precise *hour:minute:second:frame* markers that allow identifying and synchronizing frames and audio. The time code system includes a provision for "dropping" frames to ensure that the fractional frame rate of captured video (remember that a 24 fps setting actually yields 23.976 frames per second while 30 fps capture gives you 29.97 actual "frames" per second) can be matched up with actual time spans.

Using time codes and user bits is a college-level film school class on its own, but I'm going to provide a quick overview to get you started. If you're at the stage where you're using time codes, you don't need this primer, anyway. However, the a7R IV's TC/UB Settings entry, which Sony has hidden away in the Setup 3 menu, includes the following options:

- **TC Preset.** Sets the time code. If you'll be shooting 60i/50i, you can choose time codes from 00:00:00:00 (hours, minutes, seconds, frame) to 23:59:59:29 or 23:59:59:24, respectively. With 24p, you can set multiples of four from 0 to 23 frames. If you own the RMT-VP1K remote commander, the time code can be reset to zero using a button on the controller.

- **UB Preset.** Sets the user bit, which is a marker you can insert in your video, say to designate a scene or take. There are four digits in each user bit (for example, 01:02:03:04), and the digits are each hexadecimal in nature, so you could create a code like C0 FF EE if you were feeling facetious.

- **TC Format.** Sets the recording method for the time code. You can choose from DF (drop frame) or NDF (non–drop frame) formats. Drop frames are a way of compensating for the discrepancy between the nominal number of frames per second and the actual number (for example, 30 fps yields 29.97 actual frames per second, and 60 fps gives you 59.95 frames per second). In drop-frame format, the camera will skip some time code numbers at intervals to eliminate the discrepancy. The first two frame numbers are removed every minute except for every tenth minute (think of it as a leap year). You may notice a difference of several seconds per hour when using the non–drop frame option.

- **TC Run.** Sets the count-up format for the time code. You can choose Rec Run, in which the time code counts up only when you are actually capturing video; or Free Run (also known as Time of Day), which allows the time code to run up even between shooting clips. The latter is useful when you want to synchronize clips between multiple cameras that are shooting the same event. When using Free Run, even if the cameras record at different times, you'll be able to match the video that was captured at the exact same moment during editing.

- **TC Make.** Sets the recording format for the time code on the recording medium. Choose Preset to record a new time code, or Regenerate to read the previous time code setting and record the new time code consecutively. When Regenerate is selected, the time code advances no matter what TC Run setting has been selected.

- **UB Time Rec.** Sets whether or not to record the time as a user bit.

Picture Profiles

If you've been taking photos for a while, you're probably familiar with all the fixes and tweaks you can do with your still images within image editors like Photoshop. It's relatively easy to adjust color tones, contrast, sharpness, and other parameters prior to displaying or printing your photo. Movies are a little trickier, because any given video typically consists of *thousands* of individual photos, captured at 24 frames per second (or faster), with the possibility that each and every frame within a particular sequence might need fixes or creative adjustments.

Shooting video does not preclude doing post-processing during editing. Indeed, many videographers deliberately shoot relatively low-contrast video in order to capture the largest dynamic range possible, and then fine-tune the rendition later using their editing software. Picture Profiles let you do that—and also allow you to adjust your camera so that the video you capture is *pre-fine-tuned* in order to reduce or eliminate the amount of post-processing you do later.

The a7R IV camera is furnished with ten "canned" picture profiles, which you can think of as Creative Styles for movies. The parameters included in these profiles can be further adjusted by you to better suit the "look" you are striving for in your videos. You can connect your camera to a TV or monitor using the HDMI Out connector and an HDMI cable, view the image produced by the camera on the larger screen, and then make adjustments to the picture profile. I described the process in how-to form briefly in Chapter 3.

Needless to say, creating and using Picture Profiles is a highly technical aspect of video making, at least in terms of the amount of knowledge you need to have to correctly judge what changing one of the parameters will do to your video. I hope to get you started with a quick description of what those parameters do, so you'll have a starting point when you start to explore them.

Gamma, Gamma Ding Dong

The ten Picture Profile presets in the Camera Settings I-12 menu already have their own default values, each adjusted for a particular type of shooting, using various gamma and color tone settings. Thanks to our evolutionary heritage, humans don't see differences in tones in a linear manner. An absolutely smooth progression of pixels from absolute black to pure white (with 0 representing black and 256 representing white) would not look like a continuous gradient to our eyes. We'd be unable to detect differences in shadows and highlights that have the same change in tonal values as midtones. So, everything from computer monitors to printers use a correction factor (gamma) to cancel out the differences in the way we see tones.

This correction takes the form of a curve, called a *gamma curve*. If you remember your geometry, the x and y axes on a graph are used to define the shape of a curve, and in the case of gamma curves, the values use logarithmic units (ack!) to define the slope. That's where the terms S-Log2, S-Log3, HLG and other mind-numbing jargon comes from. The whole shebang is needed to reconcile the ability of sensors to capture, video systems to display, and printers to output a range of tones in a linear way with the actual tones we perceive non-linearly. Gamma correction and gamma compression are used to help make sure that what we get is what we see. While gamma correction between computer platforms (that is, between Macs and PCs) may be different, the actual gamma values defined by video standards like NTSC and PAL are fixed and well-known. Picture Profiles allow you to configure your camera to capture video using a desired amount of gamma and color tone correction.

S-Log2/S-Log3/HLG

S-Log2 is a log gamma curve that is used when the video will be processed after shooting and captures a much larger range of tones (as many as 14 stops!) than standard gamma curves. Indeed, the tones captured using S-Log2 can't be displayed in all their glory on a standard TV or monitor, which are generally adjusted for the broadcast television BT-709 standard. Instead, the unprocessed video will look darker and lower in contrast because all those tonal values have been squeezed into the BT-709 (also called REC-709) range.

Video signals normally encompass brightness levels from 0 percent to 109 percent (you read that right: modern video cameras can record detail in highlights that are actually brighter than was possible when the video age began; the old scale was retained, reminiscent of Nigel Tufnel's 11 setting on his amp). However, even the 109 percent provides too much of a limitation; cameras can capture detail in highlights that are even brighter than *that*. So, a log gamma curve (in this case one called S-Log2) is used to *compress* all that image detail to fit into the space allowed for conventional video signals. Post-processing in a video editor allows working with all that information and produces a finished video that contains the filmmaker's selection of tonal values in a form that can be displayed comfortably. The full dynamic range can be used to produce the finished movie. You might find that useful when exposing for highlights while avoiding blowing out the sky, or for capturing detail in shadows without losing mid tones and highlights.

The Picture Profile 7 (PP7) is already set up for S-Log2 and should be your choice if you want to work with that curve. I've oversimplified things a bit, because there are many other great things you can do with S-Log2, such as overexposing or "pushing" your video to reduce noise (but at the risk of losing some detail in brighter skin tones), and then output (called "grading") to produce an optimized final image. Picture Profiles 8 and 9 (PP8 and PP9) are set up for S-Log3, which is a gamma curve optimized to look more like what you would have gotten if you shot film. Both also assume your video will be processed for your final production. HLG/HLG1-HLG3 gamma curves are provided for various high-dynamic range formats.

I know this chapter doesn't tell you everything you need to know to take the next step in movie making with your a7R IV camera, but my intent was to introduce you to enough of your Sony's capabilities to spur additional exploration of this exciting creative arena.

VIEWING FIX

Movies captured using gamma profiles appear to be very low in contrast until processed using software on your computer. Because Picture Profiles extend the dynamic range of recorded video, the clips normally appear very low in contrast during review in the camera. The Gamma Display Assist entry in the Setup 1 menu allows you to adjust playback when viewing images captured using Picture Profiles, so that the appearance on the a7R IV's EVF and LCD appears more natural, which is useful if you use live view to evaluate your captures. The display is not changed if you're viewing through a device plugged into the HDMI port, and you'll still need to process the video in your video-editing software. You can turn Gamma Display Assist off, allow the camera to select an appropriate adjustment automatically, or manually set the assist feature to use the gamma you are using. Your choices include S-Log2 and S-Log3, and four HLG (Hybrid Log Gamma) settings, which are used for delivery of video to high dynamic range TVs that are currently the rage. (More on HLG later in this chapter.) These are a bit esoteric for the average a7R IV user who isn't heavily into professional-quality video capture.

More on 4K Video

It's probably a great time for you to start working with 4K video, especially since 8K video is already on the way. In practice, shooting 4K is not much different than shooting full HD or standard HD. The only changes you might make involve your realization that as long as you are capturing higher-quality video, you might as well upgrade your technique (and, perhaps, your auxiliary equipment).

While 4K video still seems new and exotic, given the usual pace of technology, it's very likely that your next HDTV will have 4K capabilities (if your current set does not), and cable/satellite/streaming systems as well as Blu-Ray discs will all make the leap sooner than any of us expect.

Shooting in 4K is still in its infancy: few of us own 4K high-definition televisions that allow playing back 4K content at its full resolution. However, the number of 4K-capable TVs is growing all the time, and there are some definite benefits to shooting ultra-high resolution now, even before the ability to take advantage of the format is widespread. Simply speaking, if you shoot 4K and then convert it to conventional full HD, your video will generally be much higher in quality than if you originated in 1920 × 1080 resolution. All you need is editing software like Adobe Premiere Pro, Final Cut Pro, or Corel Video Studio that can work with and edit your 4K clips.

The key thing to know is that your a7R IV can record 4K video internally, export 4K video to an external recorder, or to *both* simultaneously. If you want to record *only* to the memory card, you don't need to do anything special other than select XAVCS 4K under the File Format entry and your desired frame/bit rate under Record Setting (both in the Camera Settings II-1 menu).

If you prefer to output your 4K video to the HDMI port (say, to a video recorder), or HDMI port *and* the memory card, you need to visit the 4K Output Selection entry in the Setup 4 menu. Set the mode dial to Movie and attach your camera to the external device using a micro HDMI cable. Since the length of your recording time is essentially limited only by the a7R IV's ability to dissipate heat and avoid shutdown from high sensor temperatures (potentially a problem when shooting 4K video), the extra storage of an external monitor can come in handy.

As I mentioned in Chapter 10, you will probably want to use an external microphone, either plugged into the a7R IV's microphone jack or connected through the multi interface shoe on top of the camera. As I noted, a move to professional microphones using the XLR interface might also seem prudent.

 TIP If you read my Chapter 4 advice on redefining the available options in the Function menu, consider using Function Menu Set in the Camera Settings II-09 menu if you intend to shoot a lot of video. You can define *separate* Function menus for still photography and movie shooting. Among those you might consider substituting are Zebra settings, Audio levels, and Color balance/temperature settings (remember it's more difficult to adjust color in video than in individual still photos). Or, you might want to add Picture Profiles, Wind Noise Reduction, or the Movie setting (which allows you to switch among P, A, S, or M movie exposure modes). Marker Display or TC/UB settings are other entries you might want to add to your Function menu.

Using an External Recorder

If you're truly becoming an advanced videographer, you'll probably be working with the a7R IV's ability to output "clean" non-compressed HDMI video to an external monitor or video recorder, including the Atomos Shogun lineup, which includes versions that are quite affordable, at least in terms of professional video gear. You can choose models both with and without an external LCD monitor, and capture to solid-state drives (SSD), a laptop's internal or connected hard drive, or to CFast memory cards (the latter chiefly as a nod to those still using the "fast" version of Compact Flash cards). Such equipment allows very high transfer rates and is certainly your best choice if you're shooting 4K video.

Probably the best of the lot for a7R IV owners is the Atomos Ninja V, an extremely portable unit with a 5.2-inch screen and a $695 price tag that's currently the lowest for this type of device. (The only comparable monitor/recorder, the Video Devices PX-E5, costs $995.) Its size is a definite plus—if you're shooting video with a smaller, lightweight camera, you're going to need an equally compact recorder/monitor, such as the roughly 13-ounce Ninja V. Add a battery, HDMI cable, and a 2.5-inch solid-state drive, and you're ready to go.

The Ninja V has HDMI input and output jacks on its left edge, which you can see in Figure 11.4. The latter allows you to daisy-chain an even larger monitor or other device. A power button, headphone jack, microphone/audio input, and remote jack reside on the other edge. The touch screen enables you to view your video and access the monitor/recorder's menus and controls, which is convenient (except outdoors in cold weather when you're wearing gloves and might wish you had a few buttons to press instead). The only other "defect" of the unit is the noise produced by its fan; even when you're using an external microphone with your a7R IV, the fan noise may be picked up in a quiet room.

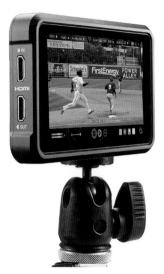

Figure 11.4 The Atomos Ninja V monitor/recorder.

Why use an external monitor/recorder like the Ninja V, when your a7R IV has its own nifty monitor and can store quite a lot of video on UHS-II-compliant memory cards? From a monitor standpoint, an external unit's screen is larger, easier to see, and offers more flexibility in positioning. The a7R IV's screen tilts up or down; mounted on a ballhead like the one in the figure, you can adjust an external screen to any angle, including reversing it to point in the same direction as the lens, so vloggers can monitor themselves as they record or stream their video blog.

But the best value may come from the recording capabilities of such a device. Internal video is saved to your memory card in the standard H.264/MPEG-4 Part 10 format, which compresses that stream of images as much as 50X. That video has only 8 bits of information: good, but somewhat limited in the dynamic range that can be included. Depending on your scene, you may lose some detail in the highlights or shadows.

Fortunately, the a7R IV can also direct its video output through the HDMI port in "clean" uncompressed 4:2:2 8-bit UHD (ultra-high-definition) resolution. That's correct. Sony still doesn't offer external 10-bit output, which is unfortunate: 8-bit output gives you 16.8 million possible colors; 10-bit output is capable of more than 108 billion hues. Nor is 60p 4K video available. However, for most of us who aren't professional videographers, the a7R IV's output should be sufficient, especially since the available Picture Profiles include four HLG (hybrid log gamma) curves suitable for HDR (high dynamic range) recording.

The HDMI port on the a7R IV accepts an HDMI mini-D cable. I prefer to purchase value-priced third-party cables, which I buy in convenient lengths of 3 feet, 6 feet, 10 feet, or longer. The cable can be connected to the monitor, recorder, or other device of your choice. (Some of the screen shots in this book were output to a Blackmagic Intensity shuttle that allowed capturing stills of the a7R IV's menus, live view, and video.)

TECH ALERT

Unless you're venturing into professional videography, you probably aren't obsessed with all those numbers in the previous paragraph. However, if you're terminally curious, the important things to keep in mind are:

- **Transfer bit rate.** This is the speed the a7R IV outputs its video to your memory card or external recorder. High transfer rates (such as 100 megabits per second) require fast memory cards; an external recorder should be able to suck up video as quickly as your camera can deliver it.
- **Encoding.** Although the "clean" video output to the HDMI port is not compressed, it is *encoded* using a procedure called *chroma subsampling,* which does reduce the amount of information that needs to be transferred. Chroma subsampling takes advantage of the fact that human beings don't detect changes in color (chroma) as easily as they do for brightness (luma). The designation 4:2:2 simply indicates that the full amount of brightness information is passed along ("4") while the two chroma values are sampled at half that rate ("2:2"). Subsampling in this way reduces the bandwidth of the otherwise uncompressed video signal by as much as one-third with no visual difference.

When it comes to saving your 4K video files, you have three destination combinations to choose from:

- **Capture to memory card (only).** You can output your 4K video to a memory card in your a7R IV, but it really should be a fast UHS-II card residing in Slots 1 or 2. Because 4K video files can be so massive, you'll want a 64GB to 128GB (or larger, when they become affordable) card to store your movies. This option is the least expensive, but it comes at a cost. The camera compresses your 4K video, using a maximum 100MB/second transfer rate, so a bit of quality is lost. If you're planning on editing the video and ending up with 1080p HD clips, you probably won't notice the difference, especially since your 4K-to-HD conversion will usually have more detail than a straight 1080p movie.
- **Capture to an external recorder (only).** If you're *really* serious about video, you'll want to consider using an external recorder, linked through the a7R IV's HDMI port. The video is *not* compressed, and you can take advantage of the fastest transfer rates to optimize quality.
- **Capture to both.** If you're equipped with a very fast memory card and external recorder, you can opt to save your video to both destinations.

And, as I noted in Chapter 6, the 4K Output Selection entry in the Setup 4 menu allows you to specify exactly where and how your 4K video is captured. To recap, you have four choices:

- **Memory Card+HDMI.** A 4K movie in 30p is saved on the camera's internal SDXC memory card *and* output to the external recorder. This option gives you two copies, including one you can review right in the camera, and a second on your external recorder.
- **HDMI Only (30p).** A 4K movie in 30p is output only to the external device, and not recorded on your memory card. HDMI Info. Display is disabled.
- **HDMI Only (24p).** A 4K movie in 24p is output only to the external device. HDMI Info. Display is disabled.
- **HDMI Only (25p).** If the NTSC/PAL Selector described earlier is set to PAL, you can use this option to shoot a 4K movie in 25p, and output only to the external device. HDMI Info. Display is disabled.

Choosing and Using Lenses | **12**

A huge number of lenses are now available in Sony FE–compatible mounts, even though only a few optics were available when the company introduced its full-frame E-mount in October 2013. Sony has played a remarkable game of catch-up, and a host of third-party lens manufacturers have joined the fray, so that today your a7R IV boasts the largest range of compatible lenses of any competing lineup. Although the number of Sony, Zeiss, and third-party FE-mount lenses is growing, there is a much larger number of APS-C format (non-full-frame) E-mount lenses available, most of which will operate with all full autofocus and autoexposure functions intact. That's a particularly good match with the a7R IV, which gives you 26-megapixel images even in APS-C crop mode.

And if you're willing to use an adapter, there are at least 100 or more different full-frame lenses in Sony/Minolta A-mount, Nikon F-mount, or Canon EF-mount—often available at bargain prices—that can be used on your a7R IV, again, with autofocus and autoexposure. And the number of lenses that can be used with *manual* focus and Aperture Priority autoexposure using adapters for Nikon, Yashica, Contex, Contarex, Alpha, and other types of lenses is mind-boggling. Indeed, Pulitzer Prize–winning photographer (and Sony guru) Brian Smith has called the Sony a7 product line the "universal mount" cameras.

This chapter will help you wend your way through the confusing world of lenses for the a7R IV. Before we get into the actual lenses themselves, it may be useful to explore some aspects that affect how you choose and use optics.

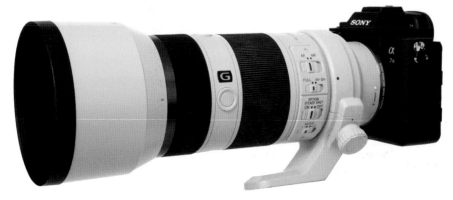

Figure 12.1 A full range of FE-mount lenses, including this Sony FE 70-200mm F4 G OSS, work well on the a7R IV.

Don't Forget the Crop Factor

If the a7R IV is your introduction to full-frame photography, you may be wondering about the term *crop factor*, or, perhaps, alternate nomenclature such as *lens multiplier* or *focal length multiplication factor*. They're used to describe the same phenomenon: the fact that cameras that do not have a full-frame sensor provide a field of view (or scene coverage) that's smaller than what you get with a camera employing the larger sensor. The a7R IV (as well as numerous other cameras of several brands) use a sensor that's approximately 24mm × 36mm (roughly 1.0 × 1.5 inches) in size. Many other digital cameras use a smaller so-called *APS-C sensor* that measures roughly 16mm × 24mm. In comparison, the APS-C sensor's field of view is *cropped*. While some interchangeable-lens cameras (ILC) from other vendors, including Olympus and Panasonic, may use even smaller sensors (with even greater cropping effect), the Sony ILC product line consists entirely of full-frame and APS-C models if you count both A-mount and E-mount variations.

In practical terms, let's say you're using a 200mm lens on a full-frame Sony a7R IV; you get a field of view (measured diagonally) of a little more than 12 degrees. But if you use a 100mm focal length lens on an APS-C camera, like the Sony a6600, the field of view is roughly 8 degrees because the smaller sensor records only a part of the image that the lens projects. Knowledgeable photographers often discuss this effect as the *crop factor* and you'll often find a reference in lens reviews to a *focal length equivalent,* such as 1.5X. In other words, a 200mm lens used on an APS-C camera (or the a7R IV when in APS-C/Super 35mm mode) is equivalent to a 300mm focal length on a full-frame camera. The most accurate expression to describe this concept might be something like *field-of-view equivalency factor.*

Figure 12.2 quite clearly shows the phenomenon at work. The outer rectangle, marked 1X, shows the field of view you might expect with a 200mm lens mounted on a full-frame digital model like the a7R IV. The rectangle marked 1.5X shows the field of view you'd get with that 200mm lens installed

Figure 12.2 This image illustrates the field of view provided by a full-frame camera like the Sony a7R IV (1X) with a 200mm lens, as well as the field of view you'd get when using a camera with the smaller sensor (1.5X crop) like the Sony a6600.

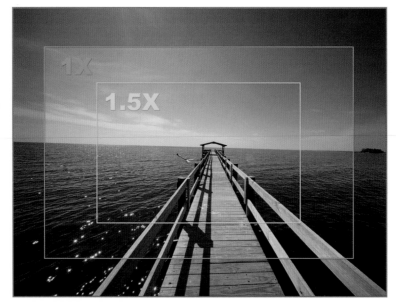

on a camera using the APS-C format (or an a7R IV in APS-C/Super 35 mode). It's easy to see from the illustration that the 1X rendition provides a wider, more expansive view, while the other view is, in comparison, *cropped*.

In any event, I strongly prefer *crop factor* to *focal length multiplier*, because nothing is being multiplied (as I said above). A 200mm lens doesn't "become" a 300mm lens; the depth-of-field and lens aperture remain the same. (I'll explain more about these later in this chapter.) Only the field of view is cropped. Of course, the term *crop factor* has a drawback: it implies that a 24mm × 36mm frame is "full" and anything else is "less than full."

I get e-mails all the time from medium-format photographers who own cameras like the Hasselblad H6D-50c, which has a 43.8mm × 32.9mm sensor that's 67 percent larger than "full frame." By their logical reckoning, the 24mm × 36mm sensors found in full-frame cameras like the Sony a7R IV are "cropped." Take a look at the outer, darkened area within the red rectangle in Figure 12.2. That represents the whopping 104-degree field of view you'd get with a Hasselblad HCD 24mm f/4.8 ($6,295; body an extra $14,495 if you're compiling a holiday gift list).

The Crop Factor and the a7R IV

So, what should the crop factor mean to you? Here's a checklist of things you should consider:

- **Lens compatibility.** Lenses designed for APS-C cameras may not cover the entire 24mm × 36mm full frame of the a7R IV, although some zoom lenses may have a large enough image circle at some focal lengths. With most APS-C lenses you will experience vignetting (darkening) in the corners and reduced sharpness along the edges of the image. For full-frame photography, these lenses will usually be less than satisfactory.

- **Crop mode.** As described in Chapter 4, you'll find the APS-C/Super 35mm crop mode in the Camera Settings I-01 menu. It has three settings:
  - **On.** The a7R IV *always* shoots in cropped mode, regardless of which lens is mounted on the camera. Both full-frame and APS-C lenses will produce images with a cropped field of view. You might use this setting to give your lenses some extra "reach" for sports or wildlife photography.
  - **Auto.** If the camera detects that an APS-C lens is mounted, it will switch to crop mode. Not all lenses will be automatically detected, so you may have to use the On setting instead to manually select crop mode.
  - **Off.** The camera *never* switches to crop mode. Even APS-C lenses will be used in full-frame mode. If you have a lens that *almost* covers the full frame at certain zoom settings, you can use this option and crop out the offending dark corners in your image editor.

- **Reduced resolution.** In crop mode, your images will have reduced resolution, producing 26MP shots with the a7R IV. However, that's still more detail than provided by other full-frame and APS-C cameras with 24MP sensors. The a7R IV allows you to take advantage of the 1.5X crop factor to increase the reach of your telephoto lenses: your 70-200mm zoom becomes a fast 105-300mm lens with plenty of resolution to spare.

- **Shoot now, crop later?** Some point out that you can always shoot everything in full-frame mode and crop your images, perhaps with greater flexibility, in an image editor. While that's true, it's not necessarily the best route. In crop mode, the a7R IV enlarges the cropped image to fill the EVF and LCD monitor, and it's more intuitive to frame and compose your images already cropped. Sports photographers and photojournalists who fire off 1,000 shots at an event won't be eager to go through their digital files and manually crop images. It's easier to crop as you shoot.

> **TIP** I used the Custom Keys entry in the Camera Settings II-09 menu to redefine the Custom 4 (C4) button to the function APS-C S35/Full Frame Select. When shooting sports, I can press the C4 button to toggle between APS-C crop mode (to give my telephoto extra reach) and full-frame mode (when I need a wider perspective) quickly and easily, on the fly. For example, if a wide receiver runs a pattern to the far side of the football field, I can switch to crop mode to get a shot, then return to full-frame mode to get set for the next play with another tap of the C4 key.

SteadyShot and You

Even the highest resolution lenses and sensors can do nothing to correct image sharpness lost due to movement. And while higher shutter speeds can counter most subject movement, when it's the *camera* that's causing blur due to vibration, other approaches have to be taken. Your a7R IV has improved technology that can help avoid blur caused by shutter movement and bounce, but when the entire camera and lens are vibrating, that's where *image stabilization* (IS) comes into play.

Image stabilization/vibration reduction can take many forms, and Sony has expertise in all of them. Electronic IS is used in video cameras and involves shifting pixels around from frame to frame so that pixels that are not moving remain in the same position, and portions of the image that *are* moving don't stray from their proper path. Optical image stabilization, which Sony calls Optical SteadyShot (OSS), is built into many FE-mount lenses and involves lens elements that shift in response to camera movement, as detected by motion sensors included in the optics. Then, Sony introduced a new (at least for its mirrorless lineup) wrinkle: in-body, anti-shake technology called SteadyShot Inside (SSI), which adjusts the position of the sensor carriage itself along five different axes to counteract movement. If you're using an OSS lens with your a7R IV camera, you actually have access to two different, complementary image stabilization systems.

The results can be spectacular. Sony claims a 4.5-stop improvement from its in-body SteadyShot technology. That is, a photograph taken at 1/30th second should have the same sharpness (at least in terms of resistance to camera shake) as one shot at 1/750th second. I've found this to be true. Figure 12.3 shows two shots of pelicans taken a few minutes apart with a 100-400mm Minolta A-mount zoom lens (using the Sony EA-LA4 adapter) at 400mm and 1/125th second hand-held. This older lens has no image stabilization built-in, so the shot at top was taken using only the camera's in-body IS. For the bottom photo, SteadyShot was turned off.

No amount of SteadyShot can eliminate blur from moving subjects, but you should find yourself less tied to a tripod when using longer lenses, or when working with wide-angle lenses under dim lighting conditions than in the past. If you're taking photos in venues where flash or tripods are forbidden, you'll find the a7R IV's image stabilization tandem invaluable. Because lens-based and in-body image stabilization work together, it's appropriate to discuss their use in this lens-oriented chapter.

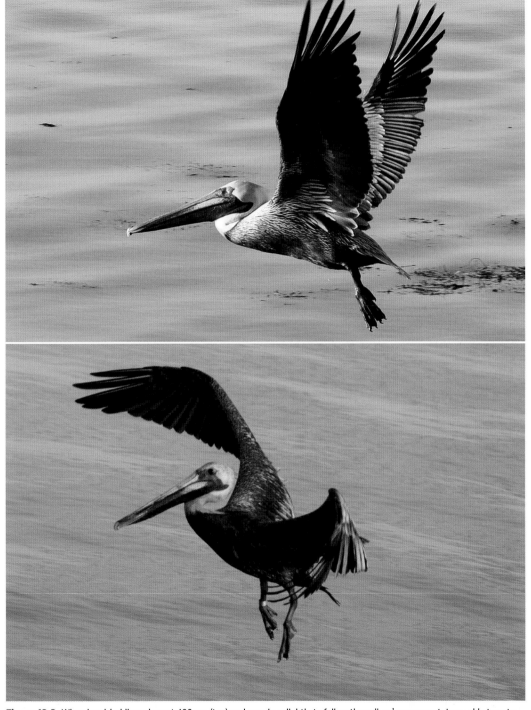

Figure 12.3 When hand-holding a lens at 400mm (top) and panning slightly to follow the pelican's movement, I was able to get a blur-free photo at 1/125th second. With SteadyShot deactivated, camera movement produced noticeable blurring (bottom).

How It Works

As I mentioned, stabilization uses gyroscope-like motion sensors to detect camera motion, which can occur along one of five different axes, as in Figure 12.4, which uses the previous a7R II for illustrative purposes. Shifts in the *x* and *y* directions are likely to occur when shooting macro images hand-held but can take place any time. *Roll* happens when you rotate the camera along the axis passing through the center of the front of the lens, say, to align the horizon while shooting a landscape. There may be a tendency to continue to "correct" for the horizon as you shoot, producing vibration along the roll axis. Roll is especially noticeable in video clips, because it's easy to see straight lines changing their orientation during a shot.

Pitch movements happen when the camera shake is such that the lens moves up or down, often because the lens itself is a front-heavy telephoto lens. The magnification of the tele only serves to exaggerate the changes in pitch. Telephotos are also a major contributor to *yaw* vibrations, in which the camera pivots slightly as if you were shooting a panorama—even when you're *not*. All five of these types of movement can be countered through image stabilization.

OSS does best in nullifying changes in pitch and yaw. SSI in the body can correct for all five types of movement. If both OSS and SSI are active at the same time, the a7R IV uses the two in tandem, allowing the lens to correct for pitch and yaw, while the in-body IS compensates for x, y, and roll movements. That makes a lot of sense, because in correcting for x, y, and roll, the camera is able to keep the sensor in the exact same plane to preserve precise focus and simply move the sensor carriage up, down, or slightly rotated to nullify the movement. If your lens does *not* have OSS, the SSI technology handles all the image stabilization tasks, in effect bringing IS to *every* lens you mount on the camera. That includes all E-mount lenses, as well as A-mount lenses attached with an EA-LA3 or EA-LA4 adapter (more on those later), and even "foreign" lenses like Canon EF optics using an appropriate adapter.

However, not all non-stabilized lenses benefit in identical ways from Sony's stabilization technology. For best results, the SSI system needs to know both focal length and focus distance to provide optimum stabilization. That's an advantage of OSS: stabilization built into the lens always knows exactly what focal length setting and focus distance is being used. For SSI, the same information has to be supplied to the smarts inside the camera body, using the SteadyShot Settings entry on the Camera Settings II-05 menu.

Figure 12.4 The five axes of in-body SteadyShot stabilization.

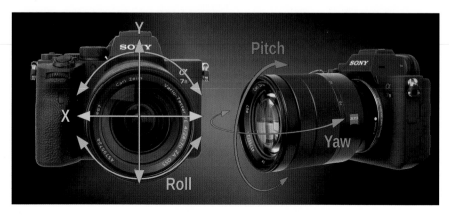

The lens may be one that can communicate this information to the camera. Focal length and distance data is also used with Sony's advanced distance integration (ADI) technology for flash exposure, as described in Chapter 13. Focal length information is needed to correct for pitch and yaw, while x and y compensation need to know the focal distance. (Roll correction needs neither type of data and can do its thing just from what SteadyShot sees happening on the sensor.)

However, when all the data is available, the full array of the a7R IV's IS capabilities can be used to correct on all five axes. If the lens *cannot* communicate this information, the focal length can still be specified using the SteadyShot Settings entry in the Camera Settings II-05 menu, as described in Chapter 3. Simply change the SteadyShot Adjustment option to Manual, then use the SteadyShot Focal Length sub-entry to specify the focal length of the lens or the zoom position you're going to use from the range 8mm to 1000mm.

Unless you're working with a non-zoom lens, going this route can be clumsy, but at least it works. When I am shooting sports with my 100-400mm Minolta lens, I set the focal length to 400mm, and get appropriate IS the majority of the time. Manually entering the focal length doesn't provide the second half of the required data—the focus distance. But with only the focal length data to work with, the IS can calculate the amount of compensation to provide to correct for pitch and yaw, and it doesn't *need* that data to fix roll. When using your non-compatible and foreign lenses, and lenses from third-party vendors like Rokinon/Samyang, you must forgo corrections along the x and y axes, but that deficit can be lived with, I've found.

One interesting variation comes when using an autofocus-compatible Metabones Canon adapter or Commlite/Fotodiox Nikon adapter with lenses that *do* have built-in image stabilization. Sony recommends turning off the lens's image stabilization/vibration reduction using the switch on the lens, because, even with an autofocus/autoexposure-compatible adapter, the foreign lens has no way of working harmoniously with the in-body stabilization (and vice versa). The result would be having *both* the lens and the a7R IV trying to correct for pitch and yaw simultaneously, and possibly overcompensating.

Here's a quick summary of some things you should keep in mind:

- **Compatible lenses.** All FE lenses and most Sony E-mount lenses should be compatible, and you can leave SteadyShot turned on. The a7R IV will identify the lens and choose how to apply the in-lens and in-body stabilization. For best results, turn off SteadyShot when the camera is mounted on a tripod.

- **SteadyShot doesn't stop action.** Unfortunately, no stabilization is a panacea to replace the action-stopping capabilities of a faster shutter speed. If you need to use 1/1000th second to freeze a high jumper in mid-air, neither type of image stabilization achieves the desired effect at a longer shutter speed.

- **Stabilization might slow you down.** The process of adjusting the lens and/or sensor to counter camera shake takes time, just as autofocus does, so you might find that SteadyShot adds to the lag between when you press the shutter and when the picture is actually taken. In a situation where you want to capture a fleeting instant that can happen suddenly, image stabilization might not be your best choice.

■ **Give SteadyShot a helping hand.** When you simply do not want to carry a tripod all day and you'll be relying on the OSS system, brace the camera or your elbows on something solid, like the roof of a car or a piece of furniture. Remember that an inexpensive monopod can be quite compact when not extended; many camera bags include straps that allow you to attach this accessory. Use a monopod for extra camera-shake compensation. Brace the accessory against a rock, a bridge abutment, or a fence and you might be able to get blur-free photos at surprisingly long shutter speeds. When you're heading out into the field to photograph wild animals or flowers and want to use longer exposures and think a tripod isn't practical, at least consider packing a monopod.

Choosing a Lens

Since the launching of the original a7R and a7, Sony has been introducing new full-frame FE lenses for the system at an admirable pace, including the Sony FE 24-105mm f/4 G OSS lens offered as a kit lens for the a7R IV. So, while I'm going to provide a quick listing of some of the lenses currently available for the a7R IV series, it will necessarily be somewhat incomplete. After all, I expect additional lenses to be introduced as this book goes into production and, with luck, during the life of the book itself.

I'm going to cover only full-frame lenses in this chapter. If you read through my explanation of the crop factor, you know that APS-C lenses can also be used with a7R IV, which still gives you a 26MP image in crop mode. But, as I noted, there are pros and cons to that approach, and the number of APS-C lenses available is vast, so I'm not going to list those options here.

In addition, most of my books rarely discuss third-party offerings, whether it's lenses, flash units, or accessories. There are so many of them, and the product churn can quickly make any recommendation obsolete during the life of this book. And, besides, for the most part the original vendor, such as Sony, provides the superior product. The situation is slightly different in the case of Sony's full-frame mirrorless cameras. In addition to Sony's own product line, produced internally from the company's own designs or with the cooperation of Zeiss, there are some excellent third-party optics you really should consider. I expect many new lenses to be introduced by third parties, so for the very latest information I urge you to consult on-line forums, such as DPReview, as they have constant updates that printed and ebook publications can't match.

Some of the best lenses are from Zeiss and some are from third parties looking to fill the vacuum caused by the initial dearth of full-fledged FE lenses, and more recently encouraged by the popularity of Sony's full-frame lineup. Samyang, Sigma, Tamron, Lensbaby, Venus Optics Laowa, Mitagon, Handevision, and others have all jumped into the Sony arena. Even *more* possibilities derive from the a7R IV's capability of using "foreign" lenses with tolerable—or better—autofocus and autoexposure features. As I noted in the introduction to this chapter, you can use a zillion A-mount lenses with the EA-LA3 and EA-LA4 adapters, Canon EF lenses and Nikon F-mount optics with an appropriate auto adapter from Metabones, Commlite, or other vendors, and adapters for virtually every other possible lens mount if you're willing to forgo autofocus and some other features.

I'll break down my overviews by vendor and provide you with my own recommendations where appropriate.

Sony FE Lenses

While the Sony-designated E-mount FE lenses should meet the needs of most photographers, you'll also find several premium-grade (and expensive) products with the Carl Zeiss ZA designation. The Carl Zeiss models all boast rugged metal construction for great durability, the very effective T* multi-layer anti-reflective coating for flare control, and one or more large high-tech optical elements for effective correction of optical aberrations. I'm going to list my favorite E-mount options for a7-series owners who want the very best.

The Affordable Trinity

First up, the trinity of (reasonably) affordable must-have lenses. These three lenses all have built-in optical image stabilization that can work in tandem with the a7R IV's in-body SteadyShot. All have a constant f/4 maximum aperture that doesn't change as you zoom and are reasonably affordable (as far as premium optics go) at $1,200–$1,500 each. (See Figure 12.5.)

- **Sony FE 16-35mm f/4 ZA OSS lens.** This is the lens you need for your architectural, landscape, and indoor photography in tight quarters. It covers an almost perfect range of focal lengths, from an ultra-wide 16mm to the street/urban photographer's favorite 35mm field of view. Some might prefer Sony's 12-24mm zoom instead (which wouldn't overlap with the 24-70mm lens described next), but I find the extra 11mm useful. I don't have to swap lenses when I need to zoom in a little tighter. One wonderful thing about this optic is that it has *curved* aperture blades, producing smooth circular defocused highlights for great *bokeh*. At around $1,350, you can afford this lens, and if you shoot a lot of wide-angle images, you can't afford *not* to have it.

Figure 12.5 Sony's three key FE lenses, left to right: 16-35mm f/4, 24-70mm f/4, and 70-200mm f/4.

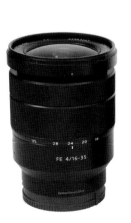
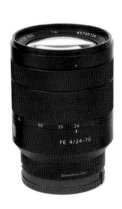
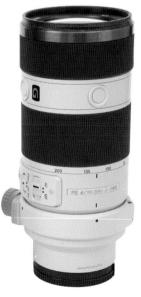

- **Sony Vario-Tessar T∗ FE 24-70mm f/4 ZA OSS lens.** This lens includes my personal least-used focal length range. I tend to see my subjects either with a wide-angle view, often with an apparent perspective distortion aspect, or with a telephoto/selective focus approach. Another Zeiss-branded product, it has excellent balance with the a7R IV, making it useful as a walk-around lens for travel photography, full-length and three-quarters portraits, and indoor sports like basketball and volleyball. Unfortunately, it won't be the sharpest optical knife in your toolkit, despite the Zeiss label. I find it perfectly acceptable when stopped down two or three stops from maximum aperture, but for $900, I expected more. You might explore the sub-$400 Sony FE 28-70mm f/3.5-5.6 OSS kit lens. It's abominably slow (f/5.6) at the 70mm zoom position, but you might find that saving $500 while filling out your trinity alleviates the pain.

- **Sony FE 70-200mm f/4 G OSS lens.** Compared to 70-200mm f/4 lenses designed for other full-frame cameras, this $1,500, 3-pound, 10.4 × 5.4 × 5.3–inch lens is almost petite, but it's quite a beast mounted on the tiny a7R IV. It's well balanced and these cameras do have the new beefed-up mounting bayonet, but you really should consider using the swiveling tripod collar, either when mounting on a tripod/monopod or as a support when hand-holding. It's a Sony premium G lens (the G stands for "Gold") and its optical performance won't disappoint.

The Elite Three

In response to professionals and others who prefer fast, super-sharp lenses with a larger maximum aperture, Sony has begun introducing what it calls its G-Master (GM) lineup; three of them span the same focal length range as the "affordable trinity." Other G-Master lenses are available now, such as the Sony FE 85mm f/1.4 GM and Sony FE 100mm f/2.8 SFT GM OSS, offering additional focal lengths.

Sony's top-of-the-line trio include:

- **Sony FE 16-35mm f/2.8 GM.** Like all G-Masters, this lens is dust- and moisture-resistant, has extra-low dispersion elements, and a price to match its high quality: in this case about $2,200. It focuses as close as 11 inches and uses 82mm filters. The downside? It's a larger lens than its f/4 cousin, and at 1.5 pounds is almost six ounces heavier.

- **Sony FE 24-70mm f/2.8 GM.** Also priced at $2,200, this lens is massive compared to its f/4 sibling, at almost 32 ounces weighing more than twice as much. It focuses down to 1.25 feet, uses 82mm filters, and is a superb lens with this focal length range.

- **Sony FE 70-200mm f/2.8 GM.** The costliest lens in the elite trinity, this one is priced at $2,600—but your cost for filters will be reduced if you already own the popular 77mm size this lens takes. It has 11 rounded aperture blades for great bokeh (the blur of the out-of-focus areas), weighs a hefty 3.26 pounds, and focuses down to about three feet for intimate telephoto close-ups.

These are my choices among the other Sony FE lenses. They include walk-around lenses, some fast primes for photojournalism and other available-light applications, and even a stellar macro. First up: additional lenses in the superb G-Master lineup:

- **Sony FE 24mm f/1.4 GM.** This is a prime lens (so to speak) for a wide variety of applications. Architectural photographers will love the $1,400 optic for hand-held interior photography under low-light conditions. Street shooters and photojournalists will find it a relatively affordable option for capturing intimate moments day or night. Landscape photographers will prize its high resolution and useful wide-angle perspective. It's a compact walk-around lens for general-purpose photography, too.

- **Sony FE 100mm f/2.8 STF GM OSS.** What do you get for $1,500? This G-Master is one of two near-ideal portrait/short telephoto lenses that Sony offers. The f/2.8 maximum aperture makes it easy to defocus the backgrounds, and the STF (Smooth Trans Focus) technology uses something called an apodization filter to produce achingly smooth bokeh with nice, round out-of-focus highlights. ("Apodization" is technical mumbo-jumbo that Sony applies to its use of a radially graduated neutral-density filter that, clear in the center and darker at its edges, in effect, counters the fade-out of those blurry round disks we call "bokeh," for a more pleasing effect.) Reduced flare for greater contrast, fast autofocus, OSS, and focus as close as 1.9 feet (you can switch focus ranges from 2.8 feet to infinity or 1.9–3.3 feet) make this a formidable lens for portraiture and other subjects.

- **Sony FE 85mm f/1.4 GM.** This is Sony's other awesome G-Master portrait lens, priced at $1,800. It's good for head-and-shoulders work, too, and a focal length shorter than the 100mm f/2.8 makes it easier to shoot full-length, couples, and group portraits. It has wonderful bokeh, weighs about 29 ounces, and can focus as close as 20 inches. I like this lens's large maximum aperture for concert and performance photography, other subjects under low light, and subjects I want to isolate with selective focus. Videographers will like the ability to de-click the actual physical lens aperture ring (most lenses these days do not have one at all) so exposure can be changed smoothly while a sequence is captured.

- **Sony 135mm f/1.8 GM.** This fast $2,100 lens is perfect for sports, portraits, and any subjects that can benefit from selective focus and world-class creamy bokeh (for smooth out-of-focus backgrounds).

- **Sony FE 100-400mm f/4.5-5.6 GM OSS.** Yet another very welcome G-Master lens, this one covers an ideal focal length range for sports and wildlife photographers, especially since it has OSS and superb weather-sealing. The price, at $2,500, is not even exorbitant considering its likely market and what you get. (Prime and zoom lenses in the 400mm and longer range can easily top $5,000 to $10,000.) It's a little over three pounds in weight, but that's normal in the long-tele-zoom territory.

- **Sony FE 400mm f/2.8 GM OSS.** This stupendous lens, announced in October 2017, was first spotted by slavering Sony photographers at the Winter Olympics in February 2018. Ordinary humans almost certainly will need at least $12,000 to buy one. It's one of several Sony telephoto lenses with a Preset switch that allows specifying a focus plane (say, home plate in a baseball game) and refocusing on that point instantly at the press of a button.

■ **Sony FE 600mm f/4 GM OSS.** A super telephoto (in many senses of the word), this G-Master has a large maximum aperture that's especially suited for field sports photography. The f/4 aperture can be used wide open at night to allow action shooters to use a motion-freezing high shutter speed, with the added benefit of shallow depth-of-field to throw distracting elements (spectators, or players not involved in the current action) out of focus. This 6.7-pound dream lens has a super price, too: expect to pay $13,000 to add this one to your gear cupboard. Optional 1.4X and 2.0X teleconverters are available. The 2.0X model transforms this optic into a 1200mm f/8 monster (or 1800mm f/8 in crop mode).

Sony has a growing lineup of G-series ("Gold") and standard lenses that will fit the needs of just about any shooting situation, and includes my own favorite walk-around lens, the Sony FE 24-105mm f/4 G OSS that leads off the list that follows:

■ **Sony FE 24-105mm f/4 G OSS.** This is the do-everything lens for me. I used to rely on the Sony FE Variao-Tessar T* 16-70mm f/4 ZA OSS, and still use it extensively indoors and for architecture, but for everyday photography I'm willing to give up a little of the wide-angle end of the zoom scale to get the extra reach and selective focus prowess at the long end of this 24-105mm optic's range. It focuses down to 16 inches, uses my full arsenal of 77mm filters, and has Optical Steady-Shot. While not petite, I find its 4.5-inch length and 24-ounce weight not burdensome to carry around. As a G lens it has great image quality. It was in short supply and back-ordered for months after the a7R IV was introduced, but if you can find one, at $1,400 it's a bargain.

■ **Sony FE 12-24mm f/4 G.** This $1,800 lens might be the most versatile walk-around lens for landscape, architectural, and, maybe, street photographers who love (or need) the wide-angle look. As I mentioned earlier, it has the added advantage of no focal length overlap with either Sony 24-70mm zoom. Roughly the same size as the 24-105mm lens, it weighs 20 ounces, but lacks image stabilization (which is less important with wide-angle lenses with most shutter speeds). I'd use this lens if the combination of the Sony 16-35mm zoom and Voigtlander 10mm f/5.6 manual focus lens didn't give me all the wide-angle flexibility I need.

■ **Sony FE 100-400mm f/4.5-5.6 GM OSS.** Yet another very welcome G-Master lens, this one covers an ideal focal length range for sports and wildlife photographers, especially since it has OSS and superb weather-sealing. The price, at $2,500, is not even exorbitant considering its likely market and what you get. (Prime and zoom lenses in the 400mm and longer range can easily top $5,000 to $10,000.) It's a little over three pounds in weight, but that's normal in the long tele-zoom territory.

■ **Sony FE 55mm f/1.8 ZA lens.** So, why get excited about a "normal" lens with an f/1.8 maximum aperture and a $1,000 price tag? After all, both Nikon and Canon offer full-frame 50mm f/1.8 prime lenses for $200 or less. In this case, your ten Benjamins buys you one of the sharpest lenses ever made, with exquisite resolution at every f/stop—including wide open. Given that perspective, this lens is actually a bargain. You'll love using it for head-and-shoulders or 3/4-length portraits using selective focus at f/1.8. It's said to rival super-costly lenses, like the 55mm f/1.4 Zeiss Otus, which has a $4,000 price tag. You owe it to yourself to get this lens.

- **Sony FE Planar T✳ 50mm f/1.4 ZA lens.** Faster, sharper, more expensive (at $1,500), and sporting a flare/ghost-reducing T✳ (T-star) coating, this mid-range ("normal") lens has the Zeiss quality you expect, a solid build, and creamy bokeh from its 11-blade circular aperture.

- **Sony FE 28-70mm f/3.5-5.6 OSS.** This lens is often bundled with Sony full-frame mirrorless cameras as a kit lens, and available separately for less than $400. As I noted above, it's slow (f/3.5) at the 28mm zoom position, and even slower (f/5.6) when zoomed to 70mm. If you favor telephoto lenses or extreme wide angles (as I do), you may find yourself not using the 28-70mm focal length range very often, in which case this lens might make an acceptable fill-in for occasional use. It's sharp enough stopped down to f/8–f/11, but really not up to the demands of the a7R IV's 61MP sensor.

- **Sony FE 24-240mm f/3.5-6.3 OSS lens.** On first glance, a 10X zoom lens stretching from a true wide-angle 24mm field of view to the edge of super telephoto range at 240mm sounds very tempting. With a second look, this optic's $1,000-plus price adds to the appeal. The reality check comes only when you realize that mating this hefty (1.72 pound), somewhat slow lens (f/6.3 at maximum zoom) to the compact a7R IV counters the best reason for toting around a tiny full-frame mirrorless camera. If you truly want to walk around with only a single lens and can justify the bulk, this optic does fill the bill. It would also be an efficient choice for photography that might call for extreme wide-angle views and telephoto reach in rapid succession. Given its modest price tag, you can expect this lens will be a jack-of-all-trades and master of none. I'd rather carry a medium-sized camera bag and fill it with the trio of lenses described in the previous section, even at a cost premium of $3,000.

- **Sony FE 28-135mm f/4 G PZ OSS lens.** The specs alone might lead you to believe this is a faster, heavier (5 pounds) walk-around lens with a more restricted zoom range. You'd be wrong. This $2,500 monster is especially designed for pro-level 4K video productions, and if heavy-duty movie making isn't on your agenda, you probably don't want or need this lens. Video shooters, though, will delight in its near-silent precision variable 8-speed power zoom, and responsive manual control rings for zoom (with direction reversal for smooth zooms), focus pulling, and aperture.

- **Sony FE 28mm f/2.0 lens.** Here's a lens that comes with its own bag of tricks. It's a compact prime lens with a fast f/2.0 aperture, so you can shoot in low light and even gain a modicum of selective focus with its (relatively) shallow depth-of-field wide open. Despite its $450 price, it boasts an advanced optical design with ED (extra-low dispersion) glass elements that improve contrast and reduce troublesome chromatic and spherical aberrations. (You'll find descriptions of lens aberrations later in this chapter.) If that's not enough, you can attach either of two adapter optics to the front. There is a wide-angle version ($250), which converts it to a 21mm f/2.8 wide angle that focuses down to eight inches, and a 16mm fisheye attachment ($300) that I personally find more interesting and fun. But then, I own eight different fisheye lenses, so I'm susceptible.

- **Sony Sonnar T✳ FE 35mm f/2.8 ZA lens.** This tiny lens is a perfect match for the compact a7R IV. At a mere eight ounces and measuring 2.42 × 1.44 inches, it makes a great walk-around lens for stealthy photographers. The image quality is great, but you'd expect that from a Zeiss lens that, at $800, is not bargain-basement cheap.

- **Sony FE 35mm f/1.8 lens.** If you need a little more speed, this compact and lightweight wide-angle prime lens has a fast f/1.8 maximum aperture. The $750 optic is especially suitable for street photography and architecture, and it is slightly cheaper than the 35mm Sonnar.

- **Sony Distagon T✱ FE 35mm f/1.4 ZA lens.** This Zeiss lens is a photojournalist's dream, with a wide-angle focal length that lets you get up close and personal with your subject, and a fast f/1.4 aperture suitable for low light and selective focus. The Zeiss T* (T-star) coating suppresses contrast loss from internal reflections among the lens elements. It's great for video, too, as the aperture ring can be de-clicked with a switch. The only drawback is the price: $1,600, which is a lot to pay for a lens that doesn't give you a range of different focal lengths to work with. However, the shooters this lens is designed for will confirm that it's worth it.

- **Sony 85mm f/1.8 lens.** At $600, this is an affordable, fast, mid-telephoto prime lens that's light-weight and portable.

- **Sony FE 90mm f/2.8 Macro G OSS lens.** While Sony will continue to make additional macro lenses available for the a7R IV, this affordable (in the Sony FE realm, anything in the $1,000 range is considered affordable) $1,100 lens is an excellent choice. Its 90mm focal length gives you a decent amount of distance between the camera and your close-up subject, even at its minimum focusing distance of 11 inches. With internal focusing such that only the internal elements move, the lens doesn't get longer as you focus, avoiding a common problem. You can add a set of auto extension tubes to get even closer. I use Fotodiox Pro 10mm and 16mm tubes. Those tubes are primarily plastic and not especially rugged but are serviceable for light-duty use.

- **Sony FE 50mm f/2.8 Macro lens.** This is a compact, lightweight standard macro lens with 1:1 (life-size) magnification, focusing as close as 6.3 inches. Priced at $550, it makes a fine, affordable standard macro lens for shooting flowers, bugs, or your coin/stamp collection. If you need to maintain some distance from your subject (say, a skittish creature, or one that requires careful lighting), you would probably prefer the 90mm macro above. But a 50mm is perfect for extreme close-up photography, particularly when mated to a set of extension tubes.

- **Sony FE 70-300mm f/4.5-5.6 G OSS lens.** This lens gives you a little more telephoto reach than either Sony FE 70-200mm optics, at the cost of a constant maximum aperture: f/4.5 at the 70mm zoom setting and f/5.6 when zoomed to its 300mm focal length. At $1,275, it's relatively affordable compared to your alternatives in the tele-zoom lineup.

- **Sony FE 200-600mm f/5.6-6.3 G OSS lens.** Most sports and wildlife photographers will find this hefty zoom lens more affordable, at roughly $2,000. Its maximum aperture varies from f/5.6 to f/6.3 as you zoom to the longest telephoto position, but if you need a 600mm focal length, setting your ISO a stop or two higher can save you $11,000. In APS-C/Super 35 mode, this lens becomes a 300-900mm ultra-tele with 26MP files. It is compatible with Sony's 1.4X and 2.0X teleconverters, too.

A-Mount Lenses

If you're coming to the Sony mirrorless world from the SLT/A-mount arena, you may already own some Sony or Minolta lenses that can work very well with your a7R IV. And even if you *don't* have any A-mount lenses now, you may want to investigate purchasing some. In some cases, they are as good as—or better—than the current roster of FE lenses. I know one professional photographer who skipped both FE mid-range zooms (the 24-70mm Zeiss and 28-70mm Sony kit lens) entirely, because he already owned the superb Sony Zeiss 24-70mm f/2.8 ZA SSM II Vario Sonar T* lens, which he used with his Sony a99. Of course, at $2,100, you'd only want to buy one if you were *very* serious about working with those particular focal lengths. You'd also need to sink another $200 to $350 into a Sony A-Mount-to-E-Mount adapter, which I'll describe later in this chapter.

However, a viable option for everyone is to buy gently *used* A-mount lenses from reliable sources, such as KEH Camera (www.keh.com). I've purchased more than a dozen lenses from them over the last few years, including the ever-popular "beercan," the Minolta AF Zoom 70-210mm f/4, an ancient optic prized for its tank-like solid build, commendable sharpness, constant maximum aperture, and smooth bokeh. Of course, my favorite is my Minolta AF 100-400mm f/4.5-6.7 APO Tele-Zoom lens. (See Figure 12.6.) It's not my sharpest lens, but I would never have been able to afford a 400mm autofocus lens otherwise.

I'm not sure where KEH gets 30-year-old lenses that are like new, but their selection is huge and the prices are a fraction of what you'd pay for new A-mount optics. Keep in mind that when it took over Konica Minolta's camera/lens technology, Sony simply rebranded quite a few of the most popular lenses, so you may find a 50mm f/1.4 Minolta lens that's identical to the Sony 50mm f/1.4 lens at a much lower price.

The only drawback to the most affordably priced A-mount lenses is that they probably use Minolta's original screw-drive autofocus technology. To use them on your a7R IV, you'll need the Sony LA-EA4 adapter, which has its own SLT (single-lens translucent) phase-detect autofocus system, similar to that used in the Sony a99.

It's highly preferable to use A-mount lenses with built-in autofocus motors of the SSM or SAM variety. These lenses work with the less expensive Sony LA-EA3 adapter and let you use the a7R IV's own hybrid phase detect/contrast detect AF system, which is typically both faster and more accurate. (Such lenses are easy to spot: they incorporate the SSM, SSM II, SAM, or SAM II designations in their official names.) SSM stands for SuperSonic motor, which uses a ring-type ultrasonic driver

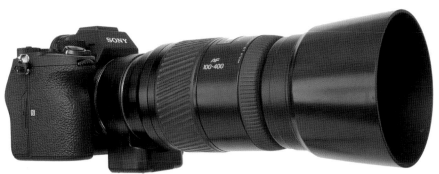

Figure 12.6 A Minolta AF 100-400mm lens mounted using the Sony EA-LA4 adapter.

that is fast and virtually silent and is found on upper-end lenses. SAM stands for Smooth Autofocus Motor, an alternate system built into some lower-end Sony optics introduced since 2009.

I won't recommend specific additional A-mount lenses here, as the selection is so vast and varied. Just keep these provisos in mind:

- **Both full-frame and APS-C.** The older Minolta lenses you'll find were designed for full-frame film cameras, but Sony has introduced both full-frame and APS-C lenses for A-mount. You can usually identify Sony APS-C A-mount lenses by the designation DT in the lens name; if DT is not included, it is a full-frame lens. Third-party lens manufacturers such as Tokina, Sigma, Vivitar, and Tamron also offer a mixture of both types. Research your lenses before you buy.

- **Motor/No Motor.** It's easy to discern Sony A-mount lenses with internal motors, as the specification is included in their name. However, specs of the offerings of third-party vendors are not always obvious. Somewhere in their catalog descriptions they will usually specify whether a particular lens includes an internal motor, and they'll also reveal whether a lens is intended for full-frame or APS-C models.

Zeiss Loxia Lenses

While the Zeiss FE lenses produced and sold by Sony all feature autofocus, Zeiss also independently sells its own optics, including the Loxia lineup designed specifically for Sony full-frame E-mount cameras.

Zeiss lenses are all premium optics, and, as I write this, the super-premium Zeiss Otus lineup (priced at $4,000 and up) is not available in Sony E-mount. Nor can you buy the new Milvus full-frame lenses to fit your a7R IV, and, just in case you're wondering, the Zeiss Touit lenses in E-mount are designed for APS-C sensors only.

However, these Loxia lenses are among the best we can get, with the five available so far all manual focus. Not including autofocus helps keep the price down on these otherwise premium-quality super-sharp lenses. Keep in mind that your a7R IV has a wealth of manual-focus-friendly features, including focus peaking and focus magnification, all described elsewhere in this book.

- **Zeiss Loxia 85mm f/2.4 T* lens.** Its maker describes this $1,400 lens as portable, inconspicuous, and powerful and urges you to use it for portrait, street, and landscape photography. It is remarkably sharp from edge to edge. Like all the Loxia lenses, the manual aperture ring can be de-clicked, using a supplied tool, for use when constantly varying apertures are desired when shooting video.

- **Zeiss Loxia 50mm f/2 Planar T* lens.** If you've been involved with photography for any length of time, you'll recognize the Zeiss Planar name, first applied to a symmetrical lens design as far back as 1896. This fast manual focus lens does a good job of correcting for chromatic aberration and distortion and is one of the best lenses you can buy for roughly $1,000.

- **Zeiss Loxia 35mm f/2 Biogon T✳ lens.** Another name out of the past, Biogon lenses have historically been some of the best wide-angle optics you can buy, and this fast 35mm f/2 lens has been optimized for use with digital cameras (that is, illumination emerges from the back of the lens at a less steep angle, as explained in Chapter 2). Your $1,300 buys you a well-corrected lens suitable for street photography, architecture, landscapes, and other subjects.

- **Zeiss Loxia 21mm f/2.8 T✳ lens.** This final lens in the trio was the last introduced in December 2015 for $1,500. It's an extra-compact lens using the famed Distagon design, which overcomes some of the drawbacks of many wide angles to provide consistent sharpness from edge to edge, with little light falloff and excellent correction for chromatic aberrations.

- **Zeiss Loxia 25mm f/2.4 T✳ lens.** Another weather-sealed, de-clickable lens, it has two low-dispersion and one aspherical element for excellent image quality, and is priced at $1,400.

Zeiss Batis Lenses

Here we have reasonably priced autofocus lenses from Zeiss, which help fill out holes in Sony's full-frame E-mount lineup. If you're looking for a futuristic touch, they each feature an illuminated OLED (organic LED) display that dynamically shows focus distance and depth-of-field. In the good old days, prime (non-zoom) lenses had etched or painted color-coded depth-of-field markers on the lens barrel, but those largely disappeared when zoom lenses became dominant. Now depth-of-field can be displayed on your lens in a more useful form. As I write this, the four available Batis lenses are as follows:

- **Zeiss Batis 135mm f/2.8 lens.** For $1,500 you get a Zeiss Sonar-design lens with OSS, fast autofocus, and impressive image quality. Some may think this lens verges on being too long for head-and-shoulders portraits, but it's a versatile lens for many types of sports, especially since it has great anti-flare and ghosting properties that are useful when shooting into sunlight.

- **Zeiss Batis 85mm f/1.8 lens.** This is a $999 medium-telephoto autofocus lens that's ideal for portraits, and a primo choice for low-light photography and selective focus. It's the first Zeiss lens that has optical image stabilization (the equivalent of Sony's trademarked OSS), giving you hybrid IS when used with the a7R IV's in-body SteadyShot Inside.

- **Zeiss Batis 25mm f/2.0 lens.** There's a bit of overlap in potential use between this autofocus lens and Sony's own 28mm f/2.0 optic. This one is more expensive at less than $1,200, sharper, and isn't compatible with Sony's wide-angle/fisheye adapters.

- **Zeiss Batis 18mm f/2.8 lens.** Featuring the famed Zeiss Distagon wide-angle design, this $1,500 optic focuses down to about 10 inches, which is useful if you like wide-angle (apparent) perspective distortion effects. (It's *apparent* rather than *real*, because the distortion is due to the placement of the subject matter within the field of view, not any defect in the lens itself.) At 12 ounces, it's not heavy and makes a good walk-around lens for those who want a prime lens with a wide field of view.

Other Third-Party Lenses

Because the a7R IV has relatively short back-focus distances (the gap between the lens mount bayonet and sensor), it's fairly easy for third parties to adapt their existing full-frame lenses to fit your camera. There are some interesting lenses available. Among them:

- **Mitakon/Zhongyi.** This company makes an ultra-fast 85mm f/1.2 manual focus lens ($630), and a hyperfast 50mm f/0.95 lens ($850) in Sony E-mount, with the latter having the distinction of being the world's fastest full-frame E-mount lens. The company also offers a 20mm f/2 super macro at a bargain $199 that can focus down to less than one inch!

- **Voigtlander.** Probably the oldest name in camera gear, dating back to its founding in Vienna in 1756 (well before the invention of photography itself), this company produces nearly a dozen interesting lenses for Sony cameras, including 10mm and 12mm f/5.6 Heliar and a 15mm f/4.5 Heliar. I own the 10mm lens, and it is one of my all-time favorites. On a full-frame camera like the a7R IV, it's the widest rectilinear (non-fisheye) prime lens available, with a breathtaking 130-degree field of view. (See Figure 12.7.)

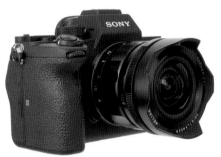

Figure 12.7 Voigtlander's 10mm f/5.6 lens is a rectilinear super-wide angle lens.

The company has an impressive array of super-sharp manual-focus full-frame macro lenses for Sony cameras, including an APO-Lanthar 50mm F2 macro introduced in late 2019 that includes electronic contacts that can report EXIF and distance information to the camera for smooth integration with the a7R IV's in-body image stabilization system and Focus Magnifier. Voigtlander's APO-Lanthar macro lineup also includes 65mm f/2 and 110mm f/2.5 models.

- **Samyang/Rokinon.** This company's manual focus 12mm f/2.8 fisheye resides in my fisheye collection, and I often alternate its use with my 15mm f/2.8 Sigma fisheye. I use them in manual focus mode with adapters, but Samyang/Rokinon also sells lenses in E-mount (sometimes under the Bower brand name). They include a 24mm f/1.4, 35mm f/1.4, 50mm f/1.4, 85mm f/1.4, 135mm f/2, and a 100mm f/2.8 macro lens that produce 1:1 (life-size) magnification at a minimum focusing distance of 12 inches. They are starting to issue autofocus lenses in Sony FE mount, including an affordable FE 35mm f/2.8 for a mere $300 and a 14mm f/2.8 for $800.

- **Tamron/Sigma.** Tamron, which is partially owned by Sony, appears to be venturing into Sony E-mount autofocus territory. Their first FE offering is the Tamron 28-75mm f/2.8 Di III RXD, which is lighter and smaller than Sony's own 24-70mm f/2.8 G-Master. With the price Tamron has announced, with luck, it will be both sharp and affordable. Sigma is also increasingly venturing into FE territory, with a 105mm f/1.4 ART lens rumored to be coming by the time this book is published. As Sony full-frame cameras gain in popularity, continue to look for additional lenses from these major manufacturers.

- **Venus Optics Laowa.** This company makes a variety of full-frame lenses for Sony E-mount cameras, including the novel Laowa 10-18mm f/4.5-5.6 FE zoom and the weirdest macro lens ever made: the Laowa 24mm f/14 2X Macro Probe, an expensive ($1,500) optic for super-close, bugs-eye views with a waterproof probe that includes a built-in LED ring light. The company also offers a compact 25mm f/2.8 ultra-macro with 2.5X to 5X life-size magnification, and focusing down to less than two inches. Other full-frame lenses from Laowa that may be of interest to discerning a7R IV owners include a 15mm f/2 "Zero D" (zero distortion) lens with a 110-degree angle of view and remarkable image quality. It's not a fisheye—it's a rectilinear lens with two aspherical elements and three extra-low dispersion (ED) elements for impressive optical quality. It focuses down to seven inches, making some interesting distorted perspective shots possible.

Using the LA-EA Series Adapters

Sony makes four A-moun-to-E-mount adapters, which allow using Sony/Minolta A-mount lenses on an Alpha E-mount camera such as the a7R IV. Why four different adapters? All four, the LA-EA1, LA-EA2, LA-EA3, and LA-EA4, allow connecting an A-mount lens to an NEX/Alpha-series camera. The two odd-numbered adapters use *only* contrast detect autofocus with lenses that have built-in AF motors and are compatible with them. The two even-numbered adapters have built-in SLT-like phase detection AF systems for fast focusing with lenses that use the original screw-drive AF system. The LA-EA1 and LA-EA2 are designed for APS-C cameras, while the LA-EA3 and LA-EA4 shown in Figure 12.8 are intended for full-frame models like the a7R IV. Table 12.1 should clear things up a bit.

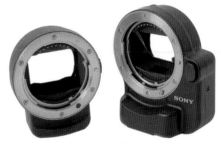

Figure 12.8 The LA-EA3 (left) and LA-EA4 (right) adapters allow using A-mount lenses on the a7R IV.

TABLE 12.1 LA-EA Series Adapters

ADAPTER	AUTOFOCUS	FORMAT
LA-EA1	Contrast detect with lenses that have built-in SSR or SAM AF motors. Lenses using a screw-drive motor in the camera body will not autofocus.	APS-C
LA-EA2	Phase detect using Translucent Mirror technology.	APS-C
LA-EA3	Contrast detect with lenses that have built-in SSM or SAM AF motors. Lenses using a screw-drive motor in the camera body will not autofocus.	Full Frame and APS-C
LA-EA4	Phase detect using Translucent Mirror technology.	Full Frame and APS-C

The LA-EA3 adapter or LA-EA4 adapter are both satisfactory, depending on the type of autofocus used in your A-mount lenses. I own both, because I have a mixture of SSM, SAM, and screw-drive lenses.

The LA-EA2 and LA-EA4 are clever because both involve, basically, building a version of Sony's Translucent Mirror Technology, found in the SLT cameras, into an adapter, as you can see in the exploded diagram shown in Figure 12.9. (In actual use, the lens must be physically mounted to the adapter.)

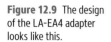

Figure 12.9 The design
of the LA-EA4 adapter
looks like this.

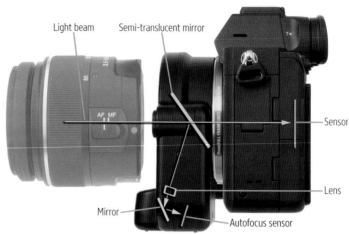

Other Lens Options

Because of the popularity of the camera line, third-party vendors have rushed to produce lenses for these models. As I mentioned earlier, because the a7-series' "flange to sensor" distance is relatively short, there's room to use various types of adapters between camera and lens and still allow focusing all the way to infinity. There are already a huge number of adapters that allow mounting just about any lens you can think of on the a7R IV cameras, if you're willing to accept manual focus and, usually, a ring on the adapter that's used to stop down the "adopted" lens to the aperture used to take the photo. You can find these from Novoflex (www.novoflex.com), Metabones (www.metabones.com), Fotodiox (www.fotodioxpro.com), Rainbow Imaging (www.rainbowimaging.biz), Cowboy Studio (www.cowboystudio.com), and others.

Some adapters of certain types and brands sell for as little as $20 to $30. With many of them you should not expect autofocus even if you're using an AF lens from some other system; as well, many of the cameras' high-tech features do not operate. However, you can usually retain automatic exposure by setting the a7R IV to Aperture Priority, stopping down to the f/stop you prefer, and firing away.

The ultra-high-grade Novoflex and Metabones adapters for using lenses of other brands sell for much higher prices. Some adapters maintain autofocus with a lens of an entirely different brand. The Metabones Canon EF-to-Sony Smart Adapter (Fifth Generation) and their similar Speed Booster (Fifth Generation) model ($400 and $650, respectively) maintain autofocus, autoexposure, and the Canon lens's image stabilizer feature when used with a camera. The "Speed Booster" part of the name comes from the adapter's ability to magically add one f/stop to the maximum aperture of the lens (thanks to the adapter's internal optics), transforming an f/4 lens into an f/2.8 speed demon.

The Metabones Smart Adapter has been especially popular, thanks to the ability to use AF-C with Canon's EF or EF-S lenses and your camera's hybrid phase detection/contrast detection autofocus system. Reports are that autofocus with these lenses is equal to or superior to that of the same lenses when mounted on their native Canon camera bodies. The Canon lenses' in-lens IS also works, but you may want to disable it and rely solely on the a7R IV's own SteadyShot capabilities. The

Metabones Smart Adapter is well made, with brass components, and costs a hefty $399, but if you are switching over from a Canon system, the ability to use your existing lenses is priceless.

Commlite, Fotodiox, and other vendors have begun offering adapters that preserve full autofocus/autoexposure/image stabilization features for Nikon AF-S and AF-D lenses. (See Figure 12.10.) The AF-S lenses have their own built-in autofocus motors; the AF-D lenses must be focused using a motor built into the lens adapter.

I love to experiment with other third-party lenses. I imported an ancient (Soviet-era) 58mm f/2 Helios 44-2 from a seller in the Ukraine for $35, so I could take advantage of this cult lens's proverbial "swirly" bokeh, which provides a wild special effect. You can find them on Amazon for $50 to $60. However, my absolute favorite lens bargain is the 35mm f/1.7 Fujian (no relation to Fuji) optic, which I purchased brand new for a total of $28, with the E-mount adapter included in the price. It's actually a tiny CCTV (closed-circuit television) lens in C-mount (a type of lens mount used for cine cameras). It's manual focus and manual f/stop, of course (and it works in Aperture Priority mode); it's a toy lens, or something like a super-cheap Lensbaby, or a great experimental lens for fooling around. It covers the full APS-C frame (more or less; expect a bit of vignetting in the corners at some f/stops), so you'll have to use it in APS-C crop mode. It is not incredibly sharp wide open and exhibits a weird kind of "bokeh" (out-of-focus rendition of highlights) that produces fantasy-like images. The only drawback (or additional drawback, if you will), is that you may have to hunt some to find one; the manufacturer doesn't sell directly in the USA. I located mine on Amazon.com.

Once you own the C-mount-to-E-mount adapter, you can use any of the host of other similar CCTV lenses on your a7R IV. Also relatively cheap, but not necessarily of equal quality, are a 25mm f/1.4, 35mm f/1.7, and 50mm f/1.4 lens (shown in Figure 12.11), as well as a Tamron 8mm f/1.4, and other lenses that I haven't tried. Some of these lenses may not even cover the APS-C image area in crop mode, but are worth borrowing to try out if you have a friend who does CCTV.

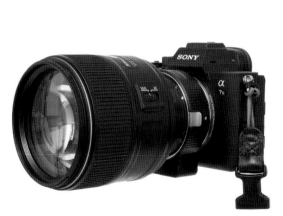

Figure 12.10 A Nikon 105mm f/1.4 lens is shown mounted using a Fotodiox Fusion adapter.

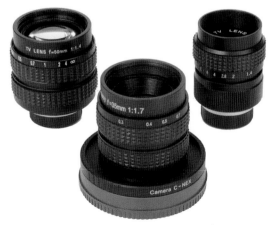

Figure 12.11 These CCTV lenses make great "toys" for your a7R IV.

Fine-Tuning the Focus of Your A-Mount Lenses

In Chapter 3, I introduced you to the a7R IV's AF Micro Adjustment feature in the Camera Settings I-08 menu, which can be manipulated *only* when you're using a Sony or a Minolta Maxxum/Dynax A-mount lens with the EA-LA2 or EA-LA4 adapters. It is not available when using the LA-EA1 or LA-EA3 adapters. (The micro adjustment may work with an A-mount lens of another brand, but Sony warns that the results may be inaccurate.) Millions of A-mount lenses have been sold over the years, and the adapter is not terribly expensive, so I will assume that many readers will eventually want to consider the fine-tuning feature.

If you do not currently have such lenses or the adapter, you cannot use AF Micro Adjustment (you can turn the feature on or off, but you cannot enter any adjustment factor). But if you do own the relevant equipment, you might find that a particular lens is not focusing properly. If the lens happens to focus a bit ahead or a bit behind the desired area (like the eyes in a portrait), and if it does that consistently, you can use the adjustment feature.

Why is the focus "off" for some lenses in the first place? There are lots of factors, including the age of the lens (an older lens may focus slightly differently), temperature effects on certain types of glass, humidity, and tolerances built into a lens's design that all add up to a slight misadjustment, even though the components themselves are, strictly speaking, within specs. A very slight variation in your lens's mount can cause focus to vary slightly. With any luck (if you can call it that) a lens that doesn't focus exactly right will at least be consistent. If a lens always focuses a bit behind the subject, the symptom is *back focus*. If it focuses in front of the subject, it's called *front focus*.

You're almost always better off sending such a lens in to Sony to have them make it right. But that's not always possible. Perhaps you need your lens recalibrated right now, or you purchased a used lens that is long out of warranty. If you want to do it yourself, the first thing to do is determine whether or not your lens has a back-focus or front-focus problem.

For a quick-and-dirty diagnosis (*not* a calibration; you'll use a different target for that), lay down a piece of graph paper on a flat surface, and place an object on the line at the middle, which will represent the point of focus (we hope). Then, shoot the target at an angle using your lens's widest aperture (smallest available f/number) and the autofocus mode you want to test. Mount the camera on a tripod so you can get accurate, repeatable results.

If your camera/lens combination doesn't suffer from front or back focus, the point of sharpest focus will be the center line of the chart, as you can see in Figure 12.12. If you do have a problem, one of the other lines will be sharply focused instead. Should you discover that your lens consistently front focuses or back focuses, it needs to be recalibrated. Unfortunately, it's only possible to calibrate a lens for a single focusing distance. So, if you use a particular lens (such as a macro lens) for close-focusing, calibrate for that. If you use a lens primarily for middle distances, calibrate for that. Close-to-middle distances are most likely to cause focus problems, anyway, because as you get closer to infinity, small changes in focus are less likely to have an effect.

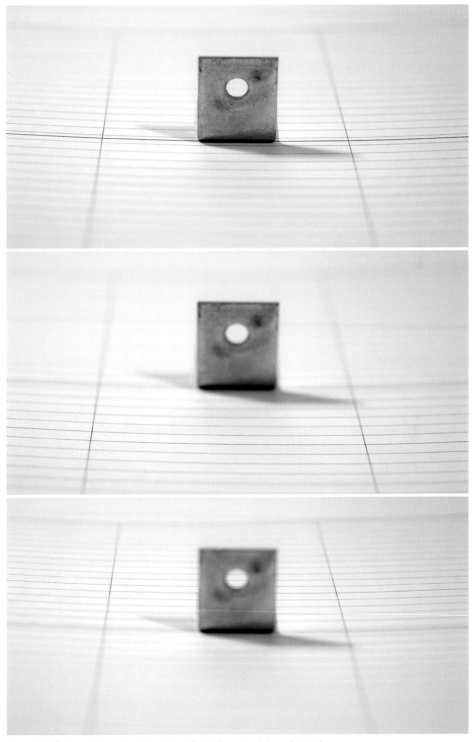

Figure 12.12 Correct focus (top), front focus (middle), and back focus (bottom).

Lens Tune-Up

The AF Micro Adj setting in the Camera Settings I-08 menu is the key tool you can use to fine-tune your A-mount lens used with the LA-EA2 or LA-EA4 adapter. Of course, this assumes you are using an A-mount lens and the adapter. You'll find the process easier to understand if you first run through this quick overview of the menu options:

- **AF Adjustment Setting. Set:** This option enables AF fine-tuning for all the lenses you've registered using this menu entry. If you discover you don't care for the calibrations you make in certain situations (say, it works better for the lens you have mounted at middle distances but is less successful at correcting close-up focus errors), you can deactivate the feature as you require. You should set this to On when you're doing the actual fine-tuning. Adjustment values range from −20 to +20. **Off:** Disables autofocus micro adjustment.

- **Amount.** You can specify values of plus or minus 20 for each of the lenses you've registered. When you mount a registered lens, the degree of adjustment is shown here. If the lens has not been registered, then +/-0 is shown. If "-" is displayed, you've already registered the maximum number of lenses—up to 30 different lenses can be registered with each camera.

- **Clear.** Erases *all* user-entered adjustment values for the lenses you've registered. When you select the entry, a message will appear. Select OK and then press the center button of the control wheel to confirm.

Evaluate Current Focus

The first step is to capture a baseline image that represents how the lens you want to fine-tune autofocuses at a particular distance. You'll often see advice for photographing a test chart with millimeter markings from an angle, and the suggestion that you autofocus on a particular point on the chart. Supposedly, the markings that actually *are* in focus will help you recalibrate your lens. The problem with this approach is that the information you get from photographing a test chart at an angle doesn't actually tell you what to do to make a precise correction. So, your lens back focuses three millimeters behind the target area on the chart. So what? Does that mean you change the Saved Value by −3 clicks? Or −15 clicks? Angled targets are a "shortcut" that don't save you time.

Instead, you'll want to photograph a target that represents what you're actually trying to achieve: a plane of focus locked in by your lens that represents the actual plane of focus of your subject. For that, you'll need a flat target, mounted precisely perpendicular to the sensor plane of the camera. Then, you can take a photo, see if the plane of focus is correct, and if not, dial in a bit of fine-tuning in the AF Fine Tuning menu, and shoot again. Lather, rinse, and repeat until the target is sharply focused.

You can use the focus target shown in Figure 12.13, or you can use a chart of your own, as long as it has contrasty areas that will be easily seen by the autofocus system, and without very small details that are likely to confuse the AF. Download your own copy of my chart from www.dslrguides.com/FocusChart.pdf. (The URL is *case sensitive*.) Then print out a copy on the largest paper your printer can handle. (I don't recommend just displaying the file on your monitor and focusing on that; it's unlikely you'll have the monitor screen lined up perfectly perpendicular to the camera sensor.)

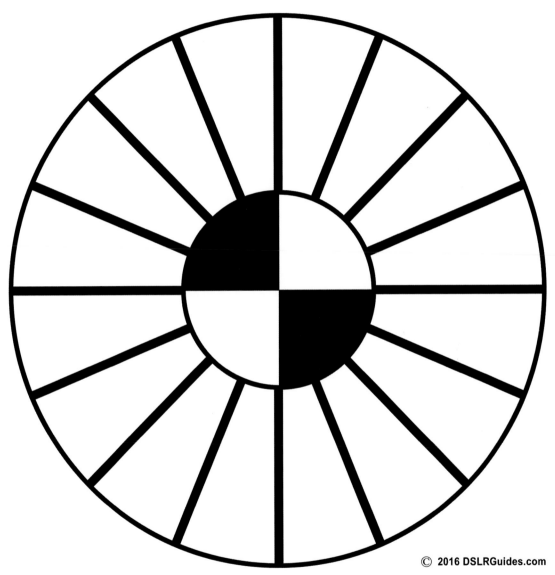

Figure 12.13 Use this focus test chart or create one of your own.

Then, follow these steps:

1. **Position the camera.** Place your camera on a sturdy tripod with a remote release attached, positioned at roughly eye-level at a distance from a wall that represents the distance you want to test for. Keep in mind that autofocus problems can be different at varying distances and lens focal lengths, and that you can enter only *one* correction value for a particular lens. So, choose a distance (close-up or mid-range) and zoom setting with your shooting habits in mind.

2. **Set the autofocus mode.** Choose the autofocus mode you want to test.

3. **Level the camera (in an ideal world).** If the wall happens to be perfectly perpendicular, you can use a bubble level, plumb bob, or other device of your choice to ensure that the camera is level to match. Many tripods and tripod heads have bubble levels built in. Avoid using the center column, if you can. When the camera is properly oriented, lock the legs and tripod head tightly.

4. **Level the camera (in the real world).** If your wall is not perfectly perpendicular, use this old trick. Tape a mirror to the wall, and then adjust the camera on the tripod so that when you look through the viewfinder at the mirror, you see directly into the reflection of the lens. Then, lock the tripod and remove the mirror.

5. **Mount the test chart.** Tape the test chart on the wall so it is centered in your camera's viewfinder.

6. **Photograph the test chart using AF.** Allow the camera to autofocus and take a test photo using the remote release to avoid shaking or moving the camera.

7. **Make an adjustment and re-photograph.** Navigate to the Camera Settings I-08 menu and choose AF Micro Adj. Make sure the feature has been turned on, then press down to Amount and make a fine-tuning adjustment, plus or minus, and photograph the target again.

8. **Lather, rinse, repeat.** Repeat steps 6 and 7 several times to create several different adjustments to check.

9. **Evaluate the image(s).** If you have the camera connected to your computer with a USB cable or through a Wi-Fi connection, so much the better. You can view the image(s) after transfer to your computer. Otherwise, *carefully* open the camera card door and slip the memory card out and copy the images to your computer.

10. **Evaluate focus.** Which image is sharpest? That's the setting you need to use for this lens. If your initial range doesn't provide the correction you need, repeat the steps between –20 and +20 until you find the best fine-tuning. Once you've made an adjustment, the –7 will automatically apply the AF fine-tuning each time that lens is mounted on the camera, as long as the function is turned on.

MAXED OUT

If you've reached the maximum number of lenses (which is unlikely—who owns 30 lenses?), mount a lens you no longer want to compensate for, and reset its adjustment value to +/-0. Or you can reset the values of all your lenses using the Clear function and start over.

What Lenses Can Do for You

A sane approach to expanding your lens collection is to consider what each of your options can do for you and then choose the type of lens that will really boost your creative opportunities. Here's a guide to the sort of capabilities you can gain by adding a lens (using an adapter, if necessary) to your repertoire.

- **Wider perspective.** A 24-70mm or 28-70mm lens can serve you well for moderate wide-angle to medium telephoto shots. Now you find your back is up against a wall and you *can't* take a step backward to take in more subject matter. Perhaps you're standing on the boulevard adjacent to the impressive domed walls of the Mirogoj Cemetery in Zagreb, Croatia, and you want to show the expanse of the walls, as I did for the photo at top in Figure 12.14, made with the Sony/Zeiss 16-35mm f/4 zoom lens. Or, you might find yourself just behind the baseline at a high school basketball game and want an interesting shot with a little perspective distortion tossed in the mix. If you often want to make images with a super-wide field of view, a wider lens is in your future.

- **Bring objects closer.** A long focal length brings distant subjects closer to you, allows you to produce images with very shallow depth-of-field, and avoids the perspective distortion that wide-angle lenses provide. If you find the traffic on the street intrusive, as I did in Zagreb, you can zoom in to eliminate the distraction, as in Figure 12.14, center. A lens like the Sony/Zeiss 24-70mm f/4 can be your best friend.

Or, perhaps you want to zoom in on one of the domes. As I write this, the longest focal length in an FE lens zooms from 100mm to 400mm. If you own such a lens, it's easy to blur the background because the maximum remains f/4 at long focal lengths. With the right adapter, you can also use a much longer super telephoto lens on your a7R IV, as I did for Figure 12.14, bottom, using my own Minolta 100-400mm lens.

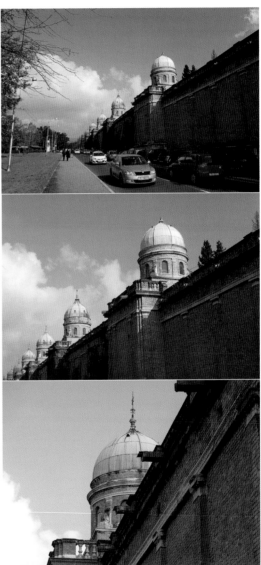

Figure 12.14 A 16mm view shows a broad expanse of wall outside the Mirogoj Cemetery in Zagreb, Croatia (top). A view at roughly the same distance at 100mm (center). A long telephoto lens at 400mm captured this image (bottom).

- **Bring your camera closer.** Sony's 90mm FE macro lens is great, but you can also use an adapter and work with other close-up lenses if you don't want to purchase the E-mount 30mm f/3.5 macro lens. Sony has two excellent A-mount macro lenses that would be fine for use with an adapter; you might own one of these or may be able to borrow one: the 50mm f/2.8 and the 100mm f/2.8 macro lens.

  Even if the autofocus speed you get isn't fast enough for you, the need to manually focus an A-mount macro lens is not a tremendous hardship. Most serious photographers use manual focus in extreme close-up photography for the most convenient method of controlling the exact subject element that will be in sharpest focus. The A-mount 100mm f/2.8 macro lens ($800) is preferable to the shorter macro lenses in nature photography because you do not need to move extremely close to a skittish subject for high magnification. And you can get a frame-filling photo of a tiny blossom without trampling all the other plants in its vicinity.

- **Look sharp.** Many lenses, particularly the higher-priced Sony and Zeiss optics, are prized for their sharpness and overall image quality. Your run-of-the-mill lens is likely to be plenty sharp for most applications at the optimum aperture (usually f/8 or f/11), but the very best optics, such as the Zeiss 55mm f/1.8, are definitely superior. You can expect to get excellent sharpness in much of the image area at the maximum aperture, high sharpness even in the corners by one stop down, more consistent sharpness at various focal lengths with a zoom, and better correction for various types of distortions (discussed shortly).

- **More speed.** Your basic lens might have the perfect focal length and sharpness for sports photography, but the maximum aperture may be small at telephoto focal lengths, such as f/5.6 or f/6.3 at the far end. That won't cut it for night baseball or football games, since you'll need to use an extremely high ISO (where image quality suffers) to be able to shoot at a fast shutter speed to freeze the action. Even outdoor sports shooting on overcast days can call for a high ISO if you're using a slow zoom lens (with small maximum apertures).

  That makes the FE-mount lenses with a very wide aperture (small f/number) such as the 24mm f/2 optic a prime choice (so to speak) for low-light photography when you can get close to the action; that's often possible at an amateur basketball or volleyball game. But, you might be happier with an adapter and an A-mount lens, such as the Carl Zeiss Sonnar T* 135mm f/1.8 lens (if money is no object; it costs $1,800). But there are lower-cost fast lens options, such as the 50mm f/1.4 lens ($400), which might be suitable for indoor sports in a gym and whenever you must shoot in dark locations, in a castle or cathedral or theater, for example.

Categories of Lenses

Lenses can be categorized by their intended purpose—general photography, macro photography, and so forth—or by their focal length. The range of available focal lengths is usually divided into three main groups: wide-angle, normal, and telephoto. Prime lenses fall neatly into one of these classifications. Zooms can overlap designations, with a significant number falling into the catchall wide-to-telephoto zoom range. This section provides more information about focal length ranges, and how they are used.

Any lens with a focal length of 10mm to 20mm is said to be an *ultra-wide-angle lens*; from about 20mm to 40mm is said to be a *wide-angle lens*. *Normal lenses* have a focal length roughly equivalent to the diagonal of the film or sensor, in millimeters, and so fall into the range of about 45mm to 60mm on a full-frame camera like your a7R IV model. *Telephoto lenses* usually fall into the 75mm and longer focal lengths, while those with a focal length much beyond 300mm are referred to as *super telephotos*.

Using Wide-Angle Lenses

To use wide-angle prime lenses and wide zooms, you need to understand how they affect your photography. Here's a quick summary of the things you need to know.

- **More depth-of-field (apparently).** Practically speaking, wide-angle lenses seem to produce more extensive depth-of-field at a particular subject distance and aperture. However, the range of acceptable sharpness actually depends on magnification: the size of the subject in the frame. With a wide-angle lens, you usually include a full scene in an image; any single subject is not magnified very much, so the depth-of-field will be quite extensive. When using a telephoto lens however, you tend to fill the frame with a single subject (using high magnification), so the background is more likely to be blurred. (I'll discuss this in more detail in the sidebar below.)

  You'll find a wide-angle lens helpful when you want to maximize the range of acceptable sharpness in a landscape, for example. On the other hand, it's very difficult to isolate your subject (against a blurred background) using selective focus unless you move extremely close. Telephoto lenses are better for this purpose and as a bonus, they also include fewer extraneous elements of the scene because of their narrower field of view.

- **Stepping back.** Wide-angle lenses have the effect of making it seem that you are standing farther from your subject than you really are. They're helpful when you don't want to back up—or can't because of impediments—to include an entire group of people in your photo, for example.

- **Wider field of view.** While making your subject seem farther away, as implied above, a wide-angle lens also provides a more expansive field of view, including more of the scene in your photos.

- **More foreground.** As background objects appear further back than they do to the naked eye, more of the foreground is brought into view by a wide-angle lens. That gives you extra emphasis on the area that's closest to the camera. Photograph your home with a 50mm focal length, for example, and the front yard probably looks fairly conventional in your photo. Switch to a wider lens, such as the 16mm setting of the 16-35mm f/4 zoom, and you'll discover that your lawn now makes up much more of the photo. So, wide-angle lenses are great when you want to emphasize that lake in the foreground, but problematic when your intended subject is located farther in the distance.

- **Super-sized subjects.** The tendency of a wide-angle lens to emphasize objects in the foreground while de-emphasizing objects in the background can lead to a kind of size distortion that may be more objectionable for some types of subjects than others. Shoot a bed of flowers up close with a 16mm or shorter focal length, and you might like the distorted effect of the nearby blossoms looming in the photo. Take a shot of a family member with the same lens from the same distance, and you're likely to get some complaints about that gigantic nose in the foreground.

- **Perspective distortion.** This type of distortion occurs when you tilt the camera so the plane of the sensor is no longer perpendicular to the vertical plane of your subject. As a result, some parts of the subject are now closer to the sensor than they were before, while other parts are farther away. This is what makes buildings, flagpoles, or NBA players appear to be leaning over backward (like the building shown in Figure 12.15). While this kind of apparent distortion is actually caused by tilting the camera/lens upward (not by a defect in the lens), it can happen with any lens, but it's most apparent when a wide angle is used.

- **Steady cam.** You'll find that it is easier to get photos without blur from camera shake when you hand-hold a wide-angle lens at slower shutter speeds than it is with a telephoto lens. And, thanks to SteadyShot stabilization, you can take sharp photos at surprisingly long shutter speeds at a long focal length without using a tripod. That's because the reduced magnification of the wide-angle lens or wide-zoom setting doesn't empha-size camera shake like a telephoto lens does.

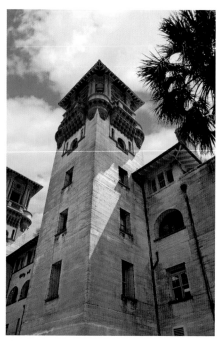

Figure 12.15 Tilting the camera produces this "falling back" look in architectural photos.

- **Interesting angles.** Many of the factors already listed combine to produce more interesting angles when shooting with wide-angle lenses. Raising or lowering a telephoto lens a few feet probably will have little effect on the appearance of a distant subject that fills the frame. The same change in elevation can produce a dramatic effect if you're using a short focal length and are close to your subject.

DOF IN DEPTH

The depth-of-field advantage of wide-angle lenses disappears when you enlarge your picture. Believe it or not, a wide-angle image enlarged and cropped to provide the same subject size as a telephoto shot will have the same depth-of-field. Try it: take a wide-angle photo of a friend from a fair distance. Then, use a longer (telephoto) zoom setting from the same shooting position to take the same picture; naturally, your friend will appear to be larger in the second because of the greater telephoto magnification.

Download the two photos to your computer. While viewing the wide-angle shot, magnify it with the zoom or magnify tool so your friend is as large as in the telephoto image. You'll find that the wide-angle photo will have the same depth-of-field as the telephoto image; for example, the background will be equally blurred.

Avoiding Potential Wide-Angle Problems

Wide-angle lenses have a few quirks that you'll want to keep in mind when shooting so you can avoid falling into some common traps. Here's a checklist of tips for avoiding common problems:

- **Symptom: converging lines.** Unless you want to use wildly diverging lines as a creative effect, it's a good idea to keep horizontal and vertical lines in landscapes, architecture, and other subjects carefully aligned with the sides, top, and bottom of the frame. To prevent undesired perspective distortion, you must take care not to tilt the camera. If your subject is very tall, like a building, you may need to shoot from an elevated position (like a high level in a parking garage) so you won't need to tilt the lens upward. And if your subject is short, like a small child, get down to a lower level so you can get the shot without tilting the lens downward.

- **Symptom: color fringes around objects.** Lenses often produce photos that are plagued with fringes of color around backlit objects, produced by *chromatic aberration*. This common lens flaw comes in two forms: *longitudinal/axial*, in which all the colors of light don't focus in the same plane, and *lateral/transverse*, in which the colors are shifted to one side. Axial chromatic aberration can be reduced by stopping down the lens (to f/8 or f/11, for example), but transverse chromatic aberration cannot.

  Better-quality lenses reduce both types of imaging defect; it's common for reviews to point out these failings, so you can choose the best performing lenses that your budget allows. The Lens Compensation feature in the Camera Settings I-02 menu can help reduce this problem. Leave it set for Auto to get the chromatic aberration reduction processing that the camera can provide.

- **Symptom: lines that bow outward.** Some wide-angle lenses cause straight lines to bow outward, an effect called barrel distortion; you'll see the strongest effect at the edges. Most fisheye (or *curvilinear*) lenses produce this effect as a feature of the lens; it's much more obvious than with any other type of lens. (See Figure 12.16.) The mild barrel distortion you get with a conventional lens

Figure 12.16 Many wide-angle lenses cause lines to bow outward toward the edges of the image. That's often not noticeable unless you use a fisheye lens; the effect is considered to be interesting and desirable.

is rarely obvious except in some types of architectural photography. If you find it objectionable, you'll need to use a well-corrected lens.

Manufacturers like Sony do their best to minimize or eliminate it (producing a *rectilinear* lens), often using *aspherical* lens elements (which are not cross-sections of a sphere). You can also minimize barrel distortion simply by framing your photo with some extra space all around, so the edges where the bowing outward is most obvious can be cropped out of the picture. The Lens Correction feature can help reduce this problem, too. Leave it set to Auto to allow the processor to minimize the slight barrel distortion that can occur with the more affordable lenses.

■ **Symptom: light and dark areas when using a polarizing filter.** You should be aware that polarizers work best when the camera is pointed 90 degrees away from the sun and have the least effect when the camera is oriented 180 degrees from the sun. This is only half the story, however. With lenses like the 16-35mm f/4 zoom, the range is extensive enough to cause problems.

Think about it: if you use the widest setting of such a zoom and point it at a part of a scene that's at the proper 90-degree angle from the sun, the areas of the scene that are at the edges of the frame will be oriented at much wider angles from the sun. Only the center of the image area will be at exactly 90 degrees. When the filter is used to darken a blue sky, the sky will be very dark near the center of your photo. Naturally, the polarizing effect will be much milder at the edges so the sky in those areas will be much lighter in tone (less polarized). The solution is to avoid using a polarizing filter in situations where you'll be including the sky with lenses that have an actual focal length of less than about 28mm.

Using Telephoto and Tele-Zoom Lenses

Telephoto lenses also can have a dramatic effect on your photography. Here are the most important things you need to know. In the next section, I'll concentrate on telephoto considerations that can be problematic—and how to avoid those problems.

■ **Selective focus.** Long lenses have reduced depth-of-field, a shallow range of acceptably sharp focus, especially at wide apertures (small f/numbers); this is useful for selective focus to isolate your subject. You can set the widest aperture to create shallow depth-of-field or close it down (to a small f/number) to allow more of the scene to appear to be in acceptably sharp focus. The flip side of the coin is that even at f/16, a 300mm and longer lens will not provide much depth-of-field, especially when the subject is large in the frame (magnified). Like fire, the depth-of-field aspects of a telephoto lens can be friend or foe.

■ **Getting closer.** Telephoto lenses allow you to fill the frame with wildlife, sports action, and candid subjects. No one wants to get a reputation as a surreptitious or "sneaky" photographer (except for paparazzi), but when applied to candids in an open and honest way, a long lens can help you capture memorable moments while retaining enough distance to stay out of the way of events as they transpire.

- **Reduced foreground/increased compression.** Telephoto lenses have the opposite effect of wide angles: they reduce the importance of things in the foreground by squeezing everything together. This so-called *compressed perspective* makes objects in the scene appear to be closer than they are to the naked eye. You can use this effect as a creative tool. You've seen the effect hundreds of times in movies and on television, where the protagonist is shown running in and out of traffic that appears to be much closer to the hero (or heroine) than it really is.

- **Accentuates camera shakiness.** Telephoto focal lengths hit you with a double whammy in terms of camera/photographer shake. The lenses themselves are bulkier, more difficult to hold steady, and may even produce a barely perceptible seesaw rocking effect when you support them with one hand halfway down the lens barrel. As they magnify the subject, they amplify the effect of any camera shake. It's no wonder that image stabilization like Optical SteadyShot (OSS) is especially popular among those using longer lenses, and why Sony includes this feature in the 18-200mm zooms (and many of the long A-mount lenses).

- **Interesting angles require creativity.** Telephoto lenses require more imagination in selecting interesting angles, because the "angle" you do get on your subjects is so narrow. Moving from side to side or a bit higher or lower can make a dramatic difference in a wide-angle shot, but raising or lowering a telephoto lens a few feet probably will have little effect on the appearance of the distant subjects you're shooting.

Avoiding Telephoto Lens Problems

Many of the "problems" that telephoto lenses pose are really just challenges and not that difficult to overcome. Here is a list of the seven most common picture maladies and suggested solutions.

- **Symptom: flat faces in portraits.** Head-and-shoulders portraits of humans tend to be more flattering when a focal length of 50mm to 85mm is used with a full-frame camera. Longer focal lengths compress the distance between features like the nose and ears, making the face look wider and flat. (Conversely, a wide-angle lens will make the nose look huge and ears tiny if you move close enough for a head-and-shoulders portrait.) So, avoid using a focal length much longer than about 60mm with your a7R IV unless you're forced to shoot from a greater distance. (Use a wide-angle lens only when shooting three-quarters/full-length portraits, or group shots.)

- **Symptom: blur due to camera shake.** Because a long focal length amplifies the effects of camera shake, make sure the SteadyShot stabilization is not turned off (with a menu item). Then, if possible, use a faster shutter speed; that may mean that you'll need to set a higher ISO to be able to do so. Of course, a firm support like a solid tripod is the most effective tool for eliminating camera shake, especially if you trip the shutter with a remote commander accessory or the self-timer to avoid the risk of jarring the camera. Of course, only the fast shutter speed option will be useful to prevent blur caused by *subject* motion; SteadyShot or a tripod won't help you freeze a race car in mid-lap.

- **Symptom: color fringes.** Chromatic aberration is the most pernicious optical problem found in tele-photo lenses. There are others, including spherical aberration, astigmatism, coma, curvature of field, and similarly scary-sounding phenomena. The best solution for any of these is to use a better lens that offers the proper degree of correction for aberrations or stop down the lens (to f/8 or f/11) to minimize the problem. But that's not always possible. Your second-best choice may be to correct the fringing in your favorite RAW conversion tool or image editor. Photoshop's Lens Correction filter offers sliders that minimize both red/cyan and blue/yellow fringing. A feature such as this (also available with some other software) can be useful in situations where the a7R IV's Lens Compensation feature doesn't fully correct for chromatic aberration.

- **Symptom: lines that curve inward.** Pincushion distortion is common in photos taken with many tele-photo lenses; lines, especially those near the edges of the frame, bow inward like the pincushion your grandma might have used. You can take photos of a brick wall at various focal lengths with your zoom lens to find out where the pincushion distortion is the most obvious; that will probably be at or near the longest focal length. Like chromatic aberration, it can be partially corrected using tools like Photoshop's Lens Correction filter (or a similar utility in some other software).

- **Symptom: low contrast from haze or fog.** When you're photographing distant objects, a long lens shoots through a lot more atmosphere, which generally is muddied up with extra haze and fog. The dust or moisture droplets in the atmosphere can reduce contrast and mute colors. Some feel that a skylight or UV filter can help, but this practice is mostly a holdover from the film days. Digital sensors are not sensitive enough to UV light for a UV filter to have much effect. A polarizer might help a bit, but only in certain circumstances. I don't consider this to be a huge problem because it's easy to boost contrast and color saturation in Picture Styles (a menu item) or later in image-editing software.

- **Symptom: low contrast from flare.** Lenses are often furnished with lens hoods for a good reason: to minimize the amount of stray light that will strike the front element causing flare or a ghost image of the diaphragm containing the aperture. A hood is effective when the light is at your side, but it has no value when you're shooting toward the sun. On the other hand, you'll often be shooting with the light striking the lens from an angle. In this situation, the lens hood is only partially effective, so minimize flare by using your hand or cap to cast a shadow over the front element of the lens. (Just be careful not to let your hand or cap intrude into the image area.)

- **Symptom: dark flash photos.** Edge-to-edge flash coverage isn't as problematic with telephoto lenses as it is with wide angles. (The built-in flash simply cannot provide light that covers the entire field of view that's recorded by a lens shorter than 16mm.) The shooting distance is the problem with longer lenses. A 210mm focal length might allow you to make a distant subject appear close to the camera, but the flash isn't fooled. You'll need extra power for distant flash shots, making a large accessory flash unit a valuable accessory.

If you do not have a powerful flash unit and cannot get closer to the subject (like Lady Gaga strutting her stuff on a dark stage), try setting the camera's ISO level to 3200. This increases the sensitivity of the sensor so less light is required to make a bright photo; of course, the photo is likely to be grainy because of digital noise. If that does not solve the problem, you will need to set an even higher ISO, but then you'll get even more obvious digital noise in your photo.

Working with Flash

13

Photography is a form of visual art that uses light to shape the finished product. The photographer may have little or no control over the subject (other than posing human subjects) but can often adjust both viewing angle *and* the nature of the light source to create a particular compelling image. The direction and intensity of the light sources create the shapes and textures that we see. The distribution and proportions determine the contrast and tonal values: whether the image is stark or high key or muted and low in contrast. The colors of the light (because even "white" light has a color balance that the sensor can detect), and how much of those colors the subject reflects or absorbs, paint the hues visible in the image.

As a Sony photographer, you must learn to be a painter and sculptor of light if you want to move from *taking* a picture to *making* a photograph. Most of the time, you'll be working with available or ambient light, perhaps with reflectors or other modifiers, or even some additional continuous light sources, such as incandescent or fluorescent lamps. But at times you'll want to turn to one of the most versatile sources of illumination you have available, the brief, but brilliant snippets of light we call *electronic flash*. This chapter will show you the differences between working with continuous illumination and working with flash and explain how to use the flash capabilities of the Sony a7R IV.

Why Flash?

Flash sometimes gets a bad rap, but that's usually prompted by photographers who make poor use of the capabilities electronic flash offers. In some respects, working with continuous lighting instead is easier and more predictable. Conventional lighting is exactly what you might think: uninterrupted illumination that is available all the time during a shooting session. Daylight, moonlight, and the artificial lighting encountered both indoors and outdoors count as continuous light sources (although all of them can be "interrupted" by passing clouds, solar eclipses, a blown fuse, or simply by switching off a lamp). Indoor continuous illumination includes both the lights that are there already (such as incandescent lamps or overhead fluorescent lights indoors) and fixtures you supply yourself, including photoflood lamps or reflectors used to bounce existing light onto your subject.

On the face of things, electronic flash may be uncomfortably *different* from what we are used to, and sometimes considered difficult to use. In practice, you can use flash in all the same ways you use continuous lighting to shape your images, and, in some cases, take advantage of its special properties, such as its action-freezing short duration. Electronic flash is notable because it can be much more intense than continuous lighting, lasts only a brief moment, and can be much more portable than supplementary incandescent sources. It's a light source you can carry with you and use anywhere.

Of course, your Sony a7R IV does not have a built-in flash of any sort. There are several reasons for that. The company wanted to make the a7-series cameras exceptionally compact, and a built-in flash would have added bulk. In addition, even though Sony upgraded the size and power of the a7R IV's NP-FZ100 battery, the features of the camera alone do a good job of consuming all that extra juice during a shooting session. With a camera like the a7R IV, a pop-up flash (which most advanced photographers would likely use only as fill or to trigger off-camera units wirelessly) would provide an unacceptable amount of extra drain. So, any electronic flash used with these cameras is necessarily an external flash with its own power supply, which happily solves the power drain situation while reducing red-eye and other effects of on-camera flash.

Before moving on to discussing flash in detail, here's a quick comparison of the pros and cons of continuous illumination versus flash:

- **Lighting preview—Pro: continuous lighting.** With continuous lighting, such as incandescent lamps or daylight, you always know exactly what kind of lighting effect you're going to get. If you're using multiple lights, you can visualize how they will interact with each other. With electronic flash, the general effect you're going to see may be a mystery until you've built some experience.

- **Lighting preview—Con: electronic flash.** Compact portable flash units often do not provide a "modeling light" function, although studio flash typically do.

- **Exposure calculation—Pro: continuous lighting.** Your camera has no problem calculating accurate exposure for continuous lighting, because the lighting remains constant and can be measured through built-in light meters that interpret the light reaching the sensor. The amount of light available just before the exposure will, in almost all cases, be the same amount of light present when the shutter mechanism is opened to take the shot. The Spot metering mode can be used to measure brightness in the bright areas of the scene and the dark areas; if you have a bit of expertise in this technique, you'll know whether it would be useful to bounce some light into the shadow areas using a reflector panel accessory.

- **Exposure calculation—Con: electronic flash.** A flash unit provides no illumination until it actually fires so the exact exposure can't be measured by the a7R IV's exposure sensor before you take a photo. Instead, the light must be measured by metering the intensity of a *pre-flash* triggered an instant before the main flash, as it is reflected back to the camera and through the lens.

- **Evenness of illumination—Pro/con: continuous lighting.** Of continuous light sources, daylight, in particular, provides illumination that tends to fill an image completely, lighting up the foreground, background, and your subject almost equally. A sunlit scene may have shadow areas too, of course, so you might need to use reflectors or fill-in light sources to even out the illumination. Barring objects that block large sections of your image from daylight, the light is spread fairly evenly. Indoors, however, continuous lighting is much less likely to be evenly distributed. The average living room, for example, has hot spots and dark corners. But on the plus side, you can *see* this uneven illumination and compensate with additional lamps.

- **Evenness of illumination—Con: electronic flash.** Electronic flash units, like the continuous light provided by lamps, don't have the advantage of being located 93 million miles from the subject as the sun is. Because of this factor, they suffer from the effects of their proximity.

The *inverse square law*, first applied to both gravity and light by Sir Isaac Newton, dictates that as a light source's distance increases from the subject, the amount of light reaching the subject falls off proportionately to the square of the distance. In plain English, that means that a flash or lamp that's 12 feet away from a subject provides only one-quarter as much illumination as a source that's 6 feet away (rather than half as much). (See Figure 13.1.) This translates into relatively shallow "depth-of-light."

■ **Action stopping—Pro: electronic flash.** When it comes to the ability to freeze moving objects in their tracks, the advantage goes to electronic flash. The brief duration of the emitted light serves as a very fast "shutter speed" when the flash is the main or only source of illumination for the photo. In other words, this effect is possible when shooting in a dark area without much, if any, lighting provided by ambient sources but assumes that the subject is not beyond the range of the flash.

In flash photography, your camera's shutter speed (called *sync speed* in flash photography) is set to 1/250th second, but when flash is the primary light source, the *effective* exposure time will be the 1/1000th to 1/50000th second or less; this is the actual duration of the flash illumination. As you can see in Figure 13.2, it's possible to freeze motion with flash of very short duration. The only fly in the ointment is that, if the ambient light is strong enough, it may produce a secondary "ghost" exposure, as I'll explain later in this chapter.

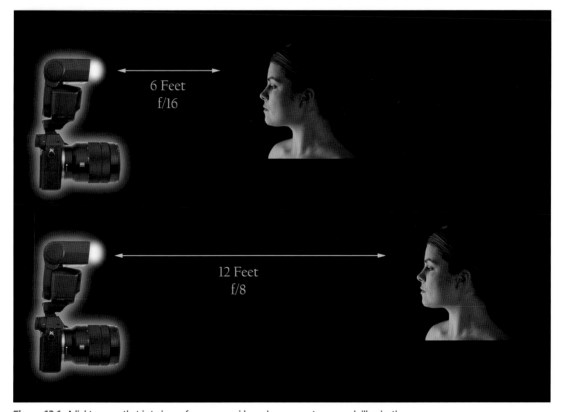

6 Feet
f/16

12 Feet
f/8

Figure 13.1 A light source that is twice as far away provides only one-quarter as much illumination.

Figure 13.2 Electronic flash can freeze almost any motion because of its extremely short duration.

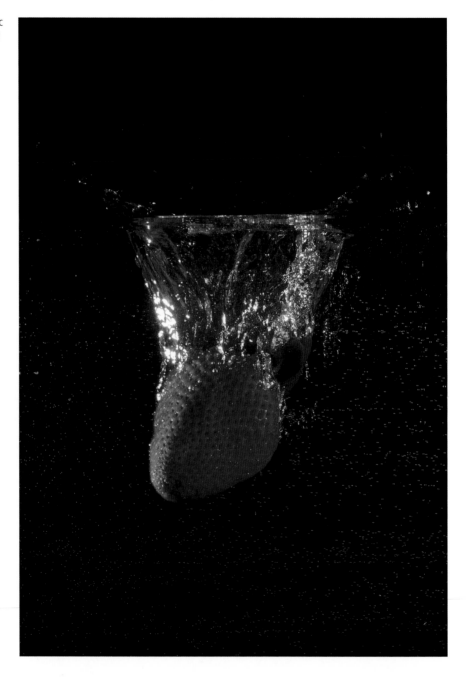

- **Action stopping—Con: continuous lighting.** Action stopping with continuous light sources is completely dependent on the shutter speed you've dialed in on the camera. And the speeds available are dependent on the amount of light available and your camera's ISO sensitivity setting. Outdoors in daylight, there will probably be enough sunlight to let you shoot at 1/2000th second and f/6.3 with a non-grainy ISO of 400. That's a fairly useful combination of settings if you're not using a super-telephoto with a small maximum aperture.

  But indoors, the reduced illumination quickly has you pushing your a7R IV to its limits. For example, if you're shooting indoor sports in a dark arena, there probably won't be enough available light to allow you to use a 1/2000th-second shutter speed unless you use a lens with an extremely wide aperture, such as f/1.8, with, say, the Sony Sonnar T* FE 55mm f/1.8 ZA. You can also specify a very high ISO setting, and accept that image quality may suffer. (In truth, the gym where I shoot indoor basketball allows me to do so at 1/500th second at f/4 using ISO 1600.) In many indoor sports situations, you may find yourself limited to a shutter speed of 1/500th second or slower.

- **Flexibility—Pro: electronic flash.** The action-freezing power of electronic flash, at least for nearby subjects in a dark location, allows you to work without a tripod; that provides extra flexibility and speed when choosing angles and positions.

- **Flexibility—Con: continuous lighting.** Because incandescent and fluorescent lamps are not as bright as electronic flash, the slower shutter speeds required (see "Action stopping," above) mean that you may have to use a tripod more often, especially when shooting portraits. The incandescent variety of continuous lighting gets hot, especially in the studio, and the side effects range from discomfort (for your human models) to disintegration (if you happen to be shooting perishable foods like ice cream).

Electronic Flash Basics

Until you delve into the situation deeply enough, it might appear that serious photographers have a love/hate relationship with electronic flash. You'll often hear that flash photos are less natural looking, and that on-camera flash in most cameras should never be used as the primary source of illumination because it provides a harsh, garish look. Some photographers strongly praise available ("continuous") lighting while denouncing electronic flash.

That bias is against *bad* flash photography. Indeed, flash—often with light modifier accessories—has become the studio light source of choice for many pro photographers. That's understandable, because the light is more intense (and its intensity can be dialed up or down by the photographer), freezes action, frees you from using a tripod (unless you want to use one to lock down a composition), and has a snappy, consistent light quality that matches daylight. (While color balance changes as the flash duration shortens, some Sony flash units can communicate to the camera the exact white balance provided for that shot.) And even conservative photographers will concede that electronic flash has some important uses as an adjunct to existing light, particularly to fill in dark shadows.

How Electronic Flash Works

The electronic flash you use will generally be connected to the camera by slipping it onto the hot shoe or linked by a cable connected to an adapter mounted on the shoe. In all cases, the flash is triggered at the instant of exposure, during a period when the sensor is fully exposed by the shutter.

The a7R IV has electronic shutter options, which I'll describe later, and a conventional vertically traveling physical shutter that consists of two curtains. The front curtain opens and moves to the opposite side of the frame, at which point the shutter is completely open. The flash can be triggered at this point (so-called *front-curtain sync,* which is the default mode), making the flash exposure. Then, after a delay that can vary from 30 seconds to 1/250th second, a second, *rear curtain* begins moving across the sensor plane, covering up the sensor again. If the flash is triggered just before the rear curtain starts to close, then the optional *rear-curtain sync* is used. In both cases, though, a shutter speed of 1/250th second is (ordinarily) the *maximum* that can be used to take a photo, because that's the speed at which both the front and rear curtains are tucked out of the way, leaving the entire full frame exposed to capture the flash burst.

Figure 13.3 illustrates how this works, with a fanciful illustration of a generic shutter (your a7R IV's shutter does *not* look like this). As an exposure is made using the conventional (non-electronic) shutter, the curtains move as follows:

1. Both curtains open. With a mirrorless camera like the a7R IV, the sensor remains completely exposed, so that the image that's being captured can be viewed on the electronic viewfinder and LCD monitor.

2. Front curtain closes. As the exposure begins, the front curtain rises to cover the sensor.

3. Prior image is dumped. When the sensor is completely covered, the preview image is dumped, resetting the pixels so that the exposure can begin.

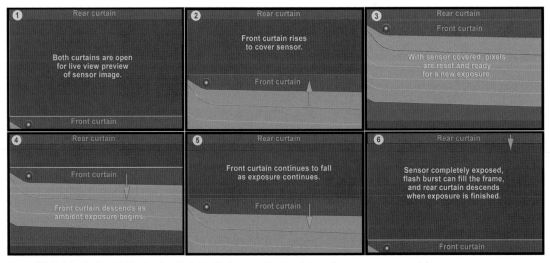

Figure 13.3 A focal plane shutter has two curtains, the lower, or front curtain, and an upper, or rear curtain.

4. Front curtain begins to descend. As the front curtain drops, the sensor is gradually exposed to light, and the *ambient* exposure (using the available light in the scene) begins.

5. Front curtain continues to descend. More of the sensor is uncovered, and the ambient exposure continues.

6. Both curtains open. With the sensor fully exposed, the electronic flash's brief burst can fill the frame.

- If this burst takes place as soon as the curtains are fully open, then *front-curtain sync*, which is the default, has been used. Following the flash, the sensor continues to be exposed for the length of the exposure, which can range from 1/250th second to 30 seconds (or longer, with a Bulb exposure).

- The burst can also take place *at the very end* of the exposure, just before the rear curtain starts to descend. This is called *rear-curtain sync.*

- When the exposure is finished, the rear curtain descends and the captured image is conveyed off the sensor to the camera's internal buffer, and thence to your memory card. The rear curtain then ascends to the top of the frame, exposing the sensor again and a preview image for the next picture appears in the EVF and LCD monitor.

Keep in mind that the a7R IV *always* defaults to front-curtain sync unless you explicitly select another sync mode using the Fn button or Flash Mode entry in the Camera Settings I-11 menu.

And Now for Something Completely Different...

If you've absorbed that, things are about to get *really* interesting. The a7R IV has special modes available from the Camera Settings II-05 menu, in which either the physical front curtain or both the physical front curtain *and* the rear curtain are simulated electronically. Only one of the two modes can be used with flash.

Here's the difference:

- **e-Front Curtain Shutter.** Recall that the sensor of a mirrorless camera is always exposed and feeding its image to the EVF and LCD monitor; in order to capture an image within a specified period of time, the sensor needs to *stop* collecting the image so the exposure can begin. In normal operation, as described above, when you press the shutter release down all the way, the shutter closes and the camera dumps the image you were previewing, resetting the pixels and leaving the sensor blank and ready to capture an exposure. When the e-Front Curtain Shutter is enabled, the physical front shutter doesn't close: the image is dumped *electronically*, and then the sensor immediately begins capturing an image. The physical rear curtain shutter then closes at the end of the exposure.

    The advantages of the electronic front curtain are that the camera can respond more quickly with less shutter lag, there is no possibility of vibration caused by the physical shutter bouncing at the end of its travel (this was a significant problem with the original a7 series), and an electronic front curtain shutter is quieter. As the a7 series is mirrorless, these cameras are already quieter than dSLR models, which have a mirror flapping about before and after the exposure.

However, an electronic front curtain shutter can exhibit problems with certain lenses and very fast shutter speeds. In such cases, when you are using an unusually wide aperture, such as f/1.8, some areas of the photo may exhibit a secondary (ghost) image. The aperture of an affected lens requires the diaphragm's "leaves" to travel a greater distance, and there may simply not be enough time. An overexposure may result. If you encounter that problem, turn the e-curtain option off; otherwise, you can do as I do and leave it on all the time.

- **Electronic shutter.** The a7R IV has an all-electronic shutter that can be activated by selecting Silent Shooting in the Camera Settings II-05 menu. In that case, both the physical front and rear curtains are replaced by electronic equivalents. Exposure is started and stopped electronically, with no curtains at all. Silent Shooting is indeed silent; I've had other photographers watching me snap away in that mode ask me whether I was really taking pictures at all. It is an excellent mode for religious ceremonies and other events where even the quiet click of the e-Front Curtain might be intrusive.

As I described in Chapter 10, silent shooting's rolling shutter captures the image line by line (as opposed to a global shutter that grabs the image in one fell swoop) and is subject to the same unwanted side effects found in video cameras, including wobble/Jell-O effect in hand-held shots, diagonal skewing, smear, and other defects. But the most important complication, in terms of the subject of this chapter, is that the electronic shutter cannot be used with flash at all. If you have a flash mounted and powered up and press the shutter release, it won't go off when the electronic shutter is active. Indeed, the Flash Mode options in the Camera Settings I-11 menu are grayed out and unavailable. (The only time your a7R IV *can* use electronic flash with the electronic shutter is during Pixel Shift exposures. However, the shutter speed is set to 1/8th second, and all speeds shorter than that are locked out.)

Avoiding Sync-Speed Problems

Using a shutter speed faster than the maximum sync speed can cause problems. Triggering the electronic flash *only* when the shutter is completely open makes a lot of sense if you think about what's going on. To obtain shutter speeds faster than 1/250th second, the a7R IV exposes only part of the sensor at one time, by starting the rear curtain on its journey before the front curtain has completely opened. That effectively provides a briefer exposure as the slit of the shutter passes over the surface of the sensor. If the flash were to fire during the time when the front and rear curtains partially obscured the sensor, only the slit that was actually open would be exposed.

You'd end up with only a narrow band, representing the portion of the sensor that was exposed when the picture was taken. For shutter speeds *faster* than the top sync speed, the rear curtain begins moving *before* the front curtain reaches the bottom of the frame. As a result, a moving slit, the distance between the front and rear curtains, exposes one portion of the sensor at a time as it moves from the top to the bottom. Figure 13.4 shows three views of our typical (but imaginary) physical focal plane shutter. At left is pictured the closed shutter; in the middle version you can see the front curtain has moved about 1/4 of the distance down from the top; and in the right-hand version, the rear curtain has started to "chase" the front curtain across the frame toward the bottom.

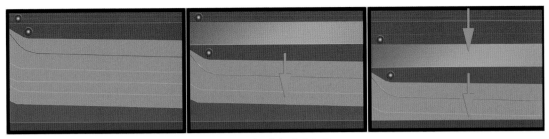

Figure 13.4 A typical exposure being made using the conventional physical shutter.

If the flash is triggered while this slit is moving, only the exposed portion of the sensor will receive any illumination. You end up with a photo like the one shown in Figure 13.5. Note that a band across the bottom of the image is black. That's a shadow of the rear shutter curtain, which had started to move when the flash was triggered. Sharp-eyed readers will wonder why the black band is at the *bottom* of the frame rather than at the top, where the rear curtain begins its journey. The answer is simple: your lens flips the image upside down and forms it on the sensor in a reversed position. You never notice that, because the camera is smart enough to show you the pixels that make up your photo in their proper orientation during picture review. But this image flip is why, if your sensor gets dirty and you detect a spot of dust in the upper half of a test photo, if cleaning manually, you need to look for the speck in the *bottom* half of the sensor.

I generally end up with sync speed problems only when shooting in the studio, using studio flash units rather than my Sony dedicated unit. That's because if you're using either type of "smart" flash, the camera knows that a strobe is attached, and remedies any unintentional goof in shutter speed settings. If you happen to set the a7R IV's shutter to a faster speed in S or M mode, the camera will automatically adjust the shutter speed down to the maximum sync speed as soon as you attach and turn on an external flash (or prevent you from choosing a faster speed if the flash is powered up).

Figure 13.5 If a shutter speed faster than 1/250th second is used with flash, you can end up photographing only a portion of the image.

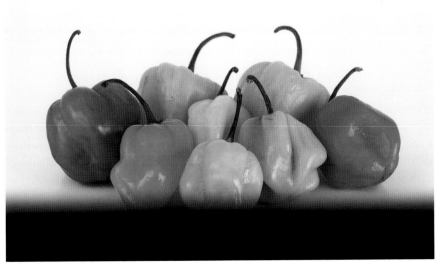

In A or P, where the a7R IV selects the shutter speed, it will never choose a shutter speed higher than 1/250th second when using flash.

But when using a non-dedicated flash, such as a studio unit plugged into the a7 IV's PC/X terminal, the camera has no way of knowing that a flash is connected, so shutter speeds faster than 1/250th second can be set inadvertently.

Note that the a7R IV can use a feature called *high-speed sync* that allows shutter speeds faster than the maximum sync speed with certain external dedicated Sony flash units. When using high-speed sync, the flash fires a continuous series of bursts at reduced power for the entire duration of the exposure, so that the illumination is able to expose the sensor as the slit moves.

HS sync is set using the controls that adjust the compatible external flash units, which include the HVL-F60M/RM, HVL-F58AM, HVL-F56AM, HVL-45RM, HVL-F43AM/HVL-F43M, HVL-F32M, and HVL-F36AM. (Note that all flashes ending in AM use the older Minolta-style foot and cannot be mounted on the a7R IV without an inexpensive Sony ADP-MAA adapter.) High-speed sync cannot be used when working with multiple flash units. When active, the message H appears on the LCD panel on the back of the flash. You'll find complete instructions accompanying those flash units.

Ghost Images

The difference might not seem like much, but whether you use front-curtain sync (the default setting) or rear-curtain sync (an optional setting) can make a significant difference to your photograph *if the ambient light in your scene also contributes to the image.* At faster shutter speeds, particularly 1/250th second, there isn't much time for the ambient light to register, unless it is very bright. It's likely that the electronic flash will provide almost all the illumination, so front-curtain sync or rear-curtain sync isn't very important.

However, at slower shutter speeds, or with very bright ambient light levels, there is a significant difference, particularly if your subject is moving, or the camera isn't steady. In any of those situations, the ambient light will register as a second image accompanying the flash exposure, and if there is movement (of the camera or subject), that additional image will not be in the same position as the flash exposure. It will show as a ghost image and, if the movement is significant enough, as a blurred ghost image trailing in front of or behind your subject in the direction of the movement.

As I mentioned earlier, when you're using front-curtain sync, the flash goes off the instant the shutter opens, producing an image of the subject on the sensor. That happens whether you're using the mechanical shutter or the optional electronic Front Curtain option from the Camera Settings II-4 menu. Then, the shutter remains open for an additional period (which, as I've noted, can be from 30 seconds to 1/250th second). If your subject is moving, say, toward the right side of the frame, the ghost image produced by the ambient light will produce a blur on the right side of the original subject image, making it look as if your sharp (flash-produced) image is chasing the ghost. For those of us who grew up with lightning-fast superheroes who always left a ghost trail *behind them*, that looks unnatural (see Figure 13.6).

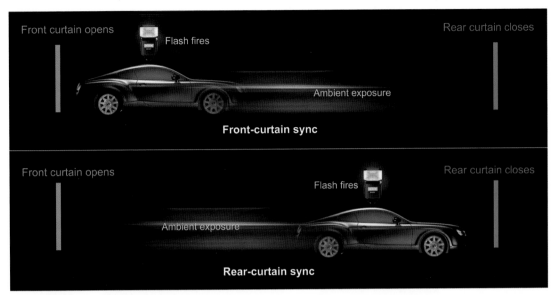

Figure 13.6 Front-curtain sync produces an image that trails in front of the flash exposure (top), whereas rear-curtain sync creates a more "natural-looking" trail behind the flash image (bottom).

So, Sony provides rear- (second-) curtain sync to remedy the situation. In that mode, the shutter opens, as before. The shutter remains open for its designated duration, and the ghost image forms. If your subject moves from the left side of the frame to the right side, the ghost will move from left to right, too. *Then*, about 1.5 milliseconds before the rear shutter curtain closes, the flash is triggered, producing a nice, sharp flash image *ahead* of the ghost image.

EVERY WHICH WAY, INCLUDING UP

Note that although I describe the ghost effect in terms of subject matter that is moving left to right in a horizontally oriented composition, it can occur in any orientation, and with the subject moving in *any* direction. (Try photographing a falling rock, if you can, and you'll see the same effect.) Nor are the ghost images affected by the fact that modern shutters travel vertically rather than horizontally. Secondary images are caused between the time the front curtain fully opens, and the rear curtain begins to close. The direction of travel of the shutter curtains, or the direction of your subject, does not matter.

Slow Sync

Another flash synchronization option is *slow sync*, which is actually an exposure option that tells the a7R IV to use slower shutter speeds when possible, to allow you to capture a scene by both flash and ambient illumination. To activate Slow Sync, press the Fn button, navigate to the flash options, and choose Slow Sync. Or, make the same selection from the Flash Mode entry in the Camera Settings I-11 menu.

Then, the exposure system will try to use longer shutter speeds with the flash, so that an initial exposure is made with the flash unit, and a secondary exposure of subjects in the background will be produced by the slower shutter speed. This will let you shoot a portrait of a person at night and, much of the time, avoid a dark background. Your portrait subject will be illuminated by the flash, and the background by the ambient light. It's a good idea to have the camera mounted on a tripod or some other support or have SteadyShot switched on to avoid having this secondary exposure produce ghost images due to camera movement during the exposure. (See Figure 13.7.)

Because Slow Sync is a type of exposure control, it does not work in Manual mode or Shutter Priority mode (because the a7R IV doesn't choose the shutter speed in those modes). It is not disabled in those modes: you can still select it using the Camera Settings menu or Function menu, but your shutter speed will not be changed.

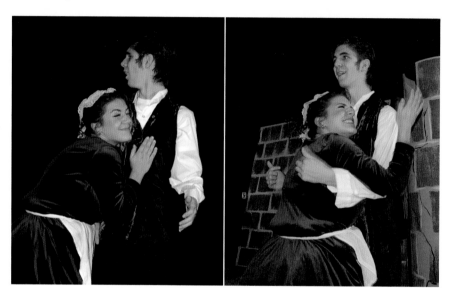

Figure 13.7 Without slow sync, ambient light may not be sufficient to balance with the flash exposure (left). When slow sync is activated, longer shutter speeds are selected, allowing the ambient light to register, too (right).

Determining Exposure

Calculating the proper exposure for an electronic flash photograph is a bit more complicated than determining the settings by continuous light. The right exposure isn't simply a function of how far away your subject is, even though the inverse square law I mentioned does have an effect: the farther away the subject is, the less light is available for the exposure. The a7R IV can calculate distance if you're using lenses with a *distance encoder chip,* which detects the position of the focusing mechanism as focus is locked in just prior to exposure. The component transmits this information to the camera, which can use it to determine the distance to the subject, and, therefore, much flash output is required to illuminate the scene. This Advanced Distance Integration (ADI) delivers high-precision flash metering that is unaffected by the reflectance of subjects or backgrounds.

But, of course, flash exposure isn't based on distance alone. Various objects reflect more or less light at the same distance so, obviously, the camera needs to measure the amount of light reflected back and through the lens. Yet, as the flash itself isn't available for measuring until it's triggered, the a7R IV has nothing to measure.

The solution is to fire the flash twice. The initial shot is a pre-flash that can be analyzed, then followed by a main flash that's given exactly the calculated intensity needed to provide a correct exposure. As a result, the primary flash may be longer for distant objects and shorter for closer subjects, depending on the required intensity for exposure. This through-the-lens evaluative flash exposure system uses distance information, and it operates whenever you have attached a Sony dedicated flash unit to the a7R IV, and a lens that provides the necessary distance integration information.

Flash Modes

There are several flash modes available in the Camera Settings I-11 menu:

- **Flash Off.** The flash never fires; this may be useful in museums, concerts, or religious ceremonies where electronic flash would prove disruptive. This option is not available in P, A, S, or M mode; if you do not want the flash to fire, turn it off.
- **Auto Flash.** The flash fires as required, depending on lighting conditions. Not available in P, A, S, or M mode because flash *always* fires in these modes if it's attached and powered up.
- **Fill-Flash.** When this option is set, the flash will always fire when set to P, A, S, or M modes, using one of the two Auto modes or in SCN modes where flash is not disabled. The camera balances the available illumination with flash to provide a balanced lighting effect. (See Figure 13.8.)
- **Slow Sync.** The camera combines flash with slow shutter speeds; the nearby subject can be illuminated by flash, but during the longer shutter speed, there's enough time for the darker surroundings (lit by ambient light) to record on the sensor.

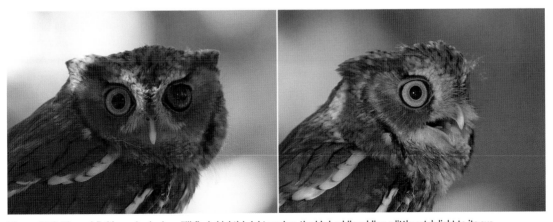

Figure 13.8 The owl (left) was in shadow. Fill flash (right) brightened up the bird, while adding a little catch light to its eye.

- **Rear Sync.** Fires the flash at the *end* of the exposure time, after the ambient light exposure has been made, producing more satisfying photos of moving subjects when using a long exposure; light trails will be behind the "ghost" image, as illustrated earlier in Figure 13.6, bottom.

- **Wireless.** This is available from a separate entry in the Camera Settings II-11 menu. (On and Off are your options.) Wireless allows an optional external flash or flash trigger mounted on the camera's multi interface shoe to activate one or more external flash units that support wireless off-camera flash; there's no need for any cable connection between the camera and the remote flash unit. I'll explain the Sony wireless system later in this chapter.

Flash Exposure Compensation

This is a feature discussed previously in Chapter 3. It's important to keep in mind how the camera's exposure compensation system works when you're using electronic flash. To activate exposure compensation for flash, visit the Flash Comp. item in the Camera Settings menu or use the Function menu, and set the amount of plus or minus compensation you want. (See Figure 13.9.) This function is not available when using Intelligent Auto mode. When you find that your flash photos are too dark even after you have set the highest amount of compensation, then the flash simply cannot provide more power; you must move closer to the subject, or use a wider aperture, or set a higher ISO, or take

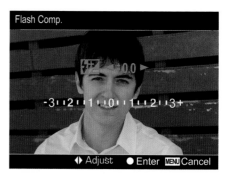

Figure 13.9 Set flash exposure compensation.

all of these steps. Note too that when a subject is extremely close to the camera, even a –3 setting may not prevent an excessively bright image. You'll probably have to *reduce* your ISO setting in that case.

Flash exposure compensation affects only the amount of light emitted by the flash. If you want to adjust the brightness of the ambient light exposure, you would also need to use the conventional exposure compensation feature. In fact, you can use both features at the same time, to get a brighter subject and a darker background, or vice versa. Let's say you're taking a photo of a friend posing against a light-toned background such as a white cabana on a beach. A plus exposure compensation setting (perhaps +1 when using multi-segment metering) will ensure that the cabana won't be under-exposed while a –1/3 or –2/3 flash exposure compensation will ensure that shadows on your friend's face will be lightened by a very gentle burst of flash. This is an advanced technique that requires some experimentation but can be valuable when used with some expertise.

Red Eye Reduction

When using semi-automatic or manual exposure modes, red-eye reduction is available if Red Eye Reduction is On in the Camera Settings I-11 menu (as described in Chapter 4). The flash will fire a burst before the photo is actually taken as you depress the shutter release button. That will theoretically cause your subjects' irises to contract (if they are looking toward the camera), thereby reducing the red-eye effect in your photograph.

Using an External Electronic Flash

As I write this, Sony offers six accessory electronic flash units that are compatible with the a7R IV's multi interface shoe: the HVL-F60M, its radio-wireless-capable sibling the HVL-F60RM, as well as the HVL-45RM, HVL-F43M, HVL-F32M, and HVL-F20M. These external units can be mounted on the camera, connected to the camera's multi interface shoe with a cable (I'll detail how later), or (except for the HVL-F20M) used off-camera with wireless connectivity when triggered by another external flash used as a controller/master. Each can also function as the controller/master mounted on an a7-series camera to trigger other flash units wirelessly.

In addition, there are earlier Sony flash units designed for the older Minolta/Sony proprietary hot shoe. They can be used with the a7-series cameras if you purchase an inexpensive adapter, such as the Sony ADP-MAA (about $25). Or, you can skip the adapter and use wireless-compatible legacy flash units off-camera in wireless mode, triggered by an on-camera master/controller. Although they are discontinued, I'll describe some of these earlier flash units because you may already own one or can find one used at a price that's hard to resist. I don't recommend the legacy flash/adapter approach, because older units operate using a more limited communication protocol, which I'll describe later. But because some of you may have an older flash or can pick one up used at a decent price, it doesn't make sense to pretend that these discontinued models don't exist, because they still can work with your a7R IV, especially as remote/slave units.

LET'S BE FRANK...

Although one of my jobs is to show you how to get the best from your wise decision to purchase a Sony camera, I'm not a cheerleader for the company. It's done a great job in responding to customer requests for features and upgraded gear, but Sony is still playing catch-up in the flash arena. It's been especially slow in providing affordable radio control flash options (as I'll note later in the chapter). The introduction of the HVL-F60RM in February 2018 added options, but at $600, many will not find it affordable.

The sheer volume of third-party options for gear makes it impossible to cover all of them in detail. So, I have generally devoted the available space to Sony products in this book, with the exception of a discussion of additional lens options. In terms of full-featured TTL-compatible third-party electronic flash units for your a7R IV, there are a number of excellent third-party products you should check out. Godox, in particular, makes good Sony-friendly flash which are marketed under the Godox name as well as rebranded for other vendors. Although I own Sony flash units, more often than not I use my Godox flash setup (which includes two Godox AD200 battery-operated studio monolights with TTL exposure metering).

Guide Numbers, Hot Shoes, and More

Before I describe the flash units themselves, there are a few aspects you need to understand in order to compare electronic flash. If you're a veteran Sony (or Minolta) shooter, you can skim over this section, or skip it entirely. Those new to photography or the Sony realm should find this information useful.

Guide Numbers

The first thing you need to learn when comparing flash units is that Sony incorporates the Guide Number (GN) of each flash in the product name. So, what's a Guide Number? The GN designation derives from the good old days prior to automatic flash units and through-the-lens flash metering, when flash exposures had to be calculated mathematically. Those days are very long ago, indeed, as Honeywell introduced Auto/Strobonar flash units way back in the 1960s.

Guide numbers are a standard way of specifying the power of a flash when used in manual, non-autoexposure mode. Divide the guide number by the distance to determine the correct f/stop to use at full power. With a GN of 197 at ISO 100, you would use an aperture of around f/19.7 for a subject that's 10 feet from the camera (197 divided by 10), or around f/9.5 for a subject at a distance of 20 feet. Because most countries in the world use metric measurements, guide numbers are given using values for both meters and feet. Thus, Sony's HVL-F60M/RM unit has a guide number of 60/197 in meters/feet, and the 60 GN is incorporated into the unit's product name.

The Guide Number data is most useful for comparing the relative power of several flash units that you're considering. According to the inverse square law, a flash unit with a GN of 200 (in feet) puts out four times the amount of light as one with a GN of about 100. If your accessory flash has a zoom head, which can change coverage to match the focal length setting of your lens, the GN will vary according to the zoom setting, as wider zoom settings spread the same light over a broader area than a telephoto zoom setting.

Hot Shoes

Starting in 1988, Minolta phased in a proprietary hot shoe, the so-called *iISO* shoe, which was supposedly more rugged and secure than the original ISO 518 shoe, based on a design that dates back to 1913, when it was used to attach viewfinders to a camera (electronic flash hadn't been invented yet). No other vendors, including Canon and Nikon, embraced Minolta's design and continued to use the industry standard shoe. The ISO 518 standard doesn't specify any electronic connections between camera and flash, other than the "dumb" triggering circuit, so when sophisticated electronic flash units with TTL metering and other capabilities were developed, each vendor created their own hot shoe version with the necessary electrical contacts for their cameras and flash units. The chief consequence for non-Minolta/Sony shooters was that you could mount dedicated flash units from one brand onto the ISO 518 shoe of another vendor's camera, and trigger that flash in manual, non-TTL mode.

When Sony purchased Konica Minolta's camera technology it began redesigning legacy features, and the old iISO hot shoe came under scrutiny. In 2012, Sony introduced a 21+3-pin hot shoe which it dubbed the *multi interface shoe,* which resembles a standard ISO 518 hot shoe with its "dumb" contacts. However, tucked away at the front of the shoe are additional electrical contacts that allow intelligent TTL flash metering communication between the camera and flash, and much more. For example, a whole series of stereo microphones from Sony and others, designed to plug into the multi interface shoe, are available. As I noted earlier, you can purchase adapters that allow you to connect older iISO flash to the a7R IV, or to attach new model flash units to a camera that has the original iISO hot shoe.

Cable Connections

In some cases, you can get your external flash off the camera without using a wireless connection by linking an HVL-F60M/RM and a7R IV with a physical cable. The gear needed for the hook-up can be costly, so I don't recommend it, but if you want to go that route, here's the way to go. Purchase the Sony FA-CS1M multi interface shoe adapter (about $40). It slides into the a7-series camera's multi interface shoe and has a four-pin TTL socket on the front. Connect that socket to a matching four-pin outlet located on the underside of the HVL-F60M/RM, beneath a protective terminal cap, using a 4.9-foot FA-MC1AM cable ($60). If you need more length, the FA-EC1AM extension cable ($50) adds another 4.9 feet to your connection. The HVL-F43M does not have the four-pin socket and connecting it to a cable requires some additional adapters, so you're better off not going that way.

HVL-F60M/RM Flash Units

Sony now has *two* top-of-the-line flash units, the HVL-F60M, which uses optical triggering only, and the HVL-F60RM, which is compatible with both optical and radio control. The F60M version is currently listed at $550, but the price will probably come down a tad now that its $600 radio-friendly sibling has been introduced. Other than optical/radio control, the two units are physically and functionally identical. The F60M model is shown in Figure 13.10. The duo are the most powerful units the company offers, with an ISO 100 guide number (GN) of 60 in meters or 197 in feet at ISO 100. As I noted earlier, the GN does not indicate actual flash range but it's useful when comparing several flash units in terms of their general power output.

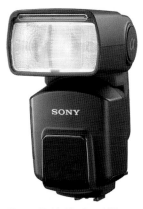

Figure 13.10 The Sony HVL-F60M is the top-of-the-line external flash unit and includes a bonus LED light for video.

Like all Sony multi interface shoe flash units except the HVL-F20M, the F60M/F60RM automatically adjust the zoom head to vary the angle of coverage to suit the lens focal length in use. You can zoom the head manually instead, if you prefer. A built-in slide-out diffuser panel boosts wide-angle coverage so it's suitable for photos taken at short focal lengths with the 10-18mm zoom. There's also a slide-out "bounce card" that can reflect some light forward even when bouncing the flash off the ceiling, to fill in shadows or add a catch light in the eyes of your portrait subjects. This dust- and moisture-resistant 21-ounce unit uses four AA batteries but can also be connected to the older FA-EB1AM external battery adapter, which has room for 6 AA batteries for increased capacity and faster recycling.

You may find the FA-EB1AM available at reduced prices, as it was recently replaced by the FA-EB1 ($250). The new pack is compatible with both the F60M and F60RM units, and capable of accepting *either* four or eight AA batteries in replaceable magazines, for up to 660 flashes with speedy recycle times of 0.6 seconds. When connected to the flash, it becomes the unit's primary power source.

ANOTHER GOODIE

Along with the F60RM flash and FA-EB1 battery pack, Sony has introduced the FA-RG1 Multi Interface Shoe Rain Guard, which prevents water from seeping into the electrical contacts of the camera.

Regardless of power source, the F60M/RM automatically communicates white balance information to your camera, allowing the a7R IV to adjust WB to match the flash output. It also offers a dedicated video light that can be useful for a bit of extra illumination if the subject is close to the camera. When you point the flash head upward, the trio of LED video illuminator lamps are revealed.

You can use this large unit as a main flash or allow it to be triggered wirelessly by another compatible flash unit. A pre-flash burst of light from the triggering master/controller unit causes a remote flash unit to fire. When using flash wirelessly, Sony recommends rotating the unit so that the flashtube is pointed to the location where light should be directed, while the front (light sensor) of the flash is pointed toward the camera. In wireless mode, you can control up to three groups of flashes, and specify the output levels for each group, giving you an easy way to control the lighting ratios of multiple flash units.

HIGH-SPEED SYNC

Those who are frustrated by an inability to use a shutter speed faster than 1/250th second will love the High-Speed Sync (HSS) mode that allows for flash at 1/500th to 1/4000th second! (HSS is also available with the HVL-F43M, HVL-F32M, and the discontinued HVL-58AM and HVL-F36AM.) This is ideal when you want to use a very wide aperture for selective focus with a nearby subject with flash; HSS at a fast shutter speed such as 1/1000th second is one way to avoid overexposure. The Mode button on the back of the flash is used to choose either TTL or Manual flash exposure. You can then use the MENU button and plus/minus keys to activate HSS mode; HSS appears in the unit's data panel as confirmation of the mode.

Keep in mind that flash output is much lower in High-Speed Sync than in conventional flash photography. That's because less than the full duration of the flash is used to expose each portion of the image as it is exposed by the slit passing in front of the sensor. As a result, the effective flash (distance) range is much shorter.

In addition, HSS will not work when using multiple flash units or when the flash unit is set for left/right/up bounce flash or when the wide-angle diffuser is being used. (If you're pointing the flash downward, say, at a close-up subject, HSS can be used.)

This flash unit can provide a simulated modeling light effect at two flashes per second or at a more useful (but more power-consuming) 40 flashes per second for 4 seconds for 160 continuous mini-bursts. In wireless off-camera flash, the HVL-60M/RM can function as the main (on-camera) flash in wireless mode or it can be the remote flash, triggered wirelessly by another compatible flash unit, as discussed earlier.

HVL-F45RM Flash Unit

If you want an on-camera flash capable of triggering external flash units optically *and* by radio control and are intimidated by the price of the HVL-F60RM, this flash is an affordable ($400) option. It also can be triggered wirelessly by an optical master, by another HVL-F45RM or an HVL-F60RM mounted on the a7R IV, or by the Sony FA-WRC1M Wireless Radio Commander mounted on the camera. When using radio control, it uses 14 channels to communicate with up to 15 flash units in five groups. It has a guide number of 45/148 (meters/feet) at ISO 100, and a fast 2.5-second recycle time. Its zoom head adjusts for the field of view from 24mm to 105mm (perfect for the a7R IV's kit lens) and has an LED video light.

HVL-F43M Flash Unit

This less pricey ($328) electronic flash (shown in Figure 13.11) shares many of the advanced features of the HVL-F60M/RM but has a lower guide number of 43/138 (meters/feet). Features shared with the high-end unit include HSS, automatic white balance adjustment, and automatic zoom with the same coverage of focal lengths and the slide-out diffuser, as well as a built-in bounce card. Its quick-shift function allows you to direct the flash upward or to the side by rotating the head. This unit also can be used in wireless mode as a master/controller or remote/slave, and it also offers the quick-shift bounce feature. The HVL-F43M is a tad lighter (at 12 ounces) than its bigger sibling and runs on four AAs. This flash replaces the similar HVL-F43AM unit, which uses the older iISO hot shoe.

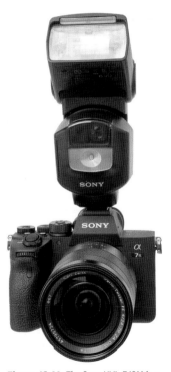

Figure 13.11 The Sony HVL-F43M is a more affordable external flash unit.

HVL-F36AM Flash Unit

Although discontinued, you can easily find this versatile flash available online or in used condition. It uses the old iISO hot shoe, so you'll need an adapter. The guide number for this lower-cost Sony flash unit is (surprise!) 36/118 (meters/feet). Although (relatively) compact at 9 ounces, you still get some big-flash features, such as wireless operation, auto zoom, and high-speed sync capabilities. Bounce flash flexibility is reduced a little, with no swiveling from side to side and only a vertical adjustment of up to 90 degrees.

HVL-F32M Flash Unit

The $300 HVL-F32M is Sony's lowest-cost wireless-compatible electronic flash unit. (See Figure 13.12.) It features a high-speed synchronization mode, wireless control, and automatic white balance compensation. In wireless mode, it can be used only on Channel 1 (as I'll describe shortly) but can function as both a master/controller and remote/slave. The flash is powered by a pair of AA batteries and it is resistant to both dust and moisture. Those who love to use bounce flash will like the built-in bounce sheet and retractable wide-angle panel that spreads the light to cover the equivalent of a 16mm lens.

HVL-F20M Flash Unit

The least-expensive Sony flash (see Figure 13.13) is the HVL-F20M ($150), designed to appeal to the budget conscious, especially those who need just a bit of a boost for fill flash, or want a small unit (just 3.2 ounces) on their camera. It has a guide number of 20 at ISO 100, and features simplified operation. For example, there's a switch on the side of the unit providing Indoor and Outdoor settings (the indoor setting tilts the flash upward to provide bounce light; with the outdoor setting, the flash fires directly at your subject). This flash can serve as a master/controller on the a7R IV to trigger off-camera flash units wirelessly but cannot be used as a remote/slave flash. There are special modes for wide-angle shooting (use the built-in diffuser to spread the flash's coverage to that of a lens with a very wide field of view or choose the Tele position to narrow the flash coverage to that of a 50mm or longer lens for illuminating more distant subjects). While it's handy for fill-flash, owners of a Sony a7R IV camera will probably want a more powerful unit as their main electronic flash.

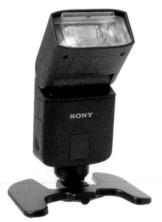

Figure 13.12 The Sony HVL-F32M is a more affordable external flash unit.

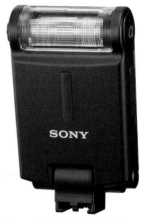

Figure 13.13 The HVL-F20M flash unit is compact and inexpensive.

BATTERY TIP

You may not use your flash very often, but when you do, you want it to operate properly. The problem with infrequent flash use is that conventional nickel-metal hydride batteries lose their charge over time, so if your flash unit is sitting in your bag for a long time between uses, you may not even be aware that your rechargeable batteries are pooped out. Non-rechargeable alkaline cells are not a solution: they generally provide less power for your flash and replacing them can be costly. The Energizer Lithium Ultimate AA batteries last up to three times longer, but they sell for about $10 for four.

I've had excellent luck with a battery developed by Panasonic called *eneloop* cells. They retain their charge for long periods of time—as much as 75 percent of a full charge over a three-year period (let's hope you don't go that long between uses of your flash). They're not much more expensive than ordinary rechargeables and can be revitalized up to 1,500 times. They're available in capacities of 1500 mAh to 2500 mAh. I use the economical models with 1900 mAh capacity.

Wireless Flash

Because the Sony a7R IV lacks a built-in flash, in order to trigger flash wirelessly, you'll need to own at least two compatible flash units, such as the HVL-F60M/RM, HVL-45RM, HVL-F43M, HVL-F32M, or HVL-F20M. One flash will be connected to the camera through the multi interface shoe and serves as the master flash or controller. A second (and additional) flash unit can be triggered wirelessly, with full exposure control. It is a limited range (about 16 feet) but a useful unit if you want your primary illumination to come from the off-camera flash, and, perhaps, use a less powerful on-camera flash as the master. In that mode, the HVL-F20M makes a workable controller/master, especially since it is the least-expensive Sony flash unit. But keep in mind that it cannot be used as a remote/slave flash unit.

To use wireless flash with optical triggering just follow these steps (I'll address radio control later):

1. **Connect the controller flash unit to the a7R IV.** Slide it all the way into the multi interface shoe so the connection is solid. Lock it in position.

2. **Position additional flash(es).** Sony flash units come with a mini-stand that lets you set the flash on a table or other surface. You can also purchase third-party adapters so the off-camera flash can be mounted on a light stand or a tripod. In a pinch, you can press a helper into service to hold your supplementary flash units. The remote units must be able to "see" the master/controller's pre-flash signal, either directly or by bouncing off another surface in the room.

3. **Power up flash and camera.** Note that when you turn off the camera, the flash turns off as well; you don't need to manually turn both on or off simultaneously if you want to save power during a shooting session.

4. **Switch camera and attached master/controller flash to wireless mode.** Use the Camera Settings menu's Flash Mode option or select Flash mode from the Function menu. Select Wireless (WL). Once the camera is set to wireless mode, press the shutter release halfway, and the attached powered-up flash automatically shifts into wireless mode as well.

5. **Set one or more remote/slave flash unit(s) to wireless mode and choose options.** Turn on the unit and follow the instructions supplied with your flash unit to switch to wireless mode, then select either controller (master) mode or remote (slave) mode. Then, choose a group and channel, which I'll explain in the next section. An alternate way of setting your off-camera flash to remote mode is to mount them on the camera, power up, choose Wireless (WL) from the Camera Settings menu's Flash Mode entry and press the shutter release halfway to transfer the setting to the flash. You can then remove the flash and a red LED on the flash will start blinking to let you know the flash is ready to use in wireless mode.

6. **Test your connection.** Press your defined AEL button, and the controller will emit a burst, which the remotes will respond to with a flash of their own about half a second later.

Key Wireless Concepts

Here are some key concepts you must understand before jumping into wireless flash photography:

- **Controllers.** The flash that communicates with and triggers all wireless flash units is called the *controller* in Sony nomenclature. It's more common within the photographic industry to use the term *master,* however, so I tend to use both terms together to avoid confusion. Because the a7R IV does not have a built-in flash, wireless communication requires one controller/master to be connected to the camera's multi interface shoe.

- **Remotes.** The flash units that are controlled wirelessly are called the *remotes* by Sony, or *slaves*. There can only be one controller/master flash, but you can have multiple remote/slave units. All the remotes triggered by a controller/master must use the same *channel*, but flashes using a particular channel can be divided into one of two *remote groups*, and their power levels specified by group.

- **Channels.** Sony's wireless flash system offers users the ability to determine on which of up to four possible channels (depending on the flash's capabilities) the units can communicate. (The pilots, ham radio operators, or scanner listeners among you can think of the channels as individual communications frequencies.) The channels are numbered 1, 2, 3, and 4, and each flash must be assigned to one of them. Moreover, in general, each of the flash units you are working with should be assigned to the *same* channel, because the remote/slave flash units will respond *only* to a controller/master flash that is on the same channel. Note that the HVL-F20M cannot be used as a remote/slave flash, and when used as a controller/master flash, you *must* use its sole channel, Channel 1.

  The channel ability is important when you're working around other photographers who are also using the same system. Photojournalists, including sports photographers, will encounter this situation frequently as Sony cameras make in-roads in these pro arenas. Each Sony photographer sets flash units to a different channel so as to not accidentally trigger other users' strobes. (At big events with more than four photographers using Sony flash, you may need to negotiate.) I use this capability at workshops I conduct where we have two different setups. Photographers working with one setup use a different channel than those using the other setup and can work independently even though we're at opposite ends of the same large room.

- **Groups.** Sony's wireless flash system lets you designate multiple flash units in two separate groups, dubbed RMT (which is selected for all flashes by default) and RMT2 (which must be specified explicitly to change individual flashes from the default RMT group). All the flashes in all the groups use the exact same *channel* and all respond to the same master controller, but you can set the output levels of each remote/slave group separately. So, flash in RMT might serve as the main light, while those in RMT2 might be adjusted to produce less illumination and serve as a fill light. It's convenient to be able to adjust the output of all the units within a given group simultaneously. This lets you create different styles of lighting for portraits and other shots.

  Note that these two groups consist *only* of remote flashes. Your on-camera controller/master flash is effectively a third group. If the controller is a low-powered unit like the HVL-F20M, it may not contribute much to the exposure at all (or, perhaps just add a little fill if pointed directly at your subject); a more powerful unit can become a potential third group. You could, for example, point the on-camera flash at a ceiling or wall to provide additional diffuse illumination.

  If you're using only one group, all the flashes in the RMT group are automatically adjusted based on the settings you specify for the controller/master, such as flash exposure bracketing and/or flash exposure compensation.

- **Flash ratios.** This ability to control the output of one flash (or set of flashes) compared to another flash or set in groups allows you to produce lighting *ratios*. You can control the power of multiple off-camera flash to adjust each unit's relative contribution to the image, for more dramatic portraits and other effects. Ratios are available with flash units that use the new CTRL+ protocol (described next).

- **Flash protocols.** Older Sony flash units, including the HVL-F20M, used a particular protocol to communicate. More recent units, such as the HVL-F60M/RM, HVL-45RM, HVL-F43M (with multi interface shoe), HVL-F58AM, HVL-F32M, and HVL-F32AM/HVL-F43AM (both with the old-style shoe) all have an enhanced protocol for communicating with compatible flash, called CTRL+. They can also revert to the older protocol (CTRL) to be compatible with older flash as well. Because the HVL-F20M uses the original Sony protocol, it cannot be used to adjust flash ratios, as described above.

- **Metering.** In wireless flash mode, advanced distance integration (ADI) is not used (the distance between the flash and subject can't be determined by the off-camera flash), and Sony's P-TTL flash metering is used instead.

Setting Channels and Remote Groups

To specify the channels and remote groups used by each flash in optical mode, you must use the flash unit's controls and menu system to do so. As an introduction to what's involved, I'm going to list the procedures for the two most commonly used flash, the HVL-F60M/RM and HVL-F43M. For the HVL-F45RM and other Sony wireless-compatible flash units, consult the manual furnished with your strobe.

Setting the HVL-F60M/RM

To choose the group on the HVL-F60M/RM, just follow these steps:

1. Press the Mode button to display the Mode screen.
2. Rotate the control wheel or use its directional buttons to highlight WL RMT.
3. Press the Fn button and use the control wheel to select the group, either TTL Remote or TTL Remote 2.
4. Press the control wheel center button to confirm your changes.

To choose the channel on the HVL-F60M/RM, just follow these steps:

1. Press the Menu button. The Menu screen appears.
2. On Page 1, select the entry to change. Use the control wheel to highlight the entry you want to adjust.
3. Select the wireless channel by highlighting WL CH and pressing the control wheel center button. Then use the control wheel to choose Channel 1, 2, 3, or 4. Press the center button again to confirm your choice.
4. You can also adjust the protocol if needed. Highlight the WL CTRL entry and press the control wheel center button. Use the wheel to select CTRL+ if you are using only compatible flash units (HVL-F60M/RM, HVL-F43M, HVL-F32M, HVL-F58AM, HVL-F32AM, or HVL-F43AM) or CTRL if you are using other flash units in your setup. Press the Menu button again to confirm your choice.

Setting the HVL-F43M

To choose the group on the HVL-F43M, just follow these steps:

1. Press the Fn button. CTRL or RMT will be blinking.
2. Press the right directional arrow on the flash as needed to highlight RMT or RMT2.
3. Press Fn to confirm your choice.

To choose the Channel on the HVL-F43M:

1. Hold down the Fn button for more than three seconds. The first Custom Setting item (CH01 HSS) is displayed.
2. Press the flash's left/right directional buttons to change to C02: Wireless Channel.
3. Press the up/down buttons to select the channel 1, 2, 3, or 4.
4. Press the Fn button again to confirm your choice.
5. You can also adjust the protocol, if needed. Hold down the Fn button for more than three seconds and use the left/right buttons to select C03: Wireless Controller Mode. You can choose 1 (CTRL, the old protocol) or 2 (CTRL+, the new protocol). Press Fn to confirm your choice.

Setting Ratios

Once you've set up one or more flash for the RMT group, and more or more for the RMT2 group, you can adjust the ratio used between them.

Ratios with the HVL-F43M

Just follow these steps when using the HVL-F43M as the controller or remote/slave. Remember that all flashes in all remote groups must be set to the same channel, as described previously:

1. The easiest way to set ratios is to mount the controller/master and remote/slave units on the camera in turn. With each flash mounted on the camera set to Wireless Flash as described earlier, press the Mode button on the flash to display WL.

2. Press the Fn button, then press the left/right directional buttons until CTRL and RATIO are *both* blinking.

3. Press the Fn button again. The line at upper right will display:

    CTRL RMT RMT1

    1 : 1 : 1

4. Use the left/right directional buttons to move the highlighting to CTRL. When CTRL is highlighted, you can press the up/down buttons to choose the relative power of that flash, compared to the others, from 1, 2, 4, 8, 16, or - - (the latter disables the flash). For example, a setting of 16:1:4 would specify that the flash mounted on the camera has 1/16th the power of the RMT group, while the RMT2 group would have 1/4 the power of the RMT group. Selecting - - disables that flash or group. You might want to do that so that the on-camera flash doesn't contribute to the exposure, even though it will still fire a pre-flash to trigger the remote/slave units (see Figure 13.14).

5. Press the TTL/M button to display TTL.

6. Repeat for each flash.

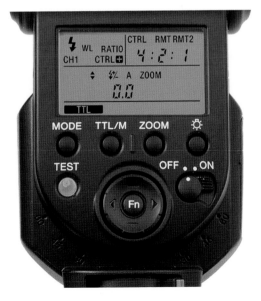

Figure 13.14 Set ratios on the HVL-F43M.

Ratios with the HVL-F60M/RM

Just follow these steps when using the HVL-F60M/RM as the controller or remote/slave. Again, all flashes in all remote groups must be set to the same channel, as described previously:

1. You can mount each flash on the camera and set the ratios. Press the Mode button to produce the Mode screen and select WL CTRL.

2. Press the Fn button to access the Quick Navi screen and use the control wheel to highlight WL CTRL. Press the control wheel center button to access the dedicated settings screen.

3. Use the control wheel to highlight RATIO. Press the center button to access your choices, Ratio: Off (the controller flash does not contribute to the exposure), TTL Ratio, and Manual Ratio. You can highlight TTL Ratio and use the control wheel to choose ON.

4. Press the center button to return to the indicator screen.

5. Press the Fn button to display the Quick Navi screen and choose the Wireless Lighting Ratio control indicator located at middle left of the screen. Press the control wheel center button, then use the control wheel to change the lighting ratio of each group. Rotate the control wheel to choose the relative power of each flash, compared to the others, from 1, 2, 4, 8, 16, or - -. The - - setting disables that group. (See Figure 13.15.)

6. Press the center button when finished.

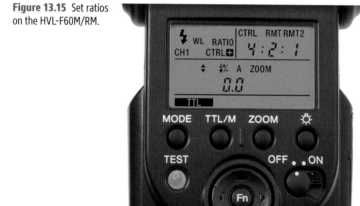

Figure 13.15 Set ratios on the HVL-F60M/RM.

Radio Control

Your Sony electronic flash communicate with each other using optical control, via the pre-flashes emitted before the actual exposure takes place. That type of linking requires line-of-sight communication between master and remote units and works only over limited distances. Early in 2016 Sony introduced its wireless radio commander/receiver duo, which gives you a much greater range, many more channels to work with, and more control. Unfortunately, Sony's radio control solution is expensive, making it impractical for all but the most avid (and well-heeled) shooters. I expect it will be more popular among professionals who can justify the expense, and those, such as photojournalists, who need the flexibility of a larger number of channels to avoid conflicts with other photographers covering the same event. To properly equip yourself, you'll need:

- **Commander.** You'll need one HVL-F60RM flash, HVL-F45RM flash, or FA-WRC1M wireless radio commander ($349) for every camera you want to equip with radio control. The radio-compatible flash or commander reside in the hot shoe of the a7R IV and are used to trigger the off-camera electronic flash.

- **Flash units.** You must have at least one Sony flash from those listed above for the wireless commander to trigger. Ideally, you'll have several to allow you to configure multi-light setups, so plan on spending $250 to $600 for each remote flash.

- **Receivers.** As I write this, only the HVL-F60RM and HVL-F45RM can be triggered by radio controls. So, if you're using any other wireless-compatible (optical only) flash, it must be connected to a FA-WRR1 wireless radio receiver ($200). The flash units are *not* sensitive to radio controls on their own.

- **Light stands or an assistant.** The wireless commander generally resides on the multi interface shoe of your camera, so you'll need light stands to accept each receiver, which has its own hot shoe your flash is attached to. Alternatively, you can enlist the aid of an assistant to hold the receiver/flash in proper position.

- **VMC-MM1 Multi Terminal cable (optional).** This $28 cable allows you to connect another one of those $200 wireless receivers to a second (or third...) *camera* so the auxiliary cameras fire in unison with the flash and main camera. This very cool feature will appeal to sports and news photographers covering events.

Each commander transmitter can support up to 15 receivers in any combination of flash units and slave cameras, with your choice of 14 different channels (reducing those conflicts at the next presidential convention you cover in 2020). All the devices on a particular channel can be divided up among as many as five different groups, so you could conceivably have a dozen or more flash units spread among all those groups to provide very sophisticated lighting effects, over a range of more than 98 feet (30 meters).

But wait! There's more. The HVL-F60RM, HVL-F45RM, and FA-WRC1M wireless radio command-ers give you Manual, TTL, and Group control of flashes, and power adjustment from full power (1/1) to 1/256th power in 1/3-stop increments. The 3.3-ounce commander and 3-ounce receiver each run on two AA batteries. While I don't expect to see many a7R IV owners springing for this system, it's nice for ambitious photographers to know that these capabilities are there for them to grow into. Eventually, Sony will introduce additional radio-capable flash units and commanders, probably at more affordable prices.

Off-Camera Flash

While using multiple flash units provides a way to work with illumination that's not locked into your a7R IV's accessory shoe, you don't need to own more than one flash unit to improve your results. Simply removing your flash from the camera and elevating it higher and off to one side can give you pleasing directional lighting, bounce lighting, and other effects.

I often use a flash connecting cable (available in 1.5- and 3-foot lengths from Vello, Metz, and other vendors) as shown in Figure 3.16. I can hold the camera in my right hand and hold and position the flash with my right hand. Such cables also offer a tripod-style mount on the bottom of the flash mount, so you can secure the off-camera flash to a light stand or tripod. The cable is compatible with the a7R IV's TTL metering system. You'll find such a plug-and-play configuration easier to use than any multi-flash setup. Remove your flash from the camera, re-connect through the cable, and shoot.

Figure 13.16 Shooting with off-camera flash.

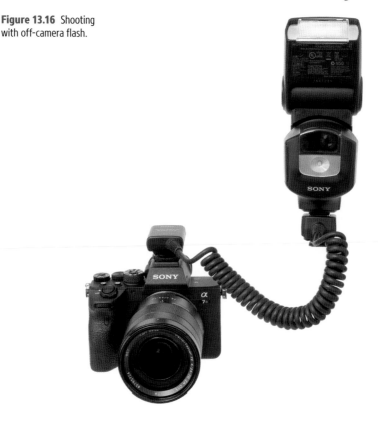

Troubleshooting and Prevention

14

One of the nice things about modern mirrorless cameras like the Sony a7R IV is that they have fewer mechanical moving parts to fail, so they are less likely to "wear out." No film transport mechanism, no wind lever or motor drive, and no complicated mechanical linkages from camera to lens to physically stop down the lens aperture. Instead, tiny, reliable motors are built into each lens (and you lose the use of only that lens should something fail).

Of course, the camera also has a moving physical shutter (which augments the electronic shutter "curtains"). It can fail, but the shutter is built rugged enough that you can expect it to last several hundred thousand shutter cycles or more. Unless you're shooting sports in continuous mode day in and day out, the shutter on your Sony a7R IV is likely to last as long as you expect to use the camera.

The only other things on the camera that move are switches, dials, buttons, and the doors that open to allow you to remove and insert the memory card and battery. I'm not fond of the removable battery door mechanism, which I have to use each time I mount the battery grip to my camera, but it hasn't failed me yet. Unless you're extraordinarily clumsy or unlucky or give your camera a good whack while it is in use, there's not a lot that can go wrong mechanically with your Sony a7R IV.

On the other hand, one of the chief drawbacks of modern electronic cameras is that they are modern *electronic* cameras. Your Sony a7R IV is fully dependent on two different batteries, the main NP-FZ100 that powers most functions, and a smaller inaccessible battery within the camera's innards that stores setup and settings information. Without them, the camera can't be used. There are numerous other electrical and electronic connections in the camera (many connected to those mechanical switches and dials), and components like the color LCD that can potentially fail or suffer damage. The camera also relies on its "operating system," or *firmware*, which can be plagued by bugs that cause unexpected behavior. Luckily, electronic components are generally more reliable and trouble-free, especially when compared to their mechanical counterparts from the pre-electronic film camera days.

Digital cameras have problems unique to their breed, too; the most troublesome being the need to clean the sensor of dust and grime periodically. This chapter will show you how to diagnose problems, fix some common ills, and, importantly, learn how to avoid some of them in the future.

Upgrading Your Firmware

As I said, the firmware in your Sony a7R IV is the camera's operating system, which handles every-thing from menu display (including fonts, colors, and the actual entries themselves), what languages are available, and even support for specific devices and features. Upgrading the firmware to a new version makes it possible to add new features while fixing some of the bugs that sneak in.

Official firmware for your Sony a7R IV is given a version number that you can view by turning the power on, pressing the MENU button, and navigating to Version in the Setup 6 menu. The first number in the string represents the major release number, while the second and third represent less significant upgrades and minor tweaks, respectively. Theoretically, a camera should have a firmware version number of 1.0 when it is introduced, but vendors have been known to do some minor fixes during testing and unveil a camera with a 1.1 firmware designation. If a given model is available long enough, it can evolve into significant upgrades, such as the current 2.0 or higher designations.

Firmware upgrades are used for both cameras and certain lenses (each listed separately in the Ver-sion entry), most frequently to fix bugs in the software, and much less frequently to add or enhance features. The exact changes made to the firmware are generally spelled out in the firmware release announcement. You can examine the remedies provided and decide if a given firmware patch is important to you. If not, you can usually safely wait a while before going through the bother of upgrading your firmware—at least long enough for the early adopters to report whether the bug fixes have introduced new bugs of their own. Each new firmware release incorporates the changes from previous releases, so if you skip a minor upgrade you should have no problems.

 WARNING Don't open the memory card door or turn off the camera while your old firmware is being overwritten. You *should* have sufficient power for the camera while upgrading, because Sony requires you to connect the camera to your computer using a USB cable, and that cable conveys power from the host computer as well as information.

Upgrading your firmware is ridiculously easy. The following is a fictitious example that may not coincide exactly with the procedure you will use, as Sony changes the process from time to time. Simply follow these steps:

1. **Search for firmware.** Visit the Sony support site for your area, such as esupport.sony.com and navigate to the Drivers and Software page for your camera. It will vary by country, but you can quickly click the Drivers and Software link, enter model information about your camera, select your operating system, such as Windows 10 64 Bit, and eventually arrive at the Firmware download page.

2. **Download firmware.** You'll see a message like the following when you reach the download page. Click the Download button.

   UPDATE: ILCE-7RM4 System Software Update.
   Release Date 10/19/2020
   Version 2.00
   File Size 236.80MB
   [Download]

3. **Check USB Connection status.** Make sure the USB Connection entry in the Setup 4 menu is set to Mass Storage. Then turn off your camera.

4. **Connect camera to your computer.** Link to a USB port on your Internet-connected computer using the USB cable that came with your camera for use when recharging the battery. Then turn on the camera.

5. **Open firmware file.** It will have a name like Update_ILCE7RM4V200.exe (for Windows) or Update_ILCE7RM4V200.dng (for Macs). The version number will vary, depending on the particular release it is.

6. **Follow the instructions** shown on the update utility, pictured in Figure 14.1.

7. **Turn off camera.** When finished, you can turn off the camera. It will have the new firmware installed the next time you power up.

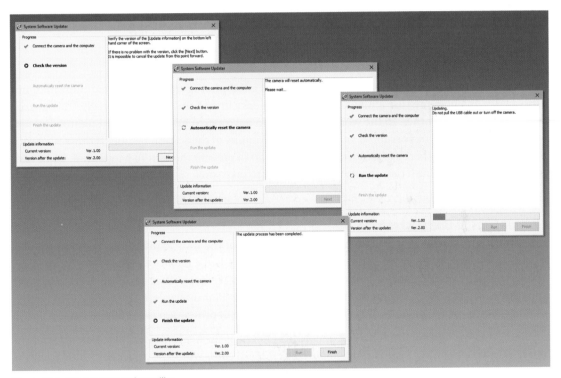

Figure 14.1 The firmware update utility.

Protecting Your LCD

The color LCD monitor on the back of your Sony a7R IV almost seems like a target for banging, scratching, and other abuse. Fortunately, it's quite rugged, and a few errant knocks are unlikely to shatter the protective cover over the LCD, and scratches won't easily mar its surface. However, if you want to be on the safe side, there are a number of protective products you can purchase to keep your LCD safe.

Sony itself offers the PCK-LG1 (about $30) semi-hard protective sheet. It's not too costly and includes an anti-fingerprint coating to reduce smudges. Like other such protectors, it fastens securely to the LCD monitor with a residue-free adhesive and can be easily removed by threading a piece of dental floss between the sheet and screen. I prefer the ultra-thin (0.3mm) glass GGS screens available on Amazon and from a variety of other sources for anywhere from around $10 to $20 for the deluxe "Larmour" version, which use a strong silicon adhesive for gapless mounting. You can also use simple plastic overlay sheets, or "skins" made for smartphones, cut to fit your LCD.

Troubleshooting Memory Cards

Sometimes good memory cards go bad. Sometimes good photographers can treat their memory cards badly. It's possible that a memory card that works fine in one camera won't be recognized when inserted into another. In the worst case, you can have a card full of important photos and find that the card seems to be corrupted and you can't access any of them. Don't panic! If these scenarios sound horrific to you, there are lots of things you can do to prevent them from happening, and a variety of remedies available if they do occur. You'll want to take some time—before disaster strikes—to consider your options.

All Your Eggs in One Basket?

The "Don't put all your eggs in one basket" myth is one of the most contentious in photography, second only to the "protective" filter myth. Most of us have had a memory card fail and have lost—or have thought we lost—some photos that we'd rather have kept. That certainly underlines the importance of backing up our pictures to other media at regular intervals, even while traveling. But whether multiple smaller cards offers an additional degree of protection is a separate issue.

Given the 42.4MB images my a7R IV produces, as I noted at the beginning of this book, I prefer the 64GB Sony G-series SDXC cards and will purchase 128GB cards when the prices come down a little. The debate about whether it's better to use one large memory card or several smaller ones has been going on since even before there were memory cards!

I can remember when computer users wondered whether it was smarter to install a pair of 200 megabyte (not *gigabyte*) hard drives in their computer, or if they should go for one of those new-fangled 500MB models. By the same token, a few years ago the conventional wisdom insisted that you ought to use 128MB memory cards rather than the huge 512MB versions. Today, most of the arguments involve 32GB cards vs. 64GB cards, with the implication that smaller cards are "better" in this regard. Conventional wisdom is often more conventional than wise.

For professional users, this does make sense. I have professional wedding photographer friends who chortle at the folly of using large memory cards (I've actually witnessed the chortling), and they have special reasons for their preference. Of course, in addition to multiple cards, they use second shooters, copy photos on-site from a full memory card to a laptop, and employ other techniques in order to avoid having to ask the bride and groom whether it would be possible to restage a wedding. When your living depends on never losing *any* pictures, different rules apply.

But most of us have no cause to fear using mature memory storage technologies. Resorting to lots of small cards instead of fewer large ones may actually increase the chances of losing some. While I don't want to be a pioneer in working with 512GB memory cards (and have no need to do so), but I'm perfectly comfortable with my 64GB and larger cards for the following reasons:

- **Memory cards don't magically wait until they are full before they fail.** You will not automatically lose 64GB worth of photos, rather than 32GB if a memory card implodes. If you typically shoot 16GB worth of images on a typical day before you have the chance to back them up to your computer or laptop, then that's the most you are at risk for under average circumstances. Whether you're using a 16GB, 32GB, 64GB, or 128GB card, the number of images you shoot in a *typical* session prior to backup will be the number you actually may lose. The only time I actually fill up my 128GB memory cards is when I am traveling, and in those instances, I have already backed up each day's shooting to multiple additional media. Most of the time, all a larger memory card does is give you greater flexibility when you want to shoot *more* in one session and don't want or don't have time to swap cards.

  Many photojournalists and sports photographers change cards when they are 80 percent full to avoid missing a crucial shot. Instead of interrupting your shoot to swap out a 16GB card that becomes full, you can go ahead and shoot 17GB or 18GB on your 32GB card and change media during lulls in the festivities. In truth, the biggest danger comes from waiting too long—say, several days—to back up your images. We all know photographers who have New Years Eve, July 4, and Thanksgiving images on a single card, and who *never* backup their photos.

- **64GB cards aren't twice as likely to fail as 32GB cards,** although many seem to feel that's so. Indeed, I've heard the same advice to use "safer" 256MB cards, 2GB cards, or 4GB cards virtually up the line as capacities have increased. Once a fabrication technology is mature, the reliability of particular sizes is the same across the board. An easy way to tell is to compare the per-gigabyte costs for the card. Once a particular card is less than twice the cost of a card with half the capacity, you can bet the technology is solid.

- **Using multiple smaller cards may increase your odds of losing photos.** Memory cards do fail, but that most often happens from user error. The first 128GB card I bought, a Sony model, failed within a few months, because I put it in my wallet for "safekeeping" and accidentally folded it nearly in half. It's also common for photographers to lose cards, put them through a wash and dry cycle, or perform other atrocities unrelated to the reliability of the card itself.

  Yes, if you use smaller cards you may lose half as many photos, but you might also find that more cards equates to a higher risk of losing one or damaging one through stupidity. I find it's better to use the minimum number of photo "baskets" and then make sure nothing happens to that basket. If all your images are important, the fact that you've lost 100 of them rather than 200 pictures isn't very comforting.

- **When your family goes on vacation, do you split up family members to travel in several smaller cars?** After all, in a terrible collision, with multiple cars you might lose only a *couple* of your kinfolk rather than all of them. Keep in mind that your family is much more important to you than your photos, and the odds of being in a traffic accident is much *greater* than encountering a faulty memory card. Humans are susceptible to the cognitive fallacy "neglect of probability." I've taken hundreds of thousands of pictures and lost two memory cards, and I know three other photographers who've had memory card problems. On the other hand, I've driven hundreds of thousands of miles and been in four traffic accidents and know a dozen people who have had auto mishaps. Should my family be riding around in different cars while I stick to 16GB memory cards?

- **The typical memory card is rated for a Mean Time Between Failures of 1,000,000 hours of use.** That's constant use 24/7 for more than 100 years! According to the manufacturers, they are good for 10,000 insertions in your camera, and should be able to retain their data (and that's without an external power source) for something on the order of 11 years. Of course, with the millions of cards in use, there are bound to be a few lemons here or there.

So, what can you do? Here are some options for preventing loss of valuable images:

- **Internal backup.** Your a7R IV has dual memory card slots, so when your photos are particularly important use the Backup feature to write copies to both cards simultaneously. Or, if you're on vacation, copy a day's shots onto another card when you get back to your hotel room.

- **External backup.** It's easy to physically transfer your images to a laptop, smart device, or other backup storage, particularly when you're on vacation. When I'm traveling, I take a tiny Mac-Book Air and at least two 1TB portable drives and copy my pictures to them frequently. (See Figure 14.2.) Ideally, one of your backups should be offsite, and that's difficult while traveling. However, offsite can be a DVD you burn and mail home, or a storage site in the cloud.

- **Transmit your images.** Another option is to transmit your images frequently over a network to your laptop or smart device. Or upload them to a cloud drive, such as iCloud, Google Drive, OneDrive, or DropBox. Many cameras have that option.

Figure 14.2 Back up your images when traveling.

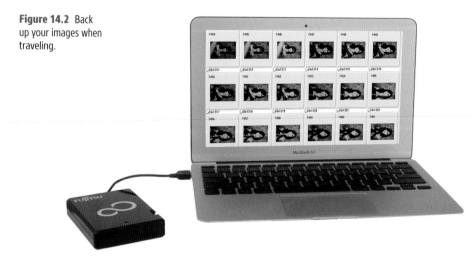

- **Interleaving.** You can also interleave your shots. Perhaps you don't shoot weddings, but you do go on vacation from time to time. Take 100 or so pictures on one card. Then, replace it with a different card and shoot another 100. Repeat these steps with diligence (you'd have to be determined to go through this degree of inconvenience), and, if you use four or more memory cards (of whatever capacity), you'll find your pictures from each location scattered among the different media. If you lose or damage one (which, alas, may be more likely because of the use of those multiple cards), you'll still have *some* pictures from all the various stops on your trip on the other cards. That's more work than I like to do, especially when it comes to sorting out the pictures back at home, but it's an option.

- **Be smart.** If you're having problems, the first thing you should do is stop using that memory card. Don't take any more pictures. Your second line of defense is to *do no harm* that hasn't already been done. If you take a picture of your business card as the first photo in a session, should the memory card be lost, your odds of having it returned to you are increased.

What Can Go Wrong?

There are lots of things that can go wrong with your memory card, but the ones that aren't caused by human stupidity are statistically very rare. Yes, a memory card's internal bit bin or controller can suddenly fail due to a manufacturing error or some inexplicable event caused by old age. However, if your memory card works for the first week or two that you own it, it should work forever. There's really not a lot that can wear out.

Given the reliability of solid-state memory, compared to magnetic memory, though, it's more likely that your memory problems will stem from something that you do. Memory cards are small and easy to misplace if you're not careful. For that reason, it's a good idea to keep them in their original cases or a "card safe" offered by Pelican (www.pelican.com), and others. Always placing your memory card in a case can provide protection from the second-most common mishap that befalls memory cards: the common household laundry. If you slip a memory card in a pocket, rather than a case or your camera bag, often enough, sooner or later it's going to end up in the washing machine and probably the clothes dryer, too. There are plenty of reports of relieved digital camera owners who've laundered their memory cards and found they still worked fine, but it's not uncommon for such mistreatment to do some damage.

Memory cards can also be stomped on, accidentally bent, dropped into the ocean, chewed by pets, and otherwise rendered unusable in myriad ways. It's also possible to force a card into your Sony a7R IV's memory card slot incorrectly if you're diligent enough. Or, if the card is formatted in your computer with a memory card reader, your Sony a7R IV may fail to recognize it. Occasionally, I've found that a memory card used in one camera would fail if used in a different camera (until I reformatted it in Windows, and then again in the camera). Every once in a while, a card goes completely bad and—seemingly—can't be salvaged.

Another way to lose images is to do commonplace things with your memory card at an inopportune time. If you remove the card from the Sony a7R IV while the camera is writing images to the card, you'll lose any photos in the buffer and may damage the file structure of the card, making it difficult or impossible to retrieve the other pictures you've taken. The same thing can happen if you remove the memory card from your computer's card reader while the computer is writing to the card (say, to erase files you've already moved to your computer). You can avoid this by *not* using your computer to erase files on a memory card but, instead, always reformatting the card in your Sony a7R IV before you use it again.

What Can You Do?

Pay attention: As mentioned, if you're having problems, the *first* thing you should do is *stop* using that memory card. Don't take any more pictures. Don't do anything with the card until you've figured out what's wrong. Your second line of defense (your first line is to be sufficiently careful with your cards that you avoid problems in the first place) is to *do no harm* that hasn't already been done. Read the rest of this section and then, if necessary, decide on a course of action (such as using a data recovery service or software described later) before you risk damaging the data on your card further.

Now that you've calmed down, the first thing to check is whether you've actually inserted a card in the camera. If you've set the camera in the Shooting menu so that Shoot w/o Card has been turned on, it's entirely possible (although not particularly plausible) that you've been snapping away with no memory card to store the pictures to, which can lead to massive disappointment later on. Of course, the No Memory Card message appears on the LCD when the camera is powered up, and it is superimposed on the review image after every shot, but maybe you're inattentive, or aren't using picture review. You can avoid all this by turning the Shoot w/o Card feature off and leaving it off.

Things get more exciting when the card itself is put in jeopardy. If you lose a card, there's not a lot you can do other than take a picture of a similar card and print up some Have You Seen This Lost Flash Memory? flyers to post on utility poles all around town.

If all you care about is reusing the card, and have resigned yourself to losing the pictures, try reformatting the card in your camera. You may find that reformatting removes the corrupted data and restores your card to health. Sometimes I've had success reformatting a card in my computer using a memory card reader (this is normally a no-no because your operating system doesn't understand the needs of your Sony a7R IV), and *then* reformatting again in the camera.

If your memory card is not behaving properly, and you *do* want to recover your images, things get a little more complicated. If your pictures are very valuable, either to you or to others (for example, a wedding), you can always turn to professional data recovery firms. Be prepared to pay hundreds of dollars to get your pictures back, but these pros often do an amazing job. You wouldn't want them working on your memory card on behalf of the police if you'd tried to erase some incriminating pictures. There are many firms of this type, and I've never used them myself, so I can't offer a recommendation. Use a Google search to turn up a ton of them. I use a software program called RescuePro, which came free with one of my SanDisk memory cards.

A more reasonable approach is to try special data recovery software you can install on your computer and use to attempt to resurrect your "lost" images yourself. They may not actually be gone completely. Perhaps your memory card's "table of contents" is jumbled, or only a few pictures are damaged in such a way that your camera and computer can't read some or any of the pictures on the card. Some of the available software was written specifically to reconstruct lost pictures, while other utilities are more general-purpose applications that can be used with any media, including floppy disks and hard disk drives. They have names like OnTrack, Photo Rescue 2, Digital Image Recovery, MediaRecover, Image Recall, and the aptly named Recover My Photos.

DIMINISHING RETURNS

Usually, once you've recovered any images on a memory card, reformatted it, and returned it to service, it will function reliably for the rest of its useful life. However, if you find a particular card going bad more than once, you'll almost certainly want to stop using it forever. See if you can get it replaced by the manufacturer, if you can, but, in the case of memory card failures, the third time is never the charm.

Cleaning Your Sensor

There's no avoiding dust. No matter how careful you are, some of it is going to settle on your camera and on the mounts of your lenses, eventually making its way inside your camera. As you take photos, the physical shutter movement causes the dust to become airborne and eventually come to rest atop your sensor. There, dust and particles can show up in every single picture you take at a small enough aperture to bring the foreign matter into sharp focus. No matter how careful you are and how cleanly you work, eventually you will get some of this dust on your camera's sensor.

Fortunately, one of the Sony a7R IV's most useful features is the automatic sensor cleaning system in the Setup 2 menu that reduces or eliminates the need to clean your camera's sensor manually. Sony has applied anti-static coatings to the sensor and other portions of the camera body interior to counter charge build-ups that attract dust. The sensor carriage vibrates ultrasonically to shake loose any dust. You can activate sensor cleaning at any time.

Dust the FAQs, Ma'am

Here are some of the most frequently asked questions about sensor dust issues.

Q. I see a bright spot in the same place in all of my photos. Is that sensor dust?

A. You've probably got either a "hot" pixel or one that is permanently "stuck" due to a defect in the sensor. A hot pixel is one that shows up as a bright spot only during long exposures as the sensor warms. A pixel stuck in the "on" position always appears in the image. Both show up as bright red, green, or blue pixels, usually surrounded by a small cluster of other improperly illuminated pixels, caused by the camera's interpolating the hot or stuck pixel into its surroundings, as shown in Figure 14.3. A stuck pixel can also be permanently dark. Either kind is likely to show up when they contrast with plain, evenly colored areas of your image.

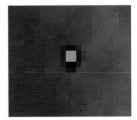

Figure 14.3 A stuck pixel is surrounded by improperly interpolated pixels created by the Sony a7R IV's demosaicing algorithm.

Bad pixels can also show up on your camera's color LCD panel, but, unless they are abundant, the wisest course is to just ignore them.

Q. I see an irregular out-of-focus blob in the same place in my photos. Is that sensor dust?

A. Yes. Sensor contaminants can take the form of tiny spots, larger blobs, or even curvy lines if they are caused by minuscule fibers that have settled on the sensor. They'll appear out of focus because they aren't actually on the sensor surface but, rather, a fraction of a millimeter above it on the filter that covers the sensor. The smaller the f/stop used, the more in-focus the dust becomes. At large apertures, it may not be visible at all.

Q. I never see any dust on my sensor. What's all the fuss about?

A. Those who never have dust problems with their Sony a7R IV fall into one of four categories: those for whom the camera's automatic dust removal features are working well; those who seldom change their lenses and have clean working habits that minimize the amount of dust that invades their cameras in the first place; those who simply don't notice the dust (often because they don't shoot many macro photos or other pictures using the small f/stops that makes dust evident in their images); and those who are very, very lucky.

Identifying and Dealing with Dust

Sensor dust is less of a problem than it might be because it shows up only under certain circumstances. Indeed, you might have dust on your sensor right now and not be aware if it. The dust doesn't actually settle on the sensor itself, but, rather, on a protective filter a very tiny distance above the sensor, subjecting it to the phenomenon of *depth-of-focus*. Depth-of-focus is the distance the focal plane can be moved and still render an object in sharp focus. At f/2.8 to f/5.6 or even smaller, sensor dust, particularly if small, is likely to be outside the range of depth-of-focus and blur into an unnoticeable dot.

However, if you're shooting at f/16 to f/22 or smaller, those dust motes suddenly pop into focus. Dust spots can easily show up in your images if you're shooting large, empty areas that are light colored. Dust motes are most likely to show up in the sky, as in Figure 14.4, or in white backgrounds of your seamless product shots and are less likely to be a problem in images that contain lots of dark areas and detail.

To see if you have dust on your sensor, take a few test shots of a plain, blank surface (such as a piece of paper or a cloudless sky) at small f/stops, such as f/22, and a few wide open. Open Photoshop, copy several shots into a single document in separate layers, then flip back and forth between layers to see if any spots you see are present in all layers. You may have to boost contrast and sharpness to make the dust easier to spot.

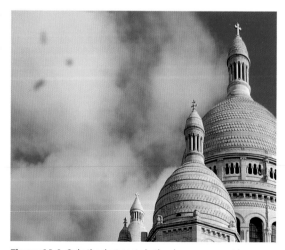

Figure 14.4 Only the dust spots in the sky are apparent in this shot.

Avoiding Dust

Of course, the easiest way to protect your sensor from dust is to prevent it from settling on the sensor in the first place. Some lenses come with rubberized seals around the lens mounts that help keep dust from infiltrating, but you'll find that dust will still find a way to get inside. Here are my tips for eliminating the problem before it begins.

- **Clean environment.** Avoid working in dusty areas if you can do so. Hah! Serious photographers will take this one with a grain of salt, because it usually makes sense to go where the pictures are. Only a few of us are so paranoid about sensor dust (considering that it is so easily removed) that we'll avoid moderately grimy locations just to protect something that is, when you get down to it, just a tool. If you find a great picture opportunity at a raging fire, during a sandstorm, or while surrounded by dust clouds, you might hesitate to take the picture, but, with a little caution (don't remove your lens in these situations and clean the camera afterward!) you can still shoot. However, it still makes sense to store your camera in a clean environment. One place cameras and lenses pick up a lot of dust is inside a camera bag. Clean your bag from time to time, and you can avoid problems.

- **Clean lenses.** There are a few paranoid types that avoid swapping lenses in order to minimize the chance of dust getting inside their cameras. It makes more sense just to use a blower or brush to dust off the rear lens mount of the replacement lens first, so you won't be introducing dust into your camera simply by attaching a new, dusty lens. Do this before you remove the lens from your camera, and then avoid stirring up dust before making the exchange.

- **Work fast.** Minimize the time your camera is lensless and exposed to dust. That means having your replacement lens ready and dusted off, and a place to set down the old lens as soon as it is removed, so you can quickly attach the new lens.

- **Let gravity help you.** Face the camera downward when the lens is detached so any dust inside the camera will tend to fall away from the sensor. Turn your back to any breezes, indoor forced air vents, fans, or other sources of dust to minimize infiltration.

- **Protect the lens you just removed.** Once you've attached the new lens, quickly put the end cap on the one you just removed to reduce the dust that might fall on it.

- **Clean out the vestibule.** From time to time, remove the lens while in a relatively dust-free environment and use a blower bulb like the ones shown in Figure 14.5 (*not* compressed air or a vacuum hose) to clean out the interior area. A blower bulb is generally safer than a can of compressed air, or a strong positive/negative airflow, which can tend to drive dust further into nooks and crannies.

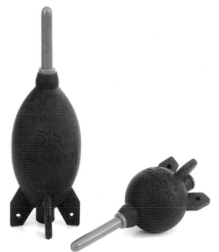

Figure 14.5 Use a robust air bulb for cleaning your sensor.

- **Be prepared.** If you're embarking on an important shooting session, it's a good idea to clean your sensor *now*, rather than come home with hundreds or thousands of images with dust spots caused by flecks that were sitting on your sensor before you even started. Before I left on my recent trip to Spain, I put both cameras I was taking through a rigid cleaning regimen, figuring they could remain dust-free for a measly 10 days. I even left my bulky blower bulb at home. It was a big mistake, but my intentions were good.

- **Clone out existing spots in your image editor.** Photoshop and other editors have a clone tool or healing brush you can use to copy pixels from surrounding areas over the dust spot or dead pixel. This process can be tedious, especially if you have lots of dust spots and/or lots of images to be corrected. The advantage is that this sort of manual fix-it probably will do the least damage to the rest of your photo. Only the cloned pixels will be affected.

- **Use filtration in your image editor.** A semi-smart filter like Photoshop's Dust & Scratches filter can remove dust and other artifacts by selectively blurring areas that the plug-in decides represent dust spots. This method can work well if you have many dust spots, because you won't need to patch them manually. However, any automated method like this has the possibility of blurring areas of your image that you didn't intend to soften.

Sensor Cleaning

Those new to the concept of sensor dust actually hesitate before deciding to clean their camera themselves. Isn't it a better idea to pack up your Sony a7R IV and send it to a service center so their crack technical staff can do the job for you? Or, at the very least, shouldn't you let the friendly folks at your local camera store do it?

Of course, if you choose to let someone else clean your sensor, they will be using methods that are more or less identical to the techniques you would use yourself. None of these techniques are difficult, and the only difference between their cleaning and your cleaning is that they might have done it dozens or hundreds of times. If you're careful, you can do just as good a job.

Of course, vendors like Sony may not tell you this, but it's not because they don't trust you. It's not that difficult for a real goofball to mess up his camera by hurrying or taking a shortcut. If Sony recommended *any* method that's mildly risky, someone would do it wrong, and then the company would face lawsuits from those who'd contend they did it exactly in the way the vendor suggested, so the ruined camera is not their fault.

You can see that vendors like Sony tend to be conservative in their recommendations, and, in doing so, make it seem as if sensor cleaning is more daunting and dangerous than it really is. Some vendors recommend only dust-off cleaning, through the use of reasonably gentle blasts of air, while condemning more serious scrubbing with swabs and cleaning fluids. However, these cleaning kits for the exact types of cleaning they recommended against are for sale in Japan only, where, apparently, your average photographer is more dexterous than those of us in the rest of the world. These kits are similar to those used by official repair staff to clean your sensor if you decide to send your camera in for a dust-up.

There are three basic kinds of cleaning processes that can be used to remove dusty and sticky stuff that settles on your dSLR's sensor. All of these must be performed with the shutter locked open. I'll describe these methods and provide instructions for locking the shutter later in this section.

- **Air cleaning.** This process involves squirting blasts of air inside your camera with the shutter locked open. This works well for dust that's not clinging stubbornly to your sensor.
- **Brushing.** A soft, very fine brush is passed across the surface of the sensor's filter, dislodging mildly persistent dust particles and sweeping them off the imager.
- **Liquid cleaning.** A soft swab dipped in a cleaning solution such as ethanol is used to wipe the sensor filter, removing more obstinate particles.

AIR CLEANING

Your first attempts at cleaning your sensor should always involve gentle blasts of air. Many times, you'll be able to dislodge dust spots, which will fall off the sensor and, with luck, out of the interior. Attempt one of the other methods only when you've already tried air cleaning and it didn't remove all the dust. Here are some tips for doing air cleaning:

- **Use a clean, powerful air bulb.** Your best bet is bulb cleaners designed for the job, like the Giottos Rocket. Smaller bulbs, like those air bulbs with a brush attached sometimes sold for lens cleaning or weak nasal aspirators, may not provide sufficient air or a strong enough blast to do much good.
- **Hold the Sony a7R IV pointed downward.** Then look up into the cavity behind the lens mount as you squirt your air blasts, increasing the odds that gravity will help pull the expelled dust downward, away from the sensor. You may have to use some imagination in positioning yourself. (See Figure 14.6.)

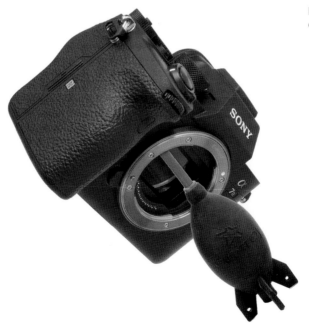

Figure 14.6 Point the camera downward.

- **Never use air canisters.** The propellant inside these cans can permanently coat your sensor if you tilt the can while spraying. It's not worth taking a chance.
- **Avoid air compressors.** Super-strong blasts of air are likely to force dust under the sensor filter.

BRUSH CLEANING

If your dust is a little more stubborn and can't be dislodged by air alone, you may want to try a brush, charged with static electricity, that can pick off dust spots by electrical attraction. One good, but expensive, option is the Sensor Brush sold at www.visibledust.com. You need a 24mm version, like the one shown in Figure 14.7, that can be stroked across the short dimension of your Sony a7R IV's sensor.

Ordinary artist's brushes are much too coarse and stiff and have fibers that are tangled or can come loose and settle on your sensor. A good sensor brush's fibers are resilient and described as "thinner than a human hair." Moreover, the brush has a wooden handle that reduces the risk of static sparks.

Brush cleaning is done with a dry brush by gently swiping the surface of the sensor filter with the tip. The dust particles are attracted to the brush particles and cling to them. You should clean the brush with compressed air before and after each use and store it in an appropriate air-tight container between applications to keep it clean and dust-free. Although these special brushes are expensive, one should last you a long time.

I like the Arctic Butterfly, shown in Figure 14.8. You activate the built-in motor that spins the brush at high speed to charge it with static electricity. Then, shut the motor off and pass the charged brush *above* the sensor surface so that dust will leap off the sensor and onto the brush.

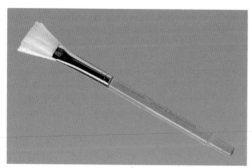

Figure 14.7 A proper brush is required for dusting off your sensor.

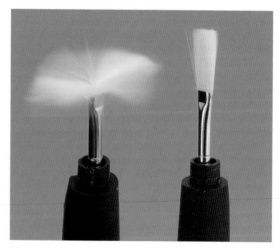

Figure 14.8 The motor in the Arctic Butterfly flutters the brush tips for a few minutes to charge them for picking up dust (left). Then, turn off the power and flick the tip above the surface of the sensor (right).

LIQUID CLEANING

Unfortunately, you'll often encounter really stubborn dust spots that can't be removed with a blast of air or flick of a brush. These spots may be combined with some grease or a liquid that causes them to stick to the sensor filter's surface. In such cases, liquid cleaning with a swab may be necessary. During my first clumsy attempts to clean my own sensor, I accidentally got my blower bulb tip too close to the sensor, and some sort of deposit from the tip of the bulb ended up on the sensor. I panicked until I discovered that liquid cleaning did a good job of removing whatever it was that took up residence on my sensor.

You can make your own swabs out of pieces of plastic (some use fast-food restaurant knives, with the tip cut at an angle to the proper size) covered with a soft cloth or Pec-Pad, as shown in Figures 14.9 and 14.10. However, if you've got the bucks to spend, you can't go wrong with good-quality commercial sensor cleaning swabs, such as those sold by Photographic Solutions, Inc. (www.photosol.com).

You want a sturdy swab that won't bend or break so you can apply gentle pressure to the swab as you wipe the sensor surface. Use the swab with methanol (as pure as you can get it, particularly medical grade; other ingredients can leave a residue), or the Eclipse solution also sold by Photographic Solutions. Eclipse is actually quite a bit purer than even medical-grade methanol. A couple drops of solution should be enough, unless you have a spot that's extremely difficult to remove. In that case, you may need to use extra solution on the swab to help "soak" the dirt off.

Once you overcome your nervousness at touching the protective cover of your Sony a7R IV's sensor, the process is easy. You'll wipe continuously with the swab in one direction, then flip it over and wipe in the other direction. You need to completely wipe the entire surface; otherwise, you may end up depositing the dust you collect at the far end of your stroke. Wipe; don't rub.

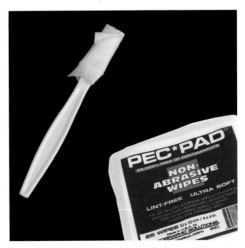

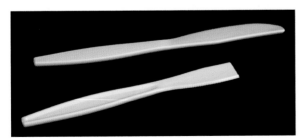

Figure 14.9 You can make your own sensor swab from a plastic knife that's been truncated.

Figure 14.10 Carefully wrap a Pec-Pad around the swab.

If you want a close-up look at your sensor to make sure the dust has been removed, you can pay $50 to $100 for a special sensor "microscope" with an illuminator. Or, you can do like I do and work with a plain old Carson MiniBrite PO-55 illuminated 5X magnifier, as seen in Figure 14.11. It has a built-in LED and, held a few inches from the lens mount with the lens removed from your Sony a7R IV, provides a sharp, close-up view of the sensor, with enough contrast to reveal any dust that remains. You can read more about this great device at http://dslrguides.com/carson.

Figure 14.11 An illuminated magnifier like this Carson MiniBrite PO-55 can be used as a 'scope to view your sensor.

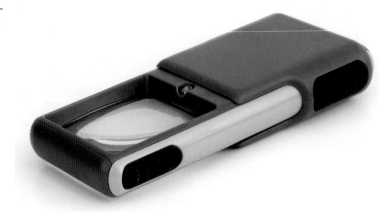

Index